Lecture Notes in Computer Science 3436

Commenced Publication in 1973
Founding and Former Series Editors:
Gerhard Goos, Juris Hartmanis, and Jan van Leeuwen

T0134777

Bruno Bouyssounouse   Joseph Sifakis (Eds.)

Embedded Systems Design

The ARTIST Roadmap
for Research and Development

 Springer

Volume Editors

Bruno Bouyssounouse
ARTIST Technical Coordinator
Joseph Sifakis
ARTIST Scientific Coordinator
Verimag Laboratory
Centre Equation, 2 avenue de Vignate, 38610 Gieres, France
E-mail: {Bruno.Bouyssounouse,Joseph.Sifakis}@imag.fr

Library of Congress Control Number: 2005921510

CR Subject Classification (1998): C.3, C.2, D.2, D.3, D.4, K.6

ISSN 0302-9743
ISBN 3-540-25107-3 Springer Berlin Heidelberg New York

Springer is a part of Springer Science+Business Media

springeronline.com

© Springer-Verlag Berlin Heidelberg 2005
Printed in Germany

Typesetting: Camera-ready by author, data conversion by Markus Richter, Heidelberg
Printed on acid-free paper   SPIN: 11400707   06/3142   5 4 3 2 1 0

Preface

Embedded systems now include a very large proportion of the advanced products designed in the world, spanning transport (avionics, space, automotive, trains), electrical and electronic appliances (cameras, toys, televisions, home appliances, audio systems, and cellular phones), process control (energy production and distribution, factory automation and optimization), telecommunications (satellites, mobile phones and telecom networks), and security (e-commerce, smart cards), etc. The extensive and increasing use of embedded systems and their integration in everyday products marks a significant evolution in information science and technology. We expect that within a short timeframe embedded systems will be a part of nearly all equipment designed or manufactured in Europe, the USA, and Asia.

There is now a strategic shift in emphasis for embedded systems designers: from simply achieving feasibility, to achieving optimality. Optimal design of embedded systems means targeting a given market segment at the lowest cost and delivery time possible. Optimality implies seamless integration with the physical and electronic environment while respecting real-world constraints such as hard deadlines, reliability, availability, robustness, power consumption, and cost. In our view, optimality can only be achieved through the emergence of embedded systems as a discipline in its own right.

Embedded systems are of strategic importance in modern economies. They are used in mass-market products and services, where value is created by supplying either functionality or quality. Europe currently has a strong position in sectors where embedded technologies play a central role. It has a lead in civil avionics where fly-by-wire technology provides an overwhelming competitive advantage in the cost of operating aircraft. Europe is also well positioned in the space sector, specifically for launch vehicles and satellites. In the automotive industry, European manufacturers and their suppliers enjoy a leading technological advantage for engine control, and emerging technologies such as brake-by-wire and drive-by-wire. Railway signalling in Europe relies on embedded systems, and allows faster, safer, and heavier traffic. Embedded applications will be extensively used to make energy distribution more flexible, especially in view of the coming market liberalization. Embedded technologies are strategic for the European telecommunications sector. Finally, Europe is also well positioned for e-services (e-banking, e-health, e-training), based on the leading edge in smart-card related technologies.

Embedded systems design raises challenging problems for research, including:

- Security
  Economic, citizenship, and societal activities in Europe rely increasingly on embedded applications. Widespread acceptance and reliance on these will depend on the availability of seamless solutions for securing rights and privacy.
- Reliable, mobile, embedded services
  Electronic commerce and e-services in a wireless world will need provably correct foundations to ensure further growth.

- Large-scale heterogeneous distributed systems
  Applications such as automated highways, advanced air traffic control, or next-generation factory automation require full-scale, industry-ready paradigms, methodologies, and advanced prototypes. These need to integrate heterogeneous elements from different, perhaps competing providers, in evolving embedded environments.
- Adaptive embedded systems
  Tomorrow's resource-constrained applications, such as image processing, telecommunications, and industrial automation, are expected to see drastic advances in performance and dependability, with the ability to adapt to dynamic changes in resource needs, including power/energy, bandwidth, memory, and computing power.
- Component-based design, validation, and tool-based certification
  Development costs and time-to-market could be vastly reduced, by enabling the incremental design and formal validation of arbitrarily complex systems.

This roadmap was written by the IST-2001-34820 ARTIST FP5 Accompanying Measure on Advanced Real-Time Systems, funded by the European Commission, and which started April 1st, 2002 and ended March 31st 2005.

The ARTIST FP5 workplan includes, in addition to providing this roadmap, advancing the state of the art and structuring research on embedded systems in Europe. It gathered together 28 leading European research institutions, as well as many top researchers in the area.

The aim of ARTIST FP5 was to coordinate the R&D effort in the area, to improve awareness of academics and industry, especially about existing innovative results and technologies, standards, and regulations, and to define innovative and relevant work directions, identify obstacles to scientific and technological progress, and propose adequate strategies for circumventing them.

ARTIST FP5 was implemented as a set of four coordinated actions, each centred on a high-priority thematic area of research on embedded systems. Correspondingly, the roadmap is organised into four parts.

Action 1: Hard Real Time. This action was led by Professor Albert Benveniste of INRIA (France), and focused on aspects of hard real-time applications, bringing together competencies from synchronous languages, time-triggered systems, and schedulers.

Action 2: Component-Based Design and Development. This action was led by Professor Bengt Jonsson of Uppsala University (Sweden), and focused on both theoretical and practical aspects of modelling complex systems with emphasis on methods (compositionality, composability) and standards (e.g. UML).

Action 3: Adaptive Real-Time Systems for QoS Management. This action was led by Professor Giorgio Buttazzo of the University of Pavia (Italy), and focused on soft real-time approaches and technology for telecommunications, large open systems, and networks. It gathered together teams with expertise in real-time operating systems and middleware.

Action 4: Execution Platforms. This action was led by Professor Lothar Thiele of the Swiss Federal Institute of Technology (ETHZ), and focused on issues at the frontier between hardware and software – and their implications for embedded systems design.

To enhance readability, each of the four parts of the roadmap follows a similar structure, although there are domain-related specificities. Also, inevitably, some topics may be treated in more than one part of the document, but the index should help the reader find the different relevant texts for a given topic.

Oversight for ARTIST FP5 was provided by the Artist Industrial Advisory Board (IAB), which reviewed the roadmap. The ARTIST IAB is chaired by Dr. Dominique Potier, Scientific Director for Software Technologies, Thalès.

We would like to thank all the contributors to the roadmap, including the engineers and researchers who participated in the various technical meetings and workshops, as well as the industrial leaders who granted interviews and/or provided information in the questionnaire. Special thanks also go to the Artist FP5 reviewers and the project officer, for constructive and stimulating comments.

The elaboration of this roadmap provided the opportunity for fertile interaction between key players in the area of embedded systems, and proved to be useful for structuring the area.

The work and the strategic orientations and conclusions of ARTIST FP5 led to the creation of the ARTIST2 FP6 Network of Excellence on Embedded Systems Design. Information about ARTIST2 is available on the web-site: http://www.artist-embedded.org/FP6.

This roadmap usefully complements other existing roadmapping work from ITEA and MEDEA+. We hope that it will be useful for both research and industry and that it will serve to advance awareness about the state of the art and provide insights on possible avenues for R&D.

Grenoble, January 2005

Bruno Bouyssounouse
ARTIST Technical Coordinator
Verimag Laboratory, France

Joseph Sifakis
ARTIST Scientific Coordinator
Verimag Laboratory, France

Editors

Bruno Bouyssounouse   Verimag Laboratory, France
ARTIST Technical Coordinator
Joseph Sifakis   Verimag Laboratory, France
ARTIST Scientific Coordinator

Contributors

Part I: Hard Real-Time Development Environments
Coordinator: Albert Benveniste   INRIA, France

Jos Baeten	Eindhoven Technical University, The Netherlands
Philippe Baufreton	Hispano-Suiza, France
Albert Benveniste	INRIA, France
Samuel Boutin	Renault, France
Bruno Bouyssounouse	Verimag Laboratory, France
Dominique Brière	Airbus, France
Paul Caspi	Verimag Laboratory, France
Werner Damm	OFFIS, Germany
Emmerich Fuchs	Vienna Technical University, Austria
Vered Gafni	Israel Aircraft Industries, Israel
Thierry Gautier	INRIA, France
Drora Goshen	Israel Aircraft Industries, Israel
Guenter Gruensteidl	Alcatel, Austria
Nicolas Halbwachs	Verimag Laboratory, France
Hermann Kopetz	Vienna Technical University, Austria
Kim Larsen	Aalborg University, Denmark
Hervé Le Berre	Airbus, France
Rainer Leupers	RWTH Aachen, Germany
Brian Nielsen	Aalborg University, Denmark
Ernst-Rüdiger Olderog	OFFIS, Germany
Yiannis Papadopoulos	University of York, UK
Philipp Peti	Vienna Technical University, Austria
Manfred Pisecky	TTTech, France
Peter Puschner	Vienna Technical University, Austria
Jörn Rennhack	Airbus, Germany
Alberto Sangiovanni-Vincentelli	PARADES, Italy
Christian Scheidler	DaimlerChrysler, Germany
Arne Skou	Aalborg University, Denmark
Yves Sorel	INRIA, France
Ulrich Virnich	Siemens, Germany
Birgit Vogel-Heuser	University of Wuppertal, Germany
Reinhard Wilhelm	Saarland University, Germany
Tim Willemse	Eindhoven Technical University, The Netherlands

Part II: Component-Based Design and Integration Platforms
Coordinator: Bengt Jonsson   University of Uppsala, Sweden

Ed Brinksma	University of Twente, The Netherlands
Geoff Coulson	Lancaster University, UK
Ivica Crnkovic	Mälardalen University, Sweden
Andy Evans	University of York, UK
Sébastien Gérard	CEA, France
Susanne Graf	Verimag Laboratory, France
Holger Hermanns	Saarland University, Germany
Jean-Marc Jézéquel	INRIA, France
Bengt Jonsson	University of Uppsala, Sweden
Noël Plouzeau	INRIA, France
Anders Ravn	Aalborg University, Denmark
Philippe Schnoebelen	LSV Laboratory, France
Francois Terrier	CEA, France
Angelika Votintseva	OFFIS, Germany

Part III: Adaptive Real-Time Systems for Quality of Service Management
Coordinator: Giorgio Buttazzo   University of Pavia, Italy

Luis Almeida	University of Aveiro, Portugal
Alejandro Alonso	Technical University of Madrid, Spain
Guillem Bernat	University of York, UK
Alan Burns	University of York, UK
Giorgio Buttazzo	University of Pavia, Italy
Antonio Casimiro	University of Lisbon, Portugal
Carlos Delgado Kloos	University Carlos III de Madrid, Spain
Johan Eker	Ericsson, Sweden
Joaquim Ferreira	Polytechnic Institute of Castelo Branco, Portugal
Gerhard Fohler	Mälardalen University, Sweden
José Alberto Fonseca	University of Aveiro, Portugal
Josep Fuertes	Technical University of Catalonia, Spain
Marisol Garcia Valls	University Carlos III de Madrid, Spain
Michael Gonzalez Harbour	University of Cantabria, Spain
Giuseppe Lipari	Scuola Superiore S. Anna of Pisa, Italy
Lucia Lo Bello	University of Catania, Italy
Evangelos Markatos	ICS Forth, Greece
Pau Marti	Technical University of Catalonia, Spain
Ernesto Martins	University of Aveiro, Portugal
Miguel de Miguel	Technical University of Madrid, Spain
Laurent Pautet	Telecom Paris, France
Paulo Pedreiras	University of Aveiro, Portugal
Julian Proenza	University of Balearic Islands, Spain
Juan Antonio de la Puente	Technical University of Madrid, Spain

Daniel Simon   INRIA, France
Liesbeth Steffens   Philips Research, The Netherlands
Paulo Verissimo   University of Lisbon, Portugal
Andy Wellings   University of York, UK
Sergio Yovine   Verimag Laboratory, France

Part IV: Execution Platforms
Coordinator: Lothar Thiele   ETHZ, Switzerland

Luca Benini   University of Bologna, Italy
Geert Deconinck   K.U.Leuven, Belgium
Petru Eles   Linköping University, Sweden
Rolf Ernst   Technical University of Braunschweig, Germany
Murali Jayapala   K.U.Leuven, Belgium
Jan Madsen   Technical University of Denmark, Denmark
Zebo Peng   Linköping University, Sweden
Marco Platzner   ETHZ, Switzerland
Paul Pop   Linköping University, Sweden
Lothar Thiele   ETHZ, Switzerland
Tom Vander Aa   K.U.Leuven, Belgium
Kashif Virk   Technical University of Denmark
Fabian Wolf   Volkswagen AG, Germany

Table of Contents

Part II: Component-Based Design and Integration Platforms

Part IV: Execution Platforms

1 Executive Overview on Hard Real-Time Development Environments

1.1 Motivation and Objectives

This is a roadmap for research in hard real-time systems. We intend it to be a roadmap for *research*, rather than for R&D in general. As such, it takes a longer view and has a more speculative approach than a typical industrial roadmap. Moreover, it shifts its focus from the topics traditionally referred to by hard real-time to topics that we believe carry the strongest research needs.

Traditionally, hard real-time includes task scheduling, real-time OS and executables, and "meeting deadlines" as the ultimate objective. These topics are indeed covered in part III of this document, but as the background for the OS needed to support Quality of Service (QoS) requirements in future real-time systems. The argument can be made that research on task scheduling should shift to adaptivity and QoS issues.

Is Research on Hard Real-Time Systems Still Needed?

We believe research on pure hard real-time systems is still needed, but that it now needs to focus on issues other than RTOS and deadlines. Hard real-time systems design has become part of a larger engineering activity: designing embedded systems for control or information processing. Said differently, Hard real-time systems are just part of intelligent devices that cannot work without being controlled and supervised by computers. Research on hard real-time must therefore shift from a single-technology research to the broader perspective of *systems design*.

Therefore, this Part I of the roadmap is about hard real-time and related issues arising in embedded systems design. It focuses on the entire design flow and the theories, methods, and tools needed to support it.

A number of theories are available: scientific engineering modelling for physical systems and their control, theories supporting verification and validation, theories supporting timing and other extra-functional analyses, theories supporting code generation, and theories supporting testing. Related tools and paradigms are also numerous and the resulting set of technologies is surprisingly rich. As we shall see, there are many subjects for difficult and relevant research in hard real-time systems design.

Who Should Read This Document?

Venture capitalists may prefer gather their data from other sources, better documented in terms of Return on Investment (RoI). However, we believe that anyone interested in future technological trends and emerging research issues in this area will benefit from this document. The reader should be warned that we have favoured depth and novelty of the information as opposed to comprehensive and balanced coverage. We have not included existing technologies that are relevant and would have found their place here. But we hope – and we do believe – that we did not miss what will be the important ideas for the next 10 years.

Artist FP5 Consortium: Embedded Systems Design, LNCS 3436, 1–9, 2005.
© Springer-Verlag Berlin Heidelberg 2005

How Should This Document Be Read?

Browsing the document can bring sources of inspiration and directions for research. The sections on advanced technologies are well documented, and provide a number of useful web links. A list of contributors is provided in the roman pages. We encourage the reader to address questions and comments to the contributors.

1.2   Essential Characteristics

There is no clear-cut definition for Embedded Systems. We will refer to Embedded Systems as electronic programmable sub-systems that are generally an integral part of a larger heterogeneous system. Embedded systems play an increasingly important role in the added value of advanced products that are designed and manufactured in Europe.

The following general statements are quoted from the Embedded Systems Roadmap 2002, published by the Technology Foundation of the Netherlands (STW), (http://www.artist-embedded.org/Intranet/Roadmaps/STW-roadmap.pdf).

> *The importance of embedded systems is undisputed. Their market size is about 100 times the desktop market. Hardly any new product reaches the market without embedded systems any more. The number of embedded systems in a product ranges from one to tens in consumer products and to hundreds in large professional systems. [...] This will grow at least one order of magnitude in this decade. [...]*
> *The strong increasing penetration of embedded systems in products and services creates huge opportunities for all kinds of enterprises and institutions. At the same time, the fast pace of penetration poses an immense threat for most of them. It concerns enterprises and institutions in such diverse areas as agriculture, health care, environment, road construction, security, mechanics, shipbuilding, medical appliances, language products, consumer electronics, etc.*

Because they are applied in a wide variety of industrial sectors, embedded systems require a large number of different skills, including principally: Skills for their design: application domain expertise, architectural design, application software, middleware, hardware design, fault tolerant design, safety techniques, verification and testing, just to name the most important areas. Embedded systems have been available for many years, yet there is a lack of a well-identified technical or academic discipline to support their design as they become more complex. The near absence of curricula in Europe dedicated to embedded systems is significant. There is indeed a strong need to establish the foundations of an engineering discipline that makes integration and multi-disciplinarily its flagship.

The increasing dependency on software is an essential characteristic of modern embedded systems and as such, it is the main focus of the Artist Roadmap.

Real-time embedded systems are of particular interest to the European community. Real-time embedded systems interact continuously with the environment and have constraints on the speed with which they react to the environment stimuli. Examples are power-train controllers for vehicles, embedded controllers for aircrafts, health monitoring systems and industrial plant controllers. Timing constraints introduce difficulties that make the design of embedded systems particularly challenging. We classify as hard real-time (HRT) the embedded systems that have tight timing constraints, i.e., they are difficult to achieve and they may not be violated, with respect to the capability of the hardware platforms used. HRT constraints challenges the way in which software is designed at its roots. Standard software development practices do not deal with physical properties of the system as a paradigm. We need a new system science where functionality is married to physical aspects. The roadmap presented here focuses on the design of distributed hard real-time embedded systems with particular emphasis on software.

We intend it to be a Roadmap for research, rather than for R&D in general and as such, it takes a longer view and has a more speculative approach than a typical industrial roadmap.

1.3   Role in Future Embedded Systems

The general trend for the future is that more systems and objects will contain computer-controlled components. The increasing role of embedded electronics in systems such as automobiles, trains, planes, power systems, military systems, consumer electronics, and other telecommunication systems is discussed in detail throughout this document. However, the set of applications that use embedded systems will continue to grow exponentially.

Emerging sensor systems technologies, often distributed and autonomous, will call for more embedded signal and information processing power. Most of it will consist in adaptive (not hard) real-time processing, however. Autonomy, adaptivity, communicating ability, and higher number crunching capability, will be the main issues. We do not expect issues of hard real-time to be central for such distributed, autonomous, sensor systems.

However, there is a trend to design more devices that will require an associated computer control system. Perhaps the most well-known such systems are aircraft: they simply could not fly without computer control, because they have inherently unstable flight modes. This trend is increasing significantly, as designing systems that would be naturally unstable opens up new possibilities and increases opportunities for better performance. Consumer electronics products including disk drives, or remote manipulators used in surgery also involves such technology. The joint design of devices with their closed-loop control will be a domain of increasing importance. Clearly, this is an area where hard real-time is central, since the computer system is responsible for the reflex capabilities of the system.

Perhaps the ultimate and most challenging domain for hard real-time in the future will be in Micro Electro-Mechanical Systems (MEMS). MEMS are considered to be a key technology for the future. MEMS devices may be able to explore blood vessels and find their path inside the human's body. As they tightly combine mechanics and electronics in both analogue and digital forms, closed loop control is an important part of their design. Therefore hard real-time aspects are also central. However, it is our opinion that most of the classical hard real-time technology will not be relevant to MEMS. Task scheduling will probably not be used. Instead, the direct mapping from specifications involving functional aspects as well as non-functional aspects related to power consumption, heat dissipation, and electro-mechanical characteristics will be likely to prevail. Methods, techniques, and tools jointly addressing these different facets of the design will be needed.

Fortunately, research efforts toward these directions are underway in both communities of EDA (with the hybrid extensions of RTL-level or system-level formalisms) and embedded control systems design (with the need to address functional specification, as well as architecture and software generation with power optimization).

1.4   Overall Challenges and Work Directions

The challenges described below point out that there is a need for a revolutionary approach to embedded software design.

Increasing Complexity of the Application Space

Overview
In the (recent) past, an embedded system would be either small or simple, or the composition of almost non-interacting imported and assembled components. The trend is that the number and complexity of functions will increase drastically. Increasing complexity is making the present design methodologies rapidly obsolete. Productivity of the order of six (or less!) lines of embedded code per day per person is common in HRT embedded systems. If we do not have a breakthrough in design methodology and tools, the inefficiency of the embedded software development process will prevent novel technology to enter the market in time. The cost of developing a new plane (of the order of several billions of Euros) is about ½ related to embedded software and electronics subsystems.

Work Directions
Research is needed to raise the levels of abstraction at which a design is entered. There is almost no hope of improving productivity substantially without this step since productivity problems originate from a number of difficulties, including verification and testing. For embedded controllers, the name of the game is to keep the control requirements orthogonal with respect to implementation. Then the strategic aspect of design is the development of control algorithms.

For low-level continuous systems or components, a rich body of theory and tools has been developed for control design. This means that control laws can be automatically synthesized from higher levels specifications related to the bandwidth of the system for control, its stability margin and its robustness margin (how much the real system is expected to deviate from the model used to synthesize control). Although mainly developed for linear systems, these techniques have been and are successfully used for nonlinear systems, by using robust control design techniques. Still, some "truly" nonlinear systems require ad-hoc designs for which existing tools provide strong assistance, not synthesis. The situation is not satisfactory for the control of more complex subsystems involving several modes of operation and switching policies between them, i.e., hybrid systems. While modellers such as Simulink/Stateflow allow for the description of such subsystems and their simulation, no synthesis technique is available yet.

From the algorithm design to implementation, we need to develop a suite of automatic synthesis tools where the implementation process is fast and at the same time highly optimized. Today, automatic code generation is available only for small parts of the design flow, mostly for embedded code generation for single components. Furthermore, even when available, this technique is not widely used in practice. Research is needed to enlarge the target of code generation to distributed architectures. Solving this problem requires the development of specification languages based on rigorous semantics, which are accepted in both the control and the software engineering communities, which unambiguously represent the behaviour of the embedded system. The semantics of Matlab/Simulink descriptions is not formally defined: the behaviour of a system is determined by the execution of the simulators! In addition, we need to develop models and methods to assess whether the performance of the final implementation meets the constraints.

Interaction with the Physical World

Overview
Hard real-time embedded systems are mostly controllers, i.e., they act on physical plants to make them behave according to a prescribed reference. This is the case for example, for industrial system control, power-train control, flight control, and environment control. The interaction with physical plants is the source of the hard real-time constraints. The interaction with the physical world also comes from the implementation side of HRT systems: the physical parameters of the implementation, e.g., timing, power, and size, are essential for fulfilling performance and cost requirements. This is what makes writing embedded software a substantially different task than "standard" software.

Work Directions
Apart from the increase in complexity, the needs for the design of embedded systems have broadened to encompass not only the functional aspects of systems, but also to capture and analyze the extra-functional ones, such as timing and energy consumption. Often the physical parameters are subject to variation. Hence, there is a link between such extra-functional aspects of systems and hybrid systems and stochastic systems that needs to be explored. The notion of time has played a fundamental role in research recently both at abstract levels and at the implementation level. Timing issues have been tackled at the abstract level introducing synchronous abstractions (e.g., the ones incorporated into synchronous languages and time-triggered protocols and architectures) but there is a growing interest in studying with the same mathematical rigor asynchronous paradigms of various sorts. These approaches tend to establish a formal relation between different levels of abstraction so that certain properties at lower levels are guaranteed to hold. More research will be needed to offer a framework where coordination policies can be traded-off and chosen with a theoretical underpinning.

However, while it is possible to achieve a certain degree of separation of concerns using theoretical approaches, the selection of implementation architecture (e.g., the number and type of processing elements, the communication mechanisms) versus another must be guided by some quantitative measure of performances that have to be abstracted at the various steps of the design. In this respect, implementation-aware control algorithms must be researched carefully. In addition, estimation and profiling models have to be derived and the appropriate tools to analyze the quality of the implementation architecture have to be further developed to allow evaluation that is solid and robust with respect to the obvious simplifications needed to obtain estimation and profiling models.

Correct deployment of designs over distributed real-time architectures involves a combination of theories and viewpoints. Correct deployment of discrete systems (say, automata or a combination of these) is feasible or will be feasible in the near future, by using recent or ongoing advances in formal methods. But how continuous control designs and even worse hybrid systems are perturbed when distributed deployment is performed is an open issue for research – unless very strict architectures such as TTA (Time Triggered) are used.

Safety-Critical Nature of Designs

Overview
Many embedded controllers operate on systems that may cause severe damages to people and property if they malfunction, i.e., they are safety critical. Clearly, the emergence of X-by-wire technologies in the transportation industry will increase their number and importance significantly. Safety has a dramatic impact on the design processes and techniques used. Because of safety concerns, the embedded systems have to have zero defects. Ideally, the design methodology should guarantee correct-by-construction implementations of a complete specification. Complete means that no constraint is left out and that the full functionality is considered. Today, some safety critical systems, e.g., embedded systems for military applications and for avionic, have to go through certification. Certification is a very expensive proposition: it requires very extensive testing, and a design and product development process that satisfy a set of tight rules on the way the development work is organized. There is, however, no guarantee that certified software is error free. A related issue is fault diagnosis and fault tolerance. When safety critical systems fail to function properly, there must be a way of tracing what went wrong (fault diagnosis) and to react accordingly, so that the system may continue to work through the fault albeit in a degraded mode (fault tolerance).

Work Directions: Diagnosis
The integration of software from different vendors into a single component demands a new approach towards fault containment, error containment and diagnosis. Hard real-time aspects raise specific problems, but offers in turn special means to fix these. Quick detection of a fault can be critical. Transient faults may reveal malfunctioning that can become fatal. Fault effect propagation requires on-line sophisticated filtering of alarms. Proper instrumentation, fault-tolerant architecture, and mechanisms for on-line probing of the system, are needed to account for these special issues. Such mechanisms can benefit in turn, from using hard real-time as an advantage for several purposes, including time as a basis for fault isolation and fault containment, and fault detection with bounded delay reaction time.

Work Directions: Certification
The trend is to move from process-based certification to process-and-tool-based certification. This calls for new trustable tools and methods. To reduce the cost of certification, it would be a great advantage if the certification can proceed in a modular fashion, i.e., if certification arguments that have been developed for a particular subsystem can be used in a modular fashion. Modular certification depends very much on the partitioning properties provided by the distributed architecture, which in turn can take advantage of the hard real-time nature of the system. So-called formal methods are an essential enabling factor in support of certification; they need to scale up to much more complex designs.

Work Directions: Dependability
Safety critical systems must achieve a dependability (a commonly used value is 1 failure in $10^{\wedge 9}$ hours) which is better than the dependability of any of its constituting components. Such systems require a safety case that must be based on a combination of experimental evidence and analytical modelling. In ultra-dependable systems even a very small correlation of failures of the replicated units can have a significant impact of the overall dependability. New approaches are needed to isolate component failures and to eliminate even very low probability error propagation. In doing this, real-time should be taken as an advantage, not as a problem.

Work Directions: Formal Methods
By formal methods, we mean fundamental techniques for analysis, validation, composition, or transformation of systems or software, in a provably sound way. Formal methods are enabling technologies for exploring specifications and models, for validating designs against requirements, for generating code, for deploying designs on architectures, and are a support for the certification of designs or tools. Formal methods include numerous technologies such as model checking, automatic test generation, proofs, automatic code generation from high level specifications, static program analysis, timing analysis, code validation, theorem proving, and more; the main ones are detailed hereafter in this document. No safety critical design will be possible in the future without a significant use of formal methods. New domains have been included during the last decade, in the scope of formal verification and validation. This includes in particular aspects of timing and hybrid systems– i.e., the mixing of discrete and continuous features.

Formal methods have scaled up drastically in the last decade, and this process is going to continue even faster. In this respect, automatic code generation from high level specifications now allows to handle quite large components or subsystems. Being more complex in nature, formal validation or analysis techniques have quite often stayed behind the needs of real life designs. Still, skilled engineers managed to use them by properly phrasing or decomposing their validation or analysis problems into tractable parts. Nevertheless, it is a constant and stringent need that formal methods and tools scale up to follow the increasing complexity of designs.

By far the most accepted means for analyzing hard real-time systems is by using automated verification techniques such as model-checking. However, the applicability of such techniques is restricted due to inherent theoretical limitations. To further improve the state of practice, existing techniques (such as model checking and symbolic reasoning) should be combined and extended to yield a common methodology.

Europe has had a leading position in this area, both for specification and programming tools, for verification and validation tools, and for provably safe distributed architectures. This rich and solid background needs to be further developed to scale up properly, and to adjust to new design methodologies, such as the ones suggested in this document.

Complexity of Design Flows and Supply Chains

Overview
Supply chains for electronic systems are changing rapidly. System companies are retrenching in core competencies that favour market access and sales channels versus product development and implementation. The electronics industry is increasingly disaggregating: new opportunities are now opening up for subsystem and component suppliers. These dynamics are stressing the interfaces among the supply chain players. Several quality problems and time-to-market delays can be traced to specification and system integration difficulties. Among the most challenging supply chains to support are the automotive and avionics chain.

Work Directions
The complexity of supply chains has several consequences. Firstly, it calls for a design approach at the level of each component (systematically investigated by the "components" action roadmap), offering means to specify components to suppliers and facilitate their subsequent integration. Secondly, the strategy of systems integrators for preserving added value will put virtual prototyping and platform-based design in the fore (see the landscape on automobile, in this document).

Research performed over the last decade has shown that notations and formalisms can be developed, that are at the same time familiar to the engineer, and still based on a solid mathematical basis – examples of such are the synchronous languages with their associated GUI. Such techniques have naturally offered specification tools associated with formal validation methods, and even certifiable code generation. Although large, the range of applicability of such results still does not encompass the whole design flow for hard real-time. The scope needs to be enlarged to cover physical systems modellers and scientific engineering tools, as well as more general system modelling techniques such as UML.

It is the essence of embedded systems design that diverse tools based on different paradigms coexist within the overall design flow. This situation will continue.

Integrating these tools has become a major concern. Scientific engineering tools and physical systems modellers, on the one hand, and formal verification, code generation over distributed architectures on the other hand, will continue to rely on different underlying paradigms. Should UML establish itself as an overall framework for the entire design process, the issue would still remain in the form of the coherence among the multi-faceted semantics supporting the different views and profiles. Thus paradigm integration emerges as the needed mathematical foundation to support the semantic integration of different tools and frameworks.

Research must be done on open semantics, to support smooth transitions between different technologies along the design flow. Paradigm integration emerges as the necessary mathematical foundation to support the semantic integration of different tools and frameworks. Paradigm integration is not the exercise of embodying different paradigms into a "most general" one, since this would require developing tools to handle this "most general" framework, something not possible due to complexity issues. The objective is rather to develop approaches that will upgrade existing tools with semantic adaptors toward tools supported by other paradigms.

1.5   Document Structure

The rest of the document is organized as follows.

Section 2 briefly reviews existing development practices, and introduces the emerging platform-based approach.

Section 3 analyses the landscape by reporting on current design practices. We have chosen to focus on selected industrial sectors, which we believe will drive the evolution of design practices: automobile, aeronautics, mobile telecommunications, and automation. For each sector, we have tried to be as specific as possible, sometimes by highlighting the design aspects of particular systems for which hard real-time is an important factor. We believe this section conveys a rich body of information. It significantly influenced the findings and recommendations.

Sections 4 – 8 review the building blocks and technologies that are available to support the design process. We review established technologies. But we have also decided to include less mature building blocks, since we believe this is the duty of an academic roadmap on research. Again, we warn the reader that our list may not be exhaustive, but we have done our best at reporting the most striking technologies available. For each building block, we give a description, its rough position in the design flow, pointers to tools; then – and most importantly – we formulate misses, needs, and detailed recommendations for research.

Section 9 presents the results from recent projects covering methodology issues. Our selection is obviously biased: while we are pretty convinced that the projects we have selected provide added value, we have certainly omitted other projects that could have been interesting.

2   Hard Real-Time System Development

2.1   Brief Discussion of Current Practice: The V-Shaped Lifecycle

The traditional hard real-time embedded system development process follows the standard V-shaped lifecycle, shown below in its simplest format.

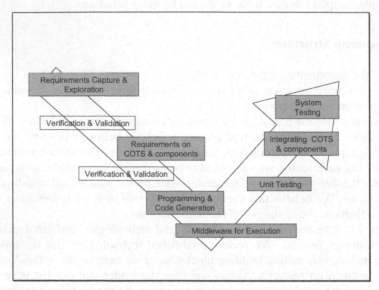

Figure 2.1. The traditional V-shaped lifecycle

Each phase can be further detailed or refined into several steps. The way the V-cycle is detailed and implemented varies significantly within the different between teams in embedded systems.

Key points are the following:

- Each phase is now supported by a well-defined methodology and supported by advanced tools with (mostly) well-accepted notations. Some of these tools and technologies are reviewed in later sections.
- Even today, a very small amount of advanced Verification and Validation (V&V) is performed. By advanced, we mean supported by formal methods or semantically-sound model checking or other similar verification techniques. Today, V&V mainly amounts to code inspection, sometimes assisted by tools, but without the added value of formal technologies. Of course, the EDA sector is far more advanced in the use of novel V&V technologies.
- The transition between the different stages requires careful manual inspection and cross-checking, and this is frequently error-prone. This is made even worse by the

Artist FP5 Consortium: Embedded Systems Design, LNCS 3436, 10–14, 2005.
© Springer-Verlag Berlin Heidelberg 2005

diverse nature of the skills, cultural backgrounds, and associated notations and tools in use by the different teams that participate in the overall design. For example, application domain engineers need to cooperate with software developers and electronics designers. They all use different tools based on different paradigms.

This situation has some important consequences. The design of unitary devices or small embedded systems is today reasonably well instrumented and does not require a strong investment from the research community. In contrast, designing complex systems where embedded computing plays an important part is still a formidable challenge. Dealing with the integration of components as well as the unavoidable heterogeneity resulting from a multidisciplinary design team requires heavy investment in research. Elements and guidelines for this are provided in the next sections.

2.2   An Emerging Approach: Platform-Based Design

In this section we present the design methodology that we like to advocate, namely: *platform-based design*. In its ultimate form that we discuss here, it originates and benefits from several sources. First and foremost, platform-based design is already in use in EDA industry. It has been promoted and advocated in the embedded systems industry, by A. Sangiovanni-Vincentelli (see references below). To put this design methodology in perspective with respect to research performed in the last years, we have collected in section 9 some projects that addressed this issue.

The reader can also refer to the MOBIES (http://www.rl.af.mil/tech/programs/ MoBIES/) project, not discussed here – Model Based Integration of Embedded Software. MOBIES is a DARPA-funded US project on application-independent methods and design tools for embedded systems.

The T-Lifecycle

The metaphor of the "V" was adequate to describe past and current practice, as it scans the design process, from highest levels down to lowest ones, and backward up to integration. Moves in the lifecycle have consisted and will consist in automating some of the steps of the V. Thus we feel that the V-metaphor is no longer adequate and we like to re-discuss it.

The study of the Setta and SafeAir projects in section 9 reveals that engineers have placed efforts in shifting the focus of the designer at higher levels of the design flow, moving towards what we call a *T-shaped* lifecycle:

- In SafeAir, the Y-cycle has been proposed as a metaphor: regard the Y as a smaller v put on top of the vertical bar of the Y; the v represents the focus on higher level phases, and the vertical bar indicates (certified) automatic code generation and automatic code validation.
- Setta recommends a VVV-cycle (or 3V-cycle), in which the first V corresponds to control engineering task with its rapid prototyping, the second V represents systems rapid prototyping, and the third V addresses system development for the final target hardware. As seen in the Fig.2 of Setta, information is extracted from elements involved at second and third V's, for feeding back as abstract parameters (e.g., related to timing) to the virtual exploration performed in the first V.

Thus the SafeAir project introduces the concept of mapping, whereas the Setta project introduces the concept of platform for virtual exploration, in which (some abstraction of) the execution infrastructure is reflected at higher levels and earlier phases of the design flow in support of the exploration.

We feel that this vision should be pushed further, by allowing for a platform-based, multi-level virtual exploration. There is no reason to require that all parts of the system be explored simultaneously with the same level of granularity. For example, when specifying a subsystem to be provided by a supplier, it is desirable to detail the considered subsystem while keeping the other subsystems it interacts with at more abstract levels. Unfortunately, neither the V, nor the 3V, nor the Y, supports the multi-level aspect as a metaphor.

The concept of the "T"-shaped lifecycle better reflects this. The horizontal bar of the T refers to the tool assisted exploration of the design space, as described below. The vertical bar of the T refers to the automatic mapping of the selected design down to the execution platform.

Platform-Based Methodology

The central principle of this methodology [San02] is a paradigm shift in design, verification, and test methodology, which has emerged recently.

- The platform-based design paradigm is a meet-in-the-middle approach. It leverages the power of top-down methods and the efficiency of bottom-up styles. The design process is viewed as a stepwise refinement of a specification into a lower level abstraction chosen from a (restricted) library of available components. Components are "computational" blocks and interconnect. This library is a platform. In this view, a platform is a family of designs and not a single design. A platform defines the design space that can be explored. Once a particular collection of components of the platform is selected, we obtain a platform instance. The choice of the platform instance and the mapping of the components of the specification into the components of the platform instance represent the top-down process. In this process, constraints that accompany the specification are mapped into constraints on the components of the platform instance. Mapping often involves budgeting, since a global constraint may have to be distributed over a set of components.
- The stepwise refinement continues by defining the selected platform instance as a specification and using a lower level platform to march towards implementation. Whenever a component is fully instantiated the stepwise refinement stops since we have an implementation for that component.
- When selecting a platform instance and mapping constraints using budgeting, it is important to guide the selection with parameters that summarize the characteristics of the components of the platform. Delay, power consumption, size and cost are examples of such parameters. When selecting a platform instance it is important to be able to evaluate quickly and with the appropriate accuracy what the performance of the design will be. The selection of the parameters to use for guiding the platform instance selection is one of the critical parts of platform-based design.
- The component selection process and the verification of the consistency between the behaviour of the specification and the one of the platform instance can be car-

ried out automatically if a common semantic domain is found where the selection process can be seen as a covering problem. The concepts of platform-based design can be used to describe the *entire* design process from specification to algorithms, from architecture selection to code generation and hardware design even when the design style chosen is ASIC. The framework is the same. The platforms are different. The number and the location of the platforms in the design abstractions, the number and the type of components that constitute a platform, the choice of parameters to represent the components are critical aspects of the method.

- Platforms form a stack, from design specification to implementation. There are platforms that demark boundaries that are critical in the electronics supply chain: these articulation points warrant particular attention. We call an architecture platform the articulation point between system architecture and micro-architecture. Micro-architecture can be seen as a platform whose components are architectural elements such as microprocessors, memories, interfaces. This articulation point is where the application engineer maps his/her design into a "physical" support. To find the common semantic domain we need to abstract these components via an operating system, device drivers and communication mechanism. In this domain the hardware components are seen as supporting the execution of the behaviour of the specification. Another essential platform is the one that corresponds to the layer that separates design from manufacturing.

The essence of the method is captured in the figure below where the articulation point shown as the vertex of the two triangles represents the common semantic domain. In particular, the figure focuses on the most important level of abstraction for our discussion: the separation between application and implementation platform. The articulation point is effective in decoupling the design of application versus the selection of architecture and the successive refinements into an implementation. It shows that if we are given a system platform then several applications can be mapped into it and the parameters obtained by the design space export can be used to estimate the performance of the application onto the platform of choice. By the same token, if the application space is known, then the "platform instance" could be optimized according to the needs of the application space.

Platform-based methodology sets some significant challenges:

- Characterizing complex components such as communication busses or sophisticated microprocessors and DSPs, in terms of their architectural behaviour and physical parameters (WCET, power consumption, heat dissipation...).
- Defining a common semantic domain where the mapping processes can be represented formally.
- Developing a framework where these principles could be effectively used. This implies also populating the framework with synthesis, formal verification and simulation tools.
- The platform-based design principles at the top-most level of abstraction call for a semantic platform where models of computation could be integrated and chosen as the first refinement step towards the final implementation. This implies that research needs to be carried out in novel terms with respect to the most popular design methods that are based on well-known models of computation and their composition.

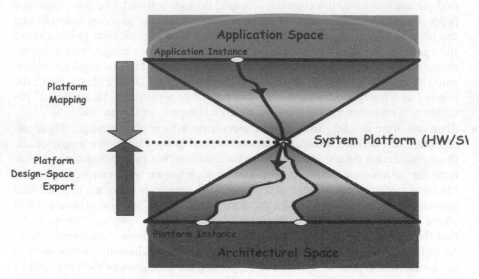

- The platform-based design approach can serve as an integration back-bone for particular design flows, tools and methodologies that are particularly suited for specific application domains.

References

[San02]   A. Sangiovanni-Vincentelli, Defining Platform-based Design, EEDesign, March 2002.

3   Current Design Practice and Needs in Selected Industrial Sectors

3.1   Automotive Systems

Industrial Landscape

The overall automotive industry structure is different in the US versus Europe and Japan that share some similarity. In the US, subsystems manufacturers are the results of spin-offs from GM (Delphi) and Ford (Visteon) and cannot be considered as independent as the European subsystem auto makers. In addition, Ford and Gm have hardly invested in the recent past to improve substantially their design methods. It is common belief, and we concur with this assessment, that the European automotive industry is the most advanced in terms of quality and design approaches.

Today, European car manufacturers provide specifications to subsystem suppliers, such as Bosch, Siemens and Magneti-Marelli, who design software and hardware subsystems that may include mechanical parts (e.g. injectors and throttle bodies) [1]. These subsystems are based on Integrated Circuits (IC) that are procured from the main IC suppliers such as Motorola, TI, Hitachi and ST and on Intellectual Property (IP) that come from a variety of sources: for example, software companies, such as WindRiver and ETAS. In general, volumes are large, and cost is a major driving force. Once the subsystems are provided back to the car manufacturers, they have to be integrated on the car and then the overall system must be tested. If the car manufacturer detects errors during the extensive testing period, which includes driving under extreme conditions, a chain of engineering changes is initiated that may (and it often does!) cause major delays in the design. The problems are today due for the most part to software errors, to incorrect understanding of the specifications and unpredictable side effects when the subsystems are interconnected. The loop is particularly painful since testing is done when the car is almost ready for its launch on the market.

Car manufacturers increasingly realize the importance of electronics in their business: Daimler-Chrysler stated that more than 90% of innovation (and hence value added!) in a car will be in electronics. BMW has indicated than more than 30% of the cost of manufacturing a car resides in the electronic components. There is a trend in the car manufacturing industry to bring more electronics competence in-house to capture added value that today is going to subsystem suppliers. The strategy calls for standards in the software and hardware domains that will allow plug-and-play of subsystems thus reducing the strategic importance of any single subsystem supplier. The OSEK [2] operating system requirements are an example of this policy. However, it is clear that without an overall understanding of the interplay of the subsystems and of the difficulties encountered in integrating very complex parts, system integration is increasingly becoming a nightmare. In addition, the subsystem suppliers are trying to enlarge the perimeter of their competence to capture more added value.

Artist FP5 Consortium: Embedded Systems Design, LNCS 3436, 15–38, 2005.
© Springer-Verlag Berlin Heidelberg 2005

Hard Real-Time Context

Today's car electronics systems can be classified into the following categories [1]:

- Infotainment/Telematics. Electronic subsystems devoted to information processing, communication with outside world and entertainment [22]. The main features
  are wide-band, adaptive real-time (ART) constraints, non-critical;
- Power train/Chassis. Main features are hard real-time constraints, safety critical,
  fault tolerant, low band (e.g. engine, brakes, steering), with subsystems being isolated from one another mostly for historical reasons;
- Cabin. Main features are real-time and non-critical (e.g., power windows, air conditioning).

We focus on the second category of applications since it has hard real-time characteristics.

Today's car real-time and safety-critical electronics systems are implemented over
distributed architectures that generally include:

- Several Electronic Control Units (ECU's) communicating via:
- One or more (for fault tolerant systems) networked broadcast buses controlled by
  communication protocols (e.g. CAN [3], TTP [5], LIN [4], and Flex Ray [6])

In turn, each ECU includes:

- Application and diagnostic software;
- System software (e.g., RTOS and Communication layers);
- One or more micro-controllers with local memories and communication control-
  ler(s) with one or multiple channels to support redundancy for fault tolerant sys-
  tems and complex bus architectures such as constellations and star couplers;
- (Optional) Dual ported RAM's for:
  - Communications between bus controllers and micro-controllers within the
    same ECU.
  - Communications between CPU's within the same ECU.

Automotive applications (e.g. X-By-Wire for steering and braking) have introduced a
new design dimension – the distributed nature of the system – that provides additional
complexities yet potentials for optimizations such as the reduction of the number of
needed ECUs, fewer mechanical parts, optimal performance, new functionalities
(including safety features). In fact, better use of each ECU may potentially reduce the
number of ECU's in the distributed architecture. Notice that the re-distribution is not
always possible since in some applications the software is tied to a specific ECU

In a nutshell, the problem, as described, for example, in [7], [8], consists of distributing a pool of functions over the target architecture with a goal of satisfying the requirements in terms of cost, safety, and real-time. Because of the distributed nature of
these applications, the communication protocol needs also to be accurately modelled.
A by-product of this methodology is that designers can experiment with new protocol
configurations.

State of the Practice

Figure 3.1 below illustrates the typical design flow for distributed systems of a car manufacturer (source BMW). The manufacturer is responsible for the overall functionality whereas the Tier 1 suppliers deliver the control algorithms and the hardware. This flow applies to BMW in particular.

In particular, the OEMs define the electrical architecture of the vehicle and the tasks that each component of the architecture must carry out. The architecture is influenced by the functionality that the OEMs want to offer the market and the availability of subsystems. The requirements for the subsystems are then discussed with Tier 1 suppliers who are responsible for delivering the entire subsystem consisting of hardware and software parts at the agreed price and performance. Often, OEMs review design practices of the suppliers, recommend (or even impose) the use of particular components of the subsystem e.g., microprocessors and real-time operating systems, and may require to include their own software modules in the solution. The Tier 1 suppliers not only deal with the electronic part of the component but deliver also mechanical components such as injectors. The integration of the subsystems is carried out at the physical level with standard communication subsystems such as CAN busses and at the software level with communication primitives offered by OSEK compliant operating systems. It is in this phase that problems may arise. Integration is becoming a nightmare especially when faulty behaviour is hard to isolate. This causes disputes with suppliers and obviously costly delays and even recalls.

Tier 1 suppliers themselves use other suppliers to deliver their products. Most of the suppliers rely upon standard parts for the computing part of their products while they design ASICs and custom chips for the power and analogue components. IC suppliers work in close collaboration with Tier 1 suppliers to define new computing

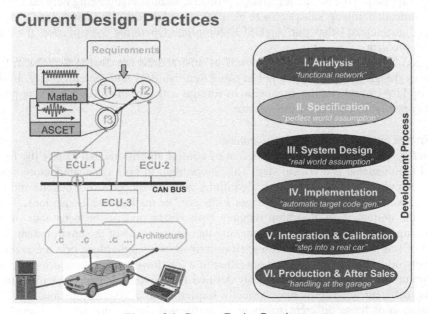

Figure 3.1. Current Design Practices

platforms and to make minor modifications to their products. Recently, Tier 1 suppliers requested Tier 2 suppliers to provide software layers (device drivers and BIOS) that tend to isolate the hardware details of peripheral devices so that application programmers can develop their software in re-usable fashion.

I. Analysis

The development process starts with the analysis phase, where a functional network (a functional network is the overall system behaviour) is developed, and continues with the specification phase, where algorithms for each of the functional components are defined. The system design phase determines the distribution of the functionality onto an architectural network. In the next phase, a composition of functional components is implemented onto the target hardware and finally the system is calibrated in the car. The design process follows the classical "V" diagram.

II. Specification

The system functionality is specified by the car manufacturer based on an overall analysis of the car performance and features. This functionality is decomposed into subsystem specifications that are passed to Tier 1 suppliers. The decomposition is performed by expert designers based on their experience and sometimes on prototypes (lab cars). The specifications are usually given in an informal fashion via natural language in a contract. The Tier 1 suppliers analyze the specifications and negotiate the terms of the contract. The car manufacturer specifications may include also implementation requirements and not only functional specifications, thus restricting the design space for Tier 1 suppliers (for example, at times the micro-controllers to use are listed in the contract). In addition, there is a growing trend for the car manufacturers to require the use of internally developed software instead of relying fully on the Tier 1 suppliers. To ease the integration problem, standards are being defined for the communication among subsystems (e.g., TTP and Flex Ray) that have clean semantics and guaranteed behaviour. An OSEK-compliant Operating System eases the integration problem.

Specifications given at different levels of abstractions are always a problem if a rigorous design methodology is not in place that can deal with heterogeneity. In the case of Tier 1 suppliers, the integration of foreign software modules is a severe problem especially for hard real-time systems.

III. System Design Algorithm Development

For safety-critical applications, the design of control algorithms that satisfy the functional requirements is a critical step. This is common to both car manufacturers and Tier 1 suppliers. In the recent past, algorithms were developed using pencils and paper and were described using languages such as C or mathematical equations. Typically, the design of an algorithm requires both abstraction of the behaviour of the remaining part of the system, and modelling the relevant part of the environment. The result of this phase is the algorithm itself described as a single block or a hierarchical sub-network. This phase is carried out either in a top down fashion (authoring) or in a bottom-up fashion (usage of previously defined IP). Given the same system requirements, different algorithms may correctly implement the system functionality. The exploration of these different solutions is performed during this phase. There is a growing trend to utilize functional design tools such as the Mathworks tool set (e.g., Matlab and Simulink [11]) to capture the algorithms and to perform simulation on a mathematical model of the plant to control.

IV. Implementation and Software Design
The algorithms are implemented on a selected architecture as software modules or hardware components. Architecture selection is often an ad hoc process based on experience and extrapolation of present products. The selection of the integrated circuits that compose an ECU is the result of a limited search among the IC providers that are active in the automotive space and often are based on commercial relations among companies more than on a technical assessment of performance/price ratio. The architecture may be adjusted during the design phase if it has problems meeting the constraints. New software needed for novel features is "grown" over existing modules to limit the risks of malfunctioning. Extensive experimentation on rapid prototyping systems or on actual cars is the preferred way to verify the correctness of the system.

Software architectures are often old fashioned and are difficult not to say impossible to port from one platform to another. The software is not cleanly partitioned into application code, communication, design drivers, and BIOS. Given the exponentially growing complexity of the features to be implemented in software, the problem of software design is becoming a serious obstacle to the development of new cars.

The most advanced Tier 1 suppliers have restructured their code so that porting becomes affordable, thus opening up new possibilities for cost reduction and performance improvement. In addition, automatic code generation from algorithmic specifications given in structured form using capture tools such as Simulink, State Charts, and ASCET [13], is becoming a reality. In this domain, several companies offer this kind of tools.

However, automatic code generation eases the problem of designing software that represents correctly a given functionality but it does not solve the timing problem. The timing aspects of the code depend on the definition of the tasks to be handled by the RTOS, the scheduling policy used and by the performance of the ECU. A number of companies and tools offers scheduling analysis. The objective of this phase is to analyze the different scheduling policies (for example cooperative and pre-emptive vs. pre-emptive only) in order to assess the near-to-optimal software architecture. The scheduling policy analysis can be carried out off-line and statically, for example via Rate Monotonic Analysis, or dynamically and on-line via interactive simulations. In this phase, the analysis relies on time budgets (task periodicity, task execution times, etc.) provided by the user.

V. Integration and Calibration
Once the Tier 1 suppliers deliver their subsystems, the car manufacturer integrates them in the car. This step is a most difficult one in absence of tools that help analyzing the behaviour and the performance of the subsystems before a prototype of the car is available.

Tools in this domain are mainly internal tools. For example, in the BMW flow, the design data are exported to a proprietary database. For example, BMW has adopted Boardnet – a customization of the Oracle database. The proprietary database data are then used to configure the downstream tools for emulation/measurement of the communication protocols (for example a TTP-Cluster Prototype board). There is a trend towards the use of communication structures that guarantee interaction patters that can be verified for correctness and do not have unexpected behaviour. TTP and Flex Ray are two approaches to this problem. However, while this approach is certainly a welcome step to improve the integration problems, it is not a panacea. The Autosar consortium has been recently founded to alleviate the integration problems by specifying appropriate standards for interfaces among different components. The aim is allowing the OEMs to decouple the tie between hardware and software that Tier 1 suppliers impose on their products making it easier to compose modules and to make sure that the best architecture for the vehicle is selected. Concerns are rampant in the automotive industry worldwide in view of recent recalls due to electrical problems in some high visibility vehicles.

In calibration, a sub-set (calibration set) of the control and regulation parameters (characteristic values, curves, maps) of the behaviour IP's (typically control algorithms) is tuned to obtain the required performance of the controlled system. This phase pertains also to the tuning of the parameters of the overall system functionality. The designer defines the calibration set selecting the tuneable parameters during the export phase. Calibration is performed on testing test-cells and on test-tracks and is a very expensive process. Calibration engineers today are more numerous that designers, a symptom of the state of the design methodology in use today. Expensive tools are available to facilitate calibration from companies such as ETAS and dSpace.

The calibration effort is large in OEMs and Tier 1 suppliers alike. This activity is heuristic and can benefit greatly from a more structured approach. For example, the parameters to set are many and they are not independent from each other. Often, calibrating a parameter to fix a problem ends up causing another problem to show up. It will be most desirable to select a set of parameters and a calibration sequence that guarantee that once a problem is corrected, it will stay that way throughout the operation. In addition, models used in today systems are based on table look-up resulting in a parameter per point in the tables. Hence, there is a strong correlation between design choices and calibration efforts. Unfortunately, because of the heuristic nature of the calibration process, it is indeed very difficult to change the methodology and go towards a more rigorous process since any change will result in the need of re-training a set of artisans of the trade.

Integration and calibration is a phase where engineers and technicians need an extensive re-training and novel skills are badly needed. We see a strong correlation between this situation and the training and education mission of the ARTIST2 Network of Excellence (http:/www.artist-embedded.org/FP6/).

Challenges and Work Directions

This design flow poses several problems [1]:

- Lack of continuity: e.g. there exists a big gap between the requirement analysis and the definition of the functional network, and between the software development phase and the overall architecture net-list definition.
- Long turnaround time: the validation of the solution can be addressed only on the car or (at best) with some physical prototyping hardware – very late in the design

cycle; the software development can only start once a hardware prototype is available and it is addressed on a single ECU.

- Suboptimal and overly conservative solutions: since the flow supports a "per-ECU" design style the design exploration concerns to exploring different scheduling policies and not to the exploration of the overall distributed system including the communication protocols. Several protocols have been introduced in the past such as CAN, TTP, LIN, and will be introduced in the future such as FlexRay], with the goal of providing more dependable and fault tolerant networks enabling the step towards X-by-Wire technologies.

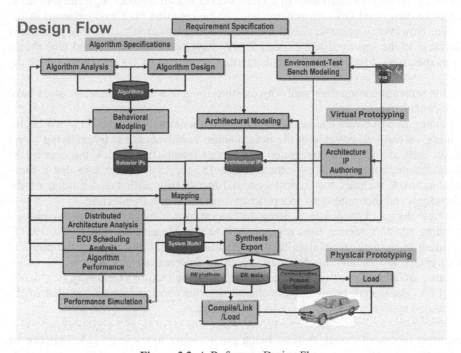

Figure 3.2. A Reference Design Flow

Because of the above issues, the development and production costs are obviously affected. As stated in [9],

Vehicle manufacturers traditionally focus on production cost rather than on development cost – the sensors and the actuators, along with the bare ECU, represent almost the entire cost for electronics in the car. However, although software does not have a "production" cost, it is not for free! The software development costs are skyrocketing: today, they are about twice as much as the development costs for hardware.

This investigation is only possible by addressing the integration step at the virtual level, and not on the car, as it is presently done. Indeed, the entire automotive industry is trying to move tests from cars to labs, where real conditions can be emulated or simulated at a much lower cost. The cost for setting up an experiment on a car is about $120-$500 per hour. The time needed to set it up is about 1 hour. The number of tests that can be performed every day is 2.

The use of a virtual environment rather than prototyping hardware for designing and testing can significantly reduce development and production costs. If designers were able to simulate the distributed application on their host workstations rather than in a test track, redundancy and fail-safe system tests could be repeated after every change in the design. Flexibility is another advantage: derivative designs (variants) can be supported more easily – there is no need to wait for the next hardware prototype to run the application software. Hence, car manufacturer goals, such as better time-to-market and reduction of development and component costs can be achieved. As BMW management pointed out:

One of the focuses and values of a system-level design methodology and tool set is that redundancy and fail-safe system tests can be repeated after every change in the design. However, a valuable use of any methodology and tool set is only possible if interfaces to the approved and existing BMW development methods and tool chains (from specifying functionality to implementing it onto an ECU) are supported by the flow.

This sentence summarizes well why existing tools that are *de-facto* standards have to be considered.

Finding design errors and near-to-optimal functional networks and HW/SW architectures, as early as possible in the design stage is only possible by applying novel design methodologies and integrated tool environments that deploy the concept of virtual integration platforms (see for example [8, 14, 15]). Please note that a functional network includes the overall system functionality with the definition of the subsystems and their interfaces independent from the target architecture.

A new design methodology is being developed by a number of automotive players including BMW, Cadence, Etas, dSpace, PARADES, Magneti-Marelli, [1, 10, 19, 15] including three main steps: algorithm specification, virtual prototyping, and physical prototyping. We assume the designers, given an informal specification of the (sub)-systems, are able to specify the requirements in some (semi)-formal way (e.g. UML [16, 17]). The overall behaviour (functional network) and architecture net-list of the distributed system constitutes the output of this phase.

The most advanced design systems being put together today (e.g., [15, 18]) can be summarized as follows:

- Use of a virtual platform, for system testing and prototyping (HW/SW architecture) via simulation.
- Use of virtual models of the application software and the target HW/SW architecture (bus controllers, CPUs, RTOS schedulers, communication protocols) to create a virtual prototype of the entire distributed application. The application software models are imported from other tools [15], or can be authored within the system. The architectural models are developed within the tool (e.g. the communication protocol model is the subject of further chapters) using a standard C++ API.
- Use of virtual models of the environment/complex human-machine interactions/test-benches that provide the stimuli to the system under testing – the models are either imported from other tools such as Mathworks/Simulink or authored within the system.

The AEE project (http://aee.inria.fr) involving the French car manufacturers and suppliers has targeted the same goal by developing the AIL language. Based on UML, it allows to specify in the same framework electronic embedded architectures, from the highest level of abstraction to the lowest level: the Vehicle Project to capture requirements in terms of services taking into account vehicle variants, Functional Architecture to decompose service in functions and sub-functions, Software Architecture to describe functions with reusable software components cooperating through the ICEM (Inter Component Exchange Manager) middleware, Hardware Architecture to describe ECU's, networks, and gateways if several networks are used, and finally Operational Architecture to describe the mapping of Software Architecture onto Hardware Architecture.

This language is used with a proprietary editing tool to create or update vehicle data-bases. In addition, simulation, mapping, and code generation tools defined in the project are applied to Vehicle Projects at different architecture levels, extracted from the data-bases through API. Exchanges between car manufacturers and suppliers are also modelled in this language to simplify and clarify these complex issues. They may share parts of data-bases through a XML common format.

We believe that the major advantages of these emerging approaches are the shift from a "per-ECU" tool-supported design style, where each ECU is considered separately, the design exploration is limited to one ECU at the time and the integration step is done later in the design process directly on the car), to:

- an integrated design style, where the entire network of ECU's is modelled along with the application and base software used to customize the platform for a particular car series, the integration is done at the virtual level.
- automatic configuration of tools for protocol analysis and implementation based upon the results provided by the simulations of the virtual model. For example, once the designer has decided how to distribute the pool of functions on each ECU, a downstream code generation tool can use this information (number of tasks needed, scheduling policies, etc) to generate the RTOS scheduler. At the same time, the downstream tools for communication protocol analysis can be configured based upon the configuration data determined at the virtual level (type of protocol, frame packaging, communication cycle, redundancy management policies, etc.). Thus, a step that is currently manual or requires intensive user's intervention (e.g. the designer needs to explicitly specify the messages that are sent over the network bus) is supported automatically in our flow.
- Simplified estimation of temporal performance during earliest design phases even before implementation. Typical examples are software task execution times and network communication latencies. The provision of these estimates may considerably shorten algorithm and platform (single ECU or Network) exploration.

References

[1]   A. Sangiovanni-Vincentelli, Automotive Electronics: Trends and Challenges, Convergence 2000, Detroit (MI), USA, October 2000

[2]   OSEK, http://www.osek-vdx.org

[3]   Robert Bosch, CAN Specification, Version 2.0, Technical Report ISO 11898, Robert Bosch GmbH, 1991

[4]   LIN, http://www.lin-subbus.org

[5]   H. Kopetz and G. Gruensteidl, TTP – A Time-Triggered Protocol for Fault-Tolerant Real-Time Systems, in Proceedings of the 23rd IEEE International Symposium on Fault-Tolerant Computing (FTCS-23), 1993. Toulouse, France: IEEE Press

[6]   Flex Ray Consortium, http://www.flexray-group.com

[7]   T. Demmeler, P. Giusto, A Universal Communication Model for an Automotive System Integration Platform, Proc. Of DATE 2001, March 2001.

[8]   Stefan Poledna, Markus Novak, TTP scheme fuels safer drive-by-wire, http://www. eetimes.com/story/OEG20010306S0042, March 2001

[9]   Ulrich Freund, Alexander Burst, Graphical Programming of ECU Software – An Interface Based Approach, white paper, ETAS GMBh, 2001.

[10]   A. Ferrari, S. Garue, M. Peri, S. Pezzini, L.Valsecchi, F. Andretta, and W. Nesci, The design and implementation of a dual-core platform for power-train systems, Convergence 2000, Detroit (MI), USA, October 2000

[11]   Mathworks/Simulink, http://www.mathworks.com

[12]   Cadence Design Systems, Inc., Virtual Component Co-design (VCC), http://www. cadence.com

[13]   ETAS, Ascet-SD Homepage, http://www.etas.de

[14]   Charles J. Murray, Auto Industry faces media revolution, March 2001 http://www. eetimes.com/story/OEG20010306S0035,

[15]   Paolo Giusto, Jean-Yves Brunel, Alberto Ferrari, Eliane Fourgeau, Luciano Lavagno, and Alberto Sangiovanni-Vincentelli, Automotive virtual integration platforms: why's, what's, and how's, Proc. Of the Int. Conf. on Comp. Des., July 2002.

[16]   Automotive UML homepage, http://www.automotive-uml.com/

[17]   Grant Martin, Luciano Lavagno, Jean Louis-Guerin, "Embedded UML: a merger of real-time UML and co-design", CODES 2001, Denmark, April 2001

[18]   Paolo Giusto, Thilo Demmeler, Peter Schiele, Translating Models of Computation for Design Exploration of Real-Time Distributed Automotive Applications, DATE 2002.

[19]   G. Bombarda, G. Gaviani, P. Marceca, Power-train System Design: Functional and Architectural Specifications, Convergence 2000, Detroit (MI), USA, October 2000

3.2   Aeronautics: A Case Study

This text is the result of a meeting held at Airbus France, in Toulouse, on February 7, 2003. The objective of this meeting was to study and report the practice of embedded software development for one particular hard real-time system, namely flight control. This text has been approved by the two participants from Airbus. The discussion covers also closely related subsystems, e.g., some aspects of autopilot. Participants in the meeting were:

- ARTIST: A. Benveniste, B. Bouyssounouse, P. Caspi.
- Airbus France: Hervé Le Berre (flight control), and Dominique Brière (System senior expert).

Industrial Landscape

There are several teams organized by specific skills, which cover the entire flight control system in manual and automatic control mode. These cover all series of Airbus aircraft, over their whole lifecycle, from the upstream preliminary studies (Research) through certification, down to the subsequent upgrades over the aircraft lifetime (new aircraft versions, in service problem analysis...).

The relevant skill areas and corresponding teams are: system architecture, flight control surfaces, Certification/Validation, flight control laws, quality assurance. All these teams belong to the same organizational "domain" (EYC) of the System Centre of Competence (EY).

Flight Control System equipment (pilot controls, actuators, computers, sensors...) are designed and developed by vendors following specifications issued by the EYC. Note that flight control computers are now designed, qualified, manufactured by an internal AIRBUS supplier.

Transversal the teams, there is an organization by programmes (e.g., A380). This is an organization of integrated groups mixing different skills and focusing on one project after the program launch (preliminary studies are performed by the skill departments); while this has considerable advantages for project development, it causes difficulties in keeping background and knowledge throughout the different projects. One responsibility of the skill department is to compensate these difficulties by selecting common methods and tools, by organizing exchange of experience, reviews, by validating program main choices.

An important evolution in the A380 project consists of integrating together – in the same computer – the flight control and autopilot functions (they were separate before). Thus, more functions will be integrated together. In A380, non critical functions use IMA (Integrated Modular Avionics) modules. But critical functions still use specific hardware modules with their own architecture. There is a tendency to migrate more functions under IMA.

Problem: there is no single engineer mastering the whole Flight Control computer subsystem, due its complexity and criticality. This will not change in the future, the tendency being to introduce new functions.

State of the Practice

High-Level System Requirements
Some new technologies are available from R&D as prototypes, and one important first step is to decide which new technology to use – for example new data acquisition principle or a new CPU core, or new communication buses at aircraft level ,or computer level.

When the project is launched, some high level requirements are formulated including performance and dependability issues. A key step in the design flow is the analysis of dependability and fault containment. Quantitative dependability studies rely on dedicated in-house modelling tools. The dependability exploration deals with relatively small configuration faults. System architecture aspects are also set, for ergonomic considerations and communality with other Airbus aircraft series. For instance, the layout of the cockpit with side sticks. Energy, mass and power are considered as well. These considerations lead to design choices for system and computer architectures.

High level requirements are formulated in natural language. Nevertheless, their traceability of these requirements is finely organized and carefully tracked. Tools used are only text-and-paper. Cross-reading and cross-checking with some lightweight in-house tools is performed.

The detailed architecture is then defined, describing the number of computers, and the type of redundancy. Flight control computer is supplied by an internal airbus team, for criticality reasons.

This part of the development process takes about one year. This phase iterates until there is mutual agreement on the requirements between the Airbus and the suppliers. Requirements may be: the computer shall accept up to 10 analogue inputs of such type; the computer shall be able to handle a SCADE program of that given complexity; MTBF for the computer is stated; environment condition to sustain are defined (temperature, EMC, vibration…), requirements of maintainability (avoid that particular component, use of uploading etc.). Technical expertise for fine-tuning many of the requirements resides with the suppliers.

Other aspects of the requirements consist in stating which notation or formalism should be used; e.g., for flight control software specification, SCADE shall be used. Guidelines of how SCADE should be used are also stated – how variables should be named, how many boxes in a given diagram, and so on. Also the library of macros and algorithms for use are specified. These libraries are provided in the form of graphical notations, together with a set of math formulas (equations). The supplier would translate this into C (for ex.).

All these requirement are set in documents called PTS (Purchaser Technical Specification, ~1000 requirements), and 3S (System Software Specification, slightly shorter). They will become the common contractual documents for the aircraft manufacturer and the suppliers over the whole aircraft lifecycle, and are rigorously managed.

Additional validation documents sustain PTS and 3S. (explanation, rationale, justification…).

Design and Specification of Flight Control Laws
This is a scientific and control engineering activity, developed using Matlab/Simulink, with extended simulators. Flight simulators equipped with these control laws are run. Again, this Matlab/Simulink specification is accompanied by a functional description. Multi-level simulations are performed extensively (from a detailed level up to the encompassing the entire control law). The flight control laws are then translated into SCADE.

The combination of the different operating modes with their control laws – the hybrid systems aspects – is not well supported by automatic control synthesis techniques. Today, this is performed heuristically via extensive know-how and investigation, using SCADE notations. Other notations such as Stateflow or StateCharts could be used as well. However, this is only a support for description, not a support for assisted design (in the sense of "control design").

On the other hand, there is always the generic requirement that mode switching should be "smooth", but still it has to occur quickly; a good example is the shifting from auto to manual pilot. Fine tuning occurs at this stage, and this is the part of early design that is most important and costly. Overall, this is considered a bottleneck.

Detailed Formal Software Specification
This is launched in parallel with the former phase. There is a textual and informal description of the software functions (i.e. functions that will be implemented in the computer software code), in addition to the control laws. Software is mainly dedicated to monitoring functions (failure detection, reconfiguration) and actuator control. This is not considered as a specification, since it is regarded informal. Still it is useful to have it in parallel with the formal specifications. This is called "Functional Description" (not "Requirement" since the latter term has a strict meaning regarding certification procedures); this happens before SCADE programming. It is sort of a detailed course to teach and explain how the flight control software works and it is useful for validation/verification test writing. It is not desirable that formal traceability between these informal requirements and the SCADE specifications is granted. The intent is to help the engineer to understand why and how things work, not to specify what the software does.

In parallel with the above activity, the detailed SCADE specification is started. A coarse functional architecture is defined first. The coordination between the different computers implementing the different control laws is studied at this stage.

The Airplane Definition Document is used to support the certification of the aircraft. The SCADE specification belongs to this level of definition, it is thus part of what is identified and strictly managed to allow for the certification of the aircraft. Not everything is part of the documents supporting certification.

The story leading to the use of SCADE (formerly SAO) is interesting. To work faster, some teams would capture requirements quickly for subsystems and would prototype, in parallel with detailed system definition; then the integration of these partial prototypes turned out to cause a lot of problems. Historically, before the A320 was launched as 1st flight-by-wire transport aircraft, the integration teams spent very long time in software bug tracking and fixing. Most of the bugs found were due to incorrect interpretations of the informal specifications forwarded by control and systems engineers to software engineers. This was the motivation for creating, for the A320, the graphical notation SAO (less formal ancestor of SCADE) – a language understood by both system and software engineers. This helped reducing software bugs drastically by shifting inspection earlier in the design flow.

Airbus engineers are reluctant to create yet another formal notation above SCADE, since the problem of supporting the correctness of the translation would immediately appear. They consider that there is little risk in fact that SCADE would become too low level a notation in the future; the reason is that engineers want to keep proper understanding of the considered system, which should prevent from an excessive increase in complexity. Another important aspect is that there is no such thing like a "draft" modification, every modification is handled like a real and final modification, i.e., the software development methodology is fully uniform; this approach was taken for the A320; it slowed down the early phases but reduced the overall design time drastically. Afterwards, cross-reading by independent teams is the rule, which contributes to the validation.

When receiving the SCADE specification of the flight control laws from the flight control law department, very few modifications are performed by the systems engineering department. Modifications are discussed jointly with control engineers. Distortion between the two types of teams does not seem to be an issue.

Detailed Code

Detailed code is now produced for flight control computers by Airbus internal supplier, who shared SCADE code with system designers. The use of a qualified SCADE code generator allows to suppress unit testing, and consequently to significantly reduce the development cycle and to increase reactivity without impairing software quality. Only crude sequencers are used for critical parts, not sophisticated RTOS functionalities.

Suppliers for other control systems – not specified in detail by AIRBUS – are responsible for their development chain and validation techniques. They are encouraged, but not bound, to work with SCADE.

Deploying on Architectures

This is supported by co-simulation. The in-house desktop simulator OCASIM is used for full virtual exploration of the whole flight control system in combination with the aircraft flight mechanics' real-time model with simplified plant, the rigid body modes and, if necessary, the first flexible modes (this simulator handles only finite difference equations; time is discrete, not continuous).

Current R&D activity aims at determining appropriate, specific hardware equipment. Today only hardened special purpose machines are considered. But this is probably not going to continue. Special purpose computers and other hardware are getting rapidly obsolete. One possible idea is to consider ASICs, and have an in-house processor in the form of a SW-IP. The SW-IP would be stable, but the actual circuit could evolve (the lifetime of an aircraft can be as much as 40-50 years!). Engineers now want to reduce the risks and costs due to re-certification. They want to re-use software certification, provided it is portable; hardware will evolve to avoid obsolescence.

Dynamic behaviour of architectures is a key issue. For this, advanced methods for estimating WCET are absolutely crucial. To perform accurate timing analysis, having dedicated processor with better predictability would be desirable. These types of processors could be useful for other industries that develop real-time, safety critical systems (e.g., automotive). If this were the case, the market demand for such processors would be ensured.

The choice of a specific bus is a global design choice, not under the responsibility of the flight-control team. A chosen design constraint is that that the total loss of the AFDX bus should not be critical in the A380. This means that the aircraft may be difficult to pilot, but there is still a possibility for survival. This means that some vital functions bypass the AFDX bus (Switch Ethernet).

In flight control, communications are based on point-to-point Arinc 429. For some aircraft, the Safebus (Honeywell) is considered. The possibility of using TTP busses is also under study, which may lead to drastic architectural evolutions. Field bus technologies (e.g., CAN) become interesting and are also considered. Today, hydro/servo-controllers do not communicate through the bus. Nevertheless, new servo-controllers need power electronics; since there is electronics anyway, it becomes possible to use numerical busses, not analogue ones; this opens the route to field busses. Field busses may not be powerful enough to be used between computers. This area could be the subject for important research.

The long-term driver for R&D has always been to reduce mass, while increasing security. No new technology will be introduced if proof of improvement in these two areas is not given. For example, this meant continuing with analogue technology for large parts of the aircraft, even as the state of the art advanced far beyond this.

For deployment, the OCASIM-SCADE modeller is used for a combined architecture-function simulation, and hardware equipment is considered. Part of the design is explored in virtual but realistic detail, using a coarsely described environment. This is done successively for different aspects, e.g., the flight control system with a model of the aircraft and actual computer, and the real cockpit. In other cases, real equipment is combined with a virtual aircraft.

The validation of all below-SCADE aspects (OS, etc) is under the responsibility of the supplier.

Flight control software code is considered to be error-free, i.e. fully conform to the SCADE specification. No flight tests are scheduled for software debugging.

Integrating Subsystems from Suppliers
Subsystem suppliers provide components. There is no software-only component. The only components considered are whole equipments comprising plant+device+HW/SW, and the whole is subject to integration. The use of the current methodology has reduced the software problems in this integration phase virtually to zero regarding unit tests. Multi-equipment simulation is performed with the OCASIM tool; these simulations are not fully accurate, however, thus there can be surprises at this integration stage. Fine-tuning of some parameters related to the technique used in the deployment phase can be a cause. Testing is a combination of random testing and deterministic testing – both are needed. Testing in successively refined environments is performed – in each case, a mix of random and deterministic exploration is performed.

Adequately covering all possible scenarios is an issue. One sensitive example is full-scale testing of the start-up phases. Once deployed, the aircraft should start is dependably as an automobile. Unfortunately, the testing teams are reluctant to test all possible configurations because it is a lengthy procedure.

In-flight Tests
Next step is the test flights with a real aircraft. Flight tests are dedicated to tuning the flight control laws and procedures, flight envelope opening etc. System behaviour is deeply monitored during flight test by recording thousands of SCADE parameters. Post flight analysis is performed after all test flights. Any suspected misbehaviour is analyzed, registered, explained, and if necessary corrected by modifying the SCADE specification. In fact, during test flights, the computers themselves are instrumented. Dedicated busses are used to continuously emit messages; some internal SCADE variables are continuously monitored and checked against the expected behaviour in

the specification. A question is where to put probes in the software to properly assess the implementation with respect to the SCADE specification.

The instrumented SCADE software is preserved in commercial use; this means some code is unnecessary, but causes no harm. Removing instrumentation code would require re-certification. In fact, the bus also preserves the possibility of collecting specific data on demand.

It is worth noticing that a dedicated in-flight test computer linked to the operational flight control computers allows online switching between different predefined branches or gains within the flight control software, thus this flight "tool" allows to shorten the development cycle. Overall, the goal is to leave fewer burdens on the flight tests: rely more on simulations. This is in particular true for everything concerning the computer – flight tests should play no role in commercial use.

An important trend is reducing the number of test flights – relying more heavily on simulation for validating flight control.

In the A380, remote loading of the code will be possible. This will drastically reduce the cost of maintenance.

Links Between Airbus and the Research Community

There are four entities for R&D at Airbus. Each Airbus entity is now becoming more specialized; e.g., Toulouse is responsible for flight control, but there are other groups working in this subject.

Airbus prefers to establish links with leading laboratories, which are free to delegate as they wish to other teams. Airbus engineers would like to rely on such "reference laboratories" for carrying out R&D work. For example ONERA and the LEEI on electronics are such laboratories.

ARTIST could play such a role in its areas of expertise.

Skills and Education for the Future

Is there a need for specific skills and education for embedded software development in aeronautics? For the moment, Airbus hires specialists of aeronautics or general systems engineering, who then learn through practice how to develop the systems. Airbus does not consider hiring embedded software development specialists per se. They are careful that each newly hired engineer has the minimal skills and know-how to develop embedded systems.

Courses on "computer engineering" in schools or universities within an aeronautics curriculum is currently considered to be low level. It is acknowledged that such education and training is not sufficient for complex systems.

Nevertheless, there is a need for well trained engineers with specific skill in computer science. For instance, using SCADE Prover is in fact much more difficult than SCADE programming and requires specific skills. On the other hand, it is important that specialists of embedded software have a background for understanding the application domain specialists.

As a result of the discussion, we collected the following opinions:
- *Availability.* If embedded software specialists were available, Airbus would consider hiring them, in order to master new methods and tools. Alternately, teaching more embedded software within a system engineering curriculum could be another solution.
- *Scientific Engineering. Overall,* Airbus would be happy to hire 10% of their engineers specialized in embedded software. The main reason is their ability to perform formal proofs of their system designs. This is required for shifting from empirical engineering-through-practice to scientific engineering. The goal is to design in such a way as to ease certification and validation.

In-house Skills and Know-how. Training and education related to these skills is performed by mixing experienced and new personnel in the same teams. No in-house "school" is organized. Reuse of existing know-how is the major driving force.

A curriculum dedicated to embedded systems in aeronautics would have too limited an audience. This could make sense only if several similar industries express similar needs.

Challenges and Work Directions

The biggest issue is to improve the overall combined simulation of architecture + functions. Today, the in-house tools are considered rigorous and reliable, but they are purely discrete time, and thus do not capture all desirable aspects. Capturing continuous time with full confidence and accuracy would be important. Later on, covering partial differential equations, in particular regarding structural and aero elastic dynamics should be considered.

Another important issue is hybrid system development and exploration (discrete mode switching + continuous systems/control); developing adequate synthesis methods is an issue for longer term research.

In general, there are powerful know-how and in-house methods; and there is a need to support/criticize this know-how by the academic community. This requires cooperation in confidence and mutual understanding.

3.3   Consumer Electronics: A Case Study

In this section, we provide an overview of current practice within one particular branch of consumer electronics, namely the development of software for mobile telephones. The study is based on interviews and documentation provided by two large European manufacturers who do not want their names to be disclosed. This means that direct quotations have not been possible.

Industrial Landscape

Today's mobile phones are typically based on three major subsystems, (1) the analogue subsystem, which interfaces to the physical environment (R/F and audio/video), (2) the codec part, which handles the HRT aspects of the involved protocol standards – including the digital signal processing, (3) the application part, which handles the non-HRT parts of the protocol stacks and the end-user functionality of the phone, i.e.

connection management (audio/video dialogue), user interface, phone books, games, etc. For 1G and 2G phones, the analogue subsystem and parts of the codec system are often developed by sub-vendors, whereas parts of the codec system and the core part of the application subsystem normally is developed by the manufacturers and represents a major part of their IP. Most manufacturers are outsourcing the assembly of phones to specialist companies.

The above indicates that the mobile phone companies have strong competences within HW/SW architecture design, DSP algorithms, GSM/GPRS protocols, static HRT analysis, and also the development and integration of basic application services.

Hard Real-Time Context

In typical 1G or 2G phones, the analogue subsystem consists of hardware components, the codec part is formed by a number of DSPs, and the application part is handled by a single additional processor. This architecture also reflects the partitioning into major subtasks when a new series is developed:

- 1) Development of the codec part, i.e. assuring the conformance to current low level protocol standards and in particular guaranteeing that the HRT protocol requirements are fulfilled. This involves both a schedulability analysis at design time and a thorough simulation of the implemented DSP algorithms.
- 2) Development of the non-HRT parts of the protocol stacks – e.g. channel allocation and connection management.
- 3) Development of the application part, i.e. providing the specified services and their coordination.

Roughly speaking, the basics of part (1) and (2) were developed about a decade ago, and since then, the majority of resources have been applied on new facilities for part (3). This situation has two important consequences:

- The software architecture of the application part can be kept very simple, i.e. it consists of a simple kernel supporting a few priority levels, a few cyclic (high priority) tasks doing the time critical parts, and a large number of (low priority) tasks which implement the fast growing number of new facilities.
- The validation of a new release consists of a (simple/static) timing validation and a (complex/error prone) functional validation to make sure that the new facilities do not interact with existing features.

This means that the companies have been following a development process which is focused on the validation of functional properties. Below, we provide a summary of the method and point out some of challenges for the development of future mobile phones.

State of the Practice

For both companies, their development process contains more or less the following sequential phases:

1. System Specification
   The general purpose of the system.

2. Requirements Specification
   The requirements to software, project estimates, and the project specification with appropriate enclosures.
3. Architectural Specification
   This provides the global design, where the overall architecture and behaviour is defined. Typically a mixture of MSC's and ASN.1 definitions is the applied notation. Interfaces to the environment (normally the GUI) and other subsystems are also defined in this phase.
4. Module Specification
   (or detailed design, which defines the detailed behaviour (e.g. using SDL notation) and the detailed data structures – e.g. using class diagrams or concrete programming language notation. In this phase MSC's are used for defining test scenarios, and the detailed test environment is also defined.
5. Implementation
   Here the detailed design is transformed into actual code. The transformation may be automated by tool support. Also, may sometimes be automated. Also, the maintenance documentation is made in this phase.
6. Testing
   Where one moves 'backwards' through the phases, i.e. first the individual modules are tested using the previously defined module test scenarios (defined as MSC's). This part of the testing can sometimes be made automatically using tools. Then the different (tested) components are integrated and tested by taking the corresponding MSC's and interface definitions into account. Finally, the acceptance test is performed based on requirements from costumers and the experience of the developers.

As seen from the above description, the phases are treated according to the philosophy of the V- model, i.e. each phase results in a refined design and also a definition of the test scenarios that can be derived (manually) from the design:

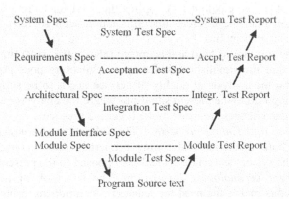

As indicated above, work is done on automating the bottom layer of the model, i.e. turning it into a Y-model.

The companies' experiences with the above process are generally good – especially for the 'downwards' path and also to some extent for the 'upwards path'. However, for the integration test and the system test, there is a lack of tool support for generation of tests with appropriate coverage (integration test) and with appropriate load and timing (stress test/system test). As for the stress test, this has not been a severe problem until now, because most of the development efforts have been concentrating on developing new application features which do not destroy the basic (low level) protocol performance – as mentioned above. However, for the integration test, this lack of appropriate tool support has forced the companies to spend a huge part of the total development costs on integration testing.

Challenges and Work Directions

Clearly, the mobile phone developers are currently faced with the following challenges:

1. The upcoming 3G and 4G systems will be much more demanding on timing properties and the signal processing algorithms will be much more complicated to develop.
2. The number of different applications will grow dramatically due to the possibilities offered by the increased bandwidth. A large amount of the applications will be installed directly from open sources.
3. The applications will partly be time critical (e.g. multimedia applications).
4. Resource consumption (speed, space, power) will be a highly competitive parameter.

This means that the requirements to their future development process will change on a number of important issues:

1. *Co-design*. The growing complexity of level1-2 protocols means that the actual distribution of HW/SW cannot be settled in the very beginning of the development of a new product line – i.e. co-design techniques are necessary.
2. *Simulation for Resource Management*. The introduction of power/space as additional resource parameters implies the need for more advanced system simulation than the discrete-time simulation seen so far – e.g. by using tools based on Simulink.
3. *QoS*. The mixture of hard and adaptive (also called soft) timing properties implies that the simplistic middleware architecture does not suffice anymore, and the analysis of quality of service needs to be supported in general as opposed to the present situation, where the analysis mostly has to be made when changes are made to the level 1-2 protocols.
4. *Functional and Timing Properties*. The validation of a new product needs to take both functional and timing properties into account. This clearly makes the system test phase critical (as opposed to the present situation).
5. *Component Technologies, Integration*. The fast growing number of new applications makes the need for reuse (i.e. component technologies) indispensable. Also, the demands on time to market will make it impossible to spend a large amount of development time on integration testing.

Based on the above observations it is clear that the developers of mobile phones have to reconsider their development process so that future requirements can be handled.

Also, the applied middleware must be revised in order to be able to handle both hard and adaptive timing requirements. This calls for new competences not seen so far in the mobile phone companies, e.g. HW/SW co-design, development of formal design models to enable test and verification, middleware platforms supporting quality of service, and real-time component technologies.

3.4   Automation Applications

Industrial Landscape

The following assessment is adapted from the study [IPA99]. Industrial automation is applied to control and optimize production processes and to provide high-quality and reliable products and services by minimizing material, cost and energy waste. Examples include systems for traffic control, chemical process control, distributed production control, machine and plant control (e.g. hydraulic presses, machine tools with several synchronized axles, coupled robots), and agent-based manufacturing. Many of these systems exhibit safety critical behaviour and have to observe real-time constraints.

Automation technology for the general public and in the service sector covers a broad spectrum of products and systems, ranging from smart products for everyday life to modular multipurpose robots for personal and industrial services, service robots interacting with the environment (e.g. for maintenance or security), or simply robots for performing an autonomous function (e.g. transport). Trends for future services are here to entertain, inform, support, and educate the members of our society (e.g. museum guide robots) and to relieve physical and mental stressing of human beings and provide assistance in carrying out tasks (e.g. for repair tasks in dangerous environments or surgery assistants).

Architectures of Automation Systems and Its Hard Real-Time Context

Automation systems rely on smart sensors, actuators and other industrial equipment like robotic and mechatronics components. Open and standardized communication networks are employed for the communication as well as configuration and control of the various automation components. The standard architecture consists of PLCs (Programmable Logic Controllers) or DCS (Distributed Control Systems), field bus systems, and PCs as man machine interfaces as well as intelligent sensor and actuators (e.g. frequency converters). The field bus systems gather the signals from process level or the sensors/actuators with field bus interfaces and are directly connected to distributed or centralized control devices (e.g. PLCs). In Europe Siemens is the market leader in PLCs (Simatic S7) and an important supplier of DCS systems (PCS7) as well as CNC (Computerized Numerical Control) equipment. Further on, groups of independent suppliers of distributed control equipment (e.g. Beckhoff, Moeller Electric, or the IDA-group [IDA]) strengthen their market share.

State of the Practice

The standard IEC 61131-3 of the International Electrotechnical Commission provides a range of programming notations suitable for implementation on PLCs [IEC93,Lew95]. It comprises basic notations close to those in electrical engineering like contact plans, instruction lists, and function plans as well as graphical and textual programming notations called sequential functions charts and structured text. Currently development of software in automation technology proceeds step by step along the lifecycle using the notations of IEC 61131-3 and different tools used in the companies and provided by different PLC vendors [FV02]. The design is done function oriented and component based. The situation is quite similar for DCS in process industry [AAF03].

A problem is that different PLC vendors use their own variants of the standard with different syntax, semantics and tool sets [BE02]. The approaches based on IEC 61131-3 are not well suited for the development of distributed applications and applications with hard real-time requirements. An attempt to overcome this shortcoming is the standard IEC 61499, which embeds IEC 61131-3 and allows describing distributed systems. The IEC 61499 architecture allows event-driven function blocks and may provide a framework to integrate run-time control and diagnosis applications and simulation for distributed automation frameworks [VH02,VHK02]. However, since IEC 61499 embeds IEC 61131-3, the semantics remains formally ambiguous [BE02]. This hampers the integration of formal methods and tools for verification.

The standard IEC 61131-3 is implementation oriented and thus lacks of notations for capturing high level requirements. Requirements engineering as such is not well established as well as reuse of functional modules (software and hardware) [AAF03]. To cope with distributed (intelligent) systems in this field the description of communication and configuration of these systems needs to be solved more efficiently [BV02]. A multi-level-multi-agents architecture which integrates all levels necessary for a comprehensive diagnosis into a diagnostic system has been developed [KDF02]. The integration of the engineering of safety aspects and aspects of functionality is not yet solved neither the proceeding, nor modelling concept, nor the tool integration [Fin02].

Challenges and Work Directions

As the applications of automation become more demanding, guaranteeing the quality of the control software becomes more and more important. However, software development in the area of automation technology is characterized by description techniques (IEC standards) that represent only a low level of abstraction from the underlying PLC hardware. Furthermore, the standards have ambiguous semantics that allows different a interpretation by each vendor. These two factors have so far hampered the use of formal techniques to specify and verify that the software meets the required behavioural properties.

Individual research projects have demonstrated that formal methods are in principle able to improve the quality of software. Some projects have build formal models of the existing description techniques of the IEC standards, e.g. of sequential function charts [BH02]. But these formal models are often too large to be checked automatically (via model checking techniques).

To overcome these difficulties we see the following research challenges:

- Building faithful and abstract models of the underlying PLC hardware and networking structures, to enable formal analysis and bridge the gap between the requirements and the implementation level. (For initial work see e.g. [BV02][Die01].)
- Investigating semantics of existing languages of the IEC standards and relate them to the abstract models.
- Using and adapting existing concepts from software development (e.g. suitable UML profiles) to the application area of automation technology. (For initial work see e.g. [K-etal02][KDF02].)
- Modularity and reusability of software development in this application area.
- Developing tools to support the methods mentioned above.

References

[Alb02]   H. Albrecht. On Meta-Modelling for Communication in Operational Process Control Engineering. Accepted dissertation. VDI Fortschritt-Bericht, Series 8, No. 975, 20 ISBN 3-18-397508-4. VDI-Verlag, Duesseldorf, Germany.

[AAF03]   R. Alznauer, K. Auer, and A. Fay. Wiederverwendung von Automatisierungs-Informationen und -Loesungen, Automatisierungstechnische Praxis 45, Oldenbourg-Verlag, 2003.

[BE02]   N. Bauer and S. Engell. A comparison of sequential function charts and statecharts and an approach towards integration. Workshop: Integration of Software Specification Techniques, pp. 58-69, ETAPS 2002.

[BH02]   N. Bauer and R. Huuck. A parametrized semantics sequential function charts. In: Semantic Foundations of Engineering Design Languages, Satellite Event of ETPAS 2002.

[BV02]   C. Biermann and B. Vogel-Heuser. Requirements of a process control description language for distributed control systems (DCS) in process industry. In: Proceedings of IECON'02, 28th Annual Conference of the IEEE Industrial Electronics Society, Sevilla, November 2002

[Buc02]   G. Buch, Verteilte Architekturen in heterogenen Umgebungen. Congress Electric Automation SPS/IPC/Drives, Nuernberg, Germany, November 2002.

[Die01]   H. Dierks. PLC-Automata: a new class of implementable real-time automata. TCS, 253:2001, 61--93.

[FV02]   K. Fischer and B. Vogel-Heuser. UML for real-time applications in automation, in German: UML in der automatisierungstechnischen Anwendung -- Staerken und Schwaechen, Automatisierungstechnische Praxis 44, Oldenbourg-Verlag, 2002.

[IDA]   IDA group: see http://www.ida-group.org

[IEC93]   IEC International Standard 1131-3, Programmable Controllers, Part 3, Programming Languages, 1993.

[K-etal02] S. Klein, X. Weng, G. Frey, J.-J. Lesage, and L.Litz. Controller design for an FMS using signal interpreted Petri Nets and SFC (I). American Control Conference, ACC 2002, Anchorage, Mai 2002.

[KDF02]   B. Koeppen-Seliger, S.X. Ding, and P.M. Frank. MAGIC – IFATIS: EC-Research Projects; IFAC World Congr., Barcelona, Spain (2002).

[Lew95]   R.W. Lewis. Programming industrial control systems using IEC 1131-3. The Institution of Electrical Engineers, 1995.

[IPA99]   J. Neugebauer, M. Hoepf, T. Skordas, and M. Ziegler. The Role of Automation and Control in the Information Society. Study supported by the EU and conducted by Fraunhofer Institut Produktionstechnik und Automatisierung (IPA), Stuttgart, October 1999.

[NDS02]   P. Neumann, C. Diedrich, and R. Simon, Engineering of Field Devices using Descriptions. 15th Triennial World Congress of the International Federation of Automatic Control (IFAC 2002), Barcelona, Juli 2002.

[Fin02]   A. Rink. Entwicklung einer Methode fueur die systemtechnische Auslegung verteilter und sicherheitskritischer Fueuhrungsfunktionen fuer Fahrzeugantriebe. Dissertation, Bergischen Universitaet Wuppertal, Fakultaet Elektrotechnik und Informationstechnik, Wuppertal, 2002.

[VH02]   V. Vyatkin and H.-M. Hanisch. Component design and validation of decentralized reconfigurable control systems with IEC 61499, Proc. of the International Symposium on Advanced Control of Industrial Processes, pp. 215-220, June 2002, Kumamoto, Japan.

[VHK02]   V. Vyatkin, H.-M. Hanisch, and S. Karras, IEC 61499 as an architectural framework to integrate formal models and methods in practical control engineering, Congress Electric Automation SPS/IPC/Drives, Nuernberg, Germany, November 2002.

4   Tools for Requirements Capture and Exploration

This part covers the tools and technologies which play a role in capturing and exploring requirements, in both functional and extra-functional aspects, for embedded systems design, with emphasis on the coupling between the functionalities and the plant for control. We propose to consider the following methods, and to classify tools accordingly:

1. Overall dependability aspects in support of architecture definition.
2. Scientific engineering tools and physical systems modellers – of course the central tool here is Matlab/Simulink.
3. System architecture modelling, using UML – and UML tools; extend the discussion to state-based modelling in general, dedicated to the discrete part of systems.

4.1   Definitions of Hard Real-Time Dependability Features

A real-time computer system must react to stimuli from the controlled object (or the operator) within time intervals dictated by its environment. The instant before which a result must be produced is called a deadline. If a result has utility even after the deadline has passed, the deadline is classified as soft, otherwise it is firm. If a catastrophe could result if a firm deadline is missed, the deadline is called hard. Consider a railway crossing a road with a traffic signal. If the traffic signal does not change to "red" before the train arrives, a catastrophe could result. A real-time computer system that must meet at least one hard deadline is called a hard real-time computer system or a safety-critical real-time computer system. If some portion of the deadlines can be missed, then the system is called an adaptive real-time computer system.

The design of a hard real-time system is fundamentally different from the design of an adaptive real-time system. While a hard real-time computer system must sustain a guaranteed temporal behaviour under all specified load and fault conditions, it is permissible for a adaptive real-time computer system to miss a deadline occasionally.

Dependability Requirements

The notion of dependability covers the meta-functional attributes of a computer system that relate to the quality of service a system delivers to its users during an extended interval of time. (A user could be a human or another technical system.) The following measures of dependability attributes are of importance [Lap92]:

Reliability
The reliability of a system is the probability that a system will provide the specified service until time t, given that the system was operational at $t = t_o$. If a system has a constant failure rate, then the reliability at time t is given by

$$R(t) = \exp(-\lambda(t - t_o)),$$

Artist FP5 Consortium: Embedded Systems Design, LNCS 3436, 39 – 53, 2005.
© Springer-Verlag Berlin Heidelberg 2005

where $t - t_0$ is given in hours. The inverse of the failure rate $1/\lambda = MTTF$ is called the *Mean-Time-To-Failure MTTF* (in hours). If the failure rate of a system is required to be in the order of 10^{-9} failures/h or lower, then we speak of a system with an *ultrahigh reliability* requirement.

Safety
This is reliability regarding *critical failure modes*. A critical failure mode is said to be *malign*, in contrast with a non-critical failure, which is *benign*. In a malign failure mode, the cost of a failure can be orders of magnitude higher than the utility of the system during normal operation. Safety-critical (hard) real-time systems must have a failure rate with regard to critical failure modes that conforms to the *ultrahigh reliability* requirement.

Maintainability
It is a measure of the time required to repair a system after the occurrence of a benign failure. Maintainability is measured by the probability $M(d)$ that the system is restored within a time interval d after the failure. In keeping with the reliability formalism, a constant repair rate μ (repairs per hour) and a *Mean-Time to Repair (MTTR)* is introduced to define a quantitative maintainability measure.

Availability
It is a measure of the delivery of correct service with respect to the alternation of correct and incorrect service, and is measured by the fraction of time that the system is ready to provide the service. In systems with constant failure and repair rates, the reliability *(MTTF)*, maintainability *(MTTR)*, and availability *(A)* measures are related by

$$A = MTTF/ (MTTF+MTTR).$$

Security
A fifth important attribute of dependability – the *security attribute* – is concerned with the ability of a system to prevent unauthorized access to information or services. Traditionally, security issues have been associated with large databases, where the concerns are confidentiality, privacy, and authenticity of information. During the last few years, security issues have also become important in real-time systems, e.g., a cryptographic theft-avoidance system that locks the ignition of a car if the user cannot present the specified access code.

Failures, Errors, and Faults

In this section, a short overview of the basic concepts that have been established in the field of fault-tolerant computing is given. The Working Group 10.4 on Fault-Tolerant Computing of the International Federation of Information Processing (IFIP) has published a five-language book [Lap92] where these concepts are explained in more detail. The core of this document details the three terms: fault, error and failure.

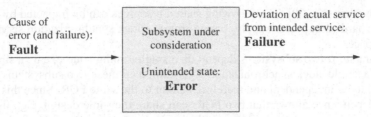

Faults and Errors are States,   Failures are Events

Computer systems are installed to provide dependable service to system users. A user can be a human user or another (higher level) system. Whenever the service of a system, as seen by the user of the system, deviates from the agreed specification of the system, the system is said to have failed.

Failures
A failure is an event that denotes a deviation between the actual service and the specified or intended service, occurring at a particular point in real-time.

Errors
Most computer system failures can be traced to an incorrect internal state of the computer, e.g., a wrong data element in the memory or a register. We call such an incorrect internal state an error. An error is thus an unintended state. If the error exists only for a short interval of time, and disappears without an explicit repair action, it is called a transient error. If the error persists permanently until an explicit repair action removes it, we call it a permanent error. In a fault-tolerant architecture, every error must be confined to a particular error containment region to avoid the propagation of the error throughout the system. The boundaries of the error containment regions must be protected by error detection interfaces.

Faults
The cause of an error, and thus indirect cause of a failure, is called fault.

Fault-Containment and Error Containment
In any fault-tolerant architecture it is important to distinguish clearly between fault containment and error containment. Fault containment is concerned with limiting the immediate impact of a single fault to a defined region, while error containment tries to avoid the propagation of the consequences of a fault, the error. It must be avoided that an error in one fault-containment region propagates into another fault-containment region that has not been directly affected by the original fault.

Fault Containment
The notion of a fault-containment region (FCR) is introduced in order to delimit the immediate impact of a single fault to a defined subsystem of the overall system. A fault-containment region is defined as the set of subsystems that share one or more common resources and may be affected by a single fault. Since the immediate consequences of a fault in any one of the shared resources in an FCR may impact all subsystems of the FCR, the subsystems of an FCR cannot be considered to be independ-

ent of each other [Kau00]. The following shared resources can be impacted by a fault: computing hardware, power supply, timing source, clock synchronization service and physical space.

For example, if two subsystems depend on a single timing source, e.g., a single oscillator or a single clock synchronization algorithm, then these two subsystems are not considered to be independent and therefore belong to the same FCR. Since this definition of independence allows that two FCRs can share the same design, e.g., the same software, design faults in the software or the hardware are not part of this fault-model.

Error Containment

An error that is caused by a fault in the sending FCR can propagate to another FCR via a message failure, i.e., a sent message that deviates from the specification. A message failure can be a message value failure or a message timing failure [Cri85]. A message value failure implies that a message is either invalid or that the data structure contained in a valid message is incorrect. A message timing failure implies that the message send instant or the message receive instant are not in agreement with the specification. In order to avoid error propagation by way of a sent message error-detection mechanisms that are in different FCRs than the message sender are needed. Otherwise, the error detection mechanism may be impacted by the same fault that caused the message failure.

The 10^{-9} Challenge

Emerging X-by-wire applications require ultra-high dependability in the order of 10^{-9} failures/h (115 000 years) or lower. Today's technology cannot support the manufacturing of electronic devices with failure rates low enough to meet the reliability requirements. Thus the reliability of an ultra-dependable system must be higher than the reliability of each of its components. This can only be achieved by utilizing fault-tolerant strategies that enable the continued operation of the system in the presence of component failures [But91].

Since systems can only be tested to dependability in the order of 10^{-4} failures/h a combination of experimental evidence and formal reasoning using a reliability model is needed to construct the safety argument. The safety argument is a set of documented arguments in order to convince experts in the field that the provided system as a whole is safe to deploy in a given environment.

The justification for building ultra-reliable systems from replicated resources rests on an assumption of failure independence among redundant units. For this reason the independence of Fault-Containment Regions (i.e. subsystems that share one or more common resources and may be affected by a single fault) is of critical importance. Thus any dependence of FCR failures must be reflected in the dependability model. Independence of FCRs can be compromised by

- Shared physical resources (hardware, power supply, time base, etc.);
- External faults (EMI, heat, shock, spatial proximity);
- Design;
- Flow of erroneous messages.

From the dependability point of view, the future unit of hardware failure is considered to be a complete chip. If complex systems constructed from components with interdependencies are modelled, the reliability model can become extremely complex and the analysis intractable [But91].

Relevant Challenges and Work Directions

Semantic Interface Specification
The behaviour of an interface is characterized by the temporal sequence of messages it accepts, the messages it produces, the internal state of the interface and the data transformations and/or actions that are performed by the interface. Whereas at the syntactic level the message specification can be performed by any type of Interface-Definition Language, e.g., the IDL of the OMG, and the temporal specification of temporal-firewall messages can be performed by making use of the global time, the proper specification of the high-level semantic properties of an interface by an interface model is a very relevant research issue.

Composability of Services
i.e., the constructive construction of complex emergent services out of simple interface services without unintended side effects, is an important property of any distributed architecture. Composability is a system issue, i.e. it must be supported at all levels of the architecture, firstly by the elimination of property mismatches at any level and secondly by the semantic integration of the interface models introduced above.

Mixed-Criticality Systems
In the future we will see the emergence of many mixed-criticality systems, i.e., systems where services of different criticalities must be integrated into a single coherent architecture. For example, in an automotive environment, safety critical drive by wire functions, body electronics and multi-media services for entertainment should be provided in single coherent architecture. Issues of service separation, integrity and independence of fault-containment region, and replica determinism for critical services under severe cost constraints are important research topics.

Security
Future embedded systems that are connected to the Internet must be concerned about security. Issues of security intrusions, authentication, denial of service attacks, and the like may become more relevant for distributed embedded systems than for many other systems that are connected to the Internet.

Modular Certification
The certification of safety-critical functions is an important cost element in the development of safety-critical applications. It would be a great advantage if the certification can proceed in a modular fashion, i.e., if certification arguments that have been developed for a particular subsystem can be used in a modular fashion. Modular certification depends very much on the partitioning properties provided by the distributed architecture.

Safety Case Analysis
The effort required for the certification of safety-critical real-time applications could be significantly reduced, if a standardized procedure for the development of the safety case is available. The safety process can be enhanced by the provision of a tool-bench with the relevant tools for safety analysis, such as failure-mode-and effect analysis (FMEA), dependability modelling, and security analysis.

Middleware Processor
In today's embedded systems it is common to execute the middleware and the application software on the same processor. The frequent interruptions of the application by middleware processes that normally have only a short execution path makes the analysis of the WCET of the application very difficult. If a separate processor is dedicated to the middleware and the interface between the middleware and the application processor is well-defined in the domains of time and value, then a more predictable node behaviour can be expected.

Dynamic Reflective Systems
Dynamic reflective systems have capability to adapt their internal structure in a way not foreseen by its developers in order to optimize the service in a dynamically changing environment. New resources, e.g., sensors and actuators must be dynamically integrated as the system becomes aware of their existence. Dynamic reflective systems must have support reflection, i.e., the capability to reason about their own behaviour. Dynamic reflective systems are expected to become relevant for the embedded system domain in the medium to long range.

Massively Parallel Systems
Massively parallel systems are distributed embedded system that consist of multitude of nodes (can be many thousand) that enter and leave the system dynamically. The nodes of massively parallel system have a high autonomy, both physical (e.g., power supply) and behavioural in the sense that they can plan on their own for goal-oriented behaviour. Research in massively parallel system is exploratory research with a long-range perspective.

References

[But91]   Butler, R.W., & Caldwell, J.L. & Di Vito, B.L. 1991. Design strategy for a formally verified reliable computing platform. In Proceedings of the Sixth Annual Conference on 'Systems Integrity, Software Safety and Process Security', COMPASS'91, 24-27 Jun 1991, pp. 125 -133

[Cri85]   Cristian, F., et al. 1985. Atomic Broadcast: From simple message diffusion to Byzantine agreement. In Proceedings of the 15th IEEE Int. Symp. on Fault-Tolerant Computing (FTCS-15). 1985. Ann Arbor, Michigan.

[Kau00]   Kaufmann, L.F., and B.W. Johnson. 2000. Modelling of Common-Mode Failures in Digital Embedded Systems. In Proceedings of the Reliability and Maintainability Symposium 2000. Los Angeles, CA, IEEE Press.

[Lap92]   Laprie, J.C. (Ed.). 1992. Dependability: Basic Concepts and Terminology – in English, French, German, and Japanese. Springer-Verlag, Vienna, Austria.

4.2   Scientific Engineering Tools and Physical Systems Modellers

Definition

Embedded software systems are generally attached to some physical system, for its control, supervision, or for data processing purposes. These include aircraft control and transport in general, manufacturing, energy production and distribution, robotics. Consideration of embedded software systems, and of the physical processes they interact with, should not be dissociated. These aspects should be addressed jointly – by both the methods, the tools, and the education and training made available to engineers. The present building block is central to address these issues. This type of technology is now considered central for key European industrial sectors, such as automobile, aeronautics, transport, energy. "XX_engineering" in general typically makes extensive use of it. It is less central, but still used, in the telecommunications sector.

Position in the Design Flow

This building block sits in the phases of specification and design. It considers the specification and design of functions in closed-loop with the plant. Related activities are detailed next.

Modelling Physical Systems
The first task to perform is the joint exploration of physical models of the different components, subsystems, or of the entire plant. The resulting models are hybrid in many ways:

- They combine models related to the physics of the (sub)system under specification, with its different modes of operation.
- They combine continuous time models (ordinary differential equations – ODE) with sampled time models, and with discrete event models (automata...).
- For some advanced systems, they involve in addition partial differential equations (PDE), or very high dimensional models. For example, modelling large, flexible aircrafts may involve finite element models with a high number of vibration modes.

In general, the designer would prefer to reuse models and assembly them, for rapid exploration – note that physical models of components or subsystems are considered an important Intellectual Property.

Modelling for Control, and Control Design
It is not possible to design control, based on the detailed, physical, model of the plant; the latter is often too detailed, and generally highly nonlinear, and involves sometimes PDEs. Therefore, it is advisable to have (possibly several) simplified models, with qualified information about the approximations or uncertainties. Such simplified models aimed at control design are again considered an important Intellectual Property, and are sometimes patented.

Virtual or Hardware-in-the-Loop Exploration and Testing
Automatic or assisted control design techniques are not comprehensive but only partial, there is a need to test and evaluate in the context of the whole system the combination of several control functions and their supervision. This can be performed in two major ways:

- Hardware-in-the-loop consists in embedding the entire digital control system on a prototype hardware, which is put in a closed loop with the real physical system. This is the solution of choice in automotive industry today, for developing the chassis or engine control functions. For other industries (e.g., aeronautics) this approach would require heavy experimental test beds (e.g., huge wind tunnels, not so much available at least in Europe).
- Virtual testing is then preferred, it consists in testing a model of the entire control system, in closed loop with a realistic physical model of the entire (sub)system. Virtual testing requires mastering very complex models and their simulation.

Exporting Control Designs
Control designs or models of (possibly closed-loop) control systems need to be exported, in the following cases:

- The physical, continuous time part, of the model can be exported for reuse as component in more powerful, possibly domain-specific, modellers.
- Since models of plants are recognized an important Intellectual Property, exporting such models is a useful service to provide. For protecting these IPs, it is often preferred to export them, not as source model, but in some kind of "compiled form", where reverse engineering is made difficult.
- Models of plants can be components in a more general system model. By "more general" system model, we mean general requirements on the overall system that are not necessarily related to scientific engineering, but can be of much larger scope. For example, the general documentation on hardware or software components requires modelling of this kind.
- Digital control specifications need to be exported and transformed into embedded software.

Description of the Technology

Modelling Physical Systems
As said before, the first task to perform is the joint exploration of physical models of the different components, subsystems, or of the entire plant. The resulting models are hybrid in many ways: They combine models related to the physics of the subsystem under specification, with its different modes of operation; they combine continuous time models with sampled time models, and with discrete event models (automata...); for some advanced systems, they involve in addition partial differential equations (PDE), or very high dimensional models. In general, the designer would prefer to reuse models and assembly them, for rapid exploration, he would like to design his control functions via a quick, tool based, exploration and tuning.

Generic scientific software for modelling and simulation (such as Matlab/Simulink or SystemBuild), have made this ideal methodology possible for the following cases:

- Small or medium size physical models, both continuous and discrete time. Modelling is performed using a sophisticated and flexible GUI, and simulation is immediate. Models can be calibrated on recorded data sets using statistical learning or identification techniques. Signal processing and system identification toolboxes assist the designer. This is the typical state of practice for the physical modelling of plant components, for each separate mode of operation. This is a major contribution of the past two decades, and progress is still ongoing both in academia and at vendors.
- Small or medium size hybrid models involving continuous/discrete time and discrete events (automata). For this more complex case, modelling and simulation is again available

The design of larger or more complex systems (e.g., in aeronautics, or even in the automobile industry for the design of engines with advanced combustion control) requires mastering much larger models involving both ODEs, PDEs, and DAEs (Differential Algebraic Equations, generalized ODEs that are relations and not input-output functions any more), possibly combined with discrete event systems for capturing mode changes. Today, only domain specific tools are available for this, no generic ones.

Modelling for Control, and Control Design
Advanced toolboxes for control design or optimization are available, to assist the design engineer. This is another major contribution of the past two decades, and progress is still ongoing both in academia and at vendors.

Virtual or Hardware-in-the-loop Exploration and Testing
Testing and evaluating in the context of the whole system the combination of several control functions and their supervision can be performed in two ways: hardware-in-the-loop testing, and virtual testing. Hardware-in-the-loop testing is typically supported by the present building block. In contrast, virtual testing requires mastering very complex models and their simulation, and is typically beyond the scope of generic tools covering the present building block.

Exporting Control Designs
Exporting control designs or models of control systems is more or less supported, depending on the cases:

- Exporting the physical, continuous time part, of the model for reuse as component in more powerful, possibly domain-specific, modellers. This service is provided by some tools, it does not seem to require specific research.
- Exporting models as IPs, in some kind of "compiled form", where reverse engineering is made difficult. This service is generally supported.
- Exporting models as components in a more general system model. There is a strong tendency that this type of engineering is supported by UML.
- Exporting digital control specifications to embedded software. This involves the whole chain of software architecture and code generation, and software testing. This is in part supported today, but this raises some difficulty we discuss below.

Existing Tools

Matlab/Simulink
Matlab/Simulink (http://www.mathworks.com/) is the de facto standard in this area. The history of its expansion is by itself of interest. Matlab started in the early eighties, as an interpreted and un-typed language for handling matrices. Everything was described as a matrix, and it was not required to declare its dimensions as they would be evaluated at run time. Matlab was targeted to students, and was a low power/low cost product. The next evolutionary step came later during the eighties, with the idea of having third-party toolboxes dedicated to a particular class of problems (system identification, control synthesis,…). This positioned Matlab as the "lego block" of the control science community, turning algorithms into software, and made its success. Modelling came as the next issue, as modellers appeared in academia in the late eighties – Simulink was issued in the early nineties. The nineties turned Matlab/Simulink to a sophisticated tool for visualization and data handling, and completed the range of services needed to perform XX_engineering. This decade (and the end of the previous one) has shown a significant move of Matlab/Simulink toward becoming a central tool for industry, not academia any more. The percentage of third party products has reduced drastically. New products addressing hardware-in-the-loop, code generation, real-time workbench, and the like, are now offered (this is further discussed later in the document). Perhaps the most interesting lesson from this is the fact that this tool became central in the whole design process, by starting from a positioning very early in the design steps. SystemBuild/MATRIXx, formerly from Wind River, is similar to the above product line, and occupies a similar segment. Due to its current unclear legal status, we do not discuss it further here.

Other tools exist in this segment, but are of much narrower scope and audience.

Scilab
The SCILAB tool is a free software tool, developed at INRIA http://www-rocq. inria.fr/scilab/ . It offers a core language comparable to Matlab, and an advanced Hybrid System modeller called SCICOS http://www-rocq.inria.fr/scilab/doc/ scicos_html. This modeller provides means to specify the synchronization of the digital part of the model without ambiguity, see below.

Modelica
The object-oriented modelling language Modelica is designed to allow convenient, component-oriented modelling of complex physical systems, e.g., systems containing mechanical, electrical, electronic, hydraulic, thermal, control, electric power or process-oriented subcomponents. The free Modelica language and free Modelica libraries are available. The development and promotion of Modelica is organized by the non-profit Modelica Association http://www.modelica.org/ . Modelica simulation tools are commercially available as part of Dymola, from Dynasim http://www.Dynasim.se/, ready-to-use and have been utilized in demanding industrial applications, including hardware-in-the-loop simulations.

Relevant Challenges and Work Directions

Scientific engineering tools and physical systems modellers are an area in which major breakthroughs, including assistance for modelling and simulation and control design and optimization have occurred in the past decade. This has been such an important step that scientific engineering tools are now at the centre of the design flow for several important industrial sectors (in particular automobile). Major challenges remain, however:

- *Medium-range physical Modelling Tools.* Regarding small or medium size physical models in both continuous and discrete time, progress is still being made towards better models, simulators, and system identification and signal processing techniques; improving the corresponding technologies is not considered to be the major issue for the coming years, however.

- *Complex Physical Modelling Tools.* Regarding models of larger or more complex systems involving both ODEs, PDEs, and DAEs (Differential Algebraic Equations, generalized ODEs that are relations and not input-output functions any more), possibly combined with discrete event systems for capturing mode changes, only domain specific tools are available today, not generic ones. In addition, these tools mainly address static aspects of the design (e.g., design of a mechanical structure), not their use for control design, where models with dynamics are required. Not surprisingly, having powerful modelling tools is a major focus of one Integrated Project proposal in the area of aeronautics for the 6th FP, dealing with the overall concept and structure of the aircraft. Having generic modelling tools for complex dynamical systems, industrially supported by a vendor, would be an important progress. However, this is somewhat beyond the scope of the present roadmap.

- *Hybrid Systems.* Whereas advanced toolboxes for control design or optimization are available, to assist the design engineer, such tools are generally only effective for each single mode of operation; there is a lack of support for the design of control in a Hybrid System context – e.g. designing jointly several control modes and their switching mechanisms. For that reason, a multi level hierarchical approach is taken, starting from a tool-assisted design of low-level closed-loop control for small components, up to a more heuristic design of the supervision of lower level functions (e.g., handling mode changes and protection). Studies in Hybrid Systems are needed to improve the assistance for this part of the design; however, no generic approach has been found yet in the academia toward getting tools for assisted modelling and control synthesis for Hybrid Systems.

- *Virtual Test beds.* Virtual testing requires mastering very complex models and their simulation. Progresses in "virtual test beds" are essential, but this topic is beyond the scope of the present roadmap.

- *Model Engineering.* There is a strong tendency that so-called Model Engineering is supported by UML; exporting to UML component models of scientific engineering type is not yet formally sound and remains a challenge for the future.

- *Timing and Synchronization Semantics of Hybrid Modelling Tools.* In most widely used hybrid system modelling tools, inadequate means are often provided to specify precisely how the different discrete times involved in the system should be synchronized. For example, suppose that you specify that signal x has frequency 100Hz and signal y has frequency 150Hz: both signals will start their first step exactly at simulation time zero. But this simulation is not representative of what will happen in the implementation, where "time zero" has no meaning. Therefore, a more canonical way of specifying synchronizations is needed. Developing hybrid system modelling tools in which the specification of discrete time/event system models is performed rigorously, without ambiguity and without over-specification, is important; advanced solvers supporting this are now available from research, and some modelling tools provide this feature.

4.3   State-Based Design: Dealing with Complex Discrete Control

Definition

If the dominant source of complexity of a controller rests in its dependency on a large set of discrete set of states, then modelling techniques supporting state-based design are the choice formalism for the specification of controllers. The need to capture complex state-behaviours for embedded system applications, in particular addressing their reactive nature, has been discussed in a series of landmark papers by David Harel, who introduced StateCharts as a succinct visual formalism to capture complex state-dependent reactive systems. Key ingredients extending the classical concept of finite state machines are the introduction of hierarchy and concurrency as modularization constructs: while states of classical finite state-machines are unstructured, State-Charts allow for

- *states to be refined to complete state-machines*: such a hierarchical state is typically used to capture some higher order mode of operation of the controller (such as "initialization", "normal operation", "exception x has occurred", "failure f has occurred"), where the detailed reactions of the controller in such a mode are specified by the state-machine attached to this hierarchical state;
- *orthogonal states* which consist of orthogonal components each being refined by a state chart, thus providing a direct modelling counterpart to the typical decomposition of controllers into sub-controllers running in parallel, each responsible for a particular aspect of the global control task (such as separate state-machines for monitoring critical sensors, for maintaining knowledge about plant states, for controlling multiple actuators;
- *communication and synchronization* between components of a state chart, by e.g. using broadcasting of events.

The basic concepts of state-charts have since been enriched by different means, including:

- using extended state-machines which in addition to explicitly modelled control states incorporate typed variables, conditions on these as guards, and means of updating variables by some form of action language;
- real-time by e.g. allowing to use time-outs as guards in conditions, or setting timers as part of the action language.

It has also been combined with such diverse modelling methods as:

- Functional Decomposition where a system is statically decomposed into subsystems and state-charts are used to capture the reactive behaviour of subsystems, as originally described in the seminal article by Harel et al;
- UML where state-charts are used to specify the behaviour of reactive classes, this again being based on pioneering work of David Harel;
- Control Modelling Tools where state-charts are used to capture modes of the controlled plant, and states can be used to select appropriate control laws depending on the current mode of the plant.

Use and Positioning in Design Flow

Typical usage of state-based specification techniques range from specification of electronic control units (in combination with modelling tools supporting functional decomposition or UML tools), or in control-law design for hybrid controllers (in conjunction with tools for modelling control laws, using a continuous time model, or with tools for code-generation, working with a discrete time model).

There a range of use-cases based on such specifications in a typical design flow. The following list follows the downward part of the V development cycle. As any executable model, state-based specifications support early validation of complex embedded systems. Of particular relevance are

- *Simulation*: including in particular co-simulation of a state-based controller with a continuous plant model, to explore and validate the specification model of the controller. Typically, modelling tools offer a range of animation capabilities supporting the exploration of the design, such as highlighting active states and active transitions, capturing traces from simulation-runs to allow re-run, generating scenarios from simulation runs, using animated panels to instrument simulation in an application-like setting, etc
- *Verification against requirements*: StateCharts are perhaps one of the best studied modelling techniques regarding interfaces to model-checkers (see the section on verification), allowing with varying degrees of richness of modelling features the verification of requirements against state-based models of reactive systems
- *Test-case generation*: there is a rich theory of test-case generation for simple models of state-based specifications, with recent extensions covering richer models
- *Automatic code generation*: today's commercial modelling tools for state-based design typically offer capabilities for automatic code generation not only for rapid prototyping but also for production code.

Existing Tools

There are too many tools supporting state-based design to allow a complete survey within this roadmap. We pick only representative examples from the different forms of integration with modelling paradigms and elaborate on these.

- *Functional Decomposition*: The StatemateMagnum Product from I-Logix Inc. (see www.ilogix.com) is widely used in avionics, space, and automotive applications for capturing system-, subsystem- and ECU specifications. From its original conception (involving with Amir Pnueli and David Harel key academic fathers) it has evolved to a comprehensive toolset allowing simulation, formal verification, automatic test-case generation, and (in conjunction with Rhapsody in MicroC) production quality code generation.

- *UML*: Since StateCharts form part of the UML standard, any UML compliant modelling tool such as RealTimeStudio Professional from Artisan (www. artisansw.com), Rational RoseRT from Rational (www.rational.com), and Rhapsody from I-Logix (www.ilogix.com) is supporting StateCharts for modelling the behaviour of reactive objects. As an example, the Rhapsody Product family provides executable UML models with animated simulation, production quality code generation with support for multiple target languages (C, C++, Java, ADA, multiple RTOS, and standard middleware layers such as Corba. Animated simulation as well as scenario based test-case generation support model validation as well as regression testing.

- *Control Modelling Tools*: Most tools for control modelling support variants of StateCharts in order to allow modelling of hybrid controllers as well as co-modelling of plants and controllers. As an example, the Matlab-Simulink product from the Mathworks Corporation (www.mathworks.com) can be enhanced with the Stateflow product to support state-dependent activation of Simulink blocks in animated simulation, as well as supporting embedded code generation through the Stateflow Coder in Combination with the RealTimeEmbeddedCoder. Product code quality code-generation for directly from Simulink-Stateflow models is also offered from dSpace (www.dspaceinc.com) with its TargetLink code generation tool. Esterel Technology (www.esterel.com) has recently acquired the Scade Product for automatic code generation from discrete-time controller models, which also includes limited capabilities for modelling state-machines. Similarly, the ASCET-SD product from ETAS (www.etas.de) allows the integration of state-machines in discrete-time controller models, offering production code quality code generation.

Relevant Challenges and Work Directions

State-based modelling techniques as such are a mature and well understood design paradigm. Research Challenges, however, originate when integrating these into richer modelling paradigms, in particular, when extending simulation, verification, test-generation, and code-generation to support this embedding. Challenging research issues include

- Co-verification: Addressing formal verification of models combining state-machines with plant models: while there is rich body of research on hybrid system verification (see the section on formal verification), efficient verification methods scalable to industrial hybrid controllers are not available.

  Addressing formal verification of UML models: the challenge here is to extend the well-studied verification methods for state chart verification to complete UML models, addressing such issues as inheritance, dynamic object creation and destruction, dynamically changing communication topologies, multiple active objects, etc.

- Distributed real-time code generation: The challenge is to extend the well understood principles of code generation from state-charts in its integration to richer
modelling paradigms to support distributed implementations using e.g. multiple
ECUs. While the time-triggered approach described in section 4.5.a is providing a
solution applicable for high-integrity components, it must be combined with more
flexible implementation schemes guaranteeing end-to-latencies or other real-time
constraints

5   Tools for Architecture Design and Capture

Although some industries perform architecture design and capture, this is not recognized a standard stage in the traditional design flow. But we believe it is an important missing piece. Since this is more exploratory, we have taken a different approach, by focusing on the important topic of architecture modelling and mapping, since it is a key step toward platform-based design as we advocate.

Definition

The essential difference between embedded software and general software is about the importance that execution time and other physical metrics bear on the quality of the design. For embedded software, execution time, power consumption and memory occupation are of paramount importance since they relate to implementation costs and performance requirements. Software per se does not carry information about execution time, memory occupation and power consumption. These quantities depend on the implementation platform that runs the software.

In traditional design methodologies, the line between functionality to implement and its software representation is often blurred: designers often think of software both as a representation of the functionality of their design and as implementation. If intended as a representation of the functionality of a design, software carries an implicit mathematical model, in general a Turing machine. In this case, the expressive power of the model is such that little can be said about its properties and yet the model does not carry any information about the physical properties of the implementation.

Following this line of reasoning, it is then natural to abstract the notion of software at a higher level. In this case then, software implies that a particular functionality will be implemented on a platform equipped with a software programmable component that can run it. Hence, software is to be intended ONLY as an implementation representation. In this case then, it is natural to decorate the representation with physical parameters summarizing the properties of the hardware platform. If we take then the higher level representation as a starting point of the design, the essential point of the design process is how to proceed towards implementation, how to trace backward the implementation against early specification, and how to choose the appropriate implementation platform.

The consensus of the system design community has evolved towards the so called Y-chart view: the functionality of the design is associated via a mapping process to elements of an architecture that is specified side-by-side. This view differs from the top-down method promoted in the 1980s where the functionality is successively refined into an implementation. In the modern view, an architecture can be defined independently of the particular functionality to be implemented. In this case then, the refinement process becomes a mapping process. This approach has become popular because of the changes in the economics of IC design and manufacturing. The increasing cost of mask making and design has been a forcing function towards the adoption of platforms that can support a rather wide range of applications to maxi-

Artist FP5 Consortium: Embedded Systems Design, LNCS 3436, 54–62, 2005.
© Springer-Verlag Berlin Heidelberg 2005

mize volume. The key to conjugate different applications and single implementation architecture is the use of programmable or reconfigurable blocks that can be customized with no need to change the mask set to support different functionality. The extension of the concept of platform has brought to the limelight platform-based design, a design methodology that exploits design re-use and formal techniques for representation and refinement of the design. In this method, a platform is a "library" of components including interconnects. Design space exploration is the process of selecting optimally the elements of the library to support a given functionality. In this view, it is clearly very important to characterize the capabilities of the elements of the library in terms of their physical properties, e.g., power consumption, speed of execution, and size. The library and its characterization is non trivial and represents the bottom-up component in platform-based design.

If a common semantic domain can be found between the higher level of abstraction and the collection of components of the lower level platform, the optimal mapping process and the corresponding selection of a platform instance can be often formalized as a unate or binate covering problem. Then the concurrent mapping and platform selection can be performed automatically, similar to what has been done for years in the area of logic synthesis, where the higher level of abstraction is represented by a Boolean network, the common semantic domain as a two-input NAND gate network and the mapping process as a binate covering problem of the network with NAND gate sub-networks representing the elements of the library. The discovery of a formal representation of two consecutive platforms and of their common semantic domain is the essence of this design method. While there are successful examples of this paradigm, much remains to be done to extend it to a large number of design problems and levels of abstraction.

Position in the Design Flow

Architecture modelling and exploration would typically occur early in the design flow, just after the specification and validation of the functions themselves. Architecture exploration should precede code generation and related activities.

Existing Tools

Warning: the reader should be warned that the following list of tools may be biased. The reason is that architecture modelling and mapping is not an established building block. Hence there is no common agreement about what it really is, and which tools are proper representatives.

- *OCASIM* (no web link available)
  OCASIM is the in-house tool used at Airbus-France for the co-simulation of SCADE designs with some abstract models of the plant for control; in performing this, essential features of the computer architecture and sensor system are captured. For example, uncertainties in timing due to sampling and delays in the communications can be handled. OCASIM is a purely discrete time modeller, meaning that important aspects related to continuous time are abstracted.

- *POLIS/VCC* http://www-cad.eecs.berkeley.edu/Respep/Research/hsc/abstract.html
  Polis was developed at the University of California, Berkeley, in the early 1990s. It
  was a tool intended to help designing automotive safety-critical systems such as
  engine controllers. The approach was based on a rigorous separation between function and architecture and it was the first incarnation of the Y-diagram. The functionality of the system was captured with a network of Co-design Finite State Machines (CFSM). CFSMs implement a globally asynchronous-locally synchronous
  model of computation. The semantics of each CFSM was captured with Esterel
  while the interaction was asynchronous with a length one buffer to deposit messages waiting to be read. Buffer overwriting and consequent loss of information
  could not be prevented a priori. This model of computation was adopted to support
  the methodology used by automotive subsystem designers that could not afford the
  loss of efficiency that would have resulted using a synchronous model of computation.

  The methodology called for mapping of the functionality on a single CPU architecture. Mapping efficiency was quickly evaluated by running a performance
  analysis based on a simple model of the execution of software on the CPU. To do
  so, the CFSMs were turned into software for the part of the system to be mapped
  on the CPU or into hardware for the parts mapped into ASIC-like logic.

  The tool supported automatic and optimized software generation with a method
  that was derived from the work on logic synthesis of the Berkeley group. The
  method that gave the best results in terms of code execution time and memory occupation was based on Binary Decision Diagrams (BDD).

  Because the structure of the code was highly optimized performance estimation
  was quite accurate with respect to final implementation. Interactions among
  CFSMs were handled by the RTOS. Polis had the possibility of automatically generating RTOS code that was tailored for the particular application thus resulting
  into small and very efficient code.

  To verify the functionality of the entire system a path to an FPGA rapid prototype board was provided. Because of the relatively small size of the board, the
  functionality could be verified directly in the car, thus eliminating the need of expensive experiments on test-benches.

  The basic ideas of the tool were the basis for a commercial offering by Cadence
  called VCC. VCC was built on the same models of computation but extended the
  applicability of the tool to multi-CPU systems such as the distributed systems
  commonly found in cars. The models for processors were extended to cover a variety of different computing cores but automatic code generation and optimization
  was not offered to the market. Mapped software is of two kinds: black box that
  cannot be estimated and white box whose performance could be estimated. Several
  architectures could be quickly evaluated by mapping the functionality to different
  subsystems. VCC is the basis for SysDesign, a complete environment for automotive system design that several other tools such as Simulink and ASCET-SD from
  ETAS to capture the functionality of the design, Mathworks, dSpace and ETAS
  tools for code generation and rapid prototyping. In this environment, different bus
  and communication schema could be analyzed and compared. In addition, fault
  analysis could be carried out at levels of abstraction as different as at the functional
  and detailed architectural level.

The tool was intended to support the design chain. In fact, it could be used by software developer to analyze the performance of their code on a virtual prototyping environment as well as by the platform developer to select the most appropriate platform for an application domain. The domain of application expanded from automotive to wireless communication and multi-media.

- *Virtio* (http://www.virtio.com)
  According to the technical leaders of the corporation, the mission of the company is the creation and distribution of virtual platforms – to both applications software people as well as Hardware-dependent software designers. Virtual prototyping is an advanced simulation technology combining high-speed instruction-set simulators with memory transaction-level peripheral models. This technology is tuned in several ways to software developers:

  * It offers execution speeds of multi-million instructions per second, allowing to boot operating systems like Windows CE in about 30 seconds.

  * It integrates with industry-standard software development tools, such as Microsoft Platform Builder and Wind River's Tornado II.

  * It features virtualized physical connections, allowing for example to connect the platform to a physical network and advanced user interfaces and 'skin' capabilities to realistically emulate the system user experience

  In addition, it features authoring tools to extend the base platform with user components, supporting the 'platform-based' design flow.

  The simulator is instruction set accurate, not cycle accurate. Because of the abstraction level supported, can certainly help software designers to understand the actual performance of their software on the execution platform but it may suffer some limitation in terms of accuracy.

- *VaST* (http://www.vastsystems.com/)
  This tool targets engineering and manufacturing of high performance, real-time electronic systems integrating software, hardware and other technology components. They provide the behavioural models (virtual processor model or VPM) for the processors, buses and a few basic peripherals (e.g. a basic interrupt); customers write the behavioural models for most of the peripherals. To be consistent with the overall performance goals of the toolset, the models must be executable at least at 5-10MIPS.

  The VPM is composed of two parts. In the first, which models the instruction execution behaviour, an analyzer builds a custom virtual processor model (VPM) based on all or some elective subset of the architectural elements required in the processor, from the target code. This task seems to be "code dependent", but it is a totally automated process. This static analysis is analogous to 'static timing analysis' in circuit simulation and the resulting model runs very fast. The code executed by a VPM may be HLL C/C++ code or assembly/object level code.

  The second part models the dynamic parts of the processor; these portions cannot be determined prior to simulation. This includes the I/O part of the processor that communicates with the hardware: cache, virtual memory, interrupts, bus signals, and the like. For obvious reasons, the simulation speed on this portion is limited by the level of detail modelled, and, where communication with hardware occurs, the speed of the hardware simulator during that communication.

With a VPM, it is also possible to select the architectural elements and the level of detail modelled in both the dynamic and static portions of the design. In this way, processors can be customized for a particular use, or modelled as cores or selectable catalogue components.

The speed of simulation is high and the accuracy good. The balance of these two factors make it an interesting tool for the development of real-time embedded software in conjunction with multi-processor architecture exploration and analysis tools.

- *AXYS* (http://www.AXYSdesign.com/)

  AXYS Design envisions that in the not too distant future semiconductor components will be offered, evaluated and purchased primarily based on virtual software prototypes of entire systems. These virtual prototypes, in form of executable, reusable models running in real-time on powerful workstations, will represent the functional behaviours and timing of the actual system-on-chip (SoC) devices. The early interactive communication between IP designers and their clients in the design of next-generation communication and entertainment devices will become crucial to their mutual success. The vision of virtual SoC prototyping and IP communication will enable a substantial reduction in time and cost compared to traditional silicon prototyping.

  AXYS Design's mission is to provide C/C++ based exploration, modelling and verification solutions and services enabling designers to efficiently specify, design, test, protect and deliver "above-RTL" models of their intellectual property and SoC designs. AXYS Design's solutions are used by hardware and software designers to explore the suitability of certain architectures and start software development before actual silicon becomes available thus reducing overall time to market for complex SoC products.

  AXYS addresses platform and hardware-aware software development (MaxSim Control Centre). AXYS offers multi-debugger support and accurate modelling. It can support DSPs, where reading and writing from and to memory in the right phases are essential for performance analysis.

  The performance is lower than VaST (and Virtio) due to their use of a compiled-code model, separate cache model, and very precise hardware timing. On the other hand, the accuracy they can offer makes its use interesting for hardware designers who develop platforms to be effective for a particular class of software applications.

- *Metropolis* http://www.gigascale.org/metropolis/

  Metropolis is an environment for design representation, analysis and synthesis under development at the University of California at Berkeley, under the sponsorship of the MARCO Gigascale System Research Center. The project involves a number of other Universities such as CMU, MIT, Politecnico di Torino, Politecnico di Milano, Cataluna Polytechnic, Scuola di Sant'Anna as well as industry such as Intel, Cypress, ST, Magneti-Marelli, PARADES and Cadence. The environment is not limited to Architecture modelling and mapping but it deals with all aspects and phases of design from conception to final implementation.

  In particular, Metropolis is designed to provide an infrastructure based on a model with precise semantics that remain general enough to support existing computation models and accommodate new ones (for this reason it is called meta-model). This meta-model can support not only functionality capture and analysis, but also architecture description and the mapping of functionality to architectural elements. Metropolis uses a logic language to capture extra-functional and declarative constraints. Because the model has a precise semantics, it can support several synthesis and formal analysis tools in addition to simulation. The first design activity Metropolis supports, communication of design intent and results, focuses on the interactions between people working at different abstraction levels and between people working concurrently at the same abstraction level. The meta-model includes constraints that represent in abstract form requirements not yet implemented or assumed to be satisfied by the rest of the system and its environment.

The second design activity, analysis, through simulation and formal verification is designed to determine how well an implementation satisfies the requirements. Proper use of abstraction can dramatically accelerate verification. The constant use of detailed representations, on the other hand, can introduce excessive dependencies between developers, reduce the interfacing requirements' understand ability, and diminish the efficiency of analysis mechanisms.

Metropolis addresses the third design activity, synthesis, throughout the abstraction levels used in a design. Setting parameters of architectural elements such as cache sizes or designing scheduling algorithms and interface blocks are typical problems, in addition to synthesis of the final implementations in hardware and software. In Metropolis, a specification may mix declarative and executable constructs of the meta-model. This is automatically translated to semantically equivalent mathematical models, to which the synthesis algorithms are applied.

One might argue that application domains and their constraints on attributes such as cost, energy, performance, design time, and safety are so different that there is insufficient economy of scale to justify developing tools to automate these design activities. The Metropolis project, however, seeks to show that this is untrue for at least a broad class of domains and implementation choices.

The choice of technique or algorithm for analysis and synthesis of a particular design depends on the application domain and the design phase. For example, safety-critical applications may need formal verification techniques, which require significant human skills for use on realistic designs. On the other hand, formal verification tools can execute simple low-level equivalence checks between various abstraction levels in hardware design—such as logic versus transistor levels.

Thus, Metropolis is not intended to provide algorithms and tools for all possible design activities. Instead, it offers syntactic and semantic mechanisms to compactly store and communicate all relevant design information, and designers can use it to plug in the required algorithms for a given application domain or design flow.

The model includes a parser that reads meta-model designs and a standard API that lets developers browse, analyze, modify, and augment additional information within those designs. For each tool integrated into Metropolis, a back-end uses the API to generate required input by the tool from the design's relevant portion. This unified mechanism makes it easy to incorporate tools developed elsewhere, as demonstrated by integrating the Spin software verification tool into Metropolis.

- *TTPMatlink* and *TTPXX*. http://www.tttech.com
  MATLAB, Simulink und Stateflow are development and simulation tools well-established and widely used in the automotive industry. TTPMatlink complements

these tools by a block set that interprets the time-triggered communication behaviour into the simulation model.

TTPMatlink supports the development of distributed control systems. Once the control application is designed and tasks are assigned to the nodes of the system, the TTP communication messages that need to be exchanged must be defined. The designer completes the cluster design process by configuring the communication system (e.g. TDMA round duration, transmission rate, type of communication controller). TTPMatlink enables the simulation of the distributed system in combination with the previously developed communication behaviour.

All design data created using TTPMatlink can be exported to TTPlan, the cluster design tool for TTP-based systems. TTPlan constructs the TDMA communication schedule and stores it in the MEDL (MEssage Descriptor List). The MEDL, which includes the entire configuration of the communication schedule, is loaded into the communication controller in the implementation phase. The node design divides the application algorithms of the subsystems into tasks and specifies them.

The design data of the tasks can be exchanged in TTPBuild, the TTP node design tool. TTPBuild calculates the timing of the task for each node and generates the fault-tolerant layer (FT-COM Layer).

In the next step the designer uses TTPMatlink and the Real-Time Workshop Embedded Coder to produce code suitable for TTP/OS, the TTP real-time operating system, and the fault-tolerant layer (FT-COM Layer). For the design of the input-output behaviour Simulink's so called I/O block library is used in order to parameterize specific hardware products (TTPBy-Wire Box, TTPSensor Box). Generating the driver code for these I/O blocks and putting it into the application code makes the implementation of the input-output behaviour in control units simple. After the C code has been compiled and linked, the machine code can be loaded into the distributed system via the application download of TTPLoad. This can be done directly from the user interface of TTPMatlink.

As evidenced by the above description, the pair of tools {Simulink/Stateflow, TTPlan} play the role of a platform in this approach.

- *ModelBuild* – now part of Sildex-V6 http://www.tni-world.com/sildex.asp
  ModelBuild was developed within the SafeAir project as an architectural description editor. It is built on top of the commercial Sildex product http://www.tnivaliosys.com/index.html marketed by TNI-Valiosys, based on the Signal synchronous language. ModelBuild provides services to perform the integration of components describing both hardware and/or software – currently, these components can be imported from Sildex, Scade, Simulink, or Statechart descriptions.

  To this end, a GALS (Globally Asynchronous Locally Synchronous) library has been developed. It contains components for use in system descriptions; any wire can be labelled with a protocol name. The GALS library contains Signal components modelling communication protocols (including a FIFO service). New protocols can be added. The following classes of components are distinguished:
  * Active (i.e. synchronous) links that carry control along with data; they provide triggering facility; triggering can be based on time.
  * Passive (i.e. asynchronous) links that do not carry control, hence cannot trigger actions.

ModelBuild through so-called "trigger" components allows to explicitly specify when an action takes place. Complex triggers have been modelled, including preemptive tasks. A task attribute contains information such as task priority, nature (cyclic, sporadic, background), timing properties like WCET (Worst Case Execution Time) or average execution time. Timing annotations are used for simulating a behaviour; in some cases they can even be used to prove its correctness. Execution time prediction is possible for RTOS-less architectures in cases that go far beyond fixed-cycle sequencers and include run-time data-dependent decisions that affect scheduling, not only from state to state, but even inside reactions (like mode changes and processing of hazardous situations and events). Such dynamic analysis gives the same level of confidence on systems with complex schedulers than what was previously achieved by hand on fixed cyclic sequencers; this drastic improvement is due to the automation of the verification process that allows schedulers with thousands of states to be analyzed exactly. A dedicated library for the industrial aeronautical ARINC653 real-time operating system standard has been provided as a result of SafeAir project.

- *Polychrony* http://www.irisa.fr/espresso/Polychrony

The Polychrony workbench is an academic platform-based design workbench which provides a reference implementation of the SIGNAL synchronous language. The goal of Polychrony is to implement mathematical models and formal methods suitable for both refinement-based and component-based design of embedded systems. To this aim, the Polychrony workbench implements the polychronous model of computation, it is proposed to provide sort of a continuum from synchrony to asynchrony. Refinement-based design is supported by formal properties of input-endochrony (controllability of a component by its environment) and flow-invariance (invariance of flow-equivalence under specification refinement via protocol insertion), implemented by either static resolution of model checking. Component-based design is implemented by the capture of existing designs (real-time JAVA classes SpecC modules and provides Polychrony with the ability to be employed as a reference workbench for platform-based design. To allow for a seamless, correct-by-construction design of embedded systems and architectures, the Polychrony workbench implements semantics-preserving model transformations (hierarchization of control, synthesis of protocols) as well as a general notion of morphism, which encompasses e.g., WCET analysis, into a generic abstract interpretation framework consisting of the projection of a design model with respect to a given, functional or extra-functional, behavioural aspect.

- SynDEx http://SynDEx.org/

This is system-level CAD software, supporting the AAA (Algorithm Architecture Adequation) methodology http://SynDEx.org/pub.htm to support the implementation of real-time embedded applications on distributed architectures. SynDEx is a graphical interactive software, which offers the following features:

* Functional specification through links to various notations, including the Synchronous Languages, Scicos, AIL, AVS;

* Abstract modelling of a distributed architecture composed of processors of different types and/or dedicated integrated circuits (ASIC, FPGA), all together interconnected by different types of network models;

* Profiling the mapping to architecture in terms of execution time for functions and for data transfers, memory, surface, power consumption, etc;
* Automatic mapping (adequation) through heuristics for the distribution and the scheduling of the algorithm onto the architecture taking into account communications, provided with a timing diagram simulating real-time performances;
* Automatic code generation of dedicated distributed real-time executives, or configuration of general purpose executives like: RT-Linux, OSEK, etc. These executives are deadlock free and based on off-line scheduling policies. Dedicated executives which induce minimal over-head are built from processor-dependent executive kernels. Presently executives kernels are provided for: ADSP216X, TMS320C4X, TMS320C6X, i80CI96, i80X86, MC68332, MPC555 and Unix/Linux workstations.

Relevant Challenges and Work Directions

Main problems for research are:

- Characterization of complex components such as sophisticated microprocessors and DSPs in terms of their physical parameters (WCET, power consumption, heat dissipation…).
- Choice of the common semantic domain where the mapping process can be represented formally.
- Performance estimation of software running on microprocessor has been the subject of intense research over the past few years. Performance estimation belongs to the general problem of characterization of mapped behaviour as expressed above. Indeed performance estimation is in our opinion essential to characterize the quality of a mapping of functionality to a microprocessor, but it has to be understood that estimation is not and cannot be 100% accurate. Being able to give an upper bound for the difference between execution time on the final implementation and its estimation is an open research issue.

From this discussion, it should be clear that mapping is central to embedded system design. We believe that embedded software design cannot be carried out in a rigorous fashion without considering mapping as a fundamental step of the methodology.

6   Tools for Programming, Code Generation, and Design

6.1   Structure

Here we consider methods to produce code, or to generate it. We do not consider the system level, but only the level of components or subsystems. To list the possible methods, we need a three-dimensional classification:

1. Nature of the targeted subsystems:

   a. continuous-dominated, e.g., power train or chassis for automobiles, and flight control for aeronautics;

   b. discrete-dominated, e.g., infotainment for automobile.

2. Considered method:

   a. code generation chains associated with requirements capture methods and tools, as listed in the corresponding section – Real-time workshop from Mathworks, ASCET, TargetLink from dSpace, Rhapsody in MicroC, UML tools supporting code generation.

   b. synchronous languages and associated code generation.

   c. direct programming in C, Ada (Hood, Spark-Ada), Java.

3. Level of code generation:

   a. high-level (e.g., from synchronous languages to C);

   b. back-end compilation (C to embedded code).

6.2   Code Generation from Synchronous Languages

Definition

Synchronous languages [SP-IEEE,Hal93,SP-IEEE03] are a family of high-level programming languages devoted to the design of reactive software. A reactive program is intended to interact permanently with its environment, at speed determined by this environment (which cannot wait nor synchronize with the program). Almost all pieces of software devoted to the control of physical devices are or contain such reactive programs. In the synchronous paradigm, the execution of a program is a sequence of atomic reactions to inputs coming from the environment.

The synchronous nature of the languages comes from the fact that they provide a logical, deterministic, notion of concurrency: basically, all the concurrent processes participate to each reaction of the program. An atomic reaction may involve a sequence of interactions between the concurrent processes. In these languages, concur-

Artist FP5 Consortium: Embedded Systems Design, LNCS 3436, 63–71, 2005.

rency is a powerful way of decomposing program activities, without paying the price of actual concurrency concerning complexity (non-determinism) and efficiency (runtime scheduling). Popular synchronous languages can be imperative (Esterel [BG92], Synccharts [André96]) or declarative (Signal [GLB87], Lustre [HCRP91], Scade). Although many research topics are still in progress in this area (concerning, e.g., semantics of synchrony, program verification and validation ...), we concentrate here on the problem of code generation from these languages.

The automatic code generation from high level descriptions is of course an important goal, both for reducing the design cost, and for increasing its quality. Synchronous languages provide both a high level, clean and formal way of describing embedded systems, and the ability to translate automatically these descriptions into efficient code. In general, the translation is made into low level languages (e.g., C), for several reasons: easy interfacing of the generated code with other pieces of program, independence of the compiler with respect to the target executable code.

The primary goal of a designer of safety-critical embedded systems is convincing him- or herself, the customer, and certification authorities that the design and its implementation are correct. At the same time, he or she must keep development and maintenance costs under control and meet extra-functional constraints on the design of the system, such as cost, power, weight, or the system architecture by itself (e.g., a physically distributed system comprising intelligent sensors and actuators, supervised by a central computer). In the 1980s, these observations lead to the following decisions for the synchronous languages:

- *Concurrency*
  The languages must support functional concurrency, and they must rely on notations that express concurrency in a user-friendly manner. Therefore, depending on the targeted application area, the languages should offer as a notation block diagrams (also called dataflow diagrams), or hierarchical automata, or some imperative type of syntax, familiar to the targeted engineering communities. Later, in the early nineties, the need appeared for mixing these different styles of notations. This obviously required that they all have the same mathematical semantics.
- *Simplicity*
  The languages must have the simplest formal model possible to make formal reasoning tractable. In particular, the semantics for the parallel composition of two processes must be the cleanest possible.
- *Synchrony*
  The languages must support the simple and frequently-used implementation models shown below, where all mentioned actions are assumed to take finite memory and time.

Combining synchrony and concurrency, while maintaining a simple mathematical model, is not so straightforward. Here, we discuss the approach taken by the synchronous languages. Synchrony divides time into discrete instants. This model is pervasive in mathematics and engineering. It appears in automata, in the discrete-time dynamical systems familiar to control engineers, and in synchronous digital logic familiar to hardware designers. Hence it was natural to decide that a synchronous program would progress according to successive atomic reactions. Combining programs then amounts to defining how to combine reactions; getting a clean mathematical concept to support this was by no means easy. It has led to a rich body of knowledge and techniques including the so-called causality analysis, automatic program scheduling generation, and finally code generation.

Position in the Design Flow

Although synchronous languages were first designed as programming languages, their compilation is generally considered as automatic code generation by industrial users. As a matter of fact, the level of expression of synchronous languages is the one of usual specification formalisms used in the industry; in the normal approach, the coding phase consists in translating manually such specifications into low level programming languages. The automatic code generation is intended to suppress not only the manual coding phase, but also – and perhaps more importantly – the expensive unit testing phase, which consists in testing the code of each module against their individual specifications, in order to detect coding errors.

Existing Tools

Code generators were first developed in academic contexts [BG92, Ber92, GLB87, BL90, HCRP91, HRR91]. Industrial versions are now commercially available: from Esterel-Technology (see http://www.esterel-technologies.com/v2/index.html) for Esterel and Lustre-Scade, and from TNI-Valiosys (see http://www.tni-valiosys.com/index.html) for Signal-Sildex.

Relevant Challenges and Work Directions

The ability of synchronous languages to be translated automatically into efficient code is a major reason for their success. However, some important issues remain more or less open.

- *Code Quality*
  In new application domains, like automotive, there is a strong need for improving the quality of the generated code, both concerning its size and its performances. Important efforts are ongoing on the compiling of Esterel [Edw02, WBC+00] into software. Moreover, in some application domains, users want to influence the scheduling of computations within a synchronous instant, by specifying, for instance, a response time between some data acquisition and a corresponding output. Such "micro-scheduling" can be performed, to some extend, in the SAXO compiler [WBC+00]. Conversely, taking into account the target architecture and/or the dependence graph, global scheduling of individual components can be computed; this contributes to reduce OS overhead. More generally static analysis techniques can be used to optimize the generated code.
- *Code Certification*
  In the domains of critical software, automatic code generation has to cope with the problem of code certification. In order to save efforts not only in manual code generation effort, but also in coding validation (unit testing), the automatically generated code must be certified, in the sense that certification authorities can accept it without further validation. It is a major industrial concern. Presently, this can be

done by qualifying the code generator, which generally implies to develop the code generator with the same norms that are applied to the embedded software development (this is what happened for the Scade-KCG code generator). This increases tremendously the cost of development of the code generator, and also the cost of any change in the language or its compiler. An alternative solution [PSS98] is to formally and automatically verify the correctness of the translation for each translated program. This very interesting track must be further explored, and is not yet admitted by certification authorities.

- *Code Distribution*
Another longstanding challenge is code generation for distributed architectures. While some specific architectures, like TTA [Kop98], are perfectly convenient to execute a synchronous program in parallel, the same problem for general architectures is difficult. Some research works [ML94, BCT99, BCG99, CGP99, GM02] concerned distributed implementations preserving the synchronous semantics, while other approaches [Cas01] accept some relaxing of these strict semantics. Finally, work on distributed fault-tolerant implementations was also conducted [DGLS01, GLSS01].

- *On the Frontier of Synchrony*
Applications suggest that the pure synchronous model should be made "less synchronous", in several ways. For instance, it is very common, in periodically sampled systems, to have several periods, with loose communication between tasks on different periods; this is not yet allowed in pure synchronous languages. Another situation is the mixing of periodic sampling and event triggered reactions. More generally, it raises the problem of implementing synchronous programs on top of a real-time OS, allowing multi-tasking, interrupts, etc. These problems have been studied in the context of polychronous model [SL97, AL96, GG99]. Research on the frontiers between synchrony, polychrony, and asynchrony must be pursued.

- *Back to the languages*
All the previous topics have some consequences on the extensions of languages. Real-time constraints, "desynchronisations", distributed implementation constraints, and so on, must be expressed in the source language. Moreover, a better expression of program and data structures enables a better code generation [Mor02]. Also, declarative specifications of properties (e.g., assertions) could be used during the compilation, through the use, for instance, of discrete control synthesis techniques [ACMR03]. So, the development of the languages is far from being terminated

References

[André 96]   C. André. Representation and analysis of reactive behaviours: a synchronous approach. In IEEE-SMC'96, Computational Engineering in Systems Applications, Lille, France, July 1996.

[ACMR03]   K. Altisen, A. Clodic, F. Maraninchi, and E. Rutten. Using controller-synthesis techniques to build property-enforcing layers. In European Symposium on Programming, ESOP'03. Warsaw, Poland, April 2003.

[AL96]   P. Aubry, P. Le Guernic. Synchronous distribution of Signal programs. In 29th Hawaii International Conference on System Sciences, IEEE Computer Society Press, Volume 1, 1996.

[BCG99]   A. Benveniste, B. Caillaud, and P. Le Guernic. From synchrony to asynchrony. In J.C.M. Baeten and S. Mauw, editors, CONCUR'99. LNCS 1664, Springer Verlag, 1999.

[BCT99]   A. Benveniste, P. Caspi, and S. Tripakis. Distributing synchronous programs on a loosely synchronous, distributed architecture. Research Report 1289, Irisa, December 1999.

[Ber92]   G. Berry. A hardware implementation of pure Esterel. ACM Workshop on Formal Methods in VLSI Design, Miami, January 1991.

[BG92]   G. Berry and G. Gonthier. The Esterel synchronous programming language: design, semantics, implementation. Science of Computer Programming, 19(2), 1992.

[BL90]   A. Benveniste and P. Le Guernic. Hybrid dynamical systems theory and the Signal language. IEEE Transactions on Automatic Control, 35(5), May 1990.

[Cas01]   P. Caspi. Embedded control: From asynchrony to synchrony and back. In 1st International Workshop on Embedded Software, EMSOFT2001, Lake Tahoe, USA, October 2001. LNCS 2211.

[CGP99]   P. Caspi, A. Girault, and D. Pilaud. Automatic distribution of reactive systems for asynchronous networks of processors. In IEEE Trans. On Software Engineering, 25:3, May-June 1999.

[DGLS01]   C. Dima, A. Girault, C. Lavarenne, and Y. Sorel. Off-line real-time fault-tolerant scheduling. In 9th Euromicro Workshop on Parallel and Distributed Processing, PDP'01. Mantova, Italy, February 2001.

[Edw02]   S. A. Edwards. An Esterel compiler for large control-dominated systems. IEEE Transactions on Computer-Aided Design of Integrated Circuits and Systems, 21, 2002.

[GG99]   T. Gautier, P. Le Guernic. Code generation in the SACRES project. In Towards System Safety, Proceedings of the Safety-critical Systems Symposium, SSS'99, Huntingdon, UK, Springer, 1999, 127-149.

[GLB87]   T. Gauthier, P. Le Guernic and L. Besnard. Signal, a declarative language for synchronous programming of real-time systems. Proc. 3rd Conf. on Functional Programming Languages and Computer Architecture, LNCS 274, Springer Verlag, 1987.

[GLSS01]   A. Girault, C. Lavarenne, M. Sighireanu, and Y. Sorel. Fault-tolerant static scheduling for real-time distributed embedded systems. In 21st IEEE International Conference on Distributed Computing Systems, ICDCS'01. Phœnix, USA, April

[GM02]   2000irault and C. Ménier. Automatic production of globally asynchronous locally synchronous systems. In 2nd International Workshop on Embedded Software, EMSOFT'02. Grenoble, France, October 2002, LNCS 2491.

[Hal93]   N. Halbwachs. Synchronous programming of reactive systems. Kluwer Academic Pub., 1993.

[HCRP91]   N. Halbwachs, P. Caspi, P. Raymond, and D. Pilaud. The synchronous dataflow programming language Lustre. Proceedings of the IEEE, 79(9), September 1991

[HRR91]   N. Halbwachs, P. Raymond, and C. Ratel. Generating efficient code from dataflow programs. 3rd Int. Symp. on Programming Language Implementation and Logic Programming, LNCS 528, Springer Verlag, August 1991.

[Kop98]   H. Kopetz. The time-triggered architecture. In ISORC '98, Kyoto, Japan, April 1998.

[ML94]   O. Maffeïs and P. Le Guernic. Distributed implementation of Signal: scheduling and graph structuring. In 3rd International School and Symposium on Formal Techniques in Real-Time and Fault-Tolerant Systems, LNCS 863, 1994.

[Mor02]   L. Morel. Efficient compilation of array iterators for Lustre. In First Workshop on Synchronous Languages, Applications, and Programming, SLAP'02, Grenoble, April 2002.

[PSS98]   A. Pnueli, M. Siegel, and O. Shtrichman. Translation validation for synchronous languages. In K.G. Larsen, S. Skyum, and G. Winskel, editors, 5th International Colloquium on Automata, Languages, and Programming, ICALP 1998. LNCS 1443, 1998.

[SL97]   I. Smarandache and P. Le Guernic. Affine transformations in Signal and their application in the specification and validation of real-time systems. In 4th International AMAST Workshop on Real-Time Systems and Concurrent and Distributed Software, LNCS 1231, 1997.

[SP-IEEE]   A. Benveniste, G. Berry Eds. Another look at real-time programming. Special Section of the Proceedings of the IEEE, 79(9), September 1991.

[SP-IEEE03] A. Benveniste, P. Caspi, S. Edwards, N. Halbwachs, P. Le Guernic, R. de Simone. The synchronous languages 12 years later. Proceedings of the IEEE, 91(1), special issue on embedded systems, 64-83,January 2003.

[WBC+00]   D. Weil, V. Bertin, E. Closse, M. Poisse, P. Venier, and J. Pulou. Efficient compilation of Esterel for real-time embedded systems. In International Conference on Compilers, Architecture, and Synthesis for Embedded System, CASES'00, San Jose, USA, 2000.

[GTL03]   Le Guernic, P., Talpin, J.-P.,Le Lann, J.-C. . Polychrony for system design. http://www.irisa.fr/prive/talpin/papers/rr-jcsc02.ps.gz . Journal for Circuits, Systems and Computers. Special Issue on Application Specific Hardware Design/. (c) World Scientific, April 2003. Available as /INRIA research report n. 4715/, December 2002.

6.3   Back-End Code Generation – Below C

Definition

Compilation of programming languages such as C and Ada to the machine language of embedded processors. The area of Compilation for Embedded Systems is largely driven by the demand for very high efficiency of compiled code. This includes design goals like high performance and low code size, but more recently also low energy code generation for portable systems. Only a small code quality overhead as compared to hand-optimized assembly code is acceptable for real-life applications. This asks for novel and aggressive code optimization technologies that make optimal use of the specialized architectures of embedded processors.

Position in the Design Flow

High-level programming languages such as C/C++ and Ada are used as targets of code generation from formal specifications (Code Generation in the SafeAir- Design Flow) and as direct coding vehicles. Their use has boosted productivity and reduced time-to-market in embedded software development.

Support for high-level language programming requires efficient compilers, mostly for C and C++. While compiler construction for general-purpose processor is a quite mature technology, the situation is different in the area of embedded systems. This is due to two reasons: (a) a large variety of domain or application specific programmable processors and (b) the need for extremely efficient code.

Retargetable Compilers
Due to the high efficiency requirements in embedded system design, there is a large variety of domain-specific processors available on the semiconductor market, e.g. special-purpose processors for audio and video signal processing (DSPs) or protocol processing in networking applications (NPUs). Moreover, more and more system houses tend to develop their own in-house processors for specific applications (ASIPs), in order to achieve a cost reduction and better product differentiation. In order to save development time and cost for C/C++ compilers for such processors, retargetable compilers [1] are needed whose back ends can be quickly adapted to new target architectures. Particularly in the case of ASIP design, retargetable compilers are critical in the design flow, since they support architecture exploration in order to determine the optimal processor architecture for a given range of applications. Incorporating the C/C++ compiler directly in the exploration flow, together with further tools like simulator, debugger, assembler, and linker, permits to achieve an optimal hardware/software match early in the design process. This idea of "compiler-in-the-loop" architecture exploration (see fig.) has also been adopted by major semiconductor vendors (e.g. Intel, STMicroelectronics, and Texas Instruments) and is expected to gain even wider importance in the future.

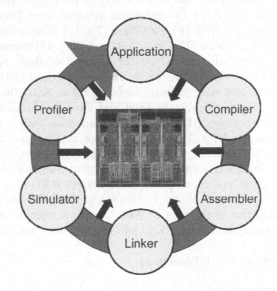

Advanced Code Optimization for Embedded Processors
Traditionally, most embedded software applications have been coded in assembly languages, a very tedious and error-prone method that results in low portability and dependability. This has been necessary, since the need for the most efficient implementation prohibited the use of high-level language compilers. Only a small overhead of compiled code versus hand-written assembly code is generally acceptable. With the advent of more sophisticated code optimization technology [2] the use of C/C++ is gaining growing importance, though. There are two major approaches to embedded code optimization. First, compiler back ends have to take the detailed characteristics of the target machines into account, e.g. hardware support in the form of SIMD in-

structions, predicated instructions, efficient use of the memory hierarchy, zero-overhead loops, etc. As opposed to general-purpose "compiler-friendly" (i.e. RISC-like) architectures, the design of an efficient optimizing compiler backend has a large impact on the code quality. This has frequently been neglected in classical compiler research and needs to be intensively addressed in the future in order to further optimize embedded code quality and to keep pace with the fast developments in processor architectures. The second approach is the use novel code optimization methodologies, e.g. based on genetic algorithms, simulated annealing, branch-and-bound, that allow obtaining high code quality even for irregular target machines by coupling different backend phases such as scheduling and register allocation. Such approaches have hardly been used in practice so far due to their comparatively high runtime requirements. However, in embedded code generation, higher compilation times are acceptable, which may lead to a paradigm shift in code optimization technology.

Existing Approaches and Systems

There exist number different approaches to retargetable and optimizing code generation for embedded processors in research and industry. From the "traditional" compiler community, there are portable compilers like gcc [3] and lcc [4] which, however, have problems with code quality for irregular targets like DSPs. Other retargetable compiler systems, more targeted to embedded systems have been developed in Europe (including CoSy [5], OCE [6], FlexWare [7]), U.S. (including SUIF [8], Expression [9], Mescal [10], Liberty [11]) and Asia (including ASIPMeister [12]). While differing significantly in their detailed concepts, many of these approaches have adopted the idea of using an architecture description language (ADL) to drive the retargeting of compilers and other software tools. Using an ADL, the target machine can be captured at a higher abstraction level and more concisely than with usual hardware description languages (HDLs). As a consequence, only a single "golden" reference model is required for the entire processor design flow. Industrial EDA products, like CoWare´s LISATek product line [13], Axys´ MaxCore [14], and Target´ Chess [15] build on this concept to explicitly support compiler-based architecture exploration and design of embedded processors. Current R&D efforts are aimed at tuning existing ADLs towards a higher automation in compiler retargeting. While a trend towards convergence in the area of ADL design is already visible, a unified ADL that best fits usual system design flows still requires more research.

Relevant Challenges and Work Directions

- *Programmable Architectures*
  Research into this direction needs to be broadened in order to explore even higher code efficiency potentials and to keep pace with new developments in programmable architectures (e.g. parallel DSPs for 3G mobile telephony or Network Processors for communication protocol processing).
- *Handling Novel Code Optimization Techniques*
  Tools are needed to support automatic compiler generation or retargeting. Further advances in this area will open up a large optimization potential for embedded system industry, since compiler retargeting will no longer be a bottleneck in both processor architecture optimization and application software development. To-

gether with novel code optimization techniques this will provide the required technology to achieve an optimal match between embedded software and the underlying processor architectures.

- *A Theory For Semantics-Preserving Program Transformations*
  Many embedded systems run in safety-critical applications. Correctness of optimizing program transformations and, in fact, proofs for this will be mandatory. A theory for semantics preserving program transformations is needed here.
- *Exploiting High-level Knowledge Present at the Specification Level*
  Automatically generated code, often encountered in Embedded Software, has specific properties. In general, it is much more disciplined than hand-written code providing for high-precision static analyses. Efficiency of the compiled code could be improved even more if high-level knowledge present at the specification level could be made known to and exploited by the compiler. On the other hand, automatically generated code often contains large amounts of redundant code. Removal of this code by provably correct optimizations is mandatory.

References

[1]   Rainer Leupers, Peter Marwedel: Retargetable Compiler Technology for Embedded Systems – Tools and Applications, Kluwer Academic Publishers. ISBN 0-7923-7578-5, November 2001.

[2]   Rainer Leupers: Code Optimization Techniques for Embedded Processors – Methods, Algorithms, and Tool, Kluwer Academic Publishers, ISBN 0-7923-7989-6, November 2000.

[3]   GNU C Compiler: http://gcc.gnu.org

[4]   LCC Compiler : http://www.cs.princeton.edu/software/lcc/

[5]   Cosy Compiler System : http://www.ace.nl

[6]   OCE: http://www.atair.co.at

[7]   P. Paulin, F. Karim, P. Bromley: Network Processors: A perspective on market requirements, processor architectures, and embedded S/W tools, Proc. DATE 2001

[8]   Stanford University: http://suif.stanford.edu

[9]   A. Halambi, P. Grun, et al. : Expression : a language for architecture exploration through compiler/simulator retargetability, Proc. DATE 1999

[10]   W. Qin, S. Malik: Automated Synthesis of Efficient Binary Decoders for Retargetable Software Toolkits, Proc. DAC 2003

[11]   M. Vachharajani, N. Vachharajani, and D. August: The Liberty Structural Specification Language: A High-Level Modeling Language for Component Reuse, ACM SIGPLAN Conference on Programming Language Design and Implementation (PLDI), June 2004

[12]   Shinsuke KOBAYASHI, Kentaro MITA, Yoshinori TAKEUCHI, Masaharu IMAI, Rapid Prototyping of JPEG Encoder using the ASIP Development System: PEAS-III, Proceedings of IEEE International Conference on Acoustics, Speech, and Signal Processing 2003, Vol. 2, pp. 485-488, Apr., 2003

[13]   CoWare Inc.: http://www.coware.com

[14]   Axys Design Automation: http://www.axys-design.com

[15]   Target Compiler Technologies: http://www.retarget.com

7   Tools for Verification and Validation

7.1   Building Blocks for Verification and Validation

Verification and validation consists in exploring the current design against side properties expressed as part of the requirements. Verification & validation can concern:

1. the specification level, at early stages of the design process, or
2. the embedded code, from C/Ada/Java, to assembly.

It includes:

1. testing, a well established technology, to be revisited based on advances in formal methods and verification,
2. model checking and methods performing an exhaustive exploration of the reachable state space, for discrete systems or systems abstracted into some discrete approximation of them,
3. static analysis to explore embedded code – static analysis is a technique to formally explore existing code, typically C or Java, by abstracting away aspects of the code that are considered "second class" for the considered purpose.
4. more exploratory techniques, such as source/object code validation, or the use of theorem proving – code validation is a tool assisted technique to formally assess the conformance of some object code against its source code, it is a proof of validity for one given compilation, not a proof of the compiler; theorem proving refers to tools and techniques for assisted reasoning on specifications or programs when undecidable properties are considered.

7.2   Model Checking

Definition

Model checking is a technique that relies on building a finite model of a system of interest and checking that a desired property holds in that model. Since the introduction of the term 'model checking' in the early eighties the technology has advanced significantly and has been applied successfully in numerous industrial case-studies. In the area of hardware verification the technology is now taken up by the industry.

The development of algorithmic techniques (e.g. partial order reduction, symmetry-reduction, cone-of-influence, compositionality, abstraction) and data structures (e.g. Binary Decision Diagrams) allows for automatic and exhaustive analysis of finite state models with more than thousand components or state variables. Existing model checkers has enabled analysis of interesting systems with more than 10400 reachable states.

Artist FP5 Consortium: Embedded Systems Design, LNCS 3436, 72–84, 2005.
© Springer-Verlag Berlin Heidelberg 2005

Finite-state model checkers support analysis of qualitative properties, in particular safety and liveness properties. However, there is a need for extensions allowing quantitative properties of embedded systems to be analyzed. These include real-time properties, properties of the evolution of the (continuous) environment of the embedded control program, and·performance properties. For real-time properties model-checking tools based on the modelling formalism of timed automata exist: the successful application of these tools to several industrial case studies demonstrates the maturity of these tools. However, there remain significant research challenges in extending some of the most successful techniques from finite-state model checking to the setting of timed automata (e.g. symbolic data structures and partial order reduction).

Whereas timed automata allows explicit modelling and analysis of real-time constraints the extended model of hybrid automata allows for more general continuous phenomena (of the environment) to be modelled. The technique of model checking is also developing in the direction of performance analysis with a number of model-checking tools based on various stochastic extensions of finite-state systems (Markov Chains, Markov Decision Processes, Semi-Markov Processes) emerging.

Position in the Design Flow

Model checking may be applied throughout the entire span from specification, through design to final implementation. MSC/LSC/sequence diagrams may be used at the early specification phases and analyzed for potential inconsistencies (e.g. race conditions) using model checking techniques. A prerequisite for applying the technique of model checking is the existence of a suitable (essentially) finite-state model. Thus the technique is directly applicable to analysis of the control structure, both at design and code level of a system. To make the technique applicable to general embedded code finite-state abstractions need to be extracted either by application of generic abstract interpretations or by other means of formal verification of the correctness of a suggested abstraction in particular with the use of theorem proving (e.g. using the theorem prover PVS). In fact the introduction of abstractions plays a key role in making model checking feasible (abstractions from infinite to finite state models) as well as efficient (abstractions from large models to smaller models). However, for model checking to truly scale up it is imperative that it is complemented with compositional methods allowing verification problems of large systems to be decomposed into verification problems of smaller systems. Lightweight theorem proving is here useful in establishing that a particular suggested decomposition is indeed correct.

Finally, model checking may also be applied in the testing phase as a method for automatically generating test suites tracking the satisfaction of a given system specification model with a good coverage/confidence.

Existing Tools

The growing application of standard modelling formalisms (e.g. UML, SDL, State-Charts, Simulink) in embedded software engineering practice provides an ideal basis for industrial take-up of the model checking technology. Below we give pointers to some main tools covering finite-state model checker, model checkers for real-time and hybrid systems, stochastic model checkers and model checking applied (via abstraction) to source code.

Finite-state Model Checkers
- *SPIN* http://www.spinroot.com
  This is a popular software tool that can be used for the formal verification of distributed software systems. The tool was developed at Bell Labs in the original Unix group of the Computing Sciences Research Center, starting in 1980. The software has been available freely since 1991, and continues to evolve to keep pace with new developments in the field. In April 2002 the tool was awarded the prestigious System Software Award for 2001 by the ACM.
- *SMV*
  Developed by Ken McMillian was the first model checker using the symbolic verification (i.e. with the use of Binary Decision Diagrams). Presently a number of variants of the tool exist including Cadence SMV (http://www-cad.eecs. berkeley.edu/~kenmcmil/), nuSMV (http://nusmv.irst.itc.it/) and SMV from CMU (http://www-2.cs.cmu.edu/~modelcheck/smv.html)
- *VisualSTATE* http://www.iar.com/Products/VS/
  This is a commercial tool supporting code generation from hierarchical state machine models compliant with UML standard. In addition the tool offer full verification of a number of generic sanity properties (e.g. absence of deadlock) and simulation capabilities. The model checker of VisualSTATE is based on the technique of Compositional Backwards Reachability exploiting the (in)dependency as well as hierarchical structure of a model.
- *StatemateMagnum ModelChecker and ModelCertifier* http://www.ilogix.com
  These are commercial products available from I-Logix, Inc. (www.ilogix.com) offering formal verification for embedded systems applications. Being tightly integrated with Statemate, the tool supports the complete range of modelling features of Statemate.
- *FormalCheck* http://www.cadence.com/datasheets/formalcheck.html
  This is a commercial tool provides formal verification of complex control units using a collection of reduction techniques providing elegant methods for dealing with the complex verification of large circuits. The tool is available from Cadence.
- *Murphi description language* http://verify.stanford.edu/dill/murphi.html
  This is based on Dijkstra's guarded commands and bears similarities to Misra and Chandy's Unity model. Murphi contains a number of strategies for reducing the number of reachable states in particular by identifying and exploiting symmetries.
- *FDR* http://www.formal.demon.co.uk/FDR2.html
  This tool is developed at Oxford University and is based on the theory of Communicating Sequential Processes, CSP and the notion of failures-divergence refinement. A key technique in the tool is the application of (fast) compositional state-minimization before analysis.

Model Checkers Based on Process Algebra
- *Caesar/Aldebaran* http://www.inrialpes.fr/vasy/cadp/
  The Caesar/Aldebaran tool suite is maintained and developed mainly in VASY/INRIA. This tool suite is built around the process algebra LOTOS. Extensions for dealing with timed extensions of LOTOS (e.g. E-LOTOS and LOTOS-NT) are currently moderately supported. The tool suite offers a range of techniques

for analyzing a system. These include various kinds of equivalence checking, simulation tools, visualization tools and model checking tools. Almost all techniques operate on finite state representations of the system.

- *muCRL*   http://www.cwi.nl/~mcrl
  The muCRL tool suite is maintained and developed mainly at the CWI and the Eindhoven University of Technology. This tool suite is built around the process algebra muCRL and timed muCRL. The tool support for timed muCRL specifications is gradually increasing. The tool suite offers tools and techniques that operate on a symbolic representation of the state space of a system, which is not necessarily finite state, and can include unbounded data types. This symbolic representation (so-called "Linear Process Equations") of a system is used by other tools to check for equivalence, simulate behaviours and verify (first order) modal mu-calculus formulae. Linear Process Equations, representing systems with a finite state space, can serve as input to the tool suite Caesar/Aldebaran.

Real-Time and Hybrid Model Checkers

- *Kronos*   http://www-verimag.imag.fr/TEMPORISE/kronos/
  This tool is developed at VERIMAG, Grenoble and is based on components of real-time systems modelled as timed automata and correctness requirements formulated in timed temporal logic.
- *UPPAAL*   www.uppaal.com
  This is a tool environment for modelling, validating and verifying real-time systems modelled as networks of timed automata extended with discrete data types. UPPAAL is developed and maintained in collaboration between DoCS, Uppsala University, Sweden and BRICS, Aalborg University, Denmark.
- *HyTech*   http://www-cad.eecs.berkeley.edu/~tah/HyTech/
  This is a tool for the analysis of embedded systems specified using linear hybrid automata. The tool is developed at UC Berkeley.
- *D/dt*   http://www-verimag.imag.fr/~tdang/ddt.htm
  This is a tool for reachability analysis of continuous and hybrids systems with linear differential inclusions; developed at VERIMAG.
- CheckMate   http://www.ece.cmu.edu/research/projects/checkmate.shtml
  This is a verification tool for hybrid dynamic systems developed at CMU, having both discrete/continuous dynamics.

Stochastic Model Checkers

- *ETMCC*   http://www7.informatik.uni-erlangen.de/etmcc/
  This is a model checker for continuous time Markov chains with requirements specified in Continuous Stochastic Logic. The tools is developed in collaboration between Erlangen University, Germany, and Twente University, The Netherlands.
- *PRISM*   http://www.cs.bham.ac.uk/~dxp/prism/
  This is a probabilistic model checker being developed at the University of Birmingham. The tool supports three models: DTMCs, CTMCs and MDPs with respect to analysis of PCTL properties.

- *RAPTURE* http://www.irisa.fr/prive/bjeannet/prob/prob_1.html
  This is a verification tool developed jointly by BRICS, Aalborg, INRIA, and Twente University. The tool is designed to verify reachability properties of Markov Decision Processes.

Model Checking for Source Code
- *BANDERA* http://www.cis.ksu.edu/santos/bandera/
  This is a toolset designed to bridge the semantic gap between a non-finite-state software system expressed as source code and the preferred input format for existing model checkers (essentially finite-state systems). The tool applies sophisticated program analysis, abstraction and transformation techniques. The tool is developed and maintained at Kansas University.
- *BLAST* http://www-cad.eecs.berkeley.edu/~tah/blast/
  This is a software model checker for C programs using counterexample-driven automatic abstraction refinement to construct an abstract model chick are model checked for safety properties. The tool is developed at Berkeley University.
- *VeriSoft* http://www.bell-labs.com/project/verisoft/
  This is a tool for systematically exploring the state spaces of systems composed of several concurrent processes executing arbitrary code written in any language (e.g. C or C++). The tool is developed and maintained by Bell Laboratories, Lucent Technologies.

Relevant Challenges and Work Directions

Some significant problems need to be solved before this take-up will be fully realized:
- *Semantic issues.*
  A necessary prerequisite in order to conduct model checking is that the given modelling formalism is provided with a formal semantics;
- *The missing link with scientific engineering formalisms.*
  The gap between the modelling formalisms currently favoured in embedded software engineering (e.g. Simulink) and the modelling formalisms supported by current verification tools should be bridged;
- *Expressing properties in a user friendly manner.*
  The various model checkers (as visualSTATE) should at least support verification of a number of generic sanity properties (e.g. absence of deadlocks, no dead code). However, to establish application specific properties these should be expressed in some suitable specification language. A challenge is to design specification languages more ergonomic and intuitive (from a software engineer's point of view) than that of temporal logic which is favoured by most existing model checkers.

7.3   Static Program Analysis

Definition

Static program analysis executes an abstract version of a program's semantics on descriptions of data (abstract data) instead of concrete data. Both data domains usually are lattices, the partial order representing precision. Often, abstraction and concretization functions exist between the two domains mapping (sets of) concrete data to their most precise description and mapping abstract data to the set of represented concrete data. The abstract semantics of the program statements is applied iteratively until a fixed point is reached. This fixed point describes properties of all program executions at each program point. Static program analysis is thus semantics based offering the chance of correctness proof, sometimes even the automatic derivation from a given semantics.

Static Program Analysis is being used for the computation of safety properties of embedded programs. Safety properties cover a host of relevant properties of safety-critical systems. They state that certain run-time errors will not occur in any execution of a program. Static analysis, by nature, is approximate. Since it often considers undecidable problems, it cannot be both correct and complete at the same time. Therefore, it is important that it "only errs on the safe side". It should be always correct, but may be incomplete. This manifests itself in the so-called "false alarms", i.e., an exceptional run-time situation is reported by the static analysis that in fact can not happen in any execution of the program. It will be a decisive property for the acceptance of static analysis tools in industry, whether the number of false alarms can be kept within reasonable limits.

The effort needed by program-analysis tools is closely related to the complexity of the program properties they try to determine. A trade-off between analysis speed and precision is often possible. The precision of analyses for a given property, i.e., the number of false alarms, often depends on, whether the used tool is a general purpose analysis tool or one that is tailored to the application and the type of software to be analyzed [BCCFMM03].

Position in the Design Flow

Static Program Analyses are mostly performed on source-level code at the S/W-Implementation and the Unit Validation stages of the design process. The support tools are partly integrated in software-development environments. Analyses are performed by software developers, often at suppliers, and by quality assurance personnel at the contractor. The necessary training effort to educate personnel to do program analysis tasks, in particular the interpretation of warnings is not low, but will amortize. Licensing of such tools will often be on project basis, often also on the basis of number of work stations, on which the tool is installed. It is meaningful to integrate such tools into environments and have a combined license.

A relevant property of a hard real-time system is whether it will always react inside the given time bounds. Often, rough estimates of the timing behaviour of a real-time system under development are useful during the development process. These can be obtained using methods based on the structure of the program; atomic statements are given some standard execution time, and composed statements receive timing estimates computed from the timing estimates of the components and a function corresponding to the type of statement. Penalties for undesirable states in modern processors, e.g. cache misses, branch misprediction can be large. As soon as the programs under consideration are rather small, the order of magnitude of these penalties can exceed the order of magnitude of the execution time of the programs. Any run-time estimation method has to be aware of this limitation.

The code implementing an embedded system may have been obtained by automatic, semi-automatic, or non-automated development phases. In any case, correctness of the result should be checked. Static program analysis on the implementation level can be used to check whether invariants of the specification level are still satisfied by the implementation. This continues for the compilation task. Compiler correctness proofs are still not feasible. Alternatives are compilation-result checks, i.e., the check whether an individual program is correctly translated, cf. CVT. This requires the use of a theorem prover with a corresponding compilation-time overhead. An alternative is to compute corresponding invariants on both the software implementation and the machine code level by static analyses. The computed invariants may be strong enough for the case under consideration and the overhead usually is much less.

Some analyses are only possible, once the machine-code level is reached. Reliable and often precise upper bounds on the execution time of embedded programs can be obtained when all the information about the hardware platform are known. The current state of the art in determining the WCET consists in a combination of micro architectural analysis predicting the behaviour of the processor components and implicit path enumeration determining a path on which the upper bound is computed. The first phase is realized using static program analysis, the second solving an integer linear program representing the control flow of the program. The advantages of this approach to WCET determination over competing approaches are the following:

- The use of program analysis for the first phase and of ILP for the second splits the task along the right border. ILP solving is the more costly task. This split leaves only ILPs of reasonable size to be solved leading to acceptable overall analysis times.
- Much precision is gained by regarding instructions in different contexts, i.e., by using context- and flow-sensitive analysis methods.
- Under certain conditions depending on the predictability of the processor behaviour, both WCET and BCET can be determined giving the developer a feel for the precision of the analysis.
- The use of ILP for the worst-case path determination allows the use of complex user annotations to express knowledge about program behaviour. These annotations can be translated into the ILP.

WCET tools, as described above, are used on the executable code. They are used by the developers, in order to see whether the code satisfies the timing constraints and to find out potential for performance improvement. The use of such tools depends on the industrial sector. They will be distributed to and used by suppliers and they will be used for in-house development and quality assurance. Technical inspection offices, like the German TÜVs, will ask their customers to use them before the certification phase and use them for the certification process itself. Licensing costs will be high, since the market is small and the development effort is high. The learning effort for users of the tools can be kept small, provided the results of the analyses are visualized adequately.

Existing Tools

- PolySpace Verifier is a general purpose tool for analyzing C and Ada programs for run-time errors. http://www.polyspace.com/product_datasheet/datasheets.htm
- The Program Analyzer Generator, PAG, is a tool supporting the automatic generation of program analyses from specifications. http://www.absint.de/pag/
- BANE is research tool for experimentation with program analyses. http://www.cs.berkeley.edu/Research/Aiken/bane.html
- The aiT WCET analyzers of AbsInt determine bounds on execution times by abstract interpretation. http://www.absint.de/wcet.htm

Relevant Challenges and Work Directions

Static analysis is certainly a new and living area, which cannot be considered fully mature and stable. Not surprisingly, research issues and advances needed are numerous, and challenging:

- *Liveness vs. progress*
  Current research on static program analysis attempts to also verify liveness properties. The approach is to combine a static analysis with a progress property. This progress property has to be proved with the help of a theorem prover.
- *Concurrency*
  The analysis of concurrent software has posed one of the biggest challenges to static program analysis, as well as to program verification. Recently, the application of Shape Analysis has advanced the limits of what could be analyzed by static analysis. Multi-threaded software even with dynamically varying number of threads and varying number of objects have been successfully tackled [YRSW03].
- *Exploiting high-level knowledge present at the specification level*
  Automatically generated code, often encountered in Embedded Software, has specific properties. In general, it is much more disciplined than hand-written code making verification easier and providing for high-precision static analysis [AAS03]. However, the situation could be improved even more if high-level knowledge present at the specification level could be made known to and exploited by the compiler.
- *Scaling-up*
  The more powerful a static analysis is the more expensive it is in general. Powerful analyses have problems of scaling-up. User annotations and assume-guarantee reasoning will be needed to solve this serious problem.
- *WCET*
  The determination of precise bounds on the execution times of real-time software critically depends on the predictability of the processor architecture. They are the more precise, the more predictable the processor architecture is. Processor architectures started to being used today reach the limit of non-deterministic behaviour that makes the computation of precise upper bounds possible. An interesting research direction is to identify principles for the design of processors that perform well both in the average and in the worst case [HLTW03].

- *Components*
  The advent of component-based design and middleware in the hard real-time domain introduces a completely new challenge. How does one guarantee real-time
  behaviour of complex systems constructed from components using middleware and
  sitting on top of a real-time operating system?

References

[BCCFMM03] B.Blanchet, P.Cousot, R.Cousot, J.Feret, L.Mauborgne, A.Miné: A Static Ana-
           lyzer for Large Safety-Critical Software, PLDI 2003
[HLTW03]   Heckmann, R., Langenbach, M., Thesing, S., Wilhelm, R.: The Influence of Proc-
           essor Architecture an the Design and the Results of WCET Tools, IEEE Transac-
           tions on Real-Time Systems, 2003, to appear
[AAS02]   Thesing, S., Souyris, J., Heckmann, R., Randimbivololona, F., Langenbach, M.,
           Wilhelm, R., Ferdinand, C.: Abstract Interpretation-Based Timing Validation of
           Hard Real Time Avionics Software Systems, submitted to the Performance and
           Dependability Symposium, 2003
[YRSW03]   Yahav, E., Reps, T., Sagiv, M., Wilhelm, R.: Verifying Temporal Heap Properties
           Specified via Evolution Logic, ESOP 2003

7.4   Testing Embedded Systems

Definition

Testing is the execution of the system under test in a controlled environment following
a prescribed procedure with the goal of measuring one or more quality characteristics
of a product. The best situation is when the required behaviour and quality is specified
in a requirements specification. The testing objective then becomes to demonstrate
whether the actual status of the product deviates from the specified status. Testing
helps finding potential defects and determining the risk of release of the product.

Testing is different from other validation techniques such as model-checking, static
analysis, review and inspection, walk-through and debugging, because it dynamically
executes the product in a realistic (but controllable) environment with actual concrete
input data, while comparing the actual and expected behaviour. The strength of testing is the execution of the actual system in a realistic environment. On the other hand
it must be stressed that a fundamental limitation of testing is that only a very small
sample of the possible system behaviours can be evaluated. In any non-trivial application the number of possible input values, input sequences, and environment conditions
is gastronomic, and often literally outnumber the atoms in the universe. Thus, the
required number of test cases needed for exhaustive (in the sense that a passing system is guaranteed to be correct) testing is practically infinite. This is the theoretical
underpinning of the well-known statement that "testing can only show the presence of
errors, not their absence". A central testing problem is therefore to engineer a suite of
effective test cases that contributes with useful knowledge (e.g. has a high likelihood
of detecting errors) about the system under test, and that can be executed in the
amount of time and resources allocated to the testing activity. Various techniques and
strategies have been formulated to aid selection of effective test cases. Examples
include boundary value analysis, equivalence class partitioning, branch and statement

coverage), fault models, mutation analysis. These test criteria can be used as test design techniques as well as heuristic measures of the thoroughness of a test suite.

Testing is used to measure several quality characteristics such as functionality (input-output behaviour, accuracy, security, compliance, interoperability), reliability (maturity, fault tolerance, recoverability), usability (understandability, learnability, operability), efficiency (performance, time behaviour, resource utilization), maintainability (analyzability, changeability, stability, testability), and portability (adaptability, installability, conformance, replaceability). Each quality characteristic is often tested separately using specialized testing procedures. This leads to several different kinds of testing, i.e., functional testing, reliability testing, usability testing, performance testing, etc.

Testing is performed at several levels during the development process: unit-level, module- or component level, module/component integration level, or system level. Different people, techniques and tools may be involved, depending on the level. Low-level testing is the process of testing individual units or integrating these, and is usually done by the developers. The source code is normally available and visible, and the goal is to construct a test suite that covers each statement or branch of the unit. High-level testing is performed when application software, system software, and hardware is integrated into a complete product. The system under test is usually treated as a black box that can be interacted with manually or using programmable environment emulators. Testing may be performed by separate testing- or quality assurance-teams. Acceptance-testing is normally performed by the customers. Regression-testing is used at all levels and involves re-executing existing test cases to check whether changes to the system under test had the desired effects and no undesired side effects. Testing is often performed to measure real-time execution time and response times e.g. to check resource utilization or obtain an estimate for the worst-case execution time. However, using this approach is very problematic because it is difficult to obtain safe and accurate bounds.

Position in the Design Flow

Testing is mainly performed in the later stages of systems development where code or integrated product is ready, but test related activities may start as soon as the project is initiated. For example, explained in terms of the V-model, preparations of test-ware and writing abstract test cases for acceptance testing can begin as soon as system requirements have been stated. Test case and test-ware design for system level testing may begin when a detailed specification exists. Similarly integration testing may start when a detailed design specification exists, and unit level testing when unit-code is available. In principle, only the execution and verdict assignment need to be done late. Indeed, the view taken by the "Test Management Approach" (TMAP) to test organization is to treat testing as a process in it self with its own phases (preparation, test generation, test execution, and completion) that are planned and controlled. Testing is thus a separate (but not independent) process that runs concurrently with the normal development process, and not merely as a phase in systems development.

Existing Tools

Testing is a very broad topic and is extremely diversified, and the required tools depend on what level is being tested, the quality aspect being measured, the specific application being tested, the programming language, etc. The tools are often very specialized and dependent on the capabilities of the specific test execution equipment. Consequently, the range of testing tools used by industry is extensive, and only a very limited selection can be discussed here.

Here we consider tools from the three main testing activities: test organization, test execution and test generation:

- *Test Organization*
  This includes management and planning of the test process, allocation of resources, test-ware management and consolidation for regression testing.
  Tools support planning and control of tests, defect management, configuration and version control to manage the system under test version, test-ware, test results and logs, etc. An example of a tool in this category is TestDirector (Mercury).
- *Test Execution*
  The means for execution of the specified tests are implemented, and the specified tests executed, and verdicts are assigned.
  Test execution of low-level tests includes tools for automatically generating test input data, controlling the execution of test cases, automatic regression testing, report generation, automatic stub generation, code-coverage analyzers, code-complexity analyzers, timing analysis, path analysis. Many tools that support the test execution activity are available. Examples of such tools include VectorCAST, Telelogic TauTester, Rational Test RealTime, Cantata, Panorama C/C++, tcov, prof, Junit.
  High-level tests are typically executed using specialized environment emulators or signal/load generators to stimulate the system under test with typical, rare, or extreme use- and load-patterns. In many cases the test cases and environment behaviour is handcrafted, and written in C or (general purpose or specialized) scripting languages. In some industrial sectors it is common to use Matlab/Simulink to specify environment behaviour. System level real-time constraints are often tested in this fashion. It is important to emphasize that the use-patterns are still generated manually in an ad-hoc fashion, although tools exist for their construction. Also the test oracle problem is not solved, and verdict assignment is done based on ad-hoc log-file analysis.
- *Test Generation*
  This activity includes analysis of the system under test and the specification basis, formulation of a test strategy, and design and construction of a set of test cases. The state-of-the-art is to manually specify test cases in natural language and then translate them into the C–language or (often ad hoc) test scripting language, to use spreadsheets to list the required test actions and expected behaviour, or to use capture-and-playback tools. Few standardized test notation languages exist; an exception is TTCN (Test and Test Control Notation) most widely deployed in the telecom sector. However, tools are emerging that utilizes design models (some form of state machine notation) as basis for automatic test case generation, so-called specification or model driven testing. These tools are not only model based input stimuli generators but also computes the expected responses. Most state-of-the-art test

automation tools emphasize test management and execution, whereas relatively few tools exist for automatic test generation. For this reason a number of examples of model based test generation tools is mentioned explicitly below:

- *Reactis Simulink Tester*   http://www.reactive-systems.com/
  This generates test suites automatically from Simulink / Stateflow diagrams. Each test consists of a sequence of stimulus / response pairs, where each stimulus assigns an input value to each in-port in the model and each response records an output value for each out-port. The test suites are generated from coverage criteria of the specification, e.g., transition or state coverage.

- *Conformiq Test Generator*   http://www.conformiq.com/
  This tool automatically generates test cases from UML state chart models. Simulations of the models can be used to generate batches of test cases that can later be executed. Alternatively, the models can be interpreted dynamically to facilitate on-the-fly testing. Similarly, the Statemate MAGNUM ATG (I-Logix) tool uses model-checking and simulation techniques to derive test sequences from state chart models.

- *RT-Tester* (Bremen) and *TorX* (University of Twente)
  http://www.verified.de/e_index.html
  http://fmt.cs.utwente.nl/tools/torx/introduction.html
  These are both tools with an underlying formal theory and are rooted in academia. Both tools are for on-the-fly test generation and execution, where the specification is continually probed for relevant input stimuli and used to check the validity of output actions. RT-tester accepts specifications in a mixture of languages, but mainly timed CSP, whereas TorX accepts Promela or LOTOS.

- *TGV* (Irisa/Verimag) and *Telelogic TestComposer*
  http://www.irisa.fr/pampa/VALIDATION/TGV/TGV.html
  http://www.telelogic.com/
  These are SDL-based test case generators. Given an SDL specification and a test purpose (or a specification coverage criterion) these tools construct a test case that meets the test purpose, and stores this in TTCN format. Phact (Philips Research) TestGen (INT, France) also produce TTCN test suites, but uses FSM checking experiment based test generation. TTCN (test and test control notation) is a standardized language dedicated to the specification of abstract test cases. Currently, TTCN mostly used in the context of telecom applications, but the new version 3 aims much broader. Given a TTCN test suite, tools exist to aid the construct the test harness, i.e. TTCN to C compilers (e.g. Telelogic Tau Tester).

A common characteristic of the few commercial tools that exists is that they are limited in the models they allow (deterministic, purely functional) and lack a theoretic foundation. Especially, explicit and systematic handling of real-time, probabilistic, and hybrid properties are missing.

As mentioned earlier, a large variety of testing tools for embedded systems exist. Some pointers can be found at:

http://www.testingfaqs.org/
http://www.cs.queensu.ca/Software-Engineering/tools.html
http://www.aptest.com/resources.html
http://www.dacs.dtic.mil/GoldPractices/practices/mbt/index.html

Relevant Challenges and Work Directions

Although testing is the by far most important practical validation technique for computer software systems employed by industry, it has long been neglected as a field of serious research. In the past decade, however, the study of the use of (formal) models for the systematic generation and execution of sound test suites, the validation of test suites, and the interpretation of test results has become an established field of research. This had led to the development of new theories and tools to support the testing of software systems that have been successfully applied in practice. In spite of this initial success the standard testing practices of the industry at large is still appallingly low. The reasons for this are:

1.   Lack of information/education: industrial teams are unaware of the nature and potential of more advanced methods and tools. This must be addressed by well-focused knowledge transfer campaigns.
2.   The current techniques have a great potential but need to be improved and address a number of practically relevant issues. A prime concern is scalability, e.g. with respect to the number of components and structure of the system, and in connection with system parameters ranging over large or infinite domains. With embedded systems this problem is aggravated by the need to take physical features of the system environment and the tight integration of electronics, mechanics and control software into account, thereby requiring handling of real-time, stochastic, and hybrid properties during modelling, test generation and execution. This requires considerable research efforts to refine and extend existing theories and tools.

Given the fact that the cost of testing is estimated to take up between 30 and 50% of the development cost of embedded systems, the potential of improvements in testing methods and tool is enormous.

The main challenges to be address include development of theory and tools for advanced model-based test-generation and execution of real-time embedded systems. Also, transfer of knowledge and practically applicable testing methods and tools to industry is highly needed. Central issues are:

- a sound theoretical basis for test generation and -execution for real-time, stochastic, and hybrid behaviours;
- the use of symbolic techniques for test data selection for system parameters with large or infinite domains;
- the study of distributed and component based observation and testing techniques;
- the development of adequate notions of test coverage;
- the development of effective tool environments for test generation, execution and interpretation;
- testable design of embedded systems.

8 Middleware for Implementing Hard Real-Time Systems

We have decided to cover selected typical middleware for hard real-time, as these are privileged targets for the design flows. Our list emphasise middleware that bring some important advantages to design flows, namely the Time-Triggered ones. The reason is that these middleware rely on a model of communication that adequately fits hard real-time. Complementary information related to more traditional and general purpose RTOS can be found in part III of this roadmap.

Aspects of real-time networks are also treated in section 24.

Approach

The Time-Triggered Architecture (TTA) provides a computing infrastructure for the design and implementation of dependable distributed embedded systems [Kop03, Mai02]. Tea's basic building block is a node, i.e. a self-contained composite hardware/software subsystem that can be used as a building block in the design of a larger system. Two replicated communication channels connect the nodes to build a cluster. To avoid medium access by a faulty node guardians are used that could be either local at the nodes, or central at hubs, if the channels are connected in star topology (see Figure 8.1).

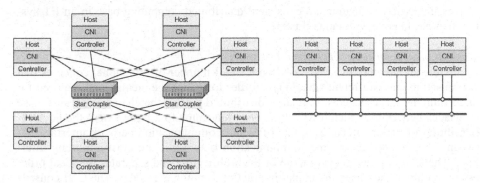

Figure 8.1. Star Topology vs. Bus Topology

Communication is performed according to a previously specified, periodic time division multiple access (TDMA) schedule. The TTA obtains its synchronous behaviour by the progression of real-time, i.e., there exists a global system time, which is used for the arbitration of the communication medium. In the TTA this global time is established using the local clocks of the nodes.

In an architecture using a TDMA scheme, time is split up into (non-overlapping) pieces of not necessarily equal durations, which are called slots. These slots are

Artist FP5 Consortium: Embedded Systems Design, LNCS 3436, 85–91, 2005.

grouped into sequences called TDMA rounds, in which every node occupies exactly one slot. The knowledge, which node occupies which slot in a TDMA round is static, available to all components a priori, and equal for all TDMA rounds. When the time of a node's slot is reached, the node is provided unique access to the communications medium for the duration of the slot. After the end of one TDMA round, the next TDMA round starts, i.e., after the sending of the node in the last slot of a TDMA round, the node that is allowed to send in the first slot sends again.

Design Principles

Consistent Distributed Computing Base

In a distributed TT system it is a priori common knowledge at which instant a message of a correct node must arrive at all other nodes. This common knowledge can be used to design a consistent distributed computing base, such as the one realized in the time-triggered architecture with the TTP protocol [Kop93]. TTP is based on a time-division-multiple-access (TDMA) strategy to replicated communication channels. The TTP protocol provides, in addition to fault-tolerant clock synchronization, a distributed membership service and a clique avoidance service. The membership service of TTP informs consistently all correct nodes about the health state of all nodes within two TDMA rounds. If a fault outside the fault hypothesis causes the formation of cliques, the clique avoidance mechanism of TTP will force the minority clique into a restart in order that a consistent distributed computing base remains available at all times. The correctness of the membership protocol of TTP has been investigated by formal methods [Rus00].

It is impossible to maintain a consistent distributed computing base in an ET system that has to cope with faults [Fis85].

Unification of Interfaces – Temporal Firewalls

A suitable architecture must be based on a small number of orthogonal concepts that are reused in many different situations in order to reduce the mental load required for understanding large systems. In a large distributed system the characteristics of these interfaces between the identified subsystems determine to a large extent the comprehensibility of the architecture. In the TTA, the communication network interface between a host computer and the communication network is the most important interface. The CNI appears in every node of the architecture and separates the local processing within a node from the global interactions among the nodes. The CNI consists of two unidirectional data-flow interfaces, one from the host computer to the communication system and the other one in the opposite direction.

We call a unidirectional data-flow interface elementary, if there is only a unidirectional control flow [Kop99] across this interface. An interface that supports periodic state messages with error detection at the receiver is an example of such an elementary interface. We call a unidirectional data-flow interface composite, if even a unidirectional data flow requires a bi-directional control flow. An event message interface with error detection is an example for a composite interface. Composite interfaces are inherently more complex than elementary interfaces, since the correct operation of the sender depends on the control signals from all receivers. This can be a problem in multicast communication where many control messages are generated for every unidirectional data transfer, and each one of the receivers can affect the operation of the sender. Multicast communication is common in distributed embedded systems. The basic TTA CNI as depicted in Figure 8.2 is an elementary interface.

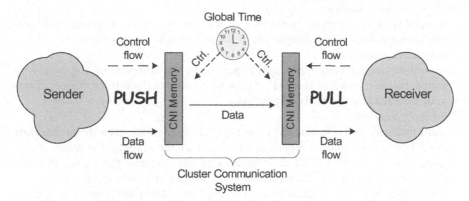

Figure 8.2. Data Flow and Control Flow at a TTA Interface

The time-triggered transport protocol carries autonomously – driven by its time-triggered schedule – state messages from the sender's CNI to the receiver's CNI. The sender can deposit the information into its local CNI memory according to the information push paradigm, while the receiver will pull the information out of its local CNI memory. From the point of view of temporal predictability, information push into a local memory at the sender and information pull from a local memory at the receiver are optimal, since no unpredictable task delays that extend the worst-case execution occur during reception of messages. A receiver that is working on a time-critical task is never interrupted by a control signal from the communication system. Since no control signals cross the CNI in the TTA (the communication system derives control signals for the fetch and delivery instants from the progress of global time and its local schedule exclusively), propagation of control errors is prohibited by design. We call an interface that prevents propagation of control errors by design a temporal firewall [Kop97]. The integrity of the data in the temporal firewall is assured by the non-blocking write (NBW) concurrency control protocol [Kop93].

From the point of view of complexity management and composability, it is useful to distinguish between three different types of interfaces of a node: the real-time service (RS) interface, the diagnostic and maintenance (DM) interface, and the configuration planning (CP) interface [Kop00]. These interface types serve different functions and have different characteristics. For the temporal composability, the most important interface is the RS interface.

Temporal Composability
In a composable architecture, the integration of a system out of components proceeds without unintended side effects. For architecture to be composable, it must adhere to the following four principles [KO02]:
- *Independent Node Development*
  Principle one of a composable architecture is concerned with design at the architecture level. A composable architecture must distinguish distinctly between architec-

ture design and node design. Components only be designed independently of each other, if the architecture supports the exact specification of all component services provided at the level of architecture design.

- *Stability of Prior Services*
  The stability-of-prior-service principle ensures that the validated service of a component is not refuted by the integration of the component into a system.
- *Constructive Integration*
  The constructive integration principle requires that if n components are already integrated, the integration of the n+1st component may not disturb the correct operation of the already integrated components.
- *Replica Determinism*
  If fault-tolerance is implemented by the replication of nodes, then the architecture and the nodes must support replica determinism. A set of replicated nodes is replica determinate [Pol95] if all the members of this set have the same externally visible state, and produce the same output messages at points in time that are at most an interval of d time units apart. The implementation of replica determinism is simplified if all nodes have access to a globally synchronized sparse time base and use the time to the mutual exclusion problem.

Time-Triggered Protocols

TTP/C
The TTP/C protocol is a fault-tolerant time-triggered protocol that provides the following services:

- Autonomous fault-tolerant message transport with known delay and bounded jitter between the CNIs of the nodes of a cluster by employing a TDMA medium access strategy on replicated communication channels.
- Fault-tolerant clock synchronization that establishes the global time base without relying on a central time server.
- Membership service to inform every node consistently about the "health-state" of every other node of the cluster. This service can be used as an acknowledgement service in multicast communication. The membership service is also used to efficiently implement the fault-tolerant clock synchronization service.
- Clique avoidance to detect and eliminate the formation of cliques in case the fault hypothesis is violated.

In TTP/C the communication is organized into rounds, where every node must send a message in every round. A particular message may carry up to 240 bytes of data. The data is protected by a 24 bits CRC checksum. The message schedule is stored in the message-descriptor list (MEDL) within the communication controller of each node. In order to achieve high data efficiency, the sender name and the message name is derived from the send instant. The clock synchronization of TTP/C exploits the common knowledge of the send schedule: every node measures the difference between the a priori known expected and the actually observed arrival time of a correct message to learn about the difference between the sender's clock and the receiver's clock. This information is used by a fault-tolerant average algorithm to calculate periodically a correction term for the local clock in order to keep the clock in synchrony with all other clocks of the cluster. The membership service employs a distributed agreement algorithm to determine whether the outgoing link of the sender or the incoming link of the receiver has failed. Nodes that have suffered a transmission fault are excluded from the membership until they restart with a correct protocol state. Before each send operation of a node, the clique avoidance algorithm checks if the node is a member of the majority clique. The detailed specification of the TTP/C protocol can be found at [TTP/C].

TTP/A
The TTP/A protocol is the time-triggered field bus protocol of the TTA. It is used to connect low-cost smart transducers to a node of the TTA, which acts as the master of a transducer cluster. In TTP/A the CNI memory element has been expanded at the transducer side to hold a simple interface file system (IFS). Each interface file contains 256 records of four bytes each. The IFS forms the uniform name space for the exchange of data between a sensor and its environment. The IFS holds the real-time data, calibration data, diagnostic data, and configuration data. The information between the IFS of the smart transducer and the CNI of the TTA node is exchanged by the time-triggered TTP/A protocol, which distinguishes between two types of rounds, the master-slave (MS) round and the multi-partner (MP) round. The MS rounds are used to read and write records from the IFS of a particular transducer to implement the DM and CP interface. The MP rounds are periodic and transport data from selected IFS records of several transducers across the TTP/A cluster to implement the RS service. MP rounds and MS rounds are interleaved, such that the time-critical real-time (RS) service and the event-based DM and CP service can coexist. It is thus possible to diagnose a smart transducer or to reconfigure or install a new smart transducer on-line, without disturbing the time-critical RS service of the other nodes. The TTP/A protocol also supports a "plug-and-play" mode where new sensors are detected, configured, and integrated into a running system on-line and dynamically. The detailed specification of the TTP/A protocol can be found at [TTP/A].

FlexRay
FlexRay [FRay] is a combination of two different protocols: a time-triggered TDMA scheme and a minislotting protocol for event-triggered transmission. FlexRay also provides a mode that makes it compatible with Byteflight [Byte] – a data bus protocol for automotive applications. FlexRay supports different modes of operation for clock synchronization:

- a distributed fault-tolerant midpoint algorithm for the TDMA mode, and
- a master-slave algorithm for the Byte-flight mode.

The master-slave algorithm in turn can establish a reference based on either time or external events. The distributed midpoint algorithm serves as a reference for a set of TDMA slots with equal length. Following this set is a dynamic segment for events. During the dynamic segment, the slot counter for the minislotting protocol is incremented. If a node wants to send any event messages, it must wait until the slot counter has reached the unique ID assigned to the message. Event messages can have different lengths. The advantage of minislotting over CSMA/CA is that minislotting has no restriction in communication speed. Similar to the TTP/C, FlexRay supports two redundant communication channels for fault tolerance. Because of the lack of published fault hypothesis information, we do not know which types and frequencies of faults the protocol intends to tolerate or how FlexRay tolerates all types of single-component failures. A consortium is developing FlexRay, and it has not yet published a specification.

TT-CAN

Time-triggered CAN [TTCAN] is an extension of the well established event-triggered CAN protocol. Communication involves periodic transmissions of a reference message by a time master. This reference message introduces a system wide reference time. Alternatively, an external event can trigger the reference message. Based on this reference, TT-CAN defines several so-called exclusive windows. These windows are equivalent to the time slots in a TDMA system. TT-CAN assigns each exclusive window to a specific node, which can send a data frame. In addition, the protocol defines arbitrating windows. Within these windows, all network nodes can transmit frames according to the event-triggered CSMA/CA access scheme used by CAN. Because CAN preserves the original CSMA/CA channel access protocol for event messages, it is inherently limited to a 1 Mbit/s data transmission rate. Because CAN provides only one communication channel and a master-slave algorithm handles clock synchronization, TT-CAN cannot tolerate arbitrary, single-component failures. An interesting feature of CAN is its acknowledgment and retransmission mechanism, which uses the CSMA/CA principle. The sender transmits an acknowledgment bit at the end of the frame, which is set to the logical true condition, and a recessive state on the channel represents this condition. If any of the receiver nodes has experienced a reception error, that node can immediately change the state to a dominant channel level, indicating the logical false condition. This mechanism can ensure consistent message delivery for most cases.

References

[Kop03]   H. Kopetz and G. Bauer. The Time-Triggered Architecture. Proceedings of the IEEE, Special Issue on Modelling and Design of Embedded Software, 2003.

[Mai02]   R. Maier, G. Bauer, G. Stöger and S. Poledna. Time-Triggered Architecture: A Consistent Computing Platform. IEEE Micro, 2002, Volume 22(4) pp. 36-45.

[KO02]   H. Kopetz and R. Obermaisser. Temporal composability [real-time embedded systems]; Computing & Control Engineering Journal, Volume 13(4), 2002, pp. 156 -162.

[Kop93]   H. Kopetz and G. Gruensteidl. TTP – A Time-Triggered Protocol for Fault-Tolerant Real-Time Systems. In Proceedings of the 23rd IEEE International Symposium on Fault-Tolerant Computing (FTCS-23). 1993. Toulouse, France: IEEE Press.

[Fis85]   M. Fischer, N. Lynch and M. Paterson. Impossibility of Distributed Consensus with one Faulty Processor. Journal of the ACM, 1985. 32(2): p. 374-382.

[Rus00]   J. Rushby. Formal Verification of Group Membership for the Time-Triggered Architecture. 2000, SRI International: Menlo Park, CA.

[Kop99]   H. Kopetz. Elementary versus Composite Interfaces in Distributed Real-Time Systems. In Proceedings 4th International Symposium on Autonomous Decentralized Systems, pages 26–33, 1999.

[Kop97]   H. Kopetz and R. Nossal. Temporal Firewalls in Large Distributed Real-Time Systems. In Proceedings of IEEE Workshop on Future Trends in Distributed Computing, pages 310–315, 1997.

[Pol95]   S. Poledna. Fault-Tolerant Real-Time Systems: The Problem of Replica Determinism. Kluwer Academic Publishers. 1995.

[Kop93]   H. Kopetz and J. Reisinger. The Non-Blocking Write Protocol NBW: A Solution to a Real-Time Synchronization Problem. In Proceedings of the 14th Real-Time Systems Symposium, pages 131–137, 1993.

[Kop00]   H. Kopetz. Software Engineering for Real-Time: A Roadmap. In Proceedings 22nd International Conference on Software Engineering, pages 201–211, 2000.

[TTP/C]   TTTech Computertechnik AG. Specification of the TTP/C Protocol.

[TTP/A]   OMG. Smart Transducer Interface. Initial Submission, Object Management Group, 2001

[Byte]   http://www.byteflight.de/homepage.htm

[FRay]   http://www.flexray.com/

[TTCAN]   http://www.can-cia.de/can/ttcan/

9 Review of Some Advanced Methodologies

9.1 The Setta Project

Authors

C. Scheidler	DaimlerChrysler
P. Puschner	TU Vienna
S. Boutin	Renault
E. Fuchs	Dependable Computer Systems
G. Gruensteidl	Alcatel Austria
Y. Papadopoulos	University of York
M. Pisecky	TTTech
J. Rennhack	EADS Airbus
U. Virnich	Siemens

Introduction

The overall goal of the project SETTA (Systems Engineering for Time Triggered Architectures) was to push time-triggered systems—an innovative European-funded technology for safety-critical, distributed, real-time applications such as fly-by-wire or drive-by-wire—into future vehicles, aircraft, and train systems. To achieve this goal, SETTA focused on the systems engineering of time-triggered systems. The SETTA consortium consisted of leading European companies in the transport and component supplier sector (DaimlerChrysler, Renault, Airbus Germany, Alcatel Austria, and Siemens VDO), innovative European high tech start-ups (TTTech, DECOMSYS), and universities with an excellent reputation in real-time (University of Technology at Vienna) and safety-critical systems (University of York).

SETTA addresses the systems engineering of safety-critical distributed real-time systems with a special focus on time-triggered architectures (Kopetz and Gruensteidl, 1994; Scheidler, et al., 1997). An innovative methodology and a corresponding engineering environment is developed which aims for a higher maturity at early development steps. Key features are the support for virtual systems integration and the tighter interconnection between the functional development process and the safety analysis process. The supporting tool components are designed and implemented in the course of the SETTA project. The methodology is evaluated by pilot applications from the automotive, aerospace, and railway domain.

The SETTA Methodology

Current Drawbacks
Figure 9.1 shows the 3V lifecycle-process model which will be used to illustrate the weaknesses in engineering of time-triggered systems. The original 3V model has been firstly published by Mosnier and Bortolazzi (1997). The 3V model in Figure 9.1 has been slightly adapted. Phases which traditionally put a major focus on the time-

Artist FP5 Consortium: Embedded Systems Design, LNCS 3436, 92–102, 2005.
© Springer-Verlag Berlin Heidelberg 2005

triggered nature of the target system are coloured in dark grey. The 3V model consists of three Vs representing the system simulation, prototyping, and product development stages.

The *first V* covers the definition and simulation of the overall system functionality. Software-in-the-loop simulation (SIL) is the primary methodology applied.

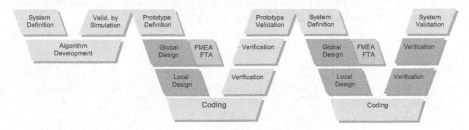

Figure 9.1. 3V process model adapted on time-triggered systems

Implementation aspects, including the "time triggered" property of the target system, are not considered in this systems-engineering phase.

The *second V* is characterized by rapid prototyping based on Hardware-in-the-loop simulation (HIL). In this phase, hardware specific parameters become important. The global design covers the mapping of tasks to computer nodes and the determination of the message scheduling between the nodes. The local design addresses the scheduling of tasks on each node.

The *third V* addresses the system development for the final target hardware. A typical problem at this stage is the limited performance of the target system. Deadlines met by the oversized prototypical hardware might not be met on the target--a situation that is not acceptable for the safety-critical systems targeted at in the SETTA project.

At least four drawbacks in this lifecycle-process model can be identified.

1. There is a gap between the first and the second V. Due to constraints of the target system, the assignment process of the second V may fail, thus invalidating the result of the preceding simulation stage of the first V. For example, a distributed control application running stable at the first V might behave differently due to the timing constraints caused by message passing between computer nodes.

2. A schedule verification tool on the global design level is lacking. The verification tool is needed to check the consistency of the message descriptor list (MEDL; the MEDL determines the message schedule and thus the runtime behaviour of the final system). A verification tool is particularly demanded for the acceptance of the time-triggered technology in the aerospace industry.

3. A timing verification tool on the local design level is lacking. Executing code and measuring its execution time on the target is the current state-of-the-art. However, this technique cannot guarantee to yield safe upper bounds of the execution time.

4. The functionnal development process and the safety analysis process are decoupled. Tools supporting Fault-Tree Analysis (FTA), Event-Tree Analysis (ETA) and Failure Mode and Effects Analysis (FMEA) are not connected to simulation tools like Matlab/Simulink.

SETTA Design Flow Model
The aim of the SETTA project is to propose a design-flow model for time-triggered systems that overcomes the four shortcomings identified before.

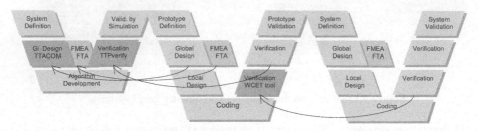

Figure 9.2. SETTA 3V design flow model

A key component in the SETTA approach is a suite of simulation-building blocks provided for the Matlab/Simulink environment. The simulation building blocks support virtual systems integration, in other words, the gap between the first V and the second V is closed. Time-triggered systems are, in contrast to event-triggered systems, fully predictable in their runtime behaviour.

SETTA exploits this predictability at the modelling stage. Simulation-building blocks model not only the core functionality of a system, but also the distributed nature and the used communication mechanisms, which both affect the system's behaviour. E.g., the effects of value discretisation, communication delays, and fault-tolerance, which are typically abstracted in a system model and are a significant source of problems in later implementation stages, are much easier dealt with, if they are already part of the system model. Based on the virtual systems integration, system manufacturers and component suppliers can co-operate in a much tighter way.

A schedule verification tool for the global design level is developed. Verification on the global design level, currently performed at the prototyping or system development stage, is mapped to the simulation stage. The verification tool developed within the SETTA project verifies the MEDL which controls the simulation building blocks. A timing verification tool for the local design level is developed. A specific WCET tool for the simulation-building block set analyses the timing behaviour of the code generated for each of the building blocks. An algorithm for fault-tree synthesis will be developed and implemented which provides an intelligent interface between a functional modelling tool (Matlab/Simulink from The Mathworks) and a fault tree analysis tool (FT+ from Isograph).

To summarize, the main goal is to achieve a high maturity at early development stages based on virtual systems integration. Activities currently performed at prototyping or product development stage are mapped to the simulation stage, as depicted by the arrows in Figure 9.2. Although the tool components are developed by four different partners, SETTA aims for a fully integrated systems engineering environment. To achieve this goal, the tool components will be linked via different interfaces which will be sketched in the following.

The simulation building blocks are triggered by a configuration file which describes the message scheduling on the bus interconnecting computer nodes. This file can be checked by the scheduling verification tool. The WCET analysis will be integrated into the Matlab/Simulink environment and is therefore also connected to the simulation building blocks. The fault-tree synthesis algorithm extracts the structural information out of Matlab/Simulink files which can be extended with the simulation building blocks.

SETTA Tool Components and Validators

Tool Components
A suite of simulation-building blocks – product name: TTACOM – is developed in the SETTA project which supports the virtual systems integration (involved partner: Dependable Computer Systems). TTACOM is a Matlab/Simulink block set that allows the development of distributed applications, including the Time-Triggered Protocol (TTP) bus. It contains blocks for configuring clusters, reading and writing messages, controlling the simulation progress over time, and a detailed graphical TTP interface.

A schedule verification tool – product name: TTPverify – is developed in the SETTA project (involved partner: TTTech). The purpose of this component is to check the message descriptor list (MEDL) of time-triggered systems. The communication in time-triggered systems is statically scheduled. The communication controllers transmit data according to a predefined schedule which is stored in dedicated data tables. To ensure correct system functionality, it is therefore of the utmost importance to verify that these automatically generated data tables satisfy the overall requirements. For this purpose, a dedicated schedule verification tool will be specified which can read the data tables and verify that they meet the requirements.

The WCET analysis tool that is being developed in the course of the SETTA project (Kirner 2000) derives the WCET by means of static code analysis (involved partner: Technical University of Vienna). This stands in contrast to the widely used method of determining the WCET by measuring the duration of representative task executions. This latter approach cannot provide a guaranteed execution-time bound.

Validators
The objective of the automotive validator is to evaluate the results of the SETTA project in the automotive domain (involved partners: DaimlerChrysler, Renault, and Siemens Automotive). The architecture chosen to be the validator for SETTA is a part of an automotive chassis control system which consists of a brake-by-wire system and an adaptive cruise control simulator. The brake-by-wire system consists of a redundant brake pedal system provided by DaimlerChrysler and a brake actuator provided by Siemens Automotive. The adaptive cruise control simulator provided by Renault models the dynamics of a vehicle on a highway. The system has strict performance, timing, and safety requirements and contains two distributed control loops.

The objective of the automotive validator is to evaluate the results of the SETTA project in the aerospace domain (involved partner: EADS Airbus). The architecture chosen to be the validator for SETTA is the cabin pressure regulation system. This system has strict performance, timing and safety requirements. Two independent pressure control functions will be realized for backup reasons and will be implemented as redundant components. Both controller functions will receive appropriate information such as planned flight profile, current position, altitude, and current cabin pressure from the air data/inertial reference system. Taking these parameters and the actual cabin pressure into account, the pressure controller will calculate and command the desired openings for the outflow valves.

In the SETTA project, Alcatel Austria provides the specific requirements from the railway domain and validates the SETTA engineering methodology and tools by using a typical railway application. The main focus of the railway validator is the evaluation of the schedule verification and timing verification tool.

References

[1]   Kirner, R., R. Lang, P. Puschner (2000). Integrating WCET Analysis into a Matlab/Simulink Simulation Model . Submitted for DCCS 2000: 16th IFAC Workshop on Distributed Computer Control Systems, Sydney, Australia, 29th November – 1st December.

[2]   Kopetz, H., G. Gruensteidl, (1994). TTP – A Protocol for Fault-Tolerant Real-Time Systems. IEEE Computer, Vol. 24 (1), pp. 14-23.

[3]   Mosnier, F., J. Bortolazzi, (1997). Prototyping Car-Embedded Applications. In Advances in Information Technologies: The Business Challenge, pp.744-751, IOS Press.

[4]   Scheidler, C., G. Heiner, R. Sasse, E. Fuchs, H. Kopetz, C. Temple. (1997). Time-Triggered Architecture– (TTA). In: Advances in Information Technologies: The Business Challenge, pp. 758-765. IOS Press.

9.2   The SafeAir Project

The SafeAir project (http://www.safeair.org) main goal was to substantially improve the design and development process of high complexity systems for aerospace and other industrial applications of similar complexity, allowing maintaining the high level of dependability in the face of an exponential growth in functionality. The project has developed tools, training and the supporting methodology for designers of embedded systems. The emphasis is on formal development of systems, providing formal specification, model checking technology, qualification analysis and validated code generation.

An ASDE (Avionics System Development Environment) tool-set implementing synchronous technologies, methods and tools, that meet the high dependability needs of real-time embedded systems with high complexity, has been developed and evaluated in the SafeAir framework. This integrated environment strongly builds on existing best in class commercial front-end tools and on the verification and validation technologies developed in the SACRES Esprit project (http://www.tni.fr/sacres/), now expanded to an open tool-set, responsive to user needs.

Authors

Drora Goshen and Vered Gafni, Israel Aircraft Industries. The author of the present version is Thierry Gautier, INRIA. The SafeAir project was headed by Philippe Baufreton, Hispano-Suiza. Other participants were: Israel Aircraft Industries, Airbus France, Airbus Deutschland GmbH, Siemens then Infineon, INRIA, OFFIS, the Weizmann Institute, TNI-Valiosys, I-Logix, Telelogic.

Architecture of the ASDE Tool-Set

The ASDE is a coordinated open tool-set, which allows:

- The creation of coherent models of the System Under Development by using in a coordinated manner various modelling and analysis tools.
- The investigation and maintenance of models created by using the coordinated tool-set.
- The formal verification of the global model and sub-models with respect to the required properties.
- The simulation of the behaviour specified by the overall model and by its sub-models.
- Code generation & validation.
- Document generation.

Following are the main building blocks of the ASDE tool-set:

- ModelBuild (http://www.tni-valiosys.com/) is the framework of the design and simulation tools (architectural description editor, Statemate, Sildex, SCADE and Simulink).
- ModelVerify is (in a conceptual view) the framework of the verification and analysis tools BOOST (http://www.infineon.com/) and HYBRID (http://www.offis.de/).
- SCADE_KCG (http://www.esterel-technologies.com/) is a compiler that generates executable C code of the design model or sub-models.
- CVT (http://www.wisdom.weizmann.ac.il) is a code validation tool applied either to the C code (with respect to the SCADE source), or to machine code (with respect to the C source).
- Polychrony http://www.irisa.fr/espresso/Polychrony is the IRISA synchronous design academic prototype (based, as Sildex, on the Signal language), provided as an added toolbox to ASDE, and that can be used for advanced experiments.

The environment allows an easy and transparent transformation of data from one tool to the next one.

Methodology

An ASDE Implementation Process Methodology has been provided during the SafeAir project to support the tool-set. The ASDE supports the following activities throughout the different phases of a typical system development cycle:

Development Cycle Phase		Activity	Activity Description
No.	description		
1	*Specification*	Not supported by ASDE	
2	*Design*	Properties Specification	Establish formal requirements
		Conceptual Modelling	Establish Functionality & Operation Concepts (Functional Analysis).
		Physical Modelling	
			Evolve alternative designs
3	*Analysis and control*	Simulation	Verify (either by simulation or formal verification) that each design meets requirements.
		Formal Verification	
4	*H/W and S/W Implementation*	Code Generation	S/W Implementation
5	*Unit integration & testing*	Code Validation	S/W unit testing
6	*System Integration & Verification*	Not supported by ASDE	

Figure 9.2 presents a top-level view of the Development cycle, the activities supported by ASDE, and their inter-relations. Each of these development activities consists of a number of sub-activities that altogether concur at getting the result. The System Engineering Process activities are used iteratively during the development cycle. Therefore, the Implementation Process Methodology does not dictate any particular method of going through these activities, however, a recommended development process is shown in Fig. 2. It shows that conceptual and physical modelling are carried out concurrently, while using simulation as an analysis feedback for the design. In parallel, properties specification is performed. A formal verification of the conceptual model can be done while an extended verification will be done on the physical model, see below for the meaning of these terms.

System Design
The System Design Phase assumes as an input the natural language system specification, and generates a global system design in terms of computational activities partitioned into a concrete physical architecture and a properties specification of the system.

The System Design process consists of the following activities (Fig. 9.1):

- *Conceptual Modelling*
  A conceptual model describes the partitioning of the system into conceptual ("logical") subsystems/objects, the behaviour and the functional capabilities provided by them, and data/signal flows between them. The Implementation Process Methodol-

ogy is intended for the development of large-scale systems that consist of a number of subsystems that operate concurrently, while interacting, to achieve the global system functionality. In terms of the operational model we call such systems "Globally Asynchronous, Locally Synchronous (GALS)".

The ASDE tool-set provides several tools for the conceptual model development and presentation (these equally apply to global behavioural and functional model views). The initial design starts with an Architectural Editor that provides for specification of asynchronous interconnected components. Then, each component is separately refined as a synchronous module. For that purpose, Sildex, SCADE, or Statemate are appropriate tools that completely support synchronous conceptual modelling. Moreover, the tool-set allows integrated specifications that employ the specific strength of each tool to generate better descriptions. It also allows the incorporation of special purpose tools such as MATLAB/Simulink.

- *Physical Modelling*
The physical design model represents the implementation of the conceptual model within a concrete physical architecture. The physical architecture describes the system partitioning into physical subsystems/components and their interconnections. The physical architecture describes the architectural modules (e.g., air-plane, engine, computer, processors, etc.), channels through which signals flow, and their connection to the physical modules. The architecture is refined by iterative decomposition of the physical system into physical subsystems. The signal channels are refined as needed by decomposition into lower-level channels, to suit the specification of lower-level architectural modules. The physical architecture is usually developed after the conceptual modelling, but it can be done concurrently.

   After review and approval of the conceptual and architectural models (see simulation and formal verification sections, below) the physical model is actually constructed by allocation of the behavioural and functional elements of the conceptual model to elements of the physical architecture, and signals flowing among them are mapped to ports and channels.

- *Properties specification*
The purpose of this activity is to provide a formal presentation of properties required for formal verification as described in the next section. State and temporal properties can be formally expressed using the Properties Specification Language (PSL) provided by ModelVerify. The input for this activity–called system formalization–is the natural language specification in the first place, but also sometimes common knowledge of the physical environment need to be formalized as well in order to enable correct verification process described in the next section. In general, properties must be classified either as "assertions" (assumed to be true in any possible behaviour of the system under development), or "requirements" (required to be true in any possible behaviour of the system under development). Naturally, assertions and requirements play different roles in the verification process (assumed versus to be verified). Hence, the correct classification of properties–under the developer responsibility–is essential to the correctness of the verification process and must be concluded by a careful analysis of the natural language specification. ModelVerify provides for managing assertions and requirements in different repositories. From a methodological point of view, since it is not realistic to have a

"total" formal verification, critical requirements must be identified and verified (this also means that only relevant assertions must be expressed formally).

A major quantitative improvement of the formal verification capabilities can be achieved by abstractions. By this technique, the data (states, etc.) are analyzed to identify equivalence classes. Thus, the size of explored graph is considerably reduced. ModelVerify is capable of performing some abstractions automatically. The major abstraction efforts, however, remain a developer due.

System Analysis
* *Formal Verification*
  Formal verification is intended for verification of temporal properties, required of the system behaviours, using algorithms rather than simulation. Formal verification is a crucial technique regarding critical systems since it results in an absolute answer whether a design satisfies the system requirements, or not (in case of refutation it also provides a counter example). This is in contrast with simulation that provides only partial coverage of the possible behaviours. However, formal verification cannot fully replace simulation due to its complexity.

  Formal verification should be carried out in various stages of the system development depending on the specific activity. Also, like simulation, formal verification can be applied to partial designs as well as to the complete model. Formal verification consists of the following activities: 1) Properties Consistency Check. 2) Model Checking.

  Properties consistency check is intended to verify that the specification expressed in the *Properties Specification Language* is consistent in the sense that it does not contain logical contradictions (e.g., requirements that contradict each other).

  Model Checking is an algorithm that gets as input the assumed properties specified in the previous stage, the System under development specification produced using ModelBuild, and a property to be verified–one of the required properties repository. Then, the model checking is activated and after a while the developer will get the result: either the required property is verified, or the required property is not satisfied in which case an example of a behaviour that falsifies the requirement will be given. Also, it should be possible to run automatically a simulation of the falsifying behaviour in order to locate the mishap. Nevertheless, it must be emphasized that often verification failures are due to under-specification of assumptions, misunderstanding of the natural text intension, or just a mistake in its formalization. In general, there are two verification stages: first, the "Formal Verification" that is carried out on the functional design; second, the "Extended Formal Verification" which considers in addition the physical architecture model.
* *Simulation*
  Simulation is intended to verify the semantic correctness, completeness and consistency of the conceptual and the physical models. It is based on running the (executable) model design through pre-defined scenarios of the (simulated) environment behaviour, and mental inspection of the results with respect to the system specification. Simulation is first applied to the functional model in order to detect conceptual errors. Then, simulation is carried out again after completion of the physical model. This time, it is intended to verify that the system functionality after physical

subsystems partitions, and insertion of communication go-betweens, is still consistent with the conceptual design. Usually, simulation is carried out in two levels: subsystem level where part of the system is isolated and locally simulated, and system level where the system is checked as a whole.

S/W Implementation
- *Code generation*
  Following verification of the model, investigation of its properties through simulation and adequate review, code is generated for architectural modules identified as modules to be implemented in software. Code is also generated for simulation purposes. The code is generated by the ASDE (SCADE/Lustre language) for each CPU, based on the allocation of activities (functions) to architectural (physical) modules, performed within the framework of the coordination of the conceptual and design models.
- *Cross compilation*
  The generated C code for each target CPU is compiled by a suitable cross compiler outside the ASDE.

S/W Unit Testing (Code Validation)
As the last step in the generation of operational software, the CVT (Code Validation Tool) validates automatically the correctness of the generated code for each processor, with respect to the SCADE/Lustre design. When the CVT is invoked to validate C code (CVT-C), the generated C code is compared to the SCADE/Lustre design for each processor: it verifies that the target C code is a correct implementation of the "source" specification in Lustre. When the CVT is invoked to validate the binary code (CVT-A), it verifies the translation from C to the assembly code.

Beyond SafeAir

Strong Points
The SafeAir methodology and its implementation through the ASDE toolset essentially rely on commercially available frameworks and tool bases; it does not require extensive developments of brand new technologies. Its strong points can be categorized as follows:

- *Moving from V-shaped to Y-shaped lifecycle.* In this metaphor, the Y is regarded as a smaller "v" put on the top of the vertical bar. The vertical bar represents automatic code generation together with automatic code validation. As a result, the "v" part of the cycle concentrates on higher level phases of the design flow.
- *Providing a strong formal basis.* All tools of the ASDE are supported by a strong formal semantic basis; the meaning of each and every notation is made very precise. This makes it possible to rely on automatic embedded code generation, even at a certified level (by using the SCADE certified code generator). As a wider and more flexible mean to qualify the generated code, very advanced procedures of automatic code cross-validation are proposed; they allow to check whether some generated code actually refines its associated source code; this is different from certifying the code generator, it rather consists of certifying a given pair of {source,

object} codes. Then, following a more established background, extensive and powerful verification tools dedicated to earlier phases of the design are available.

- *Architecture of the embedded software is addressed.* While several technologies are now commercially available to generate embedded code for individual processors, the generation of the entire embedded architecture is still far from being routine. A central difficulty is the distributed nature of such architectures, and its (frequent) hybrid synchronous/asynchronous style. The SafeAir methodology has provided a breakthrough in this respect by providing the ModelBuild service, which allows emulating the deployment of a design over a distributed, possibly asynchronous, architecture; this is again supported by a formally sound basis. This is a significant step toward virtual architecture exploration.

- *Integration of the different frameworks.* The smoothness of the design flow is recognized as a key limiting factor in all methodologies relying on the combination of different frameworks. The SafeAir project has addressed this issue by using the Lustre-SCADE formalism as a common semantic platform.

Limitations
They can be categorized into two broad classes:

- The scope of the SafeAir methodology is too narrow. The integration with higher stages of the design flow needs to be improved. Firstly, the integration with scientific engineering tools and technologies is only partial. Secondly, the issue of how to combine the advantages of the ASDE with the broader scope of UML methodologies has not been considered. Today, we see typically two concurrent progress directions:

  o Research toward integrated tool suites, from scientific engineering down to architecture;
  o Efforts aiming at extending the benefits of UML in the technical and real-time industrial areas.
  o With no doubt this concurrency is an obstacle toward progress.

- Virtual exploration is not provided to the needed level. Using the ASDE, the designer can generate models of his application deployed on his architecture. Unfortunately, he cannot back-animate his high-level specification in parallel with the modelled architecture. To say it differently, he knows his high-level spec, he sees the resulting detailed design, but he cannot see, by simulation, the link between both. This prevents the designer from having, at the same time, tightly related high-level and detailed views of his design. But it is precisely the essence of design by virtual exploration to provide this facility. On the other hand, the formal verification of programs is performed on the C code generated from these programs. This is in the most general case, a too low-level approach since it prevents from verifying properties on partial specifications, for which code cannot be generated. A more general approach would be to check properties on partial (non deterministic) designs; these partial designs would be progressively refined toward more detailed designs from which, finally, code can be generated. In this approach, the proof system should be applicable at any level of the model.

10 Executive Overview on Component-Based Design and Integration Platforms

Component-Based Design is expected to increase software productivity, by reducing the amount of effort needed to develop, update, and maintain systems. There are two main benefits expected from component technology. First, it gives structure to system design and system development, thus making system verification and maintenance more tractable. Second, it allows reuse of development effort by allowing components to be re-used across products and in the longer term by paving the way for a market for software components.

Component based technology has become widespread in general program development with platforms such as JavaBeans/EJB from Sun, .NET/COM from Microsoft, and the manufacturer independent CORBA initiative from OMG. Adoption for the development of embedded and real-time systems is significantly slower. Major reasons are that real-time systems must satisfy requirements of timeliness, quality-of-service, predictability, that they are often safety-critical, and that they must obey stringent constraints on resource usage (memory, processing power, communication). Existing wide-spread component technologies are inherently heavyweight and complex, incurring significant overheads on the run-time platform; they do not in general address timeliness, quality-of-service or similar extra-functional properties important for embedded and real-time systems. Yet, in their present form they are used in large, distributed, and not safety critical systems, e.g., in industrial automation, but they are unsuitable for deployment in most embedded real-time environments.

For small real-time systems, component technologies have been developed for particular classes of systems, often as extensions of existing real-time operating systems within specific development organizations, and their adoption outside these organizations is limited. To avoid large and resource-consuming run-time platforms, they do not in general support run-time deployment of components. Composition of components into (sub)systems is rather performed in the design environment, prior to compilation, thus enabling static prediction of system properties and global optimisation of resource utilization..

Based on a survey of selected component technologies in different industrial sectors and the needs of industry, we find two important obstacles to wider adoption of component technology for embedded and real-time systems.

- There is a lack of widely adopted standards for component technology. A complicating factor is that different industrial sectors have different priorities concerning the main characteristics offered by such a standard.
- A component technology for real-time systems should support specification and prediction of timing and QoS-properties. Solutions to these problems are not well enough developed and not well enough integrated into development tools.

Therefore we survey techniques for handling different functional and extra-functional properties of component and system behaviour. A conclusion is that techniques exist

Artist FP5 Consortium: Embedded Systems Design, LNCS 3436, 103–113, 2005.

for handling such properties, but that further research is needed to improve the theory of specifying and composing components, and to develop tool support.

After a survey of technical characteristics of main component technologies, we also survey some efforts for standardization of component models and modelling languages, paying special attention to developments pertinent to embedded and real-time systems.

The survey concludes with a summary of important issues for success of component-based development of embedded systems. Many of these are concerned with extra-functional properties, and the special characteristics of embedded systems. Satisfactory solution of these issues is considerably more challenging than the current solutions to component-based systems. We indicate possible ways to arrive at solutions.

10.1   Motivation and Objectives

Component-Based Design and Development is perceived as key for developing advanced real-time systems in a both cost- and time effective manner. It can be seen a qualitative jump in software development methodology, comparable to the transition from assembly language programming to high level problem oriented languages around 1970, or the transition from procedural programming to object oriented programming around 1990.

Component Based Design is seen to increase software productivity, by reducing the amount of effort needed to develop, update, and maintain systems. Benefits include the following:

- **Giving Structure to Systems under Development**. Component technology supports the structuring of complex systems early in the development process. In this way, many integration and maintenance problems can be addressed early, at lower cost.
- **Reuse of Development Effort**. Components can be re-used across several products or even product families. Re-use is made easer by defining product line architectures, in which components have given roles. New products can then re-use components of previous products by slight modification or parameterisation.
- **Supporting System Maintenance and Evolution**. Systems are easier to maintain if they have a clear structure, e.g., as a system composed of components. For legacy systems, it sometimes pays off to decompose them into components in order to make future upgrades and maintenance easier.
- **Enabling a Market for Software Parts**. Standardized component specifications and technologies allow to integrate components produced by different suppliers. Currently, for embedded systems, only large components are transferred between different organizations, e.g., RTOS, databases, process and control components. If a wider class of components were re-usable across a wider class of systems, it would give higher returns on development investment. One vision for the future is that application development follows a "drop & glue" approach, picking components from a library incorporating the intellectual property of the system house, as well as standardized components. This would give the system developer a range of re-usable components supporting all layers in a system architecture. This vision includes an open market of components, which are interoperable, and where integration problems are solved by standardized component frameworks.

Component technology has gained wide adoption in the area of business data processing, and is under continuous development. There are also signs of adoption for the development of embedded and real-time systems. However, the pace is significantly slower. Major reasons are that other concerns are of great importance for the development of such systems. Real-time systems must satisfy constraints on extra-functional properties such as timing (e.g., meeting deadlines), quality of service (e.g., throughput), and dependability (including reliability, safety, and security). It is important that functional and extra-functional properties be predictable, in particular if the system is safety-critical. Embedded systems must often operate with scarce resources, including processing power, memory, communication bandwidth. These concerns are not addressed by widely used component technologies.

There are many challenges to overcome in order to develop component technology that is suitable for the many particularities of embedded systems. Therefore, this roadmap presents a survey of selected topics important for component-based design of embedded systems, based on which directions for further work are outlined. Our aim is that it will serve as a guide to researchers whose work is motivated by the emergence of component-based development in embedded systems design., It assists by providing a survey of existing background work, and by providing directions for advancing the state-of-the-art. The selection of topics is, of course, coloured by the background of the authoring team, which has a strong representation of researchers particularly engaged in modelling, specification, and verification of embedded and real-time systems.

10.2   Essential Characteristics

Basic Concepts

There is some disagreement about the precise definition of basic terms in component based software development. We therefore give a short treatment of basic concepts and define how they will be understood in this document.

In component based software development a system is structured using components. In classic engineering disciplines, a component is a self-contained part or subsystem that can be used as a building block in the design of a larger system. It provides specific services to its environment across well-specified interfaces. Examples are an engine in an automobile, or the heating furnace in a home. Ideally, the development a component should be decoupled from development of the systems in which it is used. Components should be reusable in different contexts.

In software engineering, there are many different suggestions for precise definitions of components in component based software development. According to [BBB+00], advocates of software reuse equate components to anything that can be reused; practitioners using commercial off-the shelf (COTS) software equate components to COTS products; software methodologists equate components with units of project and configuration management; and software architects equate components with design abstractions.

The best accepted definition in the software industry world is based on Szyperski's work [Szy98]:

A component is a unit of composition with contractually specified interfaces and fully explicit context dependencies that can be deployed independently and is subject to third-party composition.

We largely follow this definition and in particular stress the separation between component implementation and component interface. Ideally, there should be no context dependencies that are not captured by the interface. However, in practice interfaces capture only certain aspects of a component's behaviour.

Szyperski [Szy98] tends to insist that components should be delivered in binary from, and that deployment and composition should be performed at run-time. In this report, we take a more liberal view, and consider a component as a software implementation that can be executed on a physical or logical device. This includes components delivered in high-level languages, and allows build-time (or design-time) composition. This more liberal view is partly motivated by the special requirements for embedded systems, as will be discussed in section 11.3.

There are two prerequisites that enable components to be integrated and work together:

- A *component model* specifies the standards and conventions that components must follow to enable proper interaction.
- A *component framework* is the design-time and run-time infrastructure that manages resources for components and supports component interactions.

There is an obvious correspondence between the conventions of a component model and the supporting mechanisms and services of a component framework.

Component models and frameworks can be specified at different levels of abstraction. Some component models (e.g., COM) are specified on the level of the binary executable, and the framework consists of supporting OS services. Some component models (e.g., JavaBeans, CCM, or .Net) are specified on the level of processor independent byte code. And yet other component models (e.g., Koala) are specified on the level of a programming language (such as C). The framework can contain "glue code" and possibly a runtime executive, which are bundled with the components before compilation.

In component based system development, there is a clear distinction between two perspectives of a component.

- The component *implementation* is the executable realization of a component, obeying the rules of the component model. Depending on the component model at hand, component implementations are provided in binary form, byte code, compilable C code, etc.
- The component *interface* summarizes the properties of the component that are externally visible to the other parts of the system, and which can be used when designing the system. An interface may list the signatures of operations, in which case it can be used to check that components interact without causing type mismatches. An interface may contain additional information about the component's patterns of interaction with its environment or about extra-functional properties such as execution time; this allows more system properties to be determined when the system is first designed. An interface that, in addition to information about op-

eration signatures, also specifies functional or extra-functional properties is called *a rich interface.*

The component implementations must of course conform to the properties stated in their interfaces. In principle this presupposes that there are procedures and mechanisms for checking or enforcing conformance, such as verification (simulation, testing, run-time monitoring, formal verification, etc.) and code generation.

The information in component interfaces facilitates also the check for interoperability between components. Rich interfaces enable *verification* of system requirements and *prediction* of system properties from properties of components. This allows system properties to be verified and predicted early in the development lifecycle, enables early design space exploration, and saves significant effort in the later system integration phase. A research challenge today is to develop methods for predicting system properties from component properties.

A *contract* is a specification of functional or extra-functional properties of a component, which are observable in its interface. A contract can be seen as specifying constraints on the interface of a component.

It is here important to keep in mind the role of extra-functional properties of embedded systems, and their dependence on platform characteristics. Many important properties of components in embedded systems, such as timing and performance, depend on characteristics of the underlying hardware platform. Kopetz and Suri [KS03] propose to distinguish between *software components* and *system components.* Extra-functional properties, such as performance, cannot be specified for *a software component* in isolation. Such properties must either be specified with respect to a given hardware platform, or be parameterized on (characteristics of) the underlying platform. *A system component,* on the other hand, is defined as a self-contained hardware and software subsystem, and can satisfy both functional and extra-functional properties.

Closely related with component-based development is the *software architecture* of a program or computing system, which is generally taken to denote:

> *"the structure or structures of the system, which comprise software components [and connectors], the externally visible properties of those components [and connectors] and the relationships among them."* [BCK98]

The architecture of a system is an early design decision, which to a large extent determines global system parameters such as functionality, performance, resource consumption, maintainability, etc. Descriptions of system architectures include descriptions of component properties, visible through their interfaces, and enable informed evaluations of different system architectures when selecting between them. *Architecture Definition Languages* (ADLs) have been developed as languages for expressing system architectures as compositions of software modules and/or hardware modules. Typical concepts of ADLs are *components, ports, connectors*, etc. They can also describe various classes of component properties. When used in Component-Based Development, component properties expressed using an ADL should in principle also be expressible in component interfaces. For example, Meta-H may decorate components with properties such as execution time and failure modes. Component interfaces must then be rich enough to allow description of such properties.

ADLs concentrate on the description of a system, whose properties are the composition of properties visible in component interfaces. Complementing this, a component technology specifies how such interfaces are implemented (possibly from independently developed components), so that the resulting system implementation has the properties described in its architecture. Since the purpose of this document is to concentrate on components themselves, we refrain from giving an extensive overview of ADLs. A few ADLs that are perceived as influencing the development of component technology are described in section 14.

10.3   Role in Future Embedded Systems

If the technological and organizational challenges for component based development of embedded systems are overcome, the benefits can be summarized as follows.

- **Giving Structure to System Development**. Component technology supports the structuring of complex systems early in the development process. In particular, it allows a structured resource and timing management, which is crucial for many embedded systems. In current development practice, resource and timing problems are resolved during system integration with high cost. There is a strong trend and desire to handle these problems on component level, thus solving the corresponding integration problems *a priori*. This presupposes a component technology with rich interfaces that support description of resource and timing properties.
- **Reuse of Development Effort**. Components can be re-used across several products or even product families. Re-use is made easer by defining product line architectures, in which components have given roles. Again, performance and Quality of Service properties of products can be handled when defining a system architecture, provided that component interfaces can express resource and quality-of-service properties.
- **Supporting System Maintenance and Evolution**. Systems are easier to maintain if they have a clear structure, e.g., as a system composed of components. For legacy systems, it sometimes pays to refactor into components in order to ease future upgrades and maintenance r.
- **Enabling a Market for Software Parts**. Standardized component specifications and technologies allow us to integrate components produced by different suppliers. Currently, for embedded systems, only large components are transferred between different organizations: RTOS, databases, process control components, etc. In order for a wider class of components to be re-usable across a wider class of systems, widely used component technologies must be developed that are able to cope with the specific properties of components in embedded systems.

Expectations from component technology in major industries include to gain by structuring system development; this gain is expected in the foreseeable future, and would alone justify investments in component technology, in particular if it builds on current development technology and processes There is some reluctance to make drastic changes to development processes in order to support a radically new component technology, even if it might be able to attain far greater gains, since there are high risks involved in introducing new development technology and processes.

10.4   Overall Challenges and Work Directions

Findings, Synthesis, Needs

Here is a brief summary of the findings of this roadmap, concerning the current state of the art, and needs for further development. It is structured under major headings.

Support for system development. Component technology can improve system development by supporting system design early in the development process. Many integration and maintenance problems can be addressed early, at lower cost. System properties can be predicted during system design. However, support for these activities is still not adequately developed to suit the needs of embedded system development. In particular, there is still inadequate support for the extra-functional properties that are characteristic for embedded systems. There is a need to further develop techniques that address the following issues

- **Specification of functional and extra-functional properties of components as part of their interfaces.** In particular, this concerns properties with system-wide impact, such as memory and resource consumption, timing, performance, etc. These are typically extra-functional properties characteristic for embedded systems. A complication is that extra-functional properties typically depend on the underlying platform and execution environment, and it is not well understood how to cope with this dependency in interface specifications

- **Determination of QoS, timing, and resource properties of components.** There are several existing techniques for this, including measurement, simulation, and static analysis of source code. Each technique has its advantages and limitations, so they are suitable in different contexts. For software components of embedded systems a difficult problem is that the results from measurement or simulation depend on the measurement platform, hardware platform, the particular system configuration and environment used for the measurements, etc. Such results may not be valid on other platforms or in other system configurations.

- **Prediction of system properties such as QoS, timing, and resource consumption, from component properties** expressed in component interfaces. Support for this activity can potentially solve many integration problems early in the development process, and aid in system evolution, e.g., when new modules are added. The analysis of system properties from component properties is in general an inherently complex problem; the complexity can be mitigated by more efficient analysis techniques, and by employing suitable architectures and design principles.

- **Handling interference between components.** Components have individual requirements that can be violated when composed and deployed with other components. Techniques are needed that ensure that component features do not interfere with those of other components. Such interferences can be very subtle. An important specific scenario where unexpected interferences may occur is when several components, each implementing a piece of functionality, are mapped onto one small hardware unit.

- **Handling heterogeneous system descriptions.** The interaction between components of an embedded system is typically much more extensive than between components in the business processing domain, where, e.g., interaction via method calls can suffice. Components can execute and communicate synchronously or asynchronously, sometimes using different timing models. It is not well understood how to understand systems whose components execute and communicate using different paradigms.

Wider adoption of component technologies for embedded system design is needed, in order to motivate investment in tools, platforms, component repositories, etc. Issues that must be advanced include the following.

- **Widely adopted component models.** There is currently no wide-spread component model that is suitable for the needs in embedded system development. Needs vary between industrial sectors, whence we might see a development of different models in different sectors.
- **Implementation of Component Frameworks.** There is a lack of implemented platforms that are suitable for embedded systems. Such platforms should support a suitable component model, not require a large supply of resources, and provide well-chosen generic system functionalities, e.g., for safety, reliability, and availability. Since platform requirements vary between industrial sectors, it seems plausible that different platforms will e developed for different sectors.
- **Uniformisation of interface specifications.** There is currently a variety of approaches for specifying functional and extra-functional component properties. Convergence and standardization of these approaches is necessary to motivate investment in tools for verification of component properties, prediction of system properties, etc.
- **Component Certification.** In order to transfer components across organizations, techniques and procedures should be developed for conveying trust in the quality of component implementations. This problem may need advances in component verification (including testing, simulation, formal verification), and in procedures for documenting the efforts made in verification.
- **Tool support** for different development activities, including tools to analyse and predict system properties of systems.
- **Standards** and **implementations of component frameworks** must be developed that suit different embedded systems application domains. A single technology will not suit all the various domains, and in fact domain specific standardization efforts are underway in several industrial sectors. A standard should preferably be independent of a particular platform or vendor, to avoid future dominance by a single platform provider.

Challenges and Work Directions

We conclude by summarizing some of the important research challenges, and indicate directions for further work.

Extra-functional Properties in Component-Based Development of Embedded Systems give rise to a number of hard technical problems.

- **Specification of extra-functional properties** has to meet many challenges.

o   Dependency on the underlying platform could be addressed by contracts, or specifications, that depend on properties provided by the platform interface. Such dependencies could be expressed, e.g., by letting parameters in the specification depend on parameters of the platform, or by using other mechanisms.

o   Uniformisation and Standardization of Specification formalism. This process requires a more solid understanding of how to best specify extra-functional properties at an appropriate level of understanding. Efforts are underway to extend UML notations with capabilities to express extra-functional properties.

- **Determination of QoS, timing, and resource properties of components** faces several challenges

   o   Dependency on platform, configuration parameters, etc. This problem is especially relevant when properties are obtained by measurement or simulation, since this needs a system context as driver for the measurements. Potential approaches to overcome the problem include to find ways to generate performance or timing models where the dependency on the environment is explicit, and can be determined by appropriate measurements, or to find techniques to generalize from one system environment to another. Static analysis of source code does not suffer from this problem to the same extent, and has the potential to offer stricter guarantees, important in safety-critical applications. Techniques for coping with the complexity of this technique should be further developed.

- **Prediction of extra-functional system properties** is in general an inherently complex problem, which could be addressed as follows.

   o   There is a large supply of tools that analyze system functionality, performance, timing, etc. using techniques from scheduling, formal verification, performance analysis, etc. Such tools and techniques should be linked to tools for Component Based Development; an example where this is underway is Meta-H, but there is a large untapped potential. To use this potential, techniques and notations for component and system specifications must be further uniformised and standardized.

   In the foreseeable future, an important objective should be to leverage the power of existing academic and commercial tools modelling, composition, verification, analysis, simulation, etc., by connecting existing pieces into a tool-chain for modelling and analysis of component-based real-time systems.

   o   Techniques for predicting and analyzing extra-functional system properties must take into account both the interaction between components, as well as their sharing of processing resources, making this a serious research challenge. Techniques for addressing it should include:

   –   techniques to integrate components while preserving and guaranteeing essential properties of component behaviour. Rules for composability should be developed, which guarantee that if a components meets a property in a certain context, then this property is preserved when its context changes.

   –   techniques that exploit compositionality, by developing techniques to provide or extract simple component interfaces, which enable the prediction of global properties as well as checking that each component conforms to its interface. In order for such an approach to succeed, it is essential to minimize the linking and dependencies between components.

– novel techniques for analysis of extra-functional properties that combine the strong aspects of the different disciplines of scheduling theory, performance analysis, model checking, etc.

• **Handling interference between components.** The problem of ensuring that component features do not interfere with those of other components has been termed the feature interaction problem in the telecommunications domain. We need principles for ensuring that properties of a component are still valid in a large system context.

The development of widely adopted component technologies for embedded system design should be supported by working along several directions, including the following.

• **Widely adopted component models** can be obtained in several ways.

o Parts of established component technologies, such as COM, can be adapted for embedded systems.
o Component technologies that have proven successful in specific contexts can be further developed.
o Successful techniques for handling extra-functional properties should be brought to standardization.

• **Implementation of Component Frameworks** is necessary for a wider adoption of a component technology.

o Platforms that support established component technologies and suit the needs of embedded systems by using a constrained supply of resources, and having predictable resource and timing behaviour, do not exist today, but should be developed.
o Suitable techniques by which platforms can provide services for run-time composition and replacement, failure handling, system adaptation and reconfiguration, should be developed and integrated in an RTOS.
o Small OS platforms that are used for embedded systems can be extended with new functionality and develop into a more powerful component technology. There are several examples where a small OS platform has been extended with design disciplines for component design, supported by design tools that solve integration problems prior to compilation. This trend can be further developed.

• **Development of application-specific system architectures** that support the development of components suiting specific needs in such an architecture. Such architectures are being defined in several industrial sectors.

10.5   Document Structure

This document is structured as follows. In section 11, we present a view on the development of component-based systems, as a basis for identifying key concerns for component based development, in particular for embedded systems. section 12 presents condensed reports on the state of the art, trends, and needs for component based development in different industrial application sectors. In section 13, we concentrate on presenting techniques used for specifying and analyzing important functional and extra-functional properties of systems using information about component interfaces.

Section 14 presents major component models, and assesses some of their strengths and limitations, in particular with respect to the aspects discussed in section 13. Finally, in section 15, we survey the situation with respect to standardization efforts, in particular related to OMG, that are central to component technologies for real-time systems.

11 Component-Based System Development

Component-Based Software Engineering (CBSE) uses methods, tools and principles of general software engineering. However there is one distinction: CBSE distinguishes **component development** and **system development with components**. There is a slight difference in the requirements and business goals in the two cases and there exist different approaches.

- In **component development**, the main emphasis is on *reusability*: components are built for reuse in many applications, many of them not yet existing. A component should ideally be precisely specified, easy to understand, sufficiently general, easy to adapt, easy to deliver and deploy, and easy to replace.
- **System development with components** is focused on the identification of reusable entities and relations between them, beginning from the system requirements and from the availability of already existing components [BCK98, GAO95]. Much implementation effort in system development is no longer necessary but there are efforts required in dealing with components, including locating them, selecting those most appropriate, adapting them, and verifying them [MSP+00].

We not only recognize different activities in the two processes, but also find that many activities can be performed independently. In practice the processes are often already separated, since third parties, independently of system development, develop many components. Even components developed internally within an organization that uses the same components in different products, are often treated as separate entities developed separately. For this reason we can distinguish:

- Lifecycle of component-based systems
- Lifecycle of components

11.1 Lifecycle of Component-Based Systems

Development with components builds on advanced ideas of Object Oriented Design and Pattern Based Design through its focus on the identification of reusable entities and relations between them, starting from the system requirements. Different lifecycle models, established in software engineering, can be used in Component-Based Development, but modified to emphasize component-centric activities. Let us consider, for example, the waterfall model using a component-based approach. The top half of Figure 2.1 shows the phases of the waterfall model. Underneath are shown the accompanying activities in Component-Based Development.

Characteristic features of component-based development are the following.

- Identification of **requirements** is performed as in traditional development. However in the component-based approach, the mapping between system and component requirements is important. Requirements for components should be identified during system requirements elicitation, in order to reuse existing components.

Artist FP5 Consortium: Embedded Systems Design, LNCS 3436, 114–119, 2005.
© Springer-Verlag Berlin Heidelberg 2005

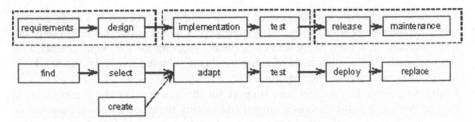

Figure 12.1. The CBD cycle compared with the waterfall model

- The early **design** phase focuses on two essential steps:
  - o The *logical view* of the system is specified by a system architecture with components and their interaction. In this view, components are represented by their interfaces, possibly including specification of relevant extra-functional properties (in real-time systems this includes timing properties). The architecture specification process is combined with finding, evaluating, selecting, and adapting components that will perform the roles defined by the interfaces. The logical design is in its essence model based development, because it focuses on composing components such that the resulting model satisfies requirements.
  - o The *structural view* refines the system architecture consisting of component implementations, to conform to a component framework, and various technology-specific services. The refined component model may support analysis of technology dependent properties usually associated with resources, such as execution times.
- The **implementation** phase includes adapting, composing, and deploying components, using a component framework.
- The **verification** (or test) phase performs system verification (e.g., by testing). Rich component interfaces enable a significant part of system verification to be performed in the design phase based on the developed models, thus saving significant effort in the test phase.
- The **maintenance** phase puts extra focus on the replacement and update of entire components, possibly during system operation.

In summary, the activities that are specific to component-based systems development are:

- *Specify logical and structural system architecture* The architecture specification process must take into account that the system requirements should be compatible with those of available components; in this way the system design becomes an interplay to match system and component requirements. Often the requirements cannot be fulfilled completely, and a trade-off analysis is needed to adjust the system architecture and to reformulate the requirements to make it possible to use existing components. In addition, the selection of a particular component technology must be taken into consideration, as a component technology may require particular frameworks with a number of specific services such as component intercommunication.
- *Find and select components that may be used in the system.* Available components are collected for further investigation. To successfully perform this procedure, a

reasonable number of candidates must be available The selection is a trade-off between requirements elicitations and system design. If the process focuses only on requirements, it is very likely that components meeting all the requirements will not be found. On the other hand, if components are selected too early, the resulting system may not meet all the requirements.

- *Component repositories* offer tool support for this process. Finding components, testing them in a particular environment and storing them in component databases are activities that can be separated from the system development, but obviously the type of categorization and the search criteria offered by such a repository influences its usability.

- *Create proprietary components to be used in the system.* In many cases, it will not be possible to define the entire system from already existing components. Core functionalities of the product are likely to be developed as they provide the competitive advantage of the product. Parts created in this way should be designed as components with well-defined interfaces to allow reuse in forthcoming applications and to facilitate maintenance. This usually requires more effort and lead-time than adapting existing components.

- *Match component requirements with system requirements and verify system properties from component properties.* A research challenge today is to predict the system properties from those of components.. Emerging properties, i.e., the (typically extra-functional) system properties not existing for the components, are of particular interest. For this purpose, rich interfaces are essential. Techniques for expressing rich interfaces and predicting system properties are discussed in section 13.

- *Adapt the selected components so that they suit the existing component model or requirement specification.* Some components can be directly integrated into the system, some need to be modified through a parameterization process, some need wrapping code for adaptation, etc.

- *Compose and deploy the components using a framework for components.* A particular function is often implemented by several components. By introducing assemblies into the system, conflicts between the basic components can occur. It may happen, for example, that assemblies include different versions of the same basic component. In such a case a mechanism for re-configuring assemblies must exist, either supported by the component framework, or used manually. The traditional V&V integration activities must be performed. However, they may become easier if some of the work has been done when specifying the system architecture (predicting system properties from component properties).

- *Replace earlier with later versions of components.* This corresponds to system maintenance. Implementations of components, and thus the entire system, may evolve over time. Bugs may be eliminated or new functionality added. Elimination of bugs in component implementations, which do not affect the interface, should be completely transparent to the system behaviour. Ideally, this requires at most a validation of the new implementation against its interface. Any evolution of the system that affects its interface requires an additional validation at system level. If functionality is added, a minimal validation consists in checking that the new functionality is not used in an undesirable manner by other components. A particular challenge is to upgrade or replace components during system operation.

11.2   Lifecycle of Components

The component development process is in many respects similar to system development; requirements must be captured, analysed and defined, the component must be designed, implemented, verified, validated and delivered. When building a new component the developers will reuse other components and will use similar procedures of component evaluation as for system development. There are however some significant differences:

- There is greater difficulty in managing requirements, caused by the interplay between component and system requirements.
- Precise component specifications are more important.
- Greater efforts are needed to develop reusable units,
- Verification against component specification must be more stringent and documented, in particular when transferring components between organizations.
- In a market for components, property rights and their protection become an issue.

The delivery result may be a component, tested and specified, perhaps even certified, stored in a component library in a package suitable for distribution and deployment. The next phase in the lifecycle is component deployment into a system. The deployment should be enabled without making changes in the rest of the system or the framework, and should be automated.

11.3   Issues Specific for Embedded Systems

The design of real-time systems must consider constraints that do not apply to large component and object-based systems such as business data processing systems. Additional constraints include the following,

- Real-time systems must satisfy constraints on extra-functional properties such as timing (e.g., meeting deadlines), quality of service (e.g., throughput), and dependability (including reliability, safety, and security).
- It is often important that functional and extra-functional properties be statically predictable, in particular if the system is safety-critical.
- Real-time systems must often operate with scarce resources (including processing power, memory, and communication bandwidth).

Therefore, observations that hold for large business data processing systems may have to be reconsidered for real-time and embedded systems.

- The definition of components by Szyperski [Szy98], emphasizes contractually specified interfaces, fully explicit context dependencies, independent deployment, and third-party composition. It seems biased towards component models where components are deployed at run-time into the system, with run-time support for component registration and composition. This fits well to the component models that are used in non-critical, non-real-time, and resource-insensitive applications. However it is not likely that this applies d to component models for embedded and real-time systems [CL02, Ch. 13]. There is a wide range of embedded systems (from very small to extremely large systems) and there is a wide range of real-time requirements (from hard real-time to adaptive real-time). While larger embedded systems may be resource insensitive and thus apply widely used component technologies, smaller embedded systems cannot afford such resources.

- In widely used component technologies, the interfaces are usually implemented as object interfaces supporting polymorphism by late binding. While late binding allows connecting of components that are completely unaware of each other beside the connecting interface, this flexibility comes with a performance penalty, which may be difficult to carry for small embedded systems. Dynamic component deployment is not be feasible for small embedded systems.

Taking into account all the constraints for real-time and embedded systems, we conclude that there are several reasons to perform component deployment and composition at design time rather than run-time:

- It allows composition tools to generate a monolithic firmware.
- It allows for global optimization,, e.g., in a static component composition known at design time, connections between components can be translated into function calls instead of using dynamic event notifications.
- Design-time composition allows specific adaptation of components and generated code towards particular micro controller families and real-time operating system..
- Verification and prediction of system requirements can be done statically from the given component properties.

Design time composition presupposes a *composition environment* that specifically provides the following functionalities.

- Component composition support;
- Component adaptation and code generation for the application;
- Building the system by including selected components and components that are part of the run-time framework;
- Static verification and prediction of system requirements and properties from the given component properties.

There may also be a need for a run-time environment, which supports the component framework. It may implement component intercommunication and control of the behaviour of the components.

11.4   Summary and Conclusions

The development of an adequate technology for component-based development faces many challenges. This is in particular true for real-time and embedded systems. Based on the exposition in this section, we structure the issues into several groups

- *Component specification*: in the context of embedded systems, it is obvious that interface specifications of components must go beyond syntactic information and include functional and extra-functional characteristics and requirements. For real-time systems the temporal attributes of components and systems are of main interest. For embedded systems the properties specifying the resources and the properties related to dependability are important. However, there is still no consensus about how components for real-time systems should be specified.

- *Prediction of system properties from component properties*: Even if we assume that we can specify all the relevant properties of components, it is not necessarily known how they will determine the corresponding properties of systems of which they are composed. Moreover, existing component models do not provide support for predictable composition. In this, one should aim for interfaces providing full functional and extra-functional specifications of components are essential.
- *Managing the interplay between achievable system requirements and component specifications*: is complex, as the possible candidate components usually lack one or more required features. Further, the relations between the system requirements and component requirements are complex.
- *Architecture specification*: the use of components has an impact on the choice of the system architecture, as it must take into account not only the requirements, but also the available components.
- *Component models*: Component models for real-time systems are still in the very early phase of development. In general, existing component models do not support the specification of functional and extra-functional properties, in particular timing and QoS properties.
- *Component evaluation and verification (possibly for certification)*: the trustworthiness of a component, which is the reliability of component in relation to its interface specification, is an important issue. The issue is difficult since the trend is to deliver components in binary form and the component development process is outside the control of component users. Protocols for component certification are of great interest
- *Component repositories*: which address the issues of how to store and retrieve components, how to index components in a component library, and how to find "similar" components.
- *Managing changes in component requirements*: an important issue are changes to components over time and possible conflicts arising from different coexisting versions of a component within the same system. A precise interface specification should allow clarifying this issue.
- *Update and replacement of components* at *run-time* is useful for many real-time systems. In the context of design-time composition, it is a challenge to combine this feature with design-time optimization across component boundaries.

For all areas, it is evident that appropriate tools are essential for a successful component-based development. In non real-time domains there exists various tools supporting model based and component-based development and they have proved to be successful, but in the real-time domains there is a lack of such tools. There is thus a unique opportunity for transferring essential results from research into industry through development of tool suites.

12 Current Design Practice and Needs in Selected Industrial Sectors

The current state of and the needs for component-based approach differ very much between industrial domains. Types of embedded systems vary from ultra small devices with simple functionality, through small systems with sophisticated functions, strong real-time requirements, and low resource consumption requirements, to large, possibly distributed systems, where the management of the complexity is the main challenge. Further we can distinguish between systems produced in large quantities, in which the low production costs are extremely important and low-volume products in which the system dependability is the most important feature. Usually for high volume products the time-to-market requirements are extremely important as well as the variation of the products. All these different requirements have impact on feasibility, on use, and on approach in component-based development. In different domains we can find very different component models and system and software architectures.

12.1 Automotive

Industrial Landscape

Cars are typically manufactured in volumes in the order of millions per year. To achieve these volumes, and still offer the customer a wide range of choices, the products are built on platforms that contain common technology that have the flexibility to adapt to different kinds of cars by adding different components or different variants of the components. Computer-based "components" built in the vehicles are control systems, infotainment (information and entertainment) systems, and diagnostic systems. Diagnostic systems are often an integrated part of the control system. Automotive systems have contained embedded controllers for more than one century. One well known example of an early embedded control system based on mechanical technology is fuel injection in combustion engines, where the camshaft, mechanisms and the cylinder valves constitute an embedded controller with parts for sensing, processing and actuation. The introduction of computer based embedded control has been motivated both by technical reasons – the need for improving performance or introducing entirely new functions – and by market demands. Moving functionality from hardware to software most notably also reduces the number of physical components and thus, at least in principle, makes the production much simpler. Another driver for the introduction of embedded control systems has been legislation. In the automotive industry, on-board diagnostics (OBD) is today regulated through legislation. Another area which has received considerably attention is the demand for increasingly efficient diagnostics, service, and production functionality.

There is a wide span of requirements on the infrastructure in today's vehicles. The vehicle industry works with demands on functionality, reliability, and safety, but also with demands related to product variation, extensibility and maintenance of delivered

Artist FP5 Consortium: Embedded Systems Design, LNCS 3436, 120–138, 2005.
© Springer-Verlag Berlin Heidelberg 2005

products, and integration of supplier components [MFN04a,MFN04b,Mer03]. This implies high requirements on flexibility in terms of adding or removing nodes or other components. Moreover, part of the functionality has stringent requirements on real-time performance and safety, e.g., safety critical control applications. Other parts of the functionality, such as the infotainment applications, have high demands on network throughput. Yet, other parts require only lightweight networks, as for example locally interconnected lights and switches. All of these varying requirements in vehicle networks are reflected in the architecture, implementation, and operation of a modern in-vehicle network.

Component-Based System Development Context

Within the automotive industry, the component-based approach has a relatively long tradition, as these systems are typically built from physical components that are either developed in-house or provided by external suppliers. Today, the physical components also include several computer nodes (or Electronic Control Units, ECUs) equipped with software that implements vehicle functions. Typical functions provided by nodes include power train controls, e.g., for fuel injection, active suspension, and combustion, safety related controls (brakes, collision warning, etc), driver assistance functions, comfort functions, and infotainment. A rapid development of electronic components and replacement of mechanical components has increased the importance of efficiency in development and production of embedded components: Modern vehicular systems contain almost hundred computer nodes, and the development costs of the electronic parts for high end models approached 40 % of the total costs [Gri03]. Even if this development is successful in many aspects, for example in the form of reuse and time-to-market, the trend cannot continue in the same way as the systems are becoming too complex and too costly with the current practice consisting essentially in having an ECU dedicated to a single functionality.

In general, there has over the last decades been a strong trend to connect standalone controllers by networks, forming distributed systems. The main driver for this has been cost reduction, since the use of networks makes reduction of the necessary cabling possible, or at least a possibility to bound the increase in length given the drastic increase in the number of control units. Another and closely related trend has been modularisation, where for example, an electronic control unit is physically integrated into an engine, forming a sort of mechatronic module. Combining the concepts of networks and mechatronic modules makes it possible to reduce both the cabling and the number of connectors, the result of which is facilitated production and increased reliability.

Notice also that the components are to a large extent provided by external suppliers, who work with many different car companies (or OEMs, original equipment manufacturers). The role of the OEM is thus to provide specifications for the suppliers, so that the component will fit a particular car, and to integrate the components into a product.

Limited resources (CPU & memory) require simple component models with as low overhead as possible. The implications of that is there a requirement for resolving of dynamic behaviour as much as possible at compilation/composition time: code generation, controlled component adaptation, generation of platform (framework) with required services. Component models should also provide a means for specification of (worst-case) execution time and memory consumption. These specific requirements exclude utilization of general-purpose component models.

State of the Practice

An example of a contemporary car electronic architecture is that of the Volvo XC90. The maximum configuration contains about 40 ECUs. They are connected mainly by two CAN networks, one for power train and one for body functionality. From some of the nodes, LIN sub networks are used to connect slave nodes into a subsystem. The other main structure is a MOST [MOS99] ring, connecting the infotainment nodes together, with a gateway to the CAN network for limited data exchange. Through this separation, the critical power train functions on the CAN network are protected from possible disturbances from the infotainment system. The diagnostics access to the entire car is via a single connection to a single ECU. The partitioning of functionality is decided by the location of the sensors and actuators used, but also by the combinations of optional variants that are possible. If a car is sold with only a subset of the full functionality, the amount of physical hardware installed is limited to the minimum necessary. Network communication software provides a layer between the hardware and the application software, so that communication can be described at a high level of abstraction in the application, regardless of the low-level mechanisms employed to send data between the nodes. Volcano [CRTM98] is a communication concept used throughout the Volvo Car Corporation for managing network traffic. Through the Volcano API the underlying network technology is hidden from the application engineer. The Volcano concept also addresses vehicle manufacturer controlled integration of components developed by suppliers. This is done through the use of the Volcano API and by separate specification of the signals used by a component and the network configuration. The network configuration is provided by the integrator and specifies how signals are to be transferred over the network. Traditional real-time operating systems are usually too resource consuming to be suitable for automotive applications, and do not provide the predictable timing that is needed. Therefore the new standard OSEK has been developed. There are several suppliers of OSEK compliant operating systems. All components interact with each other and with the application, and must therefore have standardized interfaces, and at the same time provide the required flexibility. To conserve hardware resources, the components are configurable to only include the parts that are really necessary in each particular instantiation

The main benefits of the technology used today are improved and more flexible functional behaviour of the vehicles, decreased time-to-market and production costs. The trend to replace mechanical components with electronic components will continue and even increase.

The current development trends in automotive software call also for increasing standardization of the software structure in the nodes (i.e. ECUs). In particular, the use of code generation requires a clear interface between the support software and the application, and the need to integrate software from different suppliers in the same node also calls for a well-defined structure. One approach for solving this is the new standard OSEK [OSE], which is a resource efficient and predictable real-time operating system.

Challenges and Work Directions

As the number of ECUs increases, the entire system becomes more complex. The system functions, controlling particular aspects at the system level (for example cruise control) require input and output control of many components. This requires sharing different types of resources (time, communication, memory, and CPU consumption).

While the system development is highly componentized, this is not true for software development. ECUs include proprietary software, mostly owned by subcontractors. This makes the entire system inflexible and inefficient in utilizing resources, makes it difficult to implement complex functions, and expensive to add new ECUs. The next major step in designing these systems is to go from the current situation with one node one supplier to a situation with one node several suppliers, i.e. there will be several software components of different origins executing on a typical node. Also to enable delivery of more complex applications, it must be possible to spread out software components through several nodes. This requires changes in the design process and new division of responsibilities.

- There is a need for increasing standardization of the software structure in the nodes. In particular, the use of code generation requires a clear interface between the support software and the application, and the need to integrate software from different suppliers in the same node also calls for a well-defined structure.
- An important aspect is to create a more flexible software partitioning. The main use for this is probably not to find the optimal partitioning for each car on a given platform, since that would create too much work on the verification side, but to allow parts of the software to be reused from one platform to the next. This puts even higher demands on the node architecture, since the application must be totally independent from the hardware, through a standardized interface that is stable over time. Therefore, further standardization work is needed, in particular for sensor and actuator interfaces. A standard, or de-facto standard, component model for small embedded systems in the automotive domain does not exist today. The existing component-based technologies require too many resources to be suitable for small embedded systems. Developing and establishing an appropriate component technology, including a supporting framework is one of the main research challenges.
- With increasing complexity, system reliability and safety become major problems. A satisfactory handling of safety-critical functions, such as emerging brake- and steer-by-wire systems, will require the integration of methods for establishing functional and temporal correctness for each component, as well as system-wide attributes such as safety and reliability. but also from the complexity of the involved organizations; a vehicle is composed of hardware components coming from a multitude of companies. It is not uncommon that a car manufacturer today in-house only develops a few control units – a very low percentage of some 70 control units indeed. This means that system integrators in some cases are trying to regain control and development of the control units because of their large impact on the vehicle. Systems integration is complicated by the fact that manual specifications are used, leaving room for misinterpretations, causing costly iterations, and highly difficult systems integration.

The current practice, to dedicate an ECU for each particular service can not be maintained and a need for a methodology which is more economic in resources is needed. The current approaches are only beginning to consider the deployment of model-based development processes, and current methods and tool support are available for single ECU based implementations only. In the context of high end cars, the TTA Technology [KR93] has been used. It proposes a solution for using the synchronous approach transparently in a distributed system. This is done by hiding distribution via an implementation of a time based access protocol of each node to a common bus with proven properties. It allows naturally sharing ECUs for several functionalities. Nevertheless, the underlying middleware requires very high quality, and thus expensive, components.

An example of an ongoing effort in the European automotive industry is the project EAST-EEA [EAS03] with participation of all major European car manufacturers, suppliers and software-tool providers, as well as research organizations and universities with connections to the automotive industry. The goal of EAST-EEA is to develop a structure for the next generation of electronic automotive features. There are two main activities to achieve this goal: (1) specification of middleware suitable for the automotive industry, and (2) development of an Architecture Description Language (ADL). The middleware specification will leverage on the automotive industry's positive experiences of the RTOS standard OSEK, and will support concepts and provide services on a higher abstraction level than a current OS does. The ADL will allow manufacturers and their suppliers to exchange requirements, specifications and documentation about both hardware and software characteristics. The ADL will support system-descriptions on multiple abstraction levels, ranging from very high-level feature specification to very implementation-close operational specifications.

12.2 Industrial Automation

Industrial Landscape

Industries in the industrial automation domain have long used approaches for programming control systems, which employ some elements of component based development. Typical application domains are in control of industrial processes, power supply, industrial robots, where there are many strong European companies including ABB, Siemens, Thales, etc.

Industrial automation domain comprises a large area of control, monitoring and optimization systems. They typically include large pieces of software that have been developed over many years (often several decades). Most control systems are manufactured in rather large volumes, and must to a large extent be configurable to suit a variety of customer contexts. They can be classified according to different levels of control. Each layer has a predefined set of control tasks that are typically supported by some computer system and which may or may not involve human interaction [CL02]:

- **Process level** concerns the process equipment to be controlled (for example, a valve in a water pipeline, a boiler, etc.).

- **Field level** (or single control level) concerns sensors, actuators, drivers, etc. This level comprises the interfacing equipment of a control system to the physical process.
- **Group control level** concerns controller devices and applications which control a group of related process level devices in a closed-loop fashion.
- **Process control level** concerns operator stations and processing systems with their applications for plant-wide remote supervision and control and overview the entire process to be controlled. This level may provide man-machine interface applications for different types of supervision and control activities, such as process state visualization, alarm processing, process event handling, batch preparation, etc.
- **Production or manufacturing management level** concerns systems and applications for production planning. Applications at this level support the managerial/administrative tasks in preparing for the next batch of work.
- **Enterprise management level** concerns systems which deal with enterprise-wide control activities. These tasks are usually subsumed under the term Enterprise Resource Planning (ERP). They include human resources, supply chain management, administrative order processing, finance and accounting, etc.

Notice that, even if the higher levels are not embedded, they are of uttermost importance as they need to be interoperable with the lower level which greatly influences the possible choices of the component model and in fine the design choices. The integration requirements have in many cases led to a decision to use component technologies which are not appropriate for embedded systems but provide better integration possibilities.

Depending on the level, the nature of the requirements and the implementation will be quite different. In general, the lower the level, the stronger are the real-time requirements (including timing predictability) and the resource limitations. Also, the component based approach will include different concepts at different levels. While at the lowest levels availability, timeliness, and reliability are the most important quality requirements, at higher levels it will be performance, usability, and integrability. At the process control level, the development environment is strictly separated form the run-time environment and components are usually source software modules. Typically, synchronous languages [Hal93, Ber99b] have been developed and are used to simplify the programming of reactive systems. On the basis of the synchrony hypothesis, it is possible to define components, which can easily be composed at compilation time into larger systems. The component models address extra-functional properties and constraints such as worst-case execution time and memory consumption and allow specifying efficient functional interfaces (e.g. procedural interfaces). The environment, supporting composition techniques (visual or script-based) is separated from run-time environment. At the process control level and above, the system complexity is the dominating characteristics, while hard real-time requirements are less dominant. Furthermore, systems must be open to a wide variety of other systems and standards. This allows utilizing (standard) component models, widely used in other domains: desktop applications and distributed applications.

Also, dependent on the application area the requirements on timeliness will be different. In a typical industrial process automation (manufacturing, for example), fast responses are not crucial, while in others (for example, distribution of electricity) timeliness is extremely important.

Component-Based System Development Context

The core part of a control system or a robot is typically a real-time control system that runs on a simple RTOS, or even without any OS. Other parts, such as I/O and communication protocols are in many cases provided by suppliers. The system has to be open to allow easy integration of new functionalities. Since the software usually survives many generations of hardware, it must be easy to port. Component-based development has been practised for many years by developing and using the standard IEC 61131 [IEC95].

Industrial control systems are most often part of larger systems, e.g., an assembly line for cars. Such systems are typically composed of many nodes that communicate over field buses. Thus, a system must be open to a wide variety of other systems and standards, implying that a component technology for industrial automation must be compatible with component technologies such as .NET and CORBA.

In comparison with the situation in the automotive domain, one can roughly say that the lower layers of industrial control systems have similar requirements and are similar in structure but, at least until now, the interoperability requirements are higher and the lifecycles longer. Another difference is that there is a strong tradition in software development, bound to, e.g., standards for programming PLCs and IEC 61131 [IEC95].

State of the Practice

In the last years, the use of component-based technologies has rapidly expanded and become the dominating development technologies in industrial automation. The technology mostly used in large systems is Microsoft COM, and to smaller extent different implementations of CORBA, although neither COM nor CORBA provide support for real-time. The systems using these technologies are adaptive-real-time systems. Often a component technology is used as a basis for additional abstraction level support, which is specified either as standards or proprietary solutions. Some examples of utilization of component technologies:

- **Example 1**: OPC Foundation [OPC03], an organization that consists of more than 300 member companies worldwide, is responsible for specifications that standardize the communication of acquired process data, alarm and event records, historical data, and batch data to multi-vendor enterprise systems and between production devices. The specification is based on standards DCOM [BK98], XML-DA and SOAP.
- **Example 2**: ABB Automation Products develops a next generation of automation system architecture called Aspect Integrator Platform [CL02, Chap. 17], which is the basis for the design of automation systems, such as open control systems for continuous and batch type processes, traditional supervisory control and data acquisition systems, and others. The architecture uses Microsoft's COM technology, but it determines system architecture and enables flexible system configurations. The main concept is based on AspectObjects which are treated as components. An AspectObject encapsulates all the assets called "*Aspects*" belonging to that object. In this model the aspects are treated as object attributes. The attributes (as the AspectObject itself) are implemented as special COM objects.

- **Example 3**: Component-based development has been utilized for many years by developing and using the standard IEC 61131 [IEC95]. It defines a family of languages that includes instruction lists, assembly languages, structured text, and a high level language similar to Pascal, ladder diagrams, or function block diagrams (FBD). Function blocks can be viewed as components and interfaces between blocks are released by connecting in-ports and out-ports. Function block execution may be periodic or event-driven. IEC 61131 is successfully used in development of industrial process automation systems, for example in ABB and Siemens.
- **Example 4**: Controllers that fulfil real-time requirements (either adaptive or hard) usually do not use component-based technology such as COM. However in some cases (such as for ABB controllers) a reduced version of COM has been used on a top of a real-time operating system [LCS02]. The reused version includes facilities for component specification using the interface description language of COM, and some basic services at run-time. These services have been implemented internally.

As a conclusion one can state that component-based approaches have a long tradition in automation (especially by the use IEC 6113, which is not sufficient today) and there is a clear trend to use widely spread technologies as much as possible which are not the most appropriate ones for the domain.

Benefits from Using Component Technologies

The main reason for wide use of component-based technology in the automation industry is the possibility of reusing solutions in different ranges of products, efficient development tools, standardized specifications and interoperation, and integration between different products. For example, the main advantage of OPC is the use of standard interfaces and communication protocols of control devices provided by different vendors. Another benefit is transparency of data access, provided by the middleware. Finally, component-based technologies enable seamless integration with other type of systems, for example business and office applications.

Challenges and Work Directions

The problems of growing system complexity together with the requirements on open, upgradeable, highly dependable and distributed systems pose many challenges which are in fact the central issues of component-based development in general.

- System integration is today a central problem in development. Presently, this results in a need for extensive testing and in integration problems for large systems. In fact, we are lacking well defined architectures suitable for industrial control applications. Many integration problems are caused by inadequate techniques for handling resources and timing properties in the development process. Adequate support for resource and timing properties in a component technology is a must. The problem is similar concerning predictability and quality of service. Component models including the possibility to specify quality of service and reliability related properties as well as tools supporting them are lacking.

Many systems have very high requirements on availability, which must be reflected in the development of system architecture, systems integration, etc. Support for high availability by a component framework is needed.

- Improving efficiency of the development and maintenance process. A main goal of the component-based approach is a significant improvement in the development process. An efficient use of components requires tools for system development with components; in particular tools for component composition. Controllers, usually hard real-time systems with restricted resources, cannot directly use de-facto standard technologies. They either use dedicated, in fact proprietary, component models or particular parts of de-facto standard technologies (for example, interface specification, but without run-time support).

- Increase lifetime of the products. Industrial automation systems have a long life time, they can be in operation for more than twenty years. In that period many assumptions change – the environment, the hardware platform, communication standards, component models, languages, etc. Old technologies become obsolete. This poses huge problems for maintenance. To improve and even make the maintenance possible, a means for system specification independent of the current technology is required. Concepts such as Model Driven Architecture [MDA] have the goal to allow flexible evolution of the applications and their components. These technologies should be combined with the component-based approach and be further developed.

- Because of the dependency on one component technology vendor, there is a standing risk: the current technology can become obsolete and the companies are forced to migrate to new technology even if there are no requirements for that. The controllers, usually hard real-time systems with restricted resources cannot directly use de-facto standard technologies. They either use proprietary component models or try to use particular parts of de-facto standard technologies (for example interface specification, but not run-time support). In the latter case, the challenge is to identify a proper level of reuse of the technology. The lowest level includes use of standardized interface specification, such as IDL (Interface Definition Language), or COM binary interface, and implementation of some standard interfaces.

- Improving interoperability. Systems at the process control level must be able to communicate to different types of field devices and use different protocols. For this reason, it is important to define standards that contain more information than general purpose standards or tools. OPC Foundation is one attempt to identify the interoperability standards for process data. So far it is related to particular component technologies (i.e. COM and .NET). An advantage of this is that the support in form of applications and tools comes together with the standards. A disadvantage is a dependency on a particular technology, operating system and a single vendor. Similar standards independent of particular technology should be developed. The systems on enterprise management level interoperate not only with the process control systems but also with administration enterprise resource management and similar tools. Such tools utilize in many cases successfully general-purpose component models (COM, EJB, CORBA). This means that interoperability between different application domains and different component models are required.

12.3   Consumer Electronics

Industrial Landscape

For high-volume electronics products, like TV, VCR, and DVD, cost per product unit is an important issue. These costs are largely determined by the hardware costs, and lead to constraints on the software; for example, the available memory. In addition, the diversity of these products increases, as does the complexity of the products due to convergence of functionality.

Component-Based System Development Context

Consumer electronics products are developed and delivered in form of product families which are characterized by many similarities and few differences and in form of product populations which are sets of products with many similarities but also many differences. Production is organized into product lines – this allows many variations on a central product definition [Don00,Per98,Bal98]. A product line is a top-down, planned, proactive approach to achieve reuse of software within a family or population of products. It is based on the use of a common architecture and core functions included into the product platform and basic components. The diversity of products is achieved by inclusion of different components.

Due to market requirements to launch continuously new product versions, development and production of products are separated from the development of components. Similarly as in the automotive industry, product development is integration-oriented; that is, products are built by integration of components and new features (i.e. products) are achieved by integration of new components.

Traditionally, in the consumer electronics domain the products providers are also developers of components (in difference to automotive industry). Very often, the market advantages of products are achieved by development of new, technologically advanced, components these are presently still hardware components in most cases, but importance of software components is growing rapidly.

State of the Practice

Because of the requirements for low hardware and production costs, general-purpose component technologies are not used, but rather more dedicated and simpler proprietary models have been developed.

An example of such a component model is the *Koala component model* used at Philips [vO02,vOvdLK00]. Koala is a component model and an architectural description language to build a large diversity of products from a repository of components. Koala is designed to build consumer products such as televisions, video recorders, CD and DVD players and recorders, and combinations of them. A Koala component is a piece of code that can interact with its environment through explicit interfaces only. The implementation of a Koala component is a directory with a set of C and header files that may use each other in arbitrary ways, but communication with other components is routed only through header files generated by the Koala compiler, based upon the binding between components. As Koala components are delivered in the form of *source code*, it is possible to statically analyze components and systems built by composing them.

As a rule, the component models used in consumer electronics are proprietary which requires internal support for their development and maintenance. Furthermore, it requires development of a number of development tools: ADL, component repository, composition languages, compilers, debugging and testing tools, configuration tools, etc. Such development is usually not a core business of producers of consumer electronics, and it requires an important amount of resources which could be shared amongst several producers. The use of a proprietary technology makes it also more difficult to use COTS components. There are increasing requirements for achieving interoperability between proprietary and standard component technologies.

Benefits from Using Component Technologies

There are two main benefits in a component-based product line development:

- Reuse of already existing components and common architecture for many variants of the products,
- Separation of product development from component development.

The first benefit is achieved not only through reuse of the core functionality (which includes the architecture solutions and components that build a core-functionality), but also reuse of particular components in different product families. The second benefit is realized by enabling larger development time for particular components than the time for development of a specific product. Typically, products are released two times per year, while development of a new component requires a year or a year and a half.

There are other benefits resulting from using a component-based approach. The latter forces the software to be explicitly structured. Software components can only interact through well-defined interfaces. In Koala, components can be parameterized by the use of so-called diversity interfaces – which allow describing several parameter dependent variants of interfaces. By binding components into a product, before the actual compilation of the code, the memory footprint can be reduced: optimizations, using static analysis, for example to discover unused parts, are done across components without breaking the encapsulation provided by the components.

Challenges and Work Directions

On one hand, it becomes more and more important to develop products that comprise several functions, previously being sold as separate products. Examples are TV sets that have embedded DVD and VCR, and connections to the Internet. On other hand, also interoperability requirements increase. TV sets are supposed to communicate with PCs, mobile phones and similar. Pervasive systems implementing the *"everything anytime everywhere"* paradigm, such as eHome systems are new visions of new products in which consumer electronics plays an important role. This implies high demands on interoperability. In addition to standard communication protocols, standard information models, standard component specifications and services are required. This also implies achieving interoperability of systems built on different technologies.

Presently, the component models used in consumer electronics support only rudimentary analysis and prediction of extra-functional properties of the components and systems. There are increasing requirements for developing methodologies for reasoning about system properties derived from the component properties. Typical requirements are prediction of memory, CPU and power consumptions.

Component models in this domain cover composition at development (compilation) time; runtime systems are monolithic applications, which make on-line updates of components difficult. Although requirements for plug-and-play concept are not highly prioritized, it is expected that this will be more important in the future. For this reason a support for managing components at run-time will be required.

12.4   Telecommunication Software Infrastructure

Industrial Landscape

Telecom applications involve several domains, such as commercial information systems, network management, service management and real-time network and execution platforms. There are specialized units developing particular techniques and skills (network traffic, middleware, software engineering, performance evaluation, architecture, User interfaces...). Moreover, in general, services are developed, deployed and provided by different business units. The telecommunication world is an increasingly open world involving many actors, working all on the same infrastructure.

A main requirement in the telecommunication domain is that service design and development needs to be fast, by nevertheless respecting all the actor expectations and security requirements. Many context constraints exist in the domain: the complexity of the infrastructure (middleware), the heterogeneity of the standards for protocol exchanges as well as their continuous evolution, the emergence of new standards, the absence of formal specification for many standards and many more [ITE, RNR03].

Component-Based System Development Context

In the context of telecommunication infrastructure and services, components play and have played a crucial role, and the majority of these components are embedded in core network platforms or several types of devices: mobile, fixed, etc. Components may be shared between different applications. These applications are in general not deployed at the same time but are continuously added and modified, inducing a large amount of work for functional integration, but also and even mainly, for performance integration. Furthermore, components – or their specifications – are reused when new services are developed in order to reduce the development cycle and to allow a large commercial diversity with a relatively small technical diversity [ITE] and to ensure a certain uniformity of the service behaviour.

Large telecom applications, such as switches, have to satisfy requirements on high performance, massive concurrency (handling many calls simultaneously), high availability, robustness, etc. These requirements must be addressed by a suitable architecture, which gives adequate support for all these requirements. An example of a framework which has been developed with this in mind is the Erlang Open Telecom Platform (OTP) [Erl], which is a run-time framework supporting massive concurrency and high availability of applications in the concurrent language Erlang.

State of the Practice

Currently, the application designers build new applications in a vertical fashion. A vertical structure is contradictory with the need to rapidly build and modify (customize) new services, to integrate them in a consistent way with existing ones and to share common infrastructure and platforms (core network execution platforms or embedded mobile devices), etc [KK00]. The analysis of real-time and QoS requirements, which are essential the service deployment and provision, can today not be analyzed during the early stages of design, as QoS properties are well studied and expressed only at a very low level (execution platform and network level). Consequently, time or performance problems are mainly discovered once the application is deployed and tested. This leads to expensive time to market development.

Also, due to the absence of formal specification of component interfaces and composition rules and the lack of real-time and QoS property specifications at component level, current practice consists more in creating new software components (even at the specification level) rather than in reusing existing ones.

In the domain of Telecom, UML [UML.OMG02] is extensively used in the context of commercial information systems for the static system description (class diagrams), but unfortunately it is not used for modelling of the dynamics of the application. This is mainly due to the fact that current UML tools do not handle the dynamic aspects (absence of appropriate tools and standard semantics). In the past, and still currently, for some applications model based formal approaches are used. The standards in the telecom domain, such as SDL [SDL,CCD+01,CDN01], and similar frameworks – for example ROOM [Sel96] or Erlang [Erl,OSER], a functional language are used for the specification of protocols and services. Esterel [Ber99a, CPP+01, CPP+02] or other synchronous formalisms have also been used for synchronous applications, such as software radio. For performance prediction of service platforms some commercial tools based on queuing theory – for example SES workbench [SES], Opnet [OPN]) – are used. This means that for different activities different, only informally related, models are used [MDVC03].

Challenges and Work Directions

The challenge for the telecommunication domain for the future is to enable the ubiquitous *"anything, anytime, anywhere"* concept, which means that a service should be seen for an end user as a black box – or a least a grey box – respecting functional and extra-functional properties (Quality of Service) independently of the underlying platform. Due to the openness of the telecommunication architecture, a multitude of services and service components are currently provided by several companies and must be dynamically integrated and updated. Telecommunication applications must be created in a secure and reliable way with short development times in a multi-provider environment. There is a real need to go from a vertical service development to a horizontal approach based on flexible, reliable and open software infrastructure (middleware). In order to achieve this goal, it is essential to provide service designers with a software infrastructure offering an interface layer or middleware hiding as much as possible the heterogeneity and the complexity of the underlying layers. Only such interface layers consisting of component and connectors with appropriate functional and extra-functional characterizations will allow flexible evolution of the applications and their components, as well as consistent integration of different applications developed by different providers. Concepts such as *Model Driven Architecture* [MDA, Nic02] have the objective to help the creation of such an infrastructure and provide a syntactic support for this. A research goal for software infrastructure should be to integrate Model Driven Architecture concepts with component based development approaches and provide an innovative and consistent development methodology from high level specifications towards design. Formal validation of components, which must take into account *rich* interface specifications, is crucial for a consistent composition of distributed components. It is the only way to ensure a flexible and secure interface to the telecommunication service designer.

- For service designers, the interest of components goes beyond interoperability. Service components have individual requirements that might be violated when composed and deployed with other service components. This problem, well-known in the telecommunication world as the *service interaction* problem, must be tackled taking into consideration real-time and performance aspects. Especially in the context of mobile telecommunication or WEB-services, real-time aspects, quality of service and dynamic composition are important issues.
- Another important aspect is the definition of a methodology for component based design, from the analysis steps towards implementation and testing, applied for component lifecycle and system lifecycle. There is a large consensus for the use of standards, such as UML, SDL and MDA in the telecommunication world, but research is necessary in order to take into account real-time aspects, quality of service and deployment issues and to better integrate components and composition in the software lifecycle.
- Component and system verification using formal techniques for real-time systems should be enforced. Its systematic use should enable quick and secure telecommunication service creation answering questions like how to build an architecture based on a set of components (reused and/or shared by several services) in such a way that we can guarantee the provision of complete applications respecting quality of services and safety requirements (especially security requirements).
- Specific attention should be paid to mobile devices. They have to tackle several critical constraints (memory size, energy consumption, time constraints, etc.). They require continuous adding, removing or modification of components, and different service negotiation procedures. Security and availability are requirements in any kind of environment (unreliable environment, different kinds of communication modes, different performance properties). Specific components are needed for different communication patterns.

12.5   Avionics and Aerospace

Industrial Landscape

Some of the characteristics for software development for avionics and aerospace include the following.

- Applications are highly safety- and mission-critical and must be able to satisfy very hard real-time constraints. For example, Ariane 5 is inherently instable: its position must be correctly controlled within each 10ms cycle, meaning that the loss of sensor data of a single cycle leads to the potential loss of the rocket. For this reason, such systems are inherently complex and expensive to design, upgrade, and support.
- Some of theses systems have an extremely long lifetime (over 20 years for an airplane) and will undergo several generations of upgrades and platform migrations. Also the amount of software in this kind of systems has been dramatically increasing. For example, in 1974, an Airbus 300B embedded just 500 Kbytes, tomorrow Airbus 380 will embed 64 Mbytes and at horizon of 2015, a Gbyte of embedded software is probably not a limit. In space applications, the trend is similar.
- Similar as in the telecom domain, an important difficulty, reported also in section 3.2 of this document, is that the development of avionics and space systems is divided into several teams with specialized skills, and that no single person can overlook anymore the entire flight computer and the rapid growth of the embedded software makes this worse.
- Extensive model-based simulation and validation is performed since flight testing is extremely costly.

One consequence of the facts mentioned above is that model-based approaches are more advanced and applied than in other domains, e.g., as witnessed by the prominence of the avionics application domain in many advanced technology projects (e.g., SafeAir http://www.safeair.org/project/, Mobies http://www.liacs.nl/marcello/ mobij.html, and others).

Component-Based System Development Context

Presently, the approach for building a flight controller is a synchronous approach (such as explained in section 3.2), which considers the entire system as a unique entity with a single clock. Deployment on rapidly evolving distributed architectures which might be based on different technologies (different kinds of buses,...), as well as replication for increasing reliability and other safety and security related issues are handled apart. The validation of the integrated system is a major problem. Components play a role here, but they are mainly design time components as there is no explicit notion of component based middleware used in any present development process in this domain. More emphasis appears to be placed on predictability of global system properties and global system architecture.

Nevertheless, there is a prominent desire is to continue the trend towards model-based development, supporting it by integrated tool chains that can perform analysis of properties like fault tolerance, timing, utilization, quality of service, etc. on models, and thereafter generate optimized code for target platforms. There exist some approaches which start to be used in this domain or in comparable domains (e.g. automotive):

- The TTA Technology [KR93] proposes a solution for using the synchronous approach transparently in a distributed system. This is done by hiding distribution via an implementation of a time based access protocol of each node to a common bus with proven properties. This architecture is based on the existence of redundancy of its physical nodes. It implements a particular dependability model and does not handle other extra functional aspects, as for example security issues. Moreover, its extreme requirements on the internal clocks of all components and the important computational overhead, makes this technology probably inappropriate for space applications (where high reactivity is combined with slow components due to problems with radiation).
- An example of technologies for handling component based systems that have been developed for the avionics domain is Meta-H [Met]. Meta-H is a domain-specific Architecture Description Language (ADL) dedicated to avionics systems which has been developed at Honeywell Labs since 1993 under the sponsorship of DARPA and the US Army. A significant set of tools (graphical editor, typing, safety, reliability, and timing/loading/schedulability analyzers, code generator...) has already been prototyped and used in the context of several experimentation projects. Notice however, that Meta-H is very low level. Today, it is rather a language for assembling existing pieces of code.

   Also there is an ongoing new development of a standard called AADL (Avionics Architecture Description Language [WKB04] which has emerged from Meta-H, and which will include in its forthcoming version V1 a UML profile for avionics and space system. The usefulness of this extension will depend on its ability to describe high level abstractions and the relevant properties of components.

Challenges and Work Directions

A major challenge in the domain is the adoption of a truly component based approach. The encapsulation of functionalities concerning distribution, security, replication, in a middleware consisting of components with guaranteed extra-functional properties will be the key for making existing validation methods (applied today to the synchronous model of the control) applicable to an integrated system. It makes the development of the control application independent of the actually used architecture and supports architectural changes during the lifetime of a system through the replacement of some of individual middleware components as required.

   In order to make this vision a reality, appropriate formalisms for representing high level views of a given system architecture, including properties of components need to be built. For example, in AADL, there exists a notion of connector, which needs to be made general enough to represent a middleware component guaranteeing secure or timely communication, etc. Also, the necessary infra-structure does not exist today and must be built. As an example, the EU Integrated Project ASSERT proposes to tackle this problem.

12.6   Summary and Challenges

Component-based development is practiced in several industrial domains. The component-based approach at system level, where hardware components are designed together with embedded software, has been successfully used for many years. Also large-grain generic components like protocol stacks, RTOS, etc. have been used for a long time. In addition to this, technology supporting a component-based approach has been developed either in the form of dedicated proprietary component models or by using reduced versions of some widely used component models.

- A major, short-term benefit of the component-based approach is that it imposes a beneficial structure to system development. Component technology supports the structuring of complex systems early in the development process. In this way, many integration and maintenance problems can be addressed early, at lower cost. Systems are easier to maintain if they have a clear structure, e.g., as a system composed of components. The development of product-line architectures and of standardized domain-specific architectural guidelines supports adequate system structuring. Legacy systems can sometimes be structured into components in order to make future upgrades and maintenance easier
- Component-based development allows integration problems to be handled in the earlier phases of system design. Component properties that have global system impact, notably properties of timing and resource consumption, can be specified in interfaces in such a way that global resource usage can be predicted *a priori*, avoiding hard problems in system integration.
- It is easier to achieve time-to-market requirements by separating the component development process from system development process. Components can be re-used across several products or even product families. Re-use is made easer by defining product line architectures, in which components have given roles. New products can then re-use components of previous products by modification or parameterization.

A longer-term potential of component technology is to enable a *Market for Software Parts*. However, this advantage is currently unclear, and would demand that companies make high initial investments in tools and technology.

A prerequisite for the further adoption of component technology in many sectors is to define a more standardized software structure, encompassing domain-specific guidelines for system architectures, and the functioning and interfaces of different types of components. Such developments are underway, e.g., in the automotive and avionics domains, and can lead to more efficient development processes, support for exchange of software components between organizations. Further standardization of component interfaces will support interoperability between products and between components.

Technical needs from a component technology fall into several categories:

- Composition and integration of component-based systems requires technology for specification of interfaces to be developed to the point that it can *a priori* guarantee component interoperability. This is important, e.g., in the telecommunications domain where interoperability is crucial, in domains where manufacturers have the role of system integrators, e.g., in the vehicle and industrial automation domain. Important properties for component interoperability in embedded systems are component timing and resource properties, since these properties have system-wide impact.

- Embedded systems are typically resource constrained. This is a further motivation why component technology must support specification of extra-functional properties (resources), so that system resource needs can be predicted and managed early in system development. It is furthermore important that a system composed of components can be optimized for speed and memory consumption, typically by globally optimizing compilation. This applies to industrial sectors with large volumes and small platforms that have constraints on, e.g., power consumption, such as the automotive industry and small mobile devices. To support more advanced component technologies for embedded systems, it is important to develop efficient implementations of component frameworks (i.e., middleware), which have low requirements on memory and processing power.

- Predictability of system properties, in particular concerning QoS, is crucial in many domains of embedded systems. This means that a component technology should bring solutions to the following problems.

  o Prediction of global system properties from component properties, as s specified in component interfaces. A current shortcoming is that methods for breaking down system timing requirements into component requirements are not fully developed.

  o Components have individual requirements that can be violated when composed and deployed with other components. Techniques are needed that ensure that components do not interfere with requirements of other components. Such interferences can be obvious, such as violations of memory protection, or more subtle. An important scenario where interferences will occur is when several components, each implementing a piece of functionality, are mapped onto one ECU.

  o Determination of QoS, timing, and resource properties of components, e.g., by measurement, simulation, static analysis, etc. An inherent difficulty is that these properties depend not only on the component software, but also on the underlying platform.

- Embedded systems often have high requirements on safety, reliability, availability and QoS, including their predictability. A proper solution to these generic requirements needs to include

  o Specification of relevant properties in component interfaces, together with mechanisms to check adherence to interface specifications.

  o Suitable generic mechanisms (e.g. middleware with guaranteed properties) in component frameworks that allow building systems with high requirements on safety, reliability, availability, etc.

  o Mechanisms to analyze system-wide safety, properties, potentially using techniques that are tailored for specific component frameworks.

- Reuse of components across different organizations is sometimes hampered by the lack of technology and procedures for verifying and certifying component implementations against their interface specifications.
- The adoption of component technology is hampered by the lack of widely adopted component technology standards which are suitable for real-time systems. This can to a large extent be attributed to the special needs of the embedded systems sector (resources, extra-functional properties). It may be unreasonable to expect a single standard for embedded systems to emerge; a more likely scenario – already starting to emerge – is that domain-specific component standards and frameworks will be developed. Important considerations for such solutions are as follows.
  o Interoperability between different component technologies is important. One motivation is for users not to be bound to a single vendor of platforms or integration tools. There is also a trend towards open, extensible, and upgradeable systems. Component technologies for embedded systems should therefore be compatible with existing standards. Service negotiation is a natural part of open embedded systems.
  o Frameworks and middleware implementations available to industries in a given domain.
  o Tools that allow components to be developed and integrated. Such tools must in most case provide adequate support for solving timing and resource problems when defining the system architecture. Current proprietary component models for embedded systems are typically not widely enough used to motivate the cost of developing such tool support.
- Embedded systems are typically developed over a long time, implying that support for maintenance of system evolution is an important consideration. The appropriate level of specification of component and system properties should allow system hardware and platforms to be exchanged and upgraded, as well as allowing components to be reused in different contexts. This motivates an increased interest in model based approaches to specification and development, including the MDA approach. A suitable middleware layer can hide specific problems stemming from.

13   Components and Contracts

13.1   Introduction

One of the key desiderata in component-based development for embedded systems is the ability to capture functional and extra-functional properties in component interfaces, and to verify and predict corresponding system properties. For real-time systems, this is perceived to be particularly important for properties such as timing and quality-of-service.

In this section, we review existing techniques for capturing, verifying, and predicting different properties of component and system behaviour. Properties of components can be expressed in their *contracts*, hence the title of the section. The term *contract* can very generally be taken to mean "component specification" in any form.

A contract is in practice taken to be a constraint on a given *aspect* of the interaction between a component that supplies a service, and a component that consumes this service. Component contracts differ from object contracts in the sense that to supply a service, a component often explicitly requires some other service, with its own contract, from another component. Therefore the expression of a contract on a component-provided interface might depend on another contract from one of the component-required interfaces. For instance, the throughput of component A doing some kind of computation on a data stream provided by component B clearly depends on the throughput of B.

It is indeed challenging to develop a practical framework for reasoning about complex component properties (e.g., performance properties) stated in contracts, e.g., to infer global system (performance) properties. A complete solution to this problem requires powerful mathematical reasoning, e.g., about properties of stochastic processes. A pragmatic, more modest, approach to this problem, which does not need powerful mathematical reasoning, is to agree on a small set of fixed contracts, or a small set of fixed building blocks for contracts. For each contract, one can then in advance develop techniques for monitoring or verifying that component implementations satisfy the contract, and techniques for inferring system properties from component contracts. For instance, for performance properties, one can define a fixed set of different levels of performance, and for each level define rules for run-time monitoring and for component interoperability.

In simple cases, such a scheme can be seen as constructing a type system for specifying properties. More complex cases may involve constraints expressed in some type of logic, and thus checking beforehand that components interact correctly then need some form of theorem proving techniques.

To structure the exposition into different types of component properties, we use the classification of contracts proposed by Beugnard et al. [BJP99], where a *contract hierarchy* is defined consisting of four levels.

- **Level 1**: Syntactic interface, or signature (i.e. types, fields, methods, signals, ports etc., that constitute the interface).

Artist FP5 Consortium: Embedded Systems Design, LNCS 3436, 139–159, 2005.

- **Level 2**: Constraints on values of parameters and of persistent state variables, expressed, e.g., by pre- and post-conditions and invariants.
- **Level 3**: Synchronization between different services and method calls (e.g., expressed as constraints on their temporal ordering).
- **Level 4**: Extra-functional properties (in particular real-time attributes, performance, QoS (i.e. constraints on response times, throughput, etc.). We will separate this level into two aspects
  - o **4a:** timing properties (e.g. absolute time bounds)
  - o **4b:** Quality of Service properties, typically given by performance measures, often formulated in stochastic terms (e.g. average response time).

Currently, most component models support only level 1 contracts, while some models support also other levels (see section 14). In the remainder of section 13, we will survey techniques for capturing and reasoning about component and system properties, discussing each aspect separately. We will use the four levels of the Beugnard hierarchy for structuring our treatment of different interface properties. Regarding level 4, we make a separation between timing properties (e.g. absolute time bounds) and stochastically formulated performance properties (e.g. average response time). In addition, we briefly treat reliability properties.

For each aspect, we will consider techniques for

- expressing properties of systems and components,
- predicting or verifying system properties from component properties, in particular for doing this statically at design-time,
- checking that component properties are compatible (assumptions made in one component specification are guaranteed by some other component specification),
- verifying that component implementations satisfy properties given in component specifications, and
- compile-time and run-time support for enforcing system or component properties.

13.2   Level 1 – Syntactic Interfaces

Definition

By a *syntactic interface*, we understand here a list of operations or ports, including their signatures (the types of allowed inputs and outputs), by means of which communication with a component is performed.

Generally speaking, a *type* can be understood as a set of values on which a related set of operations can be performed successfully. Belonging to a given type usually implies constraints that go beyond what value is denoted exactly, most notably *how* the value is stored (required when operations are performed). Once types have been defined, it is possible to use them in specifications of the form: if some input of type t_{in} is given, then the output will have type t_{out}.

Type safety is the guarantee that no run-time error will result from the application of some operation to the wrong object or value. A *type system* is a set of rules for checking type safety (a process usually called type checking since it is often required that enough information about the typing assumptions has been given explicitly by the designer or programmer, so that type checking becomes mostly a large bookkeeping process).

"Static" type checking is performed at compile- (or bind-) time and ensures once and for all that there is no possibility of interaction errors (of the kind addressed by the type system). Not all errors can be addressed by type systems, especially since one usually requires that type checking is easy; e.g., with static type checking it is difficult to rule out in advance all risks of division-by-zero errors.

Type systems allow checking *substitutability* when components are combined: by comparing the data types in a component's interface, and the data types desired by its environment client, one can predict whether an interaction error is possible (e.g. producing a run-time error such as "Method not understood").

Specification of System and Component Signatures

A system for specification of syntactic interfaces must include:

- A type system, together with a syntax (we can call it an Interface Description Language, or IDL) for specifying signatures of operations/ports;
- A mapping from the (abstract) interface types to component implementations. For instance, if components are given in some programming language (for example, if they are written in C), and the interface types use the type system of C, then the mapping is direct. If components are available in binary form, there must be an agreed mapping from interface types to binary formats of component implementations.
- A notion of substitutability, which describes when the interfaces of two components are compatible.

For embedded systems, the type system is usually rather simple, with a substitutability amounting to equality (i.e. one may only substitute objects whose interface is the same as the declared one). For run-time component frameworks, a little bit more flexibility is usually allowed, with substitutability based on type extension or even a more generally defined conformance relation.

For instance, every CORBA object has a type name, which is the same as the interface name assigned in its IDL declaration. The operations that it can perform, and the variables (and their types) that it understands, are all part of its type. Base types include three different precisions of integers and floating-point numbers plus fixed-point, standard and wide characters and strings, etc. Constructed types include records ("struct"s), unions, and enumerations. One can declare either fixed or variable length structs, arrays, strings, and wstrings. There is an any type that can assume any legal IDL type at runtime.

CORBA supports sub-typing by extension: one can create a subtype by extending the base type's list of operation signatures. But one must not redefine any of the base type's operations, and it only works in the absence of explicit self-reference. The advantage of this scheme is that it is easy to implement and understand, the disadvantage is that it is still quite restrictive since some safe substitutions are ruled out.

A proposal for a polymorphic type system suitable for embedded system design is given by Lee and Xiong [LX01] and incorporated in Ptolemy II. It combines several types of polymorphism, including some standard coercions between numeric data types. One design goal is that the check for substitutability should be efficient, since one may have to carry it out at run-time.

Component Interoperability

Conformance is more generally defined as the weakest (i.e., least restrictive) substitutability relation that guarantees type safety. Necessary conditions (applying recursively) are that a caller must not invoke any operation not supported by the service, and the service must not return any exception not handled by the caller. Conformance has a property called *contravariance*: the types of the input parameters of a service must conform in opposite to the types of its result parameters.

For example, if we have a type `sign` for the set of the three numbers -1, 0 and +1, it is natural to see `sign` as a subtype of `integer`. Now consider a numerical function `sign` from integers to signs: this function can be used (substituted) in contexts where a function accepting sign is expected, and in contexts where a function returning integers is expected.

At first, the contravariant rule seems theoretically appealing. However, it is less natural than covariance (where parameter types conform in the same direction), often encountered in real world modelling (animals eat food, herbivores are subtypes of animals, but they eat grass which is a subtype of food, not a super-type!), and is indeed the source of many problems. The most surprising one appears with operations combining two arguments, such as comparisons. If the contravariant rule is used, the type associated with *equal* for *Child* instances is not a subtype of the one of *equal* for *Parent* instances. As soon as this kind of feature is considered (and they are common), the contravariant rule prevents a sub-typing relation between *Child* and *Parent* (see [Cas95] for more details and solutions).

Trends and Conclusion

About 10 years after the debates on contravariance vs. covariance have peaked in the OO research community, the dust has settled down somewhat. We can now identify three main directions that have been taken to deal with this issue.

- Keep it simple: No-variance is used for IN parameters. That is the approach used in mainstream languages such as CORBA, C++, Java, C# etc. For instance, if one needs a specialized version of *x.equal(y)*, the type checking (through down casting on parameter x) must be done by hand by the programmer, and verified at runtime only.
- (ii) Model reality: Covariance is used for IN parameters. This is the approach used in Eiffel, which makes static type checking a non-local, non-incremental task. Indeed, if no other restriction is made, type checking requires extensive program analysis and looks much more like theorem proving than the simple bookkeeping process it used to be.
- (iii) Make it complex: use parametric polymorphism in conjunction with reference polymorphism, and have a type system where the types themselves can be seen as variables. This is quite appealing as far as the expressive power of the type system is concerned, but it still lacks a mainstream adoption.

The conclusion is that as soon as one wants a minimum of flexibility for defining type conformance between a provided interface and a required interface, static type checking is no longer a simple bookkeeping process. So level 1 contracts do not have a very different nature than contracts of other levels. In some cases, they can be defined with restrictive rules to allow simple tools to process them, in other cases one could be interested in having more flexibility at the price of more complex tools for static checking, or even rely on runtime monitoring.

A concern in component-based design of embedded systems is that runtime monitoring of interface types may be desirable for building reliable systems, and because one cannot completely trust component implementations. If components are deployed at run-time, the check for substitutability must be performed with available computing resources.

13.3   Level 2 – Functional Properties

Definition

Functional properties are used to achieve more than just interoperability. Level 2 in the Contract Hierarchy is concerned with the actual *values* of data that are passed between components through the interfaces, whose syntax is specified at Level 1 (the preceding section). Typical properties of interest are constraints on their ranges, or on the relation between the parameters of a method call and its return value. It is also customary to include at level 2 properties of a persistent state of a component. In level 2 contracts, transactions are described as atomic, which means they are appropriate for components with sequentialised or totally independent interactions.

Specification of System and Component Properties

Formalisms at level 2 provide means for describing partial functions or relations for representing a component (or system) step. In constraint languages, as provided by Eiffel/SCOOP [Mey91, Mey97] (dedicated to the Eiffel programming language), OCL [WK98] (Object Constraint Language dedicated to UML), LSL (Larch Shared Language) [GHG+93], JML (Java Modelling Language) [LB99], relations are expressed by means of *invariants*, *pre-* and *post conditions*. More classical notations are for example Kahn networks [Kah74]. Logical formalisms are Unity [CM88] or TLA [Lam94], with the difference that they allow also to express liveness properties, that is, additional properties of infinite sequences of steps (fix points).

In practice, pre- and post conditions are rarely used in the context of large components, but rather for small components, often describing data structures providing a set of operations considered as atomic. One reason may be that the same type of interfaces is much harder to obtain for compositions of components.

Verifying Component Properties

There exist a number of tools using constraints for *run-time monitoring* which generate exceptions in case of violation of interfaces at run-time. This is the case for example in Eiffel and for JML annotations of Java. It also exists in .NET. Run-time monitoring assumes that interface specifications are executable, and incurs a nontrivial cost. Many frameworks use assertions in a test phase, often using a constraint language. Here, aspect-oriented programming techniques [KLM+97], which allow to compose different features when generating code for testing or for final implementation, can be used to introduce some degree of automation and to facilitate maintenance.

There are research tools that perform static checking of JML, such as ESC Java at Compaq [ESC] based on (partial) static analysis methods, or in the Loop project at University of Nijmegen [Loo] which is based on the use of interactive theorem provers. Theorem provers are also used to verify invariants or temporal logic properties on TLA or Unity specifications. Such tools are primarily used in applications that require highly dependable software. Even in the future, they might not become widely used in standard component based development, but it is important that they exist for demanding applications. Certainly, component manufacturers may want to use them, to provide highly dependable component implementations conforming to contracts. To some extent, the use of theorem provers can be seen as a form of experimentation, which should result in automated procedures for various application domains.

Some of these formalisms are also used in the domain of hardware or on finite state abstractions of components, where (symbolic) composition and model-checking are applicable, and any of the many model-checkers developed in the last 2 decades can be used.

The B-Method [Abr96], is based on a formalism of the same kind, but it provides an integrated framework for systematic refinement from invariants to implementations of functional components.

Component Interoperability and System Properties

There are two aspects of interoperability: one is preservation of component properties and general system properties like absence of deadlock, and the second is verification of emerging global system properties corresponding to functional system requirements.

In the context of level 2 specifications, composition of interfaces can be seen as composition of partial relations. Therefore, *component interoperability* amounts to verify that composition does not require strengthening of preconditions (leading to additional undefinedness). In simple cases, it can be sufficient to check that preconditions are satisfied by corresponding post-conditions of connected interfaces.

The level 2 *system properties* are determined from the composed partial relation. In general, its formal calculation requires more sophisticated mathematical machinery in the form of fixed-point theory, as simpler representations in terms of invariants and pre/post conditions cannot always be synthesized.

The situation concerning existing tool support is the same as for the verification of components themselves. Run-time monitoring is the main approach, and alternative methods consist in using interactive theorem provers, or, alternatively, a top-down approach based on systematic refinement.

In the case of finite domains, the situation is more favourable, as representations of compositions can be synthesized from representations of components.

Existing academic tools for the static validation of component properties should be pushed towards more automation and integrated into professional development tools. The main problem of level 2 specifications is their applicability to distributed systems, due to the absence of means to express interactions as non atomic or to express explicit concurrency. This can be improved by considering additional level 3 specifications. In practice, level 2 specifications can be used mainly for a single level of components and when non-interference between transactions can be guaranteed by construction (in general by sequentialising access to components), as for example in the synchronous approach used in the context of safety critical applications.

13.4   Level 3 – Functional Properties

Definition

Level 3 in the Contract Hierarchy is concerned with the actual ordering between different interactions at the component interfaces and more importantly, they allow interactions between a component and its environment to be considered non atomic. Level 3 specifications provide the following facilities:

- description of transactions (input/output behaviours) not necessarily as atomic steps.
- explicit composition operators avoid the obligation to provide an explicit input/output relation taking into account all potential internal interactions. This has the further advantage that a restricted use of a component does indeed allow to derive stronger properties (only the actually occurring interactions need to be taken into account, not all hypothetical ones)
- many level 3 formalism allow to express explicit control information, which makes the expression of complex, history dependent input/output relations much easier

Indeed, formalisms at level 3 have explicit composition and communication primitives.

Specification of System and Component Properties

There are several, formally comparable families of description techniques:

- Automata, including hierarchical state machines etc. as found in SDL, UML have explicit composition operators which allow easily to represent complex components by means of the same formalism.
- Process algebras are very similar in principle, and really focus on the notion of composition.
- Temporal Logics are used for the description of global properties to be verified on a component or a system (also for components specified with level 2 interfaces), rarely as component characterizations to be used in further composition.
- Sequence Diagrams or Sequence Charts represent also global properties, but in terms of a set of interesting scenarios and are mostly used to describe test cases. They may be used to describe complete specification if the number of alternative scenarios describing a transaction is relatively small.

In order to distinguish between or the *required* and *offered* parts in the context of contract specifications, most of these formalisms use the distinction between inputs and outputs. Timeouts or explicit timing restrictions can be used in some formalism to restrict waiting for particular inputs or component reaction time. Most of these formalisms must handle unexpected inputs explicitly by providing complete specifications. A recent suggestion for extending automata-based formalisms with explicit distinction of provided and required interfaces are *interface automata* [CdAH+02].

Verifying Properties and Component Interoperability

In the context of level 3 contracts, the expression of interfaces of complex components is made possible due to explicit composition. In this case, the verification of component properties and of system properties are of the same nature. However, system verification can easily become intractable for systems consisting many complex components (cf. the state explosion problem).

In academia, in the last two decades a large number of model-checking tools have been developed, which allow to show that a composition of automata (describing behaviours of components) satisfies some property (a desired component or system property), described either as an automaton, a formula of temporal logic, or in the form of a scenario (Message Sequence Chart [Mau96, IT00] or Live Sequence Chart [DH01]). These tools can be used to verify properties of relatively small descriptions, i.e., mainly of medium-size components or systems. In order to make the verification of complex systems that are compositions of components tractable, two kinds of methods have been developed:

- abstraction, to hide the internal structure of sub-components and to synthesize the externally visible behaviour of a component by abstracting, whenever possible from interactions between internal components
- compositional verification techniques, which are similar in nature but based on characterizations of components in terms of (temporal) properties and use of deductive verification techniques

Most model-checkers work on finite-state systems only, but in the last years also tools for checking decidable or semi-decidable properties of infinite-state systems (such as parameterized systems, systems with counters or communication through lossy channels) have been developed. Nevertheless, at present these tools are not integrated with any existing tool for component-based development.

For modelling languages like SDL or UML, which can be used to describe interface behaviours, there exist case tools [USE01, Ilo, Tel] with restricted simulation and validation facilities, allowing to validate a composition of a set of components described by their interface behaviour by simulation.

Nevertheless, none of these tools provides facilities for defining observation *criteria* that are necessary to explicitly hide internal information. Industrial practice is mainly based on testing and/or on model-based simulation. The step from a complete functional model to an implementation, for example in C can be done automatically in some contexts. For synchronous languages, and for SDL, automatic code generators exist and are being used.

It should be noted that system validation is in general not done for arbitrary environments, but with a particular, restricted environment (including the underlying platform) and a restricted number of possible interaction scenarios in mind. This reduces the amount of non-determinism and makes validation more feasible, which then gets very close to testing of a restricted number of scenarios played by the environment. In this context, level 3 specification have the considerable advantage over level 2 specifications that encapsulation of internal activities need not be done a priori for all uses of a components, but after restriction to a particular environment. This allows for the derivation of stronger global properties.

Research Challenges

Currently, there exist many specialized tools, both academic and commercial, for modelling, composition, verification, analysis, simulation, or other activity in the development of component-based systems. In the foreseeable future, an important objective should be to leverage the power of these tools, by connecting existing pieces into a toolchain for modelling and analysis of component-based real-time systems. Such tool chain could, e.g., allow to model systems in a subset of UML, thereafter translate such models into formats usable by other tools, e.g., for simulation and timing analysis.

The application of model checking techniques to component-based systems has to tackle the well-known state space explosion problem. An important approach to verification large systems is to combine compositionality and abstraction techniques, by providing a simple interface for each component, and verifying that: (i) the interfaces of system components interact correctly, and (ii) that each component conforms to its interface. In order for such an approach to succeed, it is essential to minimize the linking and dependencies between components, as shown e.g., by Sharygina et al. [SBK01].

In certain applications, the interaction between components may be managed by requiring that components be strictly independent of each other, or that their interaction be in terms of access to a common data structure, under the control of, e.g., a transaction manager. For many application areas, the identification of suitable restrictions on component interaction remains a challenge.

The complexity of system complexity must also be managed by developing techniques to integrate components while preserving/guaranteeing essential properties of component behaviour. Ongoing work on composition principles that formulate conditions for guaranteeing the preservation of component properties during composition can be found in [BGS00,GS02]. Principles that allow the inference of system properties directly from component properties would certainly provide more motivation for the verification of components. An interesting research challenge is the study of architectures that support such composition principles.

13.5   Level 4a – Timing Properties

Definition

Timing requirements define constraints on the order of occurrence and on upper and/or lower bounds of durations between events. We can distinguish between *hard real-time systems*, where all the occurrences of the specified events must satisfy the specified constraints, and adaptive *real-time systems* where the distribution of the durations between the specified events over all occurrences within an execution must obey some constraints, e.g., on average and variance etc. In this section, we consider timing properties for hard real-time systems, for adaptive real-time and QoS we refer to the next section.

Specifying Timing Requirements

In the *current practice*, time bounds can be associated with the duration between events in an informal or (semi)formal requirements specification. Typical timing properties are the following ones, where time requirements are expressed using physical time, e.g., seconds, some abstract time unit, cycles of some clock or number of computation steps. When different requirements and definitions of a system are expressed using different notions of time, it is important that the relationship between these different notions is well defined.

- When called, this method is computed within 20 ms (execution time property).
- This function is computed periodically, with a period of 50 ms (periodicity property)
- packets are sent with a frequency of 50Hz and a maximal jitter of 1ms (periodicity property)
- Component C receives data requests at most every 3 ms (inter arrival time property)
- When the value of variable x exceeds 100, component C is notified within less than 10 ms (reactivity property)
- If lightning strikes, transformers is shut off within 50 microseconds (response time property)
- RPM does not exceed 50000 for more than a few seconds during the start phase.
- The response to this signal comes within 3 cycles (response time property)
- When component C gets a request every 2 to 3 cycles, it provides the response within 2 cycles (conditional response time)
- the execution time of task T is 20 to 30 ms and its overall duration should not exceed 100m.

Note that such properties can express both requirements and assumptions depending how they are used.

Existing **formalisms** that allow the expression of time bounds are in fact extensions of level 2 and level 3 formalisms extended with time. They include metric temporal logics, i.e., temporal logics with quantitative constraints on the duration between events, timed extensions of automata, sequence charts extended with time, timing diagrams or general constraint languages, like OCL, extended with time. For example, in Message Sequence Charts [IT00] and also in Sequence Diagrams in some UML tools, time bounds can be assigned to the distance between two events. In Live Sequence Charts [DH01], time dependent properties are expressed with timers, meaning that durations cannot be measured, but only constrained. Timed automata are more expressive: they specify constraints between events by means of so called "clocks" measuring durations, which are reset to zero at the occurrence of one event, and then used in "guards" to restrict the possible occurrence times of other events. A notion of *urgency* allows to distinguish between time constraints and time guards.

Temporal logics extended with time have rather limited expressive power. Sequence Diagrams define time constraints in the context of certain scenarios, and are very cumbersome if the overall number of scenarios is big. Timed-automata based formalisms naturally define constraints on all possible scenarios, but it is harder to argue about particular "interesting" scenarios.

Some programming and modelling languages have an explicit notion of time. In synchronous languages one can define behaviours occurring at certain cycles, where cycles of various lengths (all multiples of a basic cycle) can exist. In the modelling languages SDL and Room, a notion of global time and timers can be used. But all these formalisms are aimed at the definition of time dependent behaviours, rather than at expressing real-time requirements. ITU recommends time extended Message Sequence Charts for defining real-time requirements for SDL system models.

For UML, which contains both formalisms for functional behaviour descriptions and for expressing requirements and constraints, recently a "profile for real-time, scheduling and performance" has been defined [OMG01b], including notions of timers, timed events, constraints on their time of occurrence and a large number of notations for which no semantics are given. These notions are defined for all of UML, but have apparently been built with mainly timed Sequence Diagrams in mind.

A more elaborated RT-profile for UML, also based on a large number of intuitive notations, but including semantics, is being developed in the OMEGA IST project (http://www-omega.imag.fr/). Note that component timing properties depend in general on a given platform and system con- figuration. They must therefore either be properties of a system component (i.e., the running software together with platform and run-time system) be parameterized by (characteristics of) the underlying platform, compiler, etc.

Component Interoperability and System Properties

There is a vast literature on timing analysis, treating the problem of determining whether a set of given system timing requirements can be met by a collection of components with known timing parameters. The most common paradigm is schedulability analysis, which takes as input component timing properties, system timing requirements (on response times, periods, deadlines, etc.), and properties of the scheduler and platform. The output is an answer about feasibility and information about how the scheduling should be performed. In the context of hard real-time systems, it is important to answer the following questions: "to which extent a component based approach is possible?" and what kind of "components" are useful in this context. For this purpose, let us look at what is current practice:

Scheduling Periodic Tasks
Mainstream schedulability analysis assume that tasks are executed periodically or a periodically with known maximal activation frequency. For each task a worst case execution time is known or assumed, and where applicable also the worst case communication requirements, overhead for context-switching, etc. on a given platform. A simple framework is RMA, where all tasks are periodic, can be pre-empted, and have

a statically known pattern of access to shared resources. Under suitable conditions, schedulability can be analyzed in a time proportional to the number of tasks. This approach is present in Meta-H and Rubus and to some extent in PECOS. In general, an integration platform need not perform the schedulability analysis itself; this can be done by an external tool. Schedulability analysis can also be performed for distributed platforms, if communication delays have known bounds. An example is the Volcano system on CAN. This approach has also inspired the real-time profile of CORBA, and in the area of languages, Java-RT and Posix. The approach is mature and has proven practicality. In this context, a component may realize tasks or represent a shared "resource" used for the realization of certain sub-tasks. Its interface must, therefore, specify its worst-case execution time for each task (or sub-task) for the platform under consideration and the implied resource usage. It must also be stated whether preemption is allowed, and whether multiple concurrent invocations are permitted.

Synchronous Approach

This paradigm enforces a very strict scheduling policy. Globally, the system is seen as a sequential system that computes in each *step* or *cycle* a global output to a global input. The effect of a step is defined by a number of transformation rules. Scheduling is done statically by compiling the sets of rules into a sequential program implementing these rules and executing them in some statically defined order. A uniform timing bound for the execution of global steps is assumed (system requirement). In this context, components are often "design-level components", as the component-based design is compiled into a single sequential program later on. In this case the analysis of the WCET (worst case execution time) of a single step is done on the target code directly. An extension to the use of run-time components consists of generating code containing *calls* to those components. Some component models, such as IEC61131-3 use this execution paradigm. In some sense, this approach is quite close to RMA, where the "global period" plays the same role as the "global step". TTA defines a protocol for extending the synchronous languages paradigm to distributed platforms. In this context, distributed components can be made easily interoperable as long as they conform to the timing requirements imposed by the protocol. Another component view consists in considering an entire synchronous system as a "component" communicating (asynchronously) with its environment by buffering inputs from the environment and/or relying on certain continuity properties of the environment. This is sometimes called the GALS (Globally Asynchronous, Locally Synchronous) approach.

Generalizations

Currently under investigation in the research community are generalizations of schedulability analysis to distributed systems and to more dynamic task sets, e.g. with reconfiguration (this is discussed in action 3). Another extension consists in considering components with a more complex structure than entities realizing a set of periodic tasks with a global WCET, e.g., components which have an internal state, as described by a state machine, or systems with modes. Quite a number of tools have been developed recently, aiming at analysis of this kind of systems, such as Taxys [BCP+01], Prometheus [G¨os01], IF [BGM02], or Times [AFM+02] . An ambitious example of a model and framework supporting this and other paradigms is Ptolemy

[RNHL99, Lee01] or Metropolis [BLP+02]. In this context component interoperability is to some extent subsumed under the timing analysis done when checking that system requirements can be met. This analysis includes checking that the components can cooperate to satisfy the system timing requirements. In the context of adaptive real-time system, composition frameworks as proposed in [BGS00] are very promising.

Verifying Component Properties

A difficult point in timing analysis is assessment of WCETs of tasks or of the code implementing a global step of a synchronous system. In current practice, this is done by measurements (on each particular target platform), or by simulation, e.g., by using hardware simulators. Recently, there has been progress in static code-based prediction of WCET by taking into account a very precise platform model [FHL+01, FW98]. Note that WCET calculation is becoming more and more complex, since new hardware features of processors are increasingly unpredictable, and due to the sometimes complex platform dependencies. In order to make assertions about upper bounds of durations, both time-dependent characteristics of the external environment and of the platform on which the component is executed, as well as knowledge about all resource usage, need to be known. Work on extracting timing information from peripherals and other devices remains to be done.

Research Challenges

Today, it is not a problem to find a language or notation for the description of timing behaviours and timing requirements. There is a large number of formalisms (e.g. timed automata) and standards (e.g. UML SPT) available for modelling though some of them still need a formal semantics. The research challenges are in analysis. For example, the SPT notation can be used to specify requirements on UML diagrams, such as "this method should be executed within 10 milliseconds". The difficulty is really how to check that the requirement is guaranteed.

The timing behaviour of a hard real-time system depends on not only its components, but also the execution platform as well as the environment where the system is embedded. Thus the robustness and composability of analysis and implementation paradigms are of particular importance for component-based development. By robustness we mean that timing properties of a system are preserved or refined by any upgrading or reconfiguration, of components.

Much research focuses on component models for specific frameworks and platforms. Important advances have been made in the domain of execution time estimation for individual tasks, as well scheduling analysis at design time. This is supported by adapting traditional scheduling theory where parameters of some scheduling paradigm are specified in the interface of components. Such specifications are also standardized [OMG01b]. Classical scheduling theory assumes that system architectures and components have a certain structure. A number of approaches exist which go beyond the classical theories and propose techniques to extend timing analysis to less constrained forms of component specifications (e.g., as timed automata).

For short-term research, a number of important problems remain to be solved:

- Integration of the analysis capacities of the above mentioned tools for both low-level timing analysis based on abstract interpretation and for interoperability analysis based on timed automata or other more general task descriptions. The system TIMES [AFM+02] is a work in this direction.
- Extension of the well-understood, but restrictive paradigms provided by the synchronous approach or by classical RMA analysis to more general frameworks. For example, TTA is an approach extending the applicability of the synchronous approach to distributed systems. A system like Giotto [Hen01] extends it with more dynamic scheduling of the tasks making up a step.

For long-term research, a challenging research task is to develop a paradigm that encompasses the whole spectrum of approaches from the very strict synchronous approach to the fully asynchronous approach, including distributed systems. Such a paradigm must provide a semantic framework for composition of time-dependent components, based on different communication and interaction modes. This will allow the verification of compositions of time-dependent systems and their properties at modelling level.

A number of features, such as run-time update and dynamic reconfiguration of systems, which provide some of the motivation for using a component-based approach, have so far been essentially avoided in systems with hard real-time requirements. It is an interesting research question, whether such features can be reasonably included into hard real-time systems.

Essentially, what is needed is the robustness of timing analysis. There are a number of open and challenging problems in developing platform-independent analysis techniques for all levels:

- For low-level WCET analysis, existing techniques and tools are available only for specific hardware architectures and applicable under strict assumptions on the execution platform e.g. pipeline analysis will break up if pre-emption is allowed. It is not an economical solution to develop a WCET tool for every platform and re-calculate the WCET for all software components when hardware components are upgraded or replaced. It is desirable to have WCET tools where standard hardware components and features (e.g. pipeline) as input are parameters for analysis.

- For system-level analysis, a large amount of work has been done on schedulability analysis (e.g. RMA) and consistency checking of timing constraints and requirements (e.g. model checking based on timed automata). However, the existing techniques provide no guarantee that the analysis results will be valid after some change on any part of the system or environment e.g. a component is upgraded or ported to a different platform. It appears that the synchronous programming paradigm is a promising approach to construct deterministic systems that are easy to verify. But the problem is converted to check that the timing requirements from the environment are satisfied by a deterministic system, which is a difficult problem.

We should also emphasize that the components in a hard real-time system share scarce resources. Handling resource sharing induces a number of interesting and difficult research problems e.g. synthesis of schedules optimizing resource usage (e.g. power consumption) from application tasks.

13.6   Level 4b – Quality of Service

This section addresses quality of service of component-based designs related to adaptive real-time issues. Hard real-time issues have been treated in the preceding section.

Definition

A quality of a system can in general be considered as a function mapping a given system instance with its full behaviour onto some scale. The scale may be either qualitative, in particular it may be partially or totally ordered. Or the scale is quantitative, in which case the quality is a measure. The problem of realizing systems that have certain guaranteed qualities, also known as their quality of service (QoS), involves the representation of such qualities in design models or languages and techniques to implement and analyze them as properties of implemented system instances.

While some definitions of 'QoS' include concepts such as security, where the scale is not a measure, we here focus on quantitative measures, especially on those related to time. In this area, there is a common further classification of system requirements, distinguishing between hard real-time requirements, where the quality of any implemented system instance must lie in a certain interval, and adaptive real-time requirements. Typical examples of such requirements are: "The average lifetime of the battery pack is 4 hours", or "The probability of a buffer underrun is less than 0.001". This is the focus of this section; hard real-time systems are handled in the preceding section.

Embedded System Context

Embedded systems designers are usually facing many challenges if they strive for systems with predictable QoS. To incorporate these constraints in the embedded systems design process is a challenging issue, for the following reasons.

- The system dynamics is becoming ever more complex, making it more and more difficult to observe or predict the QoS properly.
- The trend towards networked embedded systems raises issues like message buffering, interdependencies due to media sharing, and communication characteristics, all influencing the system QoS.
- Applications involve more and more extra-functional features in the form of multimodal interfaces and multimedia support, having impact on the QoS.
- Modelling and analysis facilities for QoS are (if at all) not well integrated into the methods and tools available to embedded system designer, because QoS relates to different design aspects than the functional design.

For reasons such as these, encapsulation of QoS properties inside a component is very difficult. Most of the work already done focuses mainly on the definition of QoS contracts. A workable approach appears to be to attach offered QoS properties (much like post-conditions) to components, as well as required QoS properties (resembling preconditions) [Sel02].

Specifying System and Component Requirements

Contract Languages. Research has progressed in the context of languages to specify such contracts, and to attach them to component interfaces. We mention QuO/CDL (http://quo.bbn.com), AQuA (http://www.crhc.uiuc.edu/PERFORM/ AQuA.html), QML [FK98], and AQML [Nee91]. A more descriptive overview can de found in part III of this document. These languages are mostly syntactic extensions of CORBA's Interface Definition Language (IDL) tailored to express QoS properties. In order to be useful in component based systems, contract languages must include facilities for expressing properties typical of components, that is, their context dependencies [WBGP01]. A component provides a service under a given contract only if the surrounding environment offers services with adequate contracts [Reu01]. Such dependencies are much more complex than the traditional pre/post-condition contract scheme of object oriented programming. In the most general case, a component may bind together its provided contracts with its required contracts as an explicit set of equations (meaning that offered QoS is equal to required QoS).

Therefore, a component oriented contract language includes constructs for:

*   expression of QoS spaces (dimensions, units);
*   primitive bindings between these spaces and the execution model (bindings to observable events, conversion from discrete event traces to continuous flows, definition of measures);
*   constraint languages on the QoS spaces (defining the operations that can be used in the equations, form of these equations).

Verifying Component QoS Properties

In an ideal world, a component user (i.e., a designer that picks a component to include it in a design) has precise information on the QoS behaviour of the component with respect to its environment. Then, during component composition, some answers on the QoS behaviour of the composed system could be computed.

In practice, contracts written in languages such as QML or QuO are compiled to create stubs that monitor and adapt the QoS parameters when the system is operational. This QoS adaptation software is, in effect, equivalent to a controller for a discrete system. In the approaches practiced today, the following issues limit the confidence that a designer can put in QoS declarations of a component.

*   The existing QoS contract languages are not equipped with a formal meaning, thus do not provide a basis for formal proofs, nor can they be used to perform symbolic computations.
*   The QoS contracts often involve very complex dependencies.
*   There are no techniques to prove that a given component implementation abides by the QoS contracts of the component declaration.
*   The runtime monitoring cannot fully observe and measure the component's behaviour in the defined QoS space, because of technical limitations (e.g., undersampling events, distributed delay computation).

QoS Contract Negotiation and Adaptation

Components are bound to be deployed in diverse architectures. As a consequence, adaptive-real-time QoS properties are often considered as "promises", and in practice implemented with best-effort techniques. QoS contracts are thus not interpreted as final and non-negotiable constraints (differing from the classical interpretation where post condition failure means bad design). This implies that run-time violations of the contractually agreed QoS can occur. In particular, the component characteristics of "*fully explicit context dependencies*" and the possibility of being able to "*be deployed independently*" are not met by these approaches. Instead the contracts are understood as guidelines for what has to be achieved, and architectural choices by the designer must make provision for variation as well as fallback (minimal) constraints.

Classical component [Bro96] (i.e., non QoS-aware) technologies already include facilities for dynamic discovery of resource availability (in other words: level 2 contract negotiation). QoS contract models must support adaptability even further, because a contract may be valid at some instant and invalid at a later time (while level 2 contracts stay valid once "discovered" in a given component execution). Such a support requires means of specifying variation in the QoS contract model, as well as adequate contract monitoring support.

Since quality of service contracts may fail, contracted software in components must be able to cope with failure situations. This software must therefore exhibit capacities for adaptation, using techniques such as the ones described in this roadmap, in Part III. Application domains such as components for mobile computing put an emphasis on this relationship, because the highly varying quality of service of communication resources has a major impact on the software architecture of mobile applications. Although the concept of quality of service contracts is exposed in Part II, the notion of quality of service specification is shared by the QoS system development group. Such a notion of QoS contracts should be used as a pivotal concept for cooperation between these communities.

Contract Monitoring

Since contracts must be monitored during component execution, the component infrastructure must provide some support to the designer. Building contract monitors is a difficult task, often more difficult than the design and coding of a component implementation.

Typical difficulties include:

• reliable access to execution events and to precise time for sampling;
• computing with distributed events;
• coordinating distributed monitors, etc.

Therefore, monitors must now be designed by specialists. A component implementation is then augmented by specific pieces of a contract monitor. Since time is often an important factor of QoS contracts, the monitor code must be efficiently synchronized with the service code of the component. Aspect-oriented programming [KLM+97] and aspect-oriented design [CW02] may provide efficient means of extending a com-

.ponent with contract monitors when those are designed as aspects weaved with the component architecture [HJPP02].

Predicting System Properties from Component Properties

Model-Based Approaches

We here survey techniques for statically analyzing system performance properties. A workable modelling and analysis approach to embedded systems QoS is based on the observation that networks, interfaces, and even circuits on chips [Con02, Ten00, Ray02] can be understood and modelled as discrete systems exhibiting stochastic behaviour, such as error rates, response time distributions, or message queue lengths.

Mathematically speaking, the QoS characteristics of a given embedded system induce families of stochastic decision processes, e.g. Markov chains or semi-Markov decision processes. However, these mathematical objects are too fine grained to be directly specifiable by an average embedded systems designer. Therefore, one must rely on modelling techniques and tools for stochastic processes.

Stochastic modelling and analysis research has given birth to many diverse formalisms, most of them accompanied with tools supporting a QoS-oriented design. This section gives a brief account of the most prominent representatives.

Queuing Networks

Rooted in the early approaches to QoS estimation for analogue telecommunication networks, queuing networks have since then been used to quantify the quality of many communication system and multiprocessor networks. Queuing networks provide traffic-oriented modelling, where flows of jobs travel through a static structure consisting of queues and processing units [Kle75, Kle76]. Various tools for modelling and analysis of queuing networks exist, such asQnap2 (http://www.simulog.fr/eps/mod1.htm), and Opnet (http://www.opnet.com/), both being commercial products.

Stochastic Petri Nets

Stochastic Petri nets [Mol82, MCB84, SM91] are extending Petri nets with means to specify stochastic phenomena, and hence allow one to build QoS models. They can alternately be viewed as extension of *queuing networks* with dedicated means to model resource contention and several other features which are difficult to model in plain queuing networks [Chi98]. In this sense they are more appropriate for contemporary embedded and concurrent system design. Various academic tools exist, among them GreatSPN (http://www.di.unito.it/greatspn/) and Möbius (http://www.crhc.uiuc.edu/PERFORM/mobius.html).

Hierarchical Models

Modular and hierarchical design has been one of the challenges in QoS modelling. Among the first hierarchical methods is Hit [BMW89], which allows one to capture system functionalities and bind it to system resources in a layered approach (http://ls4-www.cs.uni-dortmund.de/HIT/HIT.html). Other methods, including Quest (http://www.cs.uniessen.de/SysMod/QUEST/) [DHMC96] and LQNS (http://www.sce.carleton.ca/rads/ek-rads-etc/software.html) [WHSB98] have developed this idea further. Among others [ESCW01] applies this approach to the UML setting.

Compositional Models
Another approach to construct complex QoS models is the compositional one, where systems are incrementally constructed out of smaller components. Typical representatives are Pepa [Hil96], Imc [Her02], and Spades [DKB98]. Tool support exists, e.g. as an add-on to the CADP toolkit (http://fmt.cs.utwente.nl/tools/pdac/) but is not as extensive as for the Petri net-based approaches.

Annotated Design Methods
Many formal and semiformal design notations have been decorated with QoS characteristics, in order to allow for a QoS prediction on the basis of an integrated model. This approach has been followed e.g. for MSC [Ker01], for SDL [DHMC96], and for Statechart dialects [CHK99, GLM00]. The tools that have apparently been developed for in-house case studies are not publicly available.

Reliability Modelling Methods
In the reliability analysis domain, slightly different techniques have emerged, which we briefly review here for completeness. A standard approach is to associate components with a reliability model, which involves fault events, error states, fault arrival rates, and a Markov chain model of how the component responds to fault events. If the system description describes how errors propagate between components, the reliability models of individual components can be combined into a global Markov chain, which can be analyzed using a separate tool for Markov chain analysis. This approach is used in the Meta-H toolset, where the SURE/PAVE/PAWS tool (from NASA Langley) is used to solve the resulting Markov chain.

Research Agenda

The above discussion suggests the following research strands to strengthen the development of embedded systems with predictable QoS.

- Integration into the design process.
  - o Contracts: To enable a modular reasoning about QoS, pre/post condition style contracts should be developed, allowing one to specify interfaces with *required vs. guaranteed* QoS [Sel02] along the work of e.g. QCCS [WPGS02]. Since virtually any QoS measure is a stochastic quantity, both QoS guarantees and QoS requirements must be expressible in a probabilistic setting (a simple example would be: "in 95% of the cases an answer must come within 3 seconds")– as opposed to an absolute setting ("the answer must come within 3 seconds"). In full generality one needs means to express those quantities via probability distributions which may be parameterized by the component input.
  - o Compositional reasoning. The size and complexity considerations ask for major research endeavours with respect to management of the design for predictable QoS. Efforts must be undertaken to strengthen a compositional reasoning with probabilistic quantities. Compositional methods so far focus on model construction, while truly compositional analysis has not been tackled successfully. Layered analysis methods have received some attention, for instance in the context of the SPT profile [PW03], but produce notoriously imprecise QoS results (where the inaccuracy relative to the true QoS can be unbounded). Better, and more manageable, compositional methods are needed.

- Platform & resource dependency: QoS properties of systems can in general not be deduced from the QoS characteristics of components alone. Platform dependencies such as resource constraints, and communication infrastructure aspects play an important role usually not reflected at the component level. This makes it imperative to reconsider the architectural approaches in such a way as to at least reduce the dependencies of different parts of systems, or to make the platform dependencies explicit parameters of the models.
- Semantics: A seamless QoS design process relies on a smooth but solid integration of the QoS modelling and analysis concepts into a well-designed integrated formalism, which is semantically deeper than a shallow annotational extension of the UML. The existing QoS contract languages are useful for best effort-based runtime policies, but do not possess a precise interpretation that can be used for rigid assessment of contractual obligations. Put differently, we need QoS contract languages with precise semantics.
- Tools: Industrial-strength tools supporting an integrated QoS design process are needed. On the long run, these tools are expected to emerge as extensions of existing component-oriented modelling and analysis tools. However, there is a disturbing gap between component-oriented design methods, and the mainstream QoS analysis tools which are flow oriented, as in Petri nets or queuing networks (where tokens or jobs flow through a static structure). These are closer to scenario-based notations, such as sequence diagrams, but do not fit so well to component-based design. This gap hampers a seamless integration in the design process.

13.7   Specifying and Reasoning About Contracts: Summary and Analysis

From the various information of this section 13, it is clear that the main difficulties of the contract based specification, verification and validation fall into a few general categories:

1. Specification & Monitoring
   o Harmonization of Specification Techniques: Current contract-based specification techniques use notations and models that are quite different. In order to fully support all aspects of component based design, these notations and models must be harmonized. This not a simple task: for instance, crossbreeding notations and research results on behaviour specification and performance analysis is not obvious; one needs a time model that is compatible with the behaviour notation as well as the component framework.
   o Run-Time Monitoring: Contracts must in general be monitored during component execution, unless there are guarantees that a component satisfies a contract. For embedded systems, techniques for (automatically) constructing efficient (using limited resources) monitors from contracts must be further developed. Aspect oriented programming [KLM+97] may provide structuring techniques for adding monitors to a system
2. Environment Dependency
   o Specifying Generic Contracts: Many component properties are highly dependent on the environment, including other system parts as well as the system

platform. It is highly non-trivial to express component properties in such a way that these properties can be applied in a variety of environments. As an example, properties of execution times of components depend crucially on the timing properties of the underlying platform. There are currently no widely usable solutions for specifying the timing behaviour of a component in a platform-independent way

o   Implementing Generic Contracts: Platform-independent notations, techniques and tools must be related to platform-dependent frameworks. As component infrastructures are very different from one application domain (e.g. automotive systems) to another (e.g. network based information systems), this is a nontrivial issue: e.g. a network model may not match a real protocol implementation on some platform, from both the behavioural and quality of service points of view. One potential solution to this platform dependency problem could be the implementation of architecture transformations along the lines of the MDA approach.

o   Measuring Extra-Functional Component Properties: Timing and performance properties are usually obtained from components by measurement, usually by means of simulation. Problems with this approach are that the results depend crucially on the environment (model) used for the measurements and may not be valid in other environments. Techniques should be developed for overcoming these problems to obtain more reliable component property specifications.

3. Design & Analysis

o   Adapting Well-Understood Design Principles: Many advances in component technology have been obtained by adaptation of well-understood design techniques to the component-based setting. An example is the use of classical schedulability analysis and reliability analysis in some component technologies for real-time systems. There are many other practical techniques that could potentially be adapted to and enrich component technology.

o   Formal Verification: Functional, and some extra-functional, component properties can in principle be inferred by formal analysis of the software itself, using techniques like e.g. model checking, although this is often still difficult in practice. The success of recent advances for functional and real-time system properties prompt for further work to enlarge the scope of formal analysis techniques. This should include also system diagnosis in the form of analysis techniques that can identify the "bottlenecks" in a design, i.e. the components that "cause" poor system behaviour

o   Guidelines for Tractable Analysis of System Properties: The verification and prediction of system properties from component properties is in the general case an intractable problem, i.e., general techniques can cope only with systems of small or medium complexity. To master this complexity, we need guidelines for structuring assemblies, in other words software methodologies that help the designer to build "tractable" architectures by enforcing well chosen restrictions.

4. Tool Development: Effective tool support must be developed for all the tasks listed in this section

14 Component Models and Integration Platforms: Landscape

This section provides an overview of existing component models and component integration platforms. In some cases, particularly for proprietary component models, there is a tight connection between the component model and a particular integration platform, and sometimes also a particular ADL. In such cases we combine the descriptions. Thereafter follow descriptions of (some) available toolsets and platforms that support the component model.

The section considers each model under the following headings, as discussed in the previous section:

- the component model, including its support for describing different properties in component interfaces;
- component composition;
- verification and validation tools and techniques;
- supporting integration platforms.

Aspects of real-time middleware aspects are also covered in section 23.

14.1 Widely Used Component Models

In this subsection, we survey component models and platforms that have been developed not primarily for embedded systems. The deployment and composition of components is typically performed at run-time.

Java Beans

Sun Microsystems initially introduced a client-side (or desktop) component model (JavaBeans), and subsequently a server-side (or enterprise) component model (Enterprise JavaBeans). Both of these build on the Java-based approach to distributed applications [Mic02]. In the JavaBeans specification a *bean* is a reusable software component that can be manipulated visually in a builder tool; this differentiates beans from class libraries which cannot benefit from visual manipulation even if providing the equivalent functionality. Some of the unifying features of JavaBeans are support for property customisation (to control the appearance and programmatic behaviour of beans), event handling (a communication metaphor based on delegation and event listeners), persistence (serialisation of a bean's state for later reloading or transmission over a network) and introspection (analysis and manipulation of a beans internal structure: e.g. properties, events, methods and exceptions). A key characteristic of the Java Beans component model is its simplicity – the specification of the model is only 114-pages long [Mic97].

Artist FP5 Consortium: Embedded Systems Design, LNCS 3436, 160– 193, 2005.

JavaBeans was primarily designed for the construction of graphical user interfaces (GUIs). Customization of components plays an essential role and was originally emphasised to enable incremental specialization of GUIs from generic exemplars.

Technical Description
- *Component types:* A *bean* is a self-contained, reusable software unit that can be visually composed into applets, applications, servlets, and composite components, using visual application builder tools.

  Programming a Java component requires definition of three sets of data: i) properties (similar to the attributes of a class); ii) methods; and iii) events which are an alternative to method invocation for sending data. A bean wishing to receive an event (listener) registers at the event source (the component launching the event). In Java, events are objects created by a source and propagated to all registered listeners. For example: an alarming device (listener) asks a temperature probe (source) to send it a message when the temperature value exceeds a certain threshold so that a bell can be sounded.
- *Syntactic Support in Interfaces:* The model defines four types of interaction points, referred to as *ports*:
  o methods, as in Java;
  o properties, used to parameterize the component at composition time, or as a regular attribute in the object-orientation sense of the term during run time;
  o event sources, and event sinks (called listeners) for event-based communication.
- *Other Support in Interfaces:* JavaBeans does not support behavioural or QoS properties.
- *Support for Introspection:* A bean can be dynamically queried for its characteristics (operations, attributes, etc.), through an introspection mechanism available to all Java classes.

The component programmer can restrict the amount of information made available. To do so, the Java component implements a *BeanInfo* interface whose methods return a list of properties, operations, etc.

- Supported Programming languages: code must be written in Java.
- Required "Middleware"/Framework Support: None.

Tools
There are several commercial programming environments, e.g., Sun's Net Beans, IBM's Visual Age, and Borland's JBuilder. These builders build assemblies visually as a graph of components, where ports between beans are connected. Note that the JavaBean component model by itself does not specify how to connect components; this is done by the builder tool.

EJB (Enterprise Java Beans)

The EJB model is a server-side component model, which is rather different from JavaBeans. The EJB specification defines its component architecture in terms of a scalable runtime, based on containers (see below), that provides runtime services for managing component activation, concurrency, security, persistency and transactions [JF00]. The EJB specification defines a component model by standardising the contracts (context and callback interfaces) and services offered by the runtime environment, and the patterns of interaction between components.

Technical Description

- *Component types:* There are three types of EJB beans defined:
  - o *Entity beans* are application elements that embody data and are by nature transactional and persistent; these beans may handle the persistency themselves (bean managed persistence) or delegate it to the container (container-managed persistence);
  - o *Session beans* are used to model business processes in a transactional and secure manner without the need for persistent storage (i.e. they last for the duration of a session);
  - o *Message-driven beans* are created by containers to asynchronously handle messages from the Java Messaging Service (JMS) sent, for example, to a queue transparently associated with the bean.
- *Syntactic Support in Interfaces:* Depending on the bean type, developers must implement associated, pre-defined, call-back interfaces (e.g. *EntityBean*, *SessionBean*, *MessageDrivenBean*).

These callback interfaces are used by containers to manage and notify beans about certain events (e.g. bean activation or passivation, instance removal, transaction completion, etc.). Moreover, each type of bean expects a specific interface or context from the container (e.g. *EntityContext*, *SessionContext*, *MessageDrivenContext*) for getting an entity bean's primary key, identifying the bean's caller, transaction demarcation, etc.

- *Other Support in Interfaces:* The container provides a uniform interface to services such as naming (Java Naming and Directory Service), security (public/private key authentication and encryption), transactions (based on the Java Transaction Service or OMG Object Transaction Service), and messaging (Java Messaging Service).
- *Support for Introspection:* A bean can be dynamically queried for its characteristics (operations, attributes, etc.), through an introspection mechanism available to all Java classes. The component programmer can, however, restrict the amount of information made available. To do so, the Java component implements a *BeanInfo* interface whose methods return a list of properties, operations, etc.
- Supported Programming languages: code must be written in Java.
- *Required "Middleware"/Framework Support:* Containers provide a level of indirection between clients and bean instances. Each container provides objects, called EJB objects, that expose bean functionality and intercept every method call before delegating it to the bean. This EJB object is automatically generated and embodies container-specific knowledge about bean activation, transactions, security and networking [RAJ01]. Additionally, each EJB object implements the remote interface that enumerates all business methods exposed/ implemented by the respective bean.

EJB relies heavily on the Java Remote Method Invocation (RMI) platform to support dynamic class loading, automatic activation, remote exceptions and distributed garbage collection [RAJ01]. RMI is a distributed architecture that uses a RPC-based protocol to support inter-process communication. For example, the *EJBHome* and *EJBObject* remote interfaces rely on the RMI infrastructure for transparent distribution of component functionality.

- *Deployment:* The deployment of beans is in terms of EJB-jar files that package bean classes, remote interfaces, home interfaces and bean property files, together with an XML-based deployment descriptor that contains information on all the packaged beans (e.g. home name, bean class name, primary key, container fields, etc.) and their dependencies. Deployment descriptors also declare the middleware services needed by components (e.g. lifecycle policy, persistence handling, transaction control), thus avoiding the non-standard manifest files that are used by JavaBeans. [RAJ01].

Tools
The Java Development Kit (JDK) includes a set of classes and development tools (e.g. an RMI compiler) to support the automatic generation of distribution classes (e.g. stubs), glue code (e.g. container policies) and deployment descriptors, thus alleviating developers' efforts and responsibilities.

Summary
EJB standardises a distributed architecture for building component-based business applications. EJB builds on the previous JavaBeans client-side component model and particularly on the Java language, and essentially realises the WORA principle (Write Once Run Anywhere) (albeit in a language-dependent manner). EJB also relies on the RMI architecture, and simplifies and automates the development and distribution process. In contrast to CORBA (see below), RMI not an open standard (although it has the advantage over CORBA that it fully supports objects passed by value (via serialisation). However, efforts have been made to make EJB portable to CORBA systems, particularly through standard connectors (vendor specific bridges that link different architectures) along with RMI-IIOP mappings [RAJ01]. Most crucially, the EJB software engineering process is grounded in a set of tools and code generators that automate the development and deployment process by hiding the cumbersome details of handling distribution and component management policies (e.g. lifecycle, security, transactions, persistence).

COM, DCOM, COM+

Microsoft's Component Object Model [Cor95] dates back to 1995, and is typical of early attempts to increase program independence and allow programming language heterogeneity. COM has roots in Microsoft's OLE (Object Linking and Embedding: first version in 1991), which provided a standard way to embed or link data objects (e.g. text, graphics, images, sound, video, etc.) inside document files, hence supporting the creation and management of compound documents. Unlike EJB and CORBA (see below), COM provides a *binary* solution to interoperability and extensibility [Bro96, Gos95] (see below). The Distributed Component Object Model (DCOM), which supported inter-process communication across distributed machines through an RPC-based protocol called Object RPC (ORPC) [Pat00], was introduced with Windows NT 4.0. More recently, the component model was extended (and renamed COM+) and integrated with Windows 2000 to support the development, configuration and administration of distributed systems with automatic and integrated (Windows-based) control over several aspects of business applications (e.g. security, synchronisation, transactions, queues and events).

The COM component model is fundamentally an intra-address space model. COM extends object-oriented design principles by hiding a component's implementation behind its interface(s) (encapsulation) and allowing components to be replaced by different implementations of the same set (or super set) of interfaces (polymorphism) without the need to recompile their clients. These principles are possible in COM because component services (collections of interfaces) are separated from their implementation through a binary-level indirection mechanism called a virtual table (cf. C++ virtual functions or vtables) [Szy98]. This is the basis of the binary solution referred to above. At runtime, an interface is a typed pointer (known as an Interface Identifier or IID) to a specific virtual table that references the functions (methods) implementing the services exposed by the interface. This binary interface convention allows interoperability between software components written in different languages as long as compilers can translate language structures into this binary form [Gos95].

Technical Description
- *Component types:* A COM component can be seen as an object at the binary level; the implementation is hidden behind the component's interface(s).
- *Syntactic Support in Interfaces:* COM defines interfaces at the level of binaries, consisting of data and function declarations. There are standard protocols for calling an interface, and for dynamically discovering and creating objects and interfaces. Independent development raises the possibility of naming conflicts between interfaces and their implementations. To avoid this, COM requires developers to assign a unique Interface Identifier (IID) and Class Identifier (CLSID) to each newly specified interface and class implementation, respectively.

  COM does not support inheritance; basic component composition is available through:
  - o *containment*, in which a COM object contains other COM objects: the outer object declares some of the inner object's interfaces; at run-time it delegates calls to these interfaces to the inner objects;
  - o *delegation*, this employs wrappers that insert behaviour before or after delegating method calls to inner classes;
  - o *aggregation*, in which the interface of the inner object is exposed without the overhead of call indirection; aggregation requires the source code of both the inner and outer objects to be changed.
- *Other Support in Interfaces:* COM does not support behavioural or QoS properties.
- *Support for Introspection:* components can be queried to discover their supported interfaces.
- *Supported Programming languages:* code can be written in any programming language as long as its compiler generates code that follows the binary interopera-

bility convention. Component interfaces are defined using Microsoft's Interface Definition Language (MIDL) which is an OSF/DCE-based adaptation of CORBA IDL. The MIDL compiler generates marshalling classes and the type-related information (e.g. proxies, stubs, header files, type libraries) needed to accomplish binary compatibility – i.e. joint deployment of components developed in different languages.

- *Required "Middleware"/Framework Support:* component interfaces are separated from their implementation through an indirection mechanism called a virtual table (cf. C++ virtual functions or vtables) [Szy98]. At runtime, an interface is a typed pointer to a specific virtual table that references the functions (methods) implementing the services exposed by the interface. The framework employs a run time engine that creates COM objects. COM objects are also automatically garbage collected.

DCOM (1996) extends COM with distribution, based on the DCE RPC mechanism. The component model itself is unchanged.

COM+ (1999) is an extension of DCOM that employs the container approach (see text on EJB and CCM in sections 14.2.2 and 14.2.5), using the Microsoft Transaction Server (MTS) runtime platform. The container intercepts calls to a component, and can execute pre- and post-processing actions to implement various services. Typical services offered include transactions, concurrency control, load balancing and role-based security checks.

COM/COM+ Tools

The COM framework is rather specific to Windows platforms (although it is also implemented on VxWorks). It is supported by several development tools on Windows platforms, such as Visual Studio.

Summary. The COM+ component model focuses on the construction of enterprise distributed applications. It tries to take domain-neutral aspects out of source code and expose them through declarative attributes that can be used to control service context (e.g. process synchronisation, security profiles, automatic transactions) [Box00]. Nevertheless, it is not possible to add new attributes, hence limiting this mechanism for the majority of COM developers. Additionally, COM+ type information management is rather cumbersome, i.e. it uses disparate information formats (e.g. IDL, type libraries, MIDL-generated strings embedded in proxy DLLs), sometimes with no mappings between them. Furthermore, COM+ runtime type information (in the type library) permits us to advertise only the types exported by a component but not component dependencies [Box00].

.NET

Microsoft's .NET component model and framework supports the development of distributed applications in different programming languages, and provides a run-time platform with a number of services. .NET departs from the binary-level interoperability adopted by COM/ COM+ as this was felt to be too limiting. Instead, a .NET compiler translates source code into an intermediate language called the Microsoft Intermediate Language (MSIL), which is similar to Java Byte Code. The common language runtime (CLR), which is similar to a Java Virtual Machine then takes the intermediate language and, on the fly, converts it into machine-specific instructions.

The CLR is able to recognise and execute portable executable (PE) files, which are image files that combine MSIL code with metadata (stored in metadata tables and heaps). This approach avoids the need for multiple and disparate metadata formats (e.g. type libraries, headers and IDL files) and enables the generic use of reflection, serialisation and dynamic code generation in a type safe manner [MG02].

MSIL compilers are responsible for automatically emitting metadata into the PE file (e.g. information describing types, members, references, inheritance, etc.). The runtime environment then uses this binary metadata information (cf. managed data) to locate and load classes, control memory usage, resolve invocation targets, manage runtime context boundaries, enforce security and compile to a particular computer architecture by using specific just-in-time (JIT) compilers. Metadata is .NET's language-neutral way of providing binary information describing: assemblies (e.g. unique identification, dependencies on other assemblies, security permissions), types (e.g. base classes, implemented interfaces, visibility), members (e.g. methods, fields, properties, events) and attributes (i.e. extra metadata that modifies the properties of types and members).

.NET particularly addresses the programming of services for Web-based software development. For this purpose, The .NET framework is complemented by a set of unified class libraries for standard programming (e.g. I/O, math, etc.), for accessing operating system services (e.g. network, thread, cryptography, etc.), for debugging and for building enterprise services (e.g. transactions, events, messaging, etc.). These libraries include a set of classes (called ASP.NET), which are tailored to the development of Web-based applications. ASP.NET provides an infrastructure with a set of controls that simplify both the server side (web forms that mirror the typical HTML user interface, e.g. buttons, list boxes, etc.) and client-side programming (check client capabilities and choose the appropriate interface). The ASP.NET infrastructure also includes an HTTP runtime (different from the CLR) which is an asynchronous multi-threaded execution engine that processes HTTP commands. The HTTP runtime employs a pipeline of HTTP modules that route HTTP requests to a specific handler (a managed .NET class).

Technical Description

- *Component types:* the *assembly* is the .NET abstraction that most resembles a component. The *manifest* is the component descriptor; it gathers in a single place all the information about an assembly: exported and imported methods and events, code, metadata and resources. Because of the programming language approach, the main .NET programming language, C#, which looks very much like Java, includes some features of a component model: e.g., (first class) events and extensible metadata. The compiler not only produces MSIL byte code but also generates, in the manifest, the interface description of the component (the assembly), in the form of a list of import and export types.
- *Syntactic Support in Interfaces:* the Common Type System (CTS) supports the definition and use of types across different languages. Metadata provides a uniform mechanism for storing and retrieving information about types. Together, these two facilities provide the basis of multilingual integration. Additionally,

.NET provides a Common Language Specification (CLS) that describes a set of language features (e.g. primitive and composite types, natural-sized types, references, exceptions) and rules for using these features (e.g. defining, creating, binding and persisting types). This specification expresses a set of naming and designing guidelines for mapping features between different languages [Cor01].

- *Extra-functional properties:* .NET does not provide any support for analysing extra-functional properties. It supports metadata at run-time, which gives some possibilities for checking properties at run-time. For example, contract-based interfaces with pre- and post-conditions can be implemented using this feature. .NET does not provide any support for real-time applications. Further, it's memory requirements and relatively poor performance have so far excluded it from the embedded systems domain.

- *Lifecycle*: Unlike when using traditional DLLs, the .NET model includes visibility control, which allows assemblies (and their modules) to be local to an application, and thus different DLLs with same name can run simultaneously. Further, each assembly has versioning information about itself and about the assemblies it depends on, provided either in the form of attributes in the code source or as command line switches provided when building the manifest. Version control is delegated to the dynamic loader, which selects the right version, local or distant, based on the assembly's version information and on a set of default rules.

Overview of .NET Environments

- *Supported languages:* in contrast to the (open) OMG approach (see below) wherein separate formalisms (and files), are used to indicate component related information, languages and compilers being unchanged, .NET is a proprietary approach, in which the program contains information relevant to relationships with other components, and the compiler is responsible for generating the information needed at run-time. Current platforms include support for the C# and Visual Basic languages among others.

- *Availability:* .NET is used in Microsoft Windows 2000 and XP platforms. Some parts of it are ported to Windows CE. The Mono initiative (http://go-mono.com) is developing an open source implementation of the .NET Development Framework. Mono also includes a C# compiler, a runtime for the Common Language Infrastructure and a set of class libraries. In addition, Rotor is a 'shared source' CLI implementation (see http://www.microsoft.com/downloads/details.aspx?Family-Id=3A1C93FA-7462-47D0-8E56-8DD34C6292F0&displaylang=en) that is supported by Microsoft.

Summary
.NET is Microsoft's new paradigm for service development. It uses self-describing components (assemblies) and a common language runtime to tackle the limitations of COM/ COM+. Each .NET assembly sets the scope for type names, and explicitly represents component dependencies. Moreover, assemblies avoid the fragmentation of disparate meta-information sources because the metadata is automatically compiled into the image PE file. Finally, .NET type information is extensible (via system attributes), can be applied to different elements (e.g. classes, methods, properties) and is available at runtime via reflection.

CORBA and CCM

The Common Object Request Broker Architecture (CORBA) is standardised by the Object Management Group (OMG) as a middleware infrastructure and programming model for assembling and deploying distributed applications. It is part of the Object Management Architecture (OMA) [St00] which consists of

- the *CORBA bus* which maintains information about the location of components and delivers requests and responses in a standard way.
- *CORBAservices* which are predefined objects supplying functions required by most distributed applications (naming, events, security, etc.).
- *CORBAfacilities* that are object frameworks that standardise data management and user interfaces.
- *domain interfaces* that are objects for specific domains such as finance, the health industry, etc.
- *application objects* that are objects specific to the application.

CORBA has evolved over the years as reflected in the release of three main versions of the standard. The first version simply defined a distributed object model that separated interfaces from implementations. CORBA v1 also specified a common set of services and facilities that aided in the development of distributed applications by integrating mechanisms for naming, event communication, lifecycle management, etc.

CORBA version 2 focused on ORB interoperability (v1 did not impose an inter-ORB protocol), and object activation management by defining the Internet Inter-ORB Protocol (IIOP) which enables interoperability across multiple ORB products, and the Portable Object Adapter (POA; see more below) which renders server objects portable and also offers various server-side configuration policies. The use of an IDL compiler combined with the runtime ORB manages cross-language, cross-platform and cross-location interoperation, while the TCP/IP-based IIOP protocol assures cross vendor interoperability.

Finally, CORBA version 3, adopted in 2001, standardises the CORBA Component Model (CCM) which adds features and services that enable the implementation, configuration, assembly and deployment of distributed component-based applications.

The first two CORBA versions tackled interoperability through a distributed object model, whereas v3 standardises a full component model. CCM increases integration and flexibility by automating tedious and error prone tasks that are usually solved by developers in ad hoc ways (e.g. deploying and installing implementations activating and configuring services, performing lifecycle management, etc.). CCM has been designed on the basis of much accumulated experience of using CORBA services.

The CCM is a server-side component model that is used to assemble and deploy multilingual components. CCM standardises and automates the component development cycle (from specification to deployment) by defining a middleware infrastructure and a set of support tools. The architecture supports the definition of interfaces supported by the components, automates their implementation and packs the components in assembly files (cf. JARs, DLLs) that can be automatically deployed on server hosts. The architecture uses proven design patterns [GHJV94] that enable the automation of code generation and associated usage of a container infrastructure that mediates component access to system services for handling security, transactions, events

and persistence [Cob00]. CCM focuses on the provision of the generic system services required by server applications and implemented by the container, thus freeing
applications from complex and error prone tasks and allowing developers to concentrate on business logic details. In short, the goals of CCM are very closely related to
those of EJB.

Technical Description

- *Component types:* these are similar to the corresponding EJB categories; i.e. session and entity categories are supported.
- *Syntactic Support in Interfaces:* A component interface is composed of ports,
  which can be of several types:
  o *facets:* named interfaces;
  o *receptacles:* named connection points representing external dependencies on
    other components' facets (cf. required interfaces);
  o *event sources:* emit events;
  o *event sinks:* consume events;
  o *attributes:* named values, intended primarily for use in component configura-
    tion.
- Other Support in Interfaces: None.
- Support for Introspection: This is available via the Interface Repository which
  maintains meta-information on available interfaces.
- Supported Programming languages: CCM is a language independent model.
- Required "Middleware"/Framework Support: CCM, like EJB, is based on the
  notion of a container. A container is automatically generated for each component
  implementation and constitutes the component's view of the surrounding environment [CCM]. The container shields components from the details of the underlying platform, and provides a framework (a standard runtime API) for seamless
  and automatic integration of core services [Cob00]. The container provides a set
  of uniform interfaces (called internal interfaces) that support communication with
  standard system services like transactions, security, persistence, and event notification). The types of internal interfaces available depends on the component category (i.e., service, session, process and entity; cf. the related EJB definitions). The
  container is also responsible for using callbacks to notify its hosted components of
  certain events (e.g. related to persistence, transactions) [WSO00].
- Extra-functional properties: CCM does not provide any support for analysing extra
  functional properties.
- Lifecycle: For each component type there is an associated 'home' component that
  is responsible for attributing primary keys and instantiating components. Furthermore, the container uses an activation framework (e.g. ServantActivater, Servant-
  Locator) that exploits CORBA's POA to control a component's lifecycle (e.g. activation, deactivation, lookup) according to a chosen policy. This way it is possible to control (depending on the component category) the activation and passivation of components, in co-operation with the persistence service, on a per-method,
  per-transaction, per-component (via specific call-backs) or per-container basis
  (this is slightly more general than the related EJB facility). Along with these lifecycle policies, CCM also standardises management policies that determine the

way containers handle (on a component's behalf) transactions, security, events and persistence. The container intercepts requests from clients and, according to requirements declared in the components XML configuration file, enables and executes pre-processing strategies (e.g. activation, transaction, persistence, pooling, caching) before delegating requests to the component. CCM explicitly supports the development process with automated mechanisms to generate and configure the runtime container [CCM]. Specifically, the CCM Component Implementation Framework (CIF) defines a set of APIs and tools that automate the code generation of several management strategies (e.g. lifecycle, transactions, security, events and persistence policies). This framework automatically exposes different aspects of the implementation that may be embedded in a component's implementation [WSO00]. CCM also standardises a declarative language, called the Component Implementation Definition Language (CIDL), that is used to describe component implementations and associated persistence requirements [WSO00]. A CIF compiler reads a component's CIDL description and generates default component behaviour (e.g. introspection, activation, state management). The resulting implementations are called executors and provide hook methods that may be used by developers to later add custom behaviour and adapt the default implementation [WSO00].

The CIDL compiler is also responsible for generating component descriptors, which are XML files used to define the component category (e.g. entity, session), features (e.g. ports), policies (e.g. lifetime, transactions, security, events and persistence) and segmentation (i.e. delineation of independently-deployable units). CCM defines several XML descriptor file-types, i.e. component descriptor, software package descriptor, assembly descriptor and property file descriptor, which conform to the WWW Consortium's Open Software Description (OSD). Component segments and descriptors are joined in a package file, i.e. a archive file that contains one or more implementations of a component and the associated UML description files. Component packages may be installed or grouped with other packages in an assembly file. Descriptor files are used at deployment-time to automatically create and configure the required POA hierarchy and to resolve component dependencies.

CCM Environments
Few commercial implementations of EJB have been developed. To date, the most prominent implementation has been developed in the context of the TAO CORBA platform by the University of Washington [WSO00].

Real-Time CORBA

Real-time CORBA (RT-CORBA) is an optional extension to CORBA that is designed for applications with real-time requirements, such as avionics mission computing, as well as those with stringent adaptive real-time requirements, such as telecommunications call processing. It is integrated with the CORBA 2.5 specification. RT-CORBA provides standard interfaces and policies that allow applications to configure and control the following system resources:

- Processor resources: thread pools, priority mechanisms, intra-process mutexes, and a global scheduling service for real-time applications with fixed priorities.
- Communication resources: protocol properties and explicit bindings to server objects using priority bands and private connections.
- Memory resources: buffering requests in queues and bounding the size of thread pools.

RT-CORBA has the advantage of being platform independent, in that a wide variety of programming languages support CORBA interfaces. RT-CORBA has a particular potential benefit to the embedded, real-time systems market, as until recently, many such systems have had to define highly platform specific approaches to implementing many of the features proposed by the CORBA standard.

Analysis
RT-CORBA in itself only supports very general and abstract control over system resources. It is up to the system designer to use the standard to configure the target system to meet application requirements in a predictable way. In addition, RT-CORBA has some shortcomings, such as not being suitable for dynamic real-time systems since it is only focused on fixed-priority based systems, and such as not addressing consistency issues.

The OMG's Dynamic Scheduling proposal [OMG01a] aims to overcome the limitations imposed by RT-CORBA in terms of dynamic scheduling. Static scheduling systems can only cope with applications for which resource requirements are known a priori. In such systems, offline analysis allows developers to predict the workload that will be imposed. In contrast, dynamic systems are susceptible to experiencing unexpected dynamic changes at runtime.

The proposal also provides a framework that allows for the development of portable schedulers.

Overall Analysis

The models described in this section represent an evolution from initial light-weight component models with support for component composition, to which support for distribution is added. Later, to support common needs in business applications, the models are extended to support an integrated container-based environment for automating the management of generic, extra-functional, properties such as transactions, security, persistence and event notification. Only one of the models discussed, CCM, is not tied to a particular language (such as Java) or operating system (such as Windows). CCM was designed to align closely with the EJB specification and, apart from language independence, these component models can broadly be considered conceptual equivalents [CCM]. Both support different types of components which automatically determine the available container interfaces and the policies for managing component state and persistence (component managed or container-managed). Furthermore, CCM and EJB define three approaches to the demarcating of transactions (i.e. client-managed, container-managed and server-managed) while COM+ supports only automatic transactions (MTS-managed). Moreover, COM+ defines only one type of component. This leads to a simpler programming model, but also leads to limited expressiveness and a deep dependence on the MTS environment. Despite being more difficult and complex to learn and manage, CCM and EJB may be considered more flexible and open than COM+ which builds of top of proprietary operating system services. Nevertheless, COM+ is a binary standard that allows the integration of several languages without compromising the performance.

Another significant aspect is the recurrent use of meta-information for describing the structure and behaviour of components. Meta-information is widely used in CCM (e.g. the interface repository), EJB (e.g. bean descriptors) and COM+ (e.g. type libraries) but is particularly visible in .NET where the metadata is embedded in the image files and then extracted using reflection to reason about the system and control assembly, enforce security, manage serialisation, perform compiler optimisations, etc. The combination of meta-information and reflection is an interesting approach for managing type evolution.

Finally, it must be emphasised that these component models are inherently heavyweight and complex. In their present form they are not suitable for deployment in most embedded environments. Nevertheless, they exhibit many potentially interesting features that would clearly be of interest to developers of embedded systems. Research is required to make such features available in component model environments that are considerably more lightweight and which, probably, can be tailored to specific environments on a highly configurable what-you-want-is-what-you-pay-for basis.

Some initial work in this area has been carried out. For example, THINK ('THINK Is Not a Kernel', http://sardes.inrialpes.fr/research/think.shtml) from Inria Alpes is a minimal, low-level, component model that has been used to flexibly build software configurations at the operating system level. This develops earlier OS-level efforts such as Knit from the University of Utah, and the Spring Kernel, but adds modern notions of independent run-time deployment of components, and support for multiple interfaces. Similarly, the OpenCOM component model from Lancaster University, UK, is a lightweight component model that is being used to develop low-level programmable networking software. This model incorporates lightweight reflective mechanisms to assist in the run-time deployment and dynamic reconfiguration of component compositions. Both of these component models (THINK and OpenCOM) have the potential to be applied in embedded environments, although work is required to validate this approach. Finally, Washington University, St Louis, has carried out interesting research on slimlining the CCM for application to embedded environments. This has also involved extending the CCM with support for QoS specification and validation.

14.2   Component Models for Embedded System Design

As the next step in this overview, we survey component models and platforms that have been developed specifically for application to embedded systems. Typically, component implementations are given in a compilable language (C being the most common) and are composed before compilation (unlike the models examined in section 14.1). Execution semantics are given by a run-time executive or a simple RTOS.

Programmable Logic Controllers: The IEC 61131-3 Standard

Introduction

In the area of Industrial Automation, PLCs (Programmable Logic Controllers) are a widely-used technology. However, for the last twenty years, the corresponding applications have been written in many different languages, resulting in problems for technicians, maintenance personnel and system designers. For instance, there are numerous versions of the so-called ladder diagram language, and furthermore this language is poorly equipped with facilities such as control over program execution, definition and manipulation of data structures, arithmetic operations, and hierarchical program decomposition.

These problems led to the constitution of a working group within the IEC (International Electrotechnical Commission), with the aim of defining a standard for the complete design of programmable logic controllers. While previous efforts have been made, IEC 61131 has received worldwide international and industrial acceptance. The first document introducing the general concepts was published in 1992 and this was followed by the definition of equipment requirements and tests. The core of the standard is now in its third part, published in 1993, which describes the harmonisation and coordination of the already existing programming languages. The eight parts of the standard are available at http://www.iec.ch.

Note that, due to the fact that there are many types of hardware, the aim is not toward a single programming system for all controllers. Instead, certified IEC 61131-3 programming systems have an agreed degree of source code compatibility and have a similar look and feel. Yet they will differ in debugging features, speed, etc.

PLCopen (www.plcopen.org) was founded in 1992 as an international organisation of users and producers, with the aim of promoting the development and use of compatible software for PLCs. PLCopen offers tests for IEC 61131-3 compliance, but also a course, designed for experienced or beginner PLC programmers who want to develop software according to IEC 61131-3 and for support and implementation engineers who modify systems programmed according to IEC 61131-3. There are also smaller user-only organisations, e.g. EXERA, which propose tests for the compliance of programming environments.

Technical Description
- *Component types:* An application is divided into a number of blocks.
- *Supported languages:* A block is written in any of the languages proposed in the standard. There are two textual languages (ST, IL) and three graphical languages (FBD, LD, SFC).
  - o *Function Block Diagram (FBD)* is used for the description and regulation of signal and data flows through function blocks. It can nicely express the interconnection of control system algorithms and logic;
  - o *Structured Text (ST)* is a high level textual language, with a Pascal-like syntax;
  - o *Instruction List (IL)* is an assembler-like language, found in a wide range of PLC's;
  - o *Ladder Diagram (LD)* is a graphical language based on relay ladder logic, which allows the connection of previously defined blocks; for historical reasons, it is the most frequently used in actual PLC programs;

o *Sequential Function Chart (SFC)* is used to combine in a structured way units defined in the four languages above; it mainly describes the sequential behaviour of a control system and defines control sequences that are time- and event-driven. It can express both high-level and low-level parts of a program.

- *Visibility of Underlying Hardware:* While it aims at enhancing portability of PLC programs, the IEC 61131-3 has several features referring to the actual underlying hardware (variables can be linked to physical addresses, etc.)

- *Syntactic Support:* Each functional block has a set of in-ports and out-ports. IEC 61131-3 also requires *strong data typing* and provides support to define data structures which can be used to transmit information as a whole between different units. More precisely, while a function simply computes its output from its input, without internal variables, a function block consists of a set of data, together with the algorithms handling these data, similarly to the definition of a class in an object-oriented framework (no further comparison can be made, though). Input and output parameters are formally defined to ensure a clean interface between different function blocks. This notion thus appears as an important feature, meant to encourage the development of well-structured software: blocks can be viewed as the basic components of a program. Since it is re-usable within a given program, but also from outside, an increased use of such blocks can lead to the construction of powerful libraries.

- *Support for Functional/Extra-Functional Properties:* Function block execution may be periodic or event-driven. There is no support for analysing properties other than syntactic properties.

Tools for the IEC 61131-3 Standard

Introduction

Today, all large suppliers of PLCs have announced IEC 61131-3 compliant development systems. They propose different programming environments for code generation for various hardware, with some architectural aspects as parameters. For instance: Siemens with STEP7; Allen Bradley with Control Logic; and Schneider-Electric with PL7PRO.

There are also smaller suppliers, either for PLCs only, or for programming platforms only. Of course, due to developments in the industrial market producers may not always be 100% standard compliant.

Assessment and Further Needs

The IEC 61131-3 standard is widely adopted. Compared with traditional programming systems, it appears to be a major step forward. The new set of languages is said [Lew98] to significantly improve the quality of PLC software, and in particular to overcome the weaknesses of previous versions, especially with respect to the above mentioned Ladder Programming. The improvement also concerns the communication and software model. Finally, a major benefit for end-users using IEC 61131-3 compliant products will be inter-system portability.

However, the IEC 61131-3 standard is not fully mature and the portability issue remains an important problem. For instance, users feel the need to have textual files that can be used to connect different platforms. Furthermore, some ambiguous semantics remain for the languages. Finally, new requirements emerge: systems will become more distributed with more parallel processing. Therefore, new standards are under development, such as the function block standard IEC 1499, not to replace the former but to work in conjunction with it.

Koala

Introduction
Koala is a component model and an architectural description language that successfully works for consumer electronics devices. Koala is developed and used at Philips. It was designed to build software control units for consumer products such as televisions, video recorders, CD and DVD players and recorders, and combinations of these (e.g. TV-VCRs). Koala is currently in use by a few hundred software engineers for the creation of a family of televisions. More information on Koala can be found in [vO02], [vOvdLK00], and [FEHC02].

Technical Description
- *Component types:* A Koala component is a piece of code that can interact with its environment through explicit interfaces only. As a consequence, a basic Koala component has no implicit dependencies to other Koala components.
  - o A *Component Implementation* is a directory containing a set of C and header files that may use each other in arbitrary ways, but communication with other components is routed only through header files generated by the Koala compiler, based upon the binding between components;
  - o The directory also contains a component definition file, describing among other things the interfaces of the component;
- *Visibility of Underlying Hardware:* The Koala component model itself is abstract and hardware-independent. Hardware dependency is encapsulated in particular components. The entire development environment is tailored for the development of particular product families which improves the efficiency of the development process at the expense of generality.
- *Syntactic Support:* Connections between components are expressed in terms of interfaces which are described as a small set of semantically related functions. Koala identifies two types of interface: *provides* interfaces and *requires* interfaces. Koala *provides* interfaces are similar to those known from COM and Java. A component may provide multiple interfaces, which is a useful way of handling evolution and diversity. Koala *requires* interfaces identify interfaces of other components and interfaces required from the environment of the component. All communication is routed through such *requires* interfaces. Koala interfaces can be optional. An optional *requires* interface need not be connected – an optional *provides* interface need not be implemented. This allows components to fine tune themselves to their environment, by observing what the environment can and cannot deliver.

  Connectors connect *requires* interfaces of one component to *provides* interfaces of another component. Naturally, in compound components it is also possible to connect *provides* interfaces of subcomponents to *provides* interfaces of the compound component, and similarly for *requires* interfaces.

o *Interface Compatibility*: it is possible to connect a *requires* interface to a *provides* interface of a wider type; the *provides* interface should implement all of the functions of the *requires* interface, but it may implement more than that;

o In addition, *glue code* can be added to the binding between interfaces. Simple glue code can be written in an expression language within Koala; more complicated code can be written in C. This allows the programmer to easily to overcome a certain category of syntactic and semantic differences. A special case of glue code is code that switches a binding between components. Such a mechanism to select between components can be implemented in C, but it occurs so frequently that a special concept for this is defined in the language: the switch. The compiler converts a switch internally to a set of Koala expressions, which has the advantage that it can perform certain optimisations, such as reducing the switch to a straight binding if the switch is set to a position that is known at compile time. The binding through the glue module and the switch are examples of connectors. The Koala language defines no other connectors.

• *Support for Behavioural Properties:* No extra-functional properties are specified in the interfaces of components. In a system design, it is possible to specify the ordering of tasks using precedence relations and mutual exclusion. There is also support for deriving some system properties from components. For example, the memory consumption of the system can be calculated form the memory consumption of the constituent components, which is a parameterised value.

• *Support for Timing Properties:* There is no support for timing properties.

• *Support for Performance Properties:* There is no support for modelling performance properties.

Koala Tools

• *Supported languages for component implementations:* A component resolves to an implementation in C language. Koala uses the "Koala language" for constructing applications from components by connecting component interfaces.

• *Supported development platforms:* A proprietary development platform exists that includes the Koala language and a C compiler which composes components.

• Supported target platforms: Proprietary platforms only.

• *Status:* The use of Koala is growing within Philips. There are plans to build additional development environment tools, such as visual composition and visual component selection.

• *Availability:* There are plans to publish Koala as an open source standard.

• *Degree of Automation:* The Koala compiler composes components and makes optimisations such as removing unused interfaces and resolving connections of conditional types. Component binding is static based on C code. The compiler can also optimise the memory usage of the application (the so-called footprint), by eliminating functionality in a component that is not used. Most of the documentation (header files, etc.) must be created manually. This has not been seen as a large overhead, although there are plans to improve this process by building a set of supporting tools.

- *Run-Time Infrastructure:* As in many small embedded systems, a system using the Koala component model is a single-process image, built on a top of a small real-time kernel with pre-emptive scheduling, which separates high frequency from low frequency tasks. Separate activities can be allocated to light-weight threads, which are managed by the kernel.
- *Analysis Support for:*
  - o *Memory Footprint:* The Koala component model and its implementation to some extent allows calculating and predicting resource consumption. For example, memory consumption can be estimated at composition time (compile time) as mentioned; and this feature is built into the Koala compiler. For technical detail see [FEHC02]. Using this calculation model it is possible to budget the memory for particular components and, by a parameterisation of the interface, to define the particular properties of the components.
  - o *Library Support:* Koala components are stored in a repository. The repository is a set of packages, where each package is a set of component and interface definitions, some of which are public, and some of which are private.

Summary
Koala is an example of the implementation of the component-based approach that works successfully in a large industrial company. It is a good example of an evolutionary approach to component-based development. The design and implementation fulfils the following requirements [CL02, Ch. 12] related to the component-based approach:

- It devises a technique with which components can be freely composed into products, as the main approach to deal with diversity in a product population. The technique must work in resource-constrained environments such as televisions and video recorders (which are typically 10 years behind PCs in computing power).
- Make the product architectures as explicit as possible, to manage complexity.
- Let components make as few assumptions as possible about their environment.
- Allow for parameterised components that are, when instantiated, as efficient as dedicated components.
- Allow for various ways of connecting components; more specifically, allow for adding glue code to connections between components.

These requirements are valid for many embedded and RT systems. Does this mean that the Koala component model is so general that it is possible to use it in other domains? In many aspects this appears to be the case. The basic principles, which are derived from widely-acknowledged principles of Component Based Development, are valid in general for embedded systems. In implementation, in some parts, domain knowledge is implicitly built in (due to various reasons, e.g. to improve development efficiency and performance). In order to use Koala as a general component-model for embedded systems, some parts should be removed or explicitly separated as domain-specific. The Koala component model provides a good basis for further improvement of achieving predictability of extra functional properties.

The strong points of Koala are:

- Separation of the *provided* from the *required* interfaces of a component.
- Interaction with the environment, including the underlying hardware-dependent services is exclusively via interfaces.
- There is a strict definition of the component development process, including quality assurance, and a form of component certification.

The weak points of Koala do not lie in the component model itself, but to a large extent in the lack of tools supporting efficient development on a large scale. Currently, Koala developers must conform to rules that can be violated, unless checked automatically. Potential tool functionality could include the following.

- tools that manage components (component repositories, component browsers, visual environments, etc.);
- checks that a component has no other dependencies than through its explicit interfaces;
- generation of glue could to some extent be automated;
- support for the analysis and composition of timing and performance (and some other properties) is rudimentary and can be further developed. One obstacle is that many of these properties are hardware and platform dependent and thus cannot be a part of a general model.

Rubus Component Model

Introduction
Rubus is a small Real-Time Operating System, developed by Arcticus Systems AB (http://www.arcticus.se/). Rubus is divided into one part supporting time-triggered execution, and one part supporting event-triggered execution. The time-triggered execution part is intended to support hard real-time applications with a deterministic execution mechanism. In order to support component-based development of hard real-time systems, Arcticus Systems AB, together with Department of Computer Engineering at Malardalen University, have developed a component model and associated development tools for use with the Rubus operating system [IN02]. The component model is used in projects within Volvo Construction Equipment Components AB. We include a short description of this model, in order to illustrate how a component model can be developed on top of a runtime execution platform.

Technical Description
- *Component types:* A basic Software Component consists of behaviour, persistent state, a set of in-ports, a set of out-ports and an entry function. The entry function provides the main functionality. A *task* provides the thread of execution for a component. The entry function takes as an argument a set of in-ports, the persistent state, and references to the out-ports. In [NGS+01], it is stated that entry function code may not contain any call to communication services. Instead, the compiler that compiles the system description automatically generates the communication infrastructure. For example, if an out-port of a component A is connected to an in-port of a component B, the generated code (system task) will copy the information automatically under given synchronisation and timing requirements.

The *attributes* of a task are *Task Id, Period, Release Time, Deadline*, and *WCET*. In addition, precedence and mutual exclusion ordering between tasks can be specified.

- *Visibility of Underlying Hardware:* System descriptions do not mention hardware configurations; they are intended to be used by a schedule synthesis tool.
- *Syntactic Support:* Each Component has in-ports and out-ports for communication. Tasks in the safety-critical part communicate without buffering. There is a type system for data.
- *Support for Behavioural Properties:* No functional properties are specified in the interfaces of components. In a system design, it is possible to specify the ordering of tasks using precedence relations and mutual exclusion.
- *Support for Timing Properties.* Timing requirements are specified by release-time, deadline, WCET and period. There is a tool for schedulability analysis.

Rubus Tools

- *Supported languages:* The functionality of a system can be mode-dependent. Temporal coordination between tasks is specified for each Mode by a *software circuit* or *dataflow model* which specifies the output-input connections between tasks, and timing constraints on tasks and their composition. Precedence/exclusion information can also be included.
- *Supported languages for component implementations:* C.
- *Supported development platforms:* Available on Windows and Linux platforms.
- *Supported target platforms:* Rubus OS is ported to a number of target and program development tools.
- *Status:* Commercial product.
- *Degree of Automation:* A tool designated "Rubus Visual Studio" exists. This manages the components available and their associated source files, so that components can be fetched from a library and instantiated into new designs.
- *Analysis Support for Timing Properties:* Scheduling is derived automatically from component descriptions, using task attributes and precedence/exclusion information. Time-triggered tasks are statically scheduled, and event-triggered tasks are scheduled on-line by fixed-priority pre-emptive scheduling. There is currently no support for performance properties, reliability or safety analysis.
- *Support for Distribution:* Rubus supports distribution over buses that support time synchronisation (such as TTP and TT-CAN)

Summary
Rubus is an example of how a component model can be developed on top of an existing RTOS. The model makes system integration easier by allowing timing analysis to be performed based on a system description. The development of the Rubus component model has been a significant improvement for software development inside Volvo CE. For future development, the Rubus platform may face a shortage of tools that support component-based system development, in a similar way as was discussed for Koala. There are currently no automated checks for:

- confirming that components use only explicit interfaces for communication;
- WCET (worst-case execution time) analysis of components;

- allocation of tasks to processing nodes.

PECOS

Introduction

The PECOS project (http://www.pecos-project.org/) [CL02, NAD+02, WZS02, PEC], funded by the EC under the IST Program (project number: IST-1999-20398), aims to enable component-based software development for embedded systems such as smart cell phones, PDAs, and industrial field devices. In order to validate component-based software development (CBSD) for embedded devices the project has developed hardware and software for a field device as a case study of embedded systems with real-time requirements.

The project has pursued four main activities:

- *CBSD processes:* The PECOS process aims to enable CBSD for embedded systems, specifically for field devices. It addresses the major technological deficiencies of state-of-the art component technology with respect to extra-functional requirements, such as limited CPU power, memory and hard real-time.
- Component Model:
  - o *Interfaces* are defined by input ports and output ports, and connectors connect compatible ports. Ports have basic types.
  - o *Component Types:* active components (with their own threads), passive components (encapsulating behaviour without threads), event components (triggered by events).
  - o The *attributes* of a component can specify memory consumption, WCET, cycle time, priority.
- *ADL:* The *CoCo Component Language* is used for the specification of components, entire embedded devices, and architecture and system families. In CoCo, a composite active component (with a thread) specifies execution rules (a so-called *schedule*) for its subcomponents.
- *Lightweight composition techniques:* CoCo provides the concept of abstract components, and composition rules to allow composition checking.
- *Platforms and tools:* A translation from CoCo to target languages such as C++ and Java has been developed. The PECOS model is mapped to a prioritised, preemptive, multithreaded system to realise the different components: passive, active and event. A technique has been introduced to enable data exchange between components. The developed tools are embedded in the open source ECLIPSE framework as plug-ins.

Other Characteristics

- *Supported Languages:* Includes a composition language CoCo that is translated to C++ and Java. A CoCo component structure is mapped to a corresponding class structure. Connectors are mapped to shared instance variables in the enclosing object. Ports map to set and get methods.

- *Scheduling:* The model does not specify anything regarding the scheduling of components, what scheduler can be used and how schedules can be checked to see if they are actually feasible. It only assumes that there is a scheduler.
- *Availability:* It is embedded in the ECLIPSE open source framework http://www.eclipse.org/ as plug-ins. It can include any proprietary integration platforms (developed by companies such as ABB, Boeing, Dassault, EADS, Thales). To date, ABB has started to integrated the model with its proprietary platform.

Summary
PECOS is unique in the sense that it addresses several aspects of component-based software engineering: development and lifecycle process, the provision of a component model that deals with temporal and other extra-functional attributes, architectural modelling and development tools. However the model is still not fully developed and it remains to be seen how successful its implementation will be.

14.3   Integration Platforms for Heterogeneous System Design

In this section, we review some platforms that are intended for the modelling of systems that are typically composed of heterogeneous components. A system design is represented as an architecture populated by interconnected components. Components can often be represented in different languages, formalisms, or even modelling paradigms.

Composition is performed at design time, and typically glue code is generated automatically. The software components are wrapped with a run-time executive, which schedules the (compiled and linked) components.

A major emphasis here is that the architecture description should be executable; so that simulation can be used as the major tool for design V&V. Analysis techniques can use information visible at the architectural level. Typical attributes could be period, deadline, and execution time for schedulability analysis, code size, etc.

Meta-H

Introduction
Meta-H (http://www.htc.honeywell.com/metah/) is a domain-specific ADL dedicated to avionics systems which was developed at Honeywell Labs in 1993 under the sponsorship of DARPA and the US Army. A significant set of tools (graphical editor, typing, safety, reliability, and timing/loading/schedulability analyzers, code generator, etc.) has already been prototyped and used in the context of several experimentation projects. In 2001, Meta-H was taken as the basis of a standardisation effort aiming at defining an Avionics Architecture Description Language (AADL) standard under the authority of SAE. This emerging AADL is a domain-specific ADL developed to meet the special needs of embedded real-time systems such as avionics systems. In particular, the language can describe standard control and data flow mechanisms used in avionics systems, and important extra-functional aspects such as timing requirements, fault and error behaviours, time and space partitioning, and safety and certification properties.

Technical Description
Meta-H in itself is only an ADL, and furthermore it is still under development. The rules for producing conformant component implementations are given by the current Toolset. In this description, we therefore describe Meta-H together with this toolset.

- Component types include:
  - *Macro*, which is a hierarchical composition of connected parts.
  - *Application*, which is the highest level composition, and combines a software architecture and a hardware architecture.
  - *processes*, units of scheduling with a protected address space in a partitioned system, and a unit of binding to a processor. The control structure of a process must have a main outer loop, which calls the Meta-H dispatcher on each iteration.
  - *packages* and *monitors* (as in Ada).
- *Visibility of Underlying Hardware:* The underlying platform can be described by means of a hardware architecture in terms of *processors, memories, channels,* and *devices*. A mapping from Component types to Hardware may be provided.
- *Syntactic Support:* The interface of a process or macro contains declarations of *ports, packages, monitors, subprograms, out events,* and *in events*. Components are connected by *connection declarations*, giving:
  - *port connections* that provide message transfer between ports.
  - *event connections* that control signals, events, to an aperiodic process (process dispatch), or to modes (for mode switch).
  - *equivalences* that offer shared data and resources in terms of monitors and packages. Connections are strongly typed. There is no inheritance.
- *Support for Behavioural Properties:* No functional properties are specified in the interface of components. A system can be described in terms of *modes* which are run-time configurations of active processes and connections. Mode interfaces contain events. The *run-time semantics* describe how the run-time executive works when invoking the processes in a system.
- *Support for Timing Properties:* Components of type process can have (worst-case) execution times specified. This is the duration of the main outer loop on one invocation. Processes can be given periods and deadlines in a given system. There is a tool for schedulability analysis.
- *Support for Performance Properties:* None.
- *Support for Reliability Analysis:* Components can be equipped with reliability models, which are Markov chains that relate fault events and error states. System descriptions must describe how errors propagate between components. A reliability analysis tool combines the reliability models of individual components into a global Markov chain, and uses a separate tool (in this case SURE/PAVE/PAWS tool from NASA Langley) or Markov chain analysis.
- *Support for Safety Analysis:* Each process has its own address space in an implementation. Safety levels and memory allocation properties can be declared for components. The Meta-H *partitioning analyzer* tool can partially verify that no error in a component with lower safety level can propagate to a process with higher safety level. In terms of safety/security modelling and analysis, the tool can check

if the safety/security mechanisms provided by Meta-H will enforce a specified safety/security policy. (e.g., rights of objects to access other objects.

Rubus Tools
Some are available at http://www.rl.af.mil/tech/programs/dasada/tools.html.

- *Supported languages:* Rubus accepts ADL specifications written in the emerging SAE standard Avionics Architecture Description Language (AADL) in both graphical and textual formats.
- *Supported languages for component implementations:* Ada, C; many concepts are closely inspired by Ada.
- *Supported development platforms:* Windows NT and Solaris.
- *Supported target platforms:* Portable Ada 95 and POSIX targets are available; application source code may be written in C or Ada.
- *Status:* Core toolset are fairly mature (beta-quality); but reliability analysis and general system safety specification/analysis are at the proof-of-concept stage; technologies for blended time driven/ event-driven workloads, dynamic reconfiguration, and distributed hard real-time scheduling are the subject of ongoing research.
- *Availability:* Available under zero fee license; ITAR.
- *Degree of Automation:* Automatic production of the executable image is possible. Rubus can perform software/ hardware allocation, and generate tailored/efficient middleware to integrate a system.
- *Analysis Support for:*
  o *Syntactic Properties:* AADL syntax/semantic checking can translate textual to graphical and graphical to textual AADL, and check compliance of source components with AADL specifications.
  o *Functional Properties:* It is currently being investigated how to (automatically) extract hybrid automata models from the generated code in order to analyse the target system.
  o *Timing Properties:* Real-time schedulability modelling and analysis.
  o *Reliability Properties:* See above.
  o *Safety Properties:* See above.

Ptolemy II

Introduction
Ptolemy (http://www.ptolemy.eecs.berkeley.edu/) is a simulation and rapid prototyping framework for heterogeneous systems. The focus is on embedded systems, particularly those that mix technologies, including for example analogue and digital electronics, hardware and software, and electronics and mechanical devices. The focus is also on systems that are complex in the sense that they mix widely different operations, such as signal processing, feedback control, sequential decision making, and user interfaces. An overview of the Ptolemy project can be found in [Hyl03].

The Ptolemy software environment has been used for a wide range of applications including signal processing, telecommunications, parallel processing, wireless communication, network design, investment management, modelling of optical communication systems, real-time systems, and hardware/ software co-design. The Ptolemy software has also been used as a laboratory tool for signal processing and communications courses. Currently, the Ptolemy software has hundreds of active users at various sites worldwide in industry, academia, and government.

The first generation of Ptolemy, now called Ptolemy Classic, was written in C++. The current version, Ptolemy II, is written in Java, and produces code in Java.

Since Ptolemy has to cater for many different modelling languages, it cannot define a component model with standardised of component interfaces and composition at the implementation level (C or Java).

Technical Description

- *Component types:* Components, called Actors, are created in different Models of Computation (MoC). Existing MoCs include:
  - o CSP with synchronous rendezvous as a communication mechanism.
  - o Continuous time, where components are described by algebraic or differential relations between inputs and outputs.
  - o Discrete Events, where Actors communicate via events (consisting of a value and a time stamp). Execution of an actor is typically event-triggered. The execution semantics is realised by a discrete-event simulator, which maintains a global time-stamp-sorted queue of pending events. There is an experimental Distributed DE model of computation, using ideas from distributed DE-simulation:
    - ▪ Finite State Machines, which can be used in different contexts.
    - ▪ Process networks: these are Kahn process networks.
    - ▪ Synchronous Dataflow: globally synchronous (discretely clocked) systems.
    - ▪ Synchronous/Reactive: this is similar to the synchronous paradigm.
    - ▪ Giotto: the time triggered approach developed in [HHK01].
- *Syntactic Support:* Actors send and receive data through *ports*. Ptolemy Classic can perform type conversions as in C. In the latest versions of Ptolemy II, there is a polymorphic type system [LX01].
- *Support for Behavioural Properties:* Each Model of Computation defines an abstract execution semantics. These can be used in simulation. Some support for specifying behavioural properties as part of interfaces has been developed [LX01].
- *Support for Timing Properties:* Some Models of Computation have an explicit notion of time. This can be used in simulation to estimate execution times.
- *Support for Performance Properties:* Simulations may also be used to assess performance.
- *Support for Reliability Analysis:* This has not been directly addressed.
- *Support for Safety Analysis:* This has not been directly addressed.

Ptolemy II Tool

- *Supported languages:* There is a rich family of notations for graphical definition of system structure.
- *Supported languages for component implementations:* In Ptolemy Classic, the implementation language is C++. In Ptolemy II, this has changed to Java.

- *Supported development platforms:* Windows, Linux, MacOS, X, Solaris. There is one installation that runs entirely in applets. There are on-going experiments with a distributed simulation platform.
- *Supported target platforms*: In Ptolemy Classic, C implementations can be derived. Ptolemy Classic can generate assembly code for some programmable DSPs. Ptolemy II can generate Java code from a design.
- *Status:* Research Prototype under development.
- *Availability:* Free for download.
- *Degree of Automation:* The Java Definitions of Components is parsed, and there is support for the construction of code generators.
- *Analysis Support:* Analysis support is mainly by the ability to simulate a system.
    - o *Functional Properties:* In principle, Models in the FSM MoC can be parsed and used by external model checking tool.
    - o *Timing Properties:* Timing properties are analysed by simulation. Some means must be devised for importing the timing properties of the actual platform. In some applications, one can use an external hardware simulator.

Analysis
Ptolemy has an important message for Model Based Development: the importance of simulation in embedded systems design. Simulation of functionality and behaviour is often the most practical approach to assess vague requirements like "pleasing" interfaces to human operators, and it may often be the only feasible way to assess performance properties, because these are emergent and not deducible from individual component properties. With respect to the latter properties, it is a research challenge to develop methods that allow us to predict actual performance from simulation results.

Another important point about Ptolemy is that it demonstrate that heterogeneous semantic models can and will exist in systems. There is no need to have a unified computational model. The various models need only be linked, when they communicate through interfaces, and they need only agree on the meaning of entities that are part of the defined interface. Such a minimal agreement is exemplified in the Ptolemy type system.

Metropolis

Introduction
Metropolis (http://www.gigascale.org/metropolis/) is a research project coordinated at UC Berkeley. It is not a mature design environment; it is included here as an example of a research effort which involves a component model, where components are composed at a model level, which is at a higher level of abstraction than C or Java. Metropolis develops an infrastructure such that heterogeneous components of a system can be represented uniformly, and tools for formal methods can be applied naturally.

The core of the infrastructure is a *meta-model of computation*, which allows one to model various communication and computation semantics in a uniform way. The meta-model is defined in a variant of timed automata. By defining different communication primitives and different ways of resolving concurrency, the user can, in effect, specify different models of computation (MoCs). The meta-model is used to represent the function of a system being designed, to generate executables for simulation, and as input to formal methods built in Metropolis for both synthesis and verification at various design stages. There are stated plans to translate specifications given in many existing languages automatically to an appropriate semantics specified using the meta-model.

A set of coordinated tools is being developed as part of the Metropolis project.

Analysis
Metropolis shares objectives with Ptolemy; but is much more ambitious with respect to integration. It aims to replace the individual Java simulation classes for different computational models with a uniform meta-model. Metropolis thus goes beyond a conventional component concept, because it takes source level components and translates them into its own meta language before any simulation, verification, or code generation takes place. Thus it eliminates some of the difficulties in specifying component properties, at the expense of requiring translators from the respective source languages.

A potential difficulty with the Metropolis approach is that the meta-model must be very rich to encompass all desirable properties that one may want to analyse, e.g., performance of a final implementation might not be directly derivable from an operational semantics.

14.4   Hardware/Software Modelling Languages

In this section, we briefly mention some languages that are not component models, but can be used to model embedded systems in a modular way. The models here are mainly included to describe a part of the landscape that is adjacent to component models.

SystemC

SystemC (http://www.systemc.org/) is intended to be a standardised, highly portable technology for system-level models: an alternative to languages such as Verilog or VHDL.

Similar to HDLs, users can construct structural designs in SystemC using modules, ports, and signals. Modules can be instantiated within other modules, enabling structural design hierarchies to be build. Ports and signals enable communication of data between modules, and all ports and signals are declared by the user to have a specific data type. Commonly used data types include bits, bit vectors, characters, integers, floating point numbers, vectors of integers, etc. As in VHDL, concurrent behaviour is modelled using processes.

SystemC 2.0 aims at enabling system-level modelling, i.e., modelling of systems above the RTL level of abstraction. One of the challenges in providing a system-level design language is that there are a wide range of design-level models of computation.

VHDL

VHDL is a hardware description language. It is used in a wide variety of contexts that range from complete systems like personal computers on one hand to the small logical gates on their internal integrated circuits on the other. It supports a module concept, such that abstract behavioural models may hide implementation details. The language VHDL covers the complete range of applications and can be used to model (digital) hardware in a general way.

14.5   Component Models and Integration Platforms: Summary and Conclusions

Current Trends

With respect to the evolution of different component technologies for real-time and embedded systems, we can observe the following: A clear trend is to use widely adopted component technologies for embedded systems. Examples are COM [LCS02] and CORBA (or its adaptation to RT-CORBA). One tries to avoid the cost (in terms of run-time resources) of these technologies by using only those parts of the technology that are necessary. An advantage is that there is already infrastructure available for these technologies, and that systems can interoperate with other system that use these technologies. A disadvantage is that these technologies do not a priori support several properties that are essential for embedded systems.

- *Specialized Technologies.* There are many efforts underway to define component technologies for embedded systems, often dedicated to applications in a certain domain. Examples are Koala and PECOS. These component models seem not to spread very rapidly outside the organisation in which they were created. They serve the purpose of improving the software development process of their organisation. Some of these models define interfaces that are not just syntactic, but include some properties that are essential for their application domain.

  An advantage of these models is that they can be tailor-made for their application domain. Disadvantages are the lack of synergy across application domains, that it is costly to develop tool support, and that such development is harder to justify for proprietary component technologies.

- *High Level Integration Platforms.* In the landscape, we have also included design tools, in which systems are designed by putting together pieces that might be termed components. Examples are Meta-H and Ptolemy. The functions of these tools are in some sense analogous to, e.g., MATLAB/Simulink. The advantage is that they support a variety of design notations. However, "components" can be assembled only in the supporting tool, meaning that different developments must all be developed in the same environment. In this perspective, these tools have similarities to tools like SCADE or UML/SDL-based tools.

- *Advanced Aspects are Still Evolving.* Many efforts are dedicated to a proper handling of extra-functional properties, including timing and QoS properties. There is a variety of developments, and no clearly identifiable "mainstream winner".

Summary and Conclusions

To summarise section 14, let us consider how the existing component technologies in this section address the industrial needs described in section 12.6.

The existing component technologies contribute to structuring of system development, but in different ways. Widely used component technologies offer infrastructure, middleware, and tool support that solve tricky problems of component composition and communication. They allow a separation between the component development and system development processes. They do not give adequate support for alleviating integration problems or support system predictability. The more specialised technologies focus on imposing a programming structure that supports reuse, the use of product-line architectures, and in some cases allow global timing problems to be handled in the system design phase.

Let us summarize technical contributions of existing component technologies.

- *Rich interfaces:* Few existing component technologies support specification of functional or extra-functional component properties. There are some solutions, developed in the context of specific operating systems, that utilise well-understood principles of real-time scheduling, but they can be used only inside specific development contexts. Some integration platforms allow components to be associated with the specification of some properties in interfaces, but systems can be assembled only in the context of a specific development environment..
- *Constrained Resources:* Widely used component technologies are not focused on implementations on small platforms. However, using only a small part of a technology, or a simple one such as COM, is feasible in some embedded systems. Some specialised technologies are built in the context of a static composition environment, where the mapping and compilation onto the target platform can be optimized with respect to resource consumption. The same holds for more advanced integration platforms, which differ in how much effort has been invested in generating small executables. Efficient implementations of component platforms for smaller systems is still not a very advanced area.
- *Predictability of system properties:*
  - o *Prediction of global system properties* has been implemented using techniques from real-time scheduling theory (e.g., in Rubus), and using simulation techniques (for integration platforms). There is quite limited use of more advanced system analysis techniques described in section 13.
  - o *Checking non-interference between components* is a problem for which support has not been adequately developed. Many technologies insist that all interaction between components happen through explicit interfaces, but this is not enough for guaranteeing component non-interference.
  - o *Determination of QoS, timing, and resource properties of components*, is mostly done by measurement and simulation. There is some progress on static analysis. The problem that these properties depend on the underlying platform has not been adequately solved.
- *Support for safety, reliability, availability, etc.* has not been properly addressed. There are implementation platforms that address these issues in specific contexts

(e.g., the TTP technology), but in many contexts, these problems are still solved in an ad hoc manner, without adequate support from generic technologies. We are still waiting for widely-applicable technologies that solve these problems in a component environment.

- *Wide adoption* of a component technology for embedded systems is still not emerging. There is a variety of developments, but no clearly identifiable "mainstream winner".

   o *Interoperability* between different component technologies has not been addressed to a large extent.
   o *Middleware implementations* for embedded systems exist in the form of operating systems, and some network technologies, but do not yet give full support to a component technology and are not really widely adopted.
   o *Tools* for component technologies in the embedded domain have not reached sufficient maturity.

14.6   Component Libraries: Approaches to Component Retrieval

Software component reuse subsumes three basic subtasks: (1) *Software component library* construction – collection, selection, homogenization of a central, well-maintained artefact repository, (2) *Component indexing* – attaching specifications to the components, (3) *Software component retrieval* – tools which mechanize the identification process. The process of the component retrieval has become especially important since the first successes of selling GUI-components via internet, when a number of internet markets have appeared with rising sizes of the component repositories ([HM02, TUC03]).

The modern component markets provide simplified ways for the specification of the search requirements, which can be easily understood and used, but hardly take into account any specific characteristics of the software [MMM98]. Since one has currently quite restricted possibilities to define technical requirements on a desired component, the search results have a quite small precision. In combination with restricted descriptions of the available components (which are often not unified, incomplete, ambiguous, and in most cases informal) this makes the task of automatic retrieval ineffective for general applications and especially for the field of embedded systems, where complicated behaviour of (reactive) components is of the most interest, not only the signatures of the provided operations.

- *Library construction.* Identification of appropriate software components by their specifications in a library has been investigated in [JC93, Mit93, YWRS92] and others. From the reuse point of view, it is important to find the correct *level of granularity*. Components of a large granularity usually require more external components than components of a small granularity. Although fine-grained components have less strong external dependencies, they introduce many unnecessary interfaces into the system (which degrades its performance). Besides, they are very specific, so less reusable.
- *Library Organization.* A premise for the search and final choice between the found components is the availability of the appropriate *abstraction*, which provides the understanding, assessment and comparison of components. A *library*

storage structure is an ordering on the (*key*, *surrogate*)-pairs, where *key* is an abstract representation of the asset's contents and *surrogate* is a unique abstract representations of an actual asset. The abstraction process from the assets to the surrogates is known as *indexing* or *classification*. *Match predicates* can be used to order components by generality and organize a library hierarchically. A. Mili, R. Mili, and R. Mittermeir [MMM97] described such library organization in which the components can be stored in a lattice-like fashion, using relational subsumption as ordering in such a way that the most specific components become maximal elements. J. Jeng and B. Cheng [JC94] described a two-tiered library organization. The lower tier uses their modified subsumption test to order the library components into disjoint clusters called sets of *lattices*. The upper tier applies a conventional hierarchical clustering algorithm to combine these sets of lattices into a single connected hierarchy. In J. Penix's feature-based indexing method [Pen98], a predefined set of features is used to construct an index. This set is checked off-line against the library, using conditional plug-in as match condition, and each component is indexed with the set of all matching features. In contrast to the other two methods, feature-based indexing is an external library organization method, because it relies on the explicit and external set of features and not on any intrinsic relation between the library components. T. Teschke [Tes03] developed a component description language (CDL), concepts of the behavioural-subtyping-relation match and introduced the specialization relation to compare the specific semantics of activities and operations. This allows to improve the results of component search in a repository by taking into account requirements from the models of business processes.

- **Component retrieval** The *retrieval policy* describes how components must be related to the original user's goal to be considered relevant. In *exact retrieval*, components are considered relevant only if they satisfy the user's goal exactly, while *proper retrieval* also allows for more general components. In an *approximate retrieval*, a component is already relevant if it satisfies the user's goal partially. A partial solution can be defined semantically or syntactically.

When comparing the component search with the classical *information retrieval* [SM83], one can observe their similarity (both are essentially the processes of the content-based, goal-directed extraction of relevant text documents – *assets* – from large collections), as well as differences between them: in the search space and in the definition of the search requirements. While the current component markets can provide at most 10 000 components in the observable search space, the information retrieval approaches can provide the access to a larger amount of information in effective way. The component search and information retrieval differ also in their requirements on the *quality* of the obtained results. Two main characteristics assessing the quality of the search results are *precision* – the rate of the relevant documents in the set of all found documents – and *recall* – the rate of the found relevant documents from the set of all available relevant documents. A task within the classical information retrieval is to reach an appropriate compromise between two measures. For the component retrieval, the precision is of the superior importance, because one is interested in the first turn on the best suitable component(s) which can be integrated with minimal adaptation efforts [BR89, GI94a, ZW97].

Most component retrieval systems use a variety of methods developed within the information retrieval which form a kind of continuum bounded, from one side, by "controlled vocabulary" of the component specification, and from other side, by "free vocabulary" ([Fis01]). For example, in *signature matching* [ZW93] the types of the applied programming language are used: a component is retrieved if its type is "compatible" under the applied type discipline to the query. The main conceptual difficulty in this approach is an adequate definition of "compatible" types which abstracts away "irrelevant" implementation details. Considering different levels of abstraction leads to different forms of signature matching, based on the specialization/generalization of parameter types or their reordering.

Since signature matching is based on the syntax of the components (i.e., syntax of their operations, attributes etc.), these methods alone are not sufficient for the usage with embedded systems. *Specification matching* [ZW97] or *deduction-based software component retrieval* exploit formal semantics extending the component signatures with specifications of pre- and post-conditions. This kind of retrieval methods uses formal specifications and an automated theorem prover to check whether a component matches a query. Deduction-based software component retrieval has a unique conceptual advantage over all other component retrieval methods – it is the only method which retrieves proven matches only. The disadvantage of this approach is their rising complexity problem. An integration approach of the deduction based retrieval into deductive synthesis is introduced in [FW99], based on a higher order logic interpretation of the deductive tableau approach.

Another existing approach to the component retrieval, *behaviour sampling* [PP93], takes the basic assumption that already a sample of a few (*input, output*)-pairs of an operation characterizes a component sufficiently. In practice, all behaviour sampling methods involve non-trivial up-front costs because the sampling process requires a controlled environment. The precision of such methods can not be guaranteed, since an operation can have unexpected behaviour on other inputs from the environment. A similar approach was proposed in [MMM97], where an additional refinement-relation is considered between the specifications as well as correctness-relation between specifications and available components. Built out of the behaviour sampling, [Poz01] proposed two-phased approach with automatic generation of the component descriptions based on the analysis of the test results. In the first phase, stateless components – individual operations – are partitioned in the repository using *generalized signature matching*. Then components with states are considered as modules with multiple operations, where *abstract behaviour sampling* is applied abstracting from the values of the corresponding inputs and outputs.

- *Adaptation phase.* It is often the case that a component has to be adapted to achieve interoperability with the environment. *Adapters* can be generated based on a finite state machine interface semantics [SR02,YS97]]. *Parameterized contracts* [Reu01]] are used to restrict a component's provides- and requires-interface, hence adapting the component to specific reuse contexts, which allows to perform automatically a certain class of component adaptations without changing the code. This also eases the granularity-reuse-problem by mapping of the functionality which is actually requested from a component by a system to the functionality which the component really requires to provide this requested functionality. By integrating deductive synthesis into the framework proposed by J. Penix [Pen98], the automatic adaptation tries to combine a component-oriented approach with a generator-oriented approach to achieve a higher degree of reuse of components.

Nevertheless, the necessity of the component adaptation seems to be unacceptable for some development processes, since it violates the main principle of the component-based methodology – allowing flexible adaptation of software to specific requirements by multiple reuse of the available components [Has02]. The modern component repositories with retrieval methods could win more efficiency by taking into consideration specific technical requirements from the development processes.

- ***Research results and tools.*** Most work on deduction-based retricval is of theoretical nature, or describes only proof-of-concept "implementations" which are experimentally validated only with a small number of selected example proofs. Mitra *et al.* [MRB96] proposed an informal algorithm to automatically map a design function to a system level component. The complexity of the algorithm was exponential in the worst case. Smith and de-Micheli [SM98] proposed methods for component matching and verification of circuits using polynomials. Also, low level component such as ALUs have been successfully reused [JD96]. In the context of embedded systems the best result has been obtained in [RS00], a polynomial-time component matching algorithm for system level components. Manna & Waldinger [MW92] have already shown that in theory a notion of component reuse can be built-into deductive tableaux.

Several component documentation systems, used in practice, show how the information retrieval technology can be applied to the component search. As an example, LaSSIE [DBSB91] developed for the telecommunication branch provides a natural language interface with a set of technical terms and compatibility-relations. The domain knowledge is represented in form of frames, ordered in a generalization/specialization hierarchy. Although the system does not allow a satisfactory representation of the "part-whole" relation and has quite weak precision of the component description, it allows to find also components which partially fit the requirements. ROSA [GI94a, GI94b] is a classification system, which provides automatic extraction of lexical, syntactic, and semantic information from the natural language descriptions used for component indexing and in the process of component search based on the similarity relation between requirements and component descriptions. OntoSeek [GMV99] combines the usage of linguistic ontology – to allow coupling between the user's vocabulary and that of the repository – and a structural formalism for the knowledge representation with a restricted expressiveness. This leads to a higher precision and recall rates, based on the keywords and (attribute, value)-pairs.

The AMPHION system [SWLPU94] follows the Manna-Waldinger-approach to combine synthesis and retrieval but works in the very domain-specific setting of astronomical subroutines. REBOUND-system [PA99] is an example of a working prototype which is a combined component retrieval and adaptation system. Its retrieval subsystem is based on feature-based indexing. The original REBOUND-system uses HOL-prover for classification, a later re-implementation (SOCCER) relies on PVS. NORA/HAMMR [SF97, Fis01] is an advanced prototype retrieval system based on the specification matching approach. To overcome the complexity problem, the authors proposed a pipeline architecture with a number of filters of increasing deductive strength. Dedicated rejection filters are used "upstream" to rule out non-matches as early as possible and thus to prevent the "downstream" confirmation filters (at the theorem proving process) from overflowing. The integration of a retrieval system with synthesis can only be semi-automatic even if retrieval works fully automatically, as shown in [FW99].

15   Standardization Efforts

This section provides an overview of standards that are relevant to the ARTIST components working group. It is broadly split into two main sections: specification standards and implementation technology standards. The aim is to distinguish between standards for specification and modelling, such as UML, that define modelling concepts related to real-time modelling and components, and implementation standards, which are focused at realizing these concepts at the implementation level.

15.1   Specification Standards

Over the last decade, there has been an increasing emphasis on the development of modelling and specification languages appropriate for describing software engineering concepts. The Unified Modelling Language (UML[TM]) was one of the first modelling languages to standardize software engineering concepts and related OMG standards are currently the de-facto route for incorporating new concepts into the software industry. This section briefly introduces some of these key standards and describes work currently being done to incorporate real-time components into existing standards such as UML.

UML 2.0

The Unified Modelling Language (UML) is now the de-facto industry language for specifying and designing software systems. Since its inception in 1997, the scope of the language has become ever wider. UML now provides support for a wide variety of modelling domains, including real-time system modelling.

Unfortunately, the success of UML has come at a cost, resulting in a bloated and complex language, as new modelling concepts have been repeatedly "mud-packed" into the definition. Furthermore, the specification of the language (a meta-model of its abstract syntax with weakly defined semantics) has also become difficult to manage and hard to understand due to its size and complexity.

The UML 2.0 effort is an attempt by the OMG to address these shortcomings. The aim is that UML should become a family of languages, each based on a common semantic core. Thus, specific variants of UML will be defined for specific application areas: e-business, real-time, systems engineering, warehouse meta-data and so on. Another important aim is that UML 2.0 should be defined more precisely in order to facilitate the more rigorous use of the language.

A number of consortia have submitted a variety of proposals to the OMG for the revised standard, and the main difficulty was then to find a consensus among every proposition. The work has been split into four main areas: infrastructure (the core modelling concepts supported by UML), superstructure (the modelling concepts that are used to model specific views of a system, e.g., state behaviour), OCL (the Object Constraint Language that supports the semi-formal specification of constraints) and diagram interchange (tool interchange of diagrammatical syntax). The intention is that

Artist FP5 Consortium: Embedded Systems Design, LNCS 3436, 194–203, 2005.
© Springer-Verlag Berlin Heidelberg 2005

the infrastructure model will define the semantics for the core concepts used by UML. The superstructure will then be defined in terms of this core, thus providing a firmer interpretation of the UML language as a whole.

The task involved in refractory UML as a family of languages is not straightforward. Much work needs to be done to define an infrastructure that will successively support the definition of a wide spectrum of languages. Furthermore, first class extension mechanisms are required to support the incremental extension and combination of language components to create new languages. Finally, defining a semantic for these language components is a significant challenge in itself – necessitating that UML has a well defined semantic domain and appropriate semantic mappings.

Beside restructuring its architecture and improving its usability, the UML 2.0 language has also been enriched with:

- Possibilities to organize interactions through interaction overview diagram. This latter are very closed to the high-level message sequence chart.
- Activity diagram was revisited and is know a language by itself and is not more a subset of usual state machines.
- Finally, the component concept was promoted and is gone from a just a peace of code to a part of models (see next section for more details).

Component-Based Modelling with the UML

Components being the now most widespread structuring entities at implementation level (seen as executables, binaries or library elements), the component paradigm tends also to play such role at the modelling stage. One of the motivations is related to the difficulty to have reusable components having totally known and mastered dynamics, in particular, on real-time and concurrency aspects. Incoming component-based approaches ([DW99, HS99, ABM00, GPJ02]) tend to use components as a higher-level modelling artefact that may be used whatever the nature of the model (specification design, implementation) and derived throughout the system development through to implementation. Implementation part of a component becomes one of its aspects only relevant for the implementation stage.

The evolution of this concept from UML1.x to UML 2.0 confirms this tendency. Components in UML 2.0 are likely to get a more extensive treatment than in previous versions of UML. Considered as a modular, deployable, and replaceable part of a system that encapsulates implementation and exposes a set of interfaces in the UML1.x, components become more abstract structuring entities in UML 2.0. They will be defined in the superstructure of UML 2.0. UML 2.0 components are then a modular part of a system that may be modelled and refined throughout the development lifecycle. A component is viewed as an autonomous unit within a system or subsystem. It has one or more ports, and its internals are hidden and inaccessible other than as provided by its interfaces. As a result, the aim is that components and subsystems can be flexibly reused and replaced by connecting ("wiring") them together via their provided and required interfaces. Components also support reuse through an import mechanism, which permits the elements of a component to be imported into another component. UML 2.0 component model is very close to the main frame of the component model described in previous section 11 allowing thus to use very easily UML as modelling language or ADL to support a CBSE methodology.

Although, this approach is not yet mature, at least due to the introduction of the concept only in the incoming version of UML standard, some proposals already introduce this notion in relation with real-time preoccupation through attaching real-time QoS to the component interfaces [GPJ02]. In this context, component composition issue at design stage becomes a question of QoS composition among the component models. This raised a strong interest on MDA techniques that facilitate: model weaving (http://www.qccs.org/) for the component composition; and the mapping and transformation of abstract models into detailed models for the implementation synthesis [GTT02].

UML Profiles for Real-Time

The UML contains in native some capabilities to support real-time aspects: either for qualitative aspects such as concurrency (Active objects, concurrent states, etc.) or for quantitative aspects such as time event. Nevertheless, these real-time features of the UML are not enough. For that reason, OMG has initiated a work dedicated to define a UML profile specific to real-time systems development.

UML Profile for Scheduling, Performance and Time Specification
The UML profile for Scheduling, Performance, and Time Specification (in short SPT) [OMG01c] defines standard paradigms of use for modelling of time-, scheduling-, and performance-related aspects of real-time systems. The intentions are to:

- Enable the construction of models that could be used to make quantitative predictions regarding these characteristics.
- Facilitate communication of design intent between developers in a standard way.
- Enable inter operability between various analysis and design tools.

To support this, the specification defines (as a meta-model) a complete, but generic model of some of the key concepts association with scheduling, performance modelling and times events. Main concepts introduced in the SPT profile are Quality-of-Service (in short QoS) and Resource. From these concepts, it then defines in specific sub-profiles more adequate concepts for performance and schedulability analysis. Thus it includes models of the semantics and mappings to common real-time middleware standards such as real-time CORBA.

To illustrate the usage of the SPT profile, one may consider the package dedicated to model time and time values. Among other concepts, this package contains both concepts of *TimeValue* and *TimedAction*.

The *TimeValue* concept is defined as follow: "It corresponds to a particular physical instant in time as measured by some reference clock in some inertial frame of reference". To use this conceptual element, the SPT profile proposes both following possibilities:

- the «RTtime» stereotype – it enables to specify that model elements (e.g. Attributes of a class) are time values. This involves that such tagged elements have a time semantics (see Figure 6.2).

- the *RTtimeValue* Tagged-Value Type (in short TVL) – this latter may be sued only to type tagged values of stereotype. For example, the tagged value *RTstart* of the stereotype *«RTaction»* denotes a time value and is also typed with the TVL *RTtimeValue* (Figure 16.2).

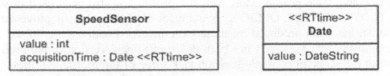

Figure 16.1. Example of usage of the stereotype «RTtime»

The *TimedAction* concept support the concept of activities that either have known start and end times or that have a known duration. Its usage in UML models is achieved through the stereotype *«RTaction»*. This latter has several tagged value: *RTstart* and *RTend* if the stereotyped element is characterized with start and end times, and *RTduration* otherwise. All these tagged values are typed as *RTtimeValue* as previously defined (Figure 16.2).

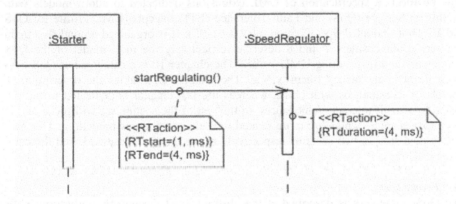

Figure 16.2. Example of usage of the stereotype «RTaction» in a sequence diagram

The *«RTaction»* stereotype may be applied on a large scale of base classes of the UML such as *Message, Action, Method*, etc. This last point is actually one of the issues of the current standard version of the SPT profile that should be solved in the next incoming version 2 of the profile (see later in this section about SPT v2). Indeed, the semantics specified for each stereotype defined I the profile applies for all the base class it can stereotyped. But sometimes it should be better to clarify some points depending of the base class on which the stereotype is applied. For example, the semantics of a *Message* element stereotyped by *«RTaction»* could mean that the action attached to the message should have the RT features specified in the stereotype attached to the message. Whereas the semantics of a Method element also stereotyped *«RTaction»* applies directly on the method itself.

UML Profile for SPT Specification
The UML profile for Scheduling, Performance and Time has been adopted and in use since mid of 2003. In parallel some other OMG standards have been adopted such as the UML profile for QoS and Fault Tolerance, UML2, etc.

All these new profiles have an influence on the current version of the Scheduling, Performance and Time profile. Moreover, the profile has also been used in various projects (AIT-WOODDES, OMEGA...) and a lot of feedback for improvement and consolidation has been produced by these experiments. Finally, some of the issues raised against the SPT version 1 has been deferred to new version of the profile because out of the scope of a simple revision task force of the profile. All these points are arguments in favour of having a new version of the UML profile for SPT.

To achieve this purpose, the SPT2 will have to solve the following mandatory requirements: (i) Express analysis profiles in terms of QoS Profile; (ii) Express profile using UML 2 profile meta-model ; (iii) Harmonize the performance and schedulability sub-profiles; (iv) Clarify Relationship with UML2; (v) And improve usability of the profile. It is expected that the new version of the UML profile for SPT will be available in the mid of 2005.

UML Profile for QoS and Fault Tolerance
This profile is a specification of UML extensions dedicated to adorn models with Quality of Service (QoS) and Fault-Tolerance (FT) concepts (UML Profile for QoS and FT Draft Adopted Specification, ptc/04-01-05). It is organized around five main chapters. Both chapters 7 and 8 describe respectively the meta-model of the QoS Framework and its resulting UML profile. The chapter 10 is a catalogue of QoS covering throughput, latency, security, etc. The chapter 12 enables the description of models of risk analysis with UML, whereas the last chapter is dedicated to the description of fault tolerant architectures. In the rest of the section we will focus on the three first chapters which are more related to real-time features modelling. This section is then split in two sections respectively related to the framework and the catalogue of QoS.

QoS Framework
The QoS framework is described at the abstract level through the definition of its meta-model in the one hand. But the framework is also described at the concrete level via a projection of its meta-model in the UML technological space. This projection is achieved by defining the UML profile matching the meta-model of the QoS framework.

The meta-model of the QoS framework consists of three sub-packages describing respectively characteristics, constraints and levels of QoS.

The QoS characteristics package provides the basics for defining specific QoS:

- QoS characteristics – this views defines the concepts enabling to model quantifiable extra-functional features (latency, safety, etc.) independently, or orthogonally, to functional features. QoS characteristics may have values that may be quantified under different dimensions (absolute values, max. or min. values, etc.). When defining one QoS characteristics for quantification of extra-functional becomes too much complex it is then possible to cluster several more basic QoS characteristics into QoS categories. This latter concept is different with characteristics in the sense that categories are not directly quantifiable, one need to go through their clustered characteristics.

- QoS values –previous concepts provide a type view of the QoS framework. QoSValue and QoSDimensionSlot defined here are respectively instances of QoSCharacteristic and QoSDimenssion.
- QoS context – this enables to describe the context of QoS characteristics, that is to say the QoS characteristics and related model elements involved in a QoS constraint. It may be useful to do so when QoS expressions or constraints involve several QoS characteristics.

The QoS constraint package provides means to limit the possible values of QoS characteristic. The generic concept of QoSContraint is reified into the three following concepts:

- QoS required – this ensures a client to specify which QoS it requires for a server when operating the required service.
- QoS offered – this ensures to define the QoS associated to services provided by model element (e.g. at the interface level of components).
- QoS contract – when linking a client and a server, respective required and offered QoS has to match or connection has at least to result from a negotiation to map the required with offered QoS. QoS contract is the proposed concept to support this king of contact modelling.

The QoS level package provides facilities to model different running modes of application in function of level of QoS it may offer or require.

The concrete syntax of the QoS meta-model is rendered under the form of a UML profile. That means that from the QoS meta-model previously described, a set of UML extensions (stereotypes and associated values) are defined in order to ensure UML modelling of the QoS framework. The architecture of the UML profile follows the architecture of the meta-model. It consists then of three sub-profiles. For example, QoS categories are modelled with package stereotyped with «QoSCategory». Our purpose is not here to describe in the minute the details of the profile but just to give enough information to understand the pros. and cons. of the profile. For more details about the UML extensions proposed in the context of the UML profile for QoS and FT, the reader is pleased to refer to the OMG' specification.

QoS Catalogue

The QoS catalogue consists in introducing specific QoS categories (e.g. performance, latency, etc.). Every category is denoted through a UML design pattern using stereotypes defined in the QoS framework.

For example, two types of latency characteristics could be:

- Latency as a generic characteristic for latency modelling on any kind of software element
- Latency as an absolute limit on the time needed to accomplish a sub-task.

MDA

The Model Driven Architecture (MDA^{TM}) is the OMG's new flagship architecture that aims to integrate its (and other) standards within a model driven approach to system development [SOM00a, SOM00b, SOM02, MM01]. MDA^{TM} encapsulates many important ideas – most notably the notion that real benefits can be obtained by using modelling languages to integrate the huge diversity of languages used in the development of systems.

In MDA^{TM}, modelling languages are categorized as being platform independent (i.e. specification oriented) and platform independent (i.e. implementation oriented). Note that a modelling language can be a language at any level of abstraction. Examples of platform independent languages include UML^{TM} itself (when used for specification). Middleware standards such as CORBA and programming level languages (e.g. Java Beans) are examples of platform specific languages.

Mappings (a key component of MDA^{TM}) define the relationships between these languages. By abstracting away from platform specific details, the intention is that system development is driven through platform independent models that can be semi-automatically translated into any platform specific language for which a standard mapping has been defined. Thus, platform independence is obtained along with greater flexibility in deployment – if a new technology emerges (e.g. .Net), then all that is required is to apply a new set of mappings.

Platform independent and platform specific mappings are good examples of vertical transformations. However, MDA^{TM} goes potentially far beyond this. For example, horizontal mappings between platform specific languages may be defined as a means of integrated different modelling perspectives at the specification level (e.g. process models, system artefacts, software specifications). In short, MDA^{TM} offers a framework that has the potential to model and integrate all aspects of system development.

Many vendors are already claiming support for MDA^{TM} (e.g. a code generator could be viewed as a mapping tool!). However, in practice there are significant issues to be addressed. Mechanisms must be defined that support executable, but declarative mappings between languages. The semantics of these languages must be defined well enough to ensure that mappings are semantic preserving, whilst more powerful extension mechanisms are required to support the reuse of mappings. These and many other issues are all currently being debated within the OMG (see www.omg.org/mda).

MDA and Current Industrial Real-Time UML Tools

In the real-time application area, this model-oriented trend is also very active and promising. Currently, there are four main model-oriented industrial approaches supported by tools: UML-RT used with Rose-RT, ROPES with Rhapsody, ARTiSAN and UML/SDL with the Tau UML/SDL suite.

Within UML-RT, an application is seen as a set of entities called "capsules"' which support logical concurrency. These capsules have a state machine as behaviour specification and may exchange signals to communicate. Models built in this way are said to be executable, meaning that at any moment in design, it is possible to produce an executable application matching the UML^{TM} model. In this case, the mapping is achieved via code generation.

For ROPES^{TM} and ARTiSAN^{TM} approaches, real-time application modelling is a 3-stage process: i) building a "functional"' model with class and state diagrams; ii) building a specific tasking model with class diagrams containing only active objects (execution tasks); iii) describing the mappings between the two models. The main drawback of this "family" of methods is that it requires advanced real-time development skills to build the tasking model and map it with the "functional" model. While there are some "shortcuts" available ([AKZ97 p. 482]) to facilitate this activity, no transformation rules are provided as could be done within a fully MDA^{TM}-based approach.

The approach proposed by Telelogic^{TM} is based on the use of both UML^{TM} and SDL^{TM} languages. It consists of building UML^{TM} models at the analysis stages using active objects as concurrency supports and SDL^{TM} within design-time. Reference document [ITU99] defines modelling rules for mapping a UML^{TM}-oriented model into an SDL-oriented model. When SDL models are finished, the engineer may generate code to produce an executable application.

All these methodologies may be considered as MDA^{TM}-based approaches for mainly two reasons. Firstly, they clearly promote the model paradigm to develop applications; and secondly, they provide code generation taking into account structural and behaviour specifications for model mapping to implementation languages such as C, C++, JAVA, etc.

Nevertheless, they do not exploit all the potentialities of MDA^{TM}. Their application models are often only PSM-like for "executable" reasons.

For modelling purposes, the user is thus led very quickly to resort, for an executable model, to a programming language such as C++. Although action semantics have been standardized by OMG [OMG02] there are still only a few tools that have integrated this feature, which allows building of executable models independently of any programming language. While these approaches are usually based on a several stage process, they do not provide the refinement mapping rules that could facilitate application development and, above all, be highly useful in promoting seamless development processes. Finally, the existing UML-based methods for real-time applications still require considerable knowledge of real-time software technology (and the different programming models promoted by these tools) to develop real-time systems.

Towards MDA Components

MDA approach has given rise to a particular interest of the RT community (e.g., editions of the Summer School on MDA for embedded systems held in Brest, Sept. 2002 and 2004, http://sancy.ensieta.fr/mda/). However, this subject remains largely open, in particular, to identify and structure the various artefacts related to MDA, such as: dedicated met models (e.g., for business domain and technical domain), specific target models (also called PSMs Platform Specific Models), transformation procedures, model weaving, mapping and transformation rules, in particular, concerning RT QoS, but also for implementation synthesis, test generation, proof synthesis.

Incoming MDA-based workbenches will consist of various parts that may interoperate:

• Documents (method book, guide lines, user guides, etc.).

- Profiles (SPT, SPEM, EDOC, etc.).
- Tools (UML modeller, code generator, model transformer, etc.).

Moreover, these MDA parts may be plug on a bus in order they interoperate. For example, the Eclipse initiative (www.eclipse.org) provides a specific plug-in, EMF (Eclipse Modelling Framework), ensuring the construction of UML-based MDA plug-ins of Eclipse.

Even if it is not well defined today, it seems logical that components will also play this structuring role [BG02]. And near future should give rise to "MDA-Components" whose nature could be clarified thanks standard stereotypes such as «Tool», «UML Profile», «Document», etc.

In fact, currently not a lot of things have been set related to MDA and it still remains a lot of work to do to clarify MDA and its related concepts. In particular, as CBSE methodologies have been developed to support more efficient use of the component artefact, model driven engineering methodologies have to be define to exploit all the potentialities of the MDA technologies and related concepts.

15.2   Implementation Technology Standards

The majority of implementation standards relevant to components tend to focus on middleware, i.e. the communication and interface aspects of components. Each of these standards emphasizes the important of independence from the technology use to implement the internal functionality of components. Because of this, we will not discuss the plethora of programming languages that can be used to implement components in this section.

SOAP

SOAP provides a simple and lightweight mechanism for exchanging structured and typed information between peers in a decentralized, distributed environment using XML. As such, SOAP can be seen as an important standard for interchanging date between distributed components. SOAP does not itself provide implementation specific semantics; rather it defines a simple mechanism for expressing application semantics by providing a modular packaging model and encoding mechanisms for encoding data within modules. This allows SOAP to be used in a large variety of systems ranging from messaging systems to RPC.

SOAP consists of three parts:

- The SOAP envelope defines an overall framework for expressing what the content of a message is.
- The SOAP encoding rules defines a serialization mechanism that can be used to exchange instances of application-defined data types. These may be simple or structured data types.
- The SOAP RPC representation defines a convention that can be used to represent remote procedure calls and responses. Just as with CORBA, the key advantage of SOAP is that it is platform independent and is not tied to any implementation specific messaging mechanism or software architecture.

15.3   Conclusions and Challenges

All the above standards are relevant to the ARTIST component working group as they each attempt to standardize a variety of aspects of real-time and component based design in isolation. As a result, there are many opportunities for additional work to unify both the real-time and component perspectives and also to provide a stronger foundation for their definition and deployment. These include the following:

- Integration of real-time and embedded QoS within the UML2 component model: Currently, little consideration has been given to the expression of real-time and QoS aspects in UML component models. Such an approach would require the definition of additional notational facilities to facilitate the capture of these aspects, along with a definition of their semantics.
- Traceability management/control of real-time QoS of a component all along the development process: By providing a model of change management/control it should be possible to provide support for the management of components throughout its lifetime (an essential requirement for change management and upgrades). Such a facility could potentially be based on an extension to emerging process management modelling languages being developed in the industry such as SPEM.
- Definition of performance / schedulability analysis methodology well-suited for such MDA component-based approaches: It is clear that the deployment of components within an MDA lifecycle could be developed whereby components could be specified in a platform independent way, and then mapped to various component technologies. In order to achieve this, significant work needs to be done to develop models of platform specific component languages and to define rules for mapping from platform independent components to platform specific models or to middleware standards such as CORBA and SOAP. These mappings must be shown to be correct with respect to certain semantic preserving properties, including QoS.
- Link between extra-functional engineering requirements and real-time/embedded QoS of UML-based models: By modelling extra-functional properties of real-time systems, it should be possible to build rich component based modelling languages that capture a variety of system engineering perspectives. This would tie in nicely with work going on in the OMG to define a UML profile for systems engineering.

16 References

[AAG95]   G. D. Abowd, R. Allen, and D. Garlan. Formalizing style to understand descriptions of software architecture. *ACM Trans. on Software Engineering and Methodology*, 4(4):319-364, 1995.

[ABM00]   C. Atkinson, J. Bayer, and D. Muthig. Component-based product line development : The KobrA approach. In *Software Product Lines: Experience and Research Directions, Proc. 1st Int. Software Product Line Conference (SPLC-1), Denver, CO, USA, Aug. 2000*, pages 289-309. Kluwer Academic, 2000.

[Abr96]   J.-R. Abrial. *The B book – Assigning Programs to Meanings*. Cambridge University Press, 1996.

[ACB84]   M. Ajmone Marsan, G. Conte, and G. Balbo. A class of generalised stochastic Petri nets for the performance evaluation of multiprocessor systems. *ACM Trans. on Computer Systems*, 2(2):93-122, 1984.

[AFM+02]   T. Amnell, E. Fersman, L. Mokrushin, P. Pettersson, and W. Yi. TIMES: A tool for modelling and implementation of embedded systems. In *Proc. 8th Int. Conf. Tools and Algorithms for the Construction and Analysis of Systems (TACAS'2002), Grenoble, France, Apr. 2002*, volume 2280 of *Lecture Notes in Computer Science*, pages 460-464. Springer Verlag, 2002.

[AG94]   R. Allen and D. Garlan. Formalizing architectural connection. In *Proc. 16th Int. Conf. on Software Engineering (ICSE'94), Sorrento, Italy, May 1994*, pages 71-80. IEEE Comp. Soc. Press, 1994.

[AH96]   R. Alur and T. A. Henzinger, editors. *Proc. 8th Int. Conf. Computer Aided Verification (CAV'96), New Brunswick, NJ, USA, July-Aug. 1996*, volume 1102 of *Lecture Notes in Computer Science*. Springer Verlag, 1996.

[AKZ97]   M. Awad, J. Kuusela, and J Ziegler. *Object-Oriented Technology for Real-time Systems: A Practical Approach Using OMT and Fusion*. Prentice Hall, 1997.

[Bal98]   R. Balzer. An architectural infrastructure for product families. In *Proc. 2nd Int. ESPRIT ARES Workshop on Development and Evolution of Software Architectures for Product Families, Las Palmas de Gran Canaria, Spain, Feb. 1998*, volume 1429 of *Lecture Notes in Computer Science*, pages 158-160. Springer Verlag, 1998.

[BBB+00]   F. Bachmann, L. Bass, C. Buhman, S. Comella-Dorda, F. Long, J. Robert, R. Seacord, and K. Wallnau. Technical Concepts of Component-Based Software Engineering, Volume II. Technical Report CMU/SEI-2000-TR-008, Software Engineering Institute, Carnegie-Mellon University, May 2000.

[BCK98]   L. Bass, P. Clements, and R. Kazman. *Software Architecture In Practice*. Addison Wesley, 1998.

[BCP+01]   V. Bertin, E. Closse, M. Poize, J. Pulou, J. Sifakis, P. Venier, D. Weil, and S. Yovine. Taxys = Esterel + Kronos. A tool for verifying real-time properties of embedded systems. In *Proc. 40th IEEE Conf. on Decision and Control (CDC'2001), Orlando, FL, USA, Dec. 2001*. IEEE Comp. Soc. Press, 2001.

[Ber99a]   G. Berry. The constructive semantics of Pure Esterel. Centre de Mathématiques Appliquées, École des Mines and INRIA, Sophia-Antipolis, France, July 1999.

[Ber99b]   G. Berry. The Esterel v5 language primer. Centre de Mathématiques Appliquées, École des Mines and INRIA, Sophia-Antipolis, France, April 1999.

[BG02]   J. Bézivin and S. Gérard. A preliminary identification of MDA components, 2002. Position Paper, OOPSLA 2002 Workshop: Generative Techniques in the context of Model Driven Architecture.

Artist FP5 Consortium: Embedded Systems Design, LNCS 3436, 204–215, 2005.
© Springer-Verlag Berlin Heidelberg 2005

[BGM02]   M. Bozga, S. Graf, and L. Mounier. IF-2.0: A validation environment for component-based real-time systems. In *Proc. 14th Int. Conf. Computer Aided Verification (CAV'2002), Copenhagen, Denmark, July 2002*, volume 2404 of *Lecture Notes in Computer Science*, pages 343-348. Springer Verlag, 2002.

[BGS00]   S. Bornot, G. Gössler, and J. Sifakis. On the construction of live timed systems. In *Proc. 6th Int. Conf. Tools and Algorithms for the Construction and Analysis of Systems (TACAS'2000), Berlin, Germany, Mar.-Apr. 2000*, volume 1785 of *Lecture Notes in Computer Science*, pages 109-126. Springer Verlag, 2000.

[BJP99]   A. Beugnard, J.-M. Jézéquel, and N. Plouzeau. Making components contract aware. *IEEE Computer*, 32(7):38-45, 1999.

[BK98]   N. Brown and C. Kindel. Distributed component object model protocol – dcom/1.0. Internet-draft, IETF, January 1998.

[BLP+02]   F. Balarin, L. Lavagno, C. Passerone, A. Sangiovanni-Vincentelli, Y. Watanabe, and G. Yang. Concurrent execution semantics and sequential simulation algorithms for the Metropolis meta-model. In *Proc. 10th Int. Symp. on Hardware/Software Codesign (CODES'2002), Estes Park, CO, USA, Apr. 2002*. ACM Press, 2002.

[BMW89]   H. Beilner, J. Mater, and N. Weissenberg. Towards a performance modeling environment: News on HIT. In *Proc. 4th Int. Conf. Modeling Techniques and Tools for Computer Performance Evaluation, Palma de Mallorca, Spain, Sep. 1998*, pages 57-75. Plenum Press, 1989.

[Box00]   D. Box. House of COM: Is COM dead? *MSDN Magazine*, December 2000.

[BR89]   T. J. Biggerstaff and C. Richter. Reusability framework, assessment, and directions. In T. J. Biggerstaff and A. J. Perlis, editors, *Software Reusability Volume I: Concepts and Models*, pages 1-17. ACM Press & Addison Wesley, 1989. Also appeared in IEEE Software, 4(2):41-49, 1987.

[Bro95]   K. Brockschmidt. *Inside OLE (2nd ed.)*. Microsoft Press, 1995.

[Bro96]   K. Brockschmidt. What OLE is really about, 1996.

[Cas95]   G. Castagna. Covariance and contravariance: Conflict without a cause. *ACM Trans. on Programming Languages and Systems*, 17(3):431-447, 1995.

[CCD+01]   P. Combes, L. Castaignet, F. Dubois, B. Nicolas, and D. Renard. Feature-driven service analysis and design in an open architecture. In *Proc. 7th Int. Conf. Intelligence in next Generation Networks (ICIN'2001), Bordeaux, France, Oct. 2001*, 2001.

[CCM]   The CORBA & CORBA Component Model (CCM) page. http://www.ditec.um.es/~dsevilla/ccm.

[CdAH+02]   A. Chakrabarti, L. de Alfaro, T. A. Henzinger, M. Jurdzinski, and F. Y. C. Mang. Interface compatibility checking for software modules. In *Proc. 14th Int. Conf. Computer Aided Verification (CAV'2002), Copenhagen, Denmark, July 2002*, volume 2404 of *Lecture Notes in Computer Science*, pages 428-441. Springer Verlag, 2002.

[CDN01]   P. Combes, F. Dubois, and B. Nicolas. Une démarche associant UML et SDL pour l'analyse, la conception et la validation de services de télécommunication. In *Actes 3ième Congrès Modélisation des Systèmes Réactifs (MSR'2001), Toulouse, France, Oct. 2001*, pages 309-324. Hermès Science Publications, 2001.

[Chi98]   G. Chiola. Petri nets versus queueing networks: similarities and differences. In *Performance Models for Discrete Event Systems with Synchronisations: Formalisms and Analysis Techniques*, pages 121-134. KRONOS, 1998.

[CL02]   I. Crnkovic and M. Larsson. *Building Reliable Component-Based Software Systems*. ArtechHouse, 2002.

[CM88]   K. M. Chandy and J. Misra. *Parallel Program Design*. Addison-Wesley, 1988.

[Cob00]   E. Cobb. CORBA Components: The industry's first multi-language component standard, June 2000. OMG meeting tutorial available at http://www.omg.org/cgi-bin/doc?omg/00-06-01.

[Con02]   C. Constantinescu. Impact of deep submicron technology on dependability of VLSI circuits. In *Proc. 2002 Int. Conf. on Dependable Systems and Networks (DSN'2002), June 2002, Bethesda, MD, USA*, pages 205-214. IEEE Comp. Soc. Press, 2002.

[CPP+01]   E. Closse, M. Poize, J. Pulou, J. Sifakis, P. Venier, D. Weil, and S. Yovine. Taxys: A tool for the development and verification of real-time embedded systems. In *Proc. 13th Int. Conf. Computer Aided Verification (CAV'2001), Paris, France, July 2001*, volume 2102 of *Lecture Notes in Computer Science*, pages 391-395. Springer Verlag, 2001.

[CPP+02]   E. Closse, M. Poize, J. Pulou, P. Venier, and D. Weil. SAXO-RT, interpreting Esterel semantics on a sequential execution structure. In *Proc. 1st Workshop on Synchronous Languages, Applications, and Programming (SLAP'2002), Grenoble, France, Apr. 2002*, volume 65(5) of *Electronic Notes in Theor. Comp. Sci.* Elsevier Science, 2002.

[CRTM98]   L. Casparsson, A. Rajnák, K. Tindell, and P. Malmberg. Volcano – a revolution in on-board communications. Volvo Technology Report, 1998.

[CW02]   S. Clarke and R. J. Walker. Towards a standard design language for AOSD. In *Proc. 1st Int. Conf. on Aspect-Oriented Software Development (AOSD'2002), Univ. Twente, Enschede, NL, Apr. 2002*, pages 113-119. ACM Press, 2002.

[DBSB91]   P. Devanbu, R. J. Brachman, P. G. Selfridge, and B. W. Ballard. LaSSIE: a knowledge-based software information system. *Communications of the ACM*, 34(5):34-49, 1991.

[DH01]   W. Damm and D. Harel. LSCs: Breathing life into Message Sequence Charts. *Journal of Formal Methods in System Design*, 19(1):45-80, 2001.

[DHK99]   M. Dal Cin, G. Huszerl, and K. Kosmidis. Evaluation of safety-critical systems based on guarded statecharts. In *Proc. 4th IEEE Int. Symp. on High Assurance Systems Engineering, Washington, DC, USA, Nov. 1999*, pages 37-45. IEEE Comp. Soc. Press, 1999.

[DHM96]   M. Diefenbruch, J. Hintelmann, and B. Müller-Clostermann. The QUEST-approach for the performance evaluation of SDL-systems. In *Proc. IFIP TC6 WG6.1 Int. Conf. on Formal Description Techniques IX / Protocol Specification, Testing and Verification XVI (FORTE'96), Kaiserslautern, Germany, Oct. 1996*, pages 229-244. Kluwer Academic, 1996.

[DKB98]   P. D'Argenio, J.-P. Katoen, and E. Brinksma. An algebraic approach to the specification of stochastic systems. In *Proc. IFIP Working Conference on Programming Concepts and Methods (PROCOMET'98), Shelter Island, NY, USA, June 1998*, pages 126-147. Chapman & Hall, 1998.

[Don00]   P. Donohoe, editor. *Software Product Lines: Experience and Research Directions, Proc. 1st Int. Software Product Line Conference (SPLC-1), Denver, CO, USA, Aug. 2000*. Kluwer Academic, 2000.

[Dou02]   B. P. Douglass. Model driven architecture and Rhapsody. Technical report, I-Logix, 2002.

[DW99]   D. F. D'Souza and A. C. Wills. *Objects, components, and frameworks with UML : the catalysis approach*. ACM Press and Addison-Wesley, 1999.

[EAS03]   EAST_EEA. http://www.east-eea.net, 2003.

[ECW01]   H. El-Sayed, D. Cameron, and C. M. Woodside. Automation support for software performance engineering. *ACM SIGMETRICS Performance Evaluation Review*, 29(1):301-311, 2001.

[Erl]   Erlang. http://www.erlang.org/.

[ESC]   ESC Java webpage. http://research.compaq.com/SRC/esc/.
[FEHC02]   A. V. Fioukov, E. M. Eskenazi, D. K. Hammer, and M. R. V. Chaudron. Evalua-
             tion of static properties for component-based architectures. In *Proc. 28th
             EUROMICRO Conference, Dortmund, Germany, Sep. 2002*, pages 33-39. IEEE
             Comp. Soc. Press, 2002.
[FHL⁺01]   C. Ferdinand, R. Heckmann, M. Langenbach, F. Martin, M. Schmidt, H. Theiling,
             S. Thesing, and R. Wilhelm. Reliable and precise WCET determination for a real-
             life processor. In *Proc. 1st Int. Workshop on Embedded Software (EMSOFT'2001),
             Tahoe City, CA, USA, Oct. 2001*, volume 2211 of *Lecture Notes in Computer Sci-
             ence*, pages 469-485. Springer Verlag, 2001.
[Fis01]   B. Fischer. *Deduction-Based Software Component Retrieval*. PhD thesis, Univer-
             sität Passau, Germany, November 2001.
[FK98]   S. Frolund and J. Koistinen. Quality-of-Service specifications in distributed object
             systems. *Distributed Systems Engineering*, 5(4):179-202, 1998.
[FLV00]   P. H. Feiler, B. Lewis, and S. Vestal. Improving predictability in embedded real-
             time systems. Special report CMU/SEI-2000-SR-011, Carnegie Mellon Software
             Engineering Institute, December 2000. 2000.
[FW98]   C. Ferdinand and R. Wilhelm. On predicting data cache behaviour for real-time
             systems. In *Proc. ACM SIGPLAN Workshop on Languages, Compilers, and Tools
             for Embedded Systems (LCTES'98), Montreal, Canada, June 1998*, volume 1474
             of *Lecture Notes in Computer Science*, pages 16-30. Springer Verlag, 1998.
[FW99]   B. Fischer and J. Whittle. An integration of deductive retrieval into deductive
             synthesis. In *Proc. 14th IEEE Int. Conf. on Automated Software Engineering
             (ASE'99), Cocoa Beach, Florida, USA, Oct. 1999*, pages 52-62. IEEE Comp. Soc.
             Press, 1999.
[GAO95]   D. Garlan, R. Allen, and J. Ockerbloom. Architectural mismatch: Why reuse is so
             hard. *IEEE Software*, 12(6):17-26, 1995.
[GHG⁺93]   J. V. Guttag, J. J. Horning, S. J. Garland, K. D. Jones, A. Modet, and J. M. Wing.
             Larch: Languages and Tools for Formal Specification. Texts and Monographs in
             Computer Science. Springer Verlag, 1993.
[GHJV94]   E. Gamma, R. Helm, R. Johnson, and J. Vlissides. *Design Patterns: Elements of
             Reusable Object-Oriented Software*. Addison-Wesley, 1994.
[GI94a]   M. R. Girardi and B. Ibrahim. Automatic indexing of software artifacts. In *Proc.
             3rd Int. Conf. on Software Reuse, Rio De Janeiro, Brazil, Nov. 1994*, pages 24-32.
             IEEE Comp. Soc. Press, 1994.
[GI94b]   M. R. Girardi and B. Ibrahim. A similarity measure for retrieving software arti-
             facts. In *Proc. 6th Int. Conf. on Software Engineering and Knowledge Engineering
             (SEKE'94), Jurmala, Latvia, June 1994*, pages 478-485. Knowledge Systems Insti-
             tute, 1994.
[GJS96]   J. Gosling, B. Joy, and G. L. Steele. *The Java Language Specification*. Addison-
             Wesley, 1996.
[GLM00]   S. Gnesi, D. Latella, and M. Massink. A stochastic extension of a behavioural
             subset of UML statechart diagrams. In *Proc. 5th IEEE Int. Symp. on High-
             Assurance Systems Engineering (HASE'2000), Albuquerque, NM, USA, Nov. 2000*,
             pages 55-64. IEEE Comp. Soc. Press, 2000.
[GMV99]   N. Guarino, C. Masolo, and G. Vetere. OntoSeek: Content-based access to the
             web. *IEEE Intelligent Systems*, 14(3):70-80, 1999.
[Gos95]   C. Goswell. The COM programmer's cookbook, 1995.
[Gös01]   G. Gössler. Prometheus – a compositional modeling tool for real-time systems. In
             *Proc. 1st Workshop on Real-Time Tools (RT-TOOLS'2001), Aalborg, Demark,
             Aug. 2001*, 2001. Published as Technical report 2001-014, Uppsala University,
             Department of Information Technology.

[GPJ02]   S. Gérard, P. Petterson, and B. Josko. Methodology for developing real-time embedded systems. Pub IST-1999-10069, CEE, Paris, France, 2002.

[Gri03]   K. Grimm. Software technology in an automotive company: major challenges. In *Proc. 25th Int. Conf. on Software Engineering (ICSE'2003), Portland, OR, USA, May 2003*, pages 498-505. IEEE Comp. Soc. Press, 2003.

[GS02a]   G. Gössler and A. Sangiovanni-Vincentelli. Compositional modeling in Metropolis. In *Proc. 2nd Int. Conf. on Embedded Software (EMSOFT'2002), Grenoble, France, Oct. 2002*, volume 2491 of *Lecture Notes in Computer Science*, pages 93-107. Springer Verlag, 2002.

[GS02b]   G. Gössler and J. Sifakis. Composition for component-based modeling. In *Proc. 1st Int. Symp. Formal Methods for Components and Objects (FMCO'2002), Leiden, The Netherlands, Nov. 2002*, volume 2852 of *Lecture Notes in Computer Science*, pages 443-466. Springer Verlag, 2002.

[GTT02]   F. Gérard, F. Terrier, and Y. Tanguy. Using the model paradigm for real-time systems development: ACCORD/UML. In *Proc. Workshops on Advances in Object-Oriented Information Systems (OOIS'2002), Montpellier, France, Sep. 2002*, volume 2426 of *Lecture Notes in Computer Science*, pages 260-269. Springer Verlag, 2002.

[Gur95]   Y. Gurevich. Evolving algebras 1993: Lipari guide. In E. Börger, editor, *Specification and Validation Methods*, pages 9-36. Oxford University Press, 1995.

[Hal93]   N. Halbwachs. *Synchronous Programming of Reactive Systems*. Kluwer Academic, 1993.

[Has02]   W. Hasselbring. Component-based software engineering. In S. K. Chang, editor, *Handbook of Software Engineering and Knowledge Engineering Vol. 2: Emerging Technologies*, pages 289-306. World Scientific Publishing, 2002.

[Hen01]   T. A. Henzinger. Giotto: A time-triggered language for embedded programming. In *Proc. 1st Int. Workshop on Embedded Software (EMSOFT'2001), Tahoe City, CA, USA, Oct. 2001*, volume 2211 of *Lecture Notes in Computer Science*, pages 166-184. Springer Verlag, 2001.

[Her02]   H. Hermanns. *Interactive Markov Chains and The Quest for Quantified Quality*, volume 2428 of *Lecture Notes in Computer Science*. Springer Verlag, 2002.

[Hil96]   J. Hillston. *A Compositional Approach to Performance Modeling*. Cambridge University Press, 1996.

[HJPP02]   W.-M. Ho, J.-M. Jézéquel, F. Pennaneac'h, and N. Plouzeau. A toolkit for weaving aspect oriented UML designs. In *Proc. 1st Int. Conf. on Aspect-Oriented Software Development (AOSD'2002), Univ. Twente, Enschede, NL, Apr. 2002*, pages 99-105. ACM Press, 2002.

[HM02]   M. Hau and P. Mertens. Computergestuetzte Auswahl komponentenbasierter Anwendungssysteme. *Informatik Spektrum*, 25(5):331-340, 2002.

[HS99]   P. Herzum and O. Sims. *Business Component Factory: A Comprehensive Overview of Component Based Development for the Enterprise*. John Wiley and Sons, 1999.

[Hyp]   Hyperformix. http://www.hyperformix.com.

[IEC95]   IEC. Application and implementation of IEC 61131-3. Technical report, IEC, Geneva, 1995.

[Ilo]   Ilogix rhapsody. http://www.ilogix.com.

[IN02]   D. Isovic and C. Norström. Components in real-time systems. In *Proc. 8th Int. Conf. on Real-Time Computing Systems and Applications (RTCSA'2002), Tokyo, Japan, Mar. 2002*, 2002.

[ITE]   Technology Roadmap of Software Intensive Systems, the vision of ITEA. ITEA Office Association, http://ww.itea-office.org.

[ITU96]   International Telecommunications Union, ITU-TS. Recommendation Z.120: Message Sequence Chart (MSC96), April 1996.

[ITU99a]   International Telecommunications Union, ITU-T. Recommendation Z.100: Specification and Description Language (SDL). http://www.sdl-forum.org, November 1999.

[ITU99b]   International Telecommunications Union, ITU-T. Recommendation Z.109: Languages for telecommunications applications – SDL combined with UML, November 1999.

[JC93]   J.-J. Jeng and B. H. C. Cheng. Using formal methods to construct a software component library. In *Proc. 4th European Software Engineering Conference (ESEC'93), Garmisch-Partenkirchen, Germany, Sep. 1993*, volume 717 of *Lecture Notes in Computer Science*, pages 397-417. Springer Verlag, 1993.

[JC94]   J.-J. Jeng and B. H. C. Cheng. A formal approach to reusing more general components. In *Proc. 9th Knowledge-Based Software Engineering Conference (KBSE'94), Monterey, California, USA, Sep. 1994*, pages 90-97. IEEE Comp. Soc. Press, 1994.

[JD96]   P. K. Jha and N. D. Dutt. High-level library mapping for arithmetic components. *IEEE Transactions on Very Large Scale Integration (VLSI) Systems*, 4(2):157-169, 1996.

[JF00]   H. Jubin and J. Friedrichs. *Enterprise JavaBeans by Example*. Prentice Hall, 2000.

[JKK$^+$01]   C. Jones, M.-O. Killijian, H. Kopetz, E. Marsden, N. Moffat, M. Paulitsch, D. Powell, B. Randell, A. Romanovsky, and R. Stroud. Revised version of DSoS conceptual model. Project Deliverable for DSoS (Dependable Systems of Systems), Research Report 35/2001, Technische Universität Wien, Institut für Technische Informatik, Treitlstr. 1-3/182-1, 1040 Vienna, Austria, 2001.

[Kah74]   G. Kahn. The semantics of a simple language for parallel programming. In *Proc. IFIP Congress (Information Processing'74), Stockholm, Sweden, Aug. 1974*, pages 471-475. North-Holland, 1974.

[Ker01]   L. Kerber. Scenario-based performance evaluation of SDL/MSC-specified systems. In *Performance Engineering – State of the Art and Current Trends*, volume 2047 of *Lecture Notes in Computer Science*, pages 185-201. Springer Verlag, 2001.

[KK94]   K. H. Kim and H. Kopetz. A real-time object model RTO.k and an experimental investigation of its potential. In *Proc. 18th Int. Computer Software and Applications Conference (COMPSAC'94), Taipei, Taiwan, Nov. 1994*, pages 392-402. IEEE Comp. Soc. Press, 1994.

[KK00]   M. Kolberg and K. Kimbler. Service interaction management for distributed services in a deregulated market environment. In *Proc. 6th Int. Workshop on Feature Interactions in Telecommunications and Software Systems (FIW'2000), Glasgow, Scotland, May 2000*, pages 23-37. IOS Press, 2000.

[Kle75]   L. Kleinrock. *Queueing systems – Volume 1: Theory*. John Wiley and Sons, 1975.

[Kle76]   L. Kleinrock. *Queueing systems – Volume 2: Computer Applications*. John Wiley and Sons, 1976.

[KLM$^+$97]   G. Kiczales, J. Lamping, A. Menhdhekar, C. Maeda, C. Lopes, J.-M. Loingtier, and J. Irwin. Aspect-oriented programming. In *Proc. 11th European Conf. Object-Oriented Programming (ECOOP'97), Jyväskylä, Finland, June 1997*, volume 1241 of *Lecture Notes in Computer Science*, pages 220-242. Springer Verlag, 1997.

[KM96]   B. B. Kristensen and D. C. M. May. Component composition and interaction. In *Proc. Int. Conf. on Technology of Object-Oriented Languages and Systems (TOOLS PACIFIC'96), Melbourne, Australia*, 1996.

[KR93]   H. Kopetz and J. Reisinger. The non-blocking write protocol NBW: A solution to a
           real-time synchronization problem. In *Proc. 14th Real-Time Systems Symposium
           (RTSS'93), Raleigh-Durham, NC, Dec. 1993*, pages 131-137. IEEE Comp. Soc.
           Press, 1993.
[KS03]   H. Kopetz and N. Suri. Compositional design of RT systems: A conceptual basis
           for specification of linking interfaces. In *Proc. 6th IEEE Int. Symp. on Object-
           Oriented Real-Time Distributed Computing (ISORC'2003), Hakodate, Hokkaido,
           Japan, May 2003*, pages 51-60. IEEE Comp. Soc. Press, 2003.
[Lam94]   L. Lamport. The temporal logic of actions. *ACM Trans. on Programming Lan-
           guages and Systems*, 16(3):872-923, 1994.
[LB99]   G. T. Leavens and A. L. Baker. Enhancing the pre- and postcondition technique for
           more expressive specifications. In *Proc. World Congress on Formal Methods in
           the Development of Computing Systems (FM'99), Toulouse, France, Sep. 1999,
           vol. II*, volume 1709 of *Lecture Notes in Computer Science*. Springer Verlag, 1999.
[LCS02]   F. Lüders, I. Crnkovic, and A. Sjögren. Case study: Componentization of an indus-
           trial control system. In *Proc. 26th Int. Computer Software and Applications Con-
           ference (COMPSAC'2002), Oxford, UK, Aug. 2002*, pages 67-74. IEEE Comp.
           Soc. Press, 2002.
[Lee03]   E. A. Lee. Overview of the Ptolemy project. Technical Memorandum UCB/ERL
           M03/25, University of California, Berkeley, July 2003.
[Lew98]   R. W. Lewis. *Programming industrial control systems using IEC 1131-3*. IEE,
           1998.
[Loo]   Loop project webpage. http://www.cs.kun.nl/~bart/LOOP/.
[LX01]   E. A. Lee and Y. Xiong. System-level types for component-based design. In *Proc.
           1st Int. Workshop on Embedded Software (EMSOFT'2001), Tahoe City, CA, USA,
           Oct. 2001*, volume 2211 of *Lecture Notes in Computer Science*, pages 237-253.
           Springer Verlag, 2001.
[Mau96]   S. Mauw. The formalization of message sequence charts. *Computer Networks and
           ISDN Systems*, 28(12):1643-1657, 1996.
[MDA]   Model Driven Architecture. \www.omg.org/mda/.
[MDVC03]   W. Monin, F. Dubois, D. Vincent, and P. Combes. Looking for better integration
           of design and performance engineering. In *SDL 2003: System Design, Proc. 11th
           Int. SDL Forum, Stuttgart, Germany, July 2003*, volume 2708 of *Lecture Notes in
           Computer Science*, pages 1-17. Springer Verlag, 2003.
[Mer03]   Mercedes. Innovation – Research & Technology. http://www.mercedes-
           benz.com/com/e/home/innovation/, 2003.
[Met]   Meta-H homepage. http://www.htc.honeywell.com/metah/.
[Mey91]   B. Meyer. *Eiffel: The Language*. Prentice Hall, 1991.
[Mey97]   B. Meyer. *Object-Oriented Software Construction*. Prentice Hall, 1997. Second
           edition.
[MFN04a]   A. Möller, J. Fröberg, and M. Nolin. Industrial requirements on component tech-
           nologies for embedded systems. In *Proc. Int. Symp. on Component-Based Software
           Engineering (CBSE7), Edinburgh, Scotland , May 2004*, Lecture Notes in Com-
           puter Science. Springer Verlag, 2004. To appear.
[MFN04b]   A. Möller, J. Fröberg, and M. Nolin. Requirements on component technologies for
           heavy vehicles. MRTC Report ISSN 1404-3041 ISRN MDH-MRTC-150/2004-1-
           SE, Mälardalen Real-Time Research Centre, Mälardalen Univ., January 2004.
[MG02]   E. Meijer and J. Gough. Technical overview of the Common Language Runtime,
           2002. White paper.
[Mic95]   Microsoft Corporation. The component object model specification, October 1995.
           24th ed.

[Mic01]   Microsoft Corporation. .NET framework developer's guide.
           http://msdn.microsoft.com/library/default.asp, 2001.

[MM01]   J. Miller and J. Mukerji. Model driven architecture (MDA), July 2001. OMG,
           Draft Specification ormsc/2001-07-01.

[MMM93]   R. T. Mittermeir, R. Mili, and A. Mili. Building a repository of software compo-
           nents: A formal specifications approach. In *Proc. 6th Workshop on Institutionaliz-
           ing Software Reuse (WISR'93), Owego, NY, USA, Nov. 1993*, 1993.

[MMM97]   A. Mili, R. Mili, and R. Mittermeir. Storing and retrieving software conponents: A
           refinement based system. *IEEE Transactions on Software Engineering*, 23(7):445-
           460, 1997.

[MMM98]   A. Mili, R. Mili, and R. Mittermeir. A survey of software reuse libraries. *Annals of
           Software Engineering*, 5:349-414, 1998.

[MN98]   N. Maiden and C. Ncube. Acquiring COTS software selection requirements. *IEEE
           Software*, 15(2):46-56, 1998.

[Mol82]   M. K. Molloy. Performance analysis using Stochastic Petri Nets. *IEEE Trans. on
           Computers*, C-31(9):913-917, 1982.

[MOS99]   MOST Cooperation, MOST specification framework Rev 1.1,
           http://www.oasis.com/support/downloads/mosttechnology/MOSTSpecification_Fr
           amework_1V1.pdf, 1999.

[MRB96]   R. S. Mitra, P. S. Roop, and A. Basu. A new algorithm for implementation of
           design functions by available devices. *IEEE Transactions on Very Large Scale In-
           tegration (VLSI) Systems*, 4(2):170-180, 1996.

[MS97]   L. Mikhajlov and E. Sekerinski. The fragile base class problem and its solution.
           Technical Report 117, Turku Centre for Computer Science, Turku, Finland, May
           1997.

[MSP+00]   M. Morisio, C. B. Seaman, A. T. Parra, V. R. Basili, S. E. Kraft, and S. E. Condon.
           Investigating and improving a COTS-based software development. In *Proc. 22nd
           Int. Conf. on Software Engineering (ICSE'2000), Limerick, Ireland, June 2000*,
           pages 32-41. ACM Press, 2000.

[MSZ01]   P. Müller, C. Stich, and C. Zeidler. Components work: Component technology for
           embedded systems. In *Proc. 27th EUROMICRO Conference: A Net Odyssey, War-
           saw, Poland, Sep. 2001*, pages 146-153. IEEE Comp. Soc. Press, 2001.

[MT89]   M. D. Mesarovic and Y. Takahara. *Abstract Systems Theory*, volume 116 of *Lec-
           ture Notes in Control and Information Sciences*. Springer Verlag, 1989.

[MW92]   Z. Manna and R. J. Waldinger. Fundamentals of deductive program synthesis.
           IEEE Transactions on Software Engineering, 18(8):674-704, 1992.

[NAD+02]   O. Nierstrasz, G. Arévalo, S. Ducasse, R. Wuyts, A. P. Black, P. O. Müller,
           C. Zeidler, T. Genssler, and R. van den Born. A component model for field de-
           vices. In *Proc. IFIP/ACM Working Conference on Component Deployment
           (CD'2002), Berlin, Germany, June 2002*, volume 2370 of *Lecture Notes in Com-
           puter Science*, pages 200-209. Springer Verlag, 2002.

[Nee91]   S. Neema. *System-Level Synthesis of Adaptive Computing Systems*. PhD thesis,
           Vanderbilt University, Nashville, TN, USA, May 1991.

[NGS+01]   C. Norström, M. Gustafsson, K. Sandström, J. Mäki-Turja, and N.-E. Bånkestad.
           Experiences from introducing state-of-the-art real-time techniques in the automo-
           tive industry. In *Proc. 8th IEEE Int. Conf. on Engineering of Computer-Based Sys-
           tems (ECBS'2001), Washington, DC, USA, Apr. 2001*, pages 111-118. IEEE
           Comp. Soc. Press, 2001.

[Nic02]   B. Nicolas. MDA experiment in telecom industry. 1st MDA Summer School,
           Brest, France, September 2002.

[Ome]   IST 33522 OMEGA project on Correct Development of Real-Time Embedded
           Systems. http://www-omega.imag.fr/.

[OMG01a] OMG. The COmmon Object Request Broker: Architecture and specification, February 2001.

[OMG01b] OMG. Dynamic scheduling, joint final submission, August 2001.

[OMG01c] OMG. Response to the OMG RFP for schedulability, performance, and time (revised submission), June 2001. OMG, RFP ad/2001-06-14.

[OMG01d] OMG. A UML profile for enterprise distributed object computing, June 2001. ptc/2001-12-04.

[OMG02]   OMG. UML 1.4 with action semantics, 2002. OMG ptc/02-01-09.

[OPC03]   OPC Foundation. \www.opcfoundation.org/, 2003.

[OPN]   OPNET. http://www.opnet.com/.

[OS95]   OMG and R. Soley. Object management architecture guide, revision 3.0, 1995.

[OSE]   OSEK/VDX OS 2.2. http://www.osek-vdx.org.

[PA99]   J. Penix and P. Alexander. Efficient specification-based component retrieval. *Automated Software Engineering*, 6(2):139-170, 1999.

[Pat00]   T. Pattison. *Programming Distributed Applications with COM+ and Microsoft Visual Basic 6.0, 2nd edition*. Microsoft Press, 2000.

[PEC]   PECOS project. http://www.pecos-project.org.

[Pen98]   J. Penix. *Automated Component Retrieval and Adaptation Using Formal Specifications*. PhD thesis, Univ. Cincinnati, Ohio, USA, 1998.

[Per98]   D. E. Perry. Generic architecture descriptions for product lines. In *Proc. 2nd Int. ESPRIT ARES Workshop on Development and Evolution of Software Architectures for Product Families, Las Palmas de Gran Canaria, Spain, Feb. 1998*, volume 1429 of *Lecture Notes in Computer Science*, pages 51-56. Springer Verlag, 1998.

[Pet02]   P. Peti. The concepts behind time, state, component, and interface – a literature survey. Research Report 53/2002, Technische Universität Wien, Institut für Technische Informatik, Vienna, Austria, 2002.

[PP93]   A. Podgurski and L. Pierce. Retrieving reusable software by sampling behaviour. *ACM Trans. on Software Engineering and Methodology*, 2(3):286-303, 1993.

[PW03]   D. C. Petriu and C. M. Woodside. Performance analysis with uml: layered queueing models from the performance profile. In L. Lavagno, G. Martin, and B. Selic, editors, *UML for Real: Design of Embedded Real-Time Systems*, pages 221-240. Kluwer Academic, 2003.

[RAJ01]   E. Roman, S. Ambler, and T. Jewell. *Mastering Enterprise JavaBeans*. John Wiley and Sons, 2001. 2nd edition.

[Ray02]   J. T. Rayfield. Keynote presentation. CASES/EMSOFT'2002, October 2002.

[Reu01]   R. H. Reussner. The use of parameterised contracts for architecting systems with software components. In *Proc. 6th Int. Workshop on Component-Oriented Programming (WCOP'2001), Budapest, Hungary, June 2001*, 2001.

[RL02]   H. J. Reekie and E. A. Lee. Lightweight component models for embedded systems. Technical Report UCB ERL M02/30, Electronics Research Laboratory, University of California at Berkeley, October 2002.

[RNHL99a] H. J. Reekie, S. Neuendorffer, C. Hylands, and E. A. Lee. Software practice in the Ptolemy project. Technical Report GSRC-TR-1999-01, Gigascale Silicon Research Center, April 1999.

[RNHL99b] H. J. Reekie, S. Neuendorffer, C. Hylands, and E. A. Lee. Software practice in the Ptolemy project. Gsrc-tr-1999-01, Gigascale Silicon Research Center, 1999.

[RNR03]   Positionnement du RNRT par rapport aux grandes "Roadmaps" Européennes du secteur des Télécommunications.
http://www.telecom.gouv.fr/rnrt/qdn/roadmap_technopolis.pdf, December 2003.

[RS00]   P. S. Roop and A. Sowmya. A formal approach to component-based development of embedded systems. Tech. Report UNSW-CSE-TR-0004, Univ. South Wales, Sydney, Australia, May 2000.

[SBK01]   Natasha Sharygina, James C. Browne, Robert P. Kurshan: A Formal Object-Oriented Analysis for Software Reliability: Design for Verification. In Proc. FASE 2001, Italy, April 2001 pp. 318-332. LNCS 2029, Springer Verlag, 2001.

[SD98]   J. Smith and G. De Micheli. Polynomial methods for component matching and verification. In *International Conference on Computer Aided Design (ICCAD-98), San Jose, CA, USA, Nov. 1998*, pages 678-685. ACM Press and IEEE Comp. Soc. Press, 1998.

[Sel96]   B. Selic. Real-time object-oriented modeling (ROOM). In *Proc. 2nd IEEE Real-Time Technology and Applications Symposium (RTAS'96), Boston, MA, USA, June 1996*, pages 214-219. IEEE Comp. Soc. Press, 1996.

[Sel02]   B. Selic. Physical programming: Beyond mere logic. In *Proc. 2nd Int. Conf. on Embedded Software (EMSOFT'2002), Grenoble, France, Oct. 2002*, volume 2491 of *Lecture Notes in Computer Science*, pages 399-406. Springer Verlag, 2002.

[SF97]   J. Schumann and B. Fischer. NORA/HAMMR: Making deduction-based software component retrieval practical. In *Proc. Int. Conf. on Automated Software Engineering (ASE'97), Lake Tahoe, CA, USA, Nov. 1997*, pages 246-254. IEEE Comp. Soc. Press, 1997.

[SM83]   G. Salton and M. J. McGill. *Introduction to Modern Information Retrieval*. McGraw-Hill, 1983.

[SM91]   W. H. Sanders and J. F. Meyer. Reduced base model construction methods for stochastic activity networks. *IEEE Journal on Selected Areas in Communications*, 9(1):25-36, 1991.

[SMB97]   B. Steffen, T. Margaria, and V. Braun. The Electronic Integration Platform: Concepts and design. *Journal of Software Tools for Technology Transfer*, 1(1-2):9-30, 1997.

[SOM00a]   R. Soley and the OMG Staff Strategy Group. Model Driven Architecture (Draft 3.2), November 2000. OMG, White paper.

[SOM00b]   R. Soley and the OMG Staff Strategy Group. Overview of the proposed Model Driven Architecture to augment the Object Management Architecture. omg/00-11-05, 2000.

[SOM01]   J. Siegel and the OMG Staff Strategy Group. Developing in OMG's Model-Driven Architecture, November 2001. OMG, White paper, Revision 2.6.

[SR02]   H. W. Schmidt and R. Reussner. Generating adapters for concurrent component protocol synchronisation. In *Proc. 5th Int. Conf. Formal Methods for Open Object-Based Distributed Systems (FMOODS'2002), Univ. Twente, Enschede, NL, Mar. 2002*, volume 209 of *IFIP Conference Proceedings*, pages 213-229. Kluwer Academic, 2002.

[Ste93]   J.-B. Stefani. Computational aspects of QoS in an object based distributed architecture. In *Proc. 3rd Int. Workshop on Responsive Computer Systems, Lincoln, NH, USA*, September 1993.

[Sun97]   Sun Microsystems.Javabeans.
http://java.sun.com/products/javabeans/docs/spec.html, July 1997.

[Sun02]   Sun Microsystems. Enterprise JavaBeans specification.
http://java.sun.com/products/ejb/index.html, 2002.

[SWL+94]   M. E. Stickel, R. J. Waldinger, M. R. Lowry, T. Pressburger, and I. Underwood. Deductive composition of astronomical software from subroutine libraries. In *Proc. 12th Int. Conf. Automated Deduction (CADE'94), Nancy, France, June-July 1994*, volume 814 of *Lecture Notes in Computer Science*, pages 341-355. Springer Verlag, 1994.

[Szy98]   C. Szyperski. *Component Software: Beyond Object-Oriented Programming*. ACM Press and Addison-Wesley, 1998.

[Tel99a]   Telelogic. *ObjectGEODE 4.1 Reference Manual*, 1999.

[Tel99b]   Telelogic. *TAU Reference Manual*, 1999.

[Tel02]   Telelogic. *TAU Generation 2 Reference Manual*, 2002.

[Ten00]   D. Tennenhouse. Proactive computing. *Communications of the ACM*, 43(5):43-50, 2000.

[Tes03]   T. Teschke. *Semantic Component Retrieval Based on Business Process Models (Semantische Komponentensuche auf Basis von Geschäftsprozessmodellen).* PhD thesis, Carl von Ossietzky Universität Oldenburg, Germany, September 2003. (In German).

[TG00]   F. Terrier and S. Gérard. For a full integration of real-time concern into OO models, or "how to popularize real-time programming?". In *Proc. 3rd Int. Conf. UML, The Unified Modeling Language: Advancing the Standard (UML'2000), York, Uk, Oct. 2000*, volume 1939 of *Lecture Notes in Computer Science*, pages 25-35. Springer Verlag, 2000.

[TUC03]   Information Systems & Management. Component Markets – An overview. http://www.tu-chemnitz.de/wirtschaft/wi2/projects/components/, 2003.

[U2P03]   U2 Partners. UML 2.0: Superstructure, 2nd revised submission. OMG Tech. Report ad/03-01-02, 2003.

[UML]   OMG. UML – Unified Modelling Language. http://www.omg.org/uml/.

[USE01]   *USE, a UML-based specification environment*, 2001.

[vO02]   R. C. van Ommering. Building product populations with software components. In *Proc. 22rd Int. Conf. on Software Engineering (ICSE'2002), Orlando, FL, USA, May 2002*, pages 255-265. ACM Press, 2002.

[vOvdLK00]   R. C. van Ommering, F. van der Linden, and J. Kramer. The Koala component model for consumer electronics software. *IEEE Computer*, 33(3):78-85, 2000.

[WBGP01]   T. Weis, C. Becker, K. Geihs, and N. Plouzeau. A UML meta-model for contract aware components. In *Proc. 4th Int. Conf. UML, The Unified Modeling Language: Modeling Languages, Concepts, and Tools (UML'2001), Toronto, Canada, Oct. 2001*, volume 2185 of *Lecture Notes in Computer Science*, pages 442-456. Springer Verlag, 2001.

[WHSB98]   C. M. Woodside, C. Hrischuk, B. Selic, and S. Bayarov. A wideband approach to integrating performance prediction into a software design environment. In *Proc. 1st Int. Workshop on Software and Performance (WOSP'98), Santa Fe, NM, USA, Oct. 1998*, pages 31-41. ACM Press, 1998.

[Wij01]   J. G. Wijnstra. Components, interfaces and information models within a platform architecture. In *Proc. 3rd Int. Conf. Generative and Component-Based Software Engineering (GCSE'2001), Erfurt, Germany, Sept. 2001*, volume 2186 of *Lecture Notes in Computer Science*, pages 25-35. Springer Verlag, 2001.

[WK99]   J. Warmer and A. Kleppe. *The Object Constraint Language: Precise Modelling with UML*. Addison-Wesley, 1999.

[WKB04]   M. Wirsing, A. Knapp, and S. Balsamo, editors. *Proc. 9th Monterey Software Engineering Workshop on Radical Innovations of Software and Systems Engineering in the Future (RISSEF'2002), Venice, Italy, Oct. 2002*, volume 2941 of *Lecture Notes in Computer Science*. Springer Verlag, 2004.

[WPG⁺02]   T. Weis, N. Plouzeau, K. Geihs, A.-M. Sassen, J.-M. Jézéquel, and K. Macédo de Amorim. QCCS: Quality controlled component-based software development. In F. Barbier, editor, *Business Component-Based Software Engineering*, volume 705 of *Kluwer Int. Series in Engineering and Computer Science*, chapter 9. Kluwer Academic, 2002.

[WSO00]   N. Wang, D. Schmidt, and C. O'Ryan. Overview of the CORBA Component Model, September 2000. White paper.

[WZS02] M. Winter, C. Zeidler, and C. Stich. The PECOS software process. In *Proc. Workshop on Components-based Software Development Processes, Austin, TX, USA,* April 2002.

[YS97] D. M. Yellin and R. E. Strom. Protocol specifications and component adaptors. *ACM Trans. on Programming Languages and Systems,* 19(2):292-333, 1997.

[YWRS92] Guohui Yu, L. R. Welch, W. Rossak, and A. D. Stoyenko. Automatic retrieval of formally specified real-time software components. In *Proc. 5th Workshop on Institutionalizing Software Reuse (WISR'92), Palo Alto, CA, October, 1992,* 1992.

[ZW93] A. M. Zaremski and J. M. Wing. Signature matching: A key to reuse. In *Proc. ACM SIGSOFT Symp. on the Foundations of Software Engineering, Los Angeles, CA, USA, Dec. 1993,* pages 182-190. ACM Press, 1993.

[ZW97] A. M. Zaremski and J. M. Wing. Specification matching of software components. *ACM Trans. on Software Engineering and Methodology,* 6(4):333-369, 1997.

17 Executive Overview on Adaptive Real-Time Systems for Quality of Service Management

17.1 Motivation and Objectives

The main goal for a Quality of Service management layer in an *adaptive* embedded system is to provide predictability and flexibility for systems and environments where requirements on resources are inherently unstable and difficult to predict in advance. Such a difficulty is due to different causes. First of all, modern computer architectures include several low-level mechanisms that are designed to enhance the average performance of applications, but unfortunately introduce high variations on tasks' execution times. In other situations, as in multimedia systems, processes can have highly variable execution times. As a consequence, the overall workload of a computing system is subject to significant variations, which can produce an overload and degrade the performance of the entire system in an unpredictable fashion. This situation is particularly critical for small embedded devices used in consumer electronics, telecommunication systems, industrial automation, and automotive systems. In fact, in order to satisfy a set of constraints related to weight, space, and energy consumption, these systems are typically built using small microprocessors with low processing power and limited resources.

For most of these systems, the classical real-time approach based on a rigid off-line design, worst-case assumptions and a priori guarantee would keep resources unused for most of the time, therefore is not acceptable for efficiency reasons. When resources are scarce, they cannot be wasted. On the other hand, an off-line design based on average-case behaviour is also critical, because it would be difficult to guarantee timing constraints when resources are overloaded.

To prevent unpredictable performance degradations due to overloads, a real-time system must react to load variations, degrading its performance in a controlled fashion acting on system, as well as application parameters. The process of controlling the performance of a system as a function of workload variations is referred to as Quality of Service (QoS) Management. Performing efficient QoS management requires specific support at different levels of the system architecture. Hence, new software methodologies are emerging in Embedded Systems, which strictly relates to Real-Time Operating Systems (RTOS), Middleware, and Networks.

The objective of this document is to provide a complete picture of these elements in the context of Embedded Systems, and to show how they relate to Quality of Service Management. After analyzing the state of the art of the available software and methodologies currently used in real-time applications, we describe the limitations of current solutions and the new research trends emerging to overcome them.

Before discussing the different topics in detail, we provide some definition of the main concepts recurring throughout the document, and present some examples of the most important application domains of real-time embedded systems. Then we describe the importance of adaptation in modern embedded systems, with particular emphasis on quality of service management.

Artist FP5 Consortium: Embedded Systems Design, LNCS 3436, 216–226, 2005.
© Springer-Verlag Berlin Heidelberg 2005

17.2   Essential Characteristics

Throughout this document, the concepts of real-time system, embedded system, and quality of service recur very frequently. Considering the broad use of these terms in different research and industrial communities, there is still not a universally accepted meaning for them. For this reason, we decided to provide a number of definitions that will help the reader to better understand the rest of this document.

Embedded Computer System

A computer (and its software) is considered embedded if it is an integral component of a larger system and is used to control and/or directly monitor that system, using special hardware devices. (From IEEE P1003.13/D2.1, February 2003).

Real-Time System

A real-time system is a system whose performance depends not only on the values of its outputs, but also on the time at which these values are produced.

A real-time system is a combination of one or more computers, hardware I/O devices and special purpose software in which there is a strong temporal interaction with the environment. An embedded system acts within – and in many cases on – the physical environment. Embedded Systems are, by nature, inherently real-time.

The environment changes with time and as a consequence there are timing requirements imposed on the software. Since the system simultaneously controls or reacts to different parts or subsystems of that environment, it is naturally concurrent.

A common misconception is to consider a real-time system as a fast computer. This is wrong because, no matter how fast a computer is, its control performance must always be guaranteed against the characteristics of the environment. The most important feature for a real-time system is not speed, but predictability. Typically, in a system with several concurrent activities, high-speed tends to minimize the average performance of the task set, whereas a predictable behaviour aims at guaranteeing the individual timing constraints of each task.

Depending on the consequences of missing timing constraints, real-time tasks are usually distinguished into hard and adaptive:

- A real-time task is said to be *hard* if missing a single deadline may cause catastrophic consequences on the controlled system.
- A real-time task is said to be *adaptive* if missing one or more deadlines does not jeopardize the correct system behaviour, but only causes a performance degradation. For adaptive real-time systems, the goal is typically to meet some *Quality of Service* (QoS) requirements.

Quality of Service

The quality of service is a collective effect of service performances that determine the degree of satisfaction by a user of the service. (ITU-T Recommendation E.800 – Geneva 1994).

Real-Time Operating System
A real-time operating system is an operating system able to provide a required level of service in a bounded response time. (From POSIX IEEE Std 1003.1:2001).

Hard Real-Time Operating System
A hard real-time operating system is a real-time operating system able to enforce hard timing constraints on tasks for which there exists a feasible schedule.

Another common misconception is to consider an embedded system as a small computing device. This is not precise, because many embedded systems are large in size and include several sensors, actuators and computing elements. Examples of large embedded systems include air traffic controllers, flight control systems, flight simulators, and industrial controllers for assembly chains. Examples of small embedded systems include cell phones, car engine controllers, smart sensors, and smart cards.

Most of the embedded systems considered above have a tight interaction with the environment, hence must have real-time features to perform correct operations. For example, in flight control systems, the dynamic behaviour of the aircraft imposes stringent timing constraints on the various concurrent activities related to sensing, actuation, and control. The same is true in flight simulators, with the difference that in these systems the environment is simulated through a computer program.

In some other cases, the environment is so dynamic that one or more internal mechanisms of the computing system need to be modified in order to cope with the changes and achieve the desired level of performance.

Adaptive Embedded System
An embedded system is adaptive if it is able to adjust its internal strategies in response to a change in the environment, to keep the system performance at a desired level.

The implementation of *adaptive real-time embedded systems* requires several issues to be considered at the same time. They involve predictable scheduling strategies, time-bounded operating systems mechanisms, QoS management policies, adaptive middleware software, and expressive programming languages. Moreover, most of embedded systems work under several resource constraints, due to space, weight, energy, and cost limitations imposed by the specific application. Often, such limitations also affect memory and computing power. As a consequence, efficient resource management is a critical aspect in embedded systems, that must be considered at different architecture levels,

17.3   Role in Future Embedded Systems

Since some years ago, the use of processor-based devices in our daily lives has increased dramatically. Mobile phones and PDAs are used extensively. Consumer Electronics (Set-top boxes, TVs, DVD players, etc.) are increasingly using microprocessors as a core system component, instead of using dedicated hardware. This trend is expected to continue in the near future. There are extensive research work on topics such as ambient intelligence, pervasive systems, disappearing computer, home automation, and ubiquitous computing, which deal with integrating computers in our lives even more, and in a way that they are hidden.

Most of these devices share a number of important properties, such as:

- *Limited resources.* They have limited devices, due to cost constraints related with mass production, and strong industrial competition. In order to make these devices cost-effective, it is mandatory to make a very efficient use of the computational resources.
- *Demanding quality requirements.* Unfortunately, in software industry misbehaving products are commonplace. However, this is not the case with consumer electronics, home appliances, and mobile devices. Users are accustomed to robust and well behaved devices. It is obvious that this requirement will not be relaxed because of the usage of processors in their construction.
- *Applications with time requirements.* Some of the applications to be run in these devices have time requirements. They can be related with multimedia processing, process controllers, etc.

The challenge is how to implement applications that can execute efficiently on limited resources, that meets extra-functional requirements, such as timeliness, robustness, dependability, performance etc.

This context is where the term Quality of Service applies. There is no clear and general accepted definition of this topic. The basic aim of QoS is to make it possible for applications to fulfill some extra-functional requirements or characteristics. The following two definitions can help to clarify it:

- *QoS characteristics* have been defined as a quantifiable aspect of QoS, which is defined independently of the means by which it is represented or controlled. They are extra-functional characteristics of a system or application, affecting the perceived quality results.
- *QoS mechanisms* can be defined as a specific mechanism that may use protocol elements, QoS parameters or QoS context, possibly in conjunction of other QoS mechanisms, in order to support establishment, monitoring, maintenance, control, or enquiry of QoS. Negotiation, optimization, and adaptation are examples of QoS mechanisms that are usually supported by QoS middleware.

It seems evident, that an application cannot provide a stable QoS characteristics if it has not some guarantees on available computing power. Then, resource management for providing resource reserves or budgets is basic for supporting QoS mechanisms. The operating system or middleware reserves a portion of the system resources to an application, which has to provide a predefined stable output quality. This has been precisely the goal of years of research on real-time scheduling and schedulability analysis: to ensure that are enough resources (CPU, network bandwidth, etc.) for meeting time requirements. This is the reason for the increment on the interest on real-time techniques during the last years.

Real-time techniques have been one of the bases for the implementation of resource reserves. In particular, the management of CPU has used traditional real-time scheduling policies, such as fixed priority and earliest deadline first. However, the nature of the application to run in the mentioned type of devices makes it very difficult to set an upper bound to the required resources that is usable. In most of the cases, this value will be much higher than the average case. If resource reservation is based on worst case resource usage, an important amount of computational resources may be wasted. In addition, these are not hard real-time applications.

To effectively assign system resources among applications and achieve predictability and flexibility, a number of issues should be further investigated. The most relevant ones include, at the higher abstraction level, protocols for managing quality levels of applications and for middleware QoS managers. Suitable architectures will allow obtaining flexible systems. Also, it will be an added value to aim at supporting as many types of applications as possible; therefore, generality is an issue. At a lower level, further work on resource management algorithms, new task models, admission control, monitoring, and adaptation algorithms should be done.

Also, a promising research area consists in developing hybrid methods, which integrate two complementary types of adaptation strategies: the one that is embedded in the application, and the adaptation scheme that is performed by a QoS manager. Such integration can be done by controlling the CPU bandwidth reserved to a task, but allowing each task to change its QoS requirements if the amount of reserved resources is not sufficient to accomplish the goal within a desired deadline. Using such an integrated approach, the QoS adaptation is performed in a task-specific fashion: each task can react to overloads in a different way and use different techniques to scale down its resource requirements. On the other hand, if a task does not react adequately to a lack of resources, the scheduler will slow it down in order not to influence the other tasks.

In the rest of this document, a number of techniques that are important for supporting Quality of Service are described.

17.4   Overall Challenges and Work Directions

Most of today's embedded systems are required to work in dynamic environments, where the characteristics of the computational load cannot always be predicted in advance. Still timely responses to events have to be provided within precise timing constrains in order to guarantee a desired level of performance. Hence, embedded systems are, by nature, inherently real-time.

The combination of real-time features in dynamic environments, together with cost and resource constraints, creates new problems to be addressed in the design of such systems, at different architecture levels. The classical worst-case design approach, typically adopted in hard real-time systems to guarantee timely responses in all possible scenarios, is no longer acceptable in highly dynamic environments, because it would waste the resources and prohibitively increase the cost.

Instead of allocating resources for the worst case, smarter techniques are needed to sense the current state of the environment and react as a consequence. This means that, to cope with dynamic environments, a system must be adaptive; that is, it must be able to adjust its internal strategies in response to a change in the environment, to keep the system performance at a desired level.

Implementing adaptive embedded systems requires specific support at different levels of the software architecture. The most important component affecting adaptiveness is the kernel; however, flexibility can also be introduced above the operating system, in a software layer denoted as a middleware, and also in the programming language used to develop the application. Some embedded systems are large and distributed among several computing nodes. In these cases, special network methodologies are needed to achieve adaptive behaviour and predictable response. Often such a support cannot be found in today's commercial software.

The rest of this section provides a synthesis of the roadmap, summarizing for each relevant topic those areas in which advances would clearly benefit.

Real-Time Operating Systems

The most important mechanism in the operating system affecting adaptiveness is scheduling. Unfortunately, however, the majority of today's commercial operating systems schedule tasks based on a single parameter, the priority. Recent research on flexible scheduling showed that a single parameter is not enough to express all the application requirements. In order to provide effective support to QoS management, modern operating systems should be:

- *Reflective.* That is, they should reflect the application characteristics into a set of parameters, which can be used by appropriate scheduling algorithms to optimize system performance. For example, typical parameters that may be useful for effective task management include deadlines, periodicity constraints, importance, QoS values, computation time, and so on.
- *Resource aware.* That is, they should give the possibility of partitioning the resources (e.g., the processor) among the existing activities based on their computational requirements. Such a partitioning would enforce a form of temporal protection that would prevent reciprocal interference among the tasks during overload conditions.
- *Informative.* That is, they should provide information on the current state of execution to allow the implementation of adaptive management schemes at different levels of the software architecture. Any difference between the expected and the actual behaviour of a computation can be used to adjust system parameters and achieve a better control of the performance.

To achieve these general objectives, further research is needed in the following areas:

Overload Handling
Predictability in dynamic systems is strictly related to the capability of controlling the incoming workload to prevent overload conditions. In fact, when the computation exceeds the processor capabilities, breakdown phenomena may cause abrupt performance degradation. Computational workload can be controlled using different techniques, each requiring deeper investigation:

- Selection of different QoS levels. Some computations can be performed using different algorithms, leading to different computational complexity. In some case, the complexity can be increased as a function of the desired quality of the result. Hence the workload can be controlled by selecting the proper quality level for each system activity.
- Adjustable timing constraints. In a real-time system, the workload depends not only on the amount of computation arriving per each unit of time, but also on the

timing constraints associated with the computations. Hence, another way to react to overloads is to relax the timing constraints of the application tasks in the presence of high computational requirements.

- Admission control. A third way to control the load is to filter the incoming requests of computation. This solution is the most drastic one, because is solves the overload by rejecting one or more tasks. Hence, the effect of such a rejection on the overall system performance has to be carefully evaluated.

Feedback-Based Scheduling

When application tasks or scheduling algorithms have tunable parameters, finding the most appropriate values is an important issue to optimize QoS performance. In these situations, feedback control theory can be used to estimate current workload conditions and perform proper parameter tuning. Integration of real-time and control theory just begun to be studied and is a promising research area.

Combined Scheduling Schemes

Today's computers are powerful enough to execute multiple applications at the same time. This may require partitioning the processor into several "virtual" machines, each with a proper fraction of computation power and scheduling algorithm. When different scheduling schemes are demanded in the same computer, the analysis of the entire system becomes complex and more theoretical work is needed for providing guarantee tests of multiple concurrent applications.

Energy-Aware Scheduling

In battery-powered devices, reducing energy consumption is crucial for increasing system lifetime. Modern processors can operate at variable voltage levels for trading performance vs. duration. In real-time systems, however, decreasing voltage may cause deadline misses; hence future scheduling algorithms must take voltage into account to meet timing constraints while minimize energy consumption.

In addition, with the constant evolution of hardware, portability is also a very important issue, necessary to run applications developed for a particular platform into new hardware platforms. The use of standards opens the door to the possibility of having several OS providers for a single application or company, which also promotes competition among vendors and increases quality and value. However, extensions are needed in these standards to support application-defined scheduling services and facilitate the evolution from fixed-priority scheduling towards more flexible scheduling algorithms. This additional flexibility is necessary to provide better support to systems with quality of service requirements, even though it is expected that most of the services required by these systems will continue to be implemented in a specialized middleware layer.

The ARTIST project can have an important role in this process as a driver for specifying user requirements, identifying new areas for standardization, and contributing in the production and the reviewing of these standards.

Real-Time Middleware

Currently, middleware technologies are being widely used in many application areas to mask out problems of system and network heterogeneity and alleviate the inherent complexity of distributed systems. However, the recent emergence of new application areas for middleware, such as embedded systems, real-time systems, and multimedia, has imposed new challenges which most existing middleware platforms are unable to tackle. This new application areas impose more demands in terms of resource sharing, dynamism, and timeliness. Therefore, these areas require additional properties from the underlying middleware. Some of them are current subject of study and research, such as middleware support for QoS resource management.

In the last years, some organizations have improved the specifications with respect to real-time systems issues. This is the case of the OMG with respect to CORBA. Conventional ORB (one of CORBA's backbone) specifications present some weak points. Firstly, conventional ORBs neither define a way for applications to specify their end-to-end QoS requirements nor provide support for end-to-end QoS enforcement between applications. Secondly, conventional ORBs lack real-time features; there is no standard programming language mapping for exchanging ORB requests asynchronously (blocking prone). As last point, it may be said that there is a lack of performance optimizations; current ORBs have a considerable throughput and latency overhead. This is due to internal message buffering strategies, long chains of intra-ORB virtual method calls, and lack of integration with underlying real-time operating systems and QoS mechanisms.

Over the last decade, research efforts on COTS middleware, such as Real-Time CORBA, have matured. Former key drawback points in distributed real-time systems as overhead, non-determinism, and priority inversion of the middleware are no longer the dominant factor. Recent studies argue that focus has switched to the COTS operating system and networks, which are responsible for the majority of end-to-end latency and jitter.

Whereas some important features related to middleware as software portability are being addressed with the introduction of intermediate code generation, other features as timely invocations are not resolved. On one hand, the power of software portability has been sufficiently proven. In this respect, emerging middleware technologies try to adjust to this feature. Originally Sun's Java technology and later Microsoft's .NET have developed intermediate code generation technologies to address this issue. This presents some drawbacks for real-time systems that will hopefully be addressed in the near future. On the other hand, timely invocations are of great importance for distributed real-time systems. They are not easy to achieve because they involve the network. There are studies that prove the performance QoS that certain RT-CORBA implementations may achieve for high speed and bandwidth networks. However, lower level issues that involve the operation of the network protocols to handle retransmissions and the effect they have over real-time behaviour have not been fully supported. On another side, other technologies, such as Jini, provide no specific features for real-time systems. It relies on the underlying remote method invocation mechanism (usually RMI), therefore, its capabilities for timely invocations of remote services depend on the features that RMI exhibits for real-time. Currently, there is an ongoing effort to build the specification for Real-Time RMI, which will hopefully lead to the fulfillment of some of the requirements of timely invocations for distributed real-time applications.

Lastly, QoS capabilities and adaptive resource management will play an important role in next generation middleware, especially in fields like multimedia processing. This will allow to achieve a high utilization of the system resources such as CPU, memory and network, in order to enhance the system performance. Also, it will distribute and allocate system resources according to the application requirements. Resource aware middleware systems will need to use QoS management techniques to ensure that the solicited service requirements are met.

Communication Networks

Technological advances in hardware made possible the embedding of both processing and communication functions in highly integrated, low-cost components, fostering the use of a distributed approach in the particular field of embedded systems, either breaking whole systems into separated nodes interconnected through a network or connecting together different pieces of equipment to form a new more integrated system. Both approaches led to the development of many different interconnecting networks, with protocols and services specifically tailored to embedded systems but, nevertheless, based on different paradigms and exhibiting different properties, which are in some cases specifically designed for particular applications.

Mainly along the last decade, distributed embedded systems (DESs) evolved towards highly distributed systems, with growing numbers of nodes, leading to higher connectivity and scalability requirements. However, it also resulted in higher system complexity, even with simpler individual nodes, and led to a stronger impact of the network on the global system properties.

Therefore, the network within a DES plays now a vital role since it supports all the interactions among the set of interconnected nodes and, in general all global system services. The network, or generally the communication system, determines, to a great extent, the support for properties such as composability, timeliness, flexibility and dependability as well as determines the efficiency in the use of system resources. Hence, networks with adequate protocols and throughputs must be used in order to confer those properties to the respective systems, as appropriate.

However, several limitations to the use of networks in embedded systems arise due to different options concerning conflicting concepts, taken in the design of the respective protocols. For example, static versus dynamic communication requirements, shared versus exclusive bandwidth allocation, replica determinism versus low communication overhead, retransmissions versus real-time requirements, replication versus low cost and power consumption. Proper design of the network can help solving these conflicts while at the same time keeping the cost of the final system at low level.

Several trends concerning network design for DESs have thus been identified and discussed. Namely, the continuing move towards higher distribution, the renewed interest for higher integration, dependability integrated within the lower layers, the quest for higher flexibility, the efficient integration of time-triggered and event-triggered traffic, the use of wireless connections and Internet connectivity. These trends are establishing the basis for supporting a new generation of applications that are dynamic and exhibit real-time, dependability and efficiency requirements.

Programming Languages

Embedded real-time systems are mainly small scale but can sometimes be extremely large. For small embedded applications, sequential languages like C and C++ remain the most widely used. For the larger real-time high integrity systems, Ada still dominates. In the telecommunications market, CHILL is popular. In Germany, Pearl is widely used for process control and other industrial automation applications.

Although there is little doubt that the Java language has been immensely successful in a wide range of application areas, it has yet to establish itself completely in the real-time and embedded markets. The introduction of a Real-Time Specification for Java could dramatically alter the status quo. In the future, C# programming language starts to gain momentum, extensions will inevitably be considered to make it more appropriate for real-time systems.

The future for Ada is unclear, as it is perceived to be an "old" language in many areas of computing. This makes it more difficult to obtain funding for research. However, the Ada real-time community in Europe is still very active and topics currently being addressed include: subsets for high integrity applications, kernels, and better support for scheduling. As the need to support more flexible real-time applications grows, the expressive power of the programming systems (language and OS) may become a limiting factor. The more advanced features of Ada (requeue, ATC etc) may then cause a resurgence in interest in Ada.

Interestingly although Ada is considered in some senses 'out of date', an even older language, C, remains very popular. In contrast with Ada, the future for Java augmented by its real-time extensions is more positive. However, there are still obstacles to be overcome before Java can replace its main competitors in the embedded and real-time systems application areas. The main issues are in the areas of inconsistencies in the specification, lack of profiles, lack of efficient implementations and lack of user experience. There is also a need to maintain momentum during the development of the technology. Ada suffered from high expectations that were slow to be delivered – the same could occur to Java.

While Java strives to assert itself into engineering practice, the need for a language that supports the OO paradigm has lead to increased popularity in C++ even though it is acknowledged that its definition has a number of problems. With C++ (and C) the support for concurrency and real-time comes not from the language but from the underlying operating system. The debate about language provision or OS provision (in terms of support for concurrency and real-time) continues with little sign of an early conclusion.

17.5   Document Structure

The rest of the document is structured as follows. section 18 illustrates a brief overview of the general approach used today by the industry to implement adaptive real-time system. section 19 presents some specific analysis of the current design practice in some important industrial sectors, including consumer electronics, industrial automation, and telecommunication systems. Then, the following seven sections are dedicated to specific issues that play an important role for the development of flexible real-time embedded systems:

- **Real-Time Scheduling** is devoted to task scheduling, that is, the kernel mechanism that has the most relevant impact on the performance of a real-time system.
- **Real-Time Operating Systems** presents the kernel features that have most influence for controlling the quality of service of dynamic real-time applications. It also addresses the problem of portability, by presenting the most widespread operating system standard interfaces for developing real-time applications. An important objective of Action 3 is indeed to actively propose modifications or new additions to existing standards that simplify the development of adaptive real-time applications.
- **Quality of Service Management** discusses the different approaches that can be used for controlling the QoS in a real-time system, organizing them in a hierarchical architecture.
- **Real-Time Middleware** is devoted to the software layers provided above the operating system to facilitate the development of distributed real-time applications.
- **Communication Networks** presents the problem of developing large embedded systems consisting of multiple computers connected together.
- **Programming Languages for Real-time Systems** concentrates on Ada and Real-Time Java, which are the most advanced languages used for developing embedded real-time applications.
- **Other Issues** presents aspects that are currently not addressed with sufficient depth in current embedded systems development environments, but would be useful for dealing with novel application requirements. They relate with power-aware computing, multimedia processing, operating systems and middleware support for micro embedded systems, FPGA technology, and probabilistic execution time analysis.

For each of these topics, four different aspects are discussed in dedicated subsections:

- **Landscape** describes the state of the art in the topic, the current products available in the market, their most relevant features and the existing solutions used for developing adaptive real-time systems.
- **Assessment** describes the main limitations of the current software, and identifies what would be required to overcome them.
- **Trends** illustrates the novel research directions that are being investigated to increase the flexibility and enhance the functionality of embedded real-time systems.
- **Recommendations for research** states the most important research priorities that should be investigated to make a qualitative change in the embedded system domain.

18 Adaptive Real-Time System Development

Current real-time embedded systems used in today's industrial products have very limited capabilities for adaptation. The main reason is due to the fact that they are built on top of commercial components that do not offer the possibility of being reconfigured at runtime. For example, at the operating system level, most of the internal kernel mechanisms, such as scheduling, interrupt handling, synchronization, mutual exclusion, or communication, have a precise behaviour dictated by a specific policy that cannot be changed, nor adapted.

The typical approach used today at the operating systems level to affect the execution behaviour is to modify task priorities. This method however does not always succeed and it is not trivial to predict how the QoS will change as a function of priorities. Assume, for instance, that priorities are assigned based on periods, according to the Rate Monotonic algorithm, so that tasks with shorter periods receive higher priorities. In this case, a load variation could be achieved by scaling all activation periods by a constant factor, but such an operation would not have any effect on the priority order in the task set. In other cases, decreasing the priority of a task could raise the relative priority of a longer task, so increasing the overall system workload. In addition to that, task priorities also affect the delays due to blocking on mutual exclusive resources. If the kernel uses a priority inheritance protocol for accessing shared resources, changing the priority of a task at the "wrong" time instant could interfere with the protocol and cause very undesirable effects. This examples show that today's commercial operating systems are not suited for on-line adaptation because they do not provide explicit support for QoS management.

At the network level, the notion of QoS is normally associated with two parameters, network latency and bandwidth. In domains where safety-critical issues are at stake, such as transportation systems, network protocols are typically static without any on-line adaptability, so that the QoS delivered to the application is fixed and well established in all foreseeable operating scenarios. However, in other more dynamic application domains, such as multimedia systems or even telecommunication systems the network protocols have to support high load variations thus making it impossible, or highly undesirable, to use static approaches. In this case, several protocols have been developed that handle dynamic communication requirements on-line with admission control, performing bandwidth reservation. ATM, IEEE 1394 (Firewire) and USB are just three examples. Bluetooth also supports the dynamic setup of synchronous channels with reserved bandwidth, and concerning IP networks, RSVP also supports the dynamic setup of guaranteed bit rate channels. Nevertheless, even with these protocols we cannot talk about adaptability in a full sense because they do not generally support adaptation of the current communication requirements. The situation thus, becomes very similar to the case of operating systems. Current requirements are handled according to fixed or dynamic priorities, or according to a given order such as imposed by token-based methods. The issue is that, in case of overload, there is no adaptation of the current parameters using the referred protocols. Similarly, if bandwidth is freed, it is not exploited to increase the QoS of the remaining require-

Artist FP5 Consortium: Embedded Systems Design, LNCS 3436, 227–228, 2005.
© Springer-Verlag Berlin Heidelberg 2005

ments. The needs with respect to the support for adaptability are of two types, either related with the protocol mechanisms, e.g. dynamic QoS management, or related with the definition of QoS parameters, i.e. semantic issues, that can then be exploited by those mechanisms.

At the middleware level, there are different issues to be addressed. Existing middleware technologies address application heterogeneity allowing distributed applications to communicate, and some even address some real-time characteristics of applications. However, middleware support for QoS resource management is still under research. Some specifications, such as RT-CORBA include features for managing CPU, network, and memory resources. Implementation of such specifications to really create a QoS resource management-aware middleware is still behind it and there is some work to do. Open points are, for instance, mechanisms to specify end-to-end QoS requirements of applications, QoS enforcement mechanisms from the real-time operating systems and networks, predictable and real-time underlying communication protocols, and real-time optimized memory management. Also, code mobility and its security implications is another open research point.

Some adaptation can still be done at the application level. However, it potentially incurs in low efficiency due to the higher overhead normally introduced by the application level services. For example, with some of the network protocols referred above, the application can adapt the rate of a message stream by removing the stream and adding it again with the new rate. This not only incurs in a larger overhead but may also lead to a disruption of the communication service during the process. Normally, in sake of efficiency, adaptation should be handled at the lower layers of the system architecture, as close as possible to the systems resources.

19 Current Design Practice and Needs in Selected Industrial Sectors

19.1 Industrial Sector 1: Consumer Electronics in Philips

Industrial Landscape

Consumer Electronics (CE) products range from miniature cameras and MP3 players to advanced media servers and large displays. In the CE industry, Philips is active at two levels. Philips Semiconductors (PS) is active in the OEM market, selling hardware and basic software to CE industry at large, whereas Philips CE sells end products to the consumer market.

Mainly driven by Moore's law, the evolution in the CE industry is very fast. The software content, measured in ROM size, grows one order of magnitude every 6 to 7 years. To keep up with this speed, the industry moves to families of products based on retargetable platforms: systems on chip that allow media streaming and featurization. For example, the roadmap of Philips Semiconductors centers on the Nexperia program, which comprises "Highly integrated, programmable systems-on-chip (SoC) and companion ICs, software, and reference designs for innovating next-generation multimedia appliances" [Nexperia]. Creating new systems at an ever-larger speed requires a development practice based on fast integration of sub-systems. Increasingly, these subsystems will be acquired from third-party vendors.

Traditionally, CE products have characteristics of being robust, predictable, and easy to use. These characteristics tend to get lost in new feature-rich products with lots of software; maintaining or even regaining them is vital for survival.

Many factors contribute to jeopardizing robustness and predictability. Two of them are important in the context of this chapter. First, increasing the software share in systems implies increasing the sharing of hardware resources. Second, in both hardware and software design, the main focus is on improving average-case behaviour. Countering the effects of these two factors requires manageable and analyzable resource sharing between subsystems. Moreover, the subsystems must be able to live with resource allocations that are less than fully adequate.

Development Context

The development context concerns several fields:

- **Hardware design:**
  Many constituent parts of the hardware architecture in a system on chip can be viewed as resources shared by multiple tasks. Obvious shared resources are fully programmable processors (with caches, also shared), and weakly programmable co-processors. Other important shared resources in systems on chip are the central memory (for cost reasons usually off-chip), the memory access bus, and on-chip networks.

Artist FP5 Consortium: Embedded Systems Design, LNCS 3436, 229–241, 2005.
© Springer-Verlag Berlin Heidelberg 2005

- **Software design:**
  There are at least three types of software, with different characteristics and requirements with respect to timing and resource sharing, but tightly intertwined.

  Control software is typically event driven, and uses only a fraction of the available resources. Control software is generally subject to tight hard timing requirements (deadlines much smaller than inter-arrival distance).

  Media processing software is typically data or throughput driven, and is a major
  consumer of temporal hardware resources (processing, bandwidth). Audio and
  video processing are the main examples in this category, but graphics applications,
  and metadata extraction are starting to be used as well. In general, only a few lines
  of code are responsible for most of the resource consumption. Due to the large resource consumption, close to full system utilization, the sharing of resources is
  critical. For practical purposes, high- quality audio and video (HDTV) is treated as
  hard real-time.

  Interaction software is very complex and vastly increasing in size and complexity. Typical examples are electronic program guide, internet browsing,
  photo/music browsing, broadcast enhancement (for example, player info and statistics in sports games). In a high-end TV set, the total code size currently approaches 4 Mbytes. For this software, the timing requirements are interactive-
  response requirements.

Resource management is a shared hardware/software responsibility. On the software
side, the first responsible are the operating systems. In the hardware, bus arbiters,
network routers and cache controllers are the main players.

State of the Practice

Hardware Design
The relevant hardware-design challenge in the context of this chapter is to make sure
that on-chip data communication and memory transactions meet hard real-time requirements (media I/O) and tight adaptive real-time requirements (cache misses) in a
system that is close to fully loaded. The major quantitative approaches are simulation
and spreadsheet analysis. Real-time analysis techniques are being introduced, but
have limited applicability due to the inherent stochastic behaviour of the major resources.

Software Design
The three types of software (control, media processing and interaction) are integrated
in a single application that runs on a classical third-party RTOS. Large parts of the
media processing are offloaded to media processors, increasingly supported by a
simple real-time kernel. Development support tool set, such as debuggers and analys-
ers, are increasingly integrated with the RTOS/RTK.

Realizing the desired temporal behaviour is to a large extent based on ad-hoc decisions. Quantitative analysis methods are beginning to be applied, mainly in the control and media domains. Sometimes, real-time specialists are called in for assistance.
In software media-processing algorithms, resource adaptation is beginning to be applied.

Interactive applications are typically not resource aware, but the insight that resource awareness must be an integral aspect of application design for embedded systems, is growing. Performance is not systematically addressed, mainly focused on the average case, and without solid quantitative backing.

Links Between Industry and the Research Community

In the domain of this chapter, Philips cooperates (at different levels of intensity) with several members of the academic community, in ITEA projects (Robocop and Space4You), EC-funded projects (Fabric and Betsy), or informally. The universities involved are Mälardalen University, the Technical University of Madrid, Carlos III University Madrid, the Scuola Superiora Sant'Anna, the University of Pavia, and the University of York. The subjects of cooperation are multiprocessor scheduling, reservation-based resource allocation, probabilistic analysis, QoS management (in systems on chip and in networks of consumer devices), and resource adaptation in media processing applications.

Skills and Education for the Future

Education still has to catch up with the present state of the art. In the domain of this chapter, Philips identifies two major requirements for the basic education of software engineers for embedded systems. First, resource awareness has to become a major skill of software application designers, but the resource awareness has to be well founded, and has to be molded into a consistent set of rules of thumb, which are founded on sound theory and backed up by well-tested experience. Second, the currently available quantitative real-time analysis should be integrated in the standard curriculum for embedded software engineers. An explicit effort is needed in teaching engineers to model their systems in such a way that this theory can be applied in a practical situation. For a corroboration of this second requirement, see [Lenc 03].

Challenges and Work Directions

Philips sees the following challenges to advance the state of the practice. Academia can play an important role in meeting these challenges, provided that their solutions are applicable in industrial practice.

- Development of a reference system-architecture that allows the predictable design and realization of complex media-intensive applications at low cost. Such a reference architecture is expected to include QoS-management middleware, QoS-adaptive media processing, and reservation-based resource allocation with temporal isolation [Otero 03]. To meet this challenge, the reference architecture must gain industry-wide acceptance.
- An integrated, structural approach to the sharing of resources in systems-on-chip is required to meet the low-latency and high-utilization requirements of demanding media-processing applications. Since hardware is generally optimized for throughput rather than predictability, probabilistic analysis will be required.

- A design practice supported by appropriate quantitative methods throughout the design cycle from system architecting to detailed design, and throughout the system, from low-level silicon to high-level applications.

References

[Nexperia]   http://www.semiconductors.philips.com/products/nexperia/.
[Lenc 03]   R. Lencevicius, A. Ran, "Can fixed priority work in practice?", in Proc. Real-Time systems Symposium, Cancun, Mexico, 2003.
[Otero 03]   C.M. Otero Pérez, L. Steffens, P. Van der Stok, S. Van Loo, A. Alonso, J.F. Ruiz, R.J.Bril, M. García Valls, "QoS-based resource management for Ambient Intelligence", in Twan Basten, Marc Geilen, Harmke de Groot, eds. Ambient Intelligence: Impact on Embedded System *Design*, Kluwer Academic Publishers, Boston, 2003.

19.2   Industrial Sector 2: Industrial Automation

Industrial Landscape

In the area of Industrial Automation there are two main and different focus: The focus on industrial automation solutions providers and the focus on users. About the first, there is a trend to search distributed solutions and to prepare hardware and software for connecting the general plant actuators, sensors and the controllers. Distributed solutions give a natural automation condition to common industrial needs as usually such plants are physically and topologically distributed. So, having local controllers with some kind of coordination messaging among them is quite commonly planned and deployed in actual factories. For the second, there is an increase of demands for new options and improvements in the automation results, fetching more control of plant secondary data. This imposes a continuous increment of processing power both at the equipment level and the functional level.

The continuous increment both in processing power and memory capacity in local processors gives the opportunity to add new tasks into them, although usually not all of them are automation tasks (supervision, diagnostics, presentation, communication, etc.). And also gives the opportunity to include more complex tasks, for example, in the form of functional blocs, as defined in IEC-1131-3.

Adaptive operation of the tasks execution but preserving the real-time constraints is a possible way to handle such situation and to give insight about how manage the complexity of the tight execution of the different tasks in the real-time processing.

Adaptive real-time systems technologies are very much used in many industrial applications in the area of Industrial Automation. The requirements in typical industrial automation applications, as they are used for example by Equipos Nucleares S.A., Desin Instruments S.A., MAPS S.A., SPIN S.A., Centre CIM, Lear Automotive Spain S.L. and other automation companies include:

- Distributed architecture
- Need to be able to compose the application out of different application components, independently developed

- Event-driven software architecture with different kinds of events: periodic, sporadic, bursty, unbounded, variable rate (discrete or continuous variation) within a range, ...
- Different execution time requirements: variable (discrete or continuous variation) within a range
- Execution of different forms of closed-loop control algorithms, together with different autotunning schemes
- Quality of service requirements, which can be given through a single relative value, with rapid changes
- Different kinds of timing requirements: deadlines (adaptive-real-time and hard-real-time with offline guarantee) maximize utilization (rate or computation budget), execution time budget enforcement; usually, the part of the system with hard real-time requirements has only a small percentage of utilization, and most of the CPU resources are devoted to the adaptive part of the application
- Synchronization requirements: Events and mutual exclusion
- Underlying OS is mostly POSIX (fixed priorities + immediate priority ceiling). The scheduling services used from the OS are: fixed priority scheduling, execution time budgeting, general purpose timers, mutual exclusion that is free of priority inversion

Industrial Automation System Development Context

The European Industrial Automation sector is mainly oriented to give specific automation solutions to different application needs in all the industrial areas: Process Industry, Automotive Industry, Transforming Industry, Packaging Industry, etc. A large segment of those applications are not constrained by tight hard temporal requirements. But as soon as temporal constraints are met, the automation solution requires a new orientation in its design and deployment. Such is the case when fast response is required together with coordination among different controllers is needed for the full automation solution.

After an initial period of centralized automation, the present solutions are oriented to distribute automation tasks between different embedded processors, with some kind of intercommunication providences and looking for an optimized system just by trying to optimize each one of the local processing tasks, but with little effort for the global system optimization. As it is well known, such method can expect just a suboptimal global automation operation. In this way, the resulting architecture drives to a waste of resources, as each processor executes just one (or few) automation tasks, their processing power is underused and as a consequence, an economical loose.

But using more processing both at local level (into the autonomous processor) and at the global level (by using cooperative computing resources) a better result can be devised although a better use of tasks relations has to be studied. One of the main topics to study is the way of adding new conditions and parameters at the abstract tasks definition which could be used for scheduling them in a more flexible way, reacting and adapting both the tasks execution timing and their effect on the automated system.

State of the Practice

As mentioned above, in industrial automation applications there are many requirements for adaptive and flexible timing behaviour. But there is very limited support from the commercial tools and techniques. Most systems are developed using conventional design methodologies for non real-time systems, and then the real-time behaviour is obtained and analyzed via ad-hoc methods, usually depending heavily on the particular application.

Most commercial operating systems only offer fixed priority scheduling where more flexibility would be useful. Timing analysis techniques integrated with the design methodologies are not much used primarily because of the lack of mature commercial tools.

Distributed applications with real-time requirements are difficult to design, because of the lack of support in the networks, the design methodologies, and the timing analysis tools.

In addition, automation tasks usually require some complementary conditions to be meet by the real-time operation, the most important is to have fixed or almost known intersampling periods for each one of the tasks. Other conditions usually met are preserving a timed ordering between some of the automation related tasks executions. As stated above, as more automation tasks are executed into a single processor, and as their execution conditions are tighted, more accurate the real-time analysis has to be performed to guarantee not only the deadlines but also the automation tasks interperiods and their relative ordered execution.

Actually few provisions and methodologies are prepared around about how to include several tasks into a single processor, going close to it's maximum performance operation, while some of such tasks are automation tasks. And also few results are obtained about how to manage internal tasks conditions (flexibility conditions) for accommodating automation tasks, other real-time tasks and the non-real-time tasks. Even that, there are some initiatives in this direction.

Links Between Industry and the Research Community

The University of Cantabria has strong links with the Department of Automation in Equipos Nucleares S.A. (http://www.ensa.es/), which is a Spanish company whose main products are heavy components of nuclear reactors, and which has a staff of approximately 500. The collaboration between the two institutions has been continuous for the past 15 years, and has included the development of seven special-purpose robots with their applications, and several other industrial automation applications.

The Technical University of Catalonia (UPC) has strong links with the industrial design department of DESIN S.A., that is an industrial instruments design company with their own industrial components and programable controllers development. The collaboration has been in the design of controllers both from the hardware level and the software and functional level including communications and self-adjusting automation functions.

The UPC has also largely collaborated with MAPS S.A., and SPIN S.A. both at similar levels as indicated previously. With MAPS we had a continued relation, designing different automation components, from controllers, image processing hardware, mobile robots, and other components, during almost twenty years. About SPIN we had a more sporadic collaboration in different plants and services automation.

Also the UPC has maintained an intense relation with the CIM Center, which is a local government and University spin-off, oriented to give general automation and design solutions to local industries. Through their contacts we had intense industry relations in different industrial areas, both at the automation design, at the plant design and optimization and at the industrial communications areas.

The UPC also is initiating the contacts with Lear Automotive S.A. for applying some of the above mentioned methodologies to a distributed control and supervisory system currently in the initial phase. We are facing the mentioned steps for designing some sets of tasks with some defined kind of flexibility and for designing an adaptive real-time method for optimizing the global system.

Skills and Education for the Future

- Tools and methodologies for the modelling, design, and analysis of adaptive real-time applications
- Tools for timing analysis, both hard and adaptive real-time
- Technologies for distributed adaptive real-time systems
- Methods to describe and analyze some performance characteristics depending of the specific execution instances on automation tasks.
- Methods and tools for integrating real-time scheduling approaches and performance characteristics in flexible real-time systems

Challenges and Work Directions

From the point of view of the adaptive real-time systems, the skills that will be required in the future for industrial automation systems will be in the fields of hardware integration, software design and analysis methodologies. The design techniques in adaptive real-time systems are very much *ad hoc* today, and companies requiring the development of complex applications require well engineered methodologies. Although UML based tools enable conventional software design and analysis, they yet need to be integrated with the following technologies:

- Timing analysis of the application from the design information, including schedulability analysis of the hard real-time parts of the application, and performance analysis of the behaviour of the adaptive parts of the application. A starting point for tools following this integration are the UML profiles for schedulability analysis and for performance analysis, but mature methodologies and tools need to be developed in this area.
- Adaptive and flexible scheduling mechanisms, which are not yet available in commercial operating systems. They need to be integrated into the real-time models used in the future tools for timing analysis.
- Integration of applications with different requirements, including mostly control, data sensing filtering and storing, and multimedia technologies applied in industrial automation and quality assurance. This integration requires handling of qual-

ity of service requirements at the system level, and the integration of the quality of service management services in the commercial platforms and analysis tools.

- Integration of the above technologies in the communication networks, for the development of distributed industrial control applications. Support for adaptive timing constraints in the network is not really available at the commercial level, although there are promising technologies such as RT-CORBA. Integration of real-time distribution into the design techniques and the timing analysis tools are some of the challenges for the future.
- Flexibility provisions into the specification of automation and non-automation tasks. Definition of performance indexes and quality of service requirements from the point of view of the tasks operation at the external application. And methods to analyze how such performance indexes evolve as the adaptation gives flexible operation conditions.

Web Links

Centre CIM	http://www.centrecim.com
Desin Instruments S.A.:	http://www.desin.es
Equipos Nucleares S.A.:	http://www.ensa.es/
Lear Automotive (EEDS) Spain, S.L	http://www.lear.com
MAPS S.A.:	http://www.maps.es
Spin S.A.:	http://www.spin.es

References

[1]   Giorgio Buttazzo, Manel Velasco, Pau Martí and Gerhard Fohler
        Managing Quality-of-Control Performance Under Overload Conditions. In 16th
        Euromicro Conference on Real-Time Systems (ECRTS04), Catania, Italy, July,
        2004.
[2]   Manel Velasco, Pau Martí and Josep M. Fuertes
        The Self Triggered Task Model for Real-Time Control Systems. In Work-in-
        Progress Session of the 24th IEEE Real-Time Systems Symposium (RTSS03),
        Cancun, Mexico, Decembre, 2003.
[3]   José Yépez, Pau Martí and Josep M. Fuertes
        The Large Error First (LEF) Scheduling Policy for Real-Time Control Systems. In
        Work-in-Progress Session of the 24th IEEE Real-Time Systems Symposium
        (RTSS03), Cancun, Mexico, Decembre, 2003.
[4]   José Yépez, Pau Martí and Josep M. Fuertes
        Control Loop Scheduling Paradigm in Distributed Control Systems. In 29th An-
        nual Conference of the IEEE Industrial Electronics Society (IECON03), Roanoke,
        USA, November, 2003.
[5]   Manel Velasco, Pau Martí and Josep M. Fuertes
        Modelling Self-triggered Tasks for Real-Time Control Systems. In Co-design in
        Embedded Real-time Systems (CERTS03), satellite workshop of the 15th Euromi-
        cro Conference on Real-Time Systems, Porto, Portugal, July 2003.
[6]   Pau Martí, Gerhard Fohler, Josep M. Fuertes and Krithi Ramamritham
        Improving Quality-of-Control using Flexible Timing Constraints: Metric and
        Scheduling Issues. In 23rd IEEE Real-Time Systems Symposium (RTSS02), Aus-
        tin (TX), USA, December, 2002.

[7]   José Yépez, Pau Martí and Josep M. Fuertes
           Control Loop Performance Analysis over Networked Control Systems. In 28th
           Annual Conference of the IEEE Industrial Electronics Society (IECON02), Sevilla,
           Spain, November, 2002.
[8]   Pau Martí, Josep M. Fuertes and Gerhard Fohler
           A Control Performance Metric for Real-Time Timing Constraints. In Work-in-
           progress Session, 14th Euromicro Conference on Real-Time Systems (ECRTS02),
           Vienna, Austria, June 2002.
[9]   Pau Martí, Gerhard Fohler, Krithi Ramamritham and Josep M. Fuertes
           Jitter Compensation for Real-time Control Systems. In 22nd IEEE Real-Time Sys-
           tems Symposium (RTSS01), London, UK, December, 2001
[10]   Pau Martí, Ricard Villà, Josep M. Fuertes and Gerhard Fohler
           Stability of On-line Compensated Real-Time Scheduled Control Tasks. IFAC Con-
           ference on New Technologies for Computer Control (NTCC01), Hong Kong, No-
           vember, 2001.
[11]   Pau Martí, Josep M. Fuertes and Gerhard Fohler
           An Integrated Approach to Real-time Distributed Control Systems Over Field-
           buses. In 8th IEEE International Conference on Emerging Technologies and Fac-
           tory Automation (ETFA01). Antibes Juan-les-pins. France. October 2001.

19.3   Industrial Sector 3: Consumer Electonics: Ericsson Mobile Platforms

Industrial Landscape

Ericsson Mobile Platforms offers 2.5G and 3G technology platforms to manufacturers
of mobile phones and other wireless devices. It provides a common software platform
for GSM/GPRS, EDGE and UMTS terminals, and there is a strong focus on application portability, security, power consumption and size. Utilizing available hardware
and software resources in an optimal fashion is crucial both to save costs and to keep
the competitive edge. A key to success is the design of highly configurable, reusable,
and scalable platforms.

Mobile terminals today are getting more advanced by the hour. Features are added
at an unprecedented speed and are usually there to stay. The code base is thus constantly increasing and a 3G feature phone of today typically consists of several million lines of code with use-cases involving large number of parallel activities. Getting
all this to work is the delicate task of a few highly competent craftsmen, and it is not
getting any easier.

Development Context

The possibilities for embedded systems to evolve and become more reliable, while yet
more complex, to some extent depend on what the next generation real-time operating
systems and implementation tools have to offer. The embedded world is in many
respects stuck in a time bubble, using dated technology originating in the early 70s,
e.g. fixed priority scheduling and the C programming language. The problem is not
primarily a lack of alternatives, but more that nobody has been able to make a convincing case for a transition. Every attempt to raise the level of abstraction has included unacceptable penalties in terms of memory and speed. Also from an industrial
perspective, the support for legacy code has often been weak.

Traditionally, embedded systems design has been synonymous with 8-bit controllers and small memory footprints. Mobile terminals of today with a modern 32-bit processor and several megabytes of memory are expanding outside classical embedded system territory. The core of the terminals is still traditional embedded design, but on top of this advanced multimedia features, PDA and gaming functionality are added. The same architecture should scale from entry-level terminals to feature phones and smart phones. A problem in achieving this is how resources, such as CPU and communication bandwidths, are distributed among different activities. Adding or removing features may cause a system to fail. Terminals are highly dynamic systems, and exhaustive testing and design of every possible use case is not always tractable. Therefore, tools and metrics for expressing and handling resource requirements and on-line adaptation may prove to be a key in future system design.

In the smart phone segment, these problems are often addressed by multiple CPU solutions. One CPU is dedicated for real-time tasks including communication stacks, while the other CPU runs the user applications on top of a non-RTOS. This separation between real-time and non real-time functionality simplifies resource allocation since there are multiple resource sets. A real-time task may never be disturbed by a misbehaving user application. However, the downside is the additional hardware and the inter-processor communication introduced. Still there is a need for managing resources for the activities on the individual processors, e.g. limiting the available resources for a game engine in order to save power and communication bandwidth.

A single CPU system, with proper resource management, would provide a viable alternative. A system that supports, for example, "protected timing" along the lines of protected memory would allow us to safely mix real-time and non real-time applications. The benefit of such a solution would be a much more scalable platform. Adding and removing features would become predictable and less hazardous, allowing configuring the system without worrying about unpleasant surprises.

Terminal usage scenarios include receiving and setting up a voice while at the same time handling streaming video with high quality audio. How should resources be divided and how can this be done in a predictable way? From one hand, the system should be able to handle dynamic scenarios, still keeping some spare resources, but on the other hand the final objective is to achieve the best possible quality, and often this means using all available resources. A flexible quality-of-service framework would allow the designer to solve this issue in a more appropriate fashion.

State of the Practice

Today, real-time applications are mainly configured acting on task priorities, which are set to expresses the importance of tasks. Of course, one could argue that the priority value is not about importance, but just a scheduling parameter, however, in practice that would be an academic viewpoint and not an industrial one.

This is for many reasons inadequate when configuring complex dynamic systems, because there are other system constraints that cannot be mapped into a set of priority levels. As a consequence, today, systems require extensive testing and tuning to operate optimally.

A first problem with priority assignment is that activities often consist of several tasks, which may play different roles in different scenarios, rendering the priority assignment even more difficult. Any attempt to group tasks together fails since priority is a global property and will always break any type of encapsulation. From a design point of view, a key issue would be to leave out concepts such as tasks and priorities and instead reason about resource shares and quality-of-service. For example, instead of assigning priority to the game engine, one would allocate shares for CPU bandwidth, communication bandwidth, memory etc. These shares could be firm or adapted on-line within boundaries negotiated by the game engine and the resource manager. More importantly, theses shares should *compose* well, that is, the behaviour of a composition should be predictable when summing its subcomponents and properties of subcomponents should still hold in the composition. In addition, a property might not be fixed, but may, for example, express a relation between a set of given resources and the resulting quality-of-service.

Challenges and Work Directions

The problems mentioned above could be solved by using a programming model which enable the designer to explicitly control the resources assigned to a given activity at a given point in time. Resources can be different types of memory, CPU bandwidth or communication bandwidth. Since hardware is expensive, utilization has to be maximized, and this rules out most static schemes, in favor of dynamic approaches. Power consumption is a key factor in designing software for mobile devices and is, of course, directly related to CPU bandwidth. In today's task-based programming model, the information regarding the timely behaviour of a task is not, in general, available at system level and may therefore not be accounted for by the scheduler. Lifting timing and resource configuration data up to a higher level would be instrumental in providing a superior programming model. Being able to predict utilization allows for clever energy-aware scheduling and in turn better resource management.

Pertinent research directions include adding support for CPU reservation schemes in embedded runtime systems. A major challenge here is to contain computational overhead in an implementation. Also an efficient support for handling quality-of-service properties in a uniform way, i.e., independently of task and resource type, is necessary.

For a novel embedded real-time systems paradigm to reach any level of acceptance within industry, support for legacy code is likely to be of major importance. It must be possible to reuse the many million lines of legacy C code. Standards or open specifications are important for industrial adaptation, since it allows different tool vendors to supply compatible products.

Proper resource and quality-of-service management would enable the implementation of embedded systems that are more flexible, yet more deterministic, than it is possible today. Since such systems would be better specified, their properties would also be verified more easily. By supporting explicit resource allocation and quality-of-service functionality, the system designers would regain control over the system they are set to design.

19.4   Industrial Sector 4: Telecommunications – The PT-Inovação Case Study

Industrial Landscape

In Portugal embedded systems for telecommunications applications are developed by several companies, from SMEs to companies that are part of large groups. Examples of the latter ones are *PT-Inovação* (PTI), owned by PT, the Portuguese Telecommunications company, and *ENT – Empresa Nacional de Telecomunicações*, part of a larger group of Electrical and Electronics industries called EFACEC. PTI has currently 312 employees, most of them graduate engineers or post-graduate in Telecommunications and it is the most significant of the Portuguese companies in this field.

PTI has an active role in the development and deployment of embedded systems for telecommunications applications. PTI kernel activity in this field is focused on subsystems for which there is not world wide large scale mass production and on very specific or proprietary systems, in particular those required for telecommunications systems deployed by PT. However, some systems developed at PTI are produced and deployed in large quantities (of the order of 30,000).

State of the Practice

Embedded systems developed in this field are mainly targeted to the interfaces between communication technologies or media and to coding / decoding operations. Most will work at the telecommunications company side although some are also installed in customer facilities. They may be considered real-time as they have timeliness requirements for some of the critical operations they must perform.

The referred systems are microprocessor based, ranging from 8-bit 51 systems (being abandoned now) to 68000, i386 and, currently, mainly PowerPC based systems. Sometimes (often currently) they integrate a second processor (often a DSP) devoted to specific functions, e.g., MPEG coding. The software development is mostly done recurring to the C language (e.g. GNU GCC). Depending on the system, a proprietary kernel can be used or a real-time operating system, (e.g. iRMX). Currently Linux starts to become the adopted operating system.

The verification of real-time behaviour is made by the experimental inspection of the timeliness requirements at the development phase and at the operation phase by in-situ monitoring.

Links Between Industry and the Research Community

These companies have strong connection with the academic and research community. In some cases (e.g. PTI) they have a significant research team besides the development personnel (they even participate in joint research teams such as the IT – Telecommunications Institute at Aveiro). The participation in European and national projects is also very strong, mainly in the areas of telecommunications protocols and transmission technologies. However, their connection with academia in the field of embedded systems has not been particularly strong.

Challenges and Work Directions

Although it is not a key issue at the management level of the companies, real-time operation is a concern for telecommunications embedded systems designers. The main current interest seems to be in exploring the use of real-time extensions for the Linux OS. It also seems that QoS mechanisms are starting to be recognized as important for these embedded applications, namely in order to increase the efficiency of subsystems and to support the possibility to serve more clients with similar levels of resources.

20   Real-Time Scheduling

Real-time scheduling is the kernel mechanism having the most impact on RTOS performance. After describing existing algorithms and methodologies for embedded real-time applications, we present their limitations in handling dynamic environments, and discuss new research trends for overcoming them in next generation operating systems.

20.1   Landscape

This summary is intended to give a brief overview of the status of scheduling methods, in particular with respect to flexible scheduling. It does not aim to be complete or provide in-depth literature survey. Rather, directions and issues, together with seminal algorithms are presented. Most of the presented algorithms are research prototypes.

Hard Real-Time vs. Adaptive Real-Time

There is a fundamental difference between hard and adaptive real-time systems.

- **Hard Real-Time** preserves temporal and functional feasibility, even in the worst case. Hard real-time system scheduling has been concerned with providing guarantees for temporal feasibility of task execution in all anticipated situations, focusing on the worst case. A scheduling algorithm is defined as a set of rules defining the execution of tasks at system run-time. It is provided with a schedulability or feasibility test, which determines, whether a set of tasks with parameters describing their temporal behaviour will meet their temporal constraints if executed at run-time according to the rules of the algorithm. The result of such a test is typically a yes or no answer indicating whether feasibility will be met in the worst case or not. These schemes and tests demand precise assumptions about task properties, which hold for the entire system lifetime. Examples of hard real-time systems include digital controllers for aircraft, nuclear power plants, missiles, and high-performance production lines.
- **Adaptive Real-Time** manages Quality-of-Service. Often, task parameters and constraints are known only partially beforehand or can change during system runtime; the necessary worst-case assumptions may not be available or too costly to apply. Then, standard feasibility tests cannot be applied and yes or no types of answers are not appropriate. Rather, a quantitative answer about how good or bad an algorithm will perform with the task set is needed, i.e., the Quality-of-Service provided. As feasibility in all scenarios cannot be guaranteed, only adaptive real-time behaviour can be provided. Furthermore, these tests are typically provided for a particular scheduling scheme and task model. Similar to partially known parameters, analysis needs to provide answers when scheduling schemes are combined or change during runtime, or when assumptions about task models do not suffice. Before addressing these issues, we will briefly review basic scheduling schemes and task models. Examples of adaptive real-time systems include multimedia computing, video games, virtual reality, and robotic systems.

Artist FP5 Consortium: Embedded Systems Design, LNCS 3436, 242–257, 2005.

Basic Scheduling Paradigms

Most scheduling algorithms have been developed around one of three basic schemes: table driven, fixed priority, or dynamic priority. Depending on whether a majority of scheduling issues are resolved before or during system runtime, the classified as called offline, or online.

Offline Scheduling
Also called Table driven scheduling (TDS) constructs a table determining which tasks to execute at which points in time at runtime [Kop97, Ram90]. Thus, feasibility is proven constructively, i.e., in the table, and the runtime rules are very simple, i.e., table lookup. TDS methods are capable of managing distributed applications with complex constraints, such as precedence, jitter, and end-to-end deadlines. As only a table lookup is necessary to execute the schedule, process dispatching is very simple and does not introduce large runtime overhead. On the other hand, the a priori knowledge about all system activities and events may be hard or impossible to obtain. Its rigidity enables deterministic behaviour, but limits flexibility drastically. This approach is the one usually associated with a Time-Triggered architecture, such as TTP, which is commercially available.

Online Scheduling
These methods overcome these shortcomings and provide flexibility for partially or non-specified activities. A large number of schemes have been described in the literature. These scheduling methods can efficiently reclaim any spare time coming from early completions and allow handling overload situations according to actual workload conditions. Online scheduling algorithms for real-time systems can be distinguished into two main classes: fixed-priority and dynamic-priority algorithms.

- *Fixed priority scheduling* (FPS) [Liu73, Tin94] is similar to many standard operating systems, assigning before runtime of the system priorities to tasks, and executing the task with the highest priority to execute from the set of ready tasks at runtime. Fixed priority scheduling is at the heart of commercial operating systems such as VxWorks or OSE.
- *Dynamic priority scheduling*, as applied by earliest deadline first (EDF) [Liu73,Spur96], selects that task from the set of ready tasks, which has the closest deadline at runtime; priorities do not follow a fixed patterns, but change dynamically at runtime. To keep feasibility analysis computationally tractable and runtime overhead to execute rules small, however, tasks cannot have arbitrary constraints.

Task Models and Assumptions

The temporal attributes and demands used by real-time scheduling for feasibility analysis and runtime execution form the task model an algorithm can handle. For example, a simple model for periodic tasks may consider worst-case computation times, period, and relative deadline.

Early applications, such as simple control loops, had temporal characteristics that can be represented by simple temporal constraints. Hence, most algorithms and task models are dominated by attributes such as period, computation time, and a deadline. While periods and deadlines are typically derived from application characteristics, computation time is a function of the task code.

When tasks access resources, they introduce a contention issue, which affects schedulability. Realistically, tasks will not execute in isolation; rather, the input-processing-output chain will be distributed over a set of tasks, imposing end-to-end deadlines and precedence constraints. The different importance of timely completion of tasks can be expressed as values. Distribution introduces further issues, including allocation of tasks to nodes [Ram90] and consideration of network effects [Tin92].

Scheduling schemes and feasibility tests for these task models have been presented for the three basic scheduling paradigms. It should be noted that changes in task model typically incur the development of new feasibility tests. As applications gained in complexity temporal demands do no longer fit directly into schedulers, but design needs to decompose applications into tasks and transform temporal application demands to derive timing constraints individually. Constraints handled by schedulers no long match those of applications directly, so artifacts are introduced to suit the scheduler [Ram96].

Only Partially Known Parameters

As mentioned above, the yes-or-no type of responses of feasibility tests do not suffice when task parameters are only partially known. Particular attention has been given to tasks with uncertainty about the actual arrival time, i.e., they do not occur in a periodic manner. These are called aperiodic if no assumptions at all can be made about their arrival time and sporadic if at least a minimum time between to consecutive arrivals can be given. In the latter case, a worst-case assumption, the minimum inter-arrival time, can be used to include sporadic tasks as periodic in the feasibility test [Mok83]. Aperiodic tasks are usually generated by external events and activated by interrupts, for example coming from a sensory acquisition board.

While no hard guarantees can be made about aperiodic tasks, algorithms have been presented to allocate a certain amount of processing time reserved for aperiodic tasks, which allows analysis on response times of the entire set of aperiodic tasks. Typically, this reservation is done via server tasks [Spr89], which lend their resources to aperiodics and which are included in the offline feasibility analysis as place holders, or as bandwidth [Spu94], i.e., a portion of the processing time. In the case of table driven scheduling, the amount and location of unused resources is known to serve aperiodic tasks [Foh95].

Changing Parameters at Runtime

Adapting to changing environmental situations may involve changes to task parameters at runtime. System wide changes, e.g., for changing operational modes in the system, have been addressed by mode change algorithms. Mode changes are demanded, e.g., when the system under control undergoes a number of distinct operational modes with different task sets and schedules. These modes include startup, normal operation, and shut down phases, e.g., of processes. An important mode is the *emergency* mode, when the system needs to take critical actions, overriding all normal operations. A key requirement is that the transition time, i.e., the time interval between request and completion of a mode change is predictable.[Sha89] introduces mode changes for fixed priority scheduled systems, [Foh93] for offline, table driven scheduling, providing some flexibility to static systems by providing for changes of tasks and schedules during system operation.

Changes not of the entire system, but in single tasks, in particular their periods, have to consider their effects on the rest of the tasks as well. *Feedback control scheduling* [Sta99] changes task parameters, in particular periods online to respond to variations in the environment and current load conditions of the system. As both conditions can vary frequently, too frequent responses, which in turn influence the conditions, can introduce instability in the system. Feedback control scheduling applies control theory to estimate effects of changes and to choose parameters to provide for smooth responses and avoid instability..

Elastic task models [But98] are based on the observation that some parameters, in particular periods, can tolerate some adjustments for limited time, provided the adjustments are compensated for. This reasoning follows the model mechanical springs, which can be stretched or compressed to a certain extent and time and then swing back to the normal extent. Thus, periods can be increased or decreased within certain bounds over limited times, and then are brought back to normal values. Special consideration is given to the effect of these changes on others tasks, which may have to adjust their periods in turn.

The focus of scheduling for hard real-time system is on providing offline guarantees for a known set of tasks. Should online changes in task set or parameters result in the amount of processing demanded exceeding available resources, many standard algorithm perform badly, potentially not completing any tasks in time. Adaptive systems apply overload scheduling to cope with the situation properly. Tasks have to be selected for rejection such that the most important tasks find enough resources to complete in time. Often, this selection is based on value to the system for task completion. Fixed priority scheduling algorithms can relate values to priorities directly, while other algorithms, e.g., [But95], aim at maximizing value by task selection. In a distributed system, overload may occur only on some nodes, while others have processing reserves. Then, overload handling may include task migration [Sta87] to less loaded nodes, which has to include network effects, in particular the time needed to select nodes and transmissions of control data..

When an application can tolerate "few" deadline misses, the question arises of how to quantify how many and when. *Weakly hard scheduling* [Ber99] addresses this issue and provides guarantees of the pattern of missed and met deadlines. This guaranteed can be provided off-line in line with standard off-line schedulability tests. Also, online scheduling algorithms that guarantee this minimum guarantee of missed deadlines have been also provided [Ber01a]. Probabilistic reasoning of the number of deadlines missed can be also provided [Bro02].

Combined Scheduling Schemes

Each of the basic scheduling paradigms is selected for a set of specific advantages. When advantages of different schemes are demanded in the same system, the mostly exclusive character hinders efficient exploitation of more than one scheme. Some algorithms have been presented aiming at combining features specific to more than one scheme. For example, in a complex system including hard periodic and adaptive aperiodic tasks, two scheduling schemes need to be integrated for satisfying the different requirements of each task class.

In *hierarchical scheduling* [Reg01] a meta algorithm arbitrates between a set of diverse scheduling algorithms. Thus, it can appear to the individual scheduling algorithms and their applications that they execute alone in the system. Furthermore, the amount of the CPU portion can be set individually for each scheduler and application. Special attention has to be given to shared resources In a similar way, application specific scheduling [Riv02] allows several applications to use their own scheduling algorithm.

Dual priority scheduling [Dav95] is fixed priority based, but includes a limited yet predictable dynamic priority component. Tasks with distant deadlines, are put "on hold", i.e., not considered by the scheduler, until a specified time, called promotion time. Thus, the active task set can be kept small. The Jorvik flexible scheduling framework [Ber01b] uses the Dual priority mechanism as the underlying guarantee mechanism.

Slot shifting [Foh95] combines table driven and earliest deadline first scheduling. First, a scheduling table meeting all task constraints is created offline and analysed for leeway of tasks and the amount and location of unused resources, which are represented via intervals and associated spare capacities. At runtime these are used to include and schedule additional tasks according to EDF, while maintaining the feasibility of the offline guaranteed tasks. Slot shifting can handle complex task constraints for offline tasks and include firm and adaptive aperiodic tasks at runtime, as well as offline and online handling of sporadic tasks.

More than Temporal Objectives

Quality-of-service can also encompass non temporal objectives. If computer faults are to be considered, techniques and their temporal impact for fault tolerant real-time scheduling [Gho95] have to be included. Recently, power-aware scheduling [Ayd01] has received increasing attention as the application of real-time scheduling in embedded devices has to concern energy consumption as well. This issue will be discussed in more detail in section 25.

Probabilistic Scheduling

In many real-time systems, worst-case assumptions and deterministic guarantees tend to be avoided for the sake of enhanced flexibility, better system utilization, more adaptive behaviour and QoS control. This is the case, for instance, of real-time systems featuring adaptive temporal constraints. However, the need for removing deterministic guarantees is not limited to adaptive real-time systems only. As pointed out in [Bur03], a move from a deterministic to a probabilistic framework is required for a number of reasons, which include the inherently stochastic behaviour of fault-tolerant systems, the wide variance of workflow execution patterns and the features of modern super-scalar architectures, like cache, pipelining, branch-prediction etc, which determine a significant variability in task computation times. These reasons apply to hard real-time applications as well.

Providing a task with a probabilistic guarantee on deadline meeting means that the task is guaranteed to meet its deadline with a given probability. To calculate such a probability, a stochastic analysis method is needed.

In the real-time literature, stochastic analysis of real-time systems has been addressed from different perspectives. The Probabilistic Time Demand Analysis (PTDA) [Tia95] and the Stochastic Time Demand Analysis (STDA) [Gar99-1,Gar99-2] are targeted for fixed-priority systems with tasks having arbitrary execution time distributions. The PTDA is a stochastic extension of the Time Demand Analysis [Leh89] and can only handle tasks with relative deadlines smaller than or equal to the periods. On the other hand, the STDA, which is a stochastic extension of the General Time Demand Analysis [Leh90], can handle tasks with relative deadlines greater than the periods. Both methods are based on the critical instant assumption, i.e. the task being analyzed and all the higher priority tasks are released at the same time. This pessimistic assumption simplifies the analysis, but results in only an upper bound on the deadline miss probability.

Another relevant work is [Man01], which proposes an approach which covers general priority-driven systems including both fixed-priority and dynamic-priority systems. However, to simplify the analysis, it assumes that all the tasks are non-preemptable. Moreover, to limit the analysis scope, it assumes that the relative deadlines of tasks are smaller than or equal to their periods and that all the jobs that miss the deadlines are dropped.

An interesting approach is the Real-Time Queuing Theory [Leh96, Leh97]. This analysis method is flexible, as it is not limited to a particular scheduling algorithm and can be extended to real-time queuing networks. However, such a method is applicable to systems where the heavy traffic assumption (i.e., the utilization is close to 1.0) holds.

Other relevant stochastic analysis methods include the one by Abeni and Buttazzo [Abe01], the Transform-Task Method (TTM) [Tia95] and the Statistical Rate Monotonic Scheduling (SRMS) [Atl98]. All of them assume reservation-based scheduling algorithms so that the analysis can be performed as if each task had a dedicated (virtual) processor. That is, for each task, a guaranteed budget of processor time is provided in every period [Abe01,Tia95] or super-period (an integer multiple of the tasks period in SRMS) [Atl98]. So, the deadline miss probability of a task can be analyzed independently of other tasks assuming the guaranteed budget.

The paper [Dia02] proposes a stochastic analysis method that does not put any pessimistic or restrictive assumptions into the analysis and is applicable to general priority-driven real-time systems. The method is general and uniformly covers general priority-driven systems including both fixed-priority and dynamic-priority systems such. The analysis method can handle any task set consisting of tasks with arbitrary relative deadlines (including relative deadlines greater than the periods) and arbitrary execution time distributions.

In multiprocessor environments, the works [Nis02] [Leu03] deal with a probabilistic analysis of dynamic multi-processor scheduling. While the first paper focuses on the overall performance of the scheduling environment, the second one shifts the focus to the scheduling of individual tasks.

20.2   Assessment

Real-time computing systems were originally developed to support safety critical, mission critical, or business critical control applications characterized by stringent timing constraints – and indeed, much of embedded computing is still for these types of applications. Missing a single deadline can jeopardize the entire system behaviour and even cause catastrophic consequences. Hence, these systems need to be designed under worst-case assumptions and executed with predictable kernel mechanisms to meet the required performance in all anticipated scenarios. Tasks and their properties are identified through a static design before the system is deployed, thus ensuring a correct behaviour, but preventing changes during system operation.

Often, systems are dedicated to a specific purpose, involving specific hardware and operating systems. Such systems have been focused on providing single, specific solution to single, specific applications, treating all activities with the same methods, geared towards the most demanding scenarios. While the high cost of such an approach is acceptable for applications with dramatic failure consequences, it is no longer justified in a growing number of new applications, which extend the domain of real-time systems, including multimedia computing, graphic animations, and virtual reality. In these, real-time behaviour is demanded only for a few parts of the systems, a limited number of faults can be tolerated. Instead of strict real-time behaviour for the entire system, these applications demand "also real-time", or some temporal control.

20.3   Trends

In addition to the general requirements outlined in the assessment above, a number of trends can be observed along specific areas.

Note: a number of the issues addressed here for scheduling are detailed on a system level in section 25.

Flexible Scheduling

Flexible scheduling is an underlying theme to most novel scheduling trends which go beyond the standard model of completely known tasks with timing constraints expressed as periods and deadline, providing "yes or no" answers whether all tasks meet their deadlines.

Issues addressed include probabilistic parameters, handling of applications with only partially known properties, relaxed constraints and such that cannot be expressed solely by periods and deadlines, coexistence of activities with diverse properties and demands in a system, combinations of scheduling schemes, and adaptation or changes to scheduling schemes used at run-time.

Adaptive Systems

In adaptive real-time systems, resource needs of applications are usually highly data dependent and vary over time. In this context, it is more important to obtain systems, which can very well adapt their execution to the changing environment than to apply the too pessimistic hard real-time techniques.

Reservation-Based Resource Management

There are several reasons for addressing this topic, and there are also many sometimes very different solutions. One major reason is to provide acceptable response for adaptive real-time tasks, while bounding their interference of hard-real-time tasks. Another reason is the incorporation of real-time legacy code in a larger, often safety-critical, system. A third reason is the increasing size of systems, which requires a compositional, with pre-integrated and pre-validated subsystems, that can quickly be integrated to form new systems. These two reasons imply a third one, viz. the use of hierarchical scheduling. A final reason is the advent of QoS based systems, where applications need to provide QoS guarantees, based on service contracts.

With reservation-based scheduling, a task or subsystem receives a real-time share of the system resources according to a (pre-negotiated) contract. Thus, the contract contains timing requirements. In general, such a contract boils down to some approximation of having a private processor that runs at reduced speed.

Scheduler Composition

Hierarchical scheduling means that there is not just one scheduling algorithm for a given resource, but a hierarchy of schedulers. The tasks in the system are hierarchically grouped. The root of the hierarchy is the complete system; the leaves of the hierarchy are the individual tasks. At each node in the hierarchy, a scheduling algorithm schedules the children of that node. The practical value of a 2 level-hierarchy is immediately obvious: intermediate nodes are applications that are independently developed and/or independently loaded. If the root scheduler provides guaranteed resource reservation and temporal isolation, the applications can (with some additional precautions) be viewed to be running on private processors. We see two very distinct real-time processing domains where some form of hierarchical scheduling is proposed: one is the area of adaptive real-time in personal computers; the other is the area of certified hard real-time systems. In the first domain, [Gai01][Goy96][Ald02] [Reg01][Wan02] proposed a framework for deterministic adaptive real-time scheduler composition. In the second domain, [ARI91] proposes a root scheduler that provides time slots in a recalculated schedule. In most other proposals, the root scheduler provides some form of guaranteed bandwidth allocation [Lip00], [Mok01].

Real-Time and Control Scheduling

In the traditional approach to the analysis and design of computer control systems, controllers are assumed to execute in dedicated processors and these are assumed to be fast and predictable enough to meet all the application requirements. However, when resources such as processor time or network bandwidth are limited, the analysis and design of computer control systems is a challenging task: the resource limitations must be taken into account in the controller design stage, or the controlled system may exhibit unexpected behaviour.

For example, the criteria for scheduling tasks on processors influences the timing of all tasks and can thus introduce timing variability (jitter) in the execution of control tasks. These timing variations in the execution of control algorithms – which are allowed so long as the schedulability constraints are preserved – affect performance and possibly causing instability. This degradation appears because the controller execution violates the timing assumptions of classical discrete-time controller design theory, equidistant sampling and actuation.

On the other hand, trying to reduce jitter for control tasks by over-constraining the control task specification (e.g. by very tight deadlines) reduces the degradation of the controlled systems, although this achieved at the expense of finding feasible scheduling solutions for the entire task set.

These kinds of problems can be addressed using a combination of control and real-time scheduling principles. Instead of separating the two aspects during design, control design and computer implementation have to be jointly considered early in the design.

Scheduling for Media Processing

Motion-sensitive video algorithms (MPEG (de)coding, but also temporal scaling, and (de)interlacing) may have highly varying loads with strict timing requirements: tight jitter requirements on input (broadcast) as well as output (screen), and low latencies because of separate audio processing (home theater), interactivity, and memory constraints.

The freedom of encoding choices provided by the MPEG-2 standard results in high variability inside streams, in particular with respect to frame structures and their sizes. MPEG encoding has to meet diverse demands, depending, e.g., on the medium of distribution, such as overall size in the case of DVD, maximum bit rate for DVB, or speed of encoding for live broadcasts. In the case of DVD and DVB, sophisticated provisions to apply spatial and temporal compression are applied, while a very simple, but quickly coded stream will be used for the live broadcast. Consequently, video streams, and in particular their decoding demands will vary greatly between different media.

A number of algorithms have been presented for efficient transmission and software decoding of MPEG video streams, mostly using buffering and rate adjustment based on average-case assumptions. These provide acceptable quality for applications such as video transmissions over the Internet, when drops in quality, delays, uneven motion or changes in speed are tolerable. However, in high quality consumer terminals, such as home TVs, quality losses of such methods are not acceptable. Recently, the application of real-time scheduling for quality aware MPEG decoding has been introduced [Iso04].

Another demand stems from throughput requirements, as Megabytes of data have to be pumped through the system at a very high rate.

Scheduling with Energy Considerations

The majority of scheduling algorithms focuses on temporal aspects and constraints. With the current trends towards higher integration and embedding processors in battery-powered devices, energy consumption becomes an increasingly important issue. From the scheduling perspectives, algorithms look at tradeoffs between processor speed and energy consumption.

Modelling

Modelling plays a central role in systems engineering. The existence of modelling techniques is a basis for rigorous design and should drastically ease validation. In current engineering practices in industry, models are essentially used only at the early phases of system design and at a high level of abstraction. Requirements and design constraints are spread out and they do not easily carry through the entire development lifecycle. Validation of large real-time applications is mainly done by experimentation and measurement on specific platforms, in order to adjust design parameters and, hopefully, achieve conformity with requirements. Thus, experimenting with different architectures and execution platforms becomes error-prone.

The use of models can profitably replace experimentation on actual systems with incomparable advantages.

- Enhanced modifiability of the system parameters.
- Ease of construction by integration of models of heterogeneous components.
- Generality by using abstraction and behavioural non-determinism.
- Predictability analysis by application of formal methods.

Modelling methodologies must be related to an implementation methodology for building correct real-time systems as a succession of steps involving both the development of software components and their integration in an execution and communication plate-form. These methodologies should support specifying end-to-end constraints at every step in the design process and provide means to automatically propagate them down to the implementation. To be useful in practice, they should lead to and be accompanied by the development of the appropriate middleware, QoS management support and validation tools.

Modelling systems in the large is an important research topic in both academia and industry in the area of real-time embedded systems [Sif01]. There are several trends.

- One line of research consists of the so-called model-based approaches. This research groups the study of unified frameworks for integrating different models of computation [Lee98], languages [Hen01] and abstraction-based design methodologies [Bur01].
- A key issue in a modelling methodology is the use of adequate operators to compose heterogeneous schedulers (e.g., synchronous, asynchronous, event-triggered, or time-triggered). For this reason, some researchers propose model-based theories for composing scheduling policies [Alt02].
- An obvious challenge consists in adequately relating the functional and extra-functional requirements and constraints of the application software and underlying execution platform. There are two current approaches to this problem.
  a. One relies on architecture description languages that provide means to relate software and hardware components (e.g., Meta-H [Bin01]).
  b. The other is based on the formal verification of automata-based models automatically generated from software appropriately annotated with timing constraints (e.g., Taxys [Ber01, Sif03]).

Nevertheless, building models that faithfully represent real-time systems is not a trivial problem and still requires a great amount of theoretical and experimental research.

20.4   Recommendations for Research

Flexible and Adaptive Scheduling

Issues to be addressed in flexible scheduling include handling of applications with only partially known properties, relaxed constraints and such that cannot be expressed solely by periods and deadlines, coexistence of activities with diverse properties and demands in a system, combinations of scheduling schemes, and adaptation or changes to scheduling schemes used at run-time.

While individual steps to adapt scheduling parameters to changes in application demands have been studied, a systematic approach is needed to: identify changes in application and distinguish between temporary and structural changes, determine a desired system response from these in terms of utilization, importance of activities, and temporal constraints, and methods to select and adjust appropriate scheduling parameters.

Reservation-Based Resource Management

Instead of ad hoc solutions to individual scheduling schemes, a next step in this area is providing a notion for real-time contracts that includes the rights and duties of both parties involved in a detailed way.

Currently, reservation-based scheduling is focused on the CPU only. A system wide few, however, including other system resources, in particular network is demanded.

Scheduler Composition

Novel applications combine various types of tasks (software entities) and constraints within the same system. The requirements on tasks may also change dynamically. While off-line guarantees are still essential for meeting minimum performance levels, different types of requirements and runtime changes are included in the system analysis, such as demands on quality of service (QoS) or acceptance probabilities. Often, they require the coexistence and co-operation between diverse scheduling algorithms to combine properties, e.g., to integrate deterministic and flexible activities in the same system. Algorithms might even change during system's runtime to better adapt to environment variations.

In such a new scenario, the basic assumptions made on the classical scheduling theory are no longer valid . New approaches are needed to handle these situations in a predictable fashion. They should enforce timing constraints with a certain degree of flexibility, aimed at achieving the desired trade-off between predictable performance and efficient use of resources.

Constraints Beyond Periods and Deadlines

Timing constraints, such as period and deadline, meet the demands of system models and in particular scheduling algorithms rather than application level requirements. Instead of focusing on application demands, timing constraints are chosen to suit task models mandated by system operation.

Many applications areas, notably for control and media processing, have timing requirements which cannot be expressed properly only by deadlines and periods or which restrict the system if expressed by standard timing constraints. Most current scheduling techniques are designed to handle constraints expressed on the level of periods and deadline. Consequently, they cannot exploit extra flexibility in temporal demands efficiently. One particular restriction is the assumption of timing constraints being static, i.e., they are the same and stay fixed for all instances of an activity. This prevents solving timing problems by changing the set of timing constraints for single instances, e.g., to avoid collisions with other periodic or aperiodic activities, or rearrange subtask deadlines.

While "hard" is defined as having to meet all constraints at all times, and non real-time as the opposite, the "grey area" in between, i.e., meeting timeliness requirements in a less strict way is not well understood. Notions such as "tolerating few deadline misses" are not precise e,g, when can these deadline be missed, at which times, with which concentration etc. A well understood notion to express non hard-real-time requirements, e.g., "adaptive" is needed. Probablistic scheduling algorithm can provide a basis.

Scheduling algorithms should consider more flexible ways of expressing temporal constraints, which meet the demands of application level requirements rather than system models and scheduling algorithms.

Furthermore, novel applications have to meet non temporal demands as well, such as energy consumption, high volume data throughput, or reliability.

Real-Time and Control Scheduling

A number of algorithms to combine real-time and control have been presented. They focus on either area and try to include requirements of the other, e.g., modelling scheduling jitter as control errors, resulting in degradation of both control and system performance.

Instead of separating the two aspects during design, however, control design and computer implementation have to be jointly considered early in the design.

Scheduling for Media Processing

In addition to the demands on flexible and adaptive scheduling and constraints, media processing poses challenges which have not yet been adequately addressed by real-time scheduling.

Media streams have large throughput requirements of high variability, which do not fit the standard "task/deadline" model well. In many scenarios streams are transported over networks which demands network scheduling as well as integration of CPU and network scheduling, due to the dependency of processing and transmissions.

While being fluctuating and flexible in many parts, some activities in the media processing chain, such as display, necessitate strict constraints for high quality. Approaches to accommodate the various needs in the handling of streams are needed.

Furthermore, temporal demands media processing do not fit well the standard "period/deadline" model, due to data dependencies of timing constraints.

Scheduling with Energy Considerations

The majority of scheduling algorithm with energy considerations concentrates on including dynamic voltage scaling into the scheduling problem itself. As the CPU is only one resource consuming power, approaches for a system wide energy view are needed. In particular, the "energy overhead" of scheduling algorithms with respect to CPU, but also other resources, such as memory have to be considered. The effect of scheduling on energy consumers such as displays or disks has to be studied as well.

20.5   References

[Abe01]   L. Abeni and G. Buttazzo. "Stochastic Analysis of a Reservation Based System", In *Proc. of the 9th International Workshop on Parallel and Distributed Real-Time Systems*, Apr. 2001.

[Ald02]   M. Aldea-Rivas and M. Gonzalez-Harbour, "POSIX-compatible application-defined scheduling in MARTE OS", in Proceedings of the 14th Euromicro Conference on Real-Time Systems (ECRTS02), pages 67-75, Vienna, Austria, 2002.

[Alt02]   K. Altisen, G. Goessler, and J. Sifakis. "Scheduler modeling based on the controller synthesis paradigm". Journal of Real-Time Systems, special issue on "Control Approaches to Real-Time Computing", 23:55--84, 2002.

[ARI91]   ARINC 651: Design Guidance for Integrated Modular Avionics", pub. by Airlines Electronic Engineering Committee (AEEC), November 1991.

[Atl98]   A. K. Atlas and A. Bestavros. "Statistical Rate Monotonic Scheduling", In *Proc. of the 19th IEEE Real-Time Systems Symposium*, Dec. 1998, pp. 123–132.

[Ayd01]   H. Aydin, R. Melhem, D.Mossé and Pedro Mejia Alvarez "Determining Optimal Processor Speeds for Periodic Real-Time Tasks with Different Power Characteristics", ECRTS01 (Euromicro Conference on Real-Time Systems), Delft, Holland, 2001

[Ber99]   G. Bernat, A. Burns and A. Llamosi, Weakly hard real-time systems, IEEE Transactions on Computers. 50(4). April 2001

[Ber01a]   G. Bernat, R. Cayssials. "Guaranteed on-line weakly-hard real-time systems" IEEE Real-Time Systems Symposium RTSS. London. December 2001

[Ber01b]   G.Bernat, A. Burns "Implementing a Flexible Scheduler in Ada". Proceedings of Reliable Software Technologies – Ada Europe 2001

[Ber01]   V. Bertin, E. Closse, M. Poize, J. Pulou, J. Sifakis, P. Venier, D. Weil, and S. Yovine. "Taxys = Esterel + Kronos: a tool for verifying real-time properties of embedded systems". In Conference on Decision and Control, CDC'01 , Orlando, December 2001. IEEE Control Systems Society.

[Bin01]   P. Binns and S. Vestal. "Formalizing software architectures for embedded systems". In EMSOFT'01 Springer, LNCS 2211, 2001.

[Bro02]   I. Broster, G. Bernat and A. Burns "Weakly-Hard Real-Time Constraints on Controller Area Network" 14th Euromicro Conference on Real-Time Systems. 2002. Vienna, Austria.

[Bur01]   J.R. Burch, R. Passeronne, and A. Sangiovanni-Vincentelli. "Using multiple levels of abstractions in embedded software design". In EMSOFT'01. Springer, LNCS 2211, 2001.

[Bur03]   A. Burns, G. Bernat, I. Broster, "A Probabilistic Framework for Schedulability Analysis", EmSoft 2003, Third International Conference on Embedded Software, Philadelphia, Pennsylvania, USA, October 13-15, 2003.

[But95]   G. Buttazzo and J. Stankovic, "Adding Robustness in Dynamic Preemptive Sched-
uling", in Responsive Computer Systems: Steps Toward Fault-Tolerant Real-Time
Systems, Edited by D. S. Fussell and M. Malek, Kluwer Academic Publishers,
Boston, 1995.

[But98]   G. Buttazzo, G. Lipari, and L. Abeni, "Elastic Task Model for Adaptive Rate
Control", Proceedings of the IEEE Real-Time Systems Symposium, Madrid,
Spain, pp. 286-295, December 1998

[Dav95]   R. Davis, A. Wellings, Dual priority scheduling, 16th IEEE Real-Time Systems
Symposium (RTSS '95) , Pisa, ITALY

[Dia02]   J. L. Diaz, D. F. Garcia, K. Kim, C. Lee, L. Lo Bello, J. M. Lopez, S. L. Min, O.
Mirabella, "Stochastic Analysis of Periodic Real-Time Systems", IEEE 23rd Real-
Time Systems Symposium RTSS'02,, December 3-5, Austin, TX, USA.

[Foh93]   G. Fohler. Changing operational modes in the context of pre run-time scheduling.
IEIC transactions on information and systems, special issue on responsive computer systems, Nov 1993

[Foh95]   G. Fohler, Joint scheduling of distributed complex periodic and hard aperiodic
tasks in statically scheduled systems, 16th IEEE Real-Time Systems Symposium
(RTSS '95) Dec 1995

[Gai01]   P. Gai, L. Abeni, M. Giorgi, and G. Buttazzo, "A New Kernel Approach for Modular Real-Time Systems Development", IEEE Proceedings of the 13th Euromicro
Conference on Real-Time Systems, Delft, The Netherlands, June 2001.

[Gar99-1]   M. K. Gardner and J. W.S. Liu. "Analyzing Stochastic Fixed-Priority Real-Time
Systems", in *Proc. of the 5th International Conference on Tools and Algorithms for
the Construction and Analysis of Systems,* Mar. 1999.

[Gar99-2]   M. K. Gardner. "Probabilistic Analysis and Scheduling of Critical Soft Real-Time
Systems", Ph.D. Thesis, Univ. of Illinois Urbana-Champaign, 1999.

[Gho95]   S. Ghosh, R. Melhem and D. Mosse, "Enhancing Real-Time Schedules to Tolerate
Transient Faults", Proc. of the 16th IEEE Real-Time Systems Symposium, Pisa, Italy, 1995.

[Goy96]   P. Goyal, X. Guo, and H. M. Vin, "A hierarchical CPU scheduler for multimedia
operating systems", in Proceedings of the 2nd USENIX Symposium on Operating
Systems Design and Implementation, 1996.

[Hen01]   T. A. Henzinger, B. Horowitz, and C. Meyer Kirsch. "Giotto: A time-triggered
language for embedded programming". In EMSOFT'01. Springer, LNCS 2211,
2001.

[Iso04]   Damir Isovic, Gerhard Fohler. "Quality aware MPEG-2 stream adaptation in resource constrained systems", 16th Euromicro Conference on Real-time Systems
(ECRTS 04), Catania, Sicily, Italy, July 2004

[Kop97]   H. Kopetz, H. Real-Time Systems: Design Principles for Distributed Embedded
Applications, Kluwer Academic Publishers, 1997.

[Lee98]   E. Lee and A. Sangiovanni-Vincentelli. "A unified framework for comparing
models of computation". IEEE Trans. on Computer Aided Design of Integrated
Circuits and Systems , 17(12):1217--1229, December 1998.

[Leh96]   J. P. Lehoczky. "Real-Time Queueing Theory", In *Proc. of the 17th IEEE Real-
Time Systems Symposium,* Dec. 1996, pp. 186-195.

[Leh97]   J. P. Lehoczky. "Real-Time Queueing Network Theory," In *Proc. of the 18th IEEE
Real-Time Systems Symposium,* Dec. 1997, pp. 58-67.

[Leh89]   J. P. Lehoczky, L. Sha, and Y. Ding. "The Rate-Monotonic Scheduling Algorithm:
Exact Characterization and Average Case Behaviour", In *Proc. of the 10th IEEE
Real-Time Systems Symposium,* Dec. 1989.

[Leh90]   J. P. Lehoczky. "Fixed Priority Scheduling of Periodic Task Sets with Arbitrary
Deadlines", In *Proc. of the 11th IEEE Real-Time Systems Symposium,* Dec. 1990.

[Leu03]   A. Leulseged and N. Nissanke., "Probabilistic Analysis of Multi-processor Scheduling of Tasks with Uncertain Parameters.", In 9th Int. Conf. On Real-time and
Embedded Computing Systems and Applications, Taiwan, February 2003

[Lip00]   G. Lipari and S.K. Baruah "Efficient Scheduling of Multi-Task Applications in
Open Systems" IEEE Proceedings of the 6th Real-Time Systems and Applications
Symposium, Washington DC, June 2000

[Liu73]   C.L. Liu and J.W. Layland, "Scheduling Algorithms for Multiprogramming in
Hard Real-Time Environment", Journal of the ACM, No. 1, Vol. 20, pp. 40-61,
1973.

[Man01]   S. Manolache, P. Eles, and Z. Peng. "Memory and Time-Efficient Schedulability
Analysis of Task Sets with Stochastic Execution Times", In *Proc. of the 13th Euromicro Conference on Real-Time Systems*, Jun. 2001, pp. 19-26.

[Mok01]   A. Mok, X. Feng & D. Chen , Resource Partition for Real-Time Systems, 7th IEEE
Real-Time and Embedded Technology and Applications Symposium (RTAS 2001)

[Mok83]   A.K. Mok, Fundamental Design Problems of Distributed Systems for the Hard
Real-Time Environment, PhD Thesis, Massachusetts Institute of Technology,
1983.

[Nis02]   N. Nissanke, A. Leulseged, and S. Chillara. "Probabilistic Performance Analysis in
Multiprocessor Scheduling.", In Computing and Control Journal, IEE, London,
August, 2002.

[Ram90]   K. Ramamritham: Scheduling Complex Periodic Tasks, Intl. Conference on Distributed Computing Systems, June 1990.

[Ram96:]   K. Ramamritham, Where do timing constraints come from, where do they go?,
Journal of Database Management, 7(2):4-10, Spring 1996

[Reg01]   John Regehr, John Stankovic, "HLS: a framework for composing soft real-time
systems", Proc. RTSS 2001, London 2001.

[Riv02]   Mario Aldea Rivas and Michael González Harbour, POSIX-Compatible Application-Defined Scheduling in MaRTE OS. Proceedings of 14th Euromicro Conference on Real-Time Systems, Vienna, Austria, IEEE Computer Society Press, June
2002.

[Sha89]   L. Sha, R. Rajkumar, J.P. Lehoczky, and K. Ramamritham, Mode Change Protocols for Priority-Driven Preemptive Scheduling, Journal of Real-Time Systems
1(3), 1989

[Sif01]   J. Sifakis. "Modeling real-time systems -- challenges and work directions". In
EMSOFT'01 . Springer, LNCS 2211, 2001.

[Sif03]   J. Sifakis, S. Tripakis, S. Yovine. "Building models of real-time systems from
application software". Proceedings of the IEEE,Special issue on modeling and design of embedded, 91(1):100-111, January 2003.

[Spu94]   M. Spuri and G. Buttazzo, "Efficient Aperiodic Service under Earliest Deadline
Scheduling", Proceedings of the 15th IEEE Real-Time System Symposium (RTSS
94), Portorico, pp. 2-21, December 1994.

[Spu96]   M. Spuri and G. Buttazzo, "Scheduling Aperiodic Tasks in Dynamic Priority
Systems", The Journal of Real-Time Systems, Vol. 10, No. 2, pp. 179-210, March
1996.

[Spr89]   B. Sprunt, L. Sha, and J. Lehoczky. Aperiodic task scheduling for hard real-time
systems. Journal of Real-Time Systems, 1(1):27--60, 1989.

[Sta87]   J.A. Stankovic and K. Ramamritham, "The design of the Spring kernel," In Proc.
Real-time Systems Symposium, pp.146-157, Dec. 1987

[Sta99]   J. A. Stankovic, C. Lu, S. H. Son, and G. Tao, "The Case for Feedback Control
Real-Time Scheduling," 11th EuroMicro Conference on Real-Time Systems,
York, UK, June 1999

[Tia95]   T.S. Tia, Z. Deng, M. Shankar, M. Storch, J. Sun, L.-C. Wu, and J. W.S. Liu. "Probabilistic Performance Guarantee for Real-Time Tasks with Varying Computation Times", in *Proc. of the Real-Time Technology and Applications Symposium*, May 1995, pp. 164–173.

[Tin92]   K. Tindell, A.Burns and A.J.Wellings, Allocating Real-Time Tasks: An NP-Hard Problem made Easy, Journal of Real-Time Systems, Vol 4 pp145-165, 1992

[Tin94]   K. Tindell, A. Burns and A.J. Wellings: An Extendible Approach for Analysing Fixed Priority Hard Real-Time Tasks , Real-Time Systems, Vol. 6(2), pp. 133-151 (March 1994)

[Wan02]   S. Wang, K.-J. Lin, and Y. Wang, "Hierarchical budget management in the RED-linux scheduling framework", in Proceedings of the 14th Euromicro Conference on Real-Time Systems (ECRTS02), pp. 76-83, Vienna, Austria, 2002.

21 Real-Time Operating Systems

This section is devoted to real-time operating systems (RTOS) for supporting applications with real-time requirements. In these applications, most real-time requirements are derived form the physics of the environment that is being controlled or monitored and this implies that most real-time systems are embedded computer systems, and that an RTOS has to provide facilities for supporting embedded applications. There are many commercial products that can be categorized as an RTOS, even though there is a wide range of products, from very small real-time kernels for small embedded applications with a memory footprint in the few kilobytes range, to the large multipurpose systems controlling a very complex real-time system. Despite this broad range of systems, an RTOS always has the property of being able to provide the required level of service with bounded response times.

In the past and even today, many real-time applications were built without an operating system. They were usually simple applications with a simple cyclic scheduler and some interrupt driven routines, and with all the I/O drivers written directly by the application developer. However, with the cost and power of computers today, real-time applications are much more complex, and require full concurrency support, advanced scheduling services, networking, advanced memory management, time management, and in some cases even graphical user interfaces and file systems for secondary storage. These are the services typically provided by operating systems, and this has made their use more important in real-time systems. It is expected that this tendency will continue in the future.

In this section we will present a cross section of the most important commercial RTOS's available today, and we will also discuss the standards that play a major role in operating systems for real-time embedded applications. Some of these standards are recognized by international bodies, while others are industry standards. In both cases, they belong to a community of users and developers, and not to individual companies.

The role of standards in operating systems in general is very important as it provides portability of applications from one platform to another. With the constant evolution of hardware it is very important to be able to port an application that was developed for a particular platform into new hardware platforms. The programmers are also easily transferred between platforms because the standard imposes a particular model of the system's application program interface. In addition, standards open the door to the possibility of having several OS providers for a single application or company, which promotes competition among vendors and increases quality and value.

There are few real-time operating system standards that specify or facilitate portability at the binary code level. The reason is that in real-time systems there are many kinds of processor architectures, from very small embedded systems to very large processors handling large amounts of data. Binary code portability is usually only practical for families of processors with the same programming architecture. Therefore, current operating system standards mostly specify portability at the source code

Artist FP5 Consortium: Embedded Systems Design, LNCS 3436, 258–286, 2005.
© Springer-Verlag Berlin Heidelberg 2005

level, requiring the application developer to recompile the application for every different platform.

Portability in real-time systems is not complete with current technology. The interface between the software and the hardware devices, mostly encapsulated inside the device drivers, is usually non-portable. And in embedded real-time systems it is usual to access special hardware that requires custom-developed drivers. In many systems this can be a significant part of the overall software development. Still, the majority of the application is usually outside the device drivers and can be made portable if developed to comply to one of the standards.

Another source of non portability is that in real-time systems the port from one platform to another does not imply that the timing behaviour will be unaffected; timing requirements may or may not be met in the new platform (even if it is a faster platform) and the real-time analysis must be reevaluated as part of the migration process. An evaluation of the timing behaviour of the new platform can be done before the migration, to minimize the risk.

In this section, after presenting a landscape of existing RTOS and operating system standards, we discuss their limitations and illustrate the new trends in this area.

21.1 Landscape

Although there are a large variety of real-time operating systems varying in sizes, level of provided services, and efficiency, there are some common elements that can be found in most of them [BG-EC] [BG-DS] [FAQ], giving an answer to: what makes an OS real-time?

- An RTOS usually provides support for concurrent programming via processes or threads or both. Processes usually provide protection through separate address spaces, while threads can cooperate more easily by sharing the same address space, but with no protection.
- Real-time scheduling services are provided because this is one of the keys to obtaining a predictable timing behaviour. Most current RTOS's provide the notion of a scheduling priority, usually fixed, as for the moment there are few systems providing deadline-driven or other dynamic-priority scheduling.
- Although some RTOS's designed for high-integrity applications use non preemptive scheduling, most support preemption because it leads to smaller latencies and a higher degree of utilization of the resources.
- The OS has to support predictable synchronization mechanisms, both for events or signal and wait services, as well as for mutual exclusion. In the later case some way of preventing priority inversion is required because otherwise very improbable but also very long delays may occur. The common mechanism used to prevent priority inversion is the use of some priority inheritance protocol in the mutual exclusion synchronization services. Priority inversions must also be avoided in the internal kernel implementation; among other things this requires the use of priority queues instead of regular FIFO queues in those OS services where processes or threads may be queued waiting for some resource.
- The OS has to provide time management services with sufficient precision and resolution to make it possible for the application to meet its timing requirements.

- OS behaviour should be predictable, and so metrics of the response time bounds of the services that are used in real-time loops should be clearly given by the RTOS manufacturer or obtained by the application developer. These metrics include the interrupt latency (i.e., time from interrupt to task run), the worst case execution time of the system calls used in real-time loops, and the maximum time during which interrupts are masked or disabled by the OS and by any driver.

The real-time operating systems presented in this section largely fit into this characterization.

An RTOS is generally chosen not only for its real-time characteristics, but also for the middleware that is integrated in the RTOS, such as file system, communication stack, for its portability to different platforms (i.e., the board support packages that are provided), and for the associated cross-development environment.

A commercial RTOS is usually marketed as the run-time component of an embedded development platform, which also includes a comprehensive suite of (cross-) development tools and utilities and a range of communications options for the target connection to the host, in an Integrated Development Environment (IDE). Moreover, the vendor generally provides development support. For each successful open source RTOS there is also at least one commercial distributor that provides development tools and development support.

For many embedded-systems companies, the availability of development tools and support is a major requirement for choosing a particular RTOS. The quality of the overall package deal, including service and pricing strategy is often decisive in choosing a particular RTOS.

Not all operating systems presented in this landscape satisfy the RTOS criteria given above and/or the RTOS definition in the Introduction. To get a clearer view of the landscape, we distinguish a number of subclasses. We first present the landscape on the operating system standards, then some major commercially available RTOS, then some LINUX variants, some other open source RTOS, and finally, some typically embedded operating systems that are not real-time. Before going into the detailed descriptions of the RTOS, the development and timing analysis tools will be addressed first.

Tools

In this section, a general description is given of the development tools that make up the Integrated Development Environment (IDE), and of timing-analysis tools that, in some cases, are included in or can be attached to the IDE.

Development Tools
In addition to the general programming tools, such as (graphical) editors, compilers, source code browsers, high-level debuggers, and version control systems there are a number of tools specifically aiming cross development, and run time analysis. Advanced tools in this domain not only address development and analysis of the own application code, but also third-party code and the integration with the OS. Memory analyzers show memory usage and reveal memory leaks before they cause a system failure. Performance profilers reveal code performance bottlenecks and show where a CPU is spending its cycles, providing a detailed function-by-function analysis. Real-

time monitors allow the programmer to view any set of variables, while the program is running. Execution tracers display the function calls and function calling parameters of a running program, as well as return values and execution time. Event analyzers allow the programmer to view and track application events in a graphical viewer with stretchable time scale, showing context switches, semaphores, message queues, signals, tasks, timers, etc. Simulators enable application development to begin before hardware becomes available, allowing a large portion of software testing to occur early in the development cycle.

Timing Analysis Tools
To our knowledge there are two commercially available timing analysis tools: TimeWiz from Time Sys Corporation, and RapidRMA from TriPacific. Both tools are based on Rate Monotonic Analysis (RMA, a modelling and analysis approach for fixed priority systems) [Kle93]. These tools allow designers to test software models against various design scenarios and evaluate how different implementations might optimize the performance of their systems, and isolate and identify potential scheduling bottlenecks of both adaptive and hard real-time systems. There is also a WCET analyzer, aiT, from AbsInt. This tool takes the pipelining and caching of modern processors into account when determining worst-case execution times.

Operating System Standards

In this subsection we will discuss the main four operating system standards that are available today. The main general-purpose operating system standard, POSIX, has real-time extensions that are widely used by the real-time community. It will be discussed as a general-purpose approach to real-time operating systems. We will also discuss three other real-time standards that are more specific to certain application environments: OSEK for the automotive industry, APEX for avionics systems, and µITRON for embedded systems. In a later section, an assessment is made on the main features of these standards, and their limitations and trends are presented.

RT-Posix
One of the most successful standards in the area or Real-Time Operating Systems (RTOS) is the real-time version of POSIX. Virtually all major RTOS vendors claim some level of conformance in this standard.

The POSIX standard for Portable Operating System Interfaces is based on UNIX operating systems. Its goal is the portability of applications at the source code level.

POSIX includes three categories of standards:

- **Base standards**, defining interfaces to operating system services in C. These include the basic UNIX services, and a large number of real-time extensions that achieve predictable timing behaviour and facilitate concurrent programming. With its current definition, POSIX allows portability of applications with real-time requirements [POS01] [POS03a].
- **Profiles** for different application environments, defining standardized subsets of the operating system services. In particular, there are several subsets for real-time systems, and one of them is designed for small embedded systems . The profiles

were developed in 1998 [POS98a] and they were later revised [POS03b] to include all the new interfaces defined in the 2001 version of POSIX [POS03a].
- **Bindings with interfaces** to the operating system services in different programming languages (Ada [Pos92][Pos96][Pos98b], Fortran 77).

POSIX had a large revision in 2001 [Pos03a], when it was merged with the interfaces
developed by the industrial consortium "The Open Group". With this revision there is
now a single POSIX/UNIX standard that includes all the real-time services as optional interfaces. It was later amended with some minor technical corrigenda
[POS03a].

The basic POSIX services include process and thread management, file system
management, input and output, and the notification of events through the use of signals. The real-time interfaces to POSIX are optional for general-purpose systems, and
are mandatory if one of the real-time profiles is used. They define services for the
operating system that:

- Facilitate **Concurrent Programming**
  Services include mutual exclusion synchronization with priority inheritance and
  immediate priority ceiling protocols to avoid priority inversion; signal & wait synchronization via condition variables; shared memory objects for inter-process data
  sharing; and prioritized message queues for inter-process or inter-thread communications.
- Provide **Predictable Timing Behaviour**
  for the application. Services with this objective include preemptive fixed priority
  scheduling, with several options for individual tasks such as FIFO or round robin
  order within priorities or sporadic server scheduling; time management with high
  resolution sleep operations and multipurpose timers, execution-time budgeting for
  measuring and limiting the execution times of processes and threads, and virtual
  memory management, including the ability to disconnect virtual memory for specific real-time processes.

Because the POSIX standard is so large, subsets are defined to enable implementations for small systems. The main characteristics of the four real-time profiles defined
by POSIX.13 [POS03b] are:

- Minimal Real-Time System profile (PSE51). Implementations of this profile are
  not required to support multiple processes, nor a full featured file system. The unit
  of concurrency is the thread. Input and output is possible through predefined device files, but no regular files can be created. This profile is intended for small
  embedded systems. Most of the complexity of a general purpose operating system
  is eliminated: PSE51 systems can be implemented with a few thousand lines of
  code, and with memory footprints in the tens of kilobytes range.
- Real-Time Controller profile (PSE52). This is similar to the PSE51 profile, with
  the addition of a file system in which regular files can be created and read or written. It is intended for systems like a robot controller, which may need support for a
  simplified file system.
- Dedicated Real-Time System profile (PSE53). It is intended for large embedded
  systems (e.g.: avionics). It is an extension of the PSE52 profile adding support for
  multiple processes. For this kind of system, protection boundaries are required be-

tween different parts of the application, and processes are required in this profile for that purpose.

- Multi-purpose Real-Time System profile (PSE54). This profile is intended for general-purpose computing systems running a mixture of applications with real-time and non-real-time requirements. It requires most of the POSIX functionality for general purpose systems and, in addition, most of the real-time services.

Ada bindings exist for most of the POSIX operating system services [Pos92][Pos96] [Pos98b], except those developed after 1999, for which work is ongoing. This makes it possible to access the OS services from both C and Ada language applications, and to achieve interoperability between parts of an application written in either language.

In summary, the real-time extensions to POSIX have brought portability, for the first time, to real-time applications. The real-time services support the development of fixed-priority real-time systems, and include all the services required to guarantee a real-time response, such as bounded response times, priority inheritance synchronization protocols that avoid priority inversions, and execution-time budgeting that allows temporal protection and increases robustness. As we will describe below, in the future it is expected that real-time POSIX evolves towards more flexible scheduling schemes.

OSEK

OSEK/VDX is a joint project of many automotive industries that aims at the definition of an industry standard for an open-ended architecture for distributed control units in vehicles.

The term OSEK means "Offene Systeme und deren Schnittstellen für die Elektronik im Kraftfahrzeug" (Open systems and the corresponding interfaces for automotive electronics); the term VDX means Vehicle Distributed eXecutive. This section shortly describes the specification of the Operating System Specification, release 2.2, and recalls some other OSEK documents [OSEK].

The objective of the standard is to describe an environment which supports efficient utilization of resources for automotive control unit application software. This standard can be viewed as a set of API for real-time operating system (OSEK) integrated on a network management system (VDX) that together describes the characteristics of a distributed environment that can be used for developing automotive applications.

The typical applications that have to be implemented have tight real-time constraints and an high criticality (for example, a power-train application). In addition, these applications are usually produced in high volumes. Therefore, in order to save on production costs, there is a strong push towards the optimization of the application, by reducing the memory footprint to a minimum, enhancing as much as it is possible the OS performance.

The philosophy that drove the main architectural choices of the OSEK Operating System is inspired in the following set of application requirements and characteristics:

- **Scalability**. An OSEK compatible operating system is intended for use on a wide range control units (from systems with very limited hardware resources like 8 bit microcontrollers, to more powerful hardware platforms like 32-bit microcontrollers). To support such a wide range of systems, the standard defines four conformance classes that have increasing complexity. However, memory protection is not supported at all.

- **Software portability**. The standard specifies an ISO/ANSI-C interface between the application and the operating system. The aim of this interface is to give the ability to transfer an application's software from one ECU to another ECU without big changes inside the application. Due to the wide variety of hardware where the OS has to work in, the standard does not specify any interface to the I/O subsystem. Note that this fact reduces (if not prohibits) the portability of the application source code, since the I/O system is one of the main software part that impacts on the architecture of the software. The prime focus is not to achieve 100% compatibility between the application modules, but to ease their direct portability between compliant operating systems.

- **Configurability**. Another pre-requisite needed to adapt the OS to a wide range of hardware is a high degree of modularity and configurability. This configurability is reflected by the tool chain proposed by the OSEK standard, where appropriate configuration tools help the designer in tuning the system services and the system footprint. Moreover, a language called OIL (OSEK Implementation Language) is proposed to help the definition of standardized configuration information.

- **Static allocation of software components**. All the OS objects and the application components are statically allocated. The number of application tasks, their code, the required resources and services are defined at compile time. Note that this approach simplifies the internal structure of the kernel and makes it easier to deploy the kernel and the application code on a ROM. It is completely different from a dynamic approach followed in other OS standards like for example POSIX.

- **Support for Time Triggered Architectures**. The OSEK Standard provides the specification of OSEKTime OS, a time triggered OS that can be fully integrated in the OSEK/VDX framework.

APEX (ARINC)

APEX is a standard for an operating system interface for avionics systems. Traditionally, avionics computer systems and software have followed a federated approach – separate software functions allocated to dedicated (often physically disjoint) computing "black-boxes". Such architectures often lead to inefficient resource utilization at run-time. In recent years there has been a considerable amount of effort undertaken by ARINC to define standards for Integrated Modular Avionics (IMA) [Ari91]. IMA proposes the integration of avionics software functions to save physical resources. Also, to cut development costs, IMA encompasses a number of standards for hardware and software. One such standard is the operating system interface for IMA applications (i.e. distributed multiprocessor architectures with shared memory and network communications), called the Avionics Application Software Standard Interface (APEX) [Ari96]. The goal of APEX is to allow analyzable safety critical real-time applications to be implemented, certified and executed.

APEX is envisaged to be a system layer providing a mapping between application and O/S services. The scope of the APEX layer is intended to provide the minimum functionality required by an embedded avionics application. The APEX standard also provides some indication as to the expected behaviour of the O/S services (expressed as pseudo-code). In turn, the O/S interfaces to underlying hardware via a standard interface termed COEX, sitting upon a Hardware Interface System (HWIS).The purpose of COEX/HWIS is to enable standard interfaces to be seen by the O/S and therefore to enhance portability of the O/S. It is envisaged that the COEX/HWIS layer is small – basic memory management, interrupt handling etc.

APEX supports applications structured according to the central principles of Integrated Modular Avionics (IMA):

- Physical memory is subdivided into partitions. It is envisaged that software subsystems will occupy distinct partitions at run-time.
- Each partition contains one or more processes which may communicate both with processes within the same partition and with those from other partitions.

There is no limit in APEX on the number and size of partitions and processes (within the bounds of physical memory). The unit of distribution is the partition.

Each partition has a number of properties, including the criticality level, period, duration and lock or preemption level. Whilst allocation to a partition is criticality based, allocation criteria to partitions of identical criticality could be application specific, use temporal characteristics, or components subject to change.

APEX dictates that a cyclic schedule is used to schedule partitions. The schedule is created offline containing all partitions at least once, although some may appear more times, depending upon the relationship between a partition's period and the length of the schedule. Thus, partitions are temporally isolated from each another. Consequently, a non-critical partition cannot consume more processing resources than have been allocated to it in the cyclic schedule. These facilities together with hardware memory management techniques provide the main fire-walling facilities in APEX.

Each partition contains one or more application processes, each process having attributes, including a period, time capacity, base and current priority, and running state. Processes are initially "dormant" and ineligible for execution. When the process is started, it enters the "ready" state and becomes a candidate for execution. Processes are scheduled on a fixed priority basis. That is, when a partition is scheduled, the processor is then assigned to the highest priority "ready" process amongst those in the partition current priority is used). The selected process now enters the "running" state. During the execution of a process it may enter the "waiting" state if it needs a system resource or suspends itself.

Under APEX, it is expected that all missed deadlines will be detected by checking for a missed deadline when a re-scheduling operation occurs (e.g. at a preemption). Thus, deadlines expiring outside the partition time-slice are only recognized at the start of the next time-slice for that partition.

Communication between processes in different partitions (whether on same processor or not) is via message passing over logical ports and physical channels. Currently, APEX restricts such messages to be from a single sender to a single receiver. Physical channels are established at initialization time. Ports represent the logical connections between processes (in different partitions). Many ports maybe mapped to a single channel. The application communicates via ports, which the O/S maps to an appropriate channel. Two forms of message-passing over ports are given:

- **Sampling Messages** – the port contains a single slot of message buffer, where arrival of a new message overwrites the previous contents of the buffer. The message is read non-destructively.
- **Queuing Messages** – the port contains a multi-slot message buffer, where incoming messages are stored in FIFO order. The read operation is destructive. When the buffer is full, APEX dictates that no further sends may occur (the sender waits). Also, when the buffer is empty, a process will be forced to wait if it attempts to read a message.

Messages have other attributes, including fixed or variable lengths and requirement of an acknowledgment. Processes within a partition can communicate without the overhead of the full inter-partition message passing system using a variety of facilities including conventional buffers, semaphores and events. Note that none of these are visible outside the partition.

Real-time systems have been built successfully (and certified) using APEX, for example some critical systems within the Boeing 777 aircraft. Also, a demonstration APEX implementation has also been completed where APEX (and the underlying minimal OS) is entirely written using the Ravenscar or SPARK subsets of Ada 95 [Bar97].

Micro-ITRON

The ITRON (Industrial TRON: "The Real-time Operating system Nucleus") project started in 1984, in Japan. ITRON is an architecture for real-time operating systems used to build embedded systems. The ITRON project has developed a series of de-facto standards for real-time kernels, the previous of which was the µITRON 3.0 specification [Sak98], released in 1993. It included connection functions that allow a single embedded system to be implemented over a network. There are approximately 50 ITRON real-time kernel products for 35 processors registered with the TRON association, almost exclusively in Japan. The ITRON standards primarily aim at small systems (8-16 and 32 bits).

ITRON specification kernels have been applied over a large range of embedded application domains: audio/visual equipment (TVs, VCRs, digital cameras, STBs, audio components), home appliances (Microwave ovens, rice cookers, air-conditioners, washing machines), personal information appliances (PDAs, personal organizers, car navigation systems), entertainment (game gear, electronic musical instruments), PC peripherals (printers, scanners, disk drives, CD-ROM drives), office equipment (copiers, FAX machines, word processors), communication equipment (phone answering machines, ISDN telephones, cellular phones, PCS terminals, ATM switches, broadcasting equipment, wireless systems, satellites), transportation (automobiles), industrial control (plant control, industrial robots) and others (elevators, vending machines, medical equipment, data terminals).

The µITRON 4.0 specification [Tak02] combines the loose standardization that is typical for ITRON standards with a Standard Profile that supports the strict standardization needed for portability. In defining the Standard Profile, an effort has been made to maximize software portability while maintaining scalability. As an example, a mechanism has been introduced for improving the portability of interrupt handlers while keeping overhead small. The Standard Profile assumes the following system image: high-end 16-32 bit processor, kernel code size 10 to 20 KB when all functions included, whole system linked in one module, kernel object statically generated. There is no protection mechanism. The Standard Profile supports task priorities, semaphores, message queues, and mutual exclusion primitives with priority inheritance and priority ceiling protocols.

Currently, the ITRON project is making an effort to address the English-language community as well. Supposedly, IEEE CS Press published the English version of the μITRON 3.0 specification. The μITRON4.0 specification is available in English from the ITRON website http://www.ertl.jp/ITRON/home-e.html.

Commercial Real Time Operating Systems (RTOS)

At the time of this writing, there were 101 commercial RTOS listed and described in [BG-EC] (see also [BG-DS]). Some major players in this field are VxWorks (Wind River), OSE (OSE Systems), Windows CE (Microsoft), QNX, and Integrity (Green Hills). It is not the objective of this document to describe them all. In this section, only two systems are described: VxWorks, from Wind River, the major RTOS of the largest vendor (measured in terms of turnover), and the OSE family, from OSE Systems, a Swedish company. Integrity, the RTOS with the fastest growing market share, is also mentioned briefly.

VxWorks
This RTOS is produced by Wind River Systems and comes in two flavors:

- VxWorks 5.x is a state-of-the practice RTOS that satisfies the criteria for a "good" operating system given above. The RTOS is marketed as the run-time component of the development platform Tornado. VxWorks conforms to real-time POSIX [POS03a]. Graphics, multiprocessing support, memory management unit, connectivity, Java support, and file systems are available as separate services. All major CPU platforms for embedded systems are supported.
- VxWorks AE conforms to the POSIX standard as well as to the APEX standard. The key new concept in AE is the "protection domain", which corresponds to the partition in [ARI96]. All memory-based resources, such as tasks, queues, and semaphores are local to the protected domain, which also provides the basis for automated resource reclamation. An optional Arinc-653 compatible protection domain scheduler (Arinc scheduler for short) extends the protection to the temporal domain. Such a two-level scheduler provides a guaranteed CPU time window for a protection domain (a protection domain instance) in which that protection domain's tasks will always be able to run. Actions of tasks in other protection domains can have no effect on the availability of the protection domain instance to the designated protection domain(s). Priority-based preemptive scheduling is used within a protection domain, not between protection domains. VxWorks 5.x applications can run in an AE protected domain without modifications. VxWorks AE is available for a limited set of CPUs.

Integrity
INTEGRITY is a secure real-time operating system produced by Green Hills Software Inc., intended for use in embedded systems that require maximum reliability.

This RTOS has the same design goals as VxWorks AE. It supports partitions by using the memory management hardware to isolate the elements from the different partitions. Within an individual address space, each task may be assigned a fixed budget of CPU time that it is guaranteed to have under any circumstances, and beyond which it cannot use. It provides an optional Arinc-653 two-level partition scheduler that provides a guaranteed CPU time window for an address space in which that address space's tasks always will be able to run. Actions of tasks in other address spaces can have no effect on the availability of the CPU time window to the designated address space(s). The highest locker priority protocol is used to prevent priority inversion in mutual exclusion synchronization. The design of Integrity is able to guarantee that system resources in the time (CPU time) and space (memory) domains will always be available to individual processes no matter what any other process attempts to do.

OSE

OSE comes in three flavours: OSE, OSEck and Epsilon [OSE]. OSE is the portable kernel written mostly in C, OSEck is the 'compact kernel' version aimed at digital signal processors (DSPs) and Epsilon is a set of highly optimized assembly kernels. The different kernels implement the OSE API in different levels, from level A to level D. A is the smallest set of features that is guaranteed to exist on all OSE supported platforms, while D is the full set of features including virtual memory, memory protection and concept of users.

The OSE processes can either be dynamic or static, i.e. created at compile-time or at run-time. They can be in one of three states: Running, Ready and Waiting. OSE can use different scheduling principles for different processes; priority-based, cyclic and round-robin. These principles are implemented for the different types of processes in OSE; interrupt process, timer interrupt process, prioritized process, background process and phantom process. The interrupt processes and the prioritized processes are scheduled according to their priority, while timer interrupt processes are triggered cyclically. The background processes are scheduled in a round-robin fashion. The phantom processes are not scheduled at all, they are used as signal redirectors. The processes can be grouped into 'blocks', and one such block may be treated as a single process in some ways; e.g. one can start and stop a whole block at once.

OSE processes use messages (called signals) as their primary communication method. The signals are sent from one process to another and does not use he concept of mailboxes. The data ownership follows the signal. Each process has a single input-queue from which it can read signals. It may put on a filter to read the type of message wanted. A process may also have a redirection table that forwards certain types of messages to other processes. By the use of 'link handlers' signals may be sent between OSE systems over various communication channels (network, serial lines etc). There is API functionality to get information about processes on other OSE systems so the right receiver can be determined. Sending signals to a higher-priority process, transfers the execution to the receiver. Sending to lower processes does not. Semaphores also exist, in more than on flavour, but the use of those are discouraged due to priority inversion problems associated with them.

Processes can be grouped into blocks, and to each block one can associate a memory pool the specifies the amount of memory available for that block. There is a special pool for the system. The pools can in turn be grouped into 'segments', that can feature hardware memory protection if available. Signals going between processes inside the same memory area do not undergo copying. Only when it is necessary from memory point of view, the signal buffer is copied.

An application can be written across several CPUs by use of signal IPC and link handlers. From the process point of view, it does not matter if the receiver exists on this CPU or on some other. One may mix any kernel type with any other (including 'soft kernels'). Links are monitored for hardware failures and alternate routes are automatically attempted to be established upon a link failure. Processes are notified upon link failure events.

Errors in system calls are not indicated by a traditional return code, but as a call to an error handler. The error handlers exist on several levels, process, block and system level. One an error handler on one level cannot handle the error, it is propagated to the next level until it reaches the system level.

OSE operating systems are widely used in the automotive industry and the communications industry.

Open Source RTOS: Linux Related

There has been a considerable amount of work in making Linux, the famous open source operating system, into an RTOS. The reason is, that this would make possible to use the full-power of a real operating system, included a broad range of open source development tools, for real-time applications.

A list of Linux real-time variants can be found at [RTLin]. Some of the most important ones are described below. We can distinguish two basic approaches: one is to use a small real-time executive as a base and execute Linux as a thread in this executive; the second is to directly modify the Linux internals. RT-Linux and RTAI are examples of the first approach, whereas Linux RK is an example of the second approach.

Unless it is modified, the main drawback of Linux kernel is that it is a monolithic kernel and that many parts of the kernel code are non preemptive. As a result, the latency experienced by real-time activities can be as large as hundreds of milliseconds. This makes common Linux distributions not suitable for hard real-time applications with tight timing constraints.

RT-Linux
RT-Linux is a modification (patch) to the famous open source Linux kernel. It was developed by Victor Yodaiken (University of New Mexico). It works as a small executive with a real-time scheduler that executes Linux code (the kernel and the user applications) as one of its threads. RT-Linux is distributed by Finite State Machine Labs, Inc.

The executive modifies the standard Linux interrupt handler routine and the interrupt enabling and disabling macros. When an interrupt is raised, the micro-kernel interrupt routine is executed. If the interrupt is related to a real-time activity, a real-time thread is notified and the micro-kernel executes its own scheduler. If the interrupt is not related to a real-time activity, then it is "flagged". When no real-time thread is active, Linux is resumed and executes its own code. Moreover, any pending interrupt related to Linux is served.

In this way, Linux is executed as a background activity in the real-time executive. The approach has the advantage to separate as much as possible the interactions between the Linux kernel, which is very complex and difficult to modify, and the real-time executive. By using this approach it is possible to obtain a very low latency for real-time activities and, at the same time, the full power of Linux on the same machine. However, there are several drawbacks:

- Real-Time tasks execute in the same address space as the Linux kernel; therefore, a fault in a user task may crash the kernel.
- When working with the real-time threads it is not possible to use the standard Linux device driver mechanism; as a result it is often necessary to re-write the device drivers for the real-time application. For example, if we want to use the network in real-time, it is necessary to use another device driver expressly designed for RT-Linux.
- The real-time scheduler is a simple fixed priority scheduler, which is POSIX compliant. There is no direct support for resource management facilities.
- Some Linux drivers directly disable interrupts during some portions of their execution. During this time, no real-time activities can be executed, and thus the latency is increased.

RTAI

Real-Time Application Interface (RTAI) is a modification of the Linux kernel made by Prof. Paolo Mantegazza from Dipartimento di Ingegneria Aerospaziale at Politecnico di Milano (DIAPM) [RTAI]. RTAI is a living open-source project that builds on the original idea of RT-Linux, but has been considerably enhanced. RTAI allows to uniformly mix hard and adaptive real-time by symmetrically integrating the scheduling of RTAI proper kernel tasks, Linux kernel threads and user space processes/tasks. By using Linux schedulable objects, RTAI benefits from threads protection at the price of a slight increase in latencies. RTAI offers also a native, dynamically extensible, light middleware layer based on the remote procedure call concept, that allows to use all of its APIs in a distributed way. Current releases also run on top of the Adeos nano-kernel, which makes it easier to plug in additional features such as debuggers, analyzers and standard open middleware layers, serving all operating systems running on top of it almost without any intrusion.

Linux/RK

In Linux/RK, the Linux kernel is directly modified. [Raj98, Raj00]. RK stands for "Resource Kernel", and indeed the kernel provides resource reservations directly to user processes. The use of this mechanism is transparent to the application. It is possible to assign a reservation to a legacy Linux application. Moreover, it is possible to access a specific API to take advantage of the reservations and of the quality of service management. Linux/RK is supported by TimeSys Inc.

Open Source RTOS: Others

eCos

The Embedded Configurable Operating System (eCos) [Mas02] is an open-source and royalty-free RTOS developed by RedHat, targeting embedded applications.

The kernel is modular and has been designed so different schedulers can be plugged in. The available distribution implements two schedulers: (1) a bitmap scheduler where each runnable thread is represented with a bit in a bitmap and must have a unique priority, and there is a strict upper limit on the number of threads allowed, and (2) a multi-level queue scheduler that implements a number of thread priorities and is capable of time-slicing between threads at the same priority. Concurrent execution of several schedulers is not supported by the current implementation, though future releases may allow schedulers to co-exist. This is an interesting feature that may be useful for research on scheduler composition.

The eCos kernel provides a number of mechanisms for synchronization and communication such as mutexes/condition variables, semaphores and message queues. The current eCos release provides a relatively simple implementation of mutex priority inheritance. This implementation will only work in the multi-level queue scheduler, and it does not handle the rare case of nested mutexes completely correctly. However, the available kernel primitives should allow developers to implement other mechanisms. eCos also provides mechanisms for handling exceptions, interrupts, clocks, alarms and timers.

The eCos kernel currently supports the μITRON 3.02 specification and a wide range of hardware architectures: ARM, IA32, Matsushita AM3x, MIPS, NEC V8xx, PowerPC, SPARC, and SuperH.

The open-source nature and modularity of eCos make it an interesting alternative for research purposes.

RTEMS

The Real-Time Executive for Multiprocessor Systems (RTEMS) is a general purpose real-time operating system that provides a POSIX API as well as a "Classic" API based on the Real-Time Executive Interface Definition (RTEID). RTEMS provides a robust, highly portable execution environment for a wide range of real-time embedded applications.

RTEMS was initially developed by On-Line Applications Research Corporation (OAR) [OAR], for the U.S. Army Missile Command. It was made freely available in 1990 with full source code, as required by GNU General Public License (GPL). It was the first actual Real-Time Operating Systems delivery with GPL, and was an example of technology transfer [Acu96]. RTEMS has now become an open project, for which OAR provides support. The RTEMS Project consists of developers, users, students, teachers, and OAR engineers to promote and enhance the RTEMS environment. RTEMS also constitutes an excellent benchmark for testing tools and algorithms for real-time systems [Col01]. RTEMS is used in a wide range of projects, ranging from University projects to projects for mission critical systems for the United States Military. OAR has a history of excellence in the latter.

RTEMS is free software, and thus is distributed with the full source code and the explicit permission to copy and modify it. It is integrated with other free software tools, such as the GCC compiler, the Cygnus ANSI C Library newlib and the GDB debugger. There are a variety of support components, which provide additional features required by embedded applications, such as a TCP/IP stack, networking, microWeb server and file systems. Other useful open source tools such as omniORB2 has been ported to RTEMS.

RTEMS has been ported to a wide range of microprocessor families, including Motorola M68000, Motorola PowerPC, Intel x86, Intel 960, HP-PA, MIPS and SPARC. There are available about 50 Board Support Packages for computers based in those microprocessor families which range from small Single Board Computer (SBC) based in Motorola Coldfire or CPU32 microcontrollers to modular computers based on VME bus with the latest PowerPC microprocessors. An interesting concept is the RTEMS libchip which is a library containing generic device drivers to be used with different microprocessor families and boards.

GNAT/RTEMS is the integration of the GNAT compilation system and RTEMS to provide an Ada cross development environment for embedded system. A former version of GNAT/RTEMS was validated on SPARC/ERC32 targets. The major disadvantage is that the port of GNAT to RTEMS uses the RTEMS POSIX API built on the Classic API, as is usual in many general-purpose real-time operating system. Therefore, using both GNAT/RTEMS and the bare RTEMS POSIX API involves unnecessary overheads.

ORK

Open Ravenscar Real-Time Kernel (ORK) [Pue00] [Pue01] [Zam02] is a special purpose real-time kernel that supports the Ravenscar profile of Ada tasking [Bur99] [Bur03]). The kernel has a reduced size and complexity, so that users can seek certification for mission-critical real-time applications. ORK was launched and funded by ESA/ESTEC and developed by a consortium leaded by DIT/UPM. It is intended for on-board mission-critical space systems, to replace a cyclic executive without concurrent threads of execution.

Open Ravenscar Real-time Kernel (ORK) is a special purpose real-time kernel that supports the Ravenscar profile of Ada tasking). The kernel has a reduced size and complexity, so that users can seek certification for mission-critical real-time applications. It is intended for on-board mission-critical space systems, to replace a cyclic executive without concurrent threads of execution. ORK supports the Ravenscar profile, a subset of Ada tasking defined to provide a basis for the implementation of certifiable critical systems. Therefore, ORK is the first open Real-Time kernel intended to be used for certifiable critical systems.

The Ravenscar profile defines a subset of the Ada tasking and real-time features that enable response time analysis and other static analysis techniques to be applied to real-time programs. The profile includes static tasks and protected objects at the library level, protected objects with at most one entry with a simple Boolean barrier, absolute delays, the real-time package, preemptive priority scheduling with immediate ceiling priority protocol, and protected interrupt handlers. It is aimed at the high-integrity systems domain, where predictability and reliability are of fundamental importance. The profile is being used in this domain, particularly in the aerospace area, where the European Space Agency (ESA) recommends it for on-board mission-critical software (see [ESA92]).

ORK differs from other kernels supporting the Ravenscar profile (e.g. the Raven kernel from Aonix in that is free software, and thus is distributed with the full source code and the explicit permission to copy and modify it. It is integrated with other free software tools, such as the GNAT compilation system and the GDB debugger. It differs from other real-time kernels in that it is specific to Ada and the Ravenscar profile, and cannot be used with other programming languages, including the full Ada language. This has the advantage of enhanced reliability and efficiency, as many features commonly used in other real-time kernels are not necessary. This also enables a simple implementation of the kernel, which makes it easier to validate or certify.

ORK was launched and funded by ESA/ESTEC, and developed by a consortium lead by DIT/UPM. ORK is supported by DIT/UPM, and this support is funded by ESA/ESTEC. ORK is known to be used in some projects by European space companies as Terma, Saab-Ericcson Space, Space System, eimos-Space, and Tharsys. The current version of ORK is aimed at ERC-32 computers (a radiation-hardened version of the SPARC-V7 architecture which is the standard ESA processor for on-board systems [Spa96]). A port to PC architectures is also available.

Special Purpose Embedded Operating Systems (non RT)

Symbian OS
Symbian OS, formerly known as Epoc, has over 80% market share in the OS market for mobile phones. The main target applications for Symbian OS are wireless information devices such as mobile phones and PDAs. Symbian OS is built around a 32-bit little-endian fully preemptive multitasking kernel that supports memory allocation, thread creation, semaphores and timers. It has been ported to many flavors of the ARM architecture, but also implementation for some other processors exist. The most common hardware requirements imposed by Symbian OS are: MMU availability, caches, multiple access modes (privileged vs. non-privileged) and the ability to handle interrupts and exceptions.

Symbian OS has a micro-kernel approach: only a small portion of the code is actually associated to the kernel and running in privileged mode. Applications and servers (i.e., applications without UIs) run on top of the kernel in user mode, and are implemented in different processes. They can make use of so-called 'engines' (which are basically static libraries or DLLs). Processes are the unit of protection: they have their own address space. Processes can be implemented using multiple (preemptive) threads, which can be seen as units of execution. In addition, Symbian OS implements non-preemptive multitasking by means of events: each task is essentially an event handler. Events are handled by active objects with a virtual member RunL(). Each time the event happens, the corresponding object executes its RunL() method. Symbian OS uses a client-server model: the server manages resources that the client can only access via the server. This usually involves crossing (expensive) process boundaries. To minimize the overhead, Symbian OS has implemented mechanisms so that servers can directly access the memory space of clients. Symbian OS does not implement a generic power management strategy. It is mainly the responsibility of the application writer to write them efficient (w.r.t. power). The kernel, however, provides some mechanisms to decrease power consumption. One of these mechanisms is to turn off the CPU if all threads are waiting for an external event.

Symbian programs [Tak00, Dig02] are C++ based. Several software development kits (SDK) are available (for different product ranges, e.g., smart phones and PDAs). Usually, these SDKs come with an emulator environment. Symbian claims to implement modules for the following (draft) standards and/or RFCs: TCP, UDP, IPv4, IPv6, ICMP, PPP, DNS, security protocols for secure electronic commerce, Ipsec, Telnet, FTP, Ethernet, HTTP and HTTPS, IMAP4, POP3, SMTP, message presentation.

JavaCard

Smart cards are one of the smallest computer platforms currently in use. In the size of a credit card, smart cards have both storage space for carrying information and electronic circuits to process such information. With advances in cryptography and chip technology, they are now able to store electronic cash, prevent unauthorized access to satellite broadcasts, and carry personal medical records, among others.

ISO was the first organization to standardize various aspects of smart cards. ISO 7816 standard defines aspects as physical characteristics, size and location of contact pins, transmission protocols and electric signals, commands for interoperability between manufacturers, application identifiers, data elements for interoperability between manufacturers, SCQL (Structured Card Query Language) commands, security architecture, and electronic signals and response to reset for synchronous responses. Though smart card size, shape, and communication protocols are standardized, their internals differ from one manufacturer to another. Most smart card development tools have been built by individual smart-card manufacturers. No standardized high-level application interfaces have been available. Therefore, the job of application programmers has not been easy; they have traditionally dealt with a whole lot of low-level details (communication protocols, memory management, etc.). Because applications have been implemented for proprietary platforms, coexistence of applications from different service providers in a single card has not been possible. JavaCard technology tries to overcome this. In this sense, a JavaCard is a smart card capable of executing Java programs called applets or cardlets. JavaCard technology provides a portable and multi-application smart-card platform. Also, it has security mechanisms, JavaCard firewall; it does not allow that applets access each other, unless explicitly stated with the creation of shareable objects.

JavaCard technology [Che00, Han99, JCard] essentially defines a platform on which Java applications can run. In essence, the architecture of the JavaCard platform consists of the following: the Virtual Machine (JCVM), the Runtime Environment (JCRE), and the Application Programming interface (API).

JCRE supports the smart card memory, communication, security, and application execution model. This run-time environment cleanly separates the smart card system and the applications, by encapsulating the underlying complexity and details of the smart card system; it essentially serves as the smart card's operating system. Unlike in a PC or workstation, the JCVM runs within the JCRE. The JCVM defines only a subset of the Java programming language and virtual machine definition suitable for smart card applications. Due to the small size of memory, fitting the Java system software is a hard job. The JCVM is split in two parts. One part runs on-card (bytecode interpreter among others) whereas the other part runs off-card. Parts that are not constrained to execute at run-time (class loading, bytecode verification, resolution and linking, and optimization) are assigned to the virtual machine running off-card. Therefore, the JavaCard platform is distributed among the smart card (basically running the interpreter) and desktop environment (running the converter tasks) in both space and time.

In addition to the Java language runtime model, the JCRE supports persistent and transient objects, atomic operations and transactions, and applet firewall (applet isolation), and secure object sharing. An additional security feature is the support for native methods (only for non-uploaded applets).

The JavaCard memory model is motivated by the kind of memory in smart cards (ROM, RAM, and EEPROM) and their physical characteristics. Persistent objects are stored in EEPROM whereas transient objects can be allocated in RAM. ROM holds the JCRE (virtual machine, API classes, and other software).

Garbage collection has not been usually supported. However, many advanced Java smart cards provide mechanisms for garbage collection to enable object deletion.

Some security features of the JavaCard platform include: transient and persistent object models, atomicity and transactions, applet firewall, object sharing, and native methods. One of the aspects that have not been standardized in JavaCard is the dynamic downloading of binary files know as CAP files. This process has implications on security and authorization aspects. Another open issue is the secure communication with JavaCard applets; besides preventing data interference among applets, aspects of integrity of information sent to a card and confidentiality of communications with the card should be dealt with. The Visa Open Platform standard defines security mechanisms to implement secure communication channels among the host and the card.

There are also some important features which are not supported by the JavaCard technology as dynamic class loading and cloning of objects. Also, the JCVM does not support multiple threads of control because current CPUs for smart cards do not efficiently support multithreading.

The separation between the operating system and the applications has not been clear. Former versions of JavaCard technology offered capabilities to access a card's file system. Since version 2.0, this functionality is no longer contained. Operating systems of smart cards are mostly file-system centric; the semantics and instructions to access the application data file are implemented by the operating system.

21.2   Assessment

Operating systems for embedded systems are generally viewed as the run-time component of a development environment, and that real-time kernels can be extended with additional OS services. There is a large choice in real-time operating systems, general-purpose as well as special-purpose. Many of the systems discussed here are open source, with differences in the size and structure of the development community. Not all operating systems for embedded systems can be classified as real-time. The POSIX real-time extensions are widely adopted. Several systems provide a "process" concept, with memory protection, in addition to the "thread" concept.

Operating systems can be classified according to a number of dimensions, according to the following criteria:

- *Real-Time or Non-Real-Time*
- A *single application* system has a single address space, no memory protection; and no protection against temporal interference
- A *multi-application* system provides multiple address spaces, memory protection, and in the real-time case, protection against temporal interference.
- In a *closed system*, everything is decided at initial development time;

- In an *open system*, new applications can be downloaded, and old ones replaced, in the field.
- In a *single-unit-of-failure* system, the system fails as a whole, and has to be re-booted on any failure;

    In a *multiple-units-of-failure* system, individual applications fail, and can be re-started or get back on the rail without affecting the remainder of the system.

According to the above mentioned criteria, conventional operating systems can be classified into one of two main categories, representing opposite poles of a spectrum. Conventional non-real-time operating systems are multi-application, open, multiple-units-of-failure (NMOM). Conventional real-time operating systems are single-application, closed, single-unit-of-failure (RSCS). For these systems, temporal predictability is an essential feature.

In the landscape, we see a trend towards removing the SCS restrictions for real-time operating systems. This trend will be discussed in more detail in section 19.3.1. We also see attempts to make the Linux system (an NMOM system) real-time. However, these approaches do not yet have a wide diffusion, and the most widespread one, RT-Linux, is not an RMOM system, but an NMOM+RSCS system. On the one hand, using Linux is attractive for the industry, because they see an open source product as "free of charge" with an immediate reduction of costs. On the other hand, since these approaches are far from mature, and have many drawbacks, the cost of design, development and maintenance is still high.

The operating system standards described in this section share a number of characteristics and requirements, but being addressed at different application environments they also have some differences.

- **Software portability** (at the source code level). All the standards increase portability of real-time applications. Portability in POSIX is not perfect as device drivers are non portable, and the standard leaves some behaviour unspecified or implementation defined. Although the hardware architecture is somehow more defined for the other three standards (OSEK, APEX and μITRON), the possibility of using different platforms and special I/O devices makes it difficult to have full portability.
- **Quality of service**. Operating system standards provide very limited support for applications with quality of service requirements. Most of these requirements are handled in middleware software layers that run on top of the operating system, and they use whatever low-level services the operating system is able to provide. In addition to the typical priority or deadline scheduling, real-time synchronization, and the management of time events, QoS middleware usually requires some kind of temporal protection (see below).
- **Scalability**. Support for a wide range of execution platforms is supported in POSIX, OSEK, and ITRON. POSIX does this through different standardized profiles; OSEK through the conformance classes; and ITRON through the different levels of portability (loose vs. strict). Scalability is not a goal of the APEX standard in which the hardware architecture is somehow fixed by the busses used.
- **Distributed Applications**. POSIX has full network support. μITRON does not support distribution. APEX and OSEK have their own special distribution mecha-

nism for communication among applications running in the same system, but no support for general-purpose networks.

- **Protection**. The protection mechanism in POSIX is the process, that provides a separate address space to each process. The smaller POSIX profiles intended for small embedded systems lack this mechanism as they have no processes. Temporal protection can be programmed by the application by using the sporadic server scheduling server (providing a bandwidth preserving mechanism), or execution-time timers to limit execution-time budgets.

- **Composability**. The composition of several applications in the same system is the main purpose of APEX and OSEK, which achieve it through the strict temporal protection that is imposed on their partitions. Composability is also achievable in POSIX, although the temporal protection is not so strict because it has to be programmed explicitly by all the involved applications. Composability is not one of the goals of µITRON.

- **Configurability**. Another pre-requisite needed to adapt the OS to a wide range of hardware is a high degree of modularity and configurability. All standards provide some means of configurability.

- **Dynamic vs. static scheduling**. POSIX and ITRON define fixed priorities as the basic scheduling mechanisms, while APEX and OSEK have an underlying more static time-triggered mechanism for the partitions. The upper scheduling level in APEX and OSEK.

In summary, the µITRON requirements are basically a subset of those of real-time POSIX (corresponding roughly to the smaller PSE51 POSIX minimal real-time application environment profile). Because of the level of support of POSIX among commercial kernels, it seems that unless there is a background of using ITRON in the company, POSIX is a better choice because it is more scalable and more widely supported. If composability of applications with strict temporal protection is an issue, although POSIX is usable, a more reliable solution is the use of APEX or OSEK. The first one is only intended for the hardware architectures used in avionics systems, while the second one can be used for other hardware architectures.

Neither the POSIX standard or APEX address the design and implementation of portable device drivers. Experience shows that in most real-time systems special hardware is required, and device drivers represent a significant effort in the total development cost. There is an industry standard outside the scope of POSIX, called Uniform Driver Interface (UDI) that addresses the issues of writing portable device drivers, by providing the driver an abstract view of the hardware, on the one hand, and of the operating system, on the other hand. However, the UDI standard does not address all the real-time issues and extensions to the standard would be necessary to achieve this functionality.

Although the treatment of interrupts is fully contemplated in the UDI standard, it is the case that for small embedded systems USI is probably too complex and that developers of those systems will usually prefer to integrate the device drivers with the application. Usually in these systems there is no hardware protection and the application, or part of it, is able to directly access the hardware. In this context it is necessary that the RTOS is able to provide services to ease the management of interrupts. In particular, the installation of interrupt handlers and synchronization of application threads with these interrupt handlers seem most necessary. An effort should be made in the future to standardize these services.

As real-time systems become more complex there is an increasing need for using flexible scheduling algorithms that overcome the rigidities of fixed priorities. There are many scheduling algorithms published in the literature based on dynamic priorities and/or quality of service metrics, so it would be difficult to standardize them all. Instead, a general framework for portably specifying schedulers at the application level should be supported by the RTOS. Standardization in this area needs to be carried out.

Another area that is not well addressed today in the POSIX standard is real-time scheduling for multiprocessor systems. Scheduling algorithms for shared memory multiprocessors are not well understood yet, but one simple solution that is always analyzable is to statically allocate threads to processors. The standard should be extended with interfaces to allow allocation of threads to processors, and one possibility should be to specify this allocation as static. Multiprocessor support is also a limitation of OSEK, which does not specify support for these systems.

In multiprocessor systems, the regular mutexes can work for shared-resource synchronization, but it is possible to get more efficiency out of the system by using other synchronization primitives that enhance parallelism, such as multiple-reader single-writer locks. This scheduling mechanism is already included in the POSIX standard, but no priority inheritance mechanism has been defined for it. Therefore, its use in real-time systems is not practical, because very large priority inversions could occur. Priority inheritance or priority ceiling protocols should be defined for this synchronization primitive.

Also, there is a need for more flexibility and configurability. For example the scheduling algorithm cannot be changed neither in OSEK or POSIX.

It should be noted, that although APEX allows a communication mechanism to support priority inheritance, no specific protocol is proposed. Instead, processes may include time-outs for message send/reception, buffer read/write, semaphore wait and wait event (noting that the process may not wait if the partition is non-preemptible).

It is important to realize that APEX is not an architecture-neutral definition, but must be viewed in the context of IMA architectures. In particular, IMA assumes the existence of the ARINC 659 Backplane Data Bus [Ari93] and the ARINC 629 Data Bus (i.e. network) [Ari90]. The 659 backplane bus uses a table-driven protocol providing a cyclic series of message windows of predefined lengths. The 629 bus provides periodic message windows, with proportional access times enabling the avoidance of contention amongst senders. Clearly, the use of these buses directly impacts on the scheduling scheme supported by APEX – indeed the desire to utilize 629 and 659 imply the use of cyclic scheduling at the partition and communications levels. However, implementers must link the cyclic processor schedules with those for the 659 and 629 – allocation of one or more slots in a cyclic processor schedule to a partition must be consistent with the allocation of 659 and 629 message slots in their respective schedules. This is difficult in the context of distributed multiprocessor IMA systems containing many distinct, possibly unrelated, applications. Producing such a global schedule is a major challenge.

Finally, the major limitation of μITRON is that it is intended for the smaller systems, and does not provide a scalable approach that would enable portability to larger systems, like in POSIX.

21.3   Trends

Two major trends emerge from the landscape with regard to commercial real-time operating systems. First, real-time operating systems are moving in the direction of RMOM, strongly influenced by the POSIX and ARINC standards, but also by efforts in the research community to combine hard and adaptive real-time tasks. Second, open-source systems are maturing, in terms of reliable backup and support, and Linux is slowly making its way into the real-time domain. A combination of both trends can be found in Linux/RK. The first trend is technical, and can gain a lot from focused research. The second trend has its own dynamics, and is not fully technical in nature. Both trends lead to increasing support for QoS.

Towards Multi-application, Open, Multiple-Units-of-Failure (MOM) RTOS

The standard fixed-priority scheduling paradigm used in single-application systems does not scale to multiple-application systems. In a true multi-application RTOS, the protection between "applications" (processes, partitions, groups, etc) has to be in the temporal domain as well as in the spatial domain. Memory protection alone is not enough. Moreover, memory protection should not introduce temporal unpredictability. Linux/RK, and VxWorks AE and Integrity, both with Arinc scheduler, seem to satisfy these criteria. The latter two, however, seem to aim specifically at hard real-time systems for the aerospace and defense industries. With respect to temporal protection, the guarantees that can be given to the applications seem to depend on the underlying scheduling algorithm. Linux/RK uses RMS [Mer95][Mer94], which allows periodic and sporadic reservations. The utilization it can support depends on the number of reservations, and the relative periods of the different reservations [Liu73]. The Arinc scheduler is based on an offline schedule construction, and provides precalculated time windows to the partitions. [Lip00] proposes bandwidth-preserving reservations based on deadline extension. The rate-based execution model aims at adding temporal guarantees to the fair-share scheduling paradigm [Jef95][Jef99]. When multi-threaded applications or partitions are used, two-level scheduling becomes necessary. An example of two-level scheduling can be seen in VxWorks AE, where the ARINC-compliant scheduler schedules the partitions, and the tasks within the partitions are scheduled using fixed-priority scheduling.

In an RTOS that supports *multiple units of failures*, all memory-based resources and all restart information of a application or partition are included in that application or partition, and not in kernel space. From the available description, this seems to be the case for VxWorks AE and Integrity.

An RTOS that supports an *open* system requires dynamic resource reservation. This is typically what we see in QoS management systems. *Dynamic resource reservation* requires middleware services as well as kernel services. The kernel services account for the applications' resource usage, in order to prevent them from exceeding the assigned reservations. The middleware services must include some type of admission control in order to assess whether the system has enough resource to satisfy all the resources requested by applications, and thus provide the guarantees. As a result, some requests may be rejected. Note that the resource guarantees are an emergent property that results from the combination of feasibility check and enforcement.

Linux/RK is positioned to do just this [Raj97, Che98]. This is consistent with basic OS theory, as explained in [Lis80], and accepted micro-kernel practice [Use93].

Open Issues for Quality of Service (QoS)

When hard real-time cannot be guaranteed, deterministic quality of service (QoS) seems an acceptable alternative for many application domains. One of these domains is and will increasingly be (multi)media. As a consequence of Moore's law, signal and media processing is moving from dedicated hardware to software, which fuels the need for deterministic QoS. The RT/QoS topic is quite new, not yet well understood, and barely known in the developers' community. There are basically two approaches to RT-QoS: one is to address the issue in the scheduling, for instance by using the number of missed deadlines as a QoS measure [Lu00]; the other is to provide QoS management as middleware on top of a reservation-based resource kernel [Raj97]. The first approach lends itself very well to closed systems; the second is more focused towards open systems.

To make dynamic reservation-based resource allocation for QoS a technological success, at least three issues need to be addressed:

- **Standardization of Resource Reservation Mechanisms**. Many resource reservation algorithms have been proposed in the research literature, but the differences and the commonalities are not well understood. It is necessary to identify at least a subset of properties that should be provided by a standard resource reservation service.
- **Resource Co-Scheduling**. Little research has been done on the issue of co-scheduling different resources. Most of the proposed resource reservation algorithms are for the CPU or for the network. However, it may be the case that a single task (or application) accesses several resources during its execution. Therefore, there is the need to coordinate the resource reservations for these resources.
- **Multi-Threaded Processes for Resource Reservations**. Resource reservations may have to be allocated to multi-threading processes (partitions, applications) rather than tasks, since processes are the natural candidates for memory protection. This is for instance required by the ARINC standard. Of course, a move in the opposite direction is also possible, where memory reservation is provided per task. The DROPS project at TU Dresden has recently proposed a micro-kernel for Linux-L4 that executes every task in a separate address space.
- **Monitoring facilities to support load adaptation**. In systems with highly dynamic load, reservation cannot keep up with high-frequency load variations. Such variations have to be addressed by the application themselves, using load-reduction techniques, within the limits of the allocated resources [Nat95]. To support its decision-making process, the application needs to monitor its resource consumption.

- **Monitoring facilities to support QoS managem**ent. To support their resource allocation decisions, middleware QoS resource-management services need to monitor the resource usage patterns. To support this, the resource kernels will have to maintain statistical information on the resource usage.

A proposal for application-defined scheduling has been submitted for consideration by the real-time POSIX working group. The proposal has been implemented in MaRTE OS, a Minimal Real-Time Operating System for Embedded Applications developed at Cantabria University, as well as in RT-Linux by the Technical University of Valencia as part of the OCERA IST project. Although this is a promising approach, the notion of application-defined scheduling presumes a closed system, with a static mix of applications.

The OCERA IST project is an effort at the European level to enhance RT-Linux with more flexible scheduling and with QoS management features. The goal of the OCERA IST project, started April 2002, is to enhance an open-source RTOS such as RT-Linux with the cutting-edge real-time system technology. This will disseminate real-time technology in the open source community. It will also provide a low-cost, easy-to-use standard solution for many European SMEs that cannot afford to buy a commercial RTOS license. On the one hand, the project will enhance the real-time executive of RT-Linux by providing a POSIX standard API, by providing a predictable memory allocator, and by applying resource reservation algorithms like the constant bandwidth server (CBS). On the other hand, the project will add RT features to the Linux kernel, in order to support multimedia applications. Moreover, the project addresses fault-tolerance issues and real-time communication protocols.

Operating System Standards

As a consequence of the limitations exposed, future work is required in POSIX, UDI, OSEK, and APEX to produce extensions in the following areas:

- real-time extensions to UDI
- interrupt control from the application in POSIX
- application-defined scheduling in POSIX and OSEK
- allocation of threads to processors in POSIX
- assigning priority ceilings for reader/writer locks in POSIX
- synchronization protocols in APEX
- multiprocessor scheduling in OSEK

These extensions would on the one hand fill the missing services that are necessary for many real-time applications and, through the application-defined scheduling services, would also facilitate the evolution from fixed-priority scheduling towards more flexible scheduling algorithms. This additional flexibility is necessary to provide better support to systems with quality of service requirements, even though it is expected that most of the services required by these systems will continue to be implemented in a specialized middleware layer.

The ARTIST project can have an important role in this process as a driver for specifying user requirements, identifying new areas for standardization, and contributing in the production and the reviewing of these standards.

21.4   Recommendations for Research

As a conclusion from the assessment and trends subsections, we make the following recommendations for research in the area of real-time operating systems for embedded applications:

- Flexible scheduling services. The complexity of the applications requires more flexibility in scheduling than just fixed priorities. There has been a lot of research in scheduling theory, but there needs to be an effort of bridging the gap between theory and implementation. New APIs are needed, and overheads of the different scheduling algorithms need to be tuned to meet application requirements. APIs that could make the scheduler a pluggable and interchangeable object seem the most promising research direction.

- Protection. One way of managing the complexity of applications is by providing appropriate levels of protection, both in space (memory) and time. The time protection mechanisms specified in some standards like OSEK or ARINC are somehow too rigid, and there needs to be research in ways of making this protection more flexible but still effective.

- Dynamicity. The complexity of applications requires moving from statically designed applications to a more dynamic environment where the application components can be changed on-line. Research is needed on methods and APIs for effective on-line admission tests and dynamic resource reservation.

- Quality of service. There is a need for middleware that allows the application to define quality of service requirements, using some contract mechanism that lets the application specify its minimum and desired requirements, so if the implementation accepts the contract it can guarantee the minimum requirements and try to provide de desired ones. To implement this middleware, there is a need to develop techniques and APIs in the operating system level to perform load adaptation, and monitoring and budgeting of the system resources.

- Multiprocessor support. Predictability of the timing behaviour in multiprocessor systems is still a research issue. Most multiprocessor real-time systems today require static allocation of threads to processors.

- Drivers. Portability of drivers for real-time applications is an open issue. There is a need for extending current APIs for portable drivers to support real-time requirements.

- Networks. There are few real-time networks and protocols, and support in the OS for them is very limited. There is a need to develop protocol-independent APIs that let a distributed application define its timing requirements for the network and the remote services.

- Modelling. There is a need to develop precise models of the timing behaviour of the operating system services, that could be used in timing analysis tools. It would be useful to have automatic procedures to obtain the timing model of any operating system on a given platform.

21.5 References

[Acu96]   Phillip R. Acuff and Ron O'Guin. "RTEMS: A Technology Transfer Success Story." Proc. STC96. 1996

[Ada95]   S. Tucker Taft and Robert A. Duff, Ada 95 Reference Manual: Language and Standard Libraries. International Standard ANSI/ISO/IEC-8652:1995, 1995, Available from Springer-Verlag, LNCS no. 1246.

[ARI90]   "ARINC 629: IMA Multi-transmitter Databus Parts 1-4", October 1990, pub. by Airlines Electronic Engineering Committee (AEEC)

[ARI93]   "ARINC 659: Backplane Data Bus" pub. by Airlines Electronic Engineering Committee (AEEC), December 1993.

[ARI91]   "ARINC 651: Design Guidance for Integrated Modular Avionics", pub. by Airlines Electronic Engineering Committee (AEEC), November 1991.

[ARI96]   "ARINC 653: Avionics Application Software Standard Interface (Draft 15)", Airlines Electronic Engineering Committee (AEEC), June 1996, avail. from ARINC Incorporated.

[Aud97a]   N.C. Audsley and A.J. Wellings, "Analysing APEX Applications", Proceedings IEEE Real-Time Systems Symposium, December, pp39-44, 1997.

[Aud97b]   N.C. Audsley and A. Grigg, "Timing Analysis of the ARINC 629 Databus for Real-Time Applications", Microprocessors and Microsystems, 21, pp 55-61, 1997

[Bar97]   J. Barnes, "High Integrity Ada: The SPARK Approach", pub. Addison-Wesley, 1997.

[BG-DS]   Dedicated Systems – "The RTOS Buyers Guide", available at http://www.realtime-info.be/encyc/buyersguide/rtos/Dir228.html

[BG-EC]   Embedded;Com – "The RTOS Buyers Guide", available at http://www.embedded.com/
Buyer's Guide – Software Tools for Embedded Systems Development – Real-Time Operating Systems.

[Bur03]   Alan Burns, Brian Dobbing, and Tullio Vardanega, Guide for the use of the Ada Ravenscar Profile in high integrity system, University of York Technical Report YCS-003-348, January 2003.

[Bur99]   Alan Burns, The Ravenscar Profile, Ada Letters, volume XIX, number 4, pages 49--52, 1999

[Che98]   Chen Lee and Raj Rajkumar and John Lehoczky and Dan Siewiorek, "Practical Solutions for QoS-Based Resource Allocation", Proc. IEEE Real Time Systems Symposium, Dec. 1998

[Che00]   Z. Chen, "JavaCardTM Technology for Smart Cards". Addison-Wesley, 2000.

[Col01]   A. Colin, I. Puaut. Worst-Case Execution Time Analysis of the RTEMS Real-Time Operating System. Proc.13th Euromicro Conference on Real-Time Systems, pages 191--198, Delft, The Netherlands, June 2001

[Dig02]   Digia, Programming for the Series 60 platform and Symbian OS, John Wiley & Sons; 2002

[ESA92]   ESA, 32 Bit Microprocessor and Computer System Development, 1992, Report 9848/92/NL/FM.

[FAQ]   Comp.realtime FAQ, available at http://www.faqs.org/faqs/realtime-computing/faq/

[Han99]   U. Hansmann, M. S. Nicklous, T. Schäck, and F. Seliger, "Smart Card Application Development Using Java", Springer Verlag, 1999.

[Har98]   H. Härtig, M. Hohmuth, J. Wolter. "Taming Linux", Proceedings of PART '98.

[Jcard]   Sun Microsystems, "The JavaCard Specification", http://java.sun.com/products/javacard/

[Jeff95]   Jeffay, K. and Bennett, D. (1995). A rate-based execution abstraction for multime-
             dia computing. In Proceedings of the 5th International Workshop on Network and
             Operating System Support for Digital Audio and Video, number 1018 in Lecture
             Notes on Computer Science, pages 64-75. Springer-Verlag.
[Jeff99]   Jeffay, K. and Goddard, S. (1999). The rate-based execution model. In Proceedings
             of the Real-Time Systems Symposium.
[Kle93]   Mark H. Klein, Thomas ralya, Bill Pollak, Ray Obenza, Michale Gonzalez Har-
             bour, A Practitioner's Handbook for Real-Time Analysis, Guide to Rate Mono-
             tonic Analysis for Real_Time Systems, Kluwer Academic publishers, 1993.
[Lip00]   G. Lipari and S.K. Baruah "Efficient Scheduling of Multi-Task Applications in
             Open Systems" IEEE Proceedings of the 6th Real-Time Systems and Applications
             Symposium, Washington DC, June 2000
[Lis80]   A. Lister, Fundamentals of Operating Systems, Springer-Verlag Telos, 2nd edition,
             1980
[Lu00]   C. Lu, J. Stankovic, T. Abdelzaher, G.Tao, S. Son, M. Marley, "Performance
             specification and metrics for adaptive real-time systems", In Proceedings of the
             Real-Time Systems Symposium, Orlando Fl, 2000.
[Mas02]   A. J. Massa, "Embedded Software Development with eCos", Prentice Hall, 2002.
[Mer94]   Mercer, C., Savage, S., and Tokuda, H. (1994). Processor Capacity Reserves:
             Operating System Support for Multimedia Applications. In IEEE International
             Conference on Multimedia Computing and Systems.
[Mer95]   Mercer, C. and Rajkumar, R. (1995). An Interactive Interface and RT-Mach Sup-
             port for Monitoring and Controlling Resource Management. In Proceedings of the
             Real-Time Technology and Applications Symposium.
[Nat95]   S.Natarayan ed., Imprecise and approximate Computation, Kluwer 1995.
[OSE]   http://www.ose.com/prodserv/Default.asp. OSE Systems.
[OSEK]   "OSEK/VDX Operating System Specification 2.2.1", OSEK Group,
             http://www.osek-vdx.org
[POS92]   IEEE Std 1003.5-1992, IEEE Standard for Information Technology—POSIX Ada
             Language Interfaces—Part 1: Binding for System Application Program Interface
             (API).
[POS96]   IEEE Std 1003.5b-1996, IEEE Standard for Information Technology—POSIX Ada
             Language Interfaces—Part 1: Binding for System Application Program Interface
             (API)—Amendment 1: Realtime Extensions.
[POS98a]   POSIX.13 (1998). IEEE Std. 1003.13-1998. Information Technology -Standardized
             Application Environment Profile- POSIX Realtime Application Support (AEP).
             The Institute of Electrical and Electronics Engineers, 1998
[POS98b]   IEEE Std 1003.5c-1998, IEEE Standard for Information Technology—POSIX Ada
             Language Interfaces—Part 1: Binding for System Application Program Interface
             (API)—Amendment 2: Protocol Independent Interfaces.
[POS01]   POSIX.1 (2001). IEEE Std 1003.1:2001. Standard for Information Technology -
             Portable Operating System Interface (POSIX). The Institute of Electrical and Elec-
             tronic Engineers, 2001.
[POS03a]   POSIX.1 (2003). IEEE Std 1003.1:2003. Standard for Information Technology -
             Portable Operating System Interface (POSIX). The Institute of Electrical and Elec-
             tronic Engineers, 2003.
[POS03b]   IEEE Standard 1003.13-2003, Standard for Information Technology -Standardized
             Application Environment Profile- POSIX Realtime and Embedded Application
             Support (AEP). The Institute of Electrical and Electronics Engineers, 2003.

[Pue00]   Juan A. de la Puente, José F. Ruiz, Juan Zamorano, Rodrigo García and Ramón Fernández-Marina, "ORK: An Open Source Real-Time Kernel for On-Board Software Systems", DASIA 2000 – Data Systems in Aerospace, Montreal, Canada, May 2000.

[Pue01]   Juan A. de la Puente, Juan Zamorano, José F. Ruiz, Ramón Fernández, Rodrigo García, "The Design and Implementation of the Open Ravenscar Kernel", Ada Letters, vol. XXI, no. 1, March 2001.

[Raj00]   Ragunathan (Raj) Rajkumar, Luca Abeni, Dionisio de Niz, Sourav Ghosh, Akihiko Miyoshi, and Saowanee Saewong, "Recent Developments with Linux/RK", Proc. Second Real-Time Linux Workshop, Orlando, Florida, Nov. 2000

[Raj97]   R. Rajkumar, C. Lee, J. Lechoczky and D. Siewiorek, "A Resource Allocation Model for QoS Management", Proc. Real-Time Systems Symposium. IEEE Computer Society (December 1997).

[Raj98]   Raj Rajkumar, Kanaka Juvva, Anastasio Molano, Shuichi Oikawa, "Resource Kernels: A Resource-Centric Approach to Real-Time and Multimedia Systems", Proc. SPIE/ACM Conference on Multimedia Computing and Networking, Jan 1998

[RTLin]   List of real-time Linux variants:
http://www.realtimelinuxfoundation.org/variants/variants.html

[Sak98]   Ken Sakamura, µItron 3.0: An Open and Portable Real-Time Operating System for Embedded Systems: Concept and Specification. IEEE Computer Society, April 1998

[SPA96]   TEMIC, SPARC V7 Instruction Set Manual, 1996

[Symb]   http://www.symbian.com/technology/SymbianOSv7funcdesc15.pdf

[Symb]   http://www.symbian.com/technology/SymbianOSv7funcdesc15.pdf

[Tak02]   Hiroaki Takada, ed. µITRON4.0 specification (version 4.00.00), TRON association, Japan, 2002, http://www.ertl.jp/ITRON/SPEC/home-e.html

[Tak00]   Martin Takser, Leigh Edwards, Jonathan Dixon, Mark Shackman, Tim Richardson, John Forrest, Professional Symbian Programming: Mobile solutions on the EPOC platform, Wrox Press Inc; Book and CD-ROM edition, 2000

[Use93]   Proceedings of the Usenix Symposium on Microkernels and Other Kernel Architectures, San Diego Ca, Sept 1993, Usenix Association, 1993

[Whi02]   P. Whiston and P. Goodchild, "SHIMA – Small Helicoptor IMA", ERA Avionics Conference, 2002.

[Zam01]   Juan Zamorano, José F. Ruiz, Juan A. de la Puente, "Implementing Ada.Real_Time.Clock and Absolute Delays in Real-Time Kernels", Reliable Software Technologies – Ada-Europe 2001, ed. Alfred Strohmeier and Dirk Craeynest, Springer-Verlag, LNCS 2043, pages 317-327, 2001.

[Zam02]   Juan Zamorano, Juan A. de la Puente, "GNAT/ORK: An Open Cross-Development Environment for Embedded Ravenscar-Ada Software", Proceedings of IFAC 15th world congress, 2002

Web Links

AbsInt   http://www.absint.com/wcet.htm
Aonix   http://www.aonix.com/
ARINC   http://www.arinc.com/
DROPS   The Dresden Real-Time
Operating System Project,   http://os.inf.tu-dresden.de/drops/
ESA   http://www.estec.esa.nl/
FSML   Finite State Machine Labs,   http://www.fsmlabs.com/

LynuxWorks	http://www.lynuxworks.com/
OCERA	http://www.ocera.org/
OAR On-Line Application Research,	http://www.OARcorp.com/
RTAI RTAI Home page,	http://www.aero.polimi.it/~rtai/
Time Sys	http://www.timesys.com/
TriPacific TriPacific Software Incorporated,	http://www.tripac.com/
Embedded.com	http://www.embedded.com/
Integrity	http://www.ghs.com/
VxWorks	http://www.windriver.com/
UDI	http://www.projectudi.org/

22 QoS Management

QoS has been defined as a collective effect of service and performances that determine the degree of satisfaction of the service. This satisfaction is usually associated with a number of extra-functional requirements or QoS characteristics, such as dependability, reliability, timeliness, robustness, throughput, etc.

QoS management interacts with applications and resource managers, in order to ensure an optimal system output quality, as perceived by the user. QoS-aware applications are usually structured in such a way that they can provide different quality levels (QL), which have associated estimations of the needed resources. Quality levels are usually discrete and are characterized by the quality of the output and the fulfilment degree of other extra-functional requirements. The higher quality that a QL provides, the larger are the resource needs. QoS-aware applications can dynamically change the executing QL.

QoS manager negotiates with applications the QL they have to provide. This negotiation is based on a contract model: there is trading of quality by resources. The final goal is to use resources in an efficient way and to maximize system quality. The negotiation depends on factors such as applications importance, user settings, available resources, etc.

Resource management is needed for ensuring that the resource reserves or budgets are guaranteed. For this purpose, resource usage accounting, budget enforcement, and monitoring are required mechanisms. As mentioned in the previous section, resource kernels are a basic component in this framework. In some cases there is also a resource manager on top of them, in order to handle budgets with a higher abstraction level.

In this section, different aspects of QoS management are described. It is important to note, that in order to efficiently support QoS, it is needed to consider different abstraction layers, ranging from specification to implementation. The aim of this section is to present them and to provide some relevant research directions. Finally, the current situation is briefly assessed and future research trends are shown. Research interest on QoS management is much more recent that in other topics in this document, such as real-time operating systems, real-time scheduling, and programming languages. As a consequence, it is in a very immature state and extensive research is needed to make it really usable in future industrial devices.

22.1 Landscape

In the last decade, the increased need for timely and dependable execution and communication support have established and improved the QoS facilities (e.g. QoS specification, QoS negotiation algorithms, reservation protocols, resource brokers). They have been integrated in protocol stacks, operating systems kernels and middleware systems. These facilities provide support for the development of multimedia, real-time and complex systems in general. But to put QoS facilities in practice is complex. They must be integrated with the application software. This makes the software archi-

Artist FP5 Consortium: Embedded Systems Design, LNCS 3436, 287–304, 2005.
© Springer-Verlag Berlin Heidelberg 2005

tectures and the software development process more complex. Different levels of software infrastructures and software development require the integration of QoS concepts, as described in figure 24.1 below.

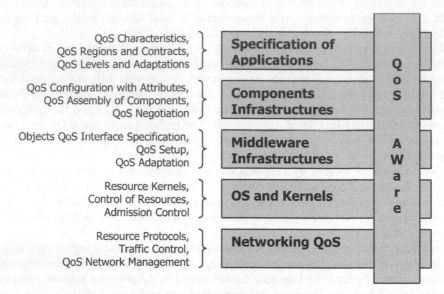

Figure 24.1. Levels of Integration of QoS

QoS-Enabled Modelling Languages and QoS Analysis

Examples of QoS-enabled modelling languages are QML (QoS Modelling Language) [Fro98] and CQML (Component Quality Modelling Language) [Aag02]. QML and CQML are languages with a BNF grammar. Other similar approaches are based on meta-models [Bor00][Ase00]. These languages provide support for the description of user defined QoS categories and characteristics, quality contracts and quality bindings. They are frameworks for the description of QoS Catalogues [Bra02] of general QoS parameters, or application specific quality parameters. They do not provide support to optimize the resource allocation, or evaluate the levels of quality provided. They address the problem from the specification point of view.

Another approach is the description of resource services quality. [OMG02][Sel00] provide support for describing quality based on resource services, and the relation with analytic methods of performances such as latencies and throughputs.

QoS-enabled modelling languages pay special attention to the specification of QoS characteristics and parameters, QoS contracts for the description of restrictions or quality values, and binding of quality between components, resources and subsystems.

In Figure 24.2, a set of components Ci provide some services with quality attributes that can affect to the component C, which provide services with quality attributes to other components. C uses a set of resources that provide services with some quality attributes.

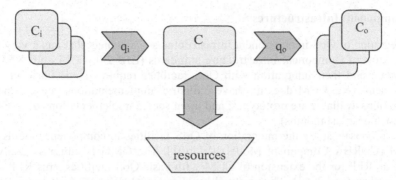

Figure 24.2. Mapping of Input/Output Qualities and Resources

Analytical models for QoS management provide support for the application of metric evaluations and resource allocation optimization. [Raj97] proposes a general QoS analytical model for the optimization of resource allocation. The model assumes a system with multiple resources and dynamic applications, each of which can operate at different levels of quality, based on the system resources available to it. Reward functions describe the interdependencies of quality levels and resource allocation, utility functions and weighted utility functions evaluate the application and system quality. The optimization of these functions provides the optimal resource distribution.

Other approaches are domain specific. [Ven97] [Sta95] are analytical models to support the QoS metrics of video and multimedia applications. They identify the QoS parameters for user satisfaction and resource consumption in these types of applications (video and multimedia), and the functions for the relationships of resources and user satisfaction.

The RFC (Request For Comments) of IETF "Specification of Guaranteed Quality of Service" [She97] introduces the basic parameters and theorems for the analysis of deadline and jitter in QoS Guaranteed mode of Integrated Services in the Internet architecture.

Some standards such as the ISO reference model for QoS [ISO98] [ISO98a] introduce some concepts (i.e., QoS Characteristics, QoS Contracts and QoS Capabilities), and a basic architecture that are basic elements of QoS specification. OMG Request for Proposals (RFP) and initial submissions provides some solutions for the integration of QoS specifications in UML [OMG02a] [OMG02b].

Three different points of view of QoS specification not combined in a common solution yet are: i) the description of user perceptible QoS characteristics and their contracts, ii) the definition of system and resource levels QoS characteristics and contracts, and iii) the analytic methods that provide support for the optimal resource allocation and quality levels identifications. A complete language for the specification of QoS must support: description of QoS characteristics, QoS contracts and QoS levels, definition of methods for the support of QoS monitoring of user defined QoS characteristics, specification of process of adaptation, and linking all these concepts with QoS analysis solutions.

QoS Component Infrastructures

The integration of QoS in component infrastructures is a subject that has a very short history. Most of Component infrastructure standards (EJB 2.0, CCM and .NET) are very recent, and their integration with QoS facilities requires some basic practical improvements (e.g. CCM does not have industrial implementations yet and the implementations available are prototypes, and open source implementations of .NET has started to appear last months).

Some proposals study the integration of QoS facilities in component models such as CCM (CORBA Component Model) [Wan01]. The OMG is currently analyzing propose an RFP for the extension of CCM with basic QoS facilities (this RFP could be proposed in June 2003). The proposal by Wang et al [Wan01] pays special attention to the QoS-enabled location transparency, reflective configuration of component server and container, and the strategies to reconfigure the component server.

Lusceta [Bla01] is a component model (it is not based on industrial component infrastructures) environment based on formal techniques, which can be simulated and analyzed. Lusceta provides support for the specification of QoS management, which can be used to synthesize (dynamic) QoS management components. The execution framework is a general QoS-aware reflective middleware. Another component modelling environment is presented in [Ras00]. It proposes solutions for the description of component architectures and for evaluation of response times. This is an architectural environment not supported by execution environments.

[Mig02] introduces a solution for the integration of QoS basic services, such as resource reservation and negotiation, in EJB (Enterprise Java Beans). The EJB containers implement some basic negotiation algorithms and isolate the business components from reservation services. The negotiation algorithms implement some basic adaptation process based on the renegotiation of resources and renegotiation with other components.

The component infrastructures introduced use two techniques for the specification of QoS:

- *application interfaces* that are part of the infrastructure;
- *component descriptors* that are used for the automatic generation of managers and containers that support the QoS aspects.

In some solutions the component descriptors are XML files with data type structures for the specification of QoS attributes. Nevertheless, they do not provide support for the description of user guided QoS attributes. The impact of QoS on component infrastructures is further analysed in section 20.6.

QoS Middleware and Interface Description Languages

The integration of QoS facilities into middleware systems has been identified as a future challenge for the middleware infrastructures [Gei01][Sch00]. QoS-aware middleware systems define general QoS frameworks to support QoS facilities:

i)   QoS Specification.
ii) QoS Negotiation and Adaptation.
iii) Resource Reservation and Admission Control.

   iv) access to basic services for the configuration of some quality attributes (e.g.
      dependability, security, mobility).
   v) QoS Monitoring.

General middleware architectures [Hou97][Nah01][Sha99] introduce the five general
facilities, but their architectures are not dependent of communication middleware
facilities. In some solutions [Hou97], QoS middleware cooperates with existing solutions at OS and network levels, and proposes the middleware layer to support other
facilities (e.g. adaptation). The architecture introduced in [Sha99] pays special attention to the quality dependencies between components. The quality level of a component depends on the quality levels provided by other components and the resources
available.

   Examples of QoS-aware middleware systems based on specific middleware are: i)
BBN's QuO project [Zin97] is a well-known framework for the integration of QoS
management in CORBA. It provides support for the specification of QoS, negotiation
and adaptation facilities, and resource reservation. QuO provides interfaces description languages for the definition of levels of quality and execute the adaptation processes. The IDL compilers integrate in stub and skeletons the management of QoS.
QuO includes a framework based on some basic services (e.g. reservation of network,
and replication of objects), and integrates the services with some ORB such as TAO.
ii) The solutions proposed in [Mig01] integrate the resource reservation and QoS IP in
Java RMI classes. This solution extends RMI basic classes that support the remote
reference and extend it with operation for reservation of resources. Java RMI libraries
and Skeletons intercept these basic extensions and handle them. Some parts of RMI
libraries are redesigned to support the reservation and to limit the resources consumption. iii) The combination of reservation protocols and Berkley Sockets and CORBA
IIOP [Wan99] is another example of practical application of QoS facilities in middleware based applications. The university of Columbia and BBN worked together to
provide an interface of socket that support QoS based on RSVP and reused this
framework in QuO with its integration in CORBA IIOP.

   Hola-QoS [Gar02] is an example of middleware independent QoS framework
based on four layers. Each one handles a different conceptual entity: i) QoS Management: Its goal is to decide which applications should be executed, according to user
wishes and feasibility. ii) Quality Control: It negotiates with the selected applications
a configuration, to find the configuration that maximizes user satisfaction, and it is
feasible. iii) Budget Control: It performs the feasibility check of the set of budgets
required to support a candidate configuration. It is in charge of creating and initialis-
ing budgets and monitoring how budgets are used. iv) Run-Time Control: This layer
can be viewed as an extension to the operating systems to provide the basic functionality of a resource kernel.

   Examples of Interface Description Languages (IDL) QoS-aware are QIDL (Quality
Interface Description Language) [Loy98] and CDL (Contract Description Language)
[Bec97]. Both are languages integrated in object-oriented middleware frameworks for
the support of QoS. QIDL is part of QuO [Zin97] and CDL is included in MAQS
[Bec97]. MAQS and QuO use CDL and QIDL for the automatic generation of stubs
and skeletons that support the management of some basic QoS functions (i.e., QoS
negotiation, adaptation, and monitoring).

The QoS-enabled IDLs support the description of regions that represent state of QoS components or objects. Constraint expressions describe the possible regions. The states have associated transitions that provide support for description of QoS adaptation. QoS-enabled IDLs include support to access the current state of system resources.

QoS Adaptation of Hard Real-Time Techniques

Traditional real-time techniques come from the hard real-time domain and are not well suited for all kinds of adaptive real-time environments, such as multimedia systems. They are usually too pessimistic to be applied directly. Such pessimism implies low use of computational resources under some situations, which is not desirable for industrial applications. In adaptive real-time systems, resource needs of applications are usually highly data-dependent and vary over time. In this context, it is more important to obtain systems which can very well adapt their execution to the changing environment than to apply the too pessimistic hard real-time techniques. Therefore, restrictive task models and scheduling algorithms are being progressively relaxed, whereas adaptation techniques based on monitoring of application execution and resource consumption are being introduced.

This is the subject of several research initiatives and different approaches.

FC-EDF (Feedback Control Earliest Deadline First) tries to apply control theory to adapt system behaviour. [Sta99] [Sta01] and SWIFT [Ste99] are two examples of this approach. One of the problems of using adaptation, to maximize the global quality of the system, is the complexity of the optimization problem.

Two proposed alternatives to simplify this problem are based on economic models for resource management [Str99] [Reu98] or using low-level parameters (in terms of generic resource models) [Lu00]. Another approach is to use middleware for cooperation between service providers and the operating system, to keep service's resource demands within the limits of available resources, while maximizing output quality. FARA [Ros98], DQM [Bra98], and Odyssey [Nob00] are works that follow this idea.

Finally, in other cases, a complete architecture for resource and quality management is defined that provides integrated mechanisms resource allocation, negotiation, and adaptation, such as AQUA [Lak97], a QoS Manager for Nemesis [Opa99], Adaptware [Abd99], and HOLA-QoS [Gar01][Gar02][Gar02a].

Networking QoS

The management of CPU and network for supporting QoS have been subject of extensive research work. For the sake of completeness, this section gives some basic ideas on networking QoS. The management of CPU is dealt with in other chapters in this document.

There are many different interpretations regarding the definition of QoS. Networking QoS is defined as: the capability to control traffic-handling mechanisms in the network such that the network meets the service needs of certain applications and user subject to network policies [Ber01a]. This objective is developed in different hardware elements. Operating systems of application computers must support: scheduling policies and access control to the network, protocols that support QoS control and configuration, application interfaces, and administration services. Other network elements such as routers and switches must provide QoS configurations mechanisms, protocols that support QoS, queuing mechanisms for quality control.

The main concepts that support networking QoS for real-time systems are:

- **Traffic control and package queuing**. Scheduling algorithms for package deliberation provide specific quality objectives [Cla92]. Some network scheduling algorithms such as Fair Queuing algorithms, Deficit Round Robin order the packets in different ways and provide different worst case deliberation times. Each algorithm has associated specific algorithms for the computation of their specific deliberation times, and their admission control. Shaping algorithms such as Token Bucket and Leaky Bucket shape the traffic of specific traffic flows with specific schemas. The shape algorithms limits the traffic congestions and improve some specific quality attributes such as jitters. Other specific algorithms control the traffic borrows between different traffic flows. Borrow algorithms control the reuse of bandwidth from idle flow to congested flows (the maximum amount of borrowed traffic, and algorithms to return the borrowed bandwidth).

- **Resource reservation protocols**. Resource reservation protocols such as RSVP [Zha97] provide support for end-to-end resource reservation for specific sessions. In RSVP the sessions are identified with the IP address and the ports of connects. Reservation is supported for specific sessions or clusters of sessions (in multicast communication). The reservation protocol includes PATH and RESV messages that make the reservation of resources (specially bandwidth reservation) in all nodes (routers, switches and computers) included in the flow path. Several routers and switches (Cisco specially) support these protocols based on configurable traffic control schemas. The basic problems associated to RSVP are the scalability (RSVP requires complex queuing algorithms and packet scheduling), and security (identification of users that make the reservation).

- **Frameworks for the integration of QoS** [Bra94]. DiffServ and IntServ are examples of IETF standards for the extension of Internet, to support real-time as well as the current non-real-time service of IP. Both standards integrate the RSVP. Each approach defines different approaches for the classification of network traffic and services and interfaces for their support. IntServ was especially ambitious for the support of internet real-time systems (remote video, multimedia and virtual reality). DiffServ is a layer 3 traffic-handling mechanism. DiffServ tries to reduce the complexity of IntServ and include new services such as SLA (service level agreement), which specify the amount of customer traffic that can be accommodated at each service level.

- **Real-Time Transport Protocols** (RTP). RTP [Jac96] is a transport protocol for carrying internet real-time traffic flows, in an IP network. It provides a standard packet header format, which gives sequence numbering, media-specific time stamp data, source identification, and playload identification, among other things. RTP is usually carried using UDP. RTP is supplemented by RTCP (Real-Time Transfer Control Protocol), which carries control information about the current RTP session. RTP do not address the issue of resource reservation, it relies on resource allocation functions such as Weighted Fair Queuing, and on reservation protocols such as RSVP.

Industrial Landscape

QoS Management is a recent technology (most of technologies that include this action has a long experimentation and research activity). Industry groups have started the QoS Management application during last five years. Some examples of this application are:

1. Boeing has developed a Weapons System Open Architecture (WSOA) that is based on CORBA middleware, pluggable protocols and Quality of Service (QoS) enforcement, management and verification. QuO is used in the development of this architecture [Gos02].
2. Another example of application of QuO is the control of video streams [Rod02] in defence applications.
3. DiffServ and IntServ have a great maturity level and are partially supported in most of last version of general purpose operating systems such as Windows 2000 and XP, and Linux kernels of versions 2.4.2 and later. RSVP that is part of these frameworks is implemented in these operating systems too. QoS IP services that implement the operating systems are used in several applications, especially multimedia applications.

QuO is open source and it has been well tested. It has been reused in industrial applications and it is integrated with middleware frameworks such as TAO and ACE, and QoS IP facilities such as RSVP and priority based real-time OS.

The application of QoS IP in real-time systems depends specially on algorithms used for packages scheduling in traffic control levels and the shaper algorithms. Some algorithms support QoS guarantee modes that has associated better predictability. Windows 2000 and XP include a limited set of algorithms. Linux implementations include a large number of algorithms and the introduction of new algorithms is not complex.

22.2   Assessment

The interest in QoS is relatively recent, especially with regard to devices such as processors, memories, etc. As a consequence, despite much ongoing research, the available techniques are not mature enough to be fully used in industrial devices. In summary, the state of development of the levels of integration shown in the figure at the start of the section is:

*   *Specification of applications*: There are some proposals for describing QoS characteristics, contracts, quality levels, etc, although none of these can be considered as really satisfactory. One of the reasons is probably that these concepts are not completely understood and it is not clear how to handle them, to achieve the desired goals. The support for this type of notation is an important requirement to making QoS more usable. In this respect, the attempts to define UML profiles for modelling Quality of Service are very relevant.
*   *Component infrastructures*: The interest in using these infrastructures is evident. There are a number of proposals for providing components frameworks with the

required QoS support. However, good approaches for describing the quality, quality composition, and QoS-aware component structure are still open issues.

- *Middleware infrastructures*: These infrastructures should provide a number of basic services for managing the quality of a number of applications. Issues such as interoperation of quality managers in different machines or distributed management are still far from being successfully solved.
- *OS and kernels*: Resource kernels have been mentioned in a previous chapter. However, it is worth to mention that they are usually an evolution of RTOS. As such, they usually fail to provide advance mechanisms for making it more efficient the execution of QoS applications, mainly adaptation facilities.
- *Networking QoS*: Techniques for providing networking QoS are the most mature. This is due to the interest on QoS, which was initially raised by communicating certain types of information.

22.3   Trends

QoS Modelling Languages and Notations

There are a number of topics in QoS modelling languages and notations that are subject of intense research. These can be summarized as follows:

- *Identification of the QoS information* that is relevant to have a complete and useful description of the target software artefacts. This information should describe QoS categories, characteristics, quality contracts and quality bindings.
- *Development of suitable notations*, which are complete and composable. They should allow the description of the QoS information with the required detail level and in a format that is portable and can be understood by different tools.
- Frameworks that allow to *static analysis* to determine whether an application fulfils a given quality specification, taking into account its components, the execution platform and other relevant information. It may be impossible to perform this operation for all the QoS characteristics, but it is certainly true that for some of them is feasible.
- *Integration of QoS descriptions in design notations*, in such a way that QoS characteristics are fully supported. This should allow to combine and analysis QoS aspects automatically.

QoS Component Infrastructures

Future systems will require dynamic infrastructures, where components can be dynamically downloaded and interconnected. In this scenario, it should be possible to find QoS-aware components, to get the QoS specification and to combine them, in such a way that a component can use those with the quality characteristics that best fit its requirements. The identification of the appropriate information to embed, its format, and its structure for being feasible its composition are open questions that should be answered.

Another important issue is how to separate the business code from that used for adding to a component functions to allow access and management of its QoS information and behaviour. The use of containers and aspect programming are two promising approaches for letting developers to clearly locate these two types of functions. QoS components are treated in greater detail in section 20.6.

QoS Adaptation: Middleware, Resource Kernels and Applications

Due to the characteristics of the applications to be run (adaptive real-time, varying resource needs), adaptation seems to be one crucial operation for maximizing system quality and optimizing their execution. Most of the ongoing research tends to address the problems according to two different approaches. In the first approach, the adaptation strategy is embedded in the application, so that each one is locally responsible for adapting its computational demand based on the available resources and the required data processing. It is important to note that in this type of adaptive real-time application, the processing demands can vary depending on the input and other factors. In the second approach, the QoS adaptation is usually performed by some system software, namely a global QoS manager, resource manager or resource kernel. This system software may vary the amount of resources assigned to each task as a function of the current workload.

The first approach has the advantage that the application can use domain specific knowledge to adapt its execution to the available resources. In this way, the application could use scalable algorithms, which quality and resource usage can be dynamically modified to adapt to the available resources or to ensure that a certain output is produced on time. This type of adaptation could not be made by a middleware layer or by the operating system, as they lack of domain specific semantic knowledge.

The QoS and resource managers, can monitor system behaviour, to detect whether applications are using the requested resources or there are free resources. In this way, it may reassign budgets, or negotiate new contracts to maximize system quality. Existing research on the system software side usually focuses on two major levels: kernel and middleware. On the kernel side, algorithms for task scheduling and resource assignment for tasks are the main issues that are covered. Middleware solutions focused on building QoS architectures, user level schedulers and protocols for managing quality levels of applications that are mapped to resource assignments.

Predictability is a characteristic of major importance. However, predictability, and flexibility cannot be addressed independently, as methods for achieving predictability will have restricting impact on flexibility and uncontrolled flexibility will reduce predictability. Historically, real-time systems have been focused on providing single, specific solution to single, specific applications, treating all activities with the same methods, geared towards the most demanding scenarios. The high cost of such a system wide approach is acceptable only for applications with dramatic failure consequences. Rather, both requirements have to be addressed not only on a system level, i.e. on individual activities as well. Typical systems demand a mix of requirements, e.g. strict predictability for the critical core of a system while other activities and application favour flexibility. A key aspect in providing predictability and flexibility on an individual level is the protection of guaranteed activities.

At both levels, kernel and middleware, it is agreed that one of the most important problems to address is effective resource assignment among applications and/or tasks. Though at different levels, either the kernel or the middleware manager should control or coordinate application execution. Execution management will be based on the quality of service that applications will receive from the system.

To effectively assign system resources among applications and achieve predictability and flexibility, a number of issues should be further investigated. The most relevant ones include, at the higher abstraction level, protocols for managing quality levels of applications and for middleware (QoS) managers. Suitable architectures will allow obtaining flexible systems. Also, it will be an added value to aim at supporting as many types of applications as possible; therefore, generality is an issue. At a lower level, further work on resource management algorithms, new task models, admission control, monitoring, and adaptation algorithms should be done.

A required research area consists of developing hybrid methods which integrate the two types of adaptation strategies described above: the one that is embedded in the application with the adaptation scheme that is performed by a QoS manager. This integration may be done by given more freedom to applications for controlling their budgets or resource reserves. For example, the QoS manager may assign coarse-grain budgets to applications, which may be responsible for sharing out these budgets to their tasks. Hence, it may need to split and merge budgets, in such a way that the coarse-grain budgets are not exceeded and the fine-grain budgets are dynamically adapted to the varying individual tasks resource needs. This is another topic that should be subject of further research: adaptation mechanisms provided by the middleware for the running applications.

Dependable QoS Assurance in Open Environments

Embedded systems are broadly used today in many application domains, both in industry and in consumer products. And a considerable amount of these applications perform critical control operations that require the use of dependable embedded systems in order to exhibit crucial attributes such as availability, reliability or safety. Furthermore, given the widespread use of embedded systems and the trend to rely more and more on them, increased demands for dependability are expected to arise.

Therefore, the issue of dependability not only plays a very important role in current embedded computer systems, but also should be regarded as key for the success of future and emerging technologies in the domain of embedded systems. Particular attention and resources must be devoted into devising what will be the future application needs and what kind of support and technologies of dependable embedded systems must be provided.

To start with, the meaning of "dependability" must be unambiguous, and systematic approaches to the problem of achieving dependability must be employed. To this end, several progresses have been made over the last decade by the dependability and fault tolerance community to agree on common definitions and systematisations. Dependability can be expressed as "the measure in which reliance can justifiably be placed on the service delivered by a system" [Lap92]. The definition implies both the knowledge of a complete system specification, and a characterization of the external operating conditions (the environment), which might influence the system behaviour. Therefore, when considering open environments or complex interactions among system entities (through that environment), it might be extremely difficult to characterize all the possible impairments to dependability and, consequently, obtain a dependable design.

This is particularly relevant when we observe that recent advances in hardware with integrated communication and networking capabilities are fostering the interest and research in distributed embedded systems and architectures. Moreover, because of the potential benefits of distribution and pervasiveness, these architectures, despite embedded, are reaching unexpected complexity and scale levels. Therefore, reconciling the dependability requirements of highly distributed embedded systems with the uncertainty of such execution environments is a difficult challenge still to be addressed in current and future research.

A promising way to go is to make embedded systems adaptable to the environment, thus capable to react to changes in the operating conditions and possibly maintain required dependability levels. When reasoning in terms of Quality of Service (QoS), which implies the establishment of contracts between clients and service providers, the idea is to design systems to be dependable with respect to these QoS contracts, using QoS adaptation and renegotiation techniques and ensuring that, despite the uncertain factors that trigger the occurrence of failures, the QoS contracts remain valid.

The provision of quality of service (QoS) guarantees in open environments, such as the Internet, is an active field of research. In fact, although there is a lot of work dealing with the problem of QoS provision in environments where resources are known and can be controlled [Xu00][Vog98], no systematic solution has been proposed for environments where there is no knowledge about the amount of available resources. In the particular case of the Internet, the IntServ [Bra94] and DiffServ [Bla98] architectures have been proposed to specifically address the problem of handling QoS requirements and differentiated service guarantees. However, they still follow the perspective of QoS management, that is, of controlling how resources are reserved by the applications.

The fundamental problem that has to be faced is the uncertainty of the environment, which does not allow the provision of guarantees for the available QoS. The way in which applications must be designed and constructed has to rely on new models and paradigms, which deal with this uncertainty. In particular, when considering real-time requirements, uncertainty means that bounds may not be met due to timing failures, producing effects such as instantaneous delays, decreased coverage over the long term or contamination of logical safety properties [Ver02]. Nevertheless, even with appropriate models, not all applications can be implemented on these uncertain environments. They need to be adaptive or time-elastic, that is, they must be able to adapt their timing expectations to the actual conditions of the environment, possibly sacrificing the quality of other (non time-related) parameters. The success of an adaptive system has to do essentially with two factors: 1) the monitoring framework, which dictates the accuracy of the observations that drive adaptation and 2) the adaptation framework, which determines how the adaptation will be realized.

Monitoring of local resources and processes is widely used [Lut01][Fos00], but it does not provide a global view of the environment. Some works propose adaptation based on network monitoring and on information exchange among hosts (using specific protocols like RTP [Bus96] or estimating delays [Cam96]) but they do not reason in terms of the confidence about the observations, which is essential for dependable adaptation. Relatively to adaptation strategies there exist various approaches in the literature. For example, we mention the work in [Abd98] that proposes adaptation among a fixed number of accepted QoS levels, and the work in [Li99], that uses control theory to enhance adaptation decisions and fuzzy logic to map adaptation values into application-specific control actions.

Some emerging approaches are based on probabilistic characterizations of the environment, that is, on the construction of pdf's that describe the expected network or execution delays [Kri01][Cas01]. The objective is then to adapt applications in order to meet a certain desired probability level of timely behaviour. Instead of trying to provide guarantees on the bounds (which can be impaired by uncertainty), such approaches provide guarantees that adaptation will be done as necessary to keep a certain desired probability of those bounds to hold. These approaches have the advantage over others that they provide dependable QoS adaptation, being QoS defined by pairs of <bound,probability>. For instance, when the environment degrades to a state that implies larger bounds, by adapting the assumed bound to a new larger value the associated probability (of satisfying that bound) can be kept constant.

A fundamentally different approach emerges from the observation that many real-time applications can execute correctly despite the occurrence of timing failures (missed deadlines), provided that the number and distribution of these failures can be precisely bounded [Ber01b]. To a certain extent, this means that applications can (dependably) operate in environments with degraded QoS. The idea is then to apply scheduling policies that enforce the desired distributions, which requires managing an amount of available resources (which must be known) that is smaller than the amount of needed resources.

22.4   Recommendations for Research

[Scha03] proposes some general ideas for the application of QoS management of next middleware generations. This paper includes a discursion about the construction of QoS infrastructures based on two different approaches: priority based services (for examples DiffServ and most of real-time OS, and a resource reservation approach (for example RSVP and most of QoS general architectures). Probably the second approach provides better results, but requires the integration of reservation facilities in low levels of software infrastructures (networking and OS).

Another line of research is the integration of QoS management in component infrastructures. This is a subject of research that has been developed during last years, but current implementations are not mature enough. OMG proposes a new standard for the integration of QoS management services in CCM, but the services included in the proposal do not provide accesses to low levels of QoS such as resource reservation facilities and QoS IP [OMG03]. The group of distributed objects in Washington University at St. Louis is currently developing CoSMIC, this is an open-source model driven tool suite implementing the CCM deployment and configuration specification. The development of analytical methods for the QoS composition (the verification of compatibility of qualities of clients and servers) is another line of work that has not been well studied yet.

There is another subject of research that as not been well studied yet and includes most of levels of integration of QoS. Currently there is none general QoS platform that support services of most of general QoS characteristics. Current solutions support general QoS management facilities (e.g. negotiation, adaptation, and admission control), and some specific services of some QoS characteristics (e.g. resource reservation, and security facilities). But currently, the general QoS requirements must be supported with some technical solutions, such as periodic and sporadic servers, redundant object replications, and specific real-time protocols. The transition from QoS platform independent solutions to the specific mitigations solutions that include the implementation platforms must be done with craft methods. These solutions are needed for the application of model-driven methods in critical systems development.

22.5   References

[Aag02]   J. Aagedal and E. Ecklund, "Modeling QoS: Toward a UML Profile", Proc. UML-2002 Conference, Springer Verlag (2002).

[Abd98]   T. F. Abdelzaher and K. G. Shin, "End-host architecture for QoS-adaptive communication", Proceedings of the 4th IEEE Real-Time Technology and Applications Symposium, Denver, Colorado, USA, June 1998.

[Abd99]   Abdelzaher, T. F. (1999). QoS Adaptation in Real-Time Systems. PhD thesis, University of Michigan.

[Ase00]   J. Asensio and V. Villagrá, "A UML Profile for QoS Management Information Specification in Distributed Object-based Applications", Proc. 7th Workshop HP Open View University Association (2000).

[Bar95]   M. Barbacci, T. Longstaff, M. Klein and C. Weinstock., Quality Attributes, CMU/SEI Technical Report No. CMU/SEI-95-TR-021 ESC-TR-95-021, (December 1995).

[Bec00]   C. Becker and K. Geihs "MAQS – Management for Adaptive QoS-enabled Services", IEEE Workshop on Middleware for Distributed Real-Time Systems and Services, (December 1997).

[Ber01a]   Y. Bernet. "Networking Quality of Service and Windows Operating Systems". New Riders (2001).

[Ber01b]   G. Bernat, A. Burns and A. Llamosí. Weakly Hard Real-Time Systems. IEEE Transactions on Computers, vol.50, n.4, Apr 2001.

[Bla01]   L. Blair, G. Blair, A. Andersen and T. Jones. "Formal Support for Dynamic QoS Management in the Development of Open Component-based Distributed Systems". IEE Proceedings Software. Vol. 148 No. 3. (June 2001).

[Bla98]   S. Blake, D. Black, M. Carlson, E. Davies, Z. Wang, and W. Weiss. An architecture for differentiated services, RFC2475, Dec. 1998.

[Bor00]   M. Born, A. Halteren and O. Kath, "Modeling and Runtime Support for Quality of Service in Distributed Component Platforms", Proc. 11th Annual IFIP/IEEE Workshop on Distributed Systems: Operations and Management, (December 2000).

[Bra94]   R. Braden, D. Clark, and S. Shenker "Integrated Services in the Internet Architecture: Overview", Internet RFC 1633, June 1994.
http://www.ietf.org/html.charters/OLD/intserv-charter.html

[Bra02]   G. Brahnmath, R. Raje, A. Olson, M. Auguston, B. Bryant and C. Bjurt, "A Quality of Service Catalog for Software Components", Proc. SESEC 2002, 2002 Southeastern Software Engineering Conference 2002, (April 2002).

[Bra98]   Brandt, S., Nutt, G., Berk, T., and Mankovich, J. (1998b). A dynamic quality of service middleware agent for mediating application resource usage. In Proceedings of the 19th IEEE Real-Time Systems Symposium (RTSS'98).

[Bus96]   I. Busse, B. Deffner, and H. Schulzrinne, "Dynamic QoS control of multimedia applications based on RTP", Computer Communications, 19(1), Jan. 1996.

[Cam96]   A. Campbell and G. Coulson, "A QoS adaptive transport system: Design, implementation and experience", In Proceedings of the Fourth ACM Multimedia Conference, pages 117-128, New York, USA, Nov. 1996.

[Cas01]   A. Casimiro and P. Veríssimo, "Using the Timely Computing Base for dependable QoS adaptation", Proceedings of the 20th IEEE Symposium on Reliable Distributed Systems, pages 208–217, New Orleans, USA, Oct. 2001.

[Cla92]   D. Clark, S. Shenker and L. Zhang. "Supporting Real-Time Applications in an Integrated Services Packet Network: Architecture and Mechanism". In Proceedings of ACM SIGCOMM. (August 1992).

[Fos00]   I. Foster, V. Sander, and A. Roy. A quality of service architecture that combines resource reservation and application adaptation. In Proceedings of the Eighth International Workshop on Quality of Service, pages 181-188, Westin William Penn, Pittsburgh, USA, June 2000.

[Fro98]   S. Frolund and J. Koistinen, "Quality of Service Specification in Distributed Object Systems", Distributed Systems Engineering Journal, Vol. 5(4), (December 1998).

[Gar01]   García-Valls, M. (2001). Calidad de Servicio en Sistemas Multimedia Empotrados Mediante Gestion Dinamica de Recursos. PhD thesis, Technical University of Madrid. In Spanish.

[Gar02]   García-Valls, M., Alonso, A., Ruiz, J. F., and Groba, A. (2002a). An architecture of a quality of service resource manager middleware for flexible multimedia embedded systems. In Proceedings of the 3rd International Workshop on Software Engineering and Middleware (SEM 2002), pages 39-57, Orlando, Florida.

[Gar02a]   García-Valls, M., Alonso, A., Ruiz, J. F., and Groba, A. (2002b). Integration of system-level policies and mechanisms for quality of service management in embedded multimedia systems for web-based environments. In Proceedings of the IADIS International Conference WWW/Internet 2002,Lisbon, Portugal.

[Gei01]   K. Geibs. "Middleware Challenges Ahead" Computer IEEE. (June 2001).

[Hou97]   C. Hou, C. Han, and Y. Min. "Communication Middleware and Software for QoS Control in Distributed Real-Time Environments". In Proceedings Computer Software and Applications Conference. COMPSAC'97. IEEE (1997).

[Gos02]   Gossett, J. Noll, D. Corman, D. "Experiences in a distributed, real-time avionics domain-Weapons System Open Architecture", Proceedings. Fifth IEEE International Symposium on Object-Oriented Real-Time Distributed Computing, ISORC 2002 (2002).

[ISO98]   International Organization for Standardization, CD15935 Information Technology: Open Distributed Processing – Reference Model – Quality of Service, ISO document ISO/IEC JTC1/SC7 N1996 (October 1998).

[ISO98a]   International Organization for Standardization, Quality of Service: Framework, ISO document ISO/IEC JTC1/SC 6 ISO/IEC 13236:1998 (December 1998).

[Jac96]   V. Jacobson. "RTP: A Transport Protocol for Real-Time Applications", IETF RFC 1889 (January 1996).

[Koi97]   J. Koistinen, "Dimensions for Reliability Contracts in Distributed Object Systems", Hewlett Packard Technical Report, HPL-97-119 (October 1997).

[Kri01]   S. Krishnamurthy, W. Sanders, and M. Cukier. A dynamic replica selection algorithm for tolerating time faults in a replicated service. In Proceedings of the International Conference on Dependable Systems and Networks, pages 107–116, Goteborg, Sweden, June 2001.

[Lak97]   K. Lakshman,, R. Yavatkar, and R. Finkel, (1997). Integrated CPU and network-
I/O qos management in an endsystem. In Proceedings of the IFIP 5th International
Workshop on Quality of Service (IWQoS '97).

[Lap92]   Laprie, J.-C., Dependability: A unifying concept for reliable, safe, secure computing. In IFIP Congress, volume 1, pages 585-593, 1992

[Li99]   B. Li and K. Nahrstedt. A control-based middleware framework for quality of
service adaptations. IEEE Journal of Selected Areas in Communications, Special
Issue on Service Enabling Platforms, 17(9):1632-1650, Sept. 1999.

[Loy98]   J. Loyall, R. Schantz, J. Zinky and D. Bakken, "Specifying and Measuring Quality
of Service in Distributed Object Systems", Proc. 5th International Symposium on
Object-Oriented Real-Time Distributed Computing, (April 1998).

[Lu00]   Lu, C., Stankovic, J. A., Abdelzaher, T. F., Tao, G., Son, S. H., and Marley, M.
(2000). Performance specifications and metrics for adaptive real-time systems. In
Proceedings of the Real-Time Systems Symposium.

[Lut01]   H. Lutfiyya, G. Molenkamp, M. Katchabaw, and M. Bauer. Issues in managing
soft QoS requirements in distributed systems using a policy-based framework. In
Proceedings of the International Workshop, POLICY 2001, LNCS 1995, pages
185-201, Bristol, UK, Jan. 2001.

[Mig01]   M. de Miguel. "Solutions to Make Java-RMI Time Predictable" In Proceedings of
4th International Symposium on Object-Oriented Real-Time Distributed Computing. ISORC'2001. IEEE, May 2001.

[Mig02]   M. de Miguel, J. Ruiz and M. García, "QoS-Aware Component Frameworks",
Proc. International Workshop on Quality of Service, (May 2002).

[Nah01]   K. Nahrstedt, D. Xu, D. Wichadakul and B. Li. "QoS-Aware Middleware for
Ubiquitous and Heterogeneous Environments". IEEE Communications Magazine.
Vol. 39, No. 11. (November 2001).

[Nob00]   Noble, B. D. (2000). System support for mobile, adaptive applications. IEEE Personal Computing Systems, 7(1):44-49.

[OMG02]   Object Management Group, UML Profile for Scheduling, Performance, and Time,
Draft Adopted Specification, OMG document number ptc/2002-11-01 (November
2002).

[OMG02a]   Object Management Group, UML Profile for Modeling Quality of Service and
Fault Tolerance Characteristics and Mechanisms RFP, OMG document number
ad/02-01-07 (January 2002).

[OMG02b]   Object Management Group, UML Profile for Modeling Quality of Service and
Fault Tolerance Characteristics and Mechanisms Initial Submission, OMG document number realtime/2002-09-01 (September 2002).

[OMG03]   Object Management Group, QoS For CORBA Components RFP and Initial
Submission, OMG document number mars/03-10-01 (October 2003).
http://www.omg.org/cgi-bin/doc?mars/03-10-01

[Opa99]   Oparah, D. (1999). A framework for adaptive resource management in a multimedia operating system. In Proceedings of the IEEE International Conference on
Multimedia Computing and Systems.

[Par92]   A. Parekh, A Generalized Processor Sharing Approach to Flow Control in Integrated Services Networks, PhD Thesis, Laboratory for Information and Decision
Systems, Massachusetts Institute of Technology, (February 1992).

[Raj97]   R. Rajkumar, K. Juvva, A. Molano, S. Oikawa, Resource Kernels: A Resource-
Centric Approach to Real-Time and Multimedia Systems, Tech. report Carnegie
Mellon University, 1997.

[Ras00]   U. Rastofer and F. Bellosa. "An Approach to Component-based Software Engineering for Distributed Real-Time Systems". In Proceedings SCI 2000 Invited Session on Generative and Component-based Software Engineering. IIIS (2000).

[Reu98]   Reumann, J. and Shin, K. G. (1998). Adaptive quality-of-service session manage-
ment for multimedia servers. In Proceedings of the 8th International Workshop on
Network and Operating Systems Support for Digital Audio and Video
(NOSSDAV98), pages 303-316.

[Rod02]   C. Rodrigues, "Using Quality Objects (QuO) Middleware for QoS Control of
Video Streams", Proceedings OMG's Third Workshop on Real-Time and Embedded Distributed Object Computing (2002).

[Ros98]   Rosu, D., Schwan, K., and Yalamanchili, S. (1998). FARA – a framework for
adaptive resource allocation in complex real-time systems. In Proceedings of the
4th IEEE Real-Time Technology and Applications Symposium (RTAS).

[Sha03]   R. Schantz, J. Loyall, C. Rodrigues, D. Schmidt, Y. Krishnamurthy, I. Pyarali,
"Flexible and Adaptive QoS Control for Distributed Real-Time and Embedded
Middleware", In Proceedings Middleware 2003. LNCS (June 2003).

[Sch00]   D. Schmidt, V. Kachroo, Y. Krishnamurthy and F. Kuhns. "Developing Next-
generation Distributed Applications with QoS-enabled DPE Middleware". IEEE
Communications Magazine. Vol. 17, No. 10. (October 2000).

[Sel00]   Selic, B., "A Generic Framework for Modeling Resources with UML," IEEE
Computer, Vol. 33(.6), (June 2000).

[Sha99]   M. Shankar, M. de Miguel, and J. Liu. "An End-to-End QoS Management Architecture". In Proceedings of Real-Time Application Symposium. RTAS'99. IEEE
(1999).

[She97]   S. Shenker, C. Partridge and R. Guerin. "Specification of Guaranteed Quality of
Service", Internet RFC 2212 (September 1997).
http://www.ietf.org/rfc/rfc2212.txt?number=2212

[Sta95]   R. Staehli, J. Walpole and D. Maier, "Quality of Service Specification for Multimedia Presentations", Multimedia Systems, Vol. 3 (5/6) (November 1995).

[Sta99]   Stankovic, J. A., Lu, C., Son, S. H., and Tao, G. (1999a). The case for feedback
control real-time scheduling. In Proceedings of the EuroMicro Conference on
Real-Time Systems.

[Sta01]   Stankovic, J. A., He, T., Abdelzaher, T., Marley, M., Tao, G., and Son, S. (2001).
Feedback control scheduling in distributed real-time systems. In Proceedings of the
22nd IEEE Real-Time Systems Symposium (RTSS 2001).

[Ste99]   Steere, D. C., Goel, A., Gruenber, J., McNamee, D., Pu, C., and Walpole, J
(1999). A feedback-driven proportion allocator for real-rate scheduling. In Proceedings of the Operating Systems Design and Implementation (OSDI).

[Str99]   Stratford, N. and Mortier, R. (1999). An economic approach to adaptive resource
management. In Proceedings of the IEEE Hot Topics in Operating Systems (HotOS) VII.

[Ven97]   N. Venkatasubramanian and K. Nahrstedt, "An Integrated Metric for Video QoS",
Proc. ACM Multimedia 97, (November 1997).

[Ver02]   P. Veríssimo and A. Casimiro. The Timely Computing Base Model and Architecture. IEEE Transactions on Computers – Special Section on Asynchronous Real-
Time Systems, vol.51, n.8, Aug 2002.

[Vog98]   C. Vogt, L. C. Wolf, R. G. Herrtwich, and H. Wittig. Heirat. Quality-of-Service
management for distributed multimedia systems. Special Issue on QoS Systems of
ACM Multimedia Systems Journal, 6(3):152.166, May 1998.

[Wan01]   N. Wang, D. Schmidt, M. Kircher, and. K. Parameswaran. "Adaptative and Reflective Middleware for QoS-Enabled CCM Applications". IEEE Distributed Systems
Online Vol 2 No. 5. (July 2001).

[Wan99]   P.Wang, Y. Yemini, D. Florissi, P. Florissi and J. Zinky. "Application QoS Provi-
sioning with Integrated Services". IEEE Communications Magazine. September
1999.

[Xu00]   D. Xu, D. Wichadakul, and K. Nahrstedt. Multimedia service configuration and reservation in heterogeneous environments. In Proceedings of International Conference on Distributed Computing Systems, Taipei, Taiwan, Apr. 2000.

[Zha97]   Zhang, S. Berson, S. Herzog, and S. Jamin. "Resource ReSerVation Protocol (RSVP)- Version 1 Function Specification". Internet RFC 2205. 1997. http://www.ietf.org/html.charters/rsvp-charter.html

[Zin97]   J. Zinky, D. Bakken, and R. Schantz. "Architecture Support for Quality of Service for CORBA Objects". Theory and Practice of Object Systems. Vol. 3 No. 1. (January

23 Real-Time Middleware

Currently, middleware technologies, such as CORBA [OMG00] and .NET [Mic00] have been widely used in many application areas to mask out problems of system and network heterogeneity and alleviate the inherent complexity of distributed systems.

The recent emergence of new application areas for middleware, such as embedded systems, real-time systems, and multimedia, has imposed new challenges which most existing middleware platforms are unable to tackle. This new application areas impose more demands in terms of resource sharing, dynamism, and timeliness. Therefore, these areas require additional properties from the underlying middleware. Some of them are current subject of study and research, such as middleware support for QoS resource management.

In the last years, the OMG (Object Management Group) has improved the CORBA standard specifications with respect to real-time systems issues. For instance, it has adopted the Minimum CORBA [OMG98a], Asynchronous Method Invocation (AMI) [OMG98], and Real-Time CORBA (RT-CORBA) specifications [OMG99]. Minimum CORBA is a subset of the CORBA specifications that removes features that are not required by real-time and embedded systems. The RT-CORBA specification includes features to manage CPU, network, and memory resources. The AMI specification defines several asynchronous method invocation models.

Also, other middleware technologies for building distributed applications have appeared more recently. Though Jini does not provide real-time capabilities to applications, it allows to build distributed embedded systems based on services that appear and disappear dynamically. Microsoft has also developed its contribution, .NET; also, it does not integrate real-time support. Even if they do not provide any real-time features, due to their increasing popularity both Jini (in the area of service discovery for embedded networked devices) and .NET (in the field of platforms for the development of distributed software systems) are also presented in this section.

This section describes some of the most relevant middleware technologies for developing distributed applications. Some of them provide real-time capabilities and some of them do not; however, they are considered to have interesting characteristics applicable to distributed and embedded networked devices. Moreover, the field of middleware technologies that provide real-time capabilities is a promising one, though it is not a mature field as opposed to other fields of real-time systems, such as real-time kernels. A considerable amount of research is being done for instance in Real-Time CORBA [OMG99], integrating real-time capabilities into Java RMI, and developing modular and open architectures for QoS resource management middleware such as in HOLA-QoS [Gar03].

Aspects of Real-Time component models are also covered in section 14.

Artist FP5 Consortium: Embedded Systems Design, LNCS 3436, 305–315, 2005.
© Springer-Verlag Berlin Heidelberg 2005

23.1   Landscape

Research Landscape

Building QoS-aware middleware that provides QoS capabilities and adaptive resource management is an active area of research, specially interesting in areas like multimedia systems. The capacity to specify end-to-end QoS requirements implies integration of system-wide policies to parameterize resource management algorithms. All this is being built into the middleware or as part of a QoS resource manager middleware.

Since middleware models were firstly aimed at general purpose distributed environments, no special real-time considerations were made. Progressively, real-time systems have acquired more protagonism, so different middleware models to tackle with the problems of introducing real-time support in distributed systems have appeared. In this sense, message-oriented middleware (MOM) is a candidate to providing a solution.

On another hand, dynamic environments, such as AI distributed systems and agent-based environments, have acquired a great popularity. They have introduced the need for providing timely support to highly dynamic invocations and, in general, predictable operation. In such systems, middleware must integrate service discovery facilities and predictability in dynamic invocations.

CORBA Technology

In the distributed systems area, CORBA is a widely accepted standard; it has also been successful in industry. A growing class of real-time systems is using CORBA among which we can mention command and control systems (Mobies/DARPA, Eurocontrol), telecommunication systems (Nokia, France Telecom) and also avionics systems (Boeing). A general web site about CORBA success stories can be found at http://www.corba.org. Also, most of the efforts to bring together real-time and distribution have come from the OMG. Therefore, this section describes different features of CORBA technology that are interesting for distributed real-time systems.

Real-Time CORBA Specification

Currently, no integrated solutions (at network, operating system, and middleware levels) currently exist to provide end-to-end QoS guarantees to distributed object applications. CORBA (Common Object Request Broker Architecture) is a widely accepted object-oriented middleware for developing distributed systems and applications. It introduces flexibility and reusability. However, many application domains need to have real-time guarantees from the underlying operating system, network, and middleware to meet their QoS requirements. In this respect, the performance levels and QoS enforcement features of current CORBA implementations are not yet suited for hard real-time systems (e.g. avionics) and constrained latency systems (e.g. teleconferencing).

Conventional ORB (one of CORBA's backbone) specifications present some weak points:

- Conventional ORBs neither define a way for applications to specify their end-to-end QoS requirements nor provide support for end-to-end QoS enforcement between applications.

- Conventional ORBs lack real-time features; there is no standard programming language mapping for exchanging ORB requests asynchronously (blocking prone).
- As last point, it may be said that there is a lack of performance optimizations; current ORBs have a considerable throughput and latency overhead. This is due to internal message buffering strategies, long chains of intra-ORB virtual method calls, and lack of integration with underlying real-time operating systems and QoS mechanisms.

Over the last decade, research efforts on COTS middleware, such as Real-Time CORBA [OMG99], have matured. Former key drawback points in distributed real-time systems as overhead, non-determinism, and priority inversion of the middleware are no longer the dominant factor. Recent studies [Sch02] argue that focus has switched to the COTS operating system and networks, which are responsible for the majority of end-to-end latency and jitter. Moreover, middleware can be configured to various runtimes profiles such as Ada Ravenscar real-time profiles [Pau01].

Real-time ORB end-systems (such as ZEN [Kle02]) require the integration with network adapters, operating system I/O subsystems, communication protocols, and common object services. Requirements of high performance, real-time ORB end-systems are mainly:

- Policies and mechanisms for specifying end-to-end application QoS requirements.
- QoS enforcement from real-time operating systems and networks.
- Optimized real-time communication protocols
- Optimized real-time request de-multiplexing and dispatching.
- Optimized memory management.
- Optimized presentation layer.

Open source implementations of Real-Time CORBA ORBs, such as ZEN [Kel02] and TAO [Sch98], have also appeared to show that it is possible to provide QoS guarantees in middleware. Currently, integration of Real-Time Java and RT-CORBA at implementation level is being performed [Kri04].

Asynchronous Message Interface
Distributed real-time applications usually exchange asynchronous requests using event-based execution models. For instance, specific devices periodically generate sensor data and the regular delivery of this data to higher level component must be guaranteed. Hence, some standard invocation models, such as the one of CORBA was too restrictive for real-time applications [Har97].

The AMI specification provides an approach to allow exchange of asynchronous requests. it allows operations to be invoked asynchronously using the Static Invocation Interface (SII) in order to eliminate the complexity inherent to the Dynamic Invocation Interface's deferred invocation model. The AMI specification defines two programming models: the Polling model and the Callback model.

In the Polling model, each two-way operation returns a local object Poller. A client can use the Poller to check the status of a request. If the server has not replied yet, the client can either block awaiting its arrival or return to the calling thread immediately. In the Callback model, when a client invokes a two-way asynchronous operation on an object, it passes an object reference for a reply handler servant as a parameter. When it receives the response, the client ORB dispatches it to the appropriate callback operation on the reply handler servant.

Events and Notification Services

Events and notification services are also an alternate approach. It is inevitable to refer to the fact that CORBA also includes this model, as it is the CORBA Event Service [OMG95]. This section uses CORBA as an example to illustrate these services.

This service has been designed to alleviate some of the restrictions with standard CORBA invocation models. In particular, the Event Service supports asynchronous message delivery and allows one or more suppliers to send messages (storing events information) to one or more consumers. Event data can be delivered from suppliers to consumers without requiring these participants to know about each other explicitly.

The CORBA Event Service defines supplier and consumer participants. Suppliers generate events and consumers process events received from suppliers. In addition, the Event Service defines an event channel, which is a mediator that propagates events to consumers on behalf of suppliers.

Suppliers and consumers collaborate separately in the Event Service architecture through the two mechanisms 'push' and 'pull'. Suppliers can either push data to an event channel or request the event channel to pull data from it. Likewise, consumers can either pull data from event channel or request the event channel to push data to it. The push mechanism on both consumer and supplier sides is commonly used in many real-time environments as it allows efficient and predictable execution of operations.

Albeit, this specification does not completely fulfil some wider requirements for event control policies. The OMG extended the COS Event Service to address these limitations, and defined the COS Notification Service. It provides a standardized API to define QoS constraints filtering or delivery policies. Besides, it defines a new object hierarchy suitable for a better event dispatching through the definition of structured events and the sharing of subscription information between event channels and consumers.

Hence, COS Notification Service defines: Proxy objects are delegates that provide complementary interfaces to clients; Admin objects that enable the logical grouping of Proxy object, and thus provide a notion of hierarchy among nodes; Filter and Mapping Filter objects that can be attached to all admin and proxy objects, they use the Trader Constraint language defined in the COS Trader to enable event filtering. These different objects, and their use when deploying the COS Notification, allow for the optimization of the critical path of event propagation.

However, this specification only define high level policies and QoS parameters that are not suitable to completely enforce hard real-time requirements [Gor01].

Jini

With the appearance of the pervasive computing paradigms and ad hoc networks, traditional distributed applications have to evolve to be used in such environments. The possibility of having a big number of devices connected to a network and physically near has to be exploited. One way of doing this is to make devices collaborate within a flexible structure, i.e., devices may advertise and export their functionality to other networked systems. Moreover, flexibility will allow devices to be come and go at a very low cost.

Jini is an architecture for distributed computing that comes from the Java world to allow network plug and play of devices. It is thought for a community of devices and systems that need support for spontaneous appearance and disappearance of devices, and the ability to self-heal. Jini is a paradigms that provides run-time use of services across address spaces. Current Sun's implementations of the Jini system rely on an underlying RMI system for communicating remote application objects. However, the Jini specification allows for any other underlying system to be used, as long as it adheres to the semantics of code mobility offered by RMI. RMI's capabilities may also be extended to be used in a Jini-like fashion. Anyway, real-time capabilities of Jini are not contemplated; in principle, they would rely on the real-time support of the underlying communication system, real-time RMI for instance.

Services of Jini are accessed through a service proxy. Proxies may be RMI stubs talking to some remote service, or they may be smart proxies. Smart ones can use any private protocol necessary to communicate with the service. It is possible to provide a Jini interface to legacy services that speak sockets or CORBA or some other protocol.

Its potential to be combined with J2ME for programming networked embedded personal devices is another of the advantages of the Jini Java technology for building communities.

.NET

Recently Microsoft announced a new initiative called .NET (pronounced dot net). .NET is the umbrella term for a) Microsoft's new vision and strategy, b) a set of products and c) a new platform for software development called the .NET Framework. The .NET Framework provides a computing platform that is programming language neutral. It comprises an extensive class library and a run-time environment. Latter is known as the Common Language Run-time (CLR). The CLR is based on the concept of a virtual machine that executes an intermediate language (IL). Code running under control of the CLR is referred to as managed code, as opposed to native code running directly on top of the operating system. The execution of managed code is a two-step process. The first step is done before deployment, in this step the program is compiled down to its intermediate representation. Apart from the intermediate code the compiler also emits an extensive set of meta-data that is needed by the CLR at run-time. The code together with the meta-data forms an assembly: the unit of deployment in .NET. In the second step the intermediate code is compiled to native code (just-in-time compilation).

.NET has many similarities to Java and as a result also many of the same problems regarding its use in real-time environments. Current implementations of the CLR build on top of the underlying operating system. As a result the characteristics of the operating system determine for a large part the ability to satisfy any real-time requirements. A real-time operating system is however perquisite but not a guaranty. The threading design of a CLR implementation and the way it maps threading related aspects to the underlying operating system remains crucial. The CLR, like Java, provides automatic memory management. Although automatic memory management can

contribute to the reliability of a system it typically introduces non-deterministic behaviour.

On the positive side, the CLR ensures type safety for managed code and supports
exception handling, which both can contribute to the reliability of a system. Furthermore, the .NET Framework provides means for managed code to interfaces to native
code (P/Invoke). Also the use of pointers is supported making it possible to access to
specific memory locations – a necessary capability for real-time embedded systems.
This opens the way to hybrid solutions where the parts of an application that need to
meet hard real-time deadlines are written in native code while other parts are written
in managed code. For resource constraint systems a compact version of the .NET
Framework is available. The .NET Framework has been submitted to the European
Computer Manufacturers (ECMA) for standardization. Open source implementations
based on this standard are currently emerging for non- Windows operating systems
(e.g. Mono an implementation for Linux).

23.2   Assessment

To compare both approaches (AMI and event and notification services), we note that
AMI does not provide a variation of group-based programming and anonymous
communication techniques. With CORBA AMI, application developers do not have
to devise their own means to send server replies to client request. AMI applications
can receive replies that include multiple IDL types when Event Service applications
communicate using a single Any argument. Although Anys can send all IDL types,
they incur significant marshalling and message footprint overhead [Aru00].

In contrast, the Event Service provides a flexible model for transmitting asynchronous events among objects. However, its specification lacks several important features required by real-time applications. Chief among these missing features include
real-time event dispatching and scheduling, periodic event processing, and centralized
event filtering and correlations. The COS Event Service interfaces have been extended by projects such as [Har97] to enable the definition of execution requirements
and characteristics using QoS parameters (such as worst-case execution time, rate,
etc.) by the application and specifically to provide real-time features.

With respect to more general features that the presented technologies exhibit, the
following characteristics are important:

- *Object orientation.* Almost all relevant middleware technologies support object
  oriented paradigms in the form of remote services (as, for instance, in CORBA
  and Jini), remote objects (as, for instance, in RMI).
- *Software portability.* The power of software portability has been sufficiently
  proven. In this respect, emerging middleware technologies try to adjust to this feature. Originally Sun's Java technology and later Microsoft's .NET have developed
  intermediate code generation technologies to address this issue. This presents
  some drawbacks for real-time systems that will hopefully be addressed in the near
  future.
- *Event based execution models.* Distributed real-time applications usually exchange
  asynchronous requests using event-based execution model. In the last years, the
  OMG has improved the standard specifications with respect to real-time systems

issues. It should be said that the OMG has made the most important effort in addressing real-time systems issues. For instance, it has adopted the Minimum CORBA [Obj98a], Asynchronous Method Invocation (AMI) [Ojb98b], and Real-Time CORBA specifications.

- *Timely invocations are of great importance for distributed real-time systems.* They are not easy to achieve because they involve the network. There are studies that prove the performance QoS that certain RTCORBA implementations may achieve for high speed and bandwidth networks. However, lower level issues that involve the operation of the network protocols to handle retransmissions and the effect they have for real-time behaviour have not been fully supported. Jini provides no specific features for real-time systems. It relies on the underlying remote method invocation mechanism (for instance RMI), therefore, its capabilities for timely invocations of remote services depend on the features that RMI exhibits for real-time. Currently, the DRTSJ is being developed, that will hopefully lead to the fulfilment of some the requirements of timely invocations for distributed real-time applications.

- *Interoperability of distributed applications.* Gateways for interoperation are being provided by the emerging middleware solutions, so that different applications are able to use each other's functionality no matter in what language they have been developed. Additional packages and cross-language compilers are generated to fulfil this goal. However, techniques to address interoperability in a more comfortable way and at a higher abstraction level could be developed.

- *Learning curve.* Some of these technologies, for instance CORBA specifications, imply a great deal of technologies and software components. Therefore, though it is a very powerful technology, its learning curve is a problem.

23.3   Trends

QoS capabilities and adaptive resource management will play an important role in next generation middleware, specially in fields like multimedia processing. This will allow to achieve a high utilization of the system resources such as CPU, memory and network, in order to enhance the system performance. Also, it will distribute and allocate system resources according to the application requirements. Resource aware middleware systems will need to use QoS management techniques to ensure that the solicited service requirements are met.

Also, distributed real-time applications often rely on event propagation around scattered logical or physical different nodes. Thus the publisher/subscriber model is often enforced as a natural solution as it provides the required features for implementation efficiency e.g. existing implementations are scalable or fault tolerant; real-time analysis, as this model is simple enough to allow complete analysis of its different components; QoS constraints enforcement or filtering capabilities. Besides, asynchronous message API enable at the lower level the efficient propagation of requests through the network.

From an industrial point of view, it is not clear that the OMG CORBA specifications and services can be considered as a definitive solution in the distributed real-time and embedded area. Both CORBA AMI and COS Event Service have their advantages and their drawbacks. One can consider that this may come from the initial design of CORBA which was not dedicated to distributed real-time and embedded applications. Besides, Jini and .NET are not designed for real-time and are outside the scope of the study.

To this respect, message-oriented middleware (MOM) may provide an alternate solution directly built upon the publisher/subscriber model. The Java Message Service (JMS) [Sun] specification provides a solid foundation for MOM architecture, and is accepted as a de facto standard for MOM API. Even if it lacks real-time features, it enables message filtering based on a SQL'92 like syntax. Thus, real-time MOM can be devised using a restricted set of this API. Nevertheless, existing projects and studies show real-time MOM are viable solutions [Raj95]; and proprietary solutions already exists [RTI00].

Such an approach should not be ignored as soon as real-time MOM industrial-strength specifications become available. This is still an ongoing effort. Hence, OMG has issued a Request For Proposal (RFP): the Data Distribution Service for Real-Time systems (DDS) RFP to establish a MDA (Model Driven Architecture) specification describing the application-visible interface and behaviour of a data-distribution service that supports a data-centric publish-subscribe for real-time systems. A revised submission is currently reviewed in the OMG specification adoption process [OMG03].

From another perspective, it is important to observe that the emergence of applications operating independently of direct human control is inevitable. In fact, with the increasing availability of technologies to support accurate and trustworthy visual, auditory, and location sensing [Hig01] as well as the availability of convenient paradigms for the acquisition of sensor data and for the actuation on the environment [Add01], a new class of large-scale decentralized and proactive applications can be envisaged.

However, research on high-level models for this class of applications--- e.g. on autonomous agents and distributed AI--- has revealed the shortcomings of current architectures and middleware interaction paradigms. Dealing with highly dynamic interactions and continuously changing environments and, at the same time, with needs for predictable operation, is still an open challenge. Since our focus is on complex real-time systems made of embedded components, then even more stringent requirements have to be taken into account, namely to achieve distributed, safe and timely process control. In this context, the provision of adequate interaction paradigms is a fundamental aspect [Bac00]. Typical characteristics of this class of applications, such as autonomy or mobility must be accommodated, while allowing the possibility to handle extra-functional requirements like reliability, timeliness or security.

In contrast with the client/server or RPC based paradigms supported by current state-of-the-art object-oriented middleware [Hor97][OMG95], event models have shown to be quite promising in this arena [Har97][Mei02]. However, the existing middleware approaches offering event services, often lack one or several of the following key points: seamless integration with a programming model; architectures with an adequate layer structure; and the provision of support for extra-functional attributes.

Therefore, we identify an emerging trend in proposing new architectural constructs that are adequate to such event-based interaction models and, at the same time, provide adequate support to address the specific requirements of real-time embedded systems. In fact, architecting such a system, namely defining the placement and composition rules for software components, when objects are embedded systems, or collections thereof, and where the differences between hardware and software are sometimes subtle, is a challenging task.

A possible research direction can be based on a component-based object model [Crn02]. This model breaks with the traditional separation between the software and hardware perspectives, pointing to seeing objects as mixed hardware/software components, although it is obviously possible to conceive an object as a software-only component. Quite interestingly, these components can be seen as sentient objects, as defined in the scope of the CORTEX project [COR02]. Sentient computing established the generic concept, presented in [Hop00], elaborated in CORTEX in the context of object components.

23.4   Recommendations for Research

Some on-going and future research lines in QoS related to middleware are the following:

System-wide resource management. Mechanisms and policies to build QoS resource management into middleware, integrating various resources, mainly: processor, memory, and network. It plays an important role to study the relation among application semantics and study the effect that this may have on such mechanisms. Also, implications of user actions are being studied with respect to the effects that they have on the system-wide policy for resource management.

Architectures for QoS resource management middleware. Some existing middleware architectures, that have become the de facto specifications, are very complete but very large. Building QoS specifications into them even increases its size, and therefore, its learning curve. In some environments, other architectural approaches to middleware are possible and they are being investigated; they aim at being lighter and more focused on QoS resource management for specific real-time environments [Gar03].

Adaptive real-time middleware. Support for highly dynamic environments. This requires integrating techniques/algorithms to monitor system behaviour, enforce resource usage, adapt to changes, and even, predict future changes.

Real-time support from communication media. Relation to real-time network protocols to achieve predictable remote invocations and packet delivery (invocation time). Though some studies focus on the OS as the bottleneck in the invocation predictability, the network also plays an obvious important role in this.

Interoperability. There are different middleware solutions for developing distributed applications. General frameworks for interoperation among different solutions are also being explored [Pau01].

New specifications for distributed middleware are also appearing such as the distributed specification for RTSJ; this is currently being worked on. Implementation of such specs is also an open research direction.

23.5   References

[Add01]   M. Addlesee, R. Curwen, S. Hodges, J. Newman, P. Steggles, A. Ward, and A. Hopper. Implementing a sentient computing system. IEEE Computer, 34(8):50–56, aug 2001.

[Aru00]   A. B. Arulanthu, C. O'Ryan, D. C. Schmidt, M. Kircher, and J. Parsons, "The Design and Performance of a Scalable ORB Architecture for CORBA Asynchronous Messaging," in Proceedings of the Middleware 2000 Conference, ACM/IFIP, Apr. 2000.

[Bac00]   J. Bacon, K. Moody, J. Bates, R. Hayton, C. Ma, A. McNeil, O. Seidel, and M. Spiteri. Generic support for distributed applications. IEEE Computer, 33(3):68–76, 2000.

[COR02]   Preliminary definition of CORTEX programming model. CORTEX project, IST-2000-26031, Deliverable D2, Mar. 2002.

[Crn02]   I. Crnkovic and M. Larsson, editors. Building Reliable Component-Based Software Systems. Artech House Publishers, 2002.

[Gar03]   M. García-Valls, A. Alonso, J. Ruiz, and A. Groba. "The Architecture of a Quality of Service Resource Manager Middleware for Flexible Embedded Multimedia Systems". Lecture Notes in Computer Science, vol. 2596. Springer Verlag, 2003.

[Gor01]   P. Gore, R. K. Cytron, D. C. Schmidt, and C. O'Ryan, "Designing and Optimizing a Scalable CORBA Notification Service," in Proceedings of the Workshop on Optimization of Middleware and Distributed Systems, (Snowbird, Utah), ACM SIGPLAN, June 2001

[Har97]   T. Harrison, D. Levine, and D. Schmidt. The design and performance of a real-time CORBA event service. In Proceedings of the 1997 Conference on Object Oriented Programming Systems, Languages and Applications (OOPSLA), pages 184–200, Atlanta, Georgia, USA, 1997. ACM Press.

[Hig01]   J. Hightower and G. Borriello. Location systems for ubiquitous computing. IEEE Computer, 34(8):57–66, aug 2001.

[Hop00]   A. Hopper. The clifford paterson lecture, 1999 sentient computing. Philosophical Transactions of the Royal Society London, 358(1773):2349–2358, Aug. 2000.

[Hor97]   M. Horstmann and M. Kirtland. DCOM Architecture. http://msdn.microsoft.com/library/, July 1997.

[Kle02]   R. Klefstad, D. C. Schmidt, and C. O'Ryan. "The Design of a Real-Time CORBA ORB using Real-Time Java", in Proceedings of the IEEE International Symposium on Object-Oriented Real-Time Distributed Computing", April 2002.

[Kri04]   A. Krishna, D. C. Schmidt, and R. Klefstad. "Enhancing Real-Time CORBA via Real-Time Java". Submitted for publication to the 24th IEEE International Conference on Distributed Computing Systems (ICDCS). Tokyo, Japan. May 2004.

[Mei02]   R. Meier and V. Cahill. Steam: Event-based middleware for wireless ad hoc networks. In Proceedings of the International Workshop on Distributed Event-Based Systems (ICDCS/DEBS'02), pages 639–644, Vienna, Austria, 2002.

[Mic00]   Microsoft. .NET Development. http://www.msdn.microsoft.com/net/ 2000.

[OMG95]   Object Management Group, CORBA Services: Common Object Services Specification, Revised Edition, 95-3-31 ed., Mar. 1995.

[OMG95]   OMG. The common object request broker: Architecture and specification. Technical Report OMG Document 96-03-04, July 1995.

[OMG98a]   Object Management Group, Minimum CORBA – Joint Revised Submission, OMG Document orbos/98-08-04 ed., August 1998.

[OMG98b]   Object Management Group, CORBA Messaging Specification, OMG Document orbos/98-05-05 ed., May 1998.

[OMG99]   Object Management Group, Real-Time CORBA Joint Revised Submission, OMG Document orbos/99-02-12 ed., March 1999.

[OMG00]   Object Management Group. The Common Object Request Broker: Architecture and Specification, 2.4 ed., October 2000.

[OMG03]   Data Distribution System RFP Roadmap; http://mars.omg.org/mars_roadmap.htm

[Pau01]   Laurent Pautet, Fabrice Kordon and Thomas Quinot, From functional to architectural analysis of a middleware supporting interoperability across heterogeneous distribution models, Proceedings of the 3rd International Symposium on Distributed Objects and Applications, 2001.

[Raj95]   R. Rajkumar, M. Gagliardi, and L. Sha, "The Real-Time Publisher/Subscriber Inter-Process Communication Model for Distributed Real-Time Systems: Design and Implementation," in First IEEE Real-Time Technology and Applications Symposium, May 1995.

[RTI00]   Real Time Innovations, Inc., "NDDS: Real-time networking made simple." http://www.rti.com/products/ndds/ndds.html, 2000.

[Sch98]   D. C. Schmidt, D. L. Levine, and S. Mungee, "The Design and Performance of Real-Time Object Request Brokers", Computer Communications, vol. 21, pp. 294-324, April 1998.

[Sch02]   Douglas C. Schmidt and Mayur Deshpande and Carlos O'Ryan, Operating System Performance in Support of Real-time Middleware, the 7th IEEE Workshop on Object-oriented Real-time Dependable Systems, San Diego, CA, January, 2002.

[Sun]   Java Message Service (JMS), Sun Microsystems; http:/java.sun.com/jms

24 Networks

During the last two decades, technological advances in hardware made possible the embedding of both processing and communication functions in highly integrated, low-cost components, fostering the use of a distributed approach in many application fields including embedded systems. This fact led to the dissemination of so-called Distributed Embedded Systems (DES), which became the core of intelligent equipment with a high degree of autonomy, from robots to machine tools, from cars to trains and planes. Another class of DES appeared from the interconnection of consumer equipment, most notably computer peripherals and portable devices, such as laptops, mobile phones, PDAs and digital cameras, as well as within intelligent home systems, either for access control, location aware services, security and distributed multimedia. In most cases, DESs have now a strong impact on human lives, either because they are used within important economic processes, e.g. complex machinery in factories, or because they control equipment that directly interacts with people, e.g. transportation systems, or simply because they became an essential part of everyday life e.g. interconnection of computer peripherals and portable devices. Current buzz words such as *X-by-wire, m2m* (machine-to-machine communication), *pervasive computing, ad-hoc networks, mobile computing, sensor networks* exhibit the current importance of networking within embedded systems.

This section starts with a description of the different networks that are typically used in distributed embedded systems found in several different application fields. Following this description, an analysis of the role that networks play within a system and of their current limitations is presented. These limitations lead to the identification of fundamental trends in current networks research, to support the requirements of new applications of distributed embedded systems. Finally, some recommendations for research are made.

Aspects of middleware for implementing hardware real-time systems are also covered in section 8.

24.1 Landscape

Today, a large variety of networks is currently available to build distributed embedded systems. Some of them are competitors for the same application market, while others are complimentary and address different requirements and application scenarios. Killer applications that are currently shaping the industrial and research interest around networks extend from the safety-critical domain, such X-by-wire, to specially time sensitive applications, such as motion control, as well as to distributed monitoring, such as sensor networks and ambient intelligence, to mobile computing and ad-hoc networks, pervasive computing, multimedia streaming and VoIP.

Therefore, to deliver a relatively horizontal view of the field as background for the remaining text, this section presents a brief description of several networks that became particularly popular in specific application fields, namely ARINC629 in avion-

Artist FP5 Consortium: Embedded Systems Design, LNCS 3436, 316–337, 2005.
© Springer-Verlag Berlin Heidelberg 2005

ics, WorldFIP in train control systems, PROFIBUS in automation equipment, CAN and TTP in automotive systems, IEEE 1394 (FireWire) and USB for multimedia devices and peripherals interconnection, Ethernet for office automation and now for industrial automation and also for multimedia devices and peripherals interconnection, LonWorks for building automation, IEEE 802.11 for wireless LANs and mobile computing, and finally Bluetooth, based on radio, and IrDA, based on infrared light, to interconnect peripherals and portable devices.

CAN

The *Controller Area Network* (CAN) protocol was developed in the mid 1980s by Robert Bosch GmbH. Despite its initial target being automotive applications, it soon expanded into different application fields such as automation and robotics. It uses a multi-master architecture on a broadcast shared bus, the transmission medium is usually a twisted pair cable and the network maximum length depends on the data rate, which imposes a fundamental limit to the maximum speed attainable (e.g. 40m @ 1 Mbps; 1300m @ 50 Kbps). The arbitration uses a CSMA non-destructive bit-wise protocol in which the controller transmitting the message with lowest identifier wins access to the medium and continues transmission. The remaining controllers detect a collision, back off and retry again as soon as the current transmission ends. Because of this arbitration scheme, each message must have a unique identifier that also establishes the message priority. The traffic scheduling at the bus access level is thus based on fixed priorities. Probably for this reason, CAN generated great interest for real-time applications. The addressing is indirect and based on the identifiers, too. The CAN protocol does not specify an application layer.

TT-CAN

The *Time-Triggered CAN* (TT-CAN) is a communication protocol based on CAN, and thus inherits many of its properties, remarkably the physical layer. TT-CAN goals are to reduce latency jitter and guarantee a deterministic communication pattern on the bus. In TT-CAN nodes are synchronized either by a specific periodic message (level 1) known as *reference message* or by executing a clock synchronization algorithm (level 2). As nodes are synchronized, time slots can be reserved to specific messages, which in this case are transmitted without contention (exclusive windows). Moreover, TT-CAN also allows to reserve time slots for shared access, in which several nodes can try to transmit on the same time slot (arbitrating windows), using the native arbitration of CAN. The bus time is organized in basic cycles, consisting of several slots. Several basic cycles may be combined to build the system matrix, which completely characterizes the sequence of slots. The TT-CAN protocol offers an application layer that includes a configuration interface for system set-up and an application interface for time, interrupt and control management.

TTP/C Protocol

The *TTP/C protocol* is a fault-tolerance oriented communication protocol, including clock synchronization and membership services, fast error detection and consistency checks. A TTP/C network consists of a set of communicating nodes connected by a replicated network. A node comprises a host computer and a TTP/C communication controller. The medium access control is based on TDMA with bus time divided into slots, each being statically assigned to one node. In each slot each node transmits one frame. The frame cycle is called a TDMA round. A distributed fault-tolerant clock synchronization algorithm establishes the global time base needed for the distributed execution of the TDMA scheme. Each node holds a data structure containing the message descriptor list (MEDL). Messages are piggybacked within the frames transmitted by each node. The MEDL contains the information relative to all messages exchanged on the system, including the respective transmission instants allowing, thus, fast detection of missing messages. Despite being static, the MEDL can hold up to 30 global pre-configured modes, which can be requested by nodes in a specified set using dedicated messages. The TTP/C protocol defines 4 transmission speed classes (500Kbps, 1Mbps, 2Mbps and more recently 25Mbps) and provides an application layer that delivers configuration and messaging services.

FlexRay

The FlexRay protocol is promoted by the FlexRay Consortium, which includes some of the top players on the automotive and electronics industries (BMW, DaimlerChrysler, Motorola, Philips, GM and Bosch), and targets specifically power train, chassis and body control on automotive applications.

The protocol supports both synchronous and asynchronous data transfers with deterministic collision-free bus access. The bus time is organized in fixed duration communication cycles, comprising a static part, where the synchronous traffic is transmitted, and a so-called dynamic part, conveying the asynchronous (on-demand) traffic. Data transmission within the static part is time-triggered, which, once combined with a time-synchronization protocol, allows for contention-free bus access. In the dynamic part the traffic is transmitted on demand, with a mini-slotting contention-resolution mechanism inherited from the BMW's ByteFlight protocol. This mechanism also supports collision-free deterministic bus access. Regarding the physical layer, the protocol supports data rates of up to 10Mbit/sec, which may grow up to 20Mbit/sec with the (optional) use of two independent communication channels. Error containment is enforced at the physical layer by the use of independent bus-guardians within each ECU. To answer the specific requirements of automotive applications, the FlexRay protocol is particularly flexible with respect to the network topology, supporting bus, star and multiple-star topologies based on electrical or optical transmission mediums.

ARINC 629

The *ARINC 629* communication standard has been developed as a successor to the ARINC 429 standard, and provides general purpose data communications between avionic subsystems. The ARINC 629 standard defines a multi-level protocol for inter-subsystem data communications, using a bi-directional multiple access data bus. Both broadcast and directed messages are supported and may have variable length. Currently 2 Mbps data transmission rate is supported, but higher bit rates, using optical fibres, are currently being considered. The standard specifies two alternative data link protocols, named basic and combined respectively. Both of these protocols support periodic and sporadic transmissions. Periodic messages are scheduled automatically according to a TDMA schedule defined at pre-run-time. Aperiodic messages are transmitted on-demand within specified temporal windows. The arbitration of aperiodic messages is based on CSMA-CA (collision avoidance), also referred to as mini-slotting, according to which one node is allowed to transmit only after sensing the bus idle for a given time window whose length is different from node to node.

WorldFIP

The *WorldFIP* protocol is part of the European Standard EN 50170 and it was developed for factory and process automation to support real-time communication. It belongs to the class of the so-called *field buses*. There is also a light version of the protocol, DWF (Device WorldFIP), which aims specifically at embedded systems offering a reduced set of services. Despite being labelled as an automation protocol, WorldFIP is particularly popular in embedded train control systems.

The protocol relies on a bus topology and can operate over copper wiring or optical fibres. Concerning the transmission speed, the WorldFIP protocol defines 3 classes for copper wire (21.25Kbps, 1Mbps and 2.5 Mbps) and a 5 Mbps class over optical fibre.

In what concerns the medium access control, WorldFIP is based on the producer-distributor-consumers (PDC) communication model. The distributor function is performed by a special node, the bus arbitrator (BA), which schedules the producers access to the bus, using master-slave transmission control. At run-time, the BA uses a static schedule table (the BAT) to schedule periodic transactions. Aperiodic message transfers are carried out in the time not used by periodic transactions. The addressing method is based on identified variables, i.e., the addressed entities are variables to be exchanged and not nodes, and both periodic and aperiodic messages are supported.

The WorldFIP protocol defines an application layer that includes PDC-based services (MPS, Periodic and Sporadic Messaging system) and messaging services (a subset of MMS, Manufacturing Message Specification).

PROFIBUS

The Profibus protocol is also a *field bus* included in the European Standard EN 50170, which aims at automation systems. There are several flavours that are better suited to different applications, such as FMS (field bus messaging specification) directed to cell control, DP (Device automation) for machine control and PA (Process Automation) meant for process control which differs from DP in what concerns the physical layer and data link interface. DP is probably the profile better suited to embedded systems.

At the physical layer, PROFIBUS (both FMS and DP) can use either RS-485 or optical cabling with transmission rates up to 12Mbps. In what concerns the data link, there are two type of nodes, master and slaves. The former ones can initiate network transactions while the latter ones just respond to master commands. The medium access control among the masters is based on token-passing, following a simplified version of the Timed Token Protocol. In Profibus, a token circulates between the masters of a logical ring, which is implemented on a physical bus. Master stations manage the token and control communications with the slave stations. Messages are transmitted in a message cycle, which comprises an action frame (request or send/request frame), a reply frame (acknowledgement or response frame) and possible retries. The Profibus protocol distinguishes between high-priority and low-priority traffic.

Unlike the Timed Token Protocol, the Profibus does not provide for a synchronous bandwidth allocation specifying the length of time a station has at its disposal to transmit, but each station can use the token for a time interval, called the Token Holding Time (TTH). The TTH is determined by the station on each token visit as TTH = TTR – TRR, where TTR is the Target Token Rotation time (a design parameter specifying the time that the token should theoretically take to make a complete round of the ring) and the TRR is the Token Real Rotation time (i.e., the time measured between two consecutive arrivals of the token in the station). In order to reduce the blocking that a station could be subject to when other stations submit heavy traffic, in each token visit it is always possible to send at least one high priority message.

IEEE 1394

The IEEE 1394 protocol is the industry-standard implementation of Apple's FireWire digital I/O system, and mainly targets the interconnection of peripherals and consumer electronics devices. This protocol provides guaranteed delivery of multiple data streams through isochronous data services, up to 1k interconnected links, up to 63 devices per link, 4.5m separation between contiguous devices (longer distances are possible using special cabling), up to 16 hops between devices, and data transfer rates of 100, 200, and 400Mbps (800Mbps and 1.2 Gbps versions in development – 1394b). The 1394 protocol is a peer-to-peer network based on a tree topology. Devices may have several ports, acting as repeaters. Configuration of the bus occurs automatically on power-on, whenever a new device is plugged in, on errors, or after explicit application request. Upon configuration, the current network topology is identified and IDs are assigned to each node. During this process a cycle master (root node), an isochronous resource manager and a bus manager are elected, possibly residing in the same node.

The 1394 protocol supports isochronous and asynchronous data transfers that take place within a cyclic framework of fixed time slots with 125μs duration. A cycle master triggers each cycle by sending a cycle start packet (CS). The isochronous transfers may use up to 100μs in each cycle and are always transmitted at a constant rate in a one-to-one or one-to-many fashion. This mode does not support error correction nor retransmission. The isochronous resource manager keeps track of the bandwidth and channels currently allocated to isochronous streams and performs an admission control of new requests. Asynchronous transfers are directed to a specific node by an explicit address, and are acknowledged, supporting error-checking and retransmission mechanisms. No bandwidth guarantees are provided to this type of traffic.

The bus operation is synchronized by the reception of the CS packet upon which all devices wishing to transmit isochronous data issue a request to the root. The root node handles these requests and grants the right to transmit. Isochronous channels can only be used once per cycle although devices can hold more than one channel. In each cycle, the bus time available after processing all pending isochronous transfers can be used for asynchronous transfers in a similar bus access scheme.

Due to its high bandwidth and bandwidth reservation scheme, the IEEE 1394 protocol is well adapted to support multimedia applications as well as bulk data transfers. It is now being considered for use within cars and planes as a backbone to support the interconnection of multimedia consumer devices.

USB

The Universal Serial Bus (USB) protocol, currently in its 2.0 revision, resulted from the joint effort of a group of major players in the telecommunications and personal computer (PC) fields. The main objective was to provide a universal solution, able to replace the vast mix of connectors usually required to interconnect peripherals to the PC. To cope with these requirements, the USB protocol supports plug and play, distinct data types and small connectors, which already include power lines. Low-power peripherals may be thus completely bus-powered. USB acceptance has been remarkable, being now a cheap, robust and efficient interconnection technology, with over 1 billion of USB-enabled products.

USB now specifies 3 distinct bus speeds: 1.5 and 12Mbps, as defined by USB revisions 1.0 and 1.1, and 480Mbps, introduced by USB revision 2.0. The USB topology is a "tiered star", with the peripherals interconnected via hubs. Hubs act as repeaters, and thus, from the logical point of view, the USB network behaves like a bus. In the network there must be one root hub, which is the system master, controlling and scheduling all the communication activities. Peripherals attached to the USB bus should only respond to the root hub commands. Upon connection, a device is polled by the host, which identifies the peripheral, assigns a unique identifier to the node and loads the appropriate device drivers, a process called enumeration. Each peripheral may have up to 16 communication endpoints. Endpoint 0 is reserved for control transfers, while the remaining ones may be used for generic data transfers. USB transactions use pipe semantics connecting the host with each one of the peripheral endpoints. When establishing a connection, each endpoint returns its communication requirements, like the type of transaction, data packet size, bandwidth, maximum latency. These communication requirements may be accepted, rejected or changed by the host, depending on the resource availability.

USB defines 4 different data transfer types, for configuration and control (**Control**), reliable transfer of large amounts of data without timeliness requirements (**Bulk**), peripheral poll for events (**Interrupt**) and isochronous data (**Isochronous**), originated e.g. from audio/video streams. The host handles these distinct data transfer types differently: Bulk transfers are carried out only whenever there are no other communication activities (background); Interrupt transfers have a guaranteed maximum latency and Isochronous transfers have a guaranteed bandwidth. Furthermore, Isochronous transfers are not protected by CRC.

USB communication occurs within 1ms or 125μs frames, for v1.1 or v2.0 respectively. All the frames start by a start of frame (SOF) field and end with a minimum period of bus idle, called end of frame (EOF). Within each frame the host may trigger different data transfers, eventually of different types, according to the system communication requirements.

Despite being master-slave, there is the "On-The-Go" supplement (OTG Supplement, Revision 1.0a, 07-09-2003), which provides a means for special devices being able to play both master and slave roles. This supplement was fostered by the need to allow portable devices to behave either as peripherals of a given root or as roots with their own peripherals, depending on the circumstances.

Ethernet

Ethernet was invented about 30 years ago, and its initial purpose was to connect office equipment. Along the time this protocol has evolved in many ways, it became adopted as an IEEE standard and achieved unprecedented acceptance mainly in the office environment. Due to its current wide acceptance, Ethernet has also been suggested for use in many diverse application fields such as automation and even embedded systems. In terms of transmission speed, Ethernet is available in 10Mbps, 100Mbps and more recently 1Gbps and 10Gbps. Concerning the network topology, Ethernet also evolved from the initial bus configuration to a more structured and fault-tolerant approach, based on a star. Ethernet uses a Carrier Sense Multiple Access with Collision Detection (CSMA/CD) arbitration mechanism, according to which a network controller having a message to be transmitted must wait for the bus to become idle and then starts transmission. Other nodes can start to transmit at the same time, originating a collision and message corruption. This is detected by all nodes that abort the transmission of the current message, wait for a random time interval as dictated by the BEB (truncated binary exponential back off) algorithm and try again. The number of retries is limited to sixteen, after which a packet is discarded. This situation becomes common when the network load grows above a given threshold, generating many chained collisions. Consequently, this protocol does not provide, by itself, predictable message transmission times.

However, during Ethernet's history, several techniques have been proposed to overcome the lack of predictability of its CSMA/CD arbitration protocol. These range from modification of the MAC to addition of transmission control layers above the original MAC. Examples of such approaches are Master/Slave, Token-passing, Timed Token, TDMA, Virtual Time Protocol and Traffic shaping, providing different degrees of efficiency, flexibility and timeliness guarantees. The low-cost, wide availability and high-bandwidth made available by this technology raised the interest of the industrial community, which has spawned several protocols, e.g. NDDS (Network Data Distribution Service) and PowerLink.

More recently, switches replaced hubs due to their capacity to create a single collision domain in each of its ports. As long as a single equipment is connected to each port (micro-segmentation) collisions never occur unless they are created on purpose for flow control. Switched Ethernet allows achieving a more predictable traffic behaviour as long as the flows of messages arriving at each port can be adequately characterized and are well behaved in the sense that they do not cause overflow in the ports queues, e.g. due to excessively long bursts, or excess of broadcast/multicast packets.

Resembling the case of shared Ethernet, a considerable amount of work has also been devoted to enhance the real-time behaviour of switched Ethernet networks, taking advantage of the better properties of this architecture. The industrial community has been particularly active on this domain, with several proposals currently active, e.g. Ethernet/IP, PROFInet/IRT and EtherCat.

LonWorks

LonWorks, and its *LonTalk* protocol, targets peer-to-peer control systems, integrating large number of nodes spanning to relatively large distances and with broad ranges of processing capability, such as the ones found in home and building automation, supporting e.g. HVAC and surveillance subsystems. The protocol supports a wide range of physical media, ranging from power-line to twisted-pair bus. However, the particular physical medium constrains the speed, distance and number of devices allowed in a system (e.g. 5.4 Kbps, 125m and 64 devices for power-line medium). The message arbitration mechanism is independent of the physical medium, and allows reducing or even completely avoiding collisions. The protocol is generally based on p-persistent CSMA with the possibility to use predictive p-persistent CSMA with acknowledged services. The predictive aspect consists on dynamically adjusting p according to the channel load and allows strongly reducing the probability of collision under heavy loads, avoiding the effect of thrashing. On the other hand, the protocol also allows defining up to 8 contention-free priority slots synchronized upon the end of the last transmission, which are statically allocated to specific devices. These slots are meant for messages with short and guaranteed response time requirements. Moreover, the protocol also provides authenticated services, which allow secure communications among system devices.

IEEE 802.11

IEEE 802.11 is a wireless LAN developed for use in the SOHO (Small Office / Home Office) environment. It has, however, been suggested for the interconnection of embedded equipment with the external world, e.g. for remote monitoring and management, as well as for the interconnection of systems formed by several mobile units such as robots. The standard defines the physical and medium access control layers. Currently, available transmission rates range from 1 and 2Mbps, as defined by the basic version to 11Mbps (802.11b) and 54Mbps (802.11a and 802.11g). The radio frequency bands are the 2.4GHz ISM license-free band for 802.11{b,g} and 5GHz for 802.11a. Comparing both high speed versions, 802.11a and 802.11g, the latter, despite its recent emergence (deployment in 2003), is finding widespread use due mainly to its retro-compatibility with 802.11b. Nevertheless, it presents a few weaknesses with respect 802.11a, namely the reduced number of channels (3 against 12) and operation in a much noisier band.

Concerning the medium access policy, the IEEE 802.11 standard defines two modes of operation: DCF (Distributed Coordination Function) and PCF (Point Coordination Function). The DCF mode employs a fully distributed arbitration mechanism of the CSMA-CA type (CSMA with collision avoidance). Stations are allowed to transmit only after sensing the medium idle for an interval called DIFS (distributed inter-frame space). If activity is detected then they wait for a random interval before starting transmission according to the BEB algorithm similarly to Ethernet. The waiting time is suspended whenever another transmission is detected. Collisions can still happen and are detected using an acknowledgement frame sent by the receiver SIFS (short inter-frame space) after a successful transmission. To further reduce collisions an optional 3-way handshake can be used. A transmitter willing to send a data packet starts by sending a reservation frame (RTF, request to send) that indicates the time needed to transmit the data packet. The receiver acknowledges the RTS issuing a control frame (CTS, clear to send). Other stations that receive one RTS or CTS refrain from transmitting during the time therein indicated, while the transmitter sends its data packet. These mechanisms become inefficient for short data packets and still do not completely prevent collisions. Therefore, DCF does not support temporal guarantees.

Time constrained traffic can be supported using the PCF mode. In this case, a special node, the PC (Point Coordinator) assumes the network management, creating traffic cycles. Each cycle is divided in two parts. In the first part, the PC explicitly controls the access to the medium, thus there is no contention. In the second part, the operation is like in DCF, and thus all nodes can compete as in the previous mode. However, most available equipment supports DCF, only, since PCF has generally received low attention. Currently, given the raising interest in streaming and interactive applications, a new specification called WME (wireless multimedia enhancements) is being proposed to provide 802.11 with prioritized traffic and queuing. These features will be integrated in the upcoming 802.11e standard.

The standard also defines encryption methodologies to protect the data exchanges such WEP (Wired Equivalent Privacy), a simple encryption method, and, more recently, WPA (Wi-Fi Protected Access), which overcomes many of the weaknesses exhibited by the former. Securities issues are addressed by the 802.11i standard, which will be released soon.

Bluetooth

Bluetooth is an industry standard for short range radio in office and home environments that aims at replacing cabling connections between personal portable devices such as mobile phones, laptops, PDAs, cameras, etc.. Bluetooth networks are ad-hoc in the sense that the network, called piconet, is set-up automatically whenever Bluetooth-enabled pieces of equipment come close enough to each other. These networks of personal devices are often referred to as *Personal Area Networks* (PANs). Several piconets in the same geographical area can be interconnected, forming a scatternet.

Bluetooth operates in distances up to 10 meter, but this range is expected to increase in upcoming extensions of the standard (a version with 100m range is under consideration). The raw bit rate is 1Mbps and it uses the 2.4GHz ISM license-free band with FHSS (frequency hopping spread spectrum) modulation. Nevertheless, the maximum achievable data rate is 723Kbps. Bluetooth uses a master-slave medium access control, with at most 7 active slaves in each piconet. More slaves may remain synchronized with the master but not engaged in active communication (parked slaves). The piconet master polls a single slave in one hop of the FHSS sequence. The slave has to answer in the next hop. The order in which slaves are polled is not defined by the protocol but depends on the pending traffic. An interesting feature of

Bluetooth is that any node can be either master or slave, depending on the automatic piconet setup procedure.

Bluetooth supports two types of communication links, SCO (synchronous connection-oriented) links and ACL (asynchronous connection-less) links. The former ones have reserved bandwidth and are meant for voice communications, with a bit rate of 64 Kbps on each direction. Each slave supports at most 3 SCOs. On the other hand, ACLs are meant for data communications and can be configured in symmetric up and downlinks with up to 433Kbps or asymmetric with up to 722Kbps in one way 57Kbps in the other way. With ACLs there are no temporal guarantees but there is a larger bandwidth that can be exploited to convey high quality audio, for example. Data exchanges can be protected by authentication and ciphering services. Moreover, Bluetooth includes a service discovery protocol that allows finding a node with specific capabilities, as well as interfaces based on a serial link emulation (RFComm), the PPP/IP/TCP-UDP suite and the object exchange protocol OBEX.

IrDA

IrDA is an industry standard defined by the Infrared Data Association (IrDA). It provides a transmission rate up to 115Kbps in asynchronous mode (SIR, serial infrared), and up to 4Mbps with synchronous transmission (FIR, fast infrared). A new version supporting up to 16 Mbps is expected soon based on the IrDA Air (Advanced Infrared) specification. Its range can cover a complete room, providing point-to-point and multipoint (IrDA Air only) connections, and its physical layer is based on modulated infra-red light.

With IrDA Air, the medium access is similar to the 802.11 DCF scheme, and thus there is no support to guaranteed traffic. The IrDA specification presents a layered architecture, comprising required and optional protocols, such as serial and parallel connection emulation (IrCOMM), object Exchange Protocol (IrOBEX) for data object transfer and a transport protocol (TinyTP), providing stream flow-control. The main interest on IrDA concerning embedded systems is as an external interface for remote monitoring, data upload/download, and management.

24.2   Assessment

Throughout the last decade, DESs have evolved towards highly distributed systems, following the concept of encapsulating different functionality in separate intelligent nodes (e.g. intelligent sensors and actuators) or simply aggregating separate pieces of equipment that were already used for specific stand-alone functionality. This resulted in a growing number of nodes, leading to higher connectivity and scalability requirements [Kop97]. However, it also resulted in higher system complexity, even with simpler individual nodes, and led to a stronger impact of the network on the global system properties.

Therefore, the network within a DES plays now a vital role since it supports all the interactions among the set of interconnected nodes and, in general all global system services. The network, or generally the communication system, determines, to a great extent, the support for properties such as composability, timeliness, flexibility and dependability as well as determines the efficiency in the use of system resources.

Hence, networks with adequate protocols and throughputs must be used in order to grant those properties to the respective systems, as appropriate [Tho99].

Currently, there is a relatively wide choice of networks adapted for embedded systems in the most diverse application domains, as expressed in the previous section. The degree at which the network supports the properties referred above is variable and must be verified against the application specific requirements. This aspect is particularly important because some properties cannot be efficiently enforced at the middleware or higher layers in the software architecture without adequate and direct support of the underlying network. For example, it is costly in bandwidth to transmit aperiodic information on time-triggered networks, or to implement multicasting on networks supporting unicasts, only.

Some of the current limitations on the use of networks in embedded systems arise from different options concerning conflicting concepts, taken in the design of the respective protocols. For example, safety concerns typically lead to protocols that use static definition of either traffic as well as system components [ARI99]. This impairs the use of such networks in more dynamic environments where the system configuration may change on-line and in which the communication requirements may also vary. Moreover, such static protocols also reduce the efficiency in the use of network bandwidth when a substantial number of information flows are of a sporadic nature (event-triggered) or when (quasi) periodic flows change their rates dynamically. If the network does not directly support consistency and replica determinism for fault masking, then implementing such mechanisms at higher software layers conflicts with low computation and communication overhead. Fault tolerance on the basis of time redundancy, such as re-transmission upon error, may conflict with real-time requirements [Bro01]. Fault tolerance on the basis of spatial redundancy, such as replicated nodes and network, typically conflicts with low cost and low power consumption.

Apart from these conflicts, the communication medium is also a source of potential limitations to the use of networks in embedded systems. For example, wireless communication is inherently open and thus non-secure. Moreover, it is also very susceptible to interferences causing errors and unavailability. The transmission rate supported by the medium can also be a limiting factor for several applications. For example, the increasing use of multimedia streams, e.g. for machine vision, might require higher bandwidth than normally offered by current networks used in the embedded domain [Dec01]. The limitations of wireless communication are particularly challenging in the field of wireless sensor networks, where the combination of real-time requirements, severe resource and cost constraints and reconfigurability and redundancy management pose problems that push the frontier of current technologies [Sta03].

Proper design of the network can help solving these conflicts while at the same time keeping the cost of the final system within bounds. This is essential to support a new generation of applications that are dynamic and exhibit real-time, dependability and efficiency requirements.

24.3 Trends

This section identifies several trends concerning networks for distributed embedded systems (DES). Emphasis is given on the trends and issues that are, somehow, related

to the general perspective of ARTIST – Action 3, i.e. adaptability in real-time applications. In particular, it will focus on the move towards higher distribution, higher
integration, integration of TT and ET traffic, dependability issues, higher flexibility,
wireless connections and Internet connectivity. The references included in the text do
not pretend to be exhaustive but illustrative, only.

Higher Distribution

One trend that has been verified for more than a decade is the evolution towards
highly distributed systems, following the concept of encapsulating different functionality in separate intelligent nodes [Kop97]. This fully distributed scenario has several
advantages: it favours dependability through easy replication of nodes and definition
of error-containment regions; composability since the system can be built by integrating nodes that constitute independent subsystems; scalability through easy addition of
new nodes to support new functionality; and maintainability due to the modularity of
the architecture and easy node replacement. Despite being witnessed in different application scenarios, this trend is particularly materialised in the field of sensor networks [Sta03], in which large numbers of simple and small communications-enabled
nodes self-organise to gather and route information on the respective environment.
Smartdust [Kah99], a project developed in the University of California at Berkeley,
USA, is just as an example of this paradigm.

Higher Integration

Following the previous trend, it became apparent that to achieve higher benefits from
fully distributed architectures it was necessary to improve the integration among the
system components. There are two main reasons: on one hand, it is necessary to integrate the information from the subsystems in order to improve the knowledge of the
global system state and improve the control over it; on the other hand, efficiency
gains can be achieved if different subsystems share information, e.g. that produced by
the respective sensors. In this latter case, functions can spawn over several components and use their local resources.

The way to higher integration has been extensively pursued in certain application
areas such as process control and factory automation [Pim90]. It has been the basis for
the architectures of modern industrial systems, structured in layers with horizontal
(within the same layer) and vertical (across different layers) communication flows.
Computer Integrated Manufacturing (CIM) is an example of such architecture.

Other application fields have been similarly pursuing higher integration, such as
home and building automation, where the objective is to integrate information from
the home or building environment in order to improve energy management, support
the remote control of devices, improve safety mechanisms, support localization-aware
applications, etc. Similarly, precision agriculture, disaster relief, pollution monitoring,
forest fire detection are all application areas that require the integration of large numbers of dispersed embedded equipment, for example using sensor networks [Sta03]. In
a different scale, the integration of peripherals and portable devices has been consistently growing, either using cabled interconnections, such as USB, or wireless such as
802.11, Bluetooth and IrDA, forming ad-hoc networks [Wu04].

Even within machines or vehicles, higher integration seems to be a hot topic, mainly due to the potential to reduce costs [Rus01]. For example, automotive industry analysts are expecting that the number of microprocessors in current high-end car models will grow more slowly in the near future than it did in recent years (current numbers account for close to 100 microprocessors). In fact, the total computing power installed is several times what is needed and the same functionality can be implemented with substantially less processors if higher integration between subsystems is used. There are several problems, however, such as how to assure a similar level of error-containment and composability [Rus01], and also how to put in practice such integration when those subsystems are built by different makers [Ell02]. These issues are deeply related with the network that supports the integration of all subsystems in the global system.

Dependability Issues

An aspect that merits particular attention in safety-critical applications is dependability. DESs are increasingly used to control systems whose failures may cause human life losses (e.g. x-by-wire applications in cars and planes). In consequence, specific dependability attributes such as reliability and safety have to reach higher values than in normal applications. Such high values of dependability are typically achieved through fault tolerance techniques, typically based on redundancy, either temporal, spatial or both. Although there has been significant work in this area, it is nevertheless important to be careful when applying existing solutions to DESs. Well-balanced designs must take into account the specificities of these systems (e.g., low cost and power consumption requirements) and still achieve the required levels of dependability.

Besides having to fulfil specific dependability requirements, the network also should play a central role as provider of low-level services, which are fundamental to help the global system to achieve the required level of dependability. If a specific service is not provided at low level, a higher-level protocol implemented in software at the various nodes has to be used. Under these circumstances the well-known problem of amplification of failures is likely to appear [Gop91]. On the other hand, if the network provides such services, the system software, system architecture and higher-level protocols are all simplified, keeping global costs within reasonable levels and preventing not only amplification of failures, but also an excessive communication overhead in the system. For instance, use of replication techniques such as active replication to tolerate node failures requires an intense communication among replicas in order to achieve replica determinism. Networks typically used in DESs offer low bandwidth. Therefore, providing consistent communication (e.g. atomic broadcast) at the data-link layer is very important to reduce the communication overhead generated [Pin01][Pro00].

In the case of systems formed by the interconnection of large numbers of relatively small embedded systems, such as sensor networks, fault-tolerance is normally based on the large scale redundancy that is inherent to such systems, thus coping with the unreliability of each individual node. In fact, it is not the information of one node that is important but the information about a given area [Sta03]. The issue of security, which is also a dependability attribute, is particularly relevant in this case because of the use of wireless transmission. This issue is addressed in the respective section further on.

Higher Flexibility

The emergence of new classes of safety-critical embedded applications, distributed in nature and operating in highly dynamic and uncertain environments (e.g., teams of autonomous robots, combat vehicles, even cars in high traffic lanes), is, however, revealing the shortcomings of current existing approaches in the dependability area. For example, the provision of safety assurances requiring the satisfaction of timeliness or security constraints, becomes considerably more difficult when at least some parts of the supporting infrastructure, namely the networks (e.g., wireless networks), do not provide the necessary baseline properties. Flexible solutions regarding communication paradigms are fundamental when it comes to the introduction of fault-tolerance or, more generically, dependability measures in such systems, to support approaches such as graceful degradation [She03] and quality-of-service (QoS) adaptation [Cas01].

Generally, the interest on flexibility comes from its potential to simplify installation, maintenance, and reconfiguration, and improve efficiency in the use of system resources, e.g. network bandwidth. This is particularly important for the situations referred above, when DESs are used in dynamic environments in which the communication requirements vary substantially during system operation. This variation might be caused, for example, by subsystems that either operate during short periods of time, e.g. the brakes in a car, or that may operate with variable levels of QoS, e.g. multimedia streaming or even feedback control in some cases [Mar02], or finally because the system may receive variable load from the environment, e.g. collision avoidance, traffic control and defence systems.

Current network protocols based on time-triggered communication, despite favouring composability, predictability and safety, consider static communication requirements, only, with at most a limited number of static modes. To circumvent this limitation while maintaining the positive properties of that paradigm, new approaches are being proposed which combine the time-triggered paradigm with operational flexibility [Alm02] supporting on-line rate adaptation of periodic message streams, according to the application instantaneous requirements.

Despite the lack of generalized consensus concerning the applicability of flexible approaches in safety-critical applications, the fact is that such issue is currently a hot topic, and there is substantial attention, for example, dedicated to the certification of real-time systems using dynamic resource management [Cha03].

Other approaches relax the safety concerns and further improve the flexibility of the network. For example, the options around the use of the IEEE 1394 (FireWire) protocol allow providing deterministic timeliness guarantees for high-quality multimedia streams together with a full support for Plug-and-Play features. Namely, it uses dynamic assignment of node IDs, network configuration upon reset and supports dynamic resource reservation. The configuration changes are, however, accomplished by means of network resets, which disrupt communication during a time window that, despite short for most multimedia streams, might be too long for control applications. The IEEE 1394 is now being proposed for backbone networks within cars and trucks to support the interconnection of consumer electronic products such as CD players, DVDs, games or computers [Col02].

Another adaptive approach to timeliness is, for example, the fuzzy traffic smoothing technique proposed in [Car02]. It controls the bursts of non-real-time traffic in an adaptive way in order to exploit the instantaneous available bandwidth and still provide probabilistic bounds on timeliness. Generally, probabilistic approaches allow higher bandwidth efficiency and flexibility than other ones based on deterministic worst-case analysis. This is also the case with the analysis of the impact of network errors, with those using probabilistic error models [Bro02] being more efficient than their deterministic counterparts. Notice that it is still possible to combine these error-modelling approaches with safety applications by considering a sufficiently small probability of failure.

Integration of TT and ET Traffic

In general, the support for composability is very important in DESs so that they can be built by integrating subsystems while keeping their properties upon integration [Kop97]. This allows coping with the complexity inherent to large systems. Particularly in the time domain, composability has been achieved by means of the time-triggered communication framework of which TTP (Time-Triggered Protocol) [TTT99] is one example. This framework supports improved system timeliness and is particularly adequate to situations with safety-critical requirements. It integrates well with synchronous approaches to system specification and modelling, supporting formal verification of system properties. Moreover, this framework supports phase control among different streams, which grants some level of control over transmission jitter. This is typically considered relevant for control applications in which the network-induced jitter may cause degradation in the quality of control.

On the other hand, the time-triggered framework is also known for its low bandwidth efficiency when a substantial part of the network traffic is of a sporadic nature (event-triggered). In fact, the mapping of event-triggered information onto time-triggered messages establishes a delicate compromise between responsiveness and allocated bandwidth. This leads to the current trend towards efficiently combining event and time-triggered traffic, in an attempt to benefit from the advantages of both frameworks, namely the flexibility and efficiency of event-triggered systems and the predictability, composability and safety of the time-triggered ones. Several efforts are being taken in this direction such as the work around TT-CAN (Time-Triggered CAN) [ISO01] and the definition of FlexRay [Bel02].

Wireless Interconnections

Advances in wireless technology made it possible to integrate it within embedded systems, either for communication with other systems [Wu04] as well as between components within large systems [Kah99]. This allows cabling to be reduced and system installation and management to become more flexible. These aspects are very interesting in industry, for example to interconnect rotating or difficult to access equipment, or even to interconnect mobile units such as AGVs to global control/information systems. Some efforts have been made with this aim, based on the extension of existing wired fieldbus protocols such as OLCHFA with WorldFIP and, more recently, R-Fieldbus with ProfiBus [Alv02]. Other protocols already include the possibility of using either wired or wireless physical layers, such as LON and FF-H1. In some other cases, when the equipments to interconnect are geographically distant, a dedicated GSM network is used instead. This is, for example, the case with the European Train Control System that aims at supporting higher track utilization and higher interoperability across Europe [Zim03].

The physical flexibility granted by wireless technology is also very interesting for consumer electronics. For example, Bluetooth and IrDA have been used extensively in PDAs and cellular phones to simplify the connection to a remote PC and synchronize personal documents and databases. Also, recent cars start to appear with Bluetooth included as an interconnection for several on-board equipments such as cell phones, PDAs and computers [Phi03]. Bluetooth provides up to 3 synchronous channels per piconet that are adequate for conveying audio streams. Its use in time-critical applications has been generating growing interest as the protocol becomes more and more widespread [Wib01]. Given the master-slave nature of medium access control within each Bluetooth piconet, the traffic timeliness is highly dependent on the way the master schedules transmissions [Joh00]. Such scheduling can also be carried out aiming at power consumption reduction as in [Gar00]. Another topic that received substantial interest is inter-piconet routing within scatternets, allowing Bluetooth networks to expand unlimitedly in an ad-hoc fashion. Ah-hoc networking is a field generating substantial interest due to its inherent flexibility. Ad-hoc networks are expected to grow in acceptance and dissemination as they will be used to interconnect ubiquitous equipment, from laptops to desktops, PDAs, cellular phones, even cars [Wu04] The main problems that these networks face include link establishment to support effective data communication, service discovery and access, and topology management to cope with nodes mobility and still support connectivity and real-time performance.

IEEE 802.11 also supports ad-hoc connectivity but its largest use is as structured networks built around base stations that connect the wireless nodes to wired backbones. Early interest in using this protocol in real-time applications led to the inclusion of a controlled medium access mode (PCF) that supports traffic timeliness guarantees. However, this has not received generalized acceptance and is now seldom supported by manufacturers, while the successful uncontrolled mode (DCF) is the basis of almost all the installed 802.11 systems. Currently, there is renewed interest on real-time support arising from delay-sensitive applications such as Voice over IP (VoIP). For this purpose, new QoS mechanisms are being proposed as part of a new standard, 802.11e, which work over DCF as well as PCF.

A negative aspect about both Bluetooth and 802.11 (b and g variants) is that they operate in a license-free band (ISM), which makes them particularly sensitive to interferences, decreasing their robustness [Dec02]. In general, there are still other drawbacks concerning wireless technology that need further attention, e.g. when compared to cabled networks, wireless adapters are still more expensive, bit error rates are higher and throughput is normally lower. Moreover, the natural openness of the wireless medium makes it more prone to security breaches, which calls upon the use of cryptographic techniques.

Another wireless related application domain that is gaining momentum is that of sensor networks, in which the problems above gain higher relevance due to the small, constrained and unreliable nature of the nodes [Kah99]. Network level issues that need further attention include the support for content addressing, location awareness and distributed routing [Sta03]. Moreover, these networks have to cope with highly variable workloads, non-uniform nodes distribution, high fault rates and energy constraints. Under these circumstances, achieving secure real-time communication is a true major challenge that still needs a substantial research effort.

Internet Connectivity

The system management and monitoring is also an important issue, particularly in large and complex systems. In this aspect, a growing pervasiveness of Internet has been witnessed so that well-known and accessible Internet technologies and protocols can be used (e.g. equipment configuration via HTTP and components description and configuration via XML). In fact, many existing networks used in embedded systems, mainly in automation, already provide a certain level of support for IP protocols, e.g. through tunnelling.

Furthermore, many distributed embedded systems also include a transparent connection to the Internet allowing real-time system diagnosis, automated software defect correction and upgrades, monitoring of operating environment conditions [Koo02], and connectivity to other systems. However, a connection to the Internet also poses many problems related to security such as unauthorized access to system management, or simply to system internal data [Pal00]. These are still open areas of research that consider, for example, adequate designs for firewalls and use of cryptography.

Another issue that gains particular relevance as embedded systems, or parts of them, become interconnected through the Internet is QoS to support time-sensitive traffic such as audio and video streaming or even streaming of control information for example related with remote virtual labs. However, the service currently offered over the Internet by the standard Internet Protocol (IP) does not provide for diversified management of real-time flows. The currently-used Internet Protocol version 4 *(IPv4)* is unable to efficiently support QoS, a task entrusted to higher-level protocols. A new version, *IPv6,* has been proposed by the IETF to overcome such and other limitations. For example, it solves the problem of limited number of available IPv4 addresses and also adds many improvements in areas such as routing, network self-configuration and QoS support. Most importantly, IPv6 offers *native* QoS support, in the sense that it provides fields in the header of IP packets that allow managing traffic flows in a differentiated fashion, according to their QoS requirements. The protocol has also been streamlined to expedite packet handling by network nodes and provides support for congestion control, reducing the need for reliable but untimely higher-level protocols (e.g. TCP) [LoB03]. Moreover, IPV6 characteristics can be exploited inside routers to entrust them with the task of providing diversified scheduling for real-time and non-real-time flows [Fic03].

Until recently, the adoption of IPv6 has been limited. More effort on the transition is necessary to make it as simple as possible and open the way for the potential of the IPv6. IPv6 is expected to gradually replace IPv4, with the two coexisting for a number of years during a transition period, thanks to Tunnelling and Dual Stack techniques. Several companies are interested in IPv6 technology to overcome IPv4 limitations for robust real-time IP-based multimedia communications [VaSt03].

24.4   Recommendations for Research

The trends identified in the previous section have in some way pointed out the main directions that are currently being pursued in the area of networks for distributed embedded systems (DESs), with special focus on the support for flexible and adaptive behaviours. These networks are required to support the growing levels of integration that will allow gathering more accurate, abundant and timely data about the environment or system, in order to better control, manage and plan, using fewer resources. This is fundamental in order to support a myriad of services upon which modern societies depend in unprecedented ways, from military systems to transportation systems, telecommunications, industrial, building and office automation, space systems, climate and assets monitoring... The development of the necessary communication infrastructures that must be flexible, real-time, dependable, pervasive and interoperable entails technological challenges that require a substantial research focus. In this section we briefly recall the open issues previously raised that need such research attention.

The limitations of current networks arise, up to a large extent, from options in the design of the respective protocols concerning conflicting requirements. Therefore, in order to support the new generation of applications referred above it is necessary to overcome current limitations and design new networks, either based on current standards or not, which do not show the conflicts that typically arise among fundamental properties, e.g. real-time behaviour and dependability. This harmonization of properties has to be achieved while, at the same time, keeping the cost of the final system low.

Providing higher integration within DESs, as referred above, is a fundamental issue to exploit the system resources more efficiently, e.g. computing resources, and to acquire a more accurate view of the system, or simply to facilitate data migration. However, this increase of integration must be done without affecting other relevant properties such as error containment and composability [Rus01]. Another challenge is to increase integration among subsystems built by different makers, calling upon strong interoperability support, and definition of adequate architectures and languages [Ell02].

For DESs used in safety-critical applications it is vital to achieve very high levels of reliability and safety, e.g. by means of fault tolerance. However, fault tolerance must be used in balance with other important properties of DESs such as low cost and low power consumption. Still in safety-critical applications, the network services that support dependability must be improved and increased. This has to be done at the lowest layers of the network in order to prevent the problem of amplification of failures and to reduce the communication overhead. Relevant services to be provided are fault-tolerant broadcast and error containment. Also, the typical bus topology used within contained embedded systems, e.g. machines, vehicles, needs to be re-evaluated with respect to other topologies, such as the star that seems more adequate for the design of future dependable networks.

Flexibility in the networks referred above is of primary interest for resource efficient operation in dynamic environments in which the communication requirements vary substantially during system operation. In the case of safety-critical applications, this must be achieved with the right balance with dependability related properties such as predictability and reliability. To improve this balance, new analysis of timing faults [Bro02] are required, probabilistic in nature, which can be integrated with the probability of system failure in general, a fundamental parameter in safety-critical systems. A hot topic in what concerns flexible mechanisms is the certification of real-time systems using dynamic resource management [Cha03]. This will allow to define base line properties, upon which global system properties can be established.

A specific type of flexibility concerns the support for different types of traffic, such as time and event-triggered [Alm02]. This particular combination has been generating substantial interest [Bel02] in order to allow benefiting from the advantages of both frameworks.

When talking about flexibility and adaptability, one fundamental issue is establishing the bounds for such adaptations in what concerns the QoS delivered to the application [Cas01]. In fact, if the adaptation is such that the QoS lowers below a minimum acceptable value for the application, then it might be wiser just to reject such service and use the released resources to improve the QoS of other services. However, establishing such QoS minimum thresholds for the application needs new paradigms for requirements specification to support appropriate QoS adaptation.

In terms of the use of wireless technology there are several open issues either in structured as well as ad-hoc networks. For example, the provision of QoS guarantees or secure transmissions are two major challenges that have to be dealt with to further explore the technologies in even wider contexts. These challenges require substantial work in traffic scheduling and medium access protocols as well as in the design of adequate cryptographic support to achieve the right combination of resource requirements and efficiency. Examples of driving applications concerning wireless communication are mobile computing, ad-hoc networks and sensor networks. In the scope of the former, further developments concerning QoS support are needed as well as prompt hand-over mechanisms to enhance the mobility capabilities without disruption of services. As for ad-hoc networks, main open issues regard the establishment of links, service discovery and topology management [Wu04]. Sensor networks are a special case of ad-hoc networks whose needs for mobility support are lower but whose nodes are highly resource constrained, e.g. CPU, memory and energy, are unreliable, but are deployed in large scale with substantial redundancy. The properties of the system arise from the ensemble and not from the individual nodes [Sta03]. Open issues that require further research efforts include content addressing, location awareness, distributed routing, highly variable workloads, non-uniform nodes distribution, high fault rates and energy constraints.

Finally, concerning embedded systems and the Internet, open issues include how to support IP functionality directly in nodes with scarce resources and how to convey IP packets on top of low bandwidth networks or, alternatively, how to design appropriate gateways. Internet connection of embedded systems allows real-time system diagnosis, automated software defect correction and upgrades, monitoring of operating environment conditions [Koo02], and connection between remote equipment. However, security issues become of major importance and require further research in the design of firewalls and use of cryptography [Pal00].

The provision of QoS and secure communication through the Internet are also ambitious objectives that need further research to support new applications such as remote virtual labs, distributed games, VoIP, video streaming and video conferencing, just to name a few that somehow exhibit some affinity with embedded systems.

24.5   References

[Alm02]   Almeida, L., Pedreiras, P., Fonseca, J. A., The FTT-CAN Protocol: Why and How, IEEE Transactions on Industrial Electronics, vol. 49, no. 6, December 2002.

[Alv02]   M. Alves, E. Tovar, F. Vasques, G. Hammer, K. Roether, Real-Time Communications over Hybrid Wired/Wireless PROFIBUS-based Networks, in Proceedings ECRTS'02 – 14th Euromicro Conference on Real-Time Systems – ECRTS'02, pp. 142-150. IEEE Press, June 2002.

[ARI99]   ARINC/RTCA-SC-182/EUROCAE-WG-48, Minimal Operational Performance Standard for Avionics Computer Resources, Washington D.C, 1999.

[Bel02]   R. Belschner et al, FlexRay Requirements Specification Version 2.0.2, FlexRay Consortium, http://www.flexray-group.com, 2002.

[Bro01]   I. Broster, A. Burns. Timely use of the CAN Protocol in Critical Hard Real-time Systems with Faults. Proceedings of ECRTS'01 – 13th Euromicro Conference in Real-time Systems, IEEE Press, June 2001.

[Bro02]   I. Broster, A. Burns, G. Rodriguez-Navas. Probabilistic Analysis of CAN with Faults. Proceedings of RTSS 2002, IEEE Press, December 2002.

[Car02]   A. Carpenzano, R. Caponetto, L. LoBello, O. Mirabella. Fuzzy Traffic Smoothing: An Approach for Real-Time Communication over Ethernet Networks. Proc of WFCS 2002 – 4th IEEE Workshop on Factory Communication Systems. IEEE Press. August 2002.

[Cas01]   A. Casimiro and P. Veríssimo. Using the Timely Computing Base for dependable QoS adaptation. In Proceedings of the 20th IEEE Symposium on Reliable Distributed Systems, pages 208–217, IEEE Press, Oct. 2001.

[Cha03]   Challenge Problem: System Certification for Real-Time Systems that Employ Dynamic Resource Management. Organized in conjunction with WPDRTS 2003, 22-23 April 2003, Nice, France. (http://wpdrts.cs.ohiou.edu)

[Col02]   Collaboration with IDB Forum Creates Flexible Network Backbone. 1394 Trade Association News Report, Dallas, USA. 17th October, 2002. http://www.1394ta.org/Press/2002Press/october/10.17.a.htm

[Dec01]   Decotignie, J.-D. A Perspective on Ethernet as a fieldbus, Proceedings of FET 2001 – 4th IFAC Conf. on Fieldbus Systems and their Applications. November 2001.

[Dec02]   Decotignie, J.-D., Wireless Fieldbusses – A Survey of Issues and Solutions, Proc of IFAC 2002 World Congress, Elsevier, July 2002.

[Ell02]   J-P Elloy, F. Simonot-Lion. An Architecture Description Language for In-Vehicle Embedded System Development. Proc of IFAC 2002 World Congress, Elsevier, July 2002.

[Fic03]   S. Fichera, S.Visalli, O. Mirabella, "QoS Support for Real-Time Flows in Internet Routers", RTLIA'03, 2nd Intl. Workshop on Real-Time LANs in the Internet Age, Satellite Workshop of the 15th Euromicro Conference on Real-Time Systems (ECRTS03), June 2003, Porto, Portugal.

[Gar00]   S. Garg, M. Kalia, R. Shorey, "MAC scheduling for power optimisation in Bluetooth: A master-driven TDD wireless system", in Proc. of *VTC 2000*, pp. 196-200, 2000.

[Gou91]   Gopal, A., Toueg, S., Inconsistency and contamination, in Proceedings of the 10th ACM Symposium on Principles of Distributed Computing, pp. 257-272, August 1991.

[ISO01]   ISO, Road vehicles – controller area network (CAN) – part 4: Time triggered communication, 2001.

[Joh00]   N. Johansson, U. Korner, P. Johansson, "Performance Evaluation of Scheduling Algorithms for Bluetooth", In Broadband Communications: Convergence of Network Technologies, Danny H. K. Tsang and Paul J. Kuhn Editors, Kluwer Academic Publishers, pp. 139-150, 2000.

[Kah99]   J. M. Kahn, R. H. Katz and K. S. J. Pister. Mobile Networking for Smart Dust. ACM/IEEE Intl. Conf. on Mobile Computing and Networking (MobiCom 99), Seattle, WA, Aug 1999.

[Koo02]   P. Koopman. Critical Embedded Automotive Networks. IEEE Micro, IEEE Press, July/August 2002.

[Kop97]   Kopetz, H. Real-Time Systems: Design Principles for Distributed Embedded Applications, Kluwer Academic Publishers, 1997.

[LoB03]   L. Lo Bello, S. Fichera, S.Visalli, O. Mirabella ,"Congestion Control Mechanisms for Multi-Hop Network Routers", IEEE Int. Conf. on Emerging Technologies and Factory Automation ETFA2003, Oct.2003, Lisbon, Portugal.

[Mar02]   P. Marti, G. Fohler, K. Ramamritham, J. M. Fuertes. Improving Quality-of-Control using Flexible Timing Constraints: Metric and Scheduling Issues. Proceedings of RTSS 2002, IEEE Press, December 2002

[Pal00]   P. Palensky; T. Sauter. Security Considerations for FAN-Internet Connections. IEEE International Workshop on Factory Communication Systems, pp 27-35, IEEE Press, Sept. 2000.

[Phi03]   P. Ross. Top 10 Techno-Cool Cars. IEEE Spectrum, February 2003.

[Pim90]   J. Pimentel. Communication Networks for Manufacturing. Prentice Hall, 1990.

[Pin01]   L. Pinho, F. Vasques. Timing Analysis of Reliable Real-Time Communication in CAN Networks. Proc. of ECRTS'01 – Euromicro Conf. on Real-Time Systems. IEEE Press, June 2001.

[Pro00]   J. Proenza, J. Miro-Julia. Major{CAN}: A Modification to the {C}ontroller {A}rea {N}etwork Protocol to Achieve {A}tomic {B}roadcast}, in Proceedings of IWGCC'00 – IEEE Int. Workshop on Group Communications and Computations. IEEE Press, April 2000.

[Rus01]   Rushby, J., Bus Architectures For Safety-Critical Embedded Systems, in Proceedings of the First Workshop on Embedded Software, Lecture Notes in Computer Science vol. 2211, pp 306-323, 2001.

[She03]   C. Shelton, Phil Koopman. A Framework for Scalable Analysis and Design of System-wide Graceful Degradation in Distributed Embedded Systems. Proc. of WORDS'03 – IEEE Workshop on Object-Oriented, Real-time and Dependable Systems, IEEE Press, January 2003.

[Sta03]   J. Stankovic, T. Abdelzaher, C. Lu, L. Sha and J. Hou. Real-Time Communication and Coordination in Embedded Sensor Networks. Proceedings of the IEEE vol. 91, no. 7, July 2003.

[Tho99]   J-P. Thomesse, M.L Chavez. Main Paradigms as a Basis for Current Fieldbus Concepts, Proc. of FeT'99, Magdeburg, Germany, September 1999.

[TTT99]   TTTech Computertechnik AG, Specification of the TTP/C protocol v0.5, July 1999.

[VaSt03]   P. Van der Stok, M. van Hartskamp. Robust real-time IP-based multimedia communication. RTLIA'03, 2nd Intl. Workshop on Real-Time LANs in the Internet Age, Satellite Workshop of the 15th Euromicro Conference on Real-Time Systems (ECRTS03), June 2003, Porto, Portugal.

[Wib03]   P-A Wiberg, U. Bilstrup. Wireless Technology in Industry – Applications and User Scenarios, Proc. of ETFA '01, IEEE Conf on Emerging Technologies for Factory Automation, IEEE Press, October 2001.

[Wu04]   J. Wu and I. Stojmenovic, Ad-Hoc Networks. IEEE Computer, vol. 37, no. 2, Feb 2004.

[Zim03]   A. Zimmermann, G. Hommel. A Train Control System Case Study in Model-Based Real-Time System Design. Proc of WPDRTS'03 – IEEE Workshop on Parallel and Distributed Real-Time Systems. IEEE Press, April 2003.

25 Programming Languages for Real-Time Systems

The real-time and embedded systems market is huge and growing all the time. It has been estimated that 100 times more processors are destined for embedded systems rather than the desktop [Egg02]. Embedded real-time systems [Bur01]:
- are mainly small (for example, mobile phones) but can also be extremely large and complex (for example air traffic control systems)
- have potentially complex mathematical models of their controlled environment
- must be dependable
- are inherently concurrent
- must interact within the time frame of the environment
- must interact with low-level mechanisms such as hardware devices and memory management faculties.

The interdependence between functional and real-time semantics of real-time software makes its design, implementation and maintenance especially difficult. Providing a programming language that directly supports the characteristics of embedded real-time software can significantly ease these difficulties. In addition, embedded software systems are not portable as they depend on the particular underlying operating system and hardware architecture. Providing implementation-independent programming models also increases the portability.

25.1 Landscape

Rather than consider all possibly real-time programming languages, this section focuses mainly on three representatives groups of the landscape: C/C++ based languages, Ada and Real-Time Java (in particular the Real-Time Specification for Java). Sequential languages such as C and C++ are not reviewed in their own right as (a) their advantages and disadvantages are well known (see Barr [Bar99] for a full discussion) (b) they do not support the main characteristics of embedded real-time systems and consequently (c) their use requires direct interaction with the facilities of an underlying operating system (which are considered in sections 21 and 22).

Ada represents the group of concurrent real-time programming languages that were developed in late 1970s and early 1980s (including Pearl and CHILL). These have been extended over the years to embrace object-oriented programming and to give better support for real-time and distributed systems. Real-time Java represents the current trend of supporting architectural neutral real-time systems potentially in an open environment (and points to the direction that languages like C# might in future take). Synchronous languages (such as Esterel, Signal or Lustre) and functional languages (such as Erlang) are not considered, as their use is either confined to a particular company (e.g. Ericsson and Erlang) or targeted at supporting only reactive systems (e.g. Esterel).

Artist FP5 Consortium: Embedded Systems Design, LNCS 3436, 338–351, 2005.

Ada 95

The development of the Ada programming language forms a unique and, at times, intriguing contribution to the history of computer languages. As all users of Ada must know, the original language design was a result of competition between a number of organizations, each of which attempted to give a complete language definition in response to a series of requirements documents. This gave rise to Ada 83. Following ten years of use, Ada was subject to a complete overhaul. Object-oriented programming features were added (through type extensibility rather than via the usual class model), better support for programming in the large was provided (via child packages) and the support for real-time and distributed programming was enhanced. The resulting language, Ada 95, is defined by an international ISO standard.

An important aspect of the Ada 95 language is the model it presents for concurrent programming. This model is both complex and wide ranging. It builds upon the original Ada 83 language features for tasking but provides many additional facilities required to meet the challenges of modern systems development particularly in the areas of real-time and embedded systems.

The Ada 95 definition has a core language design plus a number of domain-specific annexes. A compiler need not support all the annexes but it must support the core language. Most of the tasking features are contained in the core definition. But many of the important features for real-time programming are to be found in Annex D.

A listing of the key language features of Ada (for real-time programming) would contain: protected objects for efficient encapsulation of shared data and interrupt handling, fixed priority scheduling integrated with a priority ceiling protocol, the requeue statement that eliminates many sources of race condition in application code, a monotonic clock with associated abstract data types for time with absolute and relative delay primitives, dynamic priorities and an asynchronous transfer of control capability that is integrated into the syntax of the core language. These features provide an expressive environment for programming both hard real-time systems and flexible applications [Ber01].

A complete technical description of the Ada language can be found at http://www.adahome.com/.

Real-Time Java

Since its inception in the early 1990s, there is little doubt that Java has been a great success. The Java environment provides attributes that make it a powerful platform to develop embedded real-time applications. Since embedded systems normally have limited memory, an advantage that some versions of Java (for instance J2ME) present is the small size of both the Java runtime environment and the Java application programs. Dynamic loading of classes also facilitates the dynamic evolution of the applications. Additionally, the Java platform provides classes for building multithreaded applications and automatic garbage collection; these make it an attractive environment to develop embedded real-time applications. Unfortunately, the problem with garbage collection is that it introduces random pauses in the execution of applications. Consequently, Java does not guarantee determinism nor bounded resource usage, which are needed in embedded real-time systems.

For these reasons, Java was initially treated with disdain by much of the real-time community. Although the language was interesting from a number of perspectives the whole notion of Java as a real-time programming language was laughable. "Java and Real-time" was considered by many as an oxymoron.

In spite of the real-time community's misgivings, Java's overall popularity led to several attempts to extend the language so that it is more appropriate for a wide range of real-time and embedded systems. Much of the early work in this area was fragmented and lacked clear direction. In the late 1990s, under the auspices of the US National Institute of Standards and Technology (NIST), approximately 50 companies and organizations pooled their resources and generated several guiding principles and a set of requirements for real-time extensions to the Java platform [Car99]. Among the guiding principles was that Real-Time Java (RTJ) should take into account current real-time practices and facilitate advances in the state of the art of real-time systems implementation technology. The following facilities were deemed necessary to support the current state of real-time practice [Car99].

- Fixed priority and round robin scheduling.
- Mutual exclusion locking (avoiding priority inversion).
- Inter-thread communication (e.g. semaphores).
- User-defined interrupt handlers and device drivers – including the ability to manage interrupts (e.g., enabling and disabling).
- Timeouts and aborts on running threads.

The NIST group recognized that profiles (subsets) of RTJ were necessary in order to cope with the wide variety of possible applications, these included: safety critical, no dynamic loading, and distributed real-time profiles. There was also an agreement that any implementation of RTJ should provide the following.

- A framework for finding available profiles.
- Bounded pre-emption latency on any garbage collection.
- A well-defined model for real-time Java threads.
- Communication and synchronization between real-time and non real-time threads.
- Mechanisms for handling internal and external asynchronous events.
- Asynchronous thread termination.
- Mutual exclusion without blocking.
- The ability to determine whether the running thread is real-time or non real-time.
- A well-defined relationship between real-time and non real-time threads.

Solutions that comply with the NIST requirements are API-based extensions. There are three proposed approaches.

1. The Real-Time Specification for Java [Bol00], gives a new and very different specification to meet the requirements.
2. The Real-Time Core Extension for the Java Platform (RT Core) [J-C00] consists of two separate APIs: the Baseline Java API for non real-time Java threads, and the Real-Time Core API for real-time tasks.
3. The Basic RT JavaO specification [Kra99] is very simple extension, is presented as an alternative or a complement to this last solution.

There are some API-based solutions that were introduced before the NIST document. The simplest one is the Real-Time Java Threads (RTJT) [Miy97], a prototype that introduces tasks support. Another proposal is the Portable Executive for Reliable Control (PERC) [Nil98] that subdivides into two packages: the Real-Time package provides abstractions for real-time systems, whereas the Embedded package provides low-level abstractions to access the hardware. This solution is close to RT Core, which is actually an evolution of PERC. Finally, a very different solution is the Communication Threads for Java (CTJ) [Hil98], that is based on the CSP algebra, the Occam2 language and the Transputer microprocessor. Another type of solutions is to integrate the JVM into the operating system. This approach is undertaken by GVM [Bac98], a prototype centred around resource management. Another option to improve Java performance is to integrate the JVM in a microprocessor. picoJava-I [McG98] is a standard specification for the design of Java micro controllers. An implementation is the JEM-1 microprocessor of Rockwell Collins.

Perhaps the attempt with the highest profile is the one backed by Sun and produced by The Real-Time for Java Expert Group [Bol00]. This effort now has considerable momentum. In contrast, progress with the J-consortium's CORE-Java has been hampered by the lack of a reference implementation and poor support from potential users.

The approach taken by the Real-Time Specification for Java (RTSJ) has been to extend the concurrency model so that it support real-time programming abstractions, and to provide a complementary approach to memory management that removes the temporal uncertainties of garbage collection. In particular, the RTSJ enhances Java in the following areas:

- memory management
- time values and clocks
- schedulable objects and scheduling
- real-time threads
- asynchronous event handlers and timers
- asynchronous transfer of control
- synchronization and resource sharing
- physical memory access

It should be stressed that the RTSJ only really addresses the execution of real-time Java programs on a single processor systems. It attempts not to preclude execution on shared-memory multiprocessor systems but it has no facilities directly to control, say, allocation of threads to processors. A reference implementation is now available from the TimeSys Corporation (http://www.timesys.com).

A complete technical description of the Real-Time Specification for Java can be found at http://www.rtj.org.

Research Landscape

Research in real-time programming languages has focused on providing language-level support for the main characteristics of embedded real-time systems outlined in the introduction to this section.

Size and Complexity
Although addressing issues associated with scale and complexity requires more than just programming language support, most modern real-time programming languages have settled for supporting the object-oriented programming paradigm within a module/package framework. Unfortunately, the dynamic nature of this approach has had a impact on the analyzability of the program source and resulted in language subsets being used in high-integrity systems (see section 26.3). Although some research has attempted to support component-oriented real-time programming [Fra00], this has not had a major impact.

Complex Mathematical Modelling
Support for real and floating point numbers are accepted components of all modern real-time languages.

Dependability
There are many aspects to dependability (reliability, availability, safety, confidentiality, integrity, maintainability), however real-time embedded programming languages have focused on support for reliability and error recovery. The early attempts to introduce language support for backward error recovery (recovery blocks) [Shr78] failed to get support from other languages and forward error recovery within an exception-handling framework became the dominant approach. Similarly, the attempts to introduce reliable cooperation between groups of processes via atomic actions and conversations [Ran75] gave way to language support for more primitive operations, such as asynchronous transfer of control in Ada and the *Real-time Specification for Java*. Today research focuses on the appropriate exception handling facilities for modern concurrent distributed real-time programming languages [Rom01].

Concurrency
Whether a programming language should support concurrency is a debate that has rumbled on for over three decades. Those that do, have typically supported explicit language-level processes (tasks, threads etc) and allowed the programmer to develop their own high-level abstractions (for example, Ada). Early attempts by languages like Real-Time Euclid [Kli86] and Pearl [Wer85] to provide higher-level abstraction directly in the language failed to gain widespread support. However, given that many real-time activities can be classified as periodic, sporadic or aperiodic, there is growing acceptance that having direct representation of these in programs can lead to more reliable and maintainable systems. This is illustrated in both pure research languages like the C-based Alert language [Pal99] and the emerging *Real-time Specification for Java* standard.

Real-Time and Scheduling
The specification of timing constraints and their means of implementation is clearly the defining attribute of a real-time programming language. Historically, timing constraints have been associated with processes although some attempts have been made to provide them at a finer granularity (e.g., DPS [Lee85] and Timber [Bla02]). The notions of time and event triggered processes with periodic, sporadic and aperiodic release (or arrival) profiles have become commonplace. In some languages (like Ada)

these constraints and profiles have to be programmed directly (and may not be explicitly visible in the program source). In others, like the Real-Time Specification for Java and Alert [Pal99] they have explicit representation. Implementing timing constraints is the realm of the scheduler (see section 20). Whilst this aspect is crucial, it currently has little impact on the design of language features. Rather, the attributes of priority or deadline are used to provide information to a language's run-time support system. As flexible scheduling becomes more prevalent, so the impact on the program structures will increase and the need to develop abstractions that allow interactions with the scheduler will become a driving force (for example, alternative modules or optional components).

Device Driving and Memory Management
The pioneering research on high-level language support for device driving and interrupt handling was done by Wirth in the context of the Modula language [Wir77] during the 1970s. Ada extended the approach to allow a programmer to provide details to the compiler on how to map programmer-defined types onto the underlying hardware resources. In recent years, embedded programming languages have attempted to influence more directly the code generation of the compiler, for example 'C [Pol99] in order to get better control over the use of low level resources.

Memory is a scarce and costly low-level resource in embedded systems. Thus, it needs to be carefully managed. As well as considering how types and objects in high-level language can be mapped to bits and words in memory, attention has also focused on the allocation and deallocation of memory in general. The goal of allowing the programming to allocate memory when required and providing automatic reclamation via garbage collection has not been fully embraced by the real-time community; particularly in those systems where timing constraints are stringent and the penalties for missing deadlines are severe. The execution time of software with dynamic memory reclaiming is notoriously difficult to predict. This is why the use of dynamic memory is actually forbidden in software required to be certified according to high-level safety standards such as DO178-B, EN-50128, IEC-880. Furthermore, many garbage collection techniques need large amounts of extra memory. This is a serious drawback that prevents using them in embedded applications with scarce memory space. Whilst there have been attempts to provide real-time garbage collections [Hen99, Kim99, Sie99, Siel00, Hui02, Rit01, Bac03], the real-time versions of Java have also sought to provide other mechanism (such as stackable objects in Core Java [J-C00] and Scoped Memory regions in the *Real-time Specification for Java* [Sal01, Det02]).

More general, real-time systems programs are no longer destined to be implemented solely in software. Recent advances in reconfigurable hardware means that the flexibility provided by software can now be matched by Field Programmable Gate Arrays (FPGA). Initially, a version for the C language has been used (Handle C [Pag96]) to program such systems. More recently an Ada compiler has been produced which compiles Ada down to FPGAs [War02].

Industrial Landscape

For small embedded applications, use of sequential languages like C and C++ reign supreme albeit with the help of an underlying real-time operating system. For the larger real-time high integrity systems (such as air traffic control, or flight control software), Ada still dominates. In the telecommunications market, CHILL is popular. In Germany, Pearl is widely used for process control and other industrial automation applications. Older real-time languages such as Coral 66, Jovial and RTL/2 have fallen from favour and can now only be found in legacy systems.

Although there is little doubt that the Java language has been immensely successful in a wide range of application areas, it has yet to establish itself completely in the real-time and embedded markets. The introduction of a Real-Time Specification for Java could dramatically alter the status quo. In the future, if MicroSoft's C# programming language starts to gain momentum, extensions will inevitably be considered to make it more appropriate for real-time systems.

Industrial use of modern languages is in general conservative, particularly in the high-integrity application area where subsets and programming guidelines are used. Complex or costly language features are usually forbidden, as is the use of garbage collection. The typical approach is to ensure all resourced (including memory) are allocated during the initialization phase and freed during termination.

25.2   Assessment

Although there is a wide variety of language that have been used to implement real-time systems only Ada has been successful in providing language-level support for the defining characteristic of the domain. The Real-Time Specification for Java (RTSJ) hopes in the near future to compete at this level. For these reasons, this section focuses its assessment on these two languages.

Ada 95

The Ada 95 programming language addresses most of the issues associated with building fixed-priority real-time systems. Although Ada has not had the same commercial success as Java, it is widely accepted (even by its opponents) that Ada has a good technical solution for a wide range of real-time problems (for example, see the Preface to [Bol00]).

The definition of Ada benefits from being an international standard. Currently the definition is being reviewed (as ISO requires every ten years). Major changes will not be made to Ada but a number of amendments will update the definition. Many of these will be in the real-time domain and are likely to include the incorporation of timing events [Bur02] support for a wider range of scheduling paradigms [Ald02] and execution-time budgeting.

One important new addition to the language is support for high-integrity concurrent real-time programs. Ada 95, via the introduction of restrictions on the use of the language, allows different execution profiles to be defined. However, in the past the language has shied away from profiles. In recent years, the real-time Ada community has developed its own profile called Ravenscar [Bur03]. This profile defines a subset of the tasking and real-time features, and is aimed at the high integrity real-time domain where predictability, efficiency and reliability are all crucial. Ravenscar is now being used in this domain with a number of vendors offering Ravenscar-specific run-time kernels (including one open-source version). As a consequence of its success, it has been decided to incorporate the profile into the language definition.

Clearly Ada is not as popular as it was in the 90s. Although it does support object-oriented programming, languages such as C++ and Java have been more successful in propagating this form of programming. This is partly a result of choosing the type extensibility model, but also because Ada has never been able to regain the momentum it lost during the early years when compilers were expensive and efficiency of code execution was perceived to be poor. As a result there is a shortage of Ada programmers, and Ada is taught less in universities.

Ada remains the language of choice in many high integrity domains and often these are also real-time. Arguable Ada provides greater support than any other main stream engineering language for producing real-time and embedded code. By taking a language focus (rather than an API approach) Ada enables significant static analysis to be undertaken by the compiler and associated tools. This leads to high quality code and cost-effective code production.

RTSJ

In section 26.1, the NIST core requirements for real-time Java extensions were identified. It is possible to review these requirements to see the extent to which the RTSJ has met them [Wel04]. Firstly, the facilities needed to support the current state of real-time practice:

- Fixed priority and round robin scheduling – RTSJ supports fixed priority scheduler and allows implementations to provide other schedulers.
- Mutual exclusion locking (avoiding priority inversion) – the RTSJ supports priority inheritance algorithms of synchronized objects and requires that all RTSJ implementations avoid priority inversion.
- Inter-thread communication (e.g. semaphores) – schedulable objects can communicate using the standard Java mechanisms.
- User-defined interrupt handlers and device drivers (including the ability to manage interrupts; e.g. enabling and disabling) – the RTSJ allows interrupts to be associated with asynchronous events.
- Timeouts and aborts on running threads – the RTSJ allows asynchronous transfer of controls via asynchronous exceptions; they can be event triggered or time triggered.

In terms of implementation requirements:

- A framework for finding available profiles – the RTSJ does not explicitly address the issues of profiles other than by allowing an implementation to provide alternative scheduling algorithms (e.g., EDF) and allowing the application to locate the scheduling algorithms. There is no identification of, say, a safety critical systems profile or a profile that prohibits dynamic loading of classes. Distributed real-time systems are not addressed but there is another Java Expert Group that is considering this issue [Jav00][Wel02].
- Bounded pre-emption latency on any garbage collection – supported by the GarbageCollector class.
- A well-defined model for real-time Java threads – supported by the RealtimeThread and NoHeapRealtimeThread classes.

- Communication and synchronization between real-time and non real-time threads – supported by the wait free communication classes.
- Mechanisms for handling internal and external asynchronous events – supported by the AsyncEvent, AsyncEventHandler and POSIXSignalhandler classes.
- Asynchronous thread termination – supported by the AsynchronouslyInterrupt-edException class and the Interruptible interface.
- Mutual exclusion without blocking – supported by the wait free communication classes.
- The ability to determine whether the running thread is real-time or non real-time – supported by the RealtimeThread class.
- A well-defined relationship between real-time and non real-time threads – supported by the real-time thread, the scheduling and memory management models.

Overall then, it can be seen that the RTSJ addresses all the NIST top-level requirements in some form or other. It is, however, a little weak in its support for profiles.

25.3   Trends

The future for Ada is unclear, as it is perceived to be an "old" language in many areas of computing. This makes it more difficult to obtain funding for research. However, the Ada real-time community in Europe is still very active (see the latest International Real-Time Ada Workshop proceedings [Var03] for a summary) and topics currently being addressed include: subsets for high integrity applications, kernels, and hardware implementations. Arguably there has never been a better time to do real-time research using Ada technology.

In contrast with Ada, the future for Java augmented by the RTSJ is more positive. However, there are still obstacles to be overcome before Java can replace its main competitors in the embedded and real-time systems application areas. The main issues are in the following areas [Wel04, Dib04]:

- *Specification problems and inconsistencies* – A preliminary version was released in June 2000 in parallel with the development of a "reference implementation" (RI). Inevitably, the completion of the RI showed up errors and inconsistencies in the specification. Many of these will be removed in the 1.01 version that is due for released in 2004. However, some outstanding issues remain whose resolution may require more significant changes. [Wel04, Dib04].
- *Profiles* – There is a need to consider RTSJ in the context of J2ME and, in particular, to produce a profile for use in high-integrity (and possibly safety-critical) systems. The Ravenscar-Java [Kwo03] profile is perhaps the first step along this road. Currently, the Open Group is attempting to create a Java Specification Request to address this important application domain.
- *Implementation* – to generate efficient implementations of real-time virtual machines (both open source and propriety ones) for the full specification and the profiles;
- *Maintaining Momentum* – to stimulate evolution of the specification in a controlled and sustained manner to add new functionality (new schedulers, multiple schedulers, multiple criticalities, alternative interrupt handling models, real-time

concurrency utilities) and to address new architectures (multiprocessor and distributed systems). Currently, the Distributed Real-Time Specification for Java (DRTSJ) group is extending RMI and integrating these extensions in the RTSJ specification, to provide support for predictability of end-to-end timeliness of trans-node activities [Wel02].

Concurrency is an integral part of most real-time embedded systems. Efforts have been underway that attempt to ameliorate some of the well-known problems in this area. The improvements to the Java Memory Model [Java Community Process, JSR 133, 2001] will allow more precise semantics to be given to concurrent Java programs. The provision of a full set of concurrency utilities [Jav02] will ease the difficult task of constructing correct multi-thread programs. These improvements are scheduled for introduction into the forthcoming Java 1.5 release.

25.4   Recommendations for Research

The introduction for this section identified the defining characteristics of a real-time embedded system. This section identifies possible research avenues to explore within some of those characteristics.

Size and Complexity
Object-oriented programs are now highly dynamic. In contrast real-time systems must be predictable. Usually the more dynamic a system, the less predictable it is. A compromise is needed that allows the advantages of object-oriented programming without the drawbacks. This compromise may lie in allowing programmers to annotate their code with application-specific knowledge so that other tools in the programming environment (such as worst-case execution time analysis tools) can produce more reliable results. Although techniques for introducing this metadata into programs will appear in the next version of Java (Java 1.5) and is available in C#, it is typically not available at the statement level but only the class and method level. Current approaches rely on the introduction of formal comments to provide such information. There is a need for a standard set of annotations that are properly typed checked and semantically coherent. Although, composability of large real-time systems is a key area, it is unlikely that the issues will be initially addressed at the programming language level.

Dependability
The integration of support for dependability and real-time continues to be an important research topic (both from a timing specification and scheduling perspective). Now that the low-level mechanisms for asynchronous transfer of control, budget timers and processing groups are understood, the time is ripe to re-consider the high-level abstractions that can provide a better integration for reliable real-time atomic actions and their introduction into high-integrity applications.

Concurrency
The model of concurrency is the core component of a real-time program. Processes facilitate parallel execution, the placement of timing specification and the handling of

faults. Whilst the concurrency model (often called Ravenscar) of high-integrity systems is now well understood and has found representation in subsets of languages like Ada and Java, the model is conservative. There is a need for more expressive subsets.

Real-Time and Scheduling
As mentioned earlier, as flexible scheduling becomes more prevalent, so the impact on the program structure will increase and the need to develop language abstractions which allow interactions with the scheduler will become a driving force (for example, alternative modules or optional components).

Memory Management
There is still no satisfactory solution to real-time memory management that is both predictable and efficient yet does not require the programmer to be concerned with low-level allocation and deallocation issues. One possible solution in this area is to provide abstractions that allow the lifetime of objects to be specified in the program. Inevitably these will be related to the scope rules of the language but a one-to-one relationship is too constraining.

In addition to the above, two driving forces can be identified for future real-time systems that will inevitably have an impact on real-time programming languages. The first is the need for more architecture neutral real-time systems. An architecture-neutral real-time system is a real-time system whose target architecture is unknown at system design time. The term "architecture-neutral" includes the properties of both "pervasive" (embedded but not mobile) and "ubiquitous" (embedded and mobile) computing. Architecture-neutral real-time systems are at odds with traditional real-time systems because traditional systems typically need:

Known (or Bounded) Processing Resource Demand
by definition the resources needed by an architecture-neutral system will depend on the power of the site hosting its execution;

Efficient and Predictable Execution
Most architecture-neutral systems are interpreted where efficiency is often a secondary concern; techniques such as Just-In-Time compilation lead to better average-case executions but have less predictability and poorer worst-case behaviour;

Static Allocation
Predictability in a real-time multiprocessor or distributed environment is often achieved by sacrificing flexibility; for example, statically allocating threads to processors; by definition static allocation is not possible in an architecture-neutral system.

The second driving force is the introduction of reconfigurable hardware that allows more flexible co-design of real-time embedded system. This coupled with the need for architecture-neutral system provides a challenging environment for real-time programming language research.

25.5 References

[Riv02] Aldea Rivas, M. and Gonzalez Harbour, M. (2002), "Application-Defined Scheduling in Ada", IRTAW 11, Ada Letters, XXII(4), pp 77-84.

[Bac2003] Bacon, D.F, Cheng, P., and Rajan, V.T. (2003), "A Real-Time Garbage Collector with Low Overhead and Consistent Utilization", Proceedings of the 30th ACM SIGPLAN-SIGACT Symposium on Principles of Programming Languages, pp 285-298.

[Bar99] Bar, M (1999), "Programming Embedded Systems in C and C++", O'Riely.

[Bla02] Black, A.P. et al [2002], "Timber: A Programming Language for Real-Time Embedded Systems", PacSoft Technical Report, Department of Computer Science and Engineering, Oregon Health and Science University,
http://www.cse.ogi.edu/PacSoft/publications/2002/Timber-2002-04.pdf

[Ber01] Bernat, G and Burns, A (2001), "Implementing a Flexible Scheduler in Ada", Proceedings of Reliable Software Technologies – Ada Europe, LNCS, vol 2043, pp 179-190.

[Bla98] Back, G., Tullmann, P., Stoller, L., W.C. Hsieh, W.C., and Lepreau, J. (1998), "Java Operating Systems: Design an Implementation", Department of Computer Science, University of Utah.

[Bol00] Bollella, G., Brosgol, B., Dibble, P., Furr, S., Gosling, J., Hardin, D., and Turnbull, M. (2000), "The Real-Time Specification for Java", Addison Wesley.

[Bur01] Burns, A. and Wellings, A.J. (2001), "Real-Time Systems and Programming Languages", 3rd Edition, Addison Wesley.

[Bur02] Burns, A. and Wellings, A.J. (2002), "Accessing Delay Queue", Proceedings of IRTAW11, Ada Letters, vol XXI(4), ppn 72-76.

[Bur03] Burns, A, Dobbing and Vardanega, T. (2003), "Guide for Using the Ravenscar Profile in High Integrity Systems", YCS-2003-348, University of York.

[Car99] Carnahan, L., and Ruark, M. (Eds) (1999), "Requirements for Real-time Extensions for the Java Platform", NIST Publication 5000-243, http://www.nist.gov/rt-java, last accessed 20/8/2002.

[Det02] Deters, M. and Cytron, R.K. "Automated Discovery of Scoped Memory Regions for RealTime Java". ACM ISMM'02. Berlin, Germany, 2002.

[Dib04] Dibble, P. and Wellings, A.J. (2004), "The Real-Time Specification for Java: Current Status and Future Directions", Proceedings of the Seventh International Symposium on Object-Oriented Real-time Distributed Computing, ISORC 2004.

[Egg02] Eggermont, L.D.J. (Ed) (2002), "Embedded Systems Roadmap 2002, Technology Foundation (STW), STW-2002, ISBN: 90-73461-30-8.

[Fra00] Franz, M., Fröhlich, P.H., and Kistker, T. (2000), "Towards Language Support for Component-Oriented Real-Time Programming", 5th Workshop on Object-Oriented Real-Time Dependable Systems, WORDS 00, pp 125-130.

[Hen98] Henriksson, R. (1998), "Scheduling Garbage Collection in Embedded Systems", PhD Thesis, Department of Computer Science, Lund University, Sweden.

[Hil98] Hilderink, G., (1998), "A New Java Thread Model for Concurrent Programming of Real-Time Systems", Real-Time Magazine

[Hui02] Higuera, T. et al (2002). "Memory Management for Real-time Java: an Efficient Solution using Hardware Support". Real-Time Systems Journal. Kluwer Academic Publishers.

[Jav00] Java Community Process, JSR50 (2000), "JSR 50: Distributed Real-Time Specification", http:// www.jcp.org/jsr/detail/50.jsp, last accessed 20/8/2002.

[Jav01] Java Community Process, JSR133 (2001), "JSR 133: Java Memory Model and Thread Specification Revision", http://www.jcp.org/jsr/detail/133.jsp, last accessed 20/8/2002.

[Jav02]   Java Community Process, JSR166 (2002), "JSR 166: Concurrency Utililities", http:// www.jcp.org/jsr/detail/166.jsp, last accessed 20/8/2002.

[J-C00]   J-Consortium (2000), "Realtime Core Extensions", Revision 1.0.14, http://www.j-consortium.org/rtjwg/index.html, last accessed 20/8/2002.

[Kim99]   Kim, T. et al (1999), "Scheduling Garbage Collection for Embedded Real-Time Systems", ACM Workshop on Language, Compilers and Tools for Embedded Systems (LCTES 99), pp 55-64.

[Kli86]   Kligerman, E. and Stoyenko, A. (1986), "Real-Time Euclid, A Language for Relaible Real-Time Systems", IEEE Transactions on Software Engineering, SE-12(9), 941-949.

[Kra99]   Krause, K.H. and Hartmann, W (1999), "RT JAVA Proposal", http://www.j-consortium.org/rtjw

[Kwo02]   Kwon, J., Wellings, A.J., and King, S. (2002), "Ravenscar-Java: A High-Integrity Profile for Real-Time Java, Java Grande, pp 131-140.

[Lee85]   Lee, I and Gehlot, V (1985), "Language Constructs for Distributed Real-Time Programming", Proceedings of the Real-Time Systems Symposium, IEEE Computer Socitey, pp 57-66.

[McG98]   McGhan, H. and O'Connor, M. (1998) "picoJava: a Direct Execution Engine for Java Bytecode", IEEE Computer.

[Miy97]   Miyoshi, A., Tokuda, H and Kitayama T., (1997) "Implementation and Evaluation of Real-Time Java Threads", Real-Time Systems Symposium, IEEE Computer Society.

[Nil98]   Nilsen,K. (1998) "Adding Real-Time Capabilities to Java", Communications of the ACM.

[Pag96]   Page, I. (1996), "Constrcuting Hardware-Software Systems from a Single Decription", Journal of VLSI Signal Processing, 12(1), pp 87-107.

[Pal99], Palopoli, L, Buttazzo, B. and Ancilotti, P. (1999), "A C Language Extension for Programming Real-Time Applications", 6th International Conference on Real-Time Computing Systems and Applications, IEEE, pp 103-110.

[Pol99]   Poletto, M et al (1999), " 'C and tcc: A Language and Compiler for Dynamic Code Generation", ACM Transactions on Programming Languages and Systems, 21(2), pp 324-369.

[Ran75]   Randell, B. (1975), "System Structure for Software Fault Tolerance", IEEE Transactions on Software Engineering, SE-1(2), 65-75.

[Rit02]   Ritzau, T. and Fritzon, P. (2002). "Decreasing memory over-head in hard real-time garbage collection". EMSOFT'02, LNCS 2491.

[Rom01]   Romanovsky A, et al (Eds) (2001), "Advances in Exception Handling Techniques", LNCS 2022, Springer.

[Sal01]   Salcianu, A. and M. C. Rinard, M.C. (2001). "Pointer and Escape Analysis for Multithreaded Programs". Proceedings of the 8th ACM SIGPLAN Symposium on Principles and Practice of Parallel Programming.

[Shi78]   Shrivastava, S. (1979), "Concurrent Pascal with Backward Error Recovery", Software-Practice and Experience, 9(12), pp 1001-1020.

[Sie99]   Siebert, F. (1999), "Real-Time Garbage Collection in Multi-Threaded Systems on a Single Microprocessor", IEEE Real-Time Systems Symposium, pp 277-278.

[Sie00]   Siebert, F. (2000). "Hard Realtime Garbage Collection in Modern Object Oriented Programming Languages". AICAS, 2002. ISBN: 3-8311-3893-1.

[Var03]   Vardanega, T. (Ed) (2003), Proceedings of the 12th International Real-Time Ada Workshop, Ada letters, XXIII (4).

[War02]   Ward, M. and Audsley (2202), N.C., "Hardware Implementation of Programming Languages for Real-Time", Proceedings of the 8th IEEE Real-Time and Embedded Technology and Applications Symposium, pp 276-285.

[Wel02]   Wellings, A.J., Clark, R., Jenson, D. and Wells, D. (2002), "A Framework for Integrating the Real-Time Specification for Java and Java's Remote Method Invocation", Proceedings of the Fifth International Symposium on Object-Oriented Real-time Distributed Computing, ISORC 2002, pp 13-23.

[Wel04]   Wellings, A.J., "Concurrent and Real-Time Programming in Java", Wiley, 2004 (to appear).

[Wer85]   Werun, W. and Windauer, H. (1985), "Intrdouction to PEARL: Process and Experiment Realtime Language", Friedr. Vieweg Sohn.

[Wir77]   Wirth, N. (1977), "Modula: A Language for Modular Multiprogramming", Software-Practice and Experience, 7(1), pp 3-35.

26 Other Issues

26.1 Power Awareness

Power management and power awareness are active research topics, which main focus, in the context of this document, lies in the area of dynamic techniques (techniques applied at run-time). The purpose is to control power consumption, while providing a reasonably good output or service. Power awareness is relevant to augment battery life, reduce consumption in stationary systems and to limit temperature of hardware devices. This is a fundamental topic for the increasing number of mobile devices in the consumer-electronics market. In addition, the power consumption of stationary devices augments continuously and techniques to reduce it will be very much welcome.

Power-awareness is an area of intensive research. Power reduction can be done at different levels and with different techniques. As a consequence, there are a large number of approaches to this topic:

- Low power electronics
- Power conscious CAD tools.
- Architecture-level power reduction.
- Compilation techniques that generates low consuming code [Cheng98].
- Power efficient data structures and energy efficient software [Naik01].
- Power conscious OS/drivers [Zeng02].

In the context of this document, the relevant techniques are those that allow the real-time system to adapt to the environment, which is characterized information such as current workload, user settings, external events and quality characteristics of the running applications. DPM (Dynamic Power Management) is a set of techniques that achieves energy-efficient computation by selectively turning off (or reducing the performance of) system components when they are idle, partially unexploited or when battery level or device temperature requires a reduction in the consumption. [Unsal03] provides an excellent overview of power-aware techniques that can be applied at different levels of abstraction in the development of real-time systems.

Currently, electronic systems are designed to be able to deliver peak performance when requested. However, the workload applied to the system is usually variable and peak performance is only required during some time intervals. Consequently, system components are not always required to be in the active state.

Traditionally, systems have been designed to operate at fixed supply voltage and frequency. However, the interest on power management has motivated the integration of power management facilities in the hardware devices that can be controlled by software. Two examples of these facilities are DVS (Dynamic Voltage Scaling) and device power states. DVS refers to runtime change in the voltage levels supplied to various components in a system so as to reduce the overall system power dissipation while maintaining total computation time and/or throughput requirement. Implementation of DVS requires substantial software support such as development of schedul-

Artist FP5 Consortium: Embedded Systems Design, LNCS 3436, 352–372, 2005.
© Springer-Verlag Berlin Heidelberg 2005

ing techniques with a dynamic recalculation of task priorities based on average energy dissipation. DVS is becoming a mainstream technology in the industry. Several commercial CPUs featuring DVS (Intel Xscale, Transmeta) are already on the market.

In addition, it is increasingly common to find hardware devices with different power states, which are characterized by the functions that the device performs and the associated power consumption. As an example, a communication device can be turned off, fully operational, or suspended waiting to get a connection request. The power state of the device can be managed taking into account how the running applications are using it. In this way, it is possible to save power.

In summary, the contents of this section are based on DPM (Dynamic Power Management) techniques that take into account system environment to drive the power settings of the hardware. The final goal is to adapt system behaviour to the available hardware devices, including power, and to the applications launched by the user. As has been described above, the topic of power management can be dealt with from different points of view and at different hardware and software levels. In order to make an optimal power management it is necessary to exploit all of them. For this reason, this topic is addressed in another part of this document, although with a different point of view.

Aspects of power-awareness are also covered in section 30.

Landscape

The Shift Towards Managing Power with Software
Power management previously was implemented in hardware FSM or firmware. However, there is now a general trend to shift control from hardware to software layers. A promising software layer where dynamic techniques can be implemented is the operating system. OS-based power management has the advantage that the power/performance dynamic control is performed by the software layer that manages the computational, storage and I/O tasks of the system. The Advanced Configuration and Power Interface [ACPI02] standard proposed by Compaq, Intel, Microsoft, Toshiba and Phoenix is a recent example of this trend.

It is worth mentioning the ECOSystem [Zeng02] that is based on Linux and supports energy as a first-class operating system resource. They propose the Currency Model that unifies energy accounting over diverse hardware devices and enables fair allocation of available energy among applications. This work is integrated in the Milly Watt project that investigates power management techniques [MillyWatt].

[PARTS] PARTS (Power-Aware Real-Time Systems) is another relevant project which tries to minimize power consumption while still meeting deadlines. Its approach for achieving the power/deadlines objective is to develop new schemes for power-aware real-time systems, including scheduling algorithms, power control of memory resources, speed control of CPUs, and dynamic power monitoring and mode changes, mainly at the operating system level.

The middleware layer is another level where power management can be efficiently performed. The advantage of this approach is that it is possible to use additional information to decide on the policy to follow. In particular, it is possible to know which the running applications are, their importance, domain knowledge, context information, etc. This approach is compatible with a research project promoted by IBM and MontaVista Software [DPM02] for the definition of a proposal for dynamic power management in embedded systems, which attempts to standardize a dynamic power management and policy framework that supports different power management strategies. Although policies reside in the kernel, the policy manager could be outside it and it can be integrated in an appropriate middleware layer.

In summary, the final goal is to try to optimize power consumption, while maintaining the quality of service and functionality expected by the user. Generally speaking, it is possible to group research on power management in adaptive real-time systems in three areas, although these approaches are not only targeted to this type of applications:

- *Power consumption managed in a middleware layer.* This is the best option for using power management strategies that considers system level information in the decision process.
- *Power consumption managed exploiting idleness periods.* Hardware devices are not always used at its maximum performance. Then it is possible to detect idle periods and reduce power consumption during their duration.
- *Power consumption managed via scheduling.* In this case, scheduling information is used to identify slack time where the device can be powered off or scaled, while guaranteeing the fulfilment of the time requirements.

Power Management in Middleware
Power management is important for system behaviour because certain settings can reduce the available resources. This is specially the case with systems based on resource reservation for letting applications provide an appropriate and satisfactory quality output. In this type of systems, there is an special manager in the middleware layer in charge of negotiating with the applications the trade-off between quality and resources. Applications receive a set of resources reserves that are sufficient for accomplishing the requested functionality. If the CPU voltage is reduced, then the processing power is also reduced. As a consequence, the resource reserves need to be renegotiated.

It seems reasonable to advocate the need for a system level power management approach. The global system state is considered to make the appropriate power settings. Among the relevant information that is worth to consider are user preferences, resource requirements of the running applications, system workload, power status (battery level, current power source, device temperature, etc.), and context knowledge. Then, it is possibly to decide power settings that are consistent with this information. This is the approach followed in the power management activities in the Space4U project [S4Uweb], where power management is integrated in the resource management framework within a component-based environment. The operating system can make additional power savings, for example taking advantage of idleness periods in hardware devices, but in such a way that resource reserves committed during negotiation are guaranteed.

[Yua01] describes a middleware framework for coordinating processor and power management. Application admission control is based on a power-aware resource reservation mechanism. The processor speed is adjusted according to external or internal events. Reserves are updated to follow changes in the available processing capabilities. This approach is suitable for adaptive real-time systems.

There are other examples of research works that use system global information for power management in middleware. Context information taken by sensors is used for managing power in [Dalton03].

Power Consumption Managed by Exploiting Idle Periods
Since DPM is based on idleness exploitation, it requires prediction, with a certain degree of confidence, the fluctuations of the workload. Typically, a DPM implementation includes a control procedure (called policy) based on some observation and/or assumptions of the workload. An example of a simple policy, which shuts down a component after a fixed inactivity time, under the assumption that is highly likely that a component remains idle if it has been idle for the timeout time. Other examples of policies embrace stochastic, predictive, learning, task-based policies. This problem is known as policy optimization and considered to be an open research topic.

Power Management via Scheduling
An alternative line of research is to consider the system as a number of real-time tasks that must fulfil the time requirements. The power management is based on detecting slack periods to reduce power consumption while keeping the guaranteed deadlines. Although this line of work can be viewed as an special case of the previous one, its relevance for the real-time community advises to treat it separately.

[Lu00] proposes ordering task execution to adjust the length of idle periods, when it is possible to shut down the processor or other devices. [Pil01] presents extensive simulation results of a number of RT-DVS mechanisms that show that the voltage and frequency setting available and the task set CPU utilization profoundly affect their performance. [Sin01] proposes the Slacked Earliest Deadline First algorithm and shows that that it is optimal in minimizing processor energy consumption and maximum lateness. [Ayd01] proposed a solution based on three parts: a static off-line solution to compute optimal speed, an on-line speed reduction mechanism to reclaim energy by adapting to the actual workload, and an online adaptive and speculative speed adjustment mechanism to anticipate early completions of future executions by using the average-case workload information.

[Lee03] proposes a couple of algorithms for voltage-scaling. Voltages are set in such a way that deadlines are met while reducing the total amount of energy consumption. In [Lee03a] simple scheduling techniques are proposed with the goal of reducing the *leakage energy can be reduced by an order of magnitude.* [Qadi03] presents a dynamic voltage scaling *algorithm that can be used with sporadic tasks in conjunction with pre-emptive EDF scheduling. The algorithm is proven to guarantee each task meets its deadline while saving the maximum amount of energy possible with processor frequency scaling.*

Summary
Power is another system resource that has to be managed. This resource is taking primary importance due to the market expectations of mobile devices. The best way to really maximize system operation is to make an integrated resource management,

in such a way that when taking decisions on one resource, the effect on others is also considered. The approaches described should be made compatible, as they are related to decisions at different abstraction layers. Hence, solutions that combine them are expected to be the way to explore in future research works.

Assessment

There is an increasing interest on power management techniques. The research efforts have produced a large number of techniques at different abstraction levels. However, in general the power management techniques are very recent and lacks of the necessary testing in real-life systems. Although they certainly allows for power savings, most of them are not mature enough for their extensive use in industrial products. In addition, there have been few, if any, attempts to combine and use them in a system in an integrated and compatible way.

This panorama is especially true in the case of real-time systems, where in addition to the common requirements, it is necessary to develop techniques that save power without precluding applications from meeting their time requirements. Finally, there is a lack of standards for letting software and hardware power management facilities interact with a certain portability level. ACPI is certainly a standard in this way, but it adequacy for embedded and real-time systems is very much discussed.

Trends

The obvious interest on saving power in the future computer devices, and in particular in real-time systems, will cause an increasing research on power management techniques. In the context of the adaptive real-time systems, power management will also be a primary research concern. Power is a part of the context information that will require the execution algorithms for adapting system behaviour to the power status. On the other hand, power is one of the mechanisms that can be used for adapting system behaviour to the environment.

The trend for the near future is to continue research in the same areas as described in this section. It is necessary to develop more mature scheduling policies that take into account power in the task scheduling and setting power parameters of the processor, ensuring the fulfilment of the time requirements. CPU is not the only device to consider when dealing with power. On the contrary, it has been demonstrated that other hardware devices consume even more power. In consequence, it is required to develop drivers that take into account device usage scheme for driving its power states in such a way that power consumption is optimized and quality and time requirements are met.

Global system power management seems to be the way to follow. Power management will be at different levels, (application, middleware and operating system) based on global information and in a way that the decisions of each level are compatible. The leading power management policies should reside in the middleware layer, as at this level is where information about the other levels, external context, and information on the operating system can be gathered and handled.

References

[ACPI02]   Compaq, Intel, Microsoft, Phoenix, Toshiba, "Advanced Configuration and Power Interface Specification, Revision 2.0b, http://www.acpi.info/spec.htm, October 11, 2002

[Ayd01]   Hakan Aydin, Rami Melhem, Daniel Mosse, Pedro-Mejia Alvarez, "Dynamic and Aggressive Scheduling Techniques for Power-Aware Real-Time Systems", 22nd IEEE Real-Time Systems Symposium, 2001

[Cheng98]   S. Cheng, C. Chen, J. Hwang, "Low-Power Design for Real-Time Systems", *Journal of Real-Time Systems*, Vol. 15, Nu. 2, Kluwer Academic Publishers, September 1998

[Dalton03]   Angela B. Dalton and Carla S. Ellis, "Sensing User Intention and Context for Energy Management", in HOTOS, January 2003

[DPM02]   IBM and MontaVista Software, "Dynamic Power Management for Embedded Systems", Version 1.1, November 19, 2002.
http://www.research.ibm.com/arl/projects/dpm.html.

[Lee03]   Y. Lee, C. Krishna, "Voltage-Clock Scaling for Low Energy Consumtion in Fixed-Priority Real-Time Systems", *Journal of Real-Time Systems*, Vol. 24, Nu. 3, Kluwer Academic Publishers, May 2003

[Lee03a]   Yann-Hang Lee, Krishna P Reddy, C. M. Krishna, "Scheduling Techniques for Reducing Leakage Power in Hard Real-Time Systems", Proceedings of the 15th Euromicro Conference on Real-Time Systems, 2003.

[Lu00]   Yung-Hsiang Lu, Luca Benini, Giovanni De Micheli, "Low-Power Task Scheduling for Multiple Devices", 8th International Workshop on Hardware/Software Codesign, 2000

[MillyWatt]   Milly Watt Project, Duke University, http://www.cs.duke.edu/ari/millywatt.

[Naik01]   K. Naik, D. Wei, "Software Implementation Strategies for Power-Conscious Systems", Mobile Networks and Applications, vol. 6, pp. 291–305, Kluwer Academic Publishers, 2001.

[PARTS]   Power-Aware Real-Time Systems Project, University of Pittsburg, http://www2.cs.pitt.edu/PARTS/.

[Pil01]   Padmanabhan Pillai, Kang G. Shin, "Real-Time Dynamic Voltage Scaling for Low-Power Embedded Operating Systems", pages 89-102, 18th ACM Symposium on Operating System Principles, 2001.

[Qadi03]   Ala Qadi, Steve Goddard, Shane Farritor, "A Dynamic Voltage Scaling Algorithm for Sporadic Tasks", Proceedings of the IEEE Real-Time Systems Symposium, 2003.

[Sin01]   Amit Sinha, Anantha Chandrakasan, "Energy Efficient Real-Time Scheduling", Proceedings of the International Conference on Computer Aided Design (ICCAD), San Jose, Nov. 2001.

[S4Uweb]   Space4U web homepage http://www.extra.research.philips.com/euprojects/space4u

[Unsal03]   O. S. Unsal, I. Koren, "System-Level Power-Aware Design Techniques in Real-Time Systems", Proceedings of the IEEE, Vol. 91, NO. 7, July 2003

[Yua01]   Wanghong Yuan and Klara Nahrstedt, "A Middleware Framework Coordinating Processor/Power Resource Management for Multimedia Applications", in Proc. of IEEE Globecom 2001, San Antonio, Texas, November, 2001

[Yua02]   Wanghong Yuan and Klara Nahrstedt, "Integration of Dynamic Voltage Scaling and Soft Real-Time Scheduling for Open Mobile Systems", Proc. of 12th International Workshop on Network and Operating Systems Support for Digital Audio and Video (NOSSDAV '02), pp. 105-114, Miami Beach, Florida, May, 2002.

[Zeng02]   Heng Zeng, Carla S. Ellis, Alvin R. Lebeck, Amin Vahdat, "ECOSystem: managing energy as a first class operating system resource", ACM SIGOPS Operating Systems Review, Volume 36, Issue 5, December 2002

26.2   Media-Processing Applications

The transition from analogue to digital, and from hardware to software, in the wide array of control, audio, and video processing, have been a lasting feature of the past 30 years. This is due to the increased speed and capacity of digital equipment. Currently, video is also moving from analogue to digital to software. In the areas of television and stored video, the transition is currently taking place. The (writeable) DVD is taking over the prominent role of the videocassette, and digital satellite television is taking over from terrestrial analogue television. Even so, digital does not necessarily mean software yet. The bulk of digital video processing is still performed in dedicated hardware, because software decoding is still too expensive. With Moore's law, this is expected to change in the future. How near that future will be is still unclear, but that it will happen is generally accepted.

At some point in the future, digital video processing in software will become the state of the practice. Motion-sensitive video algorithms (MPEG (de)coding, but also temporal scaling, and (de)interlacing) may have highly varying loads. These video algorithms are generally embedded in video flow graphs with strict timing requirements: tight jitter requirements on input (broadcast) as well as output (screen), and low latencies because of separate audio processing (home theatre), interactivity, and memory constraints.

Decoding MPEG-2 video streams imposes hard real-time constraints for consumer devices such as television. The freedom of encoding choices provided by the MPEG-2 standard results in a high degree of variability inside the streams, in particular with respect to frame structures and their sizes. MPEG encoding has to meet diverse demands, depending, for example, on the medium of distribution, such as overall size for DVD, maximum bit rate for DVB, or encoding speed for live broadcasts. In the case of DVD and DVB, sophisticated provisions to apply spatial and temporal compression are applied, while a very simple, but quickly coded stream will be used for the live broadcast. Consequently, video streams, and in particular their decoding demands will vary greatly between different media.

A number of algorithms have been presented for efficient transmission and software decoding of MPEG video streams, mostly using buffering and rate adjustment based on average-case assumptions. These provide acceptable quality for applications such as video transmissions over the Internet, when drops in quality, delays, uneven motion or changes in speed are tolerable. However, in high quality consumer terminals, such as home television, quality losses of such methods are not acceptable.

Another major difference between digital media processing and real-time control processing arises from the throughput requirements. Megabytes of data need to be pumped through the system at a very high rate. Computation is only one of the issues – in some cases, communication may be even more important.

26.3   Integrating Real-Time and Control Theory

Current real-time design methods and associated analysis tools do not provide a model flexible enough to fit well with control systems engineering requirements. In addition, classic control theory does not give advice on how to include resource constraints into the controller, both at the design and implementation stage.

Most feedback control systems are essentially periodic, where the inputs (reading sensors) and the outputs (posting on actuators) of the controller are sampled/hold at a fixed rate. While basic digital control theory deals with systems sampled at a single rate, [Sim98] has shown that the control performance of a non-linear system like a robot can be improved using a multi-rate controller. Some parts of the control algorithm, such as updating parameters or controlling slow modes, can be executed at a slower pace. In fact, a complex system involves sub-systems with different dynamics, which must be further coordinated. Therefore the controller must run several control laws in parallel with different sampling rates inside a hierarchy of more or less tightly coordinated layers.

Digital control systems are often implemented as a set of tasks running on top of an off-the-shelf real-time operating system (RTOS) using fixed-priority and pre-emption. The performance of the control, e.g. measured by the tracking error, and even more importantly its stability, strongly relies on the respect of the specified sampling rates and computing delays (latencies) [Ast90]. As the value of the control gains depends on these temporal attributes, it is essential that the implementation of the controller respects the specified temporal behaviour at run-time.

Usually, real-time systems are modelled by a set of recurrent tasks assigned to one or several processors. A worst case response time technique is used to analyze fixed-priority real-time systems. The analysis provided in [Liu73] assumes that all the tasks are periodic, run on a single processor, have a common first release instant, have a deadline equal to their period and that there are no precedence constraints between the tasks. These assumptions have been progressively released [Aud95] to compute results for more general systems, e.g. with precedence constraints, aperiodic tasks or release jitter.

Indeed the timing requirements of a control system deserve to be accurately captured. In particular it appears that closed-loop systems have a "stability margin" which make them robust with respect to parameters deviations, including timing parameters like jitter and sample-induces delays [Cer03]. The timing constraints thus can be relaxed, e.g. as "weakly hard" constraints to specify a range of allowed deviations around nominal values [Ber01] or through a quality model gathering performance, computing cost and robustness indexes [San00].

Such control systems thus can be implemented using flexible scheduling techniques and a fault-tolerant QoS based management.

Landscape

Traditional discrete controller design uses as main paradigm the constant and equidistant sampling period and usually assumes sufficient computing resources and negligible sampling to actuation computation time. Sampling period is constrained by the Shannon Sampling Theorem, which essentially states that sampling frequency has to be at least double than the highest significant frequency which the controlled system can pass through [Ast90]. A common rule of thumb is to use a sampling frequency between 4 and 20 times this highest significant frequency. Low sampling frequencies (close to the 4x) give reasonable control objectives but at the low region of some performance measurement. High sampling frequencies (in the vicinity of 20x or larger) allows better performance measurements but imposes higher computing resource utilization. This flexibility in the selection of the sampling frequency can be modelled and used as a way to share the common tasks resources in a multitask environment.

From the real-time side, it can be used the controller design flexibility in two different ways: first, to specify the more favourable sampling frequency for a given multitask condition in a more or less static scheduling scenario; second, to dynamically change the sampling condition and the real-time scheduling as the multitask computing resources are in high load conditions.

Although the first case is almost a classical scenario, some care has to be taken as the inter-sampling period can exhibit jitters, driving to potential instability of the controlled system [Mar01]. Some work has been done to overcame this situation by reducing the jitter through acting on the scheduler design [Bal02], [Bal04], or by introducing such jitters into the controller [Mar02].

The second case is where the flexibility can take it's most interesting view. As there is some kind of performance measurement of the controlled system, it can be searched an optimal condition [Yep03a], [Yep03], [Vel03a], by scheduling the most beneficial task at each iteration. Such approaches require a careful analysis of the closed loop system performance in front of such sampling frequency changes [Vel03b]. If in addition to the control tasks the non control tasks have flexibility and performance parameters, a global cost function can be designed where to find the optimal scheduling solution.

Assessment

Design Process
In the traditional approach to the analysis and design of computer control systems, controller design and implementation are two separate stages. In the design stage, sampling and actuation are generally assumed synchronous and periodic, and a highly deterministic timing of an implementation is assumed. However, when a control algorithm is executed by a task (or by a set of subtasks) in a multitasking real-time system, those assumptions may not be met, causing control performance degradation and even instability. These problems can be addressed using a combination of control theoretic and scheduling principles so that control systems can exploit new (and more flexible) scheduling approaches and scheduling approaches can take advantage of control systems properties [Mar01].

WCET Estimation and Computing Load
Design and off-line schedulability analyses rely on a accurate estimation of the tasks' worst case execution time. Even in embedded systems the processors use caches and pipelines to improve the average computing speed while decreasing the timing predictability. Another source of uncertainty may come from the control algorithm. For example, the duration of a vision process highly depends on incoming data from a dynamic scene. Also some algorithms are iterative with a badly known convergence rate, so that the time needed to reach a predefined threshold is unknown (and must be bounded by a timeout). Finally, in a dynamic environment, some control activities can be suspended or resumed and control algorithms with different costs can be scheduled

according to various control modes leading to large variations in the computing load. Thus, real-time control design based on worst case execution and strict deadlines inevitably leads to a low average usage of the computing resource.

Timing Assignment and Support from Control Theory
Once a control algorithm has been designed, the first job consists of partitioning it into tasks, then assigning timing parameters, in the form of periods and latencies to real-time tasks so that the controller's implementation satisfies the control objective. Control theory for linear systems sampled at fixed rates, including fixed delays, has long been established. More recent results, e.g. [Lee02] or [Mar01], deal with varying delays and sampling rates in control loops, still in the framework of linear systems. Unfortunately real-life systems are non-linear. The extrapolation of timing assignment through linearizing often gives rough estimations of allowable periods and latencies and can even be meaningless. Thus slicing the control algorithm and setting adequate values for the timing parameters rapidly falls into case studies based on simulation and experimentation.

Priority Assignment and Scheduling Policy
Well known scheduling policies, such as Rate Monotonic for fixed priorities and EDF for dynamic priorities, assign priorities according to timing parameters such as deadlines or sampling periods. These methods tend to maximize the computing resource usage or the number of tasks which meet their deadline. They hardly take into account precedence and synchronization constraints, which naturally appear in a control algorithm. Finally the relative urgency or criticality of the control tasks can be unrelated with the timing parameters. [Eke99] has shown that blind use of scheduling policy based purely on computing parameters can lead to an inefficient controller implementation while a scheduling policy based on application requirements gives better results. Another example of unsuitability between computing and control requirements arise when using priority inheritance or priority ceiling protocols to bypass priority inversion due to synchronization and mutual exclusion. Such protocols jeopardize the initial run-time schedule which was carefully designed to meet control requirements, e.g. minimizing sensor to actuator latencies along some control paths and assigning priorities according to the task's criticality with respect to the control performance and stability.

Robustness of the Control Scheme
Control systems are often cited as examples of "hard real-time systems" where deadline-missed violations are forbidden. In fact, experiments show that this assumption is false for closed-loop control. Any practical feedback system must have some stability margin to have insensitivity and robustness with respect to the plant parameters uncertainty. As observed by control practitioners, this stability margin also provides robustness with respect to timing uncertainties: the controllers are able to tolerate some variations in sampling period, computing delays, output jitter and occasional data loss with no loss of stability or integrity, but only disturbances. The hard real-time assumption should be changed for a "weakly hard" one, where absolute deadlines are replaced by statistical one, e.g. the allowable output jitter compliant with the desired control performance. Even if computing such statistics is out of the scope of

current control theory, this intrinsic robustness of closed-loop controllers gives an additional degree of freedom which can serve QoS computation and flexible scheduling design.

Trends

Off-line Control/Scheduling Co-design

Taking into account the unsuitability of current real-time design techniques to capture feedback control system requirements naturally leads to the use of control/scheduling co-design. While basic implementations use a periodic sequential loop to handle the control algorithm components, the control performance can be improved by slicing the controller according to the relative criticality and timing requirements of its components. A rather general scheme for control systems consists in splitting the controller into a high priority "CalculateOutput" thread and a less critical "UpdateState" thread [Arz99]. Thus, these threads can be scheduled separately with the advantage of a lower sensitivity of critical tasks, with respect to pre-emption from concurrent processes. More specialized structures of control tasks can be found for specific application domains, such as robot control [Sim02]. A second step consists in finding adequate values for the scheduling parameters. This can be done off-line for a particular application as described in [Ryu97], where cost functions relating the timing parameters to the control performance are first experimentally identified. In a second step, these cost functions are used in iterative heuristics to set the scheduling parameters under constraint of available computing power. However, while these off-line and application-based methods can handle control requirements, they cannot easily handle timing uncertainties and dynamic reconfigurations. For dynamics systems, [Foh95] and [But98] presented scheduling algorithms that can be used to schedule control tasks that need to be dynamically accommodated according to different application requirements.

Feedback Scheduling

Timing uncertainties due to varying computing loads call for on-line adaptation of the tasks scheduling parameters according to measures of the computing resource activity. This new approach has been initiated from both the real-time computing side [But00], [LuS00] and from the control side [Cer00]. The idea consists of adding to the scheduler an outer sampled feedback loop ("scheduling regulator") to control the scheduling parameters as a function of a QoC (Quality of Control) measure. The QoC criterion captures the control performance requirements and the problem can be stated as QoC optimization under constraint of available computing resources, which usage can be measured e.g. through laxities or deadlines violations. The output of this scheduling controller triggers the scheduling parameters such as task periods or priorities. Preliminary studies [Eke00] suggest that a direct synthesis of the scheduling regulator as an optimal control problem will lead, when tractable, to a solution that is too costly to be implemented in real-time. Practical solutions will be found in the available control toolbox or in enhancements and adaptations of current control theory. Note that this approach is not limited to the design of plant control systems but can be used to manage real-time systems with varying and unpredictable loads such as multimedia servers: in such a case the QoC criterion will be computed only from computing activity measurements.

To accommodate with a dynamic environment leading to system reconfigurations this feedback loop must be supervised by a decisional process: the "scheduling manager" will be in charge of admission/rejection of incoming tasks, anticipation of the computing load variations and exception handling due to deviations from the specified QoS. In particular it will be able to use different variants of the control algorithms (with different computing costs and QoS) as an additional degree of freedom to accommodate the computing load at run-time. Obviously, to cope with control requirements the decisions made by the scheduling manager must rely on knowledge about control, real-time computing and on the controlled process itself.

Quality-of-Control Scheduling
When the responsibility of maximizing the performance of closed-loop systems relies on both the controller design and the scheduler, a new scheduling problem appears. As it has been shown in [Mar02], dynamic optimization of the quality of the controlled system response calls for

- flexible control task timing constraints that deliver effective control performance; flexible constraints allow us to achieve faster reaction by adaptively choosing the controller sampling rate and completion time upon transient perturbations;
- a Quality-of-Control (QoC) metric; it associates with each control task timing a quantitative value expressing control performance (in terms of the closed-loop system error), and
- new scheduling approaches; their goal is to quickly react to perturbations by dynamically scheduling tasks based on the chosen control task execution parameters to maximize the QoC.

This combination offers the possibility of taking scheduling decisions based on the control information for each control task invocation, rather than using fixed timing constraints with constant periods and deadlines.

References

[Arz99]   K.E. Arzen and B. Bernhardsson and J. Eker and A. Cervin and P. Persson and K. Nilsson and L. Sha, "Integrated Control and Scheduling", Department of Automatic Control, Lund Institute of Technology, ISRN LUFTD2/TFRT--7686--SE, August 1999.

[Arz00]   K.-E. Årzén and A. Cervin and J. Eker and L. Sha, "An Introduction to Control and Scheduling Co-Design",39th IEEE Conference on Decision and Control, Sydney, Australia, December 2000.

[Ast90]   K.J. Åström and B. Wittenmark, Computer-Controlled Systems – Theory and Design, Prentice Hall, Englewood Cliffs, NJ, 1990.

[Aud95]   N.C. Audsley and A. Burns and R.I Davis and K.W Tindell and A.J. Wellings, "Fixed Priority Preemptive Scheduling: An Historical Perspective", Real-Time Systems, Vol. 8, pp. 173-198, 1995.

[Bal02]   P. Balbastre, I. Ripoll, A. Crespo, "Schedulability analysis of window-constrained execution time tasks for real-time control", Euromicro Conference on Real-Time Systems 2002

[Bal04]   P. Balbastre, I. Ripoll, J. Vidal, A. Crespo, "A Task Model to Reduce Control Delays", Real-Time Systems Journal, 2004

[Ber01]   G. Bernat. A. Burns and A. Llamos, "Weakly Hard Real-Time Systems", IEEE Transactions on Computers, Vol. 50, No. 4, pp.308-321, 2001.

[But98]   G. Buttazzo, G. Lipari and L. Abeni, "Elastic Task Model for Adaptive Rate Control", IEEE Real-Time Systems Symposium, Madrid, Spain, December, 1998

[But00]   G. Buttazzo and L. Abeni, "Adaptive Rate Control through Elastic Scheduling", 39th Conference on Decision and Control, Sydney, Australia, December 2000.

[Cer00]   A. Cervin and J. Eker, "Feedback Scheduling of Control Tasks", 39th IEEE Conference on Decision and Control, Sydney, Australia, December, 2000.

[Cer03]   Anton Cervin, "Integrated Control and Real-Time Scheduling", Department of Automatic Control, Lund Institute of Technology, Sweden, ISRN LUTFD2/TFRT-1065-SE, April 2003.

[Eke99]   J. Eker and A. Cervin, "A Matlab Toolbox for Real-Time and Control Systems Co-Design", 6th Int. Conf. on Real-time Computing Systems and Applications, Hong Kong, pp. 320-327, December, 1999.

[Eke00]   J. Eker and P. Hagander and K-E. Årzén, "A feedback scheduler for real-time controller tasks", Control Engineering Practice, Vol. 8, No. 12, pp. 1369--1378, 2000.

[Foh95]   G. Fohler, "Joint Scheduling of Distributed Complex Periodic and Hard Aperiodic Tasks in Statically Scheduled Systems", in IEEE Real-Time Systems Symposium, December, 1995.

[Foh97]   G. Fohler, "Dynamic Timing Constraints -Relaxing Over-constraining Specifications of Real-Time Systems", in Proceedings of Work-in-Progress Session, 18th IEEE Real-Time Systems Symposium, December, 1997

[Lee02]   Y.S. Lee and W.H. Kwon, "Delay-dependent robust stabilization of uncertain discrete discrete-time state-delayed systems", IFAC 15th World Congress, Barcelone, Spain, 2002.

[Liu73]   C.L. Liu and J.W. Layland, "Scheduling Algorithms for Multiprogramming in Hard Real-Time Environment", Journal of the ACM, No. 1, Vol. 20, pp. 40-61, 1973.

[LuS00]   C. Lu and J. Stankovic and T. Abdelzaher and G. Tao and S. Son and M. Marley, "Performance Specifications and Metrics for Adaptive Real-Time Systems", Proc. of IEEE Real-Time Systems Symposium, December, 2000.

[Mar01]   P. Marti, J.M. Fuertes, G. Fohler and K. Ramamritham, "Jitter Compensation for Real-Time Control Systems", 22nd IEEE Real-Time Systems Symposium, London, UK, 2001.

[Mar02]   P. Marti, G. Fohler, K. Ramamritham, J.M. Fuertes, "Improving Quality-of-Control using Flexible Timing Constraints: Metric and Scheduling Issues", 23rd IEEE Real-time System Symposium, Austin, TX, USA , December 2002.

[Ryu97]   M. Ryu and S. Hong and M. Saksena, "Streamlining Real-Time Controller Design – From Performance Specifications to End-to-End Timing Constraints", Proc. of IEEE Real-Time Technology and Applications Symposium, Montreal, June 1997,

[San00]   Martin Sanfridson, "Problem Formulations for QoS Management in Automatic Control", TRITA-MMK 2000:3, ISSN 1400-1179, ISRN KTH/MMK-00/3-SE, KTH, Stockholm, 2000.

[Sim98]   D. Simon and E. Castillo and P. Freedman, "Design and Analysis of Synchronization for Real-time Closed-loop Control in Robotics", IEEE Trans. on Control Systems Technology, No. 4, Vol. 6, pp. 445-461, July 1998,

[Sim02]   D. Simon and F. Benattar, "Design of real-time periodic control systems through synchronisation and fixed priorities", INRIA, RR4677, December 2002.

[Vel03a]   M. Velasco, P. Marti, J.M. Fuertes "Modelling Self-triggered Tasks for Real-Time Control Systems", in workshop on Co-design in Embedded Real-time Systems (CERTS03), satellite Euromicro Conference on Real-Time Systems, Porto, Portugal, July 2003

[Vel03b]   M. Velasco, P. Marti, J.M. Fuertes "The Self Triggered Task Model for Real-Time Control Systems", in WiP IEEE Real-Time Systems Symposium (RTSS03), Cancun, Mexico, December 2003.

[Yep03a]   J. Yépez, P. Martí and J.M. Fuertes "A Control Loop Scheduling Paradigm in Distributed Control Systems", in Proc. IEEE Conf. Industrial Electronics Society IECON03, Virginia, November 2003

[Yep03b]   J. Yépez, P. Martí and J.M. Fuertes "The Large Error First (LEF) Scheduling Policy for Real-Time Control Systems", in WiP IEEE Real-Time Systems Symposium (RTSS03), Cancun, Mexico, December 2003.

26.4   Probabilistic Time Analysis

Scheduling work in real-time systems is traditionally dominated by the notion of absolute guarantee. The load on a system is assumed to be bounded and known, worst-case conditions are presumed to be encountered, and static analysis is used to determine that all timing constraints (deadlines) are met in all circumstances. This deterministic framework has been very successful in providing a solid engineering foundation to the development of real-time systems in a wide range of applications, from avionics to consumer electronics. The limitations of this approach are, however, now beginning to pose serious research challenges.

Flexible scheduling has addressed some of this rigidity in the model by providing more powerful mechanisms for designing and analysing systems. However, the notion of absolute guarantee is still hardwired into the basic assumptions. With increased complexity and less predictable systems a move from a more deterministic to a more probabilistic framework is required in future real-time systems. The sources of the need for probabilistic analysis are threefold [BBB03]:

1. Fault tolerant systems are inherently stochastic and cannot be subject to absolute guarantees.
2. Application needs are becoming more flexible and/or adaptive – work-flow does not follow pre-determined patterns, and algorithms with a wide variance in computation times are becoming more commonplace.
3. Modern super-scalar processor architectures with features such as cache, pipelines, branch-prediction, out-of-order execution etc. result in computation times for even straight-line code that exhibits significant variability. Also, execution time analysis techniques are pessimistic and can only provide upper bounds on the execution time of programs.

These characteristics are not isolated to so called 'adaptive (also called soft) real-time systems' but are equally relevant to the most stringent hard real-time application. Contributions on these three areas are fundamental to the advance of real-time systems in the future.

Current and future research on probabilistic timing analysis can be structured in these three categories [BBB03].

Transient faults are more frequent than permanent faults, a probabilistic argument is the right tool to reason about these systems. The issues to address are random arrivals of faults and overheads of recovery procedures. The problems are then to derive minimum fault arrival rates that guarantee schedulability [BPSW99].

In the real-time literature, stochastic analysis of real-time systems has been addressed from different perspectives. The Probabilistic Time Demand Analysis (PTDA) [Tia95] and the Stochastic Time Demand Analysis (STDA) [Gar99a][Gar99b] are targeted for fixed-priority systems with tasks having arbitrary execution time distributions. The PTDA is a stochastic extension of the Time Demand Analysis [Leh89] and can only handle tasks with relative deadlines smaller than or equal to the periods. On the other hand, the STDA, which is a stochastic extension of the General Time Demand Analysis [Leh90], can handle tasks with relative deadlines greater than the periods. Both methods are based on the critical instant assumption, i.e. the task being analyzed and all the higher priority tasks are released at the same time. This pessimistic assumption simplifies the analysis, but results in only an upper bound on the deadline miss probability.

Another relevant work is [Man01], which proposes an approach which covers general priority-driven systems including both fixed-priority and dynamic-priority systems. To simplify the analysis, it assumes that all the tasks are non-pre-emptable. Moreover, to limit the analysis scope, it assumes that the relative deadlines of tasks are smaller than or equal to their periods and that all the jobs that miss the deadlines are dropped.

An interesting approach is the Real-Time Queuing Theory [Leh96, Leh97]. This analysis method is flexible, as it is not limited to a particular scheduling algorithm and can be extended to real-time queuing networks. Such a method is applicable to systems where the heavy traffic assumption (i.e., the utilization is close to 1.0) holds.

Other relevant stochastic analysis methods include the one by Abeni and Buttazzo [Abe01], the Transform-Task Method (TTM) [Tia95] and the Statistical Rate Monotonic Scheduling (SRMS) [Atl98]. All of them assume reservation-based scheduling algorithms so that the analysis can be performed as if each task had a dedicated (virtual) processor. That is, for each task, a guaranteed budget of processor time is provided in every period [Abe01][Tia95] or super-period (an integer multiple of the tasks period in SRMS) [Atl98]. So, the deadline miss probability of a task can be analyzed independently of other tasks assuming the guaranteed budget.

The paper [Dia02] proposes a stochastic analysis method that does not put any pessimistic or restrictive assumptions into the analysis. The method is general and uniformly covers general priority-driven systems including both fixed-priority systems such as RM [Liu73] and DM [Leu82] and dynamic-priority systems such as EDF [Liu73]. The analysis method can handle any task set consisting of tasks with arbitrary relative deadlines (including relative deadlines greater than the periods) and arbitrary execution time distributions. Probabilistic schedulability analysis was also addressed to deal with scheduling in the presence of overload [Kim02].

In multiprocessor environments, the work [Nis03] deals with a probabilistic analysis of dynamic multi-processor scheduling. The paper focuses on the scheduling of individual tasks. Finally, in [MPP02] an approach based on Generalised Stochastic Petri Nets (GSPN) to deal with schedulability analysis of multiprocessor real-time applications with stochastic task execution times is presented.

Any analysis technique relies on the execution time of programs. Current WCET estimates are too pessimistic and provide a single value. The previous techniques use probability distributions of the execution times but they do not describe how these probability distributions are obtained. One simple approach is to use measurement values, however, end-to-end measurements are not adequate for the estimation of the WCET of real-time programs. The work on probabilistic WCET analysis (pWCET) [BCP02, CP03] addresses this issue in detail. PWCET allows engineers the determination of probability distributions of the execution time of the longest path in a program. Initial results indicate that there is in general a large difference between the execution time observed in average and the estimated WCET and that the WCET happens with very low probability. PWCET allows the determination of probability distributions of arbitrary code.

A very important issue that needs to be addressed by any probabilistic analysis technique applied to real-time systems is that the hypothesis of independence usually made in the analysis does not correspond with the behaviour observed in real systems [BCP02]. Initial work by Bernat et.al [BCP03] on the application of the theory of copulas [Nel98] to real-time systems shows how this theory is suitable to address this problem and how can it be incorporated in the analysis. Initial work has only been applied to the computation of the WCET, however the same results could be extended to other types of analysis, including schedulability analysis.

A different approach is the use of the theory of extreme value statistics to model the tail of the distribution of execution times [BuEd00, EdBu01].

Summary

In order to analyse the next generation of real-time systems, real-time analysis techniques have to be extended to include a probabilistic aspect. This new view can take the form of manipulation of probability distributions or the association for each result of the analysis its probability. Some important initial steps have been taken on this direction however a more general approach for a probabilistic centric view of the analysis of real-time systems needs to be developed to be able to analyse future real-time systems.

References

[Abe01]   L. Abeni and G. Buttazzo. "Stochastic Analysis of a Reservation Based System", In *Proc. of the 9th International Workshop on Parallel and Distributed Real-Time Systems*, Apr. 2001.

[Atl98]   A. K. Atlas and A. Bestavros. "Statistical Rate Monotonic Scheduling", In *Proc. of the 19th IEEE Real-Time Systems Symposium*, Dec. 1998, pp. 123–132.

[BBB03]   Burns, A, G. Bernat, I. Broster, "A Probabilistic Framework for Schedulability Analysis". *EMSOFT,* Philadelphia, 2003.

[BBR02]   I. Broster, A. Burns, and G. Rodriguez-Navas. "Probabilistic analysis of CAN with faults". *In Proceedings of the 23rd Real-time Systems Symposium (RTSS)*, 2002. Austin, Texas, USA..

[BCP02]   Bernat,G., A. Colin, S. Petters, "WCET Analysis of Probabilistic Hard Real-Time Systems". *In Proceedings of the 23rd   Real-Time Systems Symposium (RTSS)* 2002. Austin, Texas, USA.

[BCP03]   Bernat,G. A. Colin, S. Petters "pWCET: a Tool for Probabilistic Worst-Case Exe-
            cution Time Analysis of Real-Time Systems" Department of computer Science.
            University of York. Technical Report YCS-2003-353. January 2003.

[BPSW99]   A. Burns, S. Punnekkat, L. Strigini, and D.R. Wright. "Probabilistic scheduling
            guarantees for fault-tolerant real-time systems". *In Proceedings of the 7th Interna-
            tional Working Conference on Dependable Computing for Critical Applications.*
            San Jose, California, pages 339–356, 1999.

[BuEd00]   A. Burns and S. Edgar. "Predicting computation time for advanced processor
            architectures". *In Proceedings 12th EUROMICRO conference on Real-time Sys-
            tems,* 2000.

[CP03]   Colin, A, S. Petters "Experimental Evaluation of Code Properties for WCET
            Analysis" *In Proceedings of the 24th Real-Time Systems Symposium (RTSS)* 2003.
            Cancun, Mexico.

[Dia02]   J. L. Diaz, D. F. Garcia, K. Kim, C. Lee, L. Lo Bello, J. M. Lopez, S. L. Min, O.
            Mirabella, "Stochastic Analysis of Periodic Real-Time Systems", *In Proceedings
            of the 23rd Real-Time Systems Symposium (RTSS)* 2002. Austin, Texas, USA.

[EdBu01]   S. Edgar and A. Burns. "Statistical Analysis of WCET for Scheduling". *In Pro-
            ceedings of the 22nd Real-Time Systems Symposium (RTSS)* 2001. London, Eng-
            land,

[Gar99a]   M. K. Gardner and J. W.S. Liu. "Analyzing Stochastic Fixed-Priority Real-Time
            Systems", in *Proc. of the 5th International Conference on Tools and Algorithms for
            the Construction and Analysis of Systems,* Mar. 1999.

[Gar99b]   M. K. Gardner. "Probabilistic Analysis and Scheduling of Critical Soft Real-Time
            Systems", Ph.D. Thesis, Univ. of Illinois Urbana-Champaign, 1999.

[Kim02]   K.H. Kim, L. Lo Bello, S. L. Min, O. Mirabella, "On Relaxing Task Isolation in
            Overrun Handling to Provide Probabilistic Guarantees to Soft Real-Time Tasks
            with Varying Execution Times", *In Proceedings of 14th Euromicro Conference on
            Real- Time Systems,* June 19-21, 2002, Vienna, Austria.

[Leh89]   J. P. Lehoczky, L. Sha, and Y. Ding. "The Rate-Monotonic Scheduling Algorithm:
            Exact Characterization and Average Case Behaviour", In *Proc. of the 10th IEEE
            Real-Time Systems Symposium,* Dec. 1989.

[Leh90]   J. P. Lehoczky. "Fixed Priority Scheduling of Periodic Task Sets with Arbitrary
            Deadlines", In *Proc. of the 11th IEEE Real-Time Systems Symposium,* Dec. 1990.

[Leh96]   J. P. Lehoczky. "Real-Time Queueing Theory", In *Proc. of the 17th IEEE Real-
            Time Systems Symposium,* Dec. 1996, pp. 186-195.

[Leh97]   J. P. Lehoczky. "Real-Time Queueing Network Theory," In *Proc. of the 18th IEEE
            Real-Time Systems Symposium,* Dec. 1997, pp. 58-67.

[LeNi03]   A. Leulseged, N. Nissanke. "Probabilistic Analysis of Multi-processor Scheduling
            of Tasks with Uncertain Parameters". In Proceedings of the 9th International Con-
            ference on Real-Time and Embedded Computing Systems and Applications, Feb-
            ruary 2003.

[Leu82]   J. Leung and J.M. Whitehead. "On the Complexity of Fixed Priority Scheduling of
            Periodic Real-Time Tasks", *Performance Evaluation,* Vol. 2, No. 4, 1982, pp. 237-
            250.

[Liu73]   L. Liu and J. Layland. "Scheduling algorithms for Multiprogramming in a Hard
            Real-Time Environment", *Journal of ACM,* Vol. 20, No. 1, 1973, pp. 46-61.

[Man01]   S. Manolache, P. Eles, and Z. Peng. "Memory and Time-Efficient Schedulability
            Analysis of Task Sets with Stochastic Execution Times", In *Proc. of the 13th Eu-
            romicro Conference on Real-Time Systems,* Jun. 2001, pp. 19-26.

[MPP02]   S. Manolache, P. Eles, Z. Peng, "Schedulability Analysis of Multiprocessor Real-Time Applications with Stochastic Task Execution Times", 20th International Conference on Computer Aided Design (ICCAD 2002), pp. 699-706, November 2002, San Jose, California

[Nel98]   R.B. Nelsen. *An introduction to Copulas.* Springer, 1998.

[Tia95]   T.S. Tia, Z. Deng, M. Shankar, M. Storch, J. Sun, L.-C. Wu, and J. W.S. Liu. "Probabilistic Performance Guarantee for Real-Time Tasks with Varying Computation Times", in *Proc. of the Real-Time Technology and Applications Symposium,* May 1995, pp. 164–173.

26.5   Hardware Trends

Real-time embedded systems strongly depend on the target hardware, in order to achieve the required functional, and as importantly, the required extra-functional properties of the system. For example, analysis of the timing properties of a system is dependent upon the hardware upon which the functionality is implemented, often a complex CPU that is difficult to model for execution-time analysis.

Given that real-time embedded systems implementations are highly dependent upon the target hardware, it is useful to examine the trends in the hardware available for embedded system implementations.

Adaptive real-time embedded systems dynamically self modify in response to changes in the environment. This could be handled purely at the software level, although there are performance advantages if at least some adaptability is handled at the hardware level.

The following sections examine specific trends, namely System-on-a-Chip, conventional processor technologies, dedicated hardware and integrated communications.

System-on-Chip

An important development over the last few years has been that of System on a Chip (SoC), a term that is now explained. Ever decreasing minimum feature sizes in integrated circuit technology (already below the 100nm realm) now allow a single device to be allocated to multiple functions, e.g. processor, memory and communications functions can be placed within a single chip (usually a bus-based architecture is used within the chip for connectivity). This has the result of reducing the component count and hence unit cost of the system.

Initially, the mix of functionality on SoC devices was defined by the silicon vendor. More recently, customers have been able (to a limited extent) to define the functionality mix by selecting from a number of available IP cores. IP Core or Intellectual Property Core, is an expression (usually in a high level hardware development language such as VHDL) of a component device such as a communications interface or CPU.

Although more complex to design, SoCs can be more suitable to certain applications due to the possibility to include analogue subsystems such as A/D, D/A converters and drivers. For real-time systems these dedicated circuits will promote the integration in a single package of specialized devices such as intelligent sensors, actuators and network nodes (including communication controllers, drivers, bus-guardians).

Microprocessors / Microcontrollers

The performance of microprocessors and microcontrollers, is becoming less important [Bas02] due to the current availability of low cost devices with enough processing power for most practical embedded applications. This implies that current microprocessors and microcontrollers will remain usable much longer than initially anticipated. However, there is greater need for such devices to have other properties such as reliability and predictability. For example, some performance-oriented architectural techniques, such as caches and pipelines, will see their relative importance decreased while the possibility of in-circuit testing is becoming essential.

The micro-controller concept, in which the required peripherals and subsystems are integrated with the microprocessor, is increasingly important (see SoC discussion above). However, the growth in the number of different versions, already enormous, will probably stop. Then, the customization will not be done by picking a different version but by integrating a microprocessor core (i.e. IP – core) with the required interfaces and subsystems.

Dedicated Hardware

With the advent of Field Programmable Logic Devices (FPLDs) it has become possible to implement software systems directly as hardware circuits, without the need for a CPU (although one could be used) and without the development cost of an application specific circuit [Com02]. Time-to-market can be very short with the design processes supported by industrial CAD tools. It is possible to integrate IP-cores and increase reusability. Some techniques such as dynamic reconfiguration can help in enlarging the application domain of such circuits.

Initially FPLDs were used for implementing unique, and usually relatively simple, digital circuits and for prototyping. Such devices were adequate for prototypes, small series and projects without stringent cost restrictions, as well as products expected to benefit from hardware upgrades during their lifetime. The effectiveness of FPLDs has generated enormous research efforts in this area.

New and more powerful generations of FPLDs are becoming widely available. In addition, the price per CLB has been reduced substantially. Field Programmable Gate Arrays (FPGAs) are a direct development of early PLDs such as PAL and GAL arrays. Unlike the program once, logic-term architecture of these devices, FPGAs provide reprogrammability and logic functions to the system designer. This allows FPGAs to provide more complex functionality than an equivalently sized programmable logic device. For example the Virtex 812E FPGA (Field Programmable Gate Array) contains an array of 56*84: 4704 CLBs, 1Mbit of block RAM, 300Kbit of distributed RAM, more than 500 user I/Os and can operate with clock frequencies up to 240 MHz.

The key property of an FPGA is that it is inherently parallel. Thus, it is relatively easy to map a concurrent program in Ada to a truly concurrent implementation on an FPGA such that each task is executed in parallel [War02]. If required, soft processor cores can be implemented on FPGAs that are instruction level equivalent to a conventional processor [URL1]. Further technology developments combine one or more conventional processors together with a large area of reconfigurable logic on a single chip. For example, recent chips by Xilinx combine up to four PowerPC cores with reconfigurable logic [URL2]; other manufacturers are combining smaller microprocessors with different on chip devices (e.g. communications) together with reprogrammable logic.

Another key property of an FPGA is dynamic reconfigurability, which can occur in a matter of milliseconds. The entire configuration, or part of a configuration, of the device can be changed in little more than the usual context switch time of a CPU. This makes an FPGA an ideal candidate for use in adaptive systems where the functionality of the system needs to change as the environment changes.

Technologies such as FPGAs enable different implementation strategies to be evaluated. For example, a single FPGA could be a combination of one or more soft cores executing conventional compiled code, together with areas of circuit directly implementing application functionality – perhaps for functionality with extremely tight timing requirements.

Integrated Communications

Finally, a particular issue that deserves mentioning, because of its deep consequences, is the hardware advances that allowed a generalized availability of low-cost hardware components with integrated processing and communications capabilities. This fact has been fostering the large-scale use of distributed architectures in embedded systems, with positive impact on systems scalability, composability and dependability. Particularly, the trend is towards highly distributed architectures with high number of nodes, most of which will be relatively simple, dedicated to specific functions, e.g. intelligent sensors. On its turn, this trend also influences the hardware design itself, simplifying it at the node level, and transferring a substantial part of the overall complexity to the network.

On the other hand, the deployment of distributed architectures in embedded systems introduces new challenges (e.g., coordination of activities, provision of timeliness guarantees) that must be addressed also taking into account the available hardware infrastructures. The availability of simple hardware components to perform essential functionalities, possibly in a distributed way, such as failure detection or timely execution of recovery procedures, will be extremely helpful to address these new challenges and improve the overall system dependability.

Summary

Hardware trends for future real-time embedded systems are largely structural, in terms of the increased use of SoC style technologies, where greater functionality is placed onto a single device. The precise functionality mix of a device is often defined by the vendor, but is increasingly being defined by the customer selecting the functions required for a particular target system.

Conventional implementations have, until recently, used one or more processors as the main part of their target architecture. This is essentially an implementation strategy. The key requirement is to map the functional and extra-functional characteristics of the design (represented in some concurrent programming language) onto the target hardware. The advent of reprogrammable FPLDs enables a more flexible mapping of the design to target hardware.

The design can be implemented as a mixture of dedicated hardware circuits, that may or may not include a conventional processor. The benefits for real-time embedded systems are many, including target hardware designed for predictability and to support the specialized needs of real-time systems.

References

[Bas02]   Bass, M., Christensen, C., "The Future of the Microprocessor Business", IEEE Spectrum, April 2002.

[Com02]   Compton, K., Hauck, S., "Reconfigurable Computing: A Survey of Systems and Software" ACM Computing Surveys (vol. 34, no. 2, June 2002).

[War02]   Ward, M., Audsley, N.C., "Hardware Implementation of Programming Languages for Real-Time" Proceedings of the 8th IEEE Real-Time and Embedded Technology and Applications Symposium

[URL1]   www.opencores.org

[URL2]   www.xilinx.com

27 Executive Overview on Execution Platforms

Professor Hugo De Man of the IMEC research centre in Leuven, Belgium, calls the rise of embedded systems the 'third innovation wave' in ICT. First there was the period of the main frames, where many users shared one computer. Then we have seen the period of the personal computers, with each user having one computer, and now we enter the period with many computers for each 'user'. These networked computers form new, sophisticated architectures, consisting of large numbers of interconnected programmable devices and ASICs.

Heterogeneity is an important characteristic of modern, complex, embedded systems. Such systems are heterogeneous in at least two respects. They contain different types of processors, such as microcontrollers, general-purpose processors (CPUs), reconfigurable processors (FPGAs), and dedicated hardware components (ASICs), and they contain unusual means of input/output, such as sensors, actuators, antennas, and cameras. The second respect in which they are heterogeneous is in their means of communication, both on-chip and off-chip. Many different modes of communication are employed, including multi-hop strategies, which should be taken into account in the performance modelling.

A second important characteristic is the need for *low power*. This need occurs over the whole range of embedded systems, from large, cubic meter-size systems to small cubic millimetre-size (or even smaller) ones. It is obvious that the current, spectacular growth of the number of processors per person can only continue if we succeed in dramatically lowering the power consumption per processor. Many applications, such as in-clothing or in-body devices, can only be successful if they are *energy-autonomous*, meaning that they can scavenge their own energy. It is clear that this requires extreme energy-efficiency.

In this document we survey the use of (heterogeneous) execution platforms and low-power techniques in two different industrial sectors: the automotive industry and the mechatronics industry. These sectors have been chosen because they provide rather challenging and trying environments for the application of embedded systems. Automobiles require an extreme level of reliability, but as consumer goods they also have to be cost-effective. This makes traditional reliability engineering less applicable. Mechatronic systems are extremely heterogeneous in that they span a very wide technology spectrum, ranging from motion control and robotics to administrative transactions with stock-control and resource-planning systems. Both automotive and mechatronics are industrial sectors in which innovative companies (such as Daimler-Chrysler, BMW, and ASML) have extensive experience with complex embedded systems. Other companies in these and other sectors will be able to learn from these experiences.

27.1 Motivation and Objectives

Embedded systems are executed on increasingly complex platforms. They are heterogeneous both in modes of processing and in modes of communication. They also inter-

Artist FP5 Consortium: Embedded Systems Design, LNCS 3436, 373–376, 2005.

act with physical phenomena by means of sensors, actuators and other devices. It is mandatory that future research in embedded systems takes this complexity into account.

Embedded systems enter many industrial sectors. The automotive sector is extensively discussed in this chapter, but it is only an example of a sector that was earlier confronted with these systems than others. If the complexity of modern embedded is underestimated and if tools or methods are used that are not tailored to this complexity, then we are faced with the risk that these systems will increasingly become unreliable. It is of utmost importance for industry that this problem is realized and that adequate research actions are undertaken.

27.2   Essential Characteristics

The overall characteristic of modern computing platforms for embedded systems is *complexity*. It is because of the complexity of advanced, heterogeneous systems that well-trusted methods and tools are not suited for their tasks anymore. Complexity is a many-faceted phenomenon. There are many views on complex, embedded systems, and each of such views has its own merits. We need to become these different viewpoints, and integration of this multi-view landscape is the only way out of the complexity trap.

A second characteristic has to do with energy-efficiency. Whereas traditional software design was aimed at optimizing memory usage and processing time, we have now entered an era in which (for many applications) low power and energy-efficiency are the discriminating factors. It will take a while before (embedded) software designers will realize the importance of low-power engineering.

27.3   Role in Future Embedded Systems

The era of embedded systems is the era of embedded software. Of course, embedded systems contain software components (compilers, graphical user interfaces, feedback algorithms, etc.) just like they contain mechanical, optical, and electronic components. But the software is also used to integrate components and subsystems into complete systems. Therefore, the real distinction between, for example, mechatronic systems and embedded systems is in the integrating software. The field of embedded systems is about integration and software.

This section of the roadmap contains quite adequate analyses of the landscape in the automotive sector. Automotive is an industrial sector in which Europe is the global leader. There is no automotive company in the world that is, in embedded systems, as far developed as some European players. These globally advanced companies face serious problems, problems that others in the world are not yet aware of. It is the strength of this roadmap that these global leaders are willing to share with others the problems they expect on their own roadmaps.

27.4   Overall Challenges and Work Directions

In the challenges and work directions two areas of attention are distinguished: heterogeneous platforms and low power.

We see four important directions that relate to execution platforms:

- *Models*. Models are extremely important, but different models that correspond to various viewpoints must be integrated.
- *Design Space Exploration*. Methods for design space exploration must be extended to complex, heterogeneous systems.
- *Programmable Hardware*. The challenge is to arrive at an effective set of (heterogeneous) programmable hardware components.
- *System Integration*. Modern, complex embedded systems will not reach the required level of reliability if we are not able to effectively solve the integration-and-test issue.

In the realm of low-power engineering we distinguish the following challenges and work directions:

- *Middleware*. We must investigate how the middleware can exploit the flexibility in voltage levels, clock frequencies and various sleep modes.
- *Instruction Memory*. We have to look for effective ways to compress the code size of embedded software.
- *Data Memory*. We have to find ways to transform the software code in such a way that it obeys energy/efficient access patterns.

27.5   Document Structure

Section 28 presents the current design practice and needs in two industrial sectors, the automotive industry and the mechatronics industry. In automotive the trend is towards integrating more functions into one node (or processor), while simultaneously redistributing the functionality over several nodes. To accommodate this, new open architectures and standards will be developed. Both in automotive and mechatronics research will focus on reliability improvement. Typical for the mechatronics sector is that the integration-and-test issue will have to be understood better, and that new control strategies that are better at recovering from exceptions have to be developed.

Section 29 discusses four different computing platforms. Section 29.1 addresses the modelling of multiprocessor systems. Such systems can be tightly or loosely coupled, and the levels of the models can vary from the specification to the physical level. There are many types of models (event or time-triggered, synchronous or asynchronous, continuous or discrete, etc.) that all have their merits and application areas. The modelling of complex systems usually , requires the simultaneous use of different models. Reconciling these models is an important research topic.

Section 29.2 addresses the analysis of distributed real-time systems, as they occur, for example, in automotive electronics. The redistribution of the functionality over the network nodes calls for an extensive schedulability analysis. For more complex systems, however, new techniques for Design Space Exploration will have to be developed.

Section 29.3 addresses reconfigurable hardware platforms. They are classified by means of the parameters logic block granularity and host coupling. Field-Programmable Gate Arrays (FPGAs) and Complex Programmable Logic Devices

(CPLDs) are among the fastest growing segments in the semiconductor industry. Reconfigurable hardware platforms become more heterogeneous with different types of logic blocks and special function blocks. A completely new line is molecular electronic nanotechnology, a potential candidate for the post-silicon era.

Section 29.4 addresses system integration. It is again approached from the perspective of the automotive industry. System integration is a top design issue for embedded systems. But, unfortunately, it is also an ill-understood problem area, in particular now that the integration is mostly done in software. There are presently no methods and tools that can adequately predict the behaviour of complex systems with respect to power consumption and performance. There is no clear direction to solve the integration problem. Formal performance analysis for heterogeneous architectures may be a way out.

Section 30 discusses low-power engineering. Section 30.1 addresses this issue at the level of middleware. From the technology viewpoint multiple dynamically adjustable voltages and clock frequencies will increasingly become available to the middleware. From the application-level viewpoint distributed techniques for power awareness appear extremely promising. In wireless communication selective shutdowns of interfaces look promising.

Section 30.2 addresses memory aspects in the context of low power. Code compression and access patterns that reflect the memory organization are effective means to reduce power.

28 Current Design Practice and Needs in Selected Sectors

28.1 Automotive Industry

Automotive Electronics

From the point of view of automotive manufacturers, there is a constant market demand for increased vehicle performance, more functionality, less fuel consumption and less exhausts, all of these at lower costs. Also, there is a need for shorter time-to-market and reduced development and manufacturing costs. These, combined with the advancements of semiconductor technology, which is delivering ever increasing performance at lower and lower costs, has led to the rapid increase in the number of electronically controlled functions onboard a vehicle [4].

The amount of electronic content in an average car in 1977 had a cost of $110. Currently, that cost is $1341, and it is expected that this figure will reach $1476 by the year 2005, continuing to increase because of the introduction of sophisticated electronics found until now only in high-end cars (see Figure 31.1) [1], [2]. It is estimated that in 2006 the electronics inside a car will amount to 25% of the total cost of the vehicle (35% for the high end models), a quarter of which will be due to semiconductors [3], [1]. High-end vehicles currently have up to 100 microprocessors implementing and controlling various parts of their functionality. The total market for semiconductors in vehicles is predicted to grow from $8.9 billions in 1998 to $21 billion in 2005, amounting to 10% of the total worldwide semiconductors market [1], [4].

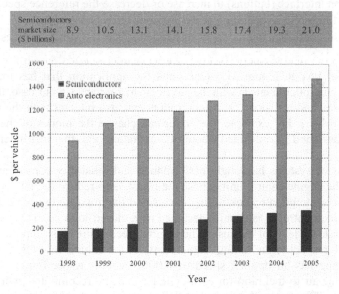

Semiconductors market size ($ billions)	8.9	10.5	13.1	14.1	15.8	17.4	19.3	21.0

Figure 31.1. Worldwide Automotive Electronics Trends [1]

Artist FP5 Consortium: Embedded Systems Design, LNCS 3436, 377–387, 2005.
© Springer-Verlag Berlin Heidelberg 2005

Applications

At the same time with the increased complexity, the type of functions implemented by embedded automotive electronics systems has also evolved. Thanks to the semiconductors revolution, in the late 50s, electronic devices became small enough to be installed on board of vehicles. In the 60s the first analogue fuel injection system appeared, and in the 70s analogue devices for controlling transmission, carburettor, and spark advance timing were developed. The oil crisis of the 70s led to the demand of engine control devices that improved the efficiency of the engine, thus reducing fuel consumption. In this context, the first microprocessor based injection control system appeared in 1976 in the USA. During the 80s, more sophisticated systems began to appear, like electronically controlled braking systems, dashboards, information and navigation systems, air conditioning systems, etc. In the 90s, development and improvement have concentrated in the areas like safety and convenience. Today, computer controlled solutions for highly critical functions like steering or braking that use electrical or electro-hydraulic actuators without any mechanical backup, like is the case in drive-by-wire and brake-by-wire systems [5], [6] have been developed and are considered for future mass production. Brake-by-wire is most developed and already used in-high end cars of DaimlerChrysler where it replaces critical mechanical parts and can provide better brake performance.

The typical automotive electronics application implements a control loop, as depicted in Figure 31.2. An example of such an automotive application is a vehicle cruise controller, which typically delivers the following functionality:

- It maintains a constant speed for speeds over 35 km/h and under 200 km/h.
- It offers an interface (buttons) to increase or decrease the reference speed.
- It is able to resume its operation at the previous reference speed.
- The cruise controller operation is suspended when the driver presses the brake pedal.

The controller box in Figure 31.2 represents the application that has to be implemented. The controller interacts with the physical environment (in our case, the vehicle) through sensors and actuators. Some controllers can also interact with the user of the vehicle (the driver). For example, the driver can change the modes of the controller using switches, and is informed about its operation via the instruments on the dashboard.

A large class of systems have tight performance and reliability constraints. A good example is the engine control unit, whose main task is to reduce the level of exhausts and the fuel consumption by controlling the air and fuel mixture in each cylinder. For this, the engine controller is usually designed as a closed-loop control system which has as feedback the level of exhausts. The engine speed is the most important factor to consider with respect to the timing requirements of the engine controller. A typical 4 cylinder engine has an optimal speed of 6,000 revolutions per minute (RPM). At 6,000 RPM the air to fuel ratio for each cylinder must be recomputed every 20 milliseconds (ms). This means that in a 4 cylinder engine a single such controller must complete the entire loop in 5 ms! For such an engine controller, not meeting the timing

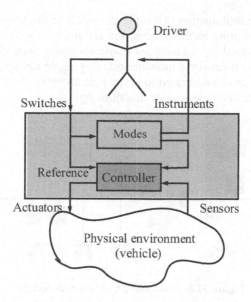

Figure 31.2. Typical Automotive Application

constraint leads to a less efficient fuel consumption and more exhausts [5]. However, for other types of systems, like drive-by-wire or brake-by-wire, not fulfilling the timing requirements can have catastrophic consequences.

In the automotive electronics area, the functionality is typically divided in two classes, depending on the level of criticalness:

- *Body electronics* refers to the functionality that controls simple devices such as the lights, the mirrors, the windows, the dashboard. The constraints of the body electronic functions are determined by the reaction time of the human operator that is in the range of 100 ms to 200 ms.
- *System Electronics* are concerned with the control of vehicle functions that are related to the movement of the vehicle. Examples of system electronics applications are engine control, braking, suspension, vehicle dynamics control. The timing constraints of system electronic functions are in the range of a couple of ms to 20 ms.

Hardware Architecture

Initially, the electronic functionality in vehicles has been implemented using analogue components wired directly to the relevant sensors and actuators. With the introduction of semiconductors and the increased reliance on more and more complex electronics, the number of micro-controllers in a high-end vehicle can today reach 100. In such a situation, if a point-to-point wiring approach is used for networking, the total length of the wires can be as much as 5 km, with a total weight of 50 kg, and a cost comparable with the cost of the engine [5], [4].

This has led to the introduction of simple in-vehicle multiplexing networks, rather than a point-to-point wiring harness. Thus, the architectures typically consist of several nodes interconnected by a broadcast communication channel. For example, in Figure 31.3 we have two networks interconnected by a gateway node. The network on the left, for example, can be dedicated to system electronics, while the network on the right can be for simple body electronics functionality.

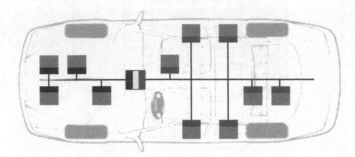

Figure 31.3. Automotive Systems Architecture

Every node (also called *electronic control unit*, ECU) in such a network is typically composed of a micro-controller with its own memory, I/O interface, and communication controller. The microcontrollers used in a node and the type of network protocol employed are influenced by the nature of the functionality and the imposed real-time, fault-tolerance and power constraints:

A typical body electronics system within a vehicle consists of a network of ten to twenty nodes that are interconnected by a low bandwidth communication network like the Local Interconnection Network (LIN) [8]. A node is usually implemented using a single-chip 8 bit micro-controller (e.g., Motorola 68HC05 or Motorola 68HC11) with some hundred bytes of RAM and Kilobytes of ROM, I/O points to connect sensors and to control actuators, and a simple network interface. Moreover, the memory size is growing by more than 25% each year [4], [5].

System electronics typically require 16-bit or 32-bit microcontrollers (e.g., Motorola 68332) with about 16 Kilobytes of RAM and 256 Kilobytes of ROM. These microcontrollers have built-in communication controllers (e.g., the 68HC11 and 68HC12 automotive family of microcontrollers have an on-chip Controller Area Network (CAN) [9] controller), I/O to sensors and actuators, and are interconnected by high bandwidth networks [4], [5].

Software Architecture

The software architecture is typically produced in an ad-hoc fashion, with limited layering and reuse. Standards can be used in order to increase the reuse and portability of software. OSEK/VDX is a standard for embedded real-time operating systems that has been proposed in the automotive area [13]. If suppliers will use operating systems implementations that are compliant with OSEK/VDX the distribution and movement of functionality across nodes will be possible and the integration task will be simpler.

However, in order to facilitate the communication of functionality provided by different suppliers, standard *communication models* are also needed. OSEK/VDX proposes two communication models:

- OSEK/VDX Communication Specification (OSEK COM) [10] provides a standardized software communication interface through a communication API, allowing the software written using OSEK COM to be used on different bus platforms. OSEK COM distinguishes between *queued* and *unqueued* messages. The former have to be serviced as soon as possible in order to prevent a buffer overflow, while the later can be overwritten by a fresher value.
- OSEK/VDX Fault-Tolerant Communication (OSEK FTCOM) [11] provides fault-tolerant services at the communication level, similar to the Time-Triggered Protocol (TTP) [12]. Each node can transmit only during a predetermined time interval, called slot. In such a slot, a node can send several messages packed in a frame.

Trends

Currently, in automotive applications, each function is running on a dedicated hardware node, allowing the system integrators to purchase nodes implementing required functions from different vendors, and to integrate them into their system. There are several problems related to this restricted mapping of functionality:

- The number of such nodes in the architecture has exploded, reaching more than 100 in a high-end car, incurring heavy cost and performance penalties.
- The resulting solutions are sub-optimal in many aspects, and do not use the available resources efficiently in order to reduce costs. For example, it is not possible to move a function from one node to another node where there are enough available resources (e.g., memory, computation power).
- Emerging functionality, such as brake-by-wire, is inherently distributed, and achieving an efficient fault-tolerant implementation is very difficult in the current setting.

This has created a huge pressure to reduce the number of nodes by integrating several functions in one node and, at the same time, certain functionality to be distributed over several nodes.

To be possible to integrate several functions in one node as well as distribute the functionality over several nodes, standards compliant operating systems, coupled with middleware software that abstracts away the hardware differences of the nodes in the heterogeneous architecture have to be available [13].

The open software architecture, which in the concept of the EAST-EEA [13] European project has to enable hardware/software independence and the efficient management of electronic functionality, is composed of a middleware and communication layer. The communication among the components of the software architecture themselves and with the applications is performed via clearly defined interfaces. For efficiency reasons, the middleware and communication layer are tightly integrated with the operating system. Also, the middleware is static, meaning that the entire configuration is done off-line. Using such a middleware architecture, the software functions become independent of the particular hardware details of a node, and thus they can be distributed on the hardware architecture. The project has influenced the new industrial AUTOSAR standardization effort [16].

In particular on the supplier side, the huge number and combinations of required features has lead to the problem of product and software variants. Modularity is seen as the solution to this problem but modularity that is oriented to variants and not only to the function is no common practice in automotive development. An example is a common controller architecture for diesel and gasoline engines that has many functions in common but with many differences in detail. The product line approach as e.g. used in the Bosch Cartronic project, is seen as a possible methodology to reach that modularity goal [15]. Such methodologies will have an impact on middleware and real-time analysis as well as safety issues.

References

[1]   P. Hansen, *The Hansen Report on Automotive Electronics*, http://www.hansenreport.com/, July–August, 2002.
[2]   G. Leen, D. Heffffernan, "Expanding Automotive Electronic Systems," in *IEEE Computer*, pages 88–93, January 2002.
[3]   K. Jost, "From Fly-by-Wire to Drive-by-Wire," *Automotive Engineering International*, 2001.
[4]   H. Kopetz, "Automotive Electronics," in *Proceedings of the 11th Euromicro Conference on Real-Time Systems*, pages 132–140, 1999.
[5]   M. Chiodo, "Automotive Electronics: A Major Application Field for Hardware-Software Co-Design," in *Hardware/Software Co-Design,* Kluwer Academic Publishers, pages 295–310, 1996.
[6]   X-by-Wire Consortium, *X-By-Wire: Safety Related Fault Tolerant Systems in Vehicles*, http://www.vmars.tuwien.ac.at/projects/xbywire/, 1998.
[7]   M. Chiodo, "Automotive Electronics: A Major Application Field for Hardware-Software Co-Design," in *Hardware/Software Co-Design,* Kluwer Academic Publishers, pages 295–310, 1996.
[8]   *Local Interconnect Network Protocol Specification*, http://www.lin-subbus.org, 2003.
[9]   R. Bosch GmbH, *CAN Specification Version 2.0*, 1991.
[10]   OSEK/VDX Communication Specification, Version 2.2.2, http://www.osek-vdx.org
[11]   OSEK/VDX Fault-Tolerant Communication Specification, Version 1.0, http://www.osek-vdx.org
[12]   H. Kopetz, *Real-Time Systems-Design Principles for Distributed Embedded Applications*, Kluwer Academic Publishers, 1997.
[13]   EAST-EEA project, *ITEA Full Project Proposal,* http://www.itea-office.org, 2002.
[14]   *OSEK/VDX Operating System Specification*, Version 2.2, http://www.osek-vdx.org
[15]   S. Thiel, A. Hein. *Modeling and Using Product Line Variability in Auto-motive Systems*. IEEE Software, pages 66–72, July/August 2002.
[16]   *Automotive Open System Architecture* www.autosar.org.

28.2   Mechatronics Industry

Industrial Landscape

Until around 1970 machinery and other industrial equipment was were mainly constructed by means of mechanical solutions. Gradually, however, several forms of electronic control started to replace these mechanical means. With the advent of programmable logic controllers (PLC) and other electronic components, the field of *mechatronics* emerged. Mechatronic systems are systems that are composed of mechanical and electronic components, which together determine the functioning of the system. Mechatronic systems typically communicate with their environment by means of *sensors* (input) and *actuators* (output).

Gradually the components in mechatronic systems have become more programmable. The PLCs are – to a certain degree -- programmable, and over the years many new programmable components have been added. Examples of these are field-programmable gate arrays (FPGA), digital signal processors (DSP), microcontrollers, and, of course, microprocessors. The use of programmable components causes the functionality of the machine to be captured more in software code than in mechanical and electronic components. Such software is called *embedded software*. An embedded system is distinct from a mechatronic system in that the functionality is mainly expressed in software. In a sense, embedded systems are the modern successors of mechatronic systems.

As a result the mechatronics industry is in the midst of the transition to the embedded systems industry, or, in order words, it is increasingly becoming a software industry. How dramatic such a change can be, may be illustrated by an example. We consider the industrial company ASML, which is the global market leader in lithographic systems for the IC (integrated circuits) industry. Until recently ASML was a simple machine construction firm with a solid know-how of the mechanical engineering involved. Now the ASML machines contain embedded software, and of the 1500 R&D employees of ASML 600 people are working in software. The remainder is: 500 in mechanics and measurement, 220 in electronics, and 180 in optics. In a short period the number of software engineers has increased from 20 to 600, and there are no signs that that development will halt. Of course, it must halt, since there are simply not enough software engineers available, and because there is an upper limit to the number of people that can work on the same product.

ASML is an example of a company that manufactures *complex machines*, but it is not unique. We witness the same trend in, for example, the medical imaging (MR, CT, X-ray, PET) industry or in the high-end digital printing industry. These companies are the ones that are currently designing complex embedded systems. For such systems the design cost of the software can account for up to half of the overall design cost, in spite of the fact that we simply design machines and that the software remains hidden (embedded) in these machines. There are many companies in the mechatronics industry that will have to face the same transition in the very near future. They work in factory automation, precision instruments, material handling systems, etc. These companies probably already have departments for embedded software, and they are at the verge of seeing these departments expand. There are many more companies, often small and medium-sized enterprises (SME) who will have to establish a software expertise now and who will witness *the embedded explosion of* ASML in 5 to 10 years from now. Such companies have to make up their minds whether they want to start an in-house software department or an alliance with a software subcontractor.

Mechatronics Development Context

Mechatronic systems communicate with their environment by means of sensors and actuators, and they are controlled by means of networks of processors, FPGAs, and microcontrollers. An ASML wafer stepper, for example, contains 50 processors and 500 FPGAs. The FPGAs are chosen in instances when processors would be too slow and microcontrollers too primitive. The latter plays, for instance, a role when there is a lot of data handling, something that microcontrollers are not too good at. The distribution over a large number of processors has to do with optimization for both speed and reliability. Often tasks are executed at separate processors to assure that their timings will not interfere.

The mechatronics industry is somewhat conservative and typically uses proven technology, such as MIPS processors, coded in C. The step to object-oriented techniques is now being made. The software, actually, fulfils two or three roles. There is software inside components, for example the components that control the user interfaces. There is also software, often called integrating software, that acts as the glue for the different subsystems and components. This software controls the subsystems and it also takes care of all the data traffic and conversions among the different subsystems

In the control of mechatronic systems there is a clear trend towards distributed control. Increasingly, intelligence is added to the sensors and actuators, so that as often as possible decisions are taken locally. Also a lot of data handling and processing is done locally at the input and output nodes.

Another trend is that mechatronic systems become networked: they communicate with other players in their environment and they start to delegate tasks to the environment. In one sense that has always been the case with machines: they are part of a factory layout and get their raw materials from other machines and deliver their finished products to yet other machines. But now these mechatronic systems become part of other networks. They can, for example, be remotely monitored via internet, GSM, or other communication means. Such machines can also be serviced and maintained (and changed, if necessary) via internet since a large fraction of their functionality is expressed as software code. Another application of networking is that machines can interact with the corporate information systems. Mechatronic systems can, for example, inspect and update the enterprise resource planning (ERP) systems.

State of the Practice

The design of mechatronic systems is typically steered from a mechanical viewpoint. First the 'iron' is designed and the control comes later. The combination of iron and control is often modelled in the mathematical package MATLAB and simulated with the corresponding tool SIMULINK. If the control turns out to be rather awkward, changes to the iron parts are still possible in this phase of the design process. Nevertheless, the iron parts of the mechatronic system are usually fixed in an early stage and are considered given from then onwards. The fact that the iron hardware is dominant in the design of mechatronic systems can lead to systems that are not well-balanced between hardware and software. It can, for example, lead to systems in which the mechanical parts are needlessly firm and heavy, because the designers were unaware how a good combination of measuring and software compensation can yield systems that are lighter, more flexible and less costly. Modern developments of mechatronic systems, such as at ASML, have shown that many imperfections of materials and constructions can be compensated (if measured correctly) within the integrating software. In a sense, embedded software can be used to compensate the imperfections of nature. In order to be able to make such trade-offs between mechanical hardware and embedded software one has to treat hardware and software at an equal footing. Probably, the software designers should be slightly given the lead, because they represent the field where the new developments come from, and they can make a change in this rather conservative field of mechatronics.

If we consider the state of practice in the mechatronics industry, we can distinguish three steps a company can make towards really coming to grips with embedded systems. They are:

- The company starts an embedded software department.
- The company realizes that, although it builds machines, it should treat its software, electronic, and mechanical departments at an equal footing.
- The company starts a systems engineering department, which is a multi-technology department that is in charge of the overall systems requirements.

It is especially the third step that determines whether a company in the mechatronics industry has realized that it has become a, software-dominated, multi-technology enterprise.

There are companies that, already for a number of years, have had systems engineering departments. They are situated in the aerospace industry, the industry that builds airplanes, rockets, and satellites. Although this is a business sector that can share its experiences with the modern mechatronics/embedded industrial sector, it is also a sector that it is just now at the verge of experiencing the software explosion described above.

Skills and Education for the Future

As described above, the field of mechatronic design is developing into one that is increasingly affected by the potentials of embedded software. It is important that future designers of mechatronic systems realize that the important design decisions are taken at the systems level. The system level is the level at which different technologies, such as software, mechanics, electronics, and optics, come together, and jointly realize system-wide requirements about cost, performance, and reliability.

It is important that future education caters to the needs of embedded systems. We need systems architects who understand this multidisciplinary field. In order to be successful in a multidisciplinary field one first has to become an expert in one of the underlying mono-disciplines. Therefore, the education for systems architects will have to build on an undergraduate education in computer science, electrical engineering, or mechanical engineering. The recent establishment in Europe of Bachelor/Master (BaMa) educational programs can be very helpful in this respect. Master's programs in Embedded Systems Engineering should be established that are aligned to Bachelor's programs in other engineering disciplines.

Many educational programs in embedded systems have the tendency to concentrate on the interface between electronics and software only. Often these programs have their origin in IC-related programs and follow the development that ICs increasingly require software to determine their functioning. It is of utmost importance that embedded systems designers also understand the realm of motion control. Without this aspect the vast world of mechatronics will be lost for the embedded systems community.

Mathematical modelling is extremely important for any engineering discipline. The problem in mechatronic systems and in embedded systems is that very many different models are required. Of course, mechanical designers use different models than software designers: differential equations versus logical assertions, for example. These models have to be reconciled with each other, so that trade-offs that run across different technologies can be addressed. But there are more types of models in systems design: models that have to do with energy dissipation, cost models, timing models, models for speed and jitter, etc. The art in systems education is to find effective ways of combining the outcomes of these models without having to resort to one overall, and therefore expressionless, model.

Challenges and Work Directions

The challenges for the mechatronics industry have been clearly outlined above. The internal challenge of this field of attention is to address multi-technology trade-offs. This is really the core of modern, mechatronic design. More important, probably, are the external challenges. There are two of them. The first one is reliability. The lack of reliability is the foremost handicap against the introduction of embedded systems in the mechatronic industry. We must succeed in constructing machines that have at least the same level of reliability as the traditional machines, while in the meantime adding the additional functionality that the advent of embedded software allows. The second external challenge is interoperability. As mentioned earlier, the fact that systems become more open to their environment poses great problems on the way in which such systems should involve. Ultimately, mechatronic systems become part of what is sometimes called a smart environment.

The challenge of reliability, mentioned above, leads to clear work directions. We mention four of them.

- *Decoupling.* It is important that failures that occur in mechatronic systems do not affect the basic functioning of the system. An error in the entertainment system of a car should not be able to interfere with the anti-lock braking system (ABS) or the cruise control.
- *Integration and Test.* A good test strategy during the integration phase of mechatronic systems can prevent many errors. Unfortunately, this is the least well-understood phase of the whole design process. This is caused by two problems: we don't know how to do multi-technology testing, and we don't know how the test the integrating software in embedded systems.

- *Aspect-oriented Design.* Object-oriented programming is not well-suited for many system-wide aspects, such as exception handling, tracing, and test facilities. The software code can become much clearer and compacter by dealing with these crosscutting concerns in an aspect-oriented fashion.
- *Recovery-oriented Control.* Often exceptions occur in mechatronic systems: the raw materials have not arrived, or they are not up to specification, or there is a power-down in part of the system. Rather than coding all these possibilities into the software, we want the system to understand what it was doing, what the purpose of the current computation is, so that it can independently find a way of recovering from the current situation.

References

[1]   De-Jiu Chen, Martin Törngren: Towards A Framework for Architecting Mechatronics Software Systems. ICECCS 2001: 170-179.

[2]   Dragan Kostic, Ron Hensen, Bram de Jager, Maarten Steinbuch: Closed-Form Kinematic and Dynamic Models of an Industrial-Like RRR Robot. ICRA 2002: 1309-1314.

[3]   M.W. Maier: System Architecture – An Emergent Discipline? IEEE Aerospace Conf. 1996: 231-245.

[4]   Gerrit Muller: Experiences in Teaching Systems Architecting. INCOSE 2004

[5]   Jan Peirs, Dominiek Reynaerts, Hendrik Van Brussel, Gudrun De Gersem, Hsiao-Wei Tang: Design of an advanced tool guiding system for robotic surgery. ICRA 2003: 2651-2656.

[6]   Martin Prins: Testing Industrial Embedded Systems – An overview. INCOSE 2004.

[7]   D.A. van Beek, Victor Bos, J.E. Rooda: Declarations of unknowns in DAE-based hybrid system specification. ACM Trans. Model. Comput. Simul. 2003: 39-61.

29 Computing Platforms

29.1 Multiprocessor Systems – Modelling and Simulation

Motivation

Modelling plays a central role in systems engineering. The use of models can profitably replace experimentation on actual systems with incomparable advantages such as:

- Enhanced modifiability of the model and its parameters.
- Ease of construction by integration of models of heterogeneous components.
- Generality by using genericity, abstraction, and behavioural non-determinism
- Enhanced observability and controllability, especially, avoidance of the probe effect and of disturbances due to experimentation.
- Possibility of analysis and predictability by the application of formal methods.

Building models which faithfully represent complex systems is a non-trivial problem and a pre-requisite to the application of formal analysis techniques. Usually, modelling techniques are applied at early phases of system development and a higher level of abstraction. Nevertheless, the need of a unified view of the various lifecycle activities and of their interdependencies have motivated the so-called model-based approaches which rely heavily on the use of modelling methods and tools to provide support and guidance for system development and validation.

Landscape

A major dividing line inevitably exists between the *discrete* embedded computing platforms and the essentially *continuous* physical environments in which they are embedded. The discrete embedded computing platforms (comprising both the hardware and the software), in turn, contribute to a number of additional dichotomies at the stage of their mathematical modelling.

The early embedded computing platforms were essentially *sequential* computing platforms but as they are extended and become more complex, a need for the concepts of hierarchy and information sharing between their sub-systems arises (as in *concurrent* systems). To mathematically characterize these concepts, a global notion of a computation step is considered. Thus the dichotomy between the *synchronous* and the *asynchronous* computation models appears. Moreover, to model the behaviour of an embedded computing platform in response to changes in inputs (as in *reactive* systems) can be described in either an *event-triggered* or a *time-triggered* fashion. In addition, timeliness can be a central issue apart from the correct functioning (as in *real-time* systems) requiring the explicit inclusion of time in the computation model.

Furthermore, the application domains contribute additional modelling preferences to the discrete embedded computing platforms. A major such division is between the control-oriented applications, leading to *state-based* computation model (where the complexity arises due to the massive numbers of control locations in a computation),

Artist FP5 Consortium: Embedded Systems Design, LNCS 3436, 388–449, 2005.
© Springer-Verlag Berlin Heidelberg 2005

and data-oriented applications, leading to *data-flow* computation model (where there is much structure in the data on which a large number of operations can be performed in a few control locations).

Most of the discrete embedded computing platforms are essentially *heterogeneous* systems composed of sub-systems that can be formalized using different models of computation. Therefore, some or all of the above-mentioned model dichotomies have to be reconciled in the same discrete embedded computation platform using appropriate meta-models. That is, the embedded computing platforms composed of continuous/discrete, synchronous/asynchronous, state-based/data-flow, event-triggered/time-triggered components have to be developed methodically based on well-defined underlying semantics to properly understand the interaction of different models of computation and to establish a solid foundation for analysis, formal verification, synthesis, and simulation.

In addition, no matter how the individual sub-systems are modelled and analyzed on their own, eventually, the composed system has to be subject to analysis to ascertain that the system exhibits the desired behaviours only in a physical environment. Thus, a very natural way to model an embedded computing platform is by including the elements of the continuous state and the discrete state in the same *hybrid* computation model.

As discussed above, another major challenge is to combine the existing analysis techniques from the various modelling paradigms and to devise a coherent verification methodology for multi-paradigm systems. In particular, to ascertain which aspects of the analysis benefit from the existing capabilities of each paradigm.

Classification of Computation Models
There are several levels at which a model of computation may exist:

- *Specification Level*: At the specification level, the model of computation provides an unambiguous description of a computational problem without any notions of its execution or implementation. Typical examples are:
  - *State Transition Models* (Finite State Machines, CFSM's, Petri Nets, Process Algebras, Duration Calculus, Pi Calculus, etc.)
  - *Data Flow Models* ({Kahn} Process Networks, Data Flow Graphs, Synchronous Data Flow Graphs, etc.)
  - *Discrete Event Models* (HDL Simulators)

- *Performance Level*: At the performance level, the model provides a basis for the evaluation and comparison of efficient methods for the solution of a computational problem. Thus, it forms the basis for the design, discussion, and prediction of the performance of algorithms. Common examples are: Turing Machines, RAM, PRAM, BSP, LogP, etc.

- *Programming Level*: At the programming level, the model provides a precise, high-level description of correct and efficient methods for the solution of the particular computational problem, e.g., Imperative Programming, Declarative Programming (Applicative Programming – Functional Programming, Predicate-based Programming – Logic Programming), etc.
  - *Communication Sub Model*: Communication is, probably, the most important aspect of a computation model. So, in any model of computation, communica-

tion needs to be accurately accounted for. Common communication abstractions are: MPI/PVM, Open MP, IPC, RPC, TCP/IP, OSI, etc.

- *Architecture Level*: At the architecture level, the model describes the characteristics of a real machine on which the computational problems will be implemented and solved, e.g., SISD (Von Neumann), SIMD (Vector, Array), MISD (Systolic), MIMD (Parallel/Distributed), Dataflow, Reduction, Neural Net, etc.
  - o *Network Sub Model*: The two basic measures of network models are latency and bandwidth. The most commonly modelled network topologies are: Butterfly, Torus, Mesh, etc.

Classification of Computing Platforms

Computing platforms may be classified into transformational, interactive, and reactive systems.

- *Transformational Computing Platforms:* compute results with the input data available right from the start of the application without any timing constraints. The computed results are usable as and when required at any given instance.
- *Interactive Computing Platforms*: operate on the environment-produced data without any timing constraints which are expected by already executing tasks. The results computed by those tasks are input to other tasks.
- *Reactive Computing Platforms*: are characterized by the fact that the results produced by the already executing tasks must be delivered at times determined by the controlled process dynamics.

Computing platforms are structured in layers. They all contain operating systems for the basic management of the processor, virtual memory, interrupt handling, and communication [1].

Most of the future embedded applications are likely to be real-time applications that will run on multiprocessor SoCs which are, essentially, distributed computing platforms. In a multiprocessor or a distributed computing platform, the processing elements can be connected through shared memory, dedicated communication links or a communication network [2].

Models of Concurrent Systems (Parallel & Distributed Computing Platforms)

A *multiprocessor* or a *parallel computing platform* is tightly coupled so that the global status and workload information on all processors can be kept current at a low cost. The system may use a centralized scheduler. When each processor has its own scheduler, the decisions and actions of the schedulers of all the processors are coherent. In contrast, a *distributed computing platform* is loosely coupled. In such a system, it is costly to keep the global status and workload information current. The schedulers on different processors may make scheduling and resource access control decisions independently. As a consequence, their decisions may be incoherent as a whole. In modelling distributed computation platforms, the operating systems have a major role.

Moreover, in a distributed computing platform, if the processors can be used interchangeably, they are identical and if a message from a source processor to a destination processor can be sent on any of the links connecting them, then the links are identical as well. In contrast, processors of different types cannot be used interchangeably. Different types of processors may either be functionally different or they may be of different types for many other reasons. A computing platform comprising such processors, which are loosely coupled, is called a distributed heterogeneous computing platform [2].

Models of parallel computation are required to act as a map between disparate programming languages and disparate architectures. Hence, an application developed according to the model is executable on the various architectures and its performance is predictable.

A model is said to be architecture-independent if it is general enough to model a range of architecture types. So, the application source code is portable to various parallel architecture classes without modification.

Despite an apparent trend towards parallel computing platforms being composed of nodes of independent processor-memory pairs connected by some interconnection network, it is by no means certain that there is a definite progression towards a single class of parallel architectures. Instead, there are numerous classes of parallel architectures. Similarly, there are numerous models of parallel computation, some specifically suited to particular architecture classes, while others are suitable across a range of parallel architecture classes.

Models of Reactive Systems

Reactive computing systems continuously interact with their environment. These systems are, in general, composed of concurrent, interacting sub-systems or processes which may cooperate, synchronize, and share resources. It is the role of a scheduler to coordinate the execution of system activities in order to guarantee a correct functioning of the system.

- *State-based vs. Data-flow Approaches*: The family of formal languages known as synchronous modelling languages have shown that they are simple enough to appeal to the engineering community and expressive enough to model non-trivial applications in embedded control. Lustre and Signal have a data-flow (declarative) style whereas Esterel and StateCharts are considered as state-based (imperative) modelling languages. Each modelling language comes with a bunch of analysis techniques and well-developed toolboxes. One of the major benefits of Signal, Lustre, and Esterel is the clearly-documented formal semantics which acts as a description of a meta-model. The *clock calculus* in Lustre and Signal and the constructive semantics of Esterel, for example, can be used for the static checking of the desired properties of an instance (an application model) based on the formal semantics of the languages the defined correctness criteria. Major such properties are the determinism in a controller and the causal consistency at every macro (computation) step. The Statemate tool based on StateCharts checks the type-coherence of the variables in a model and performs some simple consistency checks.

    These tools are finding their ways into modelling the digital components of several embedded applications such as power and digital signal processing systems (Signal), electronic design automation and aerospace systems (Esterel), and railway and aerospace systems (Lustre). These tools also provide efficient automatic code generation mechanisms. Thus, after the compilation stage, the design can be subjected to further formal verification and code optimization, eventually leading to automatically-generated controller code (C, Ada, or VHDL).

StateCharts has had its original popularity in the aerospace sector but it is gaining popularity for the embedded system design due to inclusion into the UML family of modelling languages. The tool, Rhapsody, though no longer in the framework of synchronous modelling languages, is a valuable tool for modelling object-oriented distributed embedded systems.

All of the above-mentioned tools, however, have so far been applied on an individual basis in the respective applications. Considering the growing needs of multi-paradigm modelling, two European projects have been exploring the combination potentials of these tools – SACRES for combining Signal and StateCharts, and SYRF for the combination of Signal, Lustre, and Esterel. The work in SACRES has resulted in relating synchrony with asynchrony and the conditions under which these paradigms can be combined. The work in SYRF has resulted in the development of cross-compilation tools for Lustre, Signal, and Esterel (loose integration), an environment for the multi-paradigm modelling (tight integration), and code distribution for embedded systems.

- *Event-triggered vs. Time-Triggered Approaches*: As described above, each member of the synchronous modelling language family has been extensively used for the design of embedded systems. A recent activity has been to combine the analysis of continuous systems (as modelled in Matlab) with the meta-model verification and efficient code generation capabilities of the Signal environment. This is one of the approaches in a series of attempts at the problem of analysis of hybrid systems.

  In recent years, Matlab has been extended with a modelling facility for describing a discrete controller (Stateflow – with syntax reminiscent of StateCharts). However, the underlying computation model for the simulation of the discrete part of a model is the same as the continuous part of the model. That is, all signals are defined over continuous time and the simulation is time-triggered based on the lowest sample period.

- *Synchronous vs. Asynchronous Approaches*: As discussed above, not all applications can naturally be modelled as globally synchronous systems. A recent development has been to relate the notions of synchrony and asynchrony in the context of data-flow modelling languages (in particular, Signal). This work introduces the theoretical notions that can be used to characterize an asynchronous network of locally synchronous nodes and the compositionality properties (as a meta-model property in this context). Similar ideas are developed in the context of imperative modelling languages where it is shown how constructively-checked Esterel can be used as an input modelling language to the Polis modelling environment, compiling into co-design finite state machines communicating over one-place buffers.

- *Continuous vs. Discrete Approaches*: Recent years have seen the extension of the application of formal methods to the models with both the continuous and the discrete elements. A typical goal of verification is to show that an invariance holds over a model. In particular, a bad property does not hold in any reachable state of a system. Since digital controllers are increasingly complex with mode changes and multiple inputs and outputs, and the goal of the controller is, typically, to avoid a bad state in the physical environment, the traditional methods for proving the invariance are not applicable (neither the computer science methods for proving the properties of discrete systems, nor control theory methods for the analysis of continuous systems). Several techniques for dealing with this inherently difficult problem have been proposed.

Models of Real-Time Systems
Real-time computing platforms are the systems whose correctness depends on the respect of timing constraints. Although real-time systems have become ubiquitous, their design still poses challenging problems and is a very active domain of research. Real-time systems have to reconcile functional, physical, and timing requirements that are often opposite to each other.

Currently, the validation of real-time systems is done by experimentation and measurement on specific platforms in order to adjust design parameters and, hopefully, achieve conformity to QoS requirements. The existence of modelling techniques for real-time systems is a basis for rigorous design and should drastically ease their validation. Modelling a real-time system should allow to validate its design before implementing the system, and to prove its correctness using formal methods. For reactive real-time systems, it is important to build models that faithfully represent their behaviour. In such models, the application has to be modelled together with the behaviour of its environment and dynamics [7].

A modelling framework accompanying the design process of real-time systems and providing a methodology, can guide and accelerate the design process, replace ad hoc solutions by standard constructions, and improve the quality of the model. For a modelling framework to be useful, it should meet the following requirements:

- It should be sufficiently general to allow, in a natural and comprehensive way, the specification of resource contention, synchronization, priority selection, urgency, preemption, periodic, aperiodic, and sporadic processes, and various scheduling disciplines on uni- or multiprocessor systems.
- It should be based, despite their expressiveness, on an analyzable and executable model. That is, it should be operational rather than descriptive, so as to reduce risks of errors caused by passing from one formalism to another.
- It should be founded on theoretical results ensuring well-defined semantics, supporting a modular specification, compositionality, and allowing, to some extent, correctness by construction.
- It should be practical and applicable. That is, it should provide an intuitive, high-level modelling formalism, together with a design methodology, and guidelines or standard constructions for common problems. Moreover, it should allow feasible algorithms for automatic analysis, supporting the design process, and be supported by tools.
- It should help detecting design errors by providing diagnostics at an early stage allowing debugging of the design or gain confidence in its correctness and support a predictable model, in the sense that unexpected interaction between separately modelled behavioural requirements is ruled out as far as possible.

Existing formalisms and tools are designed to meet different subsets of the requirements mentioned above. However, as some of the items seem difficult to reconcile –

for example, the generality of the model and the support for an early detection of design errors – they are not equally addressed by one framework [8].

Component-based engineering is of paramount importance for rigorous system design methodologies. It is founded on a paradigm which is common to all engineering disciplines: complex systems can be obtained by assembling components (building blocks). Components are usually characterized by abstractions that ignore implementation details and describe properties relevant to their composition e.g. transfer functions, interfaces. Composition is used to build complex components from simpler ones. It can be formalized as an operation that takes in components and their integration constraints. From these, it provides the description of a new, more complex component.

Component-based engineering is widely used in VLSI circuit design methodologies, supported by a large number of tools. Software and system component-based techniques have known significant development, especially due to the use of object technologies supported by languages such as C++, Java, and standards such as UML and CORBA. However, these techniques have not yet achieved the same level of maturity as has been the case for hardware.

- *Scheduling Theory-based Approaches*: Well established scheduling theory and scheduling algorithms have been successfully applied to real-time systems development. Schedulability analysis essentially consists in checking that the system meets the schedulability criteria prescribed by the theory, which allows efficient schedulability analysis tools. It does not require the use of a model representing the dynamic behaviour of the system to be scheduled. Current engineering practice essentially adopts this approach.

  Existing scheduling theory requires the application to be set into the mathematical framework of the schedulability criterion. Studies to relax such hypotheses have been carried out. However, most of these schedulability results apply only for particular process models or do not allow complex interaction between the components such as shared resources apart from the processor, atomicity, or communication. Generally, functional and timing properties are specified and verified separately, and no unified approach for general scheduling problems has been proposed so far.

- *Model-based Approaches*: To overcome these limitations, an alternative approach consists in building explicitly a timed computation model of the real-time application, that is, the application processes together with their possible interaction, and verifying schedulability [13] or extracting a scheduler [14], without considering particular scheduling policies. Modelling methodologies and tools for real-time systems have shifted into the focus of research in the recent years.

  The controller synthesis paradigm for discrete-event systems [15] and timed systems [16, 17, 18, 19] provides a general framework for scheduling. This is the most general approach, but the algorithmic method for synthesizing a controller is of prohibitive complexity. For this reason, sometimes, the existence of an invariant implying satisfaction of the timing constraints is explored, using real-time verification techniques [20, 21, 22, 23, 24, 25] and tools such as Kronos [26, 27], Uppaal [28, 29], Verus [30], Cospan [31], or HyTech [32]. A non-empty invariant satisfying the timing constraints is a sufficient condition for schedulability, requiring techniques of lower complexity than synthesis which do not distinguish between controllable and uncontrollable actions.

There are several other approaches to tackle the complexity of verifying real-time systems, or synthesizing schedulers. For example, [33] discusses incremental verification of communicating Time Petri Nets, based on assume-guarantee reasoning. [34] presents a scheduler synthesis tool based on constraint satisfaction for a simple process model that nevertheless allows shared resources, and a timing specification in Real-Time Logic. [35] discusses the analysis of non-deterministic real-time systems using the (max; +) algebra, which does not require exploring the state space like traditional model-checking techniques. [36] provides an algorithm synthesizing a programmable logic controller from a specification described by a fragment of the *duration calculus*.

[37] describes a formal low-level framework for real- time system models, where processes are described by sets of possible behaviours. This framework is intended as a unifying meta-model rather than to directly model real- time applications. [38] discusses modelling and verification of preemptive real-time systems with hybrid automata. Similarly, [39] describes a methodology for modelling a general class of real-time systems with resource constraints, synchronization and context switching overhead, and atomicity of code segments, as hybrid systems. The method is applied to the timing analysis of Ada programs. Adopting the same framework, [40] discusses the timing analysis of partially implemented systems, where lacking pieces of code are specified in Graphical Interval Logic. [41, 42] discuss a formal model of the Ravenscar [43] subset of Ada 95, allowing to verify applications using the model-checker Uppaal.

- *Meta-Model-based Approaches*: Among the modelling and design tools, we shall mention the Ptolemy [44] project and toolset aiming at heterogeneous modelling, simulation, and design of embedded systems by integrating different models of computation. Another tool for the integration of heterogeneous models is the SPI Workbench [45], which uses graphs of communicating processes annotated with timing intervals, as a unifying abstract representation serving as a basis for verification and hardware/software co- design. Giotto [46] is a tool-supported design methodology for distributed embedded systems based on the time-triggered paradigm. It consists of a programming language, and a platform-dependent part including a compiler and a runtime library. Taxys [47, 48] is a tool for the development and verification of embedded systems in the telecommunication domain. The system and its environment are specified in the synchronous language Esterel [49] annotated with timing constraints. The model can be verified by the model-checker Kronos, and compiled to C code by the Esterel compiler Saxo-RT [50].
- *Process Algebra-based Approaches*: There is some work aiming at integrating model-based analysis of real-time systems, and scheduling theory. The interest of considering particular scheduling policies in a model-based approach is twofold. First, it allows to verify both the functional correctness, and the timeliness, of a scheduled real-time system, whereas the same system without a scheduler, generally does not meet its timing constraints. Second, restricting the set of possible behaviours helps to manage the state explosion problem. Most of this work is based on *process algebras* extended with a notion of priority.

[51] defines a process algebra based on CCS [52] with real-time semantics and dynamic priorities. In the process algebra RTSL (Real-Time Specification Language) [53], scheduling policies such as RMS and EDF can be modelled by a function associating, with any system state, a subset of processes that remain enabled after priority choice.

The process algebra ACSR (Algebra of Communicating Shared Resources) [54, 55] provides a framework with discrete and dense-time semantics for modelling coordination between processes including shared resources, synchronization, preemption, static priorities, and exception handling. A prioritized strong bisimulation ensures compositionality. The Paragon toolset [56] for the specification and verification of real-time systems is based on ACSR. The system can be modelled in a graphical specification language. Verification is done by state-space exploration, or checking for bisimulation with a process specifying a high-level behaviour. [57] discusses the modelling of real-time schedulers in ACSR-VP, an extension of ACSR with value passing communication. Schedulability analysis amounts to symbolically checking the possibly parameterized model for bisimulation with a non-blocking process, and synthesizes the parameter values for which the system is schedulable. In [58], models of basic process specifications are given, and schedulers for EDF and the priority inheritance protocol [59] are modelled under ACSR-VP.

[60] presents a modelling methodology for fault-tolerant distributed real-time systems. Processes and fault models are specified in a process algebra based on Timed CCS; liveness properties and deadlines are expressed in logic based on modal timed-calculus. The authors give examples of a best-effort EDF scheduler, and a planning-based scheduler where processes are only scheduled if their deadlines are guaranteed to be met.

[61] model real-time processes scheduled under EDF as timed automata, and model-check the obtained representation using Uppaal. However, their modelling method is not compositional. [62] introduces I/O timed components, essentially timed automata with an interface declaration, as a modelling formalism guaranteeing non-zeno and non-blocking synchronization by construction. Information about the interface of I/O timed components is used by a relevance calculus to make abstraction from components that are irrelevant for proving a given property specified as an observer process.

Meta-H [63] is a development tool initially designed for avionics applications. It accompanies the development process of real-time systems from the specification down to code generation, and implements schedulability analysis based on the results of [64, 65] extending rate-monotonic analysis. It is also possible to specify error models, and carry out reliability analysis.

Sometimes a deductive approach is used to verify correctness of a scheduler [66, 67, 68] using theorem provers. In [69] and [70], real-time programs with timing constraints, fault models, and scheduling policies are modelled in the logic TLA [71]. Proving that scheduling the real-time system under a certain discipline, both specified in TLA, is feasible, amounts to verifying a schedulability condition similar to the results from scheduling theory.

Emerging Application Domains of Models of Multiprocessor Systems

- *Networks-on-Chip*: In the modern silicon technologies, with minimum device geometries in the nanometer range (<100nm), the on-chip interconnection fabric is a major source of delay and power consumption which is challenging the on-chip communication infrastructure and forcing a change from device-centric to inter-connect-centric design methodologies.

  A Network-on-Chip (NoC) is a disciplined approach to replace the current ad hoc wiring of the IP blocks that pairs scalable communication performance and minimal interconnect cost. It separates the computation from communication by allowing the computational blocks to communicate with one another via a uniform interface. A NoC can be based on packet switching communication to flexibly share link capacity between either homogeneous or heterogeneous network clients and to provide multiple communication services over a uniform infrastructure with fixed topology.

  An efficient combination of the best-effort and the guaranteed services in a NoC is a challenge [80]. The other key challenges for designing NoC's include automated synthesis [71, 72], low-power [73, 74], verification and testing [75, 76], and fault-tolerance [77].

  In order to address these challenges, accurate modelling of the systems and all the interrelationships among the diverse processors, software processes and physical interfaces and interconnections, is needed. One of the primary goals of the system-level modelling for networks-on-chip is to formulate a modelling framework within which a broad class of designs can be developed and explored.

  In addition, to support the designers of single-chip based embedded systems, which includes multiprocessor platforms running dedicated real-time operating systems (RTOS's) as well as the effects of on-chip interconnect network, a system-level modelling/simulation environment is required to support an analysis of the:

  o consequences of different mappings of tasks to processors (software or hardware),

  o network performance under different traffic and load conditions,

  o effects of different RTOS selections, including various scheduling, synchronization and resource allocation policies.

The traditional network models like OPNET [81] are not suited for NoC's, since they model only the abstract communication structure without any support for chip-level architecture modelling. In [78] and [79], the concept of on-chip, packet-switched micro-networks has been introduced that borrows ideas from the layered design methodology for data networks. The work on the system-level exploration of the communication architecture can be subdivided into static analysis models [82, 83] and simulation-based models [84, 85]. Lahiri et al. [86] have proposed a hybrid model combining simulation with analytical post-processing to achieve higher accuracy of the performance estimation. The SystemC Open Core Protocol (SOCP) communication channel in the StepNP simulation model [87] addresses the exploration of the communication infrastructure based on the OCP semantics. Serge Goosens et al. [88] further abstract from architecture-specific communication primitives to establish a unified modelling framework for the investigation of heterogeneous on-chip networks. The NoC modelling framework proposed in [9] deals with generalized abstract tasks, processing elements, and communication infrastructures instead of dealing with each specific application and system architecture. This not only broadens the applicability of the modelling framework, but also leads to a better understanding of the problem at hand.

The current NoC modelling approaches do not cope with the requirements introduced by the system-level design of full-fledged on-chip networks. In order to apply analytical models, enhanced algorithms are necessary to model the performance of complex network topologies with sophisticated arbitration mechanisms. Equally, current NoC simulation models fall short to provide efficient support for the exploration of on-chip networks.

- *Sensor Networks*: The recent advances in low-power embedded processors, radios, and micro-electromechanical systems (MEMS) have made possible the development of networks of wirelessly interconnected sensors. The new computing paradigm enabled by the ad hoc wireless sensor networks will be a key in making computation more proactive. The silicon-based wireless sensors and the ad hoc sensor networks represent exciting new technologies with broad societal impacts and a wide range of new commercial opportunities. As the wireless sensor technology continues to advance, one day, it will be possible to have these compact, low-cost wireless sensors embedded throughout the environment, in homes, offices, and ultimately inside people. With the continued advances in power management, these systems should find more numerous and more impressive applications. Until that day, there is a rich set of research problems associated with the distributed wireless sensors that require very different solutions than the traditional sensors and multimedia devices [70].

    With their focus on the applications requiring a tight coupling with the physical world, as opposed to the personal communication focus of conventional wireless networks, the wireless sensor networks pose significantly different design, implementation, and deployment challenges. Their application-specific nature, severe resource limitations, long network life requirements, and the presence of sensors lead to an interesting interplay between sensing, communication, power consumption, and topology that the designers need to consider. Energy dissipation, scalability, and latency must all be considered in designing network protocols for collaboration and information sharing, system partitioning, and low-power electronics design [10].

    The existing tools for modelling wireless networks focus only on the communication problem and do not support the modelling of power and sensing aspects that are essential to the design of wireless sensor networks. A model of computation is of prime importance as a clean starting point for the synthesis of modern computing platforms. The wireless sensor networks will not only require new models of computation, but also new models of the physical world.

    In the design automation domain, synthesis of the nodes for the wireless sensor networks will pose a number of new problems. Moreover, debugging and verification are the most expensive and time-consuming components in the modern design flow. Due to the heterogeneous nature and the complex interaction between the components, it is expected that the same will be true for the nodes of the wireless sensor networks. In particular, the techniques for error and fault detection and testing collaboration will be of prime importance.

Middleware will be in strong demand to enable the development of new applications. Tasks such as sensor data filtering, data compression, data fusion, data searching and profiling, exposure coverage, and tracking will be ubiquitous. It is expected that new tasks will be defined and accomplished, for example, sensor allocation and selection, sensor positioning, sensor assignment and efficient techniques for the sensor data storage [11].

In the software domain, main emphasis will be on the RTOS's (Real-Time Operating Systems). There is a need for an ultra-aggressive, low-power management due to the energy constraints and a need for comprehensive resource accounting due to the demands for privacy and security and, in a number of cases, the support for mobility-related functions as well. There is also a need for the overall energy consumption balanced architectures. Another issue is the wireless sensor organization and the development of interfaces between the components. Finally, due to the privacy, security, and authentication concerns, techniques like unique ID's for the CPU and other components can be of high importance.

Assessment

In order for a high-level modelling environment to be effective for design exploration, it must be abstract, or high enough to enable rapid design trade-offs, but detailed enough to include a time basis for performance modelling.

The development of a general theoretical modelling framework for component-based engineering is one of the few grand challenges in information sciences and technologies. The lack of such a framework is the main obstacle to mastering the complexity of heterogeneous systems. It seriously limits the current state of the practice, as attested by the lack of development platforms consistently integrating design activities and the often prohibitive cost of validation.

A major factor limiting the use of parallel computing platforms in the mainstream computing is the lack of general-purpose parallel computation models. Moreover, some specialists who believe that finding a unifying computation model is just not possible have gone in another direction, developing parallel software that lacks portability.

On the software side, the architecture differences in the parallel computing platforms correspond to a large set of different parallel models and languages often architecture-dependent and that offer only partial solutions to programming portable parallel applications in sequential computing using standard languages like C, Pascal, and Fortran. Many parallel programming languages used today are of the low-level variety that require of the programmer to face the architectural issues of the parallel computing platform on which the application executes.

On the other hand, high-level parallel languages abstract from architectural issues but deliver unpredictable performance on different architectures. Thus porting the same program to different parallel computation platforms from, say, a message-passing multi-computer to a shared-memory multi-processor can dramatically alter the platform's performance.

Existing component technologies encompass a restricted number of interaction types and execution models, for instance, interaction by method calls under asynchronous execution. We lack concepts and tools allowing integration of synchronous and asynchronous components, as well as different interaction mechanisms, such as communication via shared variables, signals, rendezvous. This is essential for modern systems engineering, where applications are initially developed as systems of interacting components, from which implementations are derived as the result of a co-design analysis.

The application of component-based design techniques raises two strongly related and hard problems. First, the development of a theory for building complex heterogeneous systems. Heterogeneity exists in the different types of component interaction, such as strict (blocking) or non strict, data driven or event driven, atomic or non atomic and in the different execution models, such as synchronous or asynchronous. Second, the development of theory for building systems which are correct by construction, especially with respect to essential and generic properties such as deadlock-freedom or progress. In practical terms, this means that the theory supplies rules for reasoning on the structure of a system and for ensuring that such properties hold globally under some assumptions about its constituents e.g. components, connectors. Tractable correctness by construction results can provide significant guidance in the design process. Their lack leaves a posteriori verification of the designed system as the only means to ensure its correctness (with the well-known limitations).

Co-design for system-level modelling has been limited by the view that all computation should be restricted to the reactive system models – mathematical models of computation unified by the event or token-based foundations. The resulting executable specifications are designed to respond to testbench-style inputs that model the external environment in which the system is intended to operate. The presumptions are that the computer system being designed is passive and it should be isolated from its operating environment.

Trends

Finding solutions to the problems and limitations in parallel computation requires two actions:

- Make the design and implementation of general-purpose parallel computing platforms capable of supporting a wide range of programming models and providing predictable performance.
- Make the definition of programming models architecture-independent, allowing abstraction and portability across different parallel computing platforms. At the same time, make these models simple and expressive.

An important step to success is the definition of high-level, architecture-independent languages to demonstrate that parallel programming is no more difficult than sequential programming.

Low-level approaches, such as Parallel Virtual Machine (PVM) and Message Passing Interface (MPI), are driven by heterogeneous parallel computing, which tries to offer, on different computers, library primitives for parallelism and communication. These approaches partly meet the portability goal but are based on tedious low-level library functions and do not free the programmer from the issues of concurrency, communication, and synchronization. In fact, even though the PVM and the MPI are the de facto standards in parallel programming, their related programming style looks in many respects like the assembler-level programming in sequential computing.

However, several proposed high-level approaches – the Bulk Synchronous Parallel (BSP), the LogP, and the Bird-Meertens Formalism – may represent good candidates for architecture-independent programming models on general-purpose computers.

Other promising models are the skeleton-based and the actor-based languages. Although these models suffer from low performance, they represent an interesting starting point toward architecture-independence because they abstract from architectural issues and allow predictable performance. If the parallel programming community convinces itself that it needs a clear strategy based on high-level languages to find a unifying model for parallel computation, these models can be used to drive this process. Adopting this strategy would unite high-level programming, generality, and high-performance, leading parallel computation to the computing mainstream [12].

Increasingly, the operating environment of a computer system is another computer system. Accordingly, next generation computer system modelling must be based not only on the reaction of a passive computer system to its operating environment, but upon the active cooperation and coordination – sharing – across model boundaries such as resources. Computer system designers must be able to capture the sharing effects or the anticipated interactions of concurrent software executing on multiple hardware resources over a range of design variations. More than understanding the response of the system, this is about understanding the response of the design.

Searching a complex design space for designs that satisfy performance criteria can be thought of as isolating and analyzing the prevalent performance models that arise between the corner cases in a design space. To fully analyze a computer system, the designers must isolate these prevalent performance models and the ranges over which they are valid. A designer can then understand the effects of software loading, resource variations, and resource sharing [5].

A grand unified approach to modelling computing platforms systems would seek a modelling framework that serves all purposes. One approach is to create the union of all the frameworks, which have been proposed so far, providing all of their services in one bundle. But the resulting framework would be extremely complex and difficult to use, and designing and synthesis and validation tools would be difficult. A more feasible alternative is to choose one concurrent framework and show that all the others are the special cases of that. This is relatively easy to do – in theory. Most of these frameworks are sufficiently expressive to subsume most of the others. The disadvantage is that this approach does not acknowledge each model's strengths and weaknesses.

A final alternative is to mix frameworks either heterogeneously but instead of forming the union of their services, preserve their distinct identity, or hierarchically where a component in one framework is actually an aggregate of components in another [6].

These are but a few of the interesting research problems for modelling computation platforms for embedded systems. There are many more. Modelling configurable computation platforms offers interesting opportunities and challenges and potentially relates strongly to the problem of selecting appropriate computational models.

As mentioned above, there are also interesting and challenging problems in the modelling of networks, particularly providing quality-of-service guarantees in the face of unreliable resources. Finally, models are required to develop appropriate hardware and software design techniques that minimize power consumption which are critical for portable devices and wireless microsensor networks.

References

[1]   Francis Cottet, Joëlle Delacroix, Claude Kaiser, and Zoubir Mammeri, Scheduling in Real-Time Systems. John Wiley & Sons Ltd., 2002.

[2]   Jane W. S. Liu, Real-Time Systems, Prentice-Hall Inc., 2000.

[3]   Duncan K. G. Campbell, A Survey of Models of Parallel Computation, University of York Report, Page 1-37, March 19, 1997.

[4]   David B. Skillicorn and Domenico Talia, Models and Languages for Parallel Computation, ACM Computing Surveys, Vol. 30, No. 2, Page 124-169, June 1998.

[5]   Neal K. Tibrewala, JoAnn M. Paul, and Donald E. Thomas, Modeling and Evaluation of Hardware/Software Designs, Proceedings of the Ninth International Symposium on Hardware/Software Codesign, 2001, Pages 11-16, 2001.

[6]   Edward A. Lee, What's Ahead for Embedded Software?, IEEE Computer, Pages 18-26, September 2000.

[7]   Joseph Sifakis, Modeling Real-Time Systems, EMSOFT01, Tahoe City, October 2001. Lecture Notes in Computer Science 2211.

[8]   Gregor Gossler, Compositional Modeling of Real-Time Systems – Theory and Practice, Ph.D. Thesis, Université Joseph Fourier, Grenoble, Pages 1-141, September 2001.

[9]   Jan Madsen, Shankar Mahadevan, and Kashif Virk, Network-on-Chip Modeling for System-level Multiprocessor Simulation, The 24th IEEE Real-Time Systems Symposium, December 3-5 2003.

[10]   Alice Wang, Rex Min, Masayuki Miyazaki, Amit Sinha, and Anantha Chanrakasan, Low-Power Sensor Networks, Book Chapter in The Applications of Programmable DSP's in Mobile Communications, John Wiley & Sons, 2002.

[11]   Jessica Feng, Farinaz Koushanfar, and Miodrag Potkonjak, System-Architectures for Sensor Networks – Issues, Alternatives, and Directions, International Conference on Computer Design (ICCD 2002), September 2002.

[12]   Domenico Talia, Parallel Computation Still not Ready for the Mainstream, ACM, July 1997, vol 40, no. 7, p 98(2).

[13]   V. Bertin, M. Poize, and J. Sifakis. Towards Validated Real-Time Software. In Proc. 12th EuroMicro Conference on Real Time Systems, pages 157-164, 2000.

[14]   P. Niebert and S. Yovine. Computing Optimal Operation Schemes for Chemical Plants in Multi-Batch Mode. In Proceedings of Hybrid Systems, Computation and Control, volume 1790 of LNCS. Springer-Verlag, 2000.

[15]   P. J. Ramadge and W. M. Wonham. Supervisory Control of a Class of Discrete-Event Processes. SIAM J. Control and Optimization, 25(1), 1987.

[16]   E. Asarin, O. Maler, and A. Pnueli. Symbolic Controller Synthesis for Discrete and Timed Systems. In Proc. Hybrid Systems II, volume 999 of LNCS. Springer-Verlag, 1995.

[17]   O. Maler, A. Pnueli, and J. Sifakis. On the Synthesis of Discrete Controllers for Timed Systems. In E.W. Mayr and C. Puech, Editors, STACS'95, volume 900 of LNCS, pages 229-242. Springer-Verlag, 1995.

[18]   K. Altisen. Génération automatique d'ordonnancements des systèmes temporisés. Master's Thesis, ENSIMAG, INPG, Grenoble, France, 1998. In French.

[19]   S. Tripakis and K. Altisen. On the Controller Synthesis for Discrete and Dense-Time Systems. In J. M. Wing, J. Woodcock, and J. Davies, Editors, Proc. Formal Methods '99, volume 1708 of LNCS, pages 233-252. Springer-Verlag, 1999.

[20]   T. A. Henzinger, X. Nicollin, J. Sifakis, and S. Yovine. Symbolic Model-Checking for Real-Time Systems. In Proc. 7th Symposium on Logics in Computer Science (LICS'92) and Information and Computation, volume 111, pages 193-244, 1994.

[21]   R. Alur, C. Courcoubetis, N. Halbwachs, T. Henzinger, P. Ho, X. Nicollin, A. Olivero, J. Sifakis, , and S. Yovine. The Algorithmic Analysis of Hybrid Systems. Theoretical Computer Science, 138:3-34, 1995.

[22]   A. Bouajjani, S.Tripakis, and S.Yovine. On-the-fly Symbolic Model-Checking for Real-Time Systems. In Proc. IEEE Real-Time Systems Symposium, RTSS'97. IEEE Computer Society Press, 1997.

[23]   H.-H. Kwak, I. Lee, A. Philippou, J.-Y. Choi, and O. Sokolsky. Symbolic Schedulability Analysis of Real-Time Systems. In Proc. RTSS 1998, pages 409-418. IEEE Computer Society Press, 1998.

[24]   S. Tripakis. L'Analyse Formelle des Systemes Temporises en Pratique. PhD Thesis, Universite Joseph Fourier, Grenoble, France, 1998.

[25]   P. Pettersson. Modeling and Verification of Real-Time Systems Using Timed Automata: Theory and Practice. PhD thesis, Uppsala University, 1999.

[26]   C. Daws, A. Olivero, S. Tripakis, and S. Yovine. The Tool Kronos. In Hybrid Systems III, Verification and Control, volume 1066 of LNCS, pages 208-219. Springer-Verlag, 1996.

[27]   S. Yovine. KRONOS: A Verification Tool for Real-Time Systems. Software Tools for Technology Transfer, 1(1+2):123-133, 1997.

[28]   K. G. Larsen, P. Pettersson, and W. Yi. Uppaal in a Nutshell. International Journal on Software Tools for Technology Transfer, 1(1-2):134-152, 1997.

[29]   H. Jensen, K.G. Larsen, and A. Skou. Scaling up Uppaal: Automatic Verification of Real-Time Systems Using Compositionality and Abstraction. In Proc. FTRTFT 2000, LNCS. Springer-Verlag, 2000.

[30]   S. Campos, E. Clarke, W. Marrero, and M. Minea. Verus: a Tool for Quantitative Analysis of Finite-State Real-Time Systems. In Proc. Workshop on Languages, Compilers and Tools for Real-Time Systems, 1995.

[31]   R. H. Hardin, Z. Har'El, and R. P. Kurshan. COSPAN. In R. Alur and T. A. Henzinger, Editors, Proc. CAV'96, volume 1102 of LNCS, pages 423-427. Springer-Verlag, 1996.

[32]   T.A. Henzinger, P.II. Ilo, and H. Wong-Toi. HyTech: A Model Checker for Hybrid Systems. In Software Tools for Technology Transfer, pages 110-122, 1997.

[33]   G. Bucci and E. Vicario. Compositional Validation of Time-Critical Systems Using Communicating Time Petri Nets. IEEE Transactions on Software Engineering, 21(12), 1995.

[34]   A. K. Mok, D.-C. Tsou, and R. C. M. de Rooij. The MSP.RTL Real-Time Scheduler Synthesis Tool. IEEE, pages 118-128, 1996.

[35]   G. P. Brat and V. K. Garg. Analyzing Non-Deterministic Real-Time Systems with (max,+) Algebra. In Proc. RTSS'98, pages 210-219, 1998.

[36]   H. Dierks. Synthesizing Controllers from Real-Time Specifications. IEEE Transactions on Computer-Aided Design of Integrated Circuits and Systems, 18(1):33-43, 1999.

[37]   E. A. Lee. Modeling Concurrent Real-Time Processes using Discrete Events. Annals of Software Engineering, Special Volume on Real-Time Software Engineering, 1998.

[38]   S. Vestal. Modeling and Verification of Real-Time Software using Extended Linear Hybrid Automata. Technical Report, Honeywell Technology Center, 1999.

[39]   J. C. Corbett. Timing Analysis of Ada Tasking Programs. IEEE Transactions on Software Engineering, 22(7), 1996.

[40]   G. S. Avrunin, J. C. Corbett, and L. K. Dillon. Analyzing Partially-Implemented Real-Time Systems. IEEE Transactions on Software Engineering, 24(8), 1998.

[41]   K. Lundqvist and L. Asplund. A Formal Model of a Run-Time Kernel for Ravenscar. In Proc. 6th International Conference on Real-Time Computing Systems and Applications – RTCSA'99, pages 504-507, 1999.

[42]   K. Lundqvist, L. Asplund, and S. Michell. A Formal Model of the Ada Ravenscar Tasking Profile; Protected Objects. In Proc. Ada-Europe '99, LNCS. Springer-Verlag, 1999.

[43]   B. Dobbing and A. Burns. The Ravenscar Tasking Profile for High-Integrity Real-Time Programs. In Proc. ACM SigAda Annual Conference, pages 1-6. ACM Press, 1998.

[44]   E. A. Lee et al. Overview of the Ptolemy Project. Technical Report UCB/ERL M01/11, University of California at Berkeley, 2001.

[45]   R. Ernst, D. Ziegenbein, K. Richter, L. Thiele, and J. Teich. Hardware/Software Co-Design of Embedded Systems – The SPI Workbench. In Proc. Int. Workshop on VLSI, Orlando, Florida, 1999.

[46]   T. A. Henzinger, B. Horowitz, and C. Meyer Kirsch. Embedded Control Systems Development with Giotto. In Proc. LCTES 2001, 2001.

[47]   E. Closse, M. Poize, J. Pulou, J. Sifakis, P. Venier, D. Weil, and S. Yovine. TAXYS = ESTEREL + KRONOS. A Tool for the Development and Verification of Real-Time Embedded Systems. In Proc. CAV'01, volume 2102 of LNCS, pages 391-395. Springer-Verlag, 2001.

[48]   G. Berry and G. Gonthier. The ESTEREL Synchronous Programming Language: Design, Semantics, Implementation. Science of Computer Programming, 19(2):87-152, 1992.

[49]   D. Weil, V. Bertin, E. Closse, M. Poize, P. Vernier, and J. Pulou. Efficient Compilation of Esterel for Real-Time Embedded Systems. In Proc. CASES'2000, 2000.

[50]   G. Bhat, R. Cleaveland, and G. Lüttgen. A Practical Approach to Implementing Real-Time Semantics. ASE, 7:127-155, 1999.

[51]   R. Milner. Communication and Concurrency. Prentice Hall, 1989.

[52]   A. N. Fredette and R. Cleaveland. RTSL: A Language for Real-Time Schedulability Analysis. In Proc. RTSS'93, pages 274-283. Computer Society Press, 1993.

[53]   I. Lee, P. Brémond-Grégoire, and R. Gerber. A Process Algebraic Approach to the Specification and Analysis of Resource-bound Real-Time Systems. Proceedings of the IEEE, Special Issue on Real-Time Systems, 1 1994.

[54]   P. Brémond-Grégoire and I. Lee. A Process Algebra of Communicating Shared Resources with Dense Time and Priorities. Theoretical Computer Science, 189, 1997.

[55]   H. Ben-Abdallah, I. Lee, and O. Sokolsky. Specification and Analysis of Real-Time Systems with Paragon. In Annals of Software Engineering, 1999.

[56]   H. Ben-Abdallah, J.-Y. Choi, D. Clarke, Y. Si Kim, I. Lee, and H.-L. Xie. A Process Algebraic Approach to the Schedulability Analysis of Real-Time Systems. Real-Time Systems, 15(3):189-219, 1998.

[57]   L. Sha, R. Rajkumar, and J. P. Lehoczky. Priority Inheritance Protocols: An Approach to Real-Time Synchronization. IEEE Transactions on Computers, 39(9):1175-1185, 1990.

[58]   T. Janowski and M. Joseph. Dynamic Scheduling and Fault-Tolerance: Specification and Verification. Int. Journal of Time-Critical Computing Systems, 20:51-81, 2001.

[59]   C. Ericsson, A. Wall, and W. Yi. Timed Automata as Task Models for Event-Driven Systems. In Proc. RTCSA'99. IEEE Computer Society Press, 1999.

[60]   V. A. Braberman. Modeling and Checking Real-Time System Designs. PhD Thesis, Departamento de Computación, Universidad de Buenos Aires, Buenos Aires, Argentina, 2000.

[61]   S. Vestal. Meta-H Support for Real-Time Multi-Processor Avionics. In Proc. IEEE Workshop on Parallel and Distributed Real-Time Systems, pages 11-21, 1997.

[62]   S. Vestal. Fixed-Priority Sensitivity Analysis for Linear Compute-Time Models. IEEE Transactions on Software Engineering, 20(4):308-317, 1994.

[63]   P. Binns. Incremental Rate Monotonic Scheduling for Improved Control System Performance. In Proc. RTSS'97, pages 80-90, 1997.

[64]   C. Fidge, O. Kearney, and M. Utting. Interactively Verifying a Simple Real-Time Scheduler. In P. Wolper, Editor, Proc. CAV'95, volume 939 of LNCS. Springer-Verlag, 1995.

[65]   B. Dutertre. Formal Analysis of the Priority Ceiling Protocol. In IEEE Real-Time Systems Symposium (RTSS'00), pages 151-160, 2000.

[66]   B. Dutertre and V. Stavridou. Formal Analysis for Real-Time Scheduling. In 19th AIAA/IEEE Digital Avionics Systems Conference, 2000.

[67]   Z. Liu and M. Joseph. Specification and Verification of Fault-Tolerance, Timing, and Scheduling. ACM Transactions on Programming Languages and Systems, 21(1):46-89, 1999.

[68]   Z. Liu and M. Joseph. Verification, Refinement and Scheduling of Real-Time Programs. TCS, 253:119-152, 2001.

[69]   L. Lamport. The Temporal Logic of Actions. ACM Transactions on Programming Languages and Systems, 16(3):872-923, 1994.

[70]   Andreas Savvides, Sung Park, and Mani B. Srivastava, On Modeling Networks of Wireless Microsensors, ACM, 2001.

[71]   Communication Architecture Synthesis of Packet-Switched Network-on-Chip

[72]   Praveen Bhojwani and Rabi Mahapatra, Interfacing Cores with On-Chip Packet-Switched Networks, IEEE, 2003.

[73]   Luca Benini and Giovanni De Micheli, Powering Networks on Chips, ISSS 2001, October 1-3, 2001, Pages 33-38.

[74]   Jingcao Hu and Radu Marculescu, Energy-Aware Mapping for Tile-based NoC Architectures under Performance Constraints.

[75]   Bart Vermeulen, John Dielissen, Kees Goosens, and Calin Ciordas, Bringing Communication Networks on Chip: Test and Verification Implications.

[76]   Mohoon Nuhvi and Andre Ivanov, A Packet Switching Communication-based Test Access Mechanism for System Chips, Pages 1-6.

[77]   Tudor Dumitras, Sam Kerner, Radu Marculescu, Towards On-Chip Fault-Tolerant Communication.

[78]   Luca Benini and Giovanni De Micheli, Networks on Chips: A New SoC Paradigm, IEEE Computer 2002, Pages 70-78.

[79]   William J. Dally and Brian Towles, Route Packets, Not Wires: On-Chip Interconnection Networks, DAC 2001.

[80]   Paul Wielage and Kees Goosens, Networks on Silicon: Blessing or Nightmare?

[81]   OPNET. http://www.opnet.com

[82]   M. Gasteiner and M. Glessner, Bus-based Communication Synthesis on System-level, AM Trans. Design Automation Electronic Systems, pages 1-11, January 1999.

[83]   Peter Voigt Knudsen and Jan Madsen, Integrating Communication Protocol Selection with Partitioning in Hardware/Software Codesign, In Proc. Int. Symp. On System Synthesis, 1998.

[84]   K. Hines and G. Borriello, Dynamic Communication Models in Embedded System Cosimulation, In Proceedings of the Design Automation Conference (DAC), 1997.

[85]   A. Baghdadi, D. Lyonnard, N.-E. Zergainoh, and A. Jerraya, An Efficient Architecture Model for Systematic Design of Application-Specific Multiprocessor SoCs. In Proc. Int. Conference on Design Automation and Test in Europe (DATE), 2001.

[86]   K. Lahiri, A. Raghunathan, and S. Dey, Performance Analysis of Systems with Multi-Channel Communication Architectures, In Proc. Int. Conf. VLSI Design, pages 530-537, 2000.

[87]   Pierre G. Paulin, Chuck Pilkington, and Essaid Bensoudane, StepNP: A System-level Exploration Platform for Network Processors, IEEE Design & Test of Computers, 19(6):17-26, Dec 2002.

[88]   Serge Goosens, Tim Kogel, Malte Doerper, Andreas Wieferink, Rainer Laupers, Gerd Ascheid, and Heinrich Meyr, A Modular Simulation Framework for Architectural Exploration of On-Chip Interconnection Networks.

29.2   Distributed Embedded Real-Time Systems – Analysis and Exploration

This section addresses the analysis and design of distributed hard real-time systems that implement safety-critical applications where timing constraints are of utmost importance to the correct behaviour of the application.

Aspects of hard real-time systems are also covered in Part I.

Hard real-time systems: Real-time systems have been classified as *hard* real-time and *adaptive* real-time systems. Basically, hard real-time systems are systems where failing to meet a timing constraint can potentially have catastrophic consequences. For example, a brake-by-wire system in a car failing to react within a given time interval can result in a fatal accident. On the other hand, a multimedia system, which is an adaptive real-time system, can, under certain circumstances, tolerate a certain amount of delays resulting maybe in a patchier picture, without serious consequences besides some possible inconvenience to the user.

Distributed architecture: Many real-time applications, following physical, modularity or safety constraints, are implemented using *distributed architectures*. Such systems are composed of several different types of hardware components (called *nodes*), interconnected in a network. For such systems, the communication between the functions implemented on different nodes has an important impact on the overall system properties such as performance, cost, maintainability, etc.

The complexity of distributed embedded real-time systems is growing at a very high pace, and the constraints—in terms of functionality, performance, reliability, cost and time-to-market—are getting tighter. Therefore, the task of designing such systems is becoming increasingly important and difficult at the same time. New design techniques are needed, which are able to:

- successfully manage the complexity of embedded systems,
- meet the constraints imposed by the application domain,
- shorten the time-to-market, and
- reduce development and manufacturing costs.

Landscape

Designing and developing an electronic system like, for example, an automotive application, is not the sole responsibility of the system integrator. Suppliers provide many of the components (*electronic control unit*, ECU), and the task of the manufacturer is to integrate the different components. The design of real-time embedded components is mainly done independently by the suppliers, which concentrate on developing components that perform as efficiently as possible their dedicated functions.

System Architecture
- **Hardware architecture:** Currently, distributed real-time systems are implemented using architectures where each node is dedicated to the implementation of a single function or class of functions. The complete system can be, in general, composed of several networks, interconnected with each other (see Figure 32.1). Each network has its own communication protocol, and inter-network communication is via a *gateway* which is a node connected to both networks. The architecture can contain several such networks, having different types of topologies.
- A network is composed of several different types of hardware components, called *nodes*. Typically, every node (ECU) has a communication controller, CPU, RAM, ROM and an I/O interface to sensors and actuators. Nodes can also have ASICs in order to accelerate parts of their functionality. The microcontrollers used in a node and the type of network protocol employed are influenced by the nature of the functionality and the imposed real-time, fault-tolerant and power constraints

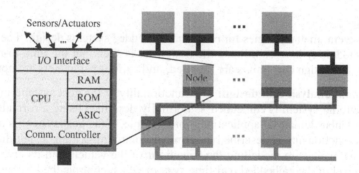

Figure 32.1. Distributed Hard Real-Time Systems

- **Real-time communication protocols:** As the communications become a critical component, new protocols are needed that can cope with the high bandwidth and predictability required.

  There are several communication protocols for real-time networks. Among the protocols that have been proposed for vehicle multiplexing only the Controller Area Network (CAN) [11], the Local Interconnection Network (LIN) [33], and SAE's J1850 [57] are currently in use on a large scale. Moreover, only a few of them are suitable for safety-critical applications where predictability is mandatory [56]. A survey and comparison of communication protocols for safety-critical embedded systems is available in [56]. Communication activities can be triggered either dynamically, in response to an event, or statically, at predetermined moments in time.

- Therefore, on one hand, there are protocols that schedule the messages statically based on the progression of time, for example, the SAFEbus [21] and SPIDER [39] protocols for the avionics industry, and the TT-CAN [22] and Time-Triggered Protocol (TTP) [28] intended for the automotive industry.
- On the other hand, there are several communication protocols where message scheduling is performed dynamically, such as Controller Area Network (CAN) used in a large number of application areas including automotive electronics, LonWorks [13] and Profibus [49] for real-time systems in general, etc. Out of these, CAN is the most well known and widespread event-driven communication protocol in the area of distributed embedded real-time systems.
- However, there is also a hybrid type of communication protocols, such as Byte-flight [10] introduced by BMW for automotive applications and the FlexRay protocol [17], that allows the sharing of the bus by event-driven and time-driven messages.

The time-triggered protocols have the advantage of simplicity and predictability, while event-triggered protocols are flexible and have low cost. Moreover, protocols like TTP offer fault-tolerant services necessary in implementing safety-critical applications. However, recent research [66] has shown that event-driven protocols like CAN are also predictable, and fault-tolerant services can also be offered on top of protocols like the TT-CAN. A hybrid communication protocol like FlexRay offers some of the advantages of both worlds.

Main Design Tasks

There are several methodologies for real-time embedded systems design. The aim of a design methodology is to coordinate the design tasks such that the time-to-market is minimized, the design constraints are satisfied, and various parameters are optimized.

- **Functional analysis and design:** The functionality of the host system, into which the electronic system is embedded, is normally described using a formalism from that particular domain of application. For example, if the host system is a vehicle, then its functionality is described in terms of control algorithms using differential equations, which are modelling the behaviour of the vehicle and its environment. At the level of the embedded real-time system which controls the host system, the functionality is typically described as a set of functions, accepting certain inputs and producing some output values.

  The typical automotive application is a control application. The controller reads inputs from sensors, and uses the actuators to control the physical environment (the vehicle). A controller can have several modes of operation, and can interact with other electronic functions, or with the driver through switches and instruments.

  During the functional analysis and design stage, the desired functionality is specified, analyzed and decomposed into sub-functions based on the experience of the designer. Several suppliers and manufacturers have started to use tools like Statemate [59], Matlab/Simulink [37], ASCET/SD [3] and SystemBuild/MatrixX

[61] for describing the functionality, in order to eliminate the ambiguities and to avoid producing incomplete or incoherent specifications.

At the level of functional analysis the exploration is currently limited to evaluating several alternative control algorithms for solving the control problem. Once the functionality has been captured using tools like Matlab/Simulink, useful explorations can involve simulations of executable specifications in order to determine the correctness of the behaviour, and to assess certain properties of chosen solutions.

- **Architecture selection**: The architecture selection task decides what components to include in the hardware architecture and how these components are connected.

  There is virtually no exploration involved, as, according to current practice, architecture selection is an *ad-hoc* process, based on the experience of the designer and previous product versions.

- **Mapping**: The mapping task has to decide what part of the functionality should be implemented on which of the selected components.

  The manufacturers integrate components from suppliers, and thus the design space is severely restricted by the fact that the mapping of functionality to an ECU is fixed.

- **Software design and implementation**: This is the phase in which the software is designed and the code is written. The code for the functions is developed manually for efficiency reasons, and thus the exploration that would be allowed by automatic code generation is limited.

  At this stage the correctness of the software is analysed through simulations, but there is no analysis of timing constraints, which is left for the scheduling and schedulability analysis stage.

- **Scheduling and schedulability analysis:** Once the functions have been defined and the code has been written, the scheduling task is responsible for determining the execution order of the functions *inside an ECU*, such that the timing constraints are satisfied.

  The analysis and exploration techniques employed depend on the scheduling paradigm and the model of the functionality used. The scheduling and mapping design tasks take as input a model of the functionality consisting of sets of interacting processes. A *process* is a sequence of computations (corresponding to several building blocks in a programming language) which starts when all its inputs are available. When it finishes executing, the process produces its output values. Processes can be pre-emptable or non pre-emptable. *Non pre-emptable* processes are processes that cannot be interrupted during their execution. *Pre-emptable* processes can be can be interrupted during their execution. For example, a higher priority process has to be activated to service an event, in this case, the lower priority process will be temporary pre-empted until the higher priority process finishes its execution.

  The aim of a schedulability analysis is to determine *sufficient* and *necessary* conditions under which an application is schedulable. An application is *schedulable* if there exists at least one scheduling algorithm that is able to produce a feasible schedule. A schedule is *feasible* if all processes can be completed within the specified constraints.

However, before such analysis techniques can be used the worst-case execution times of functions have to be determined. The designer can provide manually such worst-case times, or tools can be used in order to determine the worst-case execution time of a piece of code on a given processor [36]. For example, one such tool is the aiT analyzer [1].

There are several approaches to scheduling:

o *Static cyclic scheduling* algorithms are used to build, off-line, a schedule table with activation times for each process, such that the timing constraints of processes are satisfied.

o Fixed priority scheduling (FPS). In this scheduling approach each process has a fixed (static) priority which is computed off-line. The decision on which ready process to activate is taken on-line according to their priority.

o Earliest deadline first (EDF). In this case, that process will be activated which has the nearest deadline.

For static cyclic scheduling, if building the schedule table fulfills the timing constraints, the application is schedulable. In the context of on-line scheduling methods there are basically two approaches to the schedulability analysis: utilization-based tests, and response-time analysis.

o The *utilization tests* use the *utilization* of a process (its worst-case execution time relative to its period) in order to determine if the process set is schedulable.

o A *response time analysis* has two steps. In the first step, the analysis derives the worst-case response time of each process (the time it takes from the moment is ready for execution, until it has finished executing). The second step compares the worst case response time of each process to its deadline and, if the response times are smaller or equal to the deadlines, the system is schedulable.

Another important distinction is between two basic design approaches for real-time systems, the event-triggered and time-triggered approaches.

o *Time-Triggered:* In the time-triggered approach activities are initiated at predetermined points in time. In a distributed time-triggered system it is assumed that the clocks of all nodes are synchronized to provide a global notion of time. Time-triggered systems are typically implemented using *non-preemptive static cyclic scheduling*, where the process activation or message communication is done based on a schedule table built off-line.

o *Event-Triggered:* In the event-triggered approach activities happen when a significant change of state occurs. Event-triggered systems are typically implemented using *preemptive priority-based scheduling*, or *earliest deadline first*, where, as response to an event, the appropriate process is invoked to service it.

There has been a long debate in the real-time and embedded systems communities concerning the advantages of each approach [4], [28], [71]. Several aspects have been considered in favour of one or the other approach, such as flexibility, predictability, jitter control, processor utilization, and testability. An interesting comparison of the ET and TT approaches, from a more industrial, in particular automotive, perspective, can be found in [35]. The conclusion there is that one has to choose the right approach, depending on the particularities of the application. Thus, the automotive supplier will select, based on its own requirements, the scheduling policy to be used in their ECU.

Simulation is extensively used to determine if the timing constraints are satisfied. However, simulations are very time consuming and provide no guarantees that the timing constraints are met.

There is a large quantity of research [5], [7], [28] related to scheduling and schedulability analysis, with results having been incorporated in analysis tools such as TimeWiz [67], RapidRMA [51], RTA-OSEK Planner [55], and Aires [1]. The tools determine if the timing constraints of the functionality are met, and support the designer in exploring several design scenarios, and help to design optimized implementations.

In the context of static cyclic scheduling, deriving a schedule table is a complex design exploration problem. Static cyclic scheduling of a set of data dependent software processes on a multiprocessor architecture has been intensively researched [28], [71]. Such research has been used in commercial tools like TTP-Plan [42] which derives the static schedules for processes and messages in a time-triggered system using the time-triggered protocol for communication.

If fixed priority preemptive scheduling is used, exploration is used to determine how to allocate priorities to a set of distributed processes [20]. Their priority assignment heuristic is based on the schedulability analysis from [64]. For earliest deadline first the issue of distributing the global deadlines to local deadlines has to be addressed [23].

- **Integration:** In this phase the manufacturer has to integrate the ECUs from different suppliers. There is a lack of tools that can analyze the performance of the interacting functionality, and thus the manufacturer has to rely on simulation runs using the realistic environment of a prototype car. Detecting potential problems at such a late stage requires time-consuming extensive simulations. Moreover, once a problem is identified it takes a very long time to go through all the previous stages in order to fix it. This leads to large delays on the time-to-market.

  In order to reduce the large simulation times, and to guarantee that potential violations of timing constraints are detected, manufacturers have started to use in-house analysis tools and commercially available tools such as Volcano Network Architect (for the CAN and LIN buses) [69].

  Volcano makes inter-ECU communication transparent for the programmer. The programmer only deals with *signals* that have to be sent and received, and the details of the network are hidden. Volcano provides basic API calls for manipulating signals. To achieve interoperability between ECUs from different suppliers, Volcano uses a *publish/subscribe* model for defining the signal requirements. Published signals are made available to the system integrator by the suppliers, while subscribed signals are required as inputs to the ECU. The system integrator makes the publish/subscribe connections by creating a set of CAN frames, and creating a mapping between the data in frames and signals [50]. Volcano uses the analysis in [66] for bounding the communication delay of messages transmitted using the CAN bus.

- **Calibration, Testing, Verification**: These are the final stages of the design process. Because not enough analysis, testing and verification has been done in earlier stages of the design, these stages tend to be very time consuming, and problems identified here lead to large delays.

Assessment

Hard real-time applications are implemented using distributed architectures where, currently, each node of the architecture is responsible to implement one function. As functionality becomes more complex, in order to reduce costs and use the resources available efficiently, functions will have to be distributed over several nodes, and several functions will have to share on node.

Once a function is distributed over several nodes, communication has an important impact on the timing properties. Hence, it is imperative to use predictable, high bandwidth, communication protocols. Utilizing fully the available resources is only possible in the context of hardware/software independence, where a software function can be moved from one node to another. Such portability is achieved through the use of standards compliant operating systems and middleware.

In such a context, traditional design methodologies lead to sub-optimal implementations and large delays on the time-to-market. The limited analysis and exploration employed in the early design stages cannot handle the increasing complexity, the competing requirements in terms of cost, performance, reliability, maintainability, low power, etc., and thus severely restricts design space exploration leading to inefficient solutions. New methodologies are needed which address the design process at higher abstraction levels and encourage reuse.

In the case of mass market products cost reduction and short time-to-market is impossible without substantial reuse. The hardware architecture has to be reused, with some modifications, over several product cycles. Software functions have to be reused across product lines and over product cycles as well. Hence, new techniques are necessary which can help configure optimized hardware architectures, deal with the mapping of the distributed functionality to the hardware nodes, and handle the modification of legacy systems to support new functionality.

The success of such new design methods depends on the available analysis techniques. In order to (automatically) take informed design decisions, new, higher level, accurate analysis techniques are needed. Currently, the timing analysis at process level considers independent processes running on single processors. However, very often functionality consists of distributed processes that have data and control dependencies, exclusion constraints, etc. New schedulability analysis techniques are needed which can handle distributed applications, data and control dependencies, and accurately take into account the details of the communication protocols that have an important influence on the timing properties. Moreover, highly complex and safety critical applications can in the future be distributed across several networks, and can use different, heterogeneous, scheduling policies.

Current design practice does not take into account the impact of the communication infrastructure during the analysis and exploration. In order to improve the accuracy of the analysis and thoroughness of the exploration methods, the exact details of the communication protocols have to be considered. New, automatic analysis tools are required for the integration phase in order to handle the inter-node communication aspects.

Trends

- **Distributed functionality: As presented in section 28.1,** currently, in automotive electronics, there is a huge pressure to reduce the number of nodes by integrating several functions in one node and, at the same time, distribute certain functionality over several nodes (see Figure 32.2).

  Although an application is typically distributed over one single network, we begin to see applications that are distributed across several networks. For example, in Figure 32.2, the third application, represented as black dots, is distributed over two networks. This trend is driven by the need to further reduce costs, improve resource usage, but also by application constraints like having to be physically close to particular sensors and actuators. Moreover, not only are these applications distributed across networks, but their functions can exchange critical information through the gateway nodes.

  Such safety-critical hard real-time distributed applications running on heterogeneous distributed architectures are inherently difficult to analyze and design. Due to their distributed nature, the communication has to be carefully considered during the analysis and design in order to guarantee that the timing constraints are satisfied under the competing objective of reducing the cost of the implementation.

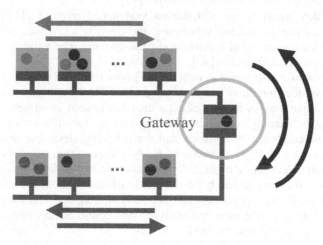

● Functions of the first application
● Functions of the second application

Figure 32.2. Distributed Safety-Critical Applications

Schedulability Analysis

- **Schedulability analysis for data dependent processes**: Current analysis tools consider a simple model of periodic independent processes, and use utilization based tests for FPS or EDF [34], depending on the type of scheduling employed. However, processes can be sporadic or aperiodic, are seldom independent, and normally they exhibit precedence and exclusion constraints. Knowledge regarding these dependencies can be used in order to improve the accuracy of schedulability analyses and the quality of the produced schedules [12].

It has been claimed [71] that static cyclic scheduling is the only approach that can provide efficient solutions to applications that exhibit data dependencies. However, advances in the area of fixed priority preemptive scheduling show that such applications can also be handled with other scheduling strategies [65].

One way of dealing with data dependencies between processes in the context of static priority based scheduling has been indirectly addressed by the extensions proposed for the schedulability analysis of distributed systems through the use of the *release jitter* [64]. Release jitter is the worst case delay between the arrival of a process and its release (when it is placed in the ready-queue for the processor) and can include the communication delay due to the transmission of a message on the communication channel.

In [65] and [73] time *offset* relationships and *phases*, respectively, are used in order to model data dependencies. Offset and phase are similar concepts that express the existence of a fixed interval in time between the arrivals of sets of processes. The authors show that by introducing such concepts into the computational model, the pessimism of the analysis is significantly reduced when bounding the time behaviour of the system. The concept of *dynamic offsets* has been later introduced and used to model data dependencies [41].

- **Schedulability analysis for distributed systems**: Tindell et al. [64] integrate processor and communication scheduling and provide a "holistic" schedulability analysis in the context of distributed real-time systems. The validity of the analysis has been later confirmed in [40].

  In the case of a distributed system the response time of a process also depends on the communication delay due to messages. In [64] the analysis for messages is done is a similar way as for processes: a message is seen as an non pre-emptable process that is "running" on a bus. The response time analyses for processes and messages are combined by realizing that the *jitter* (the delay between the *arrival* of a process—the time when becomes ready for execution—and the start of its execution) of a destination process depends on the *communication delay* (the time it takes for a message to reach the destination process, from the moment it has been produced by the sender process) between sending and receiving a message. Several researchers have provided analyses that bound the communication delay for a given communication protocol:

  o Controller area network protocol [66];
  o Time-division multiple access protocol [64];
  o Asynchronous transfer mode protocol [16];
  o Token ring protocol [60],
  o Fiber distributed data interface protocol [2];
  o Time-triggered protocol [43];
  o FlexRay protocol [45].

- **Heterogeneous scheduling policies**: Based on their own requirements, the suppliers choose one particular scheduling policy to be used. However, for certain applications, several scheduling approaches can be used together. Efficient implementation of new, highly sophisticated automotive applications, entails the use of time-triggered process sets together with event-triggered ones implemented on top of complex distributed architectures.

One approach to the design of such systems, is to allow ET and TT processes to share the same processor as well as static (TT) and dynamic (ET) communications to share the same bus. Bus sharing of TT and ET messages is supported by protocols which support both static and dynamic communication [17]. Researchers have addressed the problem of timing analysis for such systems [45].

A fundamentally different architectural approach to heterogeneous TT/ET systems is that of heterogeneous multi-clusters, where each cluster can be either TT or ET. In a *time-triggered cluster* processes and messages are scheduled according to a static cyclic policy, with the bus implementing a TDMA protocol such as, for example, the time-triggered protocol. On *event-triggered clusters* the processes are scheduled according to a priority based preemptive approach, while messages are transmitted using the priority-based CAN bus. In this context, researchers have proposed an approach to schedulability analysis for multi-cluster distributed embedded systems [46].

When several event-driven scheduling policies are used in a heterogeneous system, another approach to the verification of timing properties is to use the technique presented in [54] which couples the analysis of local scheduling strategies via an event interface model.

At the communication level, researchers have used simulation to evaluate the interplay of different scheduling approaches with a given communication protocol. The details of the communication protocol, including its arbitration policy, are described with a hierarchical tree-based language [38].

- **Extending the process model:** The current scheduling approaches capture the inter-process dependencies only in terms of dataflow.

  One drawback of dataflow process graphs is that they are not suitable to capture the control aspects of an application. For example, it can happen that the execution of some processes can also depend on conditions computed by previously executed processes. By explicitly capturing the control flow in the model, a more fine-tuned modelling and a tighter (less pessimistic) assignment of execution times to processes is possible, compared to traditional data-flow based approaches. With control dependencies, only a subset of the set of processes is executed during an invocation of the system, depending on the actual vaules of conditions.

  In the context of preemptive scheduling, *modes* have been used to model a certain class of control dependencies [18]. Such a model basically assumes that at the starting of an execution cycle, a particular functionality is known in advance and is fixed for one or several cycles until another mode change is performed. However, modes cannot handle fine grained control dependencies, or certain combinations of data and control dependencies. Careful modelling using the *periods* of processes (lower bound between subsequent re-arrivals of a process) can also be a solution for some cases of control dependencies [19]. If, for example, we know that a certain set of processes will only execute every second cycle of the system, we can set their periods to the double of the period of the rest of the processes in the system. However, using the worst case assumption on periods leads very often to unnecessarily pessimistic schedulability evaluations.

More refined process models can produce much better schedulability results. Recent works [9] aim at extending the existing models to handle control dependencies. Baruah [9] introduces the *recurring real-time task model* that is able to capture lower level control dependencies, and presents an exponential-time analysis for uniprocessor systems. Several researchers have proposed extensions to the dataflow process graph model in order to capture these control dependencies [63], [15], and show that when including control dependencies significant improvements in the quality of the resulting schedules can be obtained [15], [32], [70].

Design Space Exploration
In previous sections we have outlined the current design practice in the industry. If the presented design approach was appropriate when used for relatively small systems produced in a well defined production chain, it performs poorly for more complex systems, leading to an increase in the time-to-market. There are several reasons for this. First of all, it is very difficult, just based on the specification, to accurately determine what system architecture is appropriate and how the resources should be used. Also, the fixed allocation of functionality to the hardware components limits the function/architecture trade-offs.

New design methodologies are needed, which can handle the increasing complexity of such systems, and their competing requirements in terms of performance, reliability, low power consumption, cost, time-to-market, etc. As the complexity of the systems continues to increase, the development time lengthens dramatically, and the manufacturing costs become prohibitively high. To cope with this complexity, it is necessary to reuse as much as possible at all levels of the design process, and to work at higher and higher abstraction levels.

- **Function-architecture codesign**: *Function/architecture co-design* is a design methodology proposed in [25], [62], which addresses the design process at higher abstraction levels. Function/architecture co-design uses a top-down synthesis approach, where trade-offs are evaluated at a high level of abstraction. The main characteristic of this methodology is the use, at the same time with the top-down synthesis, of a bottom-up evaluation of design alternatives, without the need to perform a full synthesis of the design. The approach to obtaining accurate evaluations is to use an accurate modelling of the behaviour and architecture, and to develop analysis techniques that are able to derive estimates and to formally verify properties relative to a certain design alternative. The determined estimates and properties, together with user-specified constraints, are then used to drive the synthesis process.

  Thus, several architectures are evaluated to determine if they are suited for the specified system functionality. There are two extremes in the degrees of freedom available for choosing an architecture. At one end, the architecture is already given, and no modifications are possible. At the other end of the spectrum, no constraints are imposed on the architecture selection, and the synthesis task has to determine, from scratch, the best architecture for the required functionality. These two situations are, however, not common in practice. Often, a *hardware platform* is available, which can be *parameterized* (e.g., size of memory, speed of the buses, etc.). In this case, the synthesis task is to derive the parameters of the architecture such that the functionality of the system is successfully implemented. Once an architecture is determined and/or parameterized, the function/architecture co-design continues with the mapping of functionality onto the instantiated architecture.

This methodology has been used in research tools like Polis [6] and Metropolis [8], and has also led to commercial tools such as the Virtual Component Co-design (VCC) [68].

- **Platform-based design**: In order to reduce costs, especially in the case of a mass market product, the system architecture is usually reused, with some modifications, for several product lines. Such a common architecture is denoted by the term *platform*, and consequently the design tasks related to such an approach are grouped under the term *platform-based design* [26].

One of the most important components of any system design methodology is the definition of a *system platform*. Such a platform consists of a hardware infrastructure together with software components that will be used for several product versions, and will be shared with other product lines, in the hope to reduce costs and the time-to-market.

The authors in [26] have proposed techniques for deriving such a platform for a given family of applications. Their approach can be used within any design methodology for determining a system platform that later on can be parameterized and instantiated to a desired system architecture.

Considering a given application or family of applications, the system platform has to be instantiated, deciding on certain parameters, and lower level details, in order to suit that particular application(s). The search for an architecture instance starts from a certain platform, and a given application. The application is mapped and compiled on an architecture instance, and the performance numbers are derived, typically using simulation. If the designer is not satisfied with the performance of the instantiated architecture, the process is repeated.

- **Incremental design process**: A characteristic of the majority of approaches to the design of embedded systems is that it concentrates on the design, from scratch, of a new system optimized for a particular application. For many application areas, however, such a situation is extremely uncommon and only rarely appears in design practice. It is much more likely that one has to start from an already existing system running a certain application and the design problem is to implement new functionality (including also upgrades to the existing one) on this system. In such a context it is very important to operate no, or as few as possible, modifications to the already running application. The main reason for this is to avoid unnecessarily large design and testing times. Performing modifications on the (potentially large) existing application increases design time and, even more, testing time (instead of only testing the newly implemented functionality, the old application, or at least a part of it, has also to be retested) [44].

For example, if an application is remapped or rescheduled, it has to be validated again. Such a validation phase is very time consuming. In the automotive industry, for example, the time-to-market in the case of the powertrain unit is 24 months. Out of these, 5 months, representing more than 20%, are dedicated to validation. In the case of the telematic unit, the time to market is less than one year, while the validation time is two months [58]. However, if an application is not modified during implementation of new functionality, only a small part of the validation tasks have to be re-performed (e.g., integration testing), thus reducing significantly the time-to-market, at no additional hardware or development cost.

However, minimizing the modification cost is not the only aspect to be considered. Such an incremental design process, in which a design is periodically upgraded with new features, is going through several iterations. Therefore, after new functionality has been introduced, the resulting system has to be implemented such that additional functionality, later to be mapped, can easily be accommodated [44].

- **Communication synthesis:** An important design task in the context of distributed applications is the *communication synthesis* task, which decides the characteristics of the communication infrastructure and the access constraints to the infrastructure, imposed on functions initiating an inter-node communication.

Current design practices ignore or simplify aspects concerning the communication infrastructure. One typical approach is to consider communication processes as processes with a given execution time (depending on the amount of information exchanged) and to schedule them as any other process, without considering issues like communication protocol, bus arbitration, packing of messages, clock synchronization, etc. These aspects are, however, essential in the context of safety-critical distributed real-time applications and one of our objectives is to develop a strategy which takes them into consideration for process scheduling.

Many efforts dedicated to communication synthesis have concentrated on the synthesis support for the communication infrastructure. Lower level communication synthesis aspects under timing constraints have been addressed in [30].

In order to provide accurate analysis and exploration methods, the exact details of the communication protocol have to be considered. Moreover, the parameters of the communication protocol have to be carefully determined in order to obtain an optimized implementation [15].

At the level of the integration phase, an important design space exploration aspect refers to packing of messages produced by functions involved in inter-ECU communication, into frames as required by the communication protocol used.

This process is called *frame packing*, and is of utmost importance in cost-sensitive embedded systems where resources, such as communication bandwidth, have to be fully utilized [27]. Thus, messages are not sent independently, but several messages having similar timing properties are usually packed into frames. In automotive electronics, for example, messages range from one single bit (e.g., the state of a device) to a couple of bytes (e.g., vehicle speed, etc.). Transmitting such small messages one per frame would create a high communication overhead, which can cause long delays leading to an unschedulable system. For example, 48 bits have to be transmitted on CAN for delivering one single bit of application data. Moreover, a given frame configuration defines the exact behaviour of a node on the network, which is very important when integrating nodes from different suppliers.

Currently, frame packing is mostly a manual or in-house inefficient process, allowing little exploration. However, tools like Volcano [69] determine the appropriate frame packing which will guarantee that the timing properties of messages are satisfied.

When applications are distributed across several clusters, with different communication protocols, the frame configurations have an important impact on the schedulability of the application. In [47] the researchers show that by carefully considering the frame packing problem in the context of several communication protocols, the schedulability of the applications is improved, and the overall cost of the architecture can be reduced.

- **Automatic design space exploration:** Design space exploration problems are generally characterized by conflicting constraints, and can be expressed as multi-objective optimization problems, the majority of which are of NP-complete [14]. Tools are needed in order to support an efficient automatic exploration.
  There are several approaches for solving such optimization problems:
  - o The optimal solution can be found using approaches such as *integer linear programming, branch and bound, constraint programming*. However, such approaches are impractical for large design spaces, due to their prohibitively large computation times.
  - o General optimization heuristics, such as *simulated annealing, tabu search* [52] and *evolutionary* approaches [74] can be used to determine good quality solutions in reasonable time. The effectiveness of these general optimization approaches can be increased by carefully adapting them to the particular design space exploration problem that has to be solved.
  - o Polynomial-complexity heuristics, especially crafted for the particular optimization problem, can also be used to determine reasonable quality solutions.

References

[1]   Aires, http://kabru.eecs.umich.edu/aires/aiT, http://www.absint.com/ait/
[2]   G. Agrawal, B. Chen, W. Zhao, S. Davari, "Guaranteeing Synchronous Message Deadlines with the Token Medium Access Control Protocol," in IEEE Transactions on Computers, volume 43, issue 3, pages 327–339, March 1994.
[3]   Ascet/SD, http://en.etasgroup.com/products/ascet_sd/
[4]   N. C. Audsley, K. Tindell, A. Burns, "The End Of The Line For Static Cyclic Scheduling?," in *Proceedings of the 5th Euromicro Workshop on Real-Time Systems*, 36–41, 1993.
[5]   N. C. Audsley, A. Burns, R. I. Davis, K. W. Tindell, A. J. Wellings, "Fixed Priority Preemptive Scheduling: An Historical Perspective," in *Real-Time Systems*, volume 8, pages 173–198, 1995.
[6]   F. Balarin et al., Hardware-Software Co-Design of Embedded Systems: The POLIS Approach, Kluwer Academic Publishers, Boston, 1997.
[7]   F. Balarin, L. Lavagno, P. Murthy, A. Sangiovanni-Vincentelli, "Scheduling for Embedded Real-Time Systems," in *IEEE Design & Test of Computers*, volume 15, issue 1, pages 71–82, January–March 1998.
[8]   F. Balarin, Y. Watanabe, H. Hsieh, L. Lavagno, C. Paserone, A. Sangiovanni-Vincentelli, "Metropolis: An Integrated Electronic System Design Environment," *Computer* , volume 36, issue 4, pages 45–52, 2003.
[9]   S. Baruah, "A General Model for Recurring Real-Time Tasks," in *Proceedings of the IEEE Real-Time Symposium*, pages 114–122, 1998.
[10]   J. Berwanger, M. Peller, R. Griessbach, *A New High Performance Data Bus System for Safety-Related Applications*, http://www.byteflight.de, 2000.
[11]   R. Bosch GmbH, CAN Specification Version 2.0, 1991.

[12]   A. Burns, A. Wellings, *Real-Time Systems and Programming Languages*, Addison Wesley, 2001.

[13]   Echelon, LonWorks: The LonTalk Protocol Specification, http://www.eche-lon.com, 2003.

[14]   M. Eisenring, L. Thiele, E. Zilzler, "Conflicting Criteria in Embedded Systems Design", IEEE Design and Test of Computers, volume 17, number 2, pages 51–59, 2000.

[15]   P. Eles, A. Doboli, P. Pop, Z. Peng, "Scheduling with Bus Access Optimization for Distributed Embedded Systems," in *IEEE Transactions on VLSI Systems*, volume 8, number 5, pages 472–491, 2000.

[16]   H. Ermedahl, H. Hansson, M. Sjödin, "Response-Time Guarantees in ATM Networks," in *Proceedings of the IEEE Real-Time Systems Symposium*, pages 274–284, 1997.

[17]   FlexRay Requirements Specification, http://www.flexray-group.com/, 2002.

[18]   G. Fohler, "Realizing Changes of Operational Modes with Pre Run-time Scheduled Hard Real-Time Systems," in *Responsive Computer Systems*, H. Kopetz and Y. Kakuda, editors, pages 287–300, Springer Verlag, 1993.

[19]   R. Gerber, D. Kang, S. Hong, M. Saksena, "End-to-End Design of Real-Time Systems," in *Formal Methods in Real-Time Computing*, D. Mandrioli and C. Heitmeyer, editors, John Wiley & Sons, 1996.

[20]   J, J, Gutiérrez García, M. González Harbour, "Optimized Priority Assignment for Tasks and Messages in Distributed Hard Real-Time Systems," in *Proceedings of the 3rd Workshop on Parallel and Distributed Real-Time Systems*, pages 124–132, 1995.

[21]   K. Hoyme, K. Driscoll, "SAFEbus," in *IEEE Aerospace and Electronic Systems Magazine*, volume 8, number 3, pages 34–39, 1992.

[22]   International Organization for Standardization, "Road vehicles—Controller area network (CAN)—Part 4: Time-triggered communication", ISO/DIS 11898-4, 2002.

[23]   J. Jonsson, K. G. Shin, "Robust Adaptive Metrics for Deadline Assignment in Distributed Hard Real-Time Systems," *Real-Time Systems: The International Journal of Time-Critical Computing Systems*, Vol. 23, No. 3, pages 239–271, 2002.

[24]   P. B. Jorgensen, J. Madsen, "Critical Path Driven Cosynthesis for Heterogeneous Target Architectures," in *Proceedings of the International Workshop on Hardware/Software Codesign*, pages 15–19, 1997.

[25]   B. Kienhuis, E. Deprettere, K. Vissers, P. Van Der Wolf, "An Approach for Quantitative Analysis of Application-Specific Dataflow Architectures," in *Proceedings of the IEEE International Conference on Application-Specific Systems, Architectures and Processors*, pages 338 –349, 1997.

[26]   K. Keutzer, S. Malik, A. R. Newton, "System-Level Design: Orthogonalization of Concerns and Platform-Based Design," in *IEEE Transactions on Computer-Aided Design of Integrated Circuits and Systems*, volume 19, number 12, December 2000.

[27]   H. Kopez, R. Nossal, "The Cluster-Compiler—A Tool for the Design of Time Triggered Real-Time Systems," in *Proceedings of the ACM SIGPLAN Workshop. on Languages, Compilers, and Tools for Real-Time Systems*, pages 108–116, 1995.

[28]   H. Kopetz, Real-Time Systems-Design Principles for Distributed Embedded Applications, Kluwer Academic Publishers, 1997.

[29]   H. Kopetz, "Automotive Electronics," in Proceedings of the 11th Euromicro Conference on Real-Time Systems, pages 132–140, 1999.

[30]   P. V. Knudsen, J. Madsen, "Integrating Communication Protocol Selection with Hardware/Software Codesign," in *IEEE Transactions on CAD*, volume 18, number 8, pages 1077–1095, 1999.

[31]   K. Kuchcinski, "Embedded System Synthesis by Timing Constraint Solving," in *Proceedings of the International Symposium on System Synthesis*, pages 50–57, 1997.

[32]   K. Kuchcinski, "Constraints Driven Design Space Exploration for Distributed Embedded Systems," in *Journal of Systems Architecture*, volume 47, issues 3–4, pages 241–261, 2001.

[33]   Local Interconnect Network Protocol Specification, http://www.lin-subbus.org, 2003.

[34]   C. L. Liu, J. W. Layland, "Scheduling Algorithms for Multiprogramming in a Hard Real-Time Environment," in *Journal of the ACM*, volume 20, number 1, pages 46–61, 1973.

[35]   H. Lönn, J. Axelsson, "A Comparison of Fixed-Priority and Static Cyclic Scheduling for Distributed Automotive Control Applications," in *Proceedings of the 11th Euromicro Conference on Real-Time Systems*, pages 142–149, 1999.

[36]   S. Malik, M. Martonosi, Y.S. Li, "Static Timing Analysis of Embedded Software," in *Proceedings of the Design Automation Conference*, pages 147–152, 1997.

[37]   Matlab/Simulink, http://www.mathworks.com

[38]   T. Meyerowitz, C. Pinello, A. Sangiovanni-Vincentelli, "A tool for describing and evaluating hierarchical real-time bus scheduling policies", *Proceedings of the Design Automation Conference*, pages 312–317, 2003.

[39]   P. S. Miner, "Analysis of the SPIDER Fault-Tolerance Protocols," in *Proceedings of the 5th NASA Langley Formal Methods Workshop*, 2000.

[40]   J. C. Palencia, J. J. Gutiérrez García, M. González Harbour, "On the Schedulability Analysis for Distributed Hard Real-Time Systems," in *Proceedings of the Euromicro Conference on Real Time Systems*, pages 136–143, 1997.

[41]   J. C. Palencia, M. González Harbour, "Exploiting Precedence Relations in the Schedulability Analysis of Distributed Real-Time Systems," in *Proceedings of the 20th IEEE Real-Time Systems Symposium*, pages 328–339, 1999.

[42]   TTP-Plan, http://www.tttech.com/

[43]   P. Pop, P. Eles, Z. Peng, "Bus Access Optimization for Distributed Embedded Systems Based on Schedulability Analysis," in Proceedings of the Design, Automation and Test in Europe Conference, pages 567–574, 2000.

[44]   P. Pop, P. Eles, T. Pop, Z. Peng, "An Approach to Incremental Design of Distributed Embedded Systems," in *Proceedings of the Design Automation Conference*, pages 450–455, 2001.

[45]   T. Pop, P. Eles, Z. Peng, "Holistic Scheduling and Analysis of Mixed Time/ Event-Triggered Distributed Embedded Systems," in *International Symposium on Hardware/Software Codesign*, pages 187–192, 2002.

[46]   P. Pop, P. Eles, Z. Peng, "Schedulability Analysis and Optimization for the Synthesis of Multi-Cluster Distributed Embedded Systems," in *Proceedings of the Design Automation and Test in Europe Conference*, pages 184–189, 2003.

[47]   P. Pop, P. Eles, Z. Peng, "Schedulability-Driven Frame Packing for Multi-Cluster Distributed Embedded Systems," in *Proceedings of the ACM SIGPLAN Conference on Languages, Compilers and Tools for Embedded Systems*, pages 113–122, 2003.

[48]   S. Prakash, A. Parker, "SOS: Synthesis of Application-Specific Heterogeneous Multiprocessor Systems," in *Journal of Parallel and Distributed Computers*, volume 16, pages 338–351, 1992.

[49]   Profibus International, *PROFIBUS DP Specification*, http://www.profibus.com/, 2003.

[50]   A. Rajnák and M. Ramnefors, "The Volcano Communication Concept," *Convergence Conference*, 2002.

[51]   RapidRMA, http://www.tripac.com

[52]   C. R. Reevs, *Modern Heuristic Techniques for Combinatorial Problems*, Blackwell Scientific Publications, 1993.

[53]   *REVIC Software Cost Estimating Model*, User's Manual, V9.0–9.2, US Air Force Analysis Agency, 1994.

[54]   K. Richter, M. Jersak, R. Ernst, "A Formal Approach to MpSoC Performance Verification," in *Computer*, volume 36, issue 4, pages 60–67, 2003.

[55]   RTA-OSEK Planner, http://www.livedevices.com

[56]   J. Rushby, "Bus Architectures for Safety-Critical Embedded Systems," *Springer–Verlag Lecture Notes in Computer Science*, volume 2211, pages 306–323, 2001.

[57]   SAE Vehicle Network for Multiplexing and Data Communications Standards Committee, *SAE J1850 Standard*, 1994.

[58]   A. Sangiovanni-Vincentelli, "Electronic-System Design in the Automobile Industry", in *IEEE Micro*, volume 23, issue 3, pages 8–18, 2003.

[59]   Statemate, http://www.ilogix.com

[60]   J. K. Strosnider, T. E. Marchok, "Responsive, Deterministic IEEE 802.5 Token Ring Scheduling," in *Journal of Real-Time Systems*, volume 1, issue 2, pages 133–158, 1989.

[61]   SystemBuild/MatrixX, http://www.ni.com/matrixx

[62]   B. Tabbara, A. Tabbara, A. Sangiovanni-Vincentelli, *Function/Architecture Optimization and Co-Design of Embedded Systems*, Kluwer Academic Publishers, 2000.

[63]   L. Thiele, K. Strehl, D. Ziegengein, R. Ernst, J. Teich, "FunState—An Internal Design Representation for Codesign," in *International Conference on Computer-Aided Design*, pages 558–565, 1999.

[64]   K. Tindell, J. Clark, "Holistic Schedulability Analysis for Distributed Hard Real-Time Systems," in *Microprocessing and Microprogramming*, volume 40, pages 117–134, 1994.

[65]   K. Tindell, *Adding Time-Offsets to Schedulability Analysis*, Technical Report Number YCS–94–221, Department of Computer Science, University of York, 1994.

[66]   K. Tindell, A. Burns, A. J. Wellings, "Calculating Controller Area Network (CAN) Message Response Times," in *Control Engineering Practice*, volume 3, number 8, pages 1163–1169, 1995.

[67]   TimeWiz, http://www.timesys.com

[68]   Virtual Component Co-design, http://www.cadence.com/

[69]   Volcano Network Analyzer, http://www.volcanoautomotive.com/

[70]   Y. Xie, W. Wolf, "Allocation and scheduling of conditional task graph in hardware/software co-synthesis", *Proceedings of the Design, Automation and Test in Europe Conference*, pages 620–625, 2001.

[71]   J. Xu, D. L. Parnas, "On Satisfying Timing Constraints in Hard-Real-Rime Systems," in *IEEE Transactions Software Engineering*, volume 19, number 1, pages 70–84, 1993.

[72]   J. Xu, D. L. Parnas, "Priority Scheduling Versus Pre-Run-Time Scheduling," in *Journal of Real Time Systems*, volume 18, issue 1, pages 7–24, 2000.

[73]   T. Yen, W. Wolf, "Performance Estimation for Real-Time Distributed Embedded Systems," in *IEEE Transactions on Parallel and Distributed Systems*, volume 9, number 11, pages 1125–1136, 1998.

[74]   E. Zitzler, K. Deb, L. Thiele, "Comparison of Multi-Objective Evolutionary Algorithms: Empirical Results", *Evolutionary Computation*, 8(2), 173–195, 2000.

29.3 Reconfigurable Hardware Platforms

Landscape

Classification of Reconfigurable Architectures

All reconfigurable processing elements consist of an array of logic blocks and an interconnect structure. The logic blocks are used for computations and the interconnect structure is used to connect the inputs and outputs of the logic blocks. Most reconfigurable computing systems couple a reconfigurable processing element to a host system. This coupling is motivated by several reasons. First, for some operations processors are much more efficient than reconfigurable elements. For example, floating-point arithmetic is more efficiently implemented in processors than in fine-grained reconfigurable elements. Second, the host processor acts as a controller for the reconfigurable element. The host initiates and monitors the configuration process as well as data transfers. Finally, host processors allow for an easy system integration through their software layers, e.g., file systems and network interfaces.

Reconfigurable computing elements and systems have been classified according to a multitude of parameters [1] [2] [3]. We will follow a simple classification with the two parameters logic block granularity and host coupling.

Logic Block Granularity

- Fine-grained logic blocks typically operate on bit-wide data types and employ look-up tables as computing elements. Most commercial FPGAs are examples for fine-grained reconfigurable architectures.
- Medium-grained logic blocks typically operate on 2-bit and 4-bit data types and employ sets of look-up tables or small bit-width ALUs (arithmetic and logic units) as computing elements.
- Coarse-grained logic blocks operate on byte-sized and word-sized operands and employ ALUs as computing elements.

The logic block granularity is the prime design parameter of a reconfigurable computing element and determines many secondary parameters. The granularity decides on the mapping efficiency for a specific application. An efficient mapping requires a good match between the operations specified by the application and the operations offered by the logic block. Naturally, applications with many bit-level data types and operations map well to fine-grained logic blocks. Applications with many arithmetic operations on byte- and word-sized data types map well to ALU-based logic blocks. As a further consequence, coarse-grained elements require fewer bits than fine-grained ones to determine their function. This is due to two facts. First, the look-up tables in fine-grained logic blocks can be programmed to compute any function of their inputs, whereas the ALUs in coarse-grained logic blocks offer a rather limited set of meaningful arithmetic, logic, shift, and transfer operations. Therefore, coarse-grained logic blocks need fewer bits to determine their operation. Additionally, fine-grained elements require a much richer interconnect structure to utilize their logic blocks. Consequently, fine-grained logic blocks spend also more bits than coarse-grained ones to specify how the logic block connects to the interconnect structure of the device. The configuration size effects two further parameters of a reconfigurable element: the size of the configuration memory and the reconfiguration time. The configuration memory adds to the total area of the reconfigurable element and hence to the device cost. The reconfiguration time is the time required to write the configuration memory.

- **Host Coupling**: Reconfigurable systems are classified according to the tightness of the coupling between the reconfigurable processing element and the host processor into attached reconfigurable processing units, reconfigurable coprocessors, and reconfigurable functional units. The relative position of the processor core and the reconfigurable element determines the amount of computation that can be efficiently mapped to the reconfigurable element. Generally, a tighter coupling leads to a lower communication latency which allows to map a relatively small portion of code to the reconfigurable element. Loose couplings lead to higher communication latencies and require bigger amounts of computation to be assigned to the reconfigurable element. The different host couplings are shown in Figure 32.3 and are defined as follows:

  o *Attached reconfigurable processing unit*: The loosest method of coupling is to connect the reconfigurable element with the processor via the processor's memory or I/O bus. Such systems can easily be built out of off-the-shelf components, e.g., [4] [5]. The reconfigurable element and the processor can operate rather independently. Typically, tasks which implement a substantial amount of computation are mapped to the reconfigurable processing element.

  o *Reconfigurable coprocessor*: A tighter method of coupling is the coprocessor approach that couples the reconfigurable element with the processor core, e.g., [6] [7] [8]. A coprocessor coupling requires special instructions that control the coprocessor operation. Some instruction set architectures include generic coprocessor instructions that can be used to control the reconfigurable coprocessor. An alternative that requires more design effort is to extend the processor's instruction set with new instructions. The coprocessor coupling has the advantage that the processor's memory hierarchy provides a high memory bandwidth to the reconfigurable element. For streaming applications, this bandwidth is necessary to constantly feed the reconfigurable element with data. Typically, functions and runtime-intensive inner loops of functions are mapped to the reconfigurable processing element.

  o *Reconfigurable functional unit (RFU)*: The tightest coupling is achieved when the functional units of a processor core are turned into reconfigurable elements, e.g., [9] [10]. This method of coupling reduces communication between the processor core and the reconfigurable element to accesses to the common register file. However, this approach requires a complete redesign of the processor core. The redesign effects the pipeline and the instruction set. Typically, collections of a few instructions forming a new customized instruction are mapped to the reconfigurable processing element.

    Reconfigurable computing systems are built as board-level systems or as systems integrated on a single chip. The early reconfigurable computers were built as board-level systems and attached FPGAs to a PC or a workstation. This classifies early reconfigurable computers as fine-grained attached systems

[4] [5]. The next wave of reconfigurable computers included board-level systems that attached coarse-grained elements to PCs and workstations [11]. Currently, there is a strong commercial trend toward so-called (re)configurable systems on a chip (CSoC). CSoCs are single chip systems that attach fine-grained or coarse-grained reconfigurable elements to a host processor. Most current rResearch efforts concentrate on fine-grained and coarse-grained reconfigurable coprocessors and reconfigurable functional units. These devices, when fabricated, obviously integrate the reconfigurable processing element and the processor core on a single chip.

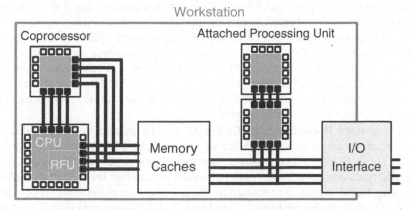

Figure 32.3. Different couplings between host processor and processing element

Reconfigurable Elements
There exists a wide variety of reconfigurable computing elements. All reconfigurable computing elements comprise an array of logic blocks and an interconnect structure. Some reconfigurable elements have configurable logic blocks, i.e., the function executed is determined by configuration data. Other reconfigurable elements have fixed logic blocks and allow the configuration of the connections between them. Most reconfigurable elements, however, allow the configuration of both the logic blocks and the interconnect. This section gives a brief survey of reconfigurable computing elements, divided into elements with fine-grained, medium-grained, and coarse-grained logic blocks. These elements have realizations as stand-alone integrated circuits, are integrated with processors on configurable systems on a chip, or form parts of reconfigurable processors.

- **Fine-grained Reconfigurable Elements**: FPGAs were introduced in the mid 1980s as a new way of implementing glue logic and were placed on the market at the high-end of programmable logic devices (PLDs). Since then, a large variety of FPGAs and complex programmable logic devices (CPLDs) evolved. In the meantime, FPGAs have found many uses other than implementing glue logic. FPGAs are used for large-scale logic emulation and rapid prototyping systems, for ASIC replacements, as building block of configurable systems on a chip, and for the construction of custom computing machines.

There are many books and papers available on CPLD and FPGA technologies and architectures, as well as on corresponding design methods and tools. For an introduction to CPLD and FPGA architectures, we refer to [12] [13]. A more recent overview over PLDs, CPLDs, and FPGAs can be found in [14]. A selection of books focusing on FPGAs includes [15] [16] [17].

SRAM-based FPGAs are reprogrammable arbitrary often in-circuit which is the central feature for their application in reconfigurable computing systems. Thus, all SRAM-based FPGAs can be used for the construction of compile-time and run-time reconfigurable systems.

- **Medium-grained Reconfigurable Elements**: Medium-grained reconfigurable elements operate on 2-bit and 4-bit data types rather than on single bits. The logic blocks are either constructed from look-up tables or small ALUs. Usually, both look-up tables and ALUs can be cascaded to implement operators for larger bit-widths. Compared to fine-grained elements, medium-grained logic blocks implement arithmetic operations more efficiently. The number of operations a block can perform is smaller which results in less configuration bits. The interconnect is organized in busses of the corresponding bit-width. In the following, we present two selected medium-grained architectures.

- **Coarse-grained Reconfigurable Elements**: Coarse-grained reconfigurable architectures are based on arrays of dedicated arithmetic and logic units (ALUs). Such arrays are intended for operations on byte-sized and word-sized operands. These operand types are common in computationally demanding areas such as multimedia and digital signal processing. In these areas, reconfigurable ALU arrays achieve a much higher performance and require less silicon area than fine-grained reconfigurable architectures. On the other hand, ALU arrays are not able to leverage optimizations in the operand sizes. If operations on few bits are required or the operands do not match the ALU bit-widths, ALU arrays suffer area and speed overheads. Coarse-grained reconfigurable elements are characterized as follows:

  o The logic blocks are based on arithmetic-logic units (ALUs) that operate on byte and multi-byte data types. Logic blocks further contain registers, multiplexers, and more specialized circuits such as barrel shifters. At the extreme end of coarse granularity we find logic blocks that contain complete processor cores with small register files and even instruction and data caches.

  o The interconnect comprises byte and word-wide busses. Due to the high regularity of digital signal processing applications, the interconnect structures of coarse-grained elements are less flexible than the interconnects for fine-grained elements. ALU arrays often use 2D-mesh interconnect structures that provide nearest neighbor connections and, additionally, vertical and horizontal array-wide global busses. Some systems are even simpler and restrict the routing to one dimension.

  o For the instruction control of coarse-grained architectures there exist several options. First, an array-wide context determines the function and interconnection of all ALUs. Second, each logic block has its own instruction memory which allows for some independence between the blocks. In such a case, the program counter can be implemented globally or locally. Global program counters result in a single instruction, multiple data (SIMD) mode of execution. Local program counters enable multiple instructions, multiple data

(MIMD) execution modes. Other sophisticated instruction control techniques include distributed control where logic blocks can define the instructions of other blocks, and wormhole routing techniques.

Reconfigurable Processors
Reconfigurable processors couple reconfigurable elements tightly with a processor core and integrate both units on the same chip. In the last years, reconfigurable processors have become the subject of many research projects.

Processor core and reconfigurable unit are two computing elements with various possible interactions. The architectural integration of these elements concerns the coupling between core and reconfigurable unit, the way instructions are issued to the reconfigurable unit, and the way operands are transferred from and to the reconfigurable unit. The design issues concerning the reconfigurable unit itself are the granularity, the interconnect and the reconfiguration technique. The last issue is the programming model for the reconfigurable processor.

- **Coupling**: The relative position of the processor core and the reconfigurable unit determines the type of applications that benefit most from the reconfigurable processor. Generally, a tighter coupling leads to a smaller communication overhead. Loose couplings thus require bigger amounts of computation assigned to the reconfigurable unit. We differentiate between reconfigurable coprocessors and reconfigurable functional units (RFUs).
- **Instructions**: Both RFU and coprocessor approaches require special instructions. In most cases, the core's instruction set is extend with a set of new instructions that handle the reconfigurable units. Some processors have generic coprocessor instructions that can be used to control the reconfigurable coprocessor. Both coprocessor and RFUs need two types of additional instructions: instructions that start the reconfiguration process, and instructions that actually execute the reconfigurable element's operation. Reconfigurable coprocessors further require instructions for data transfer and synchronization. Generally, synchronization is required whenever two computing elements operate concurrently. The simplest approach forces the processor core to stall until the execution of the reconfigurable unit has completed. More advanced techniques allow for the concurrent operation of processor core and reconfigurable coprocessor and achieve synchronization by semaphore-like mechanisms. RFUs are deeply integrated into the processor pipeline and can thus operate concurrently to other functional units. The core's control logic synchronizes activities and schedules the accesses to the register file. RFUs need thus no additional synchronization or data transfer instructions. RFUs are presently gaining interest for embedded very-long-instruction-word (VLIW) architectures, where optimized compilers extract parallelism and schedule the customized functional units at compile time.
- **Operands**: Most research prototypes for reconfigurable processors use RISC-style processor cores with load/store architectures. Hence, the RFUs may only access the core's register file in order to read and write data. Coprocessors are not integrated in the core's pipeline. They see the same memory hierarchy as the core and can thus use several techniques to read and write data. First, data may be transferred between the coprocessor and the core via special coprocessor registers.

Second, coprocessors can access caches, on-chip memories, and the external memory interface. Third, to increase the overall memory bandwidth some approaches equip the reconfigurable units with dedicated memory ports. While this certainly increases bandwidth, it potentially leads to data consistency problems.

- **Granularity**: The granularity for both coprocessors and RFUs can be fine-grained, medium-grained, or coarse-grained. Fine-grained arrays are well suited to implement bit manipulation operations and random logic. Coarse-grained architectures are better suited to implement regular arithmetic operations on byte and word-sized data found in most multimedia applications. There is obviously a trade-off involved as many real-world workloads contain both types of applications. Researchers currently investigate multi-granular elements that are well suited to implement bit manipulation operands, but can also be efficiently arranged to suite byte operations.

- **Interconnect**: All reconfigurable elements that are found in reconfigurable processors use simpler interconnect structures than the fine-grained FPGAs. Mostly, a two-dimensional interconnect structure is used that connects each element to its four neighbors horizontally and vertically. Additional busses may exist that connect all elements in a row and in a column.

- **Reconfiguration**: The actual reconfiguration process is performed either by the processor core or by a dedicated configuration controller. The latter option allows for concurrent core execution and reconfiguration and thus hides reconfiguration time. Advanced techniques allow the reconfigurable unit to request and perform its own reconfiguration. Reconfiguration time is an important parameter that is to be minimized. The reconfiguration time depends on the configuration size and on the location from where the configuration data has to be read. The clear goal is single-cycle reconfiguration, i.e., the whole reconfigurable unit is reprogrammed in a single clock cycle. This requires the configuration data to be stored on the processor, near the reconfigurable elements. Multi-context reconfigurable processors are able to store several contexts on the chip. The simplest context fetching mechanism is load on demand. This mechanism is used by single-context and multi-context units when a configuration is required which is not present in the context memory. For multi-context architectures there are more sophisticated fetching mechanisms. The context memory can be used as a cache, where recently used contexts are stored. Alternatively, a context can be prefetched concurrently to the execution of a different context.

- **Programming Model**: Programming models for reconfigurable processors have not yet received sufficient attention. This will certainly have to change as the success of reconfigurable processors strongly depends on reasonable programming models that allow for the development of automated code generation tools. Most programming environments for reconfigurable processors consist of two separate tool flows, one for the software and one for the hardware. Functions that employ the reconfigurable unit are manually constructed at the assembly language level and and wrapped together with the configuration data into library functions that are linked with the user code [18]. Recently, some projects began to touch issues of compiling from high-level languages, e.g., [19]. The goal is to develop a compiler that automatically generates code and configurations from a general-purpose programming language such as "C". Such a compiler constructs a control flow graph from the source program and then decides which operations will go into the reconfigurable unit. Generally, inner loops of programs are good candidates for reconfigurable implementation. For general-purpose code this leads to several problems. First, it is quite difficult to extract a set of operations with matching granularity at a sufficient level of parallelism. Second, inner loops of general-purpose programs often contain excess code, i.e., code that must be run on the core such as exceptions, function calls, and system calls.

Configurable Systems on a Chip (CSoCs)
CSoCs combine CPU cores with caches, memories, I/O modules, and reconfigurable elements on a single chip. During the last years, many commercial CSoCs have either entered the market or have been announced. Configurable systems on a chip are also sometimes denoted as system-on-a-programmable-chip (SoPC). We divide CSoCs into two groups, CSoCs with hard CPU cores and CSoCs with soft CPU cores:

- CSoCs with hard CPU cores include hard-wired or fixed CPUs on the chip. These devices provide the same CPU performance than their non-hybrid counterparts. The CPUs can not be configured and the coupling to the reconfigurable element is predetermined. The reconfigurable element is attached to the CPU, usually by a memory-mapped interface or some peripheral bus system.
- CSoCs with soft CPU cores employ synthesizable CPUs. The advantage of soft CPU cores is that they can be configured in a wide range of parameters. Typically, the configuration subsumes the instruction set, the number of functional units, the size of the register file, and the size of the caches. The configured soft cores are synthesized together with other system blocks either to ASIC targets or to FPGA targets. The latter variant allows for the greatest flexibility. Hence, soft CPU cores that target FPGAs are used for rapid prototyping of other CSoCs and reconfigurable processors. A CPU synthesized to an FPGA runs at a lower speed than a corresponding CPU synthesized to an ASIC or a dedicated CPU.

Assessment

Fine-Grained Reconfigurable Elements
Most current runtime reconfigurable systems are built of SRAM-based FPGAs. These systems reconfigure FPGAs during an application's runtime and rely on the FPGA's fast and partial reconfiguration capabilities:

- *Fast Reconfiguration*: The reconfiguration time is the time required to write all the SRAM configuration cells of an FPGA. This time depends on the structure and number of logic blocks, richness and flexibility of the interconnect, and on the time to transfer the configuration data to the FPGA device. While early FPGAs had rather slow configuration ports, modern FPGAs provide higher bandwidth interfaces. An example is the SelectMap interface of the Xilinx Virtex FPGA series that provides an 8-bit parallel reconfiguration port running at 50 MHz [20]. Most current FPGAs have reconfiguration times in the range of a few ms to some hundred ms.
- *Partial Reconfiguration*: Another way to keep reconfiguration time low is to reconfigure only the parts of the FPGA needed to accommodate the new function.

Most currently available FPGAs do not support partial reconfiguration. An exception is the Xilinx Virtex series that provides a limited form of partial reconfigurability. Virtex devices can be reconfigured column-wise.

Currently, all commercially available FPGAs are single-context devices that store only the context in use on the chip. Multi-context FPGAs can store several contexts on the chip. Instead of a single programmable cell per configuration point, multi-context devices provide for several planes of configuration cells. The main benefit of a multi-context FPGA is that it allows for fast, single-cycle context switches. Compared to single-context FPGAs, multi-context FPGAs better sustain their functional densities and are thus more flexible. On the other hand, multi-context devices require more silicon area than their single-context counterparts to store the contexts.

The three main issues in designing multi-context devices are number of contexts, context control, and context loading mechanisms. The question of the number of contexts and, specifically, whether a multi-context or a single-context device is preferrable, depends strongly on the application. There are two key observations: First, the description of an operation is usually much smaller than the active circuitry required to perform the operation. Data taken from a multicontext prototype [21] indicates a difference of one order of magnitude. This observation basically underlines the known fact that computation in time requires less area than computation in space. Second, many applications do not require that all logic elements perform an evaluation every cycle. The design problem of deciding on the number of contexts is basically an issue of balancing silicon area between active logic (LUTs) and context memory. In [21], DeHon presents an extensive investigation of application classes for which it is more efficient to switch between several contexts and have lesser logic blocks than to map the complete application to space.

The simplest context control mechanism is to have a single device-wide context selector that is controlled from a host processor. Using this mechanism, the reconfiguration of a multi-context device is identical to the reconfiguration of single-context device. The only but important difference lies in the single-cycle reconfiguration time. However, multi-context devices allow for more advanced mechanisms. The reconfigurable array can be divided into several regions each having an own context selector. This results in several control threads per device. A further technique is to control the context from inside the reconfigurable array, i.e., the result of some operation could determine the next context for the array. Multiple execution threads and self-controlled reconfiguration are not yet that well investigated for fine-grained reconfigurable elements.

There are several design decisions according to the handling of the context memories. The context memories of multi-context architectures can be operated either as memories or as caches. Context caches use some replacement strategy, usually least recently used (LRU). Further, the context memories are either loaded on demand or prefetched. By properly prefetching the contexts, reconfiguration times can be hidden.

Multi-context FPGAs are a natural extension to traditional FPGAs. Although FPGA manufacturers such as Xilinx produced engineering quantities of multi-context devices, they did not turn this technology into products [22]. Up to now, there are no commercially available multi-context FPGAs. In the following, we list a selection of multi-context devices that have been developed and prototyped in academic and industrial research laboratories:

- **Dynamically Programmable Gate Array (DPGA)**: The DPGA architecture [23] [24], devoloped at the M.I.T., USA, is a proof-of-concept for multi-context FPGAs. The DPGA device consists of a number of subarrays. A subarray is formed by a 4 x 4 collection of logic blocks. The DPGA logic block contains one 4-LUT. The interconnect splits into intra- and inter-subarray routing resources. A DPGA prototype with 9 subarrays has been fabricated in a 1 u CMOS process with 3 metal layers. The prototype contains a 128-bit DRAM per array element. The DRAM provides four contexts for both the look-up table and the interconnection network. A 2-bit chip-wide context selector controls the active context.
- **Dynamically Reconfigurable Logic Engine (DRLE)**: The Dynamically Reconfigurable Logic Engine (DRLE) [25] [22], developed at NEC, Japan, is a multi-context device for numerically intensive algorithms that operate on small bit-widths. The DRLE consists of an 4 x 12 array of blocks (LBs) where each block in turn is composed out of 4 x 4 so-called unified cells (UC), a reconfiguration controller (RC), a global bus switch, and bus connectors (BC). The basic computational elements in a UC are the memory columns, which contain eight memory cells, two read ports, and one write port. Each memory cell stores one configuration. A unified cell can be configured in logic mode, memory mode, or switch mode. Thus, the device allows to trade-off computational capacity for interconnect capacity. The unified cells are connected to a set of local and global busses. The minimum unit of reconfiguration is the logic block (LB) which contains a reconfiguration controller. The reconfiguration can be controlled externally or internally. NEC has presented a prototype DRLE in 0.25 u CMOS with 5.1 M transistors that stores eight contexts on the device. The context switch time is reported with 4.6 ns.

Medium-Grained Reconfigurable Elements
In the following, we present a selection of medium-grained reconfigurable architectures.

- **Garp**: The Garp architecture [6], developed at UC Berkeley, USA, couples a MIPS-II core with a reconfigurable array as a coprocessor. The bit-width of the logic block's basic data type is two bits. A logic block can perform a number of operations on up to four 2-bit inputs. Additionally, the logic blocks have special carry inputs and outputs to implement efficient arithmetic functions on larger bit-widths. A Garp block contains two 2-bit registers and several multiplexers that connect the block to the routing structure. A peculiarity of Garp is that the registers in a logic block can be read and written from an external controller via memory busses.
- **CHESS**: The CHESS architecture [26] is an array of 4-bit ALUs. A CHESS ALU has 16 instructions and can be cascaded for operations on byte and word-sized operands. The ALU instructions can either be static or dynamic. Static ALU instructions are part of the array's configuration. Dynamic instructions are signals generated by the user logic that connect to the instruction input of an ALU. CHESS uses a hierarchical two-dimensional interconnect, similar to fine-grained reconfigurable

elements. The entire routing structure is based on 4-bit busses. Each ALU is attached to an adjacent switch-box that can operate in two modes. In the standard routing mode, a switch-box implements crosspoints that connect horizontally and vertically running busses. Alternatively, the configuration points of a switch-box can be used as RAM structure. The switch-boxes contain also registers to facilitate deep pipelines. Additionally, CHESS contains a number of embedded RAM blocks.

Coarse-Grained Reconfigurable Elements
In the following, we present a selection of coarse-grained reconfigurable architectures.

- **RaPiD**: The RaPiD (Reconfigurable Pipelined Datapath) architecture [6], developed at the University of Washington, USA, is a one-dimensional array of cells. A cell comprises an integer multiplier, two integer ALUs, six registers, and three small local memories. The registers, the RAM, and the ALUs operate on 16-bit data types. The multiplier performs a 16 x 16 to 32 multiplication and outputs the 32-bit result as two 16-bit words. The ALUs can be cascaded for double-precision operations. The RAMs allow for one write and one read per clock cycle. All routing structures are 16-bit busses. Some of the routing channels are segmented. A RaPiD array is constructed by replicating identical cells from left to right, forming a linear computing pipeline. RaPiD targets highly repetitive, computationally-intensive tasks since deep, application-specific computation pipelines can be configured in RaPiD. Typical application areas are multimedia and digital signal processing.

- **KressArray**: The KressArray architecture [27], developed in the Xputer project at the University of Kaiserslautern, Germany, consists of a 3 x 3 mesh of reconfigurable DataPath Units (rDPUs). An rDPU contains a 32-bit ALU, a register file, and a set of multiplexers. The rDPUs are reconfigurable in the sense that a configuration word defines the ALU operation, the settings of the internal multiplexers that connect the ALU with the register file and the communication ports, and the mode of the local rDPU interconnections. The rDPUs are arranged in a NEWS (north, east, west, south) network where every rDPU is connected to its four neighbors. The NEWS network forms the local interconnect and contains 32-bit duplex connections. Additionally, there exists a global network which connects all nine rDPUs. The KressArray targets embedded applications which show a significant amount of parallelism, e.g., image processing.

Reconfigurable Coprocessors
In this section, we discuss reconfigurable computing elements that are integrated as coprocessors with standard processor cores on-chip.

- **NAPA**: The National Adaptive Processing Architecture (NAPA) [7], developed by National Semiconductor, USA, couples a 32-bit RISC core (CompactRISC) with a reconfigurable array of fine-grained logic elements, called Adaptive Logic Processor (ALP). The processor's instruction set is supplemented with array-specific instructions. The ALP accesses the same memory space as the processor. Additionally, the ALP has exclusive access to a set of configurable I/O pins and dedicated memory blocks. This increased flexibility in interfacing and memory allocation has been identified to be especially important for embedded systems. However, it also leads to problems of consistency and synchronization. Two programming modes are considered depending on the synchronization between the main processor and the ALP. In the first mode, the main processor initiates the ALP operation and suspends afterwards. Upon completion, the ALP reactivates the main processor by an interrupt. In the second mode, the main processor is free to perform any computation after having initiated the ALP. The execution threads of the main processor and the ALP rejoin through standard synchronization mechanisms such as status flags and interrupts.

- **Garp**: (other aspects are also described above under "Medium-grained Reconfigurable Elements") The Garp architecture [6], developed at UC Berkeley, USA, couples a MIPS-II core with a reconfigurable array as a coprocessor. For data transfers, the reconfigurable array accesses the standard memory hierarchy of the main processor via the data cache. Configurations for the array are loaded from memory via a dedicated 128-bit bus. The reconfigurable array is composed of rows of 24 medium-grained logic elements that operate on 2-bit data. The host processor's instruction set is extended to handle the reconfigurable array. This extension includes instructions for data transfer, loading and executing configurations, and synchronization. In the Garp architecture, the array execution is always controlled by the host processor. The array can be partially reconfigured and several configurations can be cached on-chip. Simulation results for three applications are reported: Data Encryption Standard (DES), image dithering, and a sorting algorithm. In this simulation, a 133 MHz Garp architecture achieves speedups from 2 to 24 over a 167 MHz UltraSPARC. The best results are achieved for DES, which maps well onto the medium-grained reconfigurable elements.

    Experiments with the Garp architecture revealed two main limitations. The first limitation is a lack of memory in the reconfigurable array to store intermediate data. Since the only memory resources in the reconfigurable array are the flip-flops inside the logic elements, intermediate data has to be written to the data cache. The limited bandwidth of the busses forms a bottleneck. Due to the caching mechanism, accesses to intermediate data may cause misses and stall array execution. To reduce such effects for data streaming applications, Garp integrates memory queues on the chip. Further, data consistency must be ensured and concurrent accesses of the core and the reconfigurable array to the cache must be resolved. The second limitation is the rather long configuration loading time of about 50 us for the entire 32-row array. Even if the array is configured from the configuration cache, the reconfiguration lasts several clock cycles.

Reconfigurable Functional Units
This section discusses reconfigurable elements that are fully integrated into a processor's execution pipeline as reconfigurable functional units (RFUs).

- **Chimaera**: The Chimaera architecture [10], developed at Northwestern University, USA, integrates an array of fine-grained reconfigurable functional units into a processor's datapath. Each column of the array corresponds to one bit of the processor's data word. Several rows of the array form one functional unit. The array is treated like a cache that stores reconfigurable functional units or, in other words, reconfigurable instructions. Recently executed instructions or instructions predicted to be needed soon are kept in the reconfigurable array. During instruction decoding, the processor determines whether a dedicated reconfigurable functional unit is to be used. If the corresponding unit is not present in the array, the caching/prefetch control logic stalls the processor and loads the proper instruction from the memory into the array. The caching logic also determines which reconfigurable instruction is overwritten by the instruction being loaded. A peculiarity of Chimaera is that the reconfigurable array contains neither state-holding elements nor pipelining latches.

- **OneChip**: The OneChip architecture [9], developed at the University of Toronto, Canada, couples fine-grained reconfigurable functional units to a RISC processor pipeline. The RFU operates concurrently to the pipeline's execution phase and has, contrary to other RFU approaches, direct access to memory. The OneChip RFU can execute functions that are much larger than typical processor instructions. However, as the RFU has its own memory interface, problems of data consistency can arise. The RFU is composed of an RFU controller and a number of FPGAs that implement reconfigurable instructions. The RFU controller contains an instruction buffer, reservation stations (RFU-RS), a reconfiguration bits table (RBT), and the memory interface. The reservation stations in the RFU controller handle data dependencies between RFU instructions and regular CPU instructions. The RFU controller is responsible for loading FPGA configurations and keeps the currently loaded instructions in the reconfiguration bits table.

Configurable Systems on a Chip (CSoCs) – Hard CPU Cores
All hard CPU CSoCs integrate a standard processor core with an array of reconfigurable elements and memory on a chip. Vendors target both low performance and high performance segments of the embedded market which is reflected by the used processor cores that range from modest 8-bit microcontrollers clocked at 40 MHz to low-power 32-bit RISCs running at speeds of up to 300 MHz. Most currently available hard CPU CSoCs base on fine-grained reconfigurable elements. Since these devices are offered by FPGA vendors, they include commercial FPGA technology. Altera's devices build on APEX20KE series, Atmel builds on the AT40K FPGA series, and Xilinx builds on the Virtex-II technology. The logic capacities of the CSoCs varies in a wide range, with the densest devices featuring up to 4M gates. An exception is Chameleon Systems' CS2000 (meanwhile, the company left the market) which employs a coarse-grained reconfigurable array. The CS2000 contains up to 84 32-bit datapath units (DPUs) of which each includes a 32-bit arithmetic-logic unit (ALU).

- **Triscend E5 and A7**: Triscend's CSoC platform consists of a processor core, the Configurable System Logic (CSL) matrix, Configurable System Interconnect (CSI) bus, CSI socket, SRAM, peripherals, and modules for test and control functions. Triscend's concept allows to integrate any processor core into the platform and to scale the size of the CSL matrix, the number of programmable I/O pins (PIOs), and the SRAM. Triscend offers two product families: the E5 based on an 8-bit 8032 microcontroller, and the A7 based on a 32-bit ARM7TDMI RISC core. Triscend's CSL matrix is arranged in an array of so called CSL banks. Number and arrangement of these banks vary and range from 2x1 to 5x5 arrays. Each bank consists of 8 columns by 16 rows of logic blocks, called CSL cells, totaling 128 cells per bank. A CSL cell consists of a flip-flop plus a look-up table (LUT) and is capable of performing various logic, arithmetic, or memory operations. The cells are surrounded by programmable interconnects which allow a signal originating from one cell to communicate with one or more cells, even those in other banks. Furthermore, the CSL matrix offers several programmable I/O (PIO) pins which can be configured to interface to the microcontroller or external devices.

Configurable Systems on a Chip (CSoCs) – Soft CPU Cores
Soft CPU cores are synthesized to ASIC or FPGA technology. This allows for configuration and customization of the core. Cores that are synthesized to ASIC technology show higher performance than FPGA cores. FPGA cores, however, can be customized to a greater extend. These cores can use hardware-assisted custom instructions in a flexible way and thus utilize trade-offs between speed and area. Soft CPU cores mapped to FPGA are especially important for rapid prototyping of reconfigurable processors and CSoCs. In the following paragraphs, we list two soft cores (XTensa and ARC cores) that target ASIC and FPGA technology, and two examples for FPGA-optimized soft cores (Nios and MicroBlaze).

- **Tensilica XTensa**: The Tensilica XTensa is a configurable low-power 32-bit RISC-like architecture that runs up to 200 MHz [28]. Among the configurable architectural parameters are hardware units that support applications from digital signal processing. Examples are a 16-bit hardware multiplier and a 16-bit DSP unit that contains a 16 bit multiplier chained with a 40-bit accumulator.
- **ARC Cores**: The ARC cores family bases on a customizable 32-bit RISC core [29] with a four-stage execution pipeline. The customization includes the instruction set, the register file, condition codes, instruction/data caches, scratchpad memory, I/O busses, and DSP extensions. The DSP extensions include three different types of multiply-accumulate (MAC) instructions, saturating addition, and subtraction. The size of the on-chip memory ranges from 512 bytes to 16 KB. Further optional modules are address-generation units that support autoincrement, autodecrement, circular, and bit-reverse addressing.
- **Altera Nios**: The Nios CPU is a five-stage pipelined RISC processor [30]. Nios uses a 16-bit instruction format but supports both 16-bit and 32-bit data bus widths. A key feature of Nios is that additional hardware can be used to increase the performance. Nios allows for two levels to use additional hardware: CPU options and custom instructions. CPU options are configurable hardware building blocks, e.g., hardware multipliers. A custom instruction is a complex sequence of operations that has been reduced to a single instruction implemented in hardware.
- **Xilinx MicroBlaze**: The Xilinx MicroBlaze is a 32-bit RISC processor core running at 150 MHz in a Xilinx FPGA [31]. The MicroBlaze processor uses a variant of a Harvard architecture, where separated instruction and data busses access internal and external memories. To connect peripheral and custom modules, the MicroBlaze offers a bus interface, called CoreConnect. CoreConnect includes a local processor bus and an on-chip peripheral bus.

Trends

Reconfigurable Elements

FPGAs and CPLDs (complex programmable logic devices) are one of the fastest growing segments of the semiconductor industry. FPGAs are general-purpose devices and thus fabricated in extraordinarily high volumes. This allows FPGAs to benefit from the latest semiconductor technologies. As a consequence, the densities and speeds of FPGAs have been improving rapidly and will continue to do so. For example, in 1997 the most densest devices delivered 100-200 Kgates. In 2002, devices with densities of 10 Mgates are on the market. Looking at the last few years, following trends in FPGAs can be observed that are especially important for the domain of reconfigurable computing:

- **Heterogeneous architectures**: Heterogeneous FPGA architectures employ different types of logic blocks. Additionally to the basic reconfigurable logic cells, heterogeneous FPGAs contain blocks specialized to specific functions for which the logic cells are not efficient. Examples for specialized blocks are embedded RAM blocks and embedded multipliers. Memory elements are required to store frequently used data and variables in the user logic. Most FPGAs allow to use the look-up tables as RAM elements. By this, custom memory structures with variable bit widths can be constructed. Building larger blocks of memory with LUTs is, however, inefficient. Therefore, more and more FPGA architectures include dedicated memory blocks. Examples are the Xilinx Virtex and Altera FLEX10K. While these memory blocks are less flexible than LUT-based RAMs, they do enable some form of customization. The embedded memory blocks in the Altera FLEX10K series, for example, provides a given number of wires to the memory and allows the designer to trade-off between the number of address lines and the data bit-width. Multiplication is another function that is difficult to efficiently achieve with traditional FPGA's logic blocks. Thus, a current trend is to embed custom multipliers into the FPGA array. An example is the Xilinx Virtex-II architecture that contains up to 168 18 x 18 multipliers.

- **Reconfiguration mechanisms**: Advanced reconfiguration mechanisms, i.e., fast reconfiguration and partial reconfiguration, are of utmost importance for reconfigurable computing systems. In the mid 1990s, the availability of the Xilinx XC6200 chip fueled many research efforts in reconfigurable computing. Today, the most widely used FPGA series for reconfigurable computing research are the Xilinx Virtex, Virtex-E, and Virtex-II. With some restrictions, these devices are partially reconfigurable. Currently, there are indications for a continued support and even for an extension of these features in future. For example, the Xilinx Virtex-II architecture allows to access the configuration port from on-chip user logic. This capability opens up the way to self-controlled, i.e., autonomous, reconfiguration.

Reconfigurable Processors

In the last years, many research projects have been started that investigate reconfigurable processors. Most of these projects target general-purpose computing and try to extend a general-purpose processor with reconfigurable logic or reconfigurable ALU arrays. Issues that are being investigated include the granularity of the reconfigurable element, the coupling between the reconfigurable element and the processor core, and reconfiguration mechanisms.

Most reconfigurable processors that have been presented so far have been designed with a specific hardware architecture in mind. Although researchers pointed to potential application domains, the specific design decisions have almost never been properly justified. In the design space that is spanned by processing performance, power consumption, and silicon area, these processors form single design points. What is needed in the future are quantitative analyses of trade-offs and design alternatives as well as design space explorations.

Reconfigurable elements are less flexible than general-purpose processors. Thus, reconfigurable processors are likely to be more successful in the embedded systems area than in the general-purpose domain. In embedded systems, the number and characteristics of applications are limited which facilitates the selection of design parameters for reconfigurable processors. The software layers for reconfigurable processors, i.e., compilers and operating systems, have not yet been sufficiently investigated. Most configurations for reconfigurable processors are either hand-crafted or are synthesized from structural hardware description languages. Although researchers have investigated compilation from high-level languages such as "C" for quite a while, compilers for hybrid processors have not yet proven successful.

Configurable Systems on a Chip
During the last few years, configurable systems on a chip have strongly gained importance. Of special interest to reconfigurable computing are hybrid processors that combine processor cores with reconfigurable logic on a chip.

Today, a large number of soft CPU cores are available that can be synthesized to FPGAs. These CPUs range from low-end 8-bit microcontrollers to 32-bit RISC processors running at 150 MHz. FPGA vendors promote to replace microprocessors with soft CPUs in embedded systems design. Although soft CPUs run slower and require more silicon area than their dedicated counterparts, they show a number of benefits. Many embedded products employ very old microprocessors for which large software bases exist. The emulation of such microprocessors in FPGAs prevents the designer from a complete system redesign in case the microprocessor is discontinued. Further, soft CPUs can be integrated with other system blocks on one FPGA. This allows for single chip systems or system with fewer chips which reduces design complexity. In research, soft CPUs will be widely used for prototyping reconfigurable processors. They also form an ideal testbed for experimenting with multiprocessor systems.

CSoCs with hard CPUs are slowly emerging on the market. Depending on the performance of the hard CPU, these devices target several application domains. The Triscend E5, for example, contains a low-end 8-bit microcontroller that can run simple control functions. The reconfigurable logic on this chip can be used for interfacing and preprocessing tasks. At the high-end, we find devices such as the Xilinx Virtex-II Pro series. These chips contain up to four PowerPC 405 cores plus 8 Mgates logic in Virtex-II technology and a set of high-speed interfaces. These multiprocessors embedded in high-performance and high-density reconfigurable logic are suitable for implementing high-end network processors and systems.

Reconfigurable Architectures in Molecular Electronics

A totally new line of research in reconfigurable architectures is molecular electronic nanotechnology, a promising technology and potential candidate for the post-silicon era. It is believed that CMOS technology will soon run into its saturation due to technical and economical reasons. However, CMOS technology is still far from the physical limits of computation. To get closer to these limits we have to move to the nanoscale regime. A number of electronic nanotechnologies are currently being investigated that take advantage of quantum-mechanical effects of nanoscale devices, including single-electron transistors, nanowire transistors, quantum dots, quantum cellular automata, resonant tunnelling devices, and reconfigurable switches. Among the most promising technologies are molecular electronic systems such as chemically assembled electronic nanotechnology (CAEN) [32]. CAEN uses the principles of self-alignment and self-assembly to construct electronic circuits. CAEN combined with nanoscale wiring technologies, such as carbon nanotubes and metal nanowires, seems to be a likely candidate for the post-silicon era. The CAEN self-assembly fabrication process is fundamentally non-deterministic and shows high defect densities. As a consequence, CAEN devices will have to be highly-regular structured and will require reconfiguration to dynamically map computations to non-defect parts of the device.

Molecular electronic nanotechnology poses many research challenges, from the construction of basic computing elements up to the programming model. Many proposals, such as the nanoFabric [33] or the NanoArrays [34], organize CAEN devices into arrays of molecular electronics and interconnects consisting of local and global nanoscale wires. The support system for the CAEN arrays, consisting of power supply, clock, configuration resources, and I/O, is implemented in CMOS. These architectures are similar to commercial fine-grained FPGAs. For this reason, researchers believe that similar techniques and methods can be applied to both FPGAs and CAEN devices.

One research issue is the role of static and dynamic reconfiguration in electronic nanotechnology. Based on a self-testing phase, CAEN devices will reconfigure the computations to non-defect CAEN blocks on the chip. It is an open question how this reconfiguration can be efficiently done and whether it effects only nanowires or also logic blocks. Another issue is whether reconfiguration should be used only statically as a defect-tolerance technique or also dynamically to optimally adapt the computation structure to the application under execution. Finally, models of computation for massively parallel nanoscale devices must be developed. Recently proposed approaches include the so-called split-phase abstract machine [33] and an execution model that has been termed computation cache [35].

References

[1]   K. Compton and S. Hauck, Reconfigurable Computing: A Survey of Systems and Software, ACM Computing Surveys, (34)2: 171-210, 2002.

[2]   T. Miyazaki, Reconfigurable Systems: A Survey, Proceedings of the Asian and South Pacific Design Automation Conference (ASP-DAC), pages 447- 452, 1998.

[3]   B. Radunovic and V. Milutinovic, A Survey of Reconfigurable Computing Architectures, Field-Programmable Logic and Applications (FPL), pages 376-385.

[4]   J.M. Arnold and D.A. Buell and E.G Davis, Splash 2, Proceedings of the Annual ACM Symposium on Parallel Algorithms and Architectures (SPAA), pages 316-322, 1992.

[5]   J.E. Vuillemin, P. Bertin, D. Roncin, M. Shand, H.H. Touati and P. Boucard, Programmable Active Memories: Reconfigurable Systems Come of Age, IEEE Transactions on Very Large Scale Integration (VLSI) Systems, (4)1: 56-69, 1996.

[6]   J.R.Hauser and J. Wawrzynek, Garp: A MIPS Processor with a Reconfigurable Coprocessor, Proceedings IEEE Symposium on Field-Programmable Custom Computing Machines (FCCM), pages 12-21, 1997.

[7]   C.R. Rupp, M. Landguth, T. Garverick, E. Gomersall, H. Holt, J.M. Arnold and M. Gokhale, The NAPA Adaptive Processing Architecture, Proceedings IEEE Symposium on Field-Programmable Custom Computing Machines (FCCM), pages 28-37, 1998.

[8]   T. Miyamori and K. Olukotun, REMARC: Reconfigurable Multimedia Array Coprocessor, IEICE Transactions on Information and Systems, (E82-D)2:389-397, 1999.

[9]   R.D. Wittig and P. Chow, OneChip: An FPGA Processor With Reconfigurable Logic, Proceedings IEEE Symposium on Field-Programmable Custom Computing Machines (FCCM), pages 126-135, 1996.

[10]   S. Hauck, T.W. Fry, M.M. Hosler and J.P. Kao, The Chimaera Reconfigurable Functional Unit, Proceedings IEEE Symposium on Field-Programmable Custom Computing Machines (FCCM), pages 87-96, 1997.

[11]   C. Ebeling, D.C. Cronquist and P. Franklin, RaPiD – Reconfigurable Pipelined Datapath, Field-Programmable Logic (FPL), pages 126-135, 1996.

[12]   S.D Brown, Field-Programmable Devices: Technology, Applications, Tools, Stan Baker Associates, 1995.

[13]   S. Brown and J. Rose, FPGA and CPLD Architectures: A Tutorial, IEEE Design & Test of Computers, pages 42-57, Summer 1996.

[14]   A.K. Sharma, Programmable Logic Handbook, McGraw-Hill, 1998.

[15]   S.M. Trimberger, Field-Programmable Gate Array Technology, Kluwer Academic Publishers, 1994.

[16]   J.V. Oldfield R.C. Dorf, Field-Programmable Gate Arrays, JohnWiley & Sons, 1995.

[17]   P.K. Chan and S. Mourad, Digital Design Using Field Programmable Gate Arrays, Prentice Hall, 1994.

[18]   T. Miyamori K. Olukotun, A Quantitative Analysis of Reconfigurable Coprocessors for Multimedia Applications, Proceedings IEEE Symposium on FPGAs for Custom Computing Machines (FCCM), pages 2-11, 1998.

[19]   T.J.Callahan, J.R. Hauser and J. Wawrzynek, The Garp Architecture and C Compiler, IEEE Computer, (33)4:62-69, April 2000.

[20]   Xilinx Inc., Virtex-II 1.5V Field Programmable Gate Arrays: Advance Product Specification, 2001.

[21]   A. DeHon, Reconfigurable Architectures for General-Purpose Computing, Massachusetts Institute of Technology, Artificial Intelligence Laboratory, PhD Thesis, 1996.

[22]   A. Cataldo, ISSCC: NEC takes leap into programmable logic, EE Times, February 15, 1999.

[23]   A. DeHon, DPGA Utilization and Application, Proceedings ACM/SIGDA International Symposium on Field Programmable Gate Arrays (FPGA), pages 115-121, 1996.

[24]   A. DeHon, DPGA-Coupled Microprocessors: Commodity ICs for the Early 21st Century, Proceedings IEEE Workshop on FPGAs for Custom Computing Machines (FCCM), pages 31-39, 1994.

[25]   T. Fujii et al., A Dynamically Reconfigurable Logic Engine with Multi-context/Multi-mode Unified-cell Architecture, IEEE International Solid-State Circuits Conference (ISSCC), pages 364-365, 1999.

[26]   A. Marshall, T. Stansfield, I. Kostarnov, J. Vuillemin and B. Hutchings, A Reconfigurable Arithmetic Array for Multimedia Applications, Proceedings ACM/SIGDA International Symposium on Field Programmable Gate Arrays (FPGA), pages 135-143, 1999.

[27]   R. W. Hartenstein, M. Herz, T. Hoffmann and U. Nageldinger, On Reconfigurable Co-Processing Units, Parallel and Distributed Processing, Proceedings of IPPS/SPDP'98 Workshops, pages 67-72, 1998.

[28]   G. Ezer, XTensa with User Defined DSP Coprocessor Microarchitectures, Proceedings International Conference on Computer Design (ICCD), pages 335-342, 2000.

[29]   ARC International, Customizing a Soft Microprocessor Core, 2002.

[30]   Altera Corporation, Nios 2.0 CPU Data Sheet, 2002.

[31]   Xilinx, Inc., MicroBlaze Hardware Reference Guide, 2002.

[32]   E. Collier et al., Electronically Configurable Molecular-based Logic Gates, Science, 285: 391-393, 1999.

[33]   C. Goldstein and M. Budiu, NanoFabrics: Spatial Computing Using Molecular Electronics, Proceedings International Symposium on Computer Architecture (ISCA), 2001.

[34]   A. DeHon, Array-Based Architecture for Molecular Electronics, Proceedings of the First Workshop on Non-Silicon Computation (NSC), 2002.

[35]   S. Swanson and M. Oskin, Towards a Universal Building Block of Molecular and Silicon Computation, Proceedings of the First Workshop on Non-Silicon Computation (NSC), 2002.

29.4   Software Integration – Automotive Applications

Landscape

Component integration is one of the tough challenges in embedded system design. Complex hardware-software architectures are a necessary result to reach design goals but significantly increase design risk. Embedded system designers search for conservative design styles and reliable techniques for interfacing and verification.

Hardware and Software Heterogeneity
With growing embedded system complexity more and more parts of a system are reused or supplied, often from external sources. These parts range from single hardware components or software processes to hardware-software (HW/SW) subsystems. They must cooperate and share resources with newly developed parts such that the design constraints are met. This, simply speaking, is the integration task. Ideally, this should be a plug-and-play procedure which does not happen in practice. Reasons are incompatible interfaces and communication standards but also specialization. Take a signal processing program that has been adapted to a specific DSP (Digital Signal Processor) architecture by carefully rewriting the source code using special functions or subword parallelism, optimizing loops, data transport, and memory access. Reusing

such a DSP program either means rewriting that code or reusing the whole DSP architecture or part of it turning the original software integration problem into a hardware-software integration problem. A crypto algorithm that runs on an application specific instruction set processor (ASIP) is another example. DSP and ASIP architectures are great to reach the performance and power consumption goals but they make portability and, thus, reuse harder. Particularly complicated are some of the specialized I/O and weakly programmable timer units, such as the TPU.

Unfortunately, compilers that could automatically adapt the code are not yet available – the designer is already happy if assembly coding can be avoided. You may continue the list with hardware accelerators, specialized memory architectures, buses, etc.. Architectural variety and adaptation seem inevitable to reach demanding design goals for competitive systems. The revival of ASIPs is driven by this observation. So, we will have to live with heterogeneous embedded system architectures and their corresponding integration problems. This holds for SoC (Systems-on-Chip) as well as for larger distributed embedded systems.

Software Integration – Automotive Perspective
On the other hand, there is a tendency towards subsystems integration. Traditionally, the automotive industry is used to a business model where the supplier provides the electronic control unit together with the software implementing a specific automotive function, such as engine control, dash board, window motors, antilock breaks (ABS), adaptive cruise control (ACC), etc.. Integration means that the zoo of often more than 50 control units is hooked up to automotive buses which have to carry the communication load. This is an increasingly difficult task due to distributed automotive functions such as ACC. There are three reasons to abandon that business model.

- To reduce the number of control units, the software shall be integrated on fewer control units
- Distributed networked functions using many different control units
- The common goals of modularity, scalability, re-usability and especially portability of software functions between different control units and cars.

These goals lead to an integration problem of different software modules on the individual control units. This integration problem is one of the aspects addressed in the AUTOSAR development partnership (http://www.autosar.org). In this international partnership, car manufacturers and first level suppliers define the future automotive system architecture as well as the software architecture and interfaces for the different control units. For the individual control units of the different domains, the integration problem can be mapped to the execution of different software functions using common resources like processing time, memory and shared variables on one control unit. This scenario requires a real-time operating system (RTOS), in the automotive environment following the OSEK standard (http://www.osek-vdx.org). The RTOS schedules the software functions and ensures consistency of the shared variables using messages. Of course, access to shared variables, message exchange as well as execution time and memory usage of the software functions need to be fixed in formal agreements to ensure system correctness. Such a formal software integration scenario for the powertrain domain has been proposed in [4]. In this approach, one of the primary concerns is the clear and coherent definition of a design process that identifies and assigns legal responsibilities that can be mapped to contracts. This is a basic requirement for a certifiable design process.

Besides hardware/software platform issues that are treated in this chapter, there is always the problem of functional correctness. The latter is approached in a platform independent modular decomposition and formal interface definition which shall improve system test. The related system function modelling and system function test is another field of top interest in AUTOSAR. One needs agreements on functions and interfaces between the software modules like exchanged variable lists and well-defined development processes as well as sophisticated testing against the functional specifications.

We summarize that the main integration tools in automotive platforms are the communication, and possibly memory, infrastructure as well as the basic software, i.e. the real-time operating system (RTOS) and communication software providing support for resource sharing and interfacing as well as application programmer interface (API) software that increases portability.

The application in the automotive industry is just one example. The same software integration challenges manifest themselves in telecommunication applications, on home platforms, or in mobile communication systems. The basic concepts are transferable and the presented methodology can be applied in different domains. In the following, the problems and concepts shall be generalized.

Assessment

Integration Challenges
In general, we can identify three main types of design tasks in embedded system integration,

- component and subsystem interfacing,
- system verification, and
- system optimization with design space exploration.

The first two tasks are general design problems, while the latter one depends on the cost and optimization pressure of an application. This roadmap chapter looks at the first two issues which are also a prerequisite to system optimization and design space exploration.

Interfacing is well developed at the RTOS level. There are software-software communication primitives such as queues (pipes) for message passing, shared variables, and semaphores for synchronization. These communication primitives separate computation from communication. The communication primitives are mapped to platform dependent functions. This way, software can be ported more easily exchanging the implementation of communication primitives. In contrast, the hardware description languages in use today (VHDL and Verilog) only support communication via electric signals. Porting hardware components to a new design requires hardware process adaptation. HW/SW communication uses drivers that, again, must be adapted to the hardware protocol. Using similar communication primitives on both sides would make hardware adaptation and driver development much easier. Therefore, newer hardware description languages, such as SpecC (a C language extension – http://www.SpecC.org) and SystemC (a C++ class library – http://www.SystemC.org)

extend hardware communication to abstract primitives comparable to RTOS communication. Using such primitives, the hardware component function can be separated
from its communication with other system components, similar to RTOS primitives.
Integration can, therefore, focus on implementing the communication primitives
which might be reused for different components to be integrated. This development of
new languages is still ongoing, but standards and first tools are out with support from
major EDA vendors.

Interfacing is necessary but not sufficient. The fact that the parts properly exchange
values and messages does not imply correctness. This is a matter of semantics and
target architecture performance. Both must be checked in system verification. Function verification focuses on the system semantics which should be implementation
independent while performance verification shall validate hardware parameters, processor resource sharing and communication performance in order to detect performance pitfalls such as transient overloads, or memory overflows.

Typically, both function and performance verification use prototyping or simulation ("virtual" prototyping). Prototyping uses a different target architecture at least for
parts of a design. For such parts, prototyping only allows function verification. Moreover, prototyping is expensive in terms of development time, and there are limitations
concerning available parts or non-reachable environment conditions (just think of
modelling a specific engine failure or car accident). So, for this article, we will focus
on simulation.

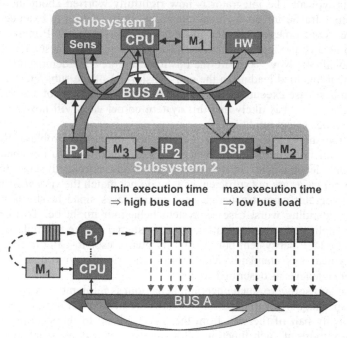

Figure 32.4. Effect of Extra-functional Dependencies on Integration

While function verification of an embedded system may use untimed simulation, performance verification relates to timing and therefore requires timed simulation, i.e. simulation where events have a time label. Because timed simulation needs far more computation time, performance verification is a bottleneck. Therefore, abstract timing models for components reducing computation time receive much attention. Such models range from so called "cycle-accurate" models which model the system behaviour clock cycle by clock cycle, to networks of abstract state machines, such as in the CADENCE VCC simulator (http://www.cadence.com/).

It is, however, not sufficient to just develop faster simulation models and simulators. Consider the example in Figure 32.4. A supplier has provided subsystem 1 consisting of a sensor ("Sens") which sends signals to a microcontroller CPU running a system of processes with preemptive scheduling (i.e. scheduling where the execution of one process can be interrupted for the execution of another process), one of them is P_1. This subsystem uses a bus A two times, to read the sensor data and to write the data to a hardware component which could be a peripheral device generating output signals periodically. The sensor signal is buffered in the CPU memory M_1. The supplier provides the working subsystem and simulation patterns stimulating the worst case CPU load situation including the worst case execution time (WCET) of P_1. The integrator decides to share bus A with a DSP subsystem 2. Subsystem 2 consists of an IP (intellectual property) component that generates periodic output data (e.g. a filter or Digital-to-Analog Converter) and a DSP processor running a fixed periodic schedule. A buffer is inserted at the DSP input to resynchronize the data stream. This integration task is typical. The integrator is now rightfully worried about the distortion that subsystem 1 traffic injects to subsystem 2 possibly leading to extended end-to-end system response times and buffer under or overflow at the DSP input. The integrator has no idea of the internal subsystem function, only the worst case simulation patterns are available. Now, compare the bus load. Figure 32.4 demonstrates that the highest transient bus load leading to the worst distortion of the subsystem 2 traffic is caused by the best case execution time (BCET) of P_1 which was not a corner case in subsystem design. So, it is likely that this system corner case will not be covered in simulation and the system might fail.

This example shows a fundamental performance simulation problem. Simulation patterns from function simulation are not sufficient, since they do not check for the extra-functional dependencies of the two functionally unrelated subsystems. The *subsystem* corner cases are not sufficient as they do not match the *system* corner cases. The system integrator cannot generate new corner cases since he/she is not aware what the corresponding worst case subsystem behaviour might be. To make things even more complicated, communication of subsystem 1 in the example is not only distorted by the DSP subsystem but also by its own sensor-to-CPU traffic. Unfortunately, the typical bus standards with arbitration priorities introduce such extra-functional dependencies as described above.

Unlike standard software, such uncertain behaviour is intolerable in embedded system design especially when life critical functions are involved. Firing an airbag 10ms late takes roughly half of the way from the driver's head to the steering wheel and there are many more of such functions in a car. But even if lives are not involved, even less frequent system failures can make products unmarketable as people are typically not willing to accept an embedded system with the quality level of PC software.

Conservative Design
One possible answer is to use integration techniques and strategies that avoid extra-functional dependencies. The TDMA (Time Division Multiple Access) protocol assigns a fixed time slot to each logic communication channel, i.e. Sens-CPU, CPU-HW, IP-DSP, and remains unused even if the communication is not active. This way, each logic communication channel receives a fixed share of the overall bandwidth irrespective of the other subsystems. The discrete time slots introduce jitter, but this jitter can be bounded and may already be considered in component design. This conservative technique is adopted both on the chip level, where it is, e.g., used by the Sonics Micronetworks, and in larger scale systems such as in the TTP architecture for safety critical automotive and aerospace applications (http://www.ttagroup.org). The TDMA technique can be applied to processor scheduling and it can be extended all the way to software development, where the elegantly simple mathematical formulation describing TDMA performance can be used for a system wide performance analysis and control, such as in the Giotto tool of UC Berkeley [2].

However, conservative design with TDMA comes at a performance (and power) price. If short response times are required, or if the system reacts to non periodic and burst events, or if the load varies depending on system scenarios, then the system must be significantly overdesigned. The problem is that even a small change in the conservative strategy dilutes the conservative properties. In, e.g., a round-robin strategy which assigns unused slots to the next process or communication in line, we see the same extra-functional dependencies, even though round-robin at least guarantees minimum performance that is equivalent to TDMA.

Performance Analysis
Instead of conservative design, one might resort to a more formal performance analysis. Statistical approaches do not seem adequate given the complex deterministic communication patterns leading. They do not capture very specific overload conditions and either be risky or lead to overly conservative design.

Today, most advanced embedded system engineers are familiar with formal methods developed for real-time computing, at least with rate-monotonic scheduling and analysis (RMS and RMA) [7]. RMA shows the principle of such formal methods. RMA abstracts from individual process activations (as used in simulation) to activation patterns. Based on these activation patterns and process worst case execution times (WCETs), it derives schedulability and worst case response times. There is a host of work in the real-time computing community on schedulability and response time tests using activation pattern and WCET as input. In contrast to the static priority assignment in RMS, another approach treats task scheduling under dynamically assigned priorities such as earliest deadline first (EDF) [15]. The basic ideas behind both RMS and EDF have been heavily extended to cover sporadic tasks [14] or more complex task activation with jitter and burst [19], arbitrary priority [1] and deadline assignments [6].The worst case execution times are typically simulated or measured. Recently there was major progress in formal program analysis with first commercial tools available modelling program execution (http://www.absint.com). There is a chapter in this roadmap dedicated to process WCET.

Cache interference introduces dependencies between process executions. As caches, today, are even used in critical real-time systems, such as automotive engine controllers, cache related inter-process dependencies require attention. In automotive control units, large sets of small, periodically executed processes with very few, if any, loops show significant cache related overhead. This has not sufficiently been investigated, so far. Current approaches either analyze cache related preemption delay [5][8] for simplified execution models that do not match the complexity of automotive engine controllers or suggest cache locking to simplify cache access strategies [11].There are still other open issues, such as best case execution time analysis (see Figure 32.4) but we may expect formal analysis solutions in the near future which could replace or complement measurement or simulation, provided that there is enough investment into the EDA technology and processor models.

If such formal methods are available, why is there a need for conservative design? The main limitation is that these methods do not easily scale to larger heterogeneous embedded systems such as Figure 32.4. They cover one processor or bus or at most a subsystem with homogeneous scheduling [3][13]. There are proposals combining few different scheduling strategies, e.g. RMS on a processor and TDMA on the bus. These are called holistic approaches and were introduced by Tindell [16]. A very good recent example that shows the power of this "holistic" approach is the work in [9], which is based on an automotive case study [10]. EDF task scheduling and TDMA bus-protocols have been considered in [15]. In general, it appears more efficient to identify solutions that encompass the whole system than to consider local scheduling individually.

On the other hand, there is an apparent scalability problem when considering the huge number of potential subsystem combinations that require adapted holistic scheduling. Not surprisingly, a general coherent approach covering, e.g., Figure 32.4 is not known to the author.

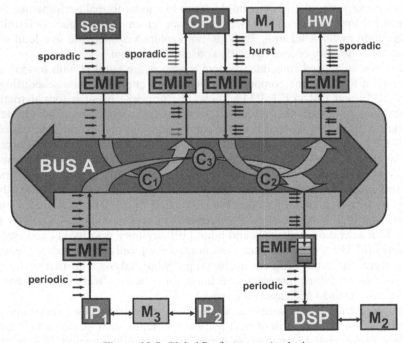

Figure 32.5. Global Performance Analysis

If we take Figure 32.4 again, then we see that we could partition the system into lo-cally scheduled communicating components grouped around bus A which has its own resource arbitration protocol. In principle, these components send and receive mes-sages which can be combined to message streams. Figure 32.5 shows Figure 32.4 highlighting these message streams. With some relatively simple math, we can trans-form the message streams to activation patterns such that the analysis results of the sending component are propagated to the analysis algorithm of the next component. This also works for buses. These transformations are called Event Model Interface (EMIF). We continue propagation and analysis until we have reached the output. Components can be analyzed if all input streams are available. This way, we turn global performance analysis into an event flow analysis problem. Loops in the flow, such as between the CPU and bus A (bidirectional flow) are solved by iteration. Even-tually, we can also calculate the required buffer size at the DSP input. For more de-tails, the interested reader is referred to [12].

Event streams can also be modelled as distribution functions that capture upper and/or lower bounds of event counts versus time. This is a more general model that is combined with new approximate analysis algorithms. Following the same principle of local analysis and event propagation, this approach has successfully been used to analyze network processor architectures [17], [18].

We can summarize that flow based analysis has been applied to first practical ex-amples from telecom, automotive and multi-media even though expert knowledge is still necessary and no easy-to-use tool is available yet.

Trends

Given the development of embedded system complexity it seems that simulation based performance verification is slowly running out of steam. This is what worries people in safety critical applications today and, with growing system complexity, will be a key problem for any integrator. Conservative techniques alone are no general solution for power consumption, cost and performance reasons. Formal methods as an alternative to simulation based performance verification have many benefits as an alternative to simulation based performance verification, but must be extended to global analysis methods adequate to heterogeneous embedded systems. It appears that the real medium to long term alternative is conservative design versus analytical per-formance verification. Conservative techniques would be used where sound perform-ance verification methods are not applicable or are for whatever reason inefficient (e.g. too wide bounds due to abstract formal models).

Timed simulation will continue to play a big role, and appears inevitable when continuous time models are included to simulate the embedded system together with its physical environment. Combinations are possible [20]. But, given the advances in analytical methods, we should reconsider if it is useful to put most energy in improv-ing timed event driven simulation or if we should invest more effort into formal meth-ods for performance analysis of complex architectures.

Systems integration is a top embedded system design issue. Platform performance verification is a key problem of systems integration. There are many hidden perform-ance dependencies and pitfalls that are not reflected in the system function. The ef-fects grow with platform complexity. Performance verification is currently primarily based on timed simulation. This approach is risky and time consuming, and it does not scale to larger systems. There is a good chance that embedded systems integration failures will become a major thread to the European industry if there is no investment in appropriate solutions.

We foresee two developments that approach integration problems from different directions, conservative design and formal performance analysis. Conservative design reduces extra-functional subsystem dependencies and supports independent subsystem development and integration. It can be used to reduce platform dependency by assigning fixed and implementation independent time slots to all processing and communication. Conservative design leads to overdesign that comes at a significant performance, cost and, possibly, power consumption price. It can, however, be the only viable choice where highly reliable design is required.

An alternative is a formal performance analysis that includes heterogeneous architectures as described in this chapter. There is major progress in that direction which enables system wide performance analysis. It has the potential to enable highly competitive and cost effective yet reliable software integration and optimization. This is currently demonstrated in several applications and has already reached industrial practice, e.g. in software integration for automotive powertrain control.

Formal performance analysis will not replace but complement simulation. Appropriate commercial tools, models and interface standards will be needed to reach a wider user base in the European embedded system design community. The automotive AUTOSAR consortium is a good example of a suitable standardization platform.

Formal architecture modelling and analysis techniques should be included in the engineering curriculum in order to raise an understanding for integration problems and for formal approaches, both for conservative design and for performance analysis. Standard university covers rarely go beyond classical real-time basics which is inappropriate to current system complexity. This is a challenge for the development of new courses.

References

[1]   N. C. Audsley, A. Burns, M. F. Richardson, and A. J. Wellings. Hard Real-Time Scheduling: The Deadline Monotonic Approach. Proceedings of the 8th IEEE Workshop on Real-Time Operating Systems, pages 133-137, 1991.

[2]   Th. Henzinger, Ch. Kirsch, R. Majumdar, and S. Matic. Time-safety checking for embedded programs. Proceedings of the Second International Workshop on Embedded Software (EMSOFT), Lecture Notes in Computer Science 2491, Springer-Verlag, 2002, pp. 76-92.

[3]   K .Jeffay and S. Goddard. A theory of rate-based execution. *In Proceedings Real-TimeSystems Symposiom*, Phoenix, Arizona, 1999.

[4]   M. Jersak, K. Richter, R. Racu, J. Staschulat, R. Ernst, J.C. Braam und F. Wolf, "Formal methods for integration of automotive software", Embedded Software for SOC, Kluwer Academic Publisher, August 2003.

[5]   C.-G. Lee, K. Lee, J. Hahn, Y-M. Seo, S. L. Min, R. Ha, S. Hong, C. Y. Park, M. Lee, C. S. Kim, "Bounding Cache-related preemption delay for real-time systems", In IEEE Transactions on software engineering, Vol 27, No. 9, pages 805-826, Sept. 2001.

[6]   J. Lehoczky. Fixed priority scheduling of periodic task sets with arbitrary deadlines. In *Proceedings Real-Time Systems Symposiom*, pages 201-209, 1990.

[7]   C. L. Liu and J. W. Layland. Scheduling algorithms for multiprogramming in a hard-real-time environment. *Journal of the ACM*, 20(1):46-61, 1973.

[8]   H. S. Negi, T. Mitra, and A. Roychoudhury, "Accurate estimation of cache-related preemption delay", Proceedings of the 1st IEEE/ACM/IFIP international conference on Hardware/software codesign & system synthesis, pages 201-206, 2003,

[9]   P. Pop, P. Eles, and Z. Peng. Bus access optimization for distributed embedded systems based on schedulability analysis. In *Proc. Design, Automation a*nd and Test in Europe (DATE 2000), Paris, France, 2000.

[10]   T. Pop, P. Eles, and Z. Peng. Holistic scheduling and analysis of mixed time/event-triggered distributed embedded systems. Proceedings of the International Symposium on Hardware/Software Codesign (CODES02), pp.187-192, Estes Park (CO), USA, 2002.

[11]   I. Puaut, "Cache analysis vs static cache locking for schedulability analysis in multitasking real-time system", Proc. of 2nd International Workshop on worst-case execution time analysis, Vienna, Austria, June 2002.

[12]   K. Richter, M. Jersak, R. Ernst. A Formal Approach to MpSoC Performance Verification, *IEEE Computer*, April 2002, or http://www.spi-project.org.

[13]   L. Sha, R. Rajkumar, and S. S. Sathaye. Generalized rate-monotonic scheduling theory: A framework for developing real-time systems. *Proceedings of the IEEE*, 82(1):68-82, January 1994.

[14]   B. Sprunt, L. Sha, and J. Lehoczky. Aperiodic task scheduling for hard real-time systems. *Journal of Real-Time Systems*, 1(1):27-60, 1989.

[15]   J. Stankovic, M. Spuri, K. Ramamritham, andG. Buttazzo. *DEADLINE SCHEDULING FOR REAL-TIME SYSTEMS – EDF and Related Algorithms*. Kluwer Academic Publishers, Boston, Massachusetts, USA, 1998.

[16]   K. W. Tindell. An extendible approach for analysing fixed priority hard real-time systems. *Journal of Real-Time Systems*, 6(2):133-152, Mar 1994.

[17]   L. Thiele, S. Chakraborty, M. Gries, S. Künzli: Design Space Exploration of Network Processor Architectures. *First Workshop on Network Processors at the 8th International Symposium on High-Performance Computer Architecture* (HPCΛ8), Cambridge MA, USA, pages 30-41, February, 2002.

[18]   L. Thiele, S. Chakraborty, and M. Naedele. Real-time Calculus For Scheduling Hard Real-Time Systems. Proceedings of International Symposium on Circuits and Systems (ISCAS 2000), pp. 101-104, Geneva, Switzerland, vol. 4, March 2000.

[19]   K. Tindell and J. Clark. Holistic schedulability analysis for distributed real- time systems. *Microprocessing and Microprogramming – Euromicro Journal (Special Issue on Parallel Embedded Real-Time Systems)*, 40:117–134, 1994.

[20]   S. Chakrabortya, S. Künzli, L. Thiele, A. Herkersdorf, P. Sagmeister. Performance evaluation of network processor architectures: Combining simulation with analytical estimation. *Computer Networks 41 (2003) 641–665.*

30   Low Power Engineering

Aspects of low power engineering are also covered in section 26.1.

30.1   Power-Aware and Energy Efficient Middleware

Landscape

Resource usage in embedded system platforms depends on application workload characteristics, desired quality of service and environmental conditions. In general, system workload is highly non-stationary due to the heterogeneous nature of information content. Quality of service depends on user requirements, which may change over time. In addition, both can be affected by environmental conditions such as network congestion and wireless link quality. For instance, consider a video streaming application based on a video capture embedded device that grabs, encodes and transmits a video stream through a wireless network to a remote video decoding and playback device. , the decoder may experience a variable input data rate due to channel quality variations such as noise level and fading. User tuneable network parameters, such as transmission power and code rate, lead to variations in error probability and latency affecting the PSNR (Peak Signal to Noise Ratio) as well as the perceived quality of the video sequence.

Power aware approaches in this context aim at reducing the power consumption of embedded systems either by controlling algorithmic and network parameters or by appropriately configuring resource power states to adapt to workload characteristics, network conditions and quality of service requirements. Power optimization policies may non-uniformly affect different parts of the system. Hence, effective techniques should be aware of the power consumption of all components of a wearable device, and ensure adequate orchestration of power management actions. For example, quantization in MPEG4 encoding algorithms may be tuned to significantly reduce communication energy (spent by the network interface card) with little loss in visual quality. On the other hand, the impact in computational energy (spent by the processor) has been shown to be very small [Zhao02]

System power can be reduced through power state configuration of processor and devices. In general-purpose architectures such as those used in modern mobile devices, resources are redundant and as they must accommodate the peak of computational, memory and I/O requirements. For this reason, resources can be put in low-power modes characterized by lower performance adapting to the workload and the required QoS. For instance, processor speed and voltage can be scaled down if applications provide information on their requirements, such as processor utilization [Yuan01]. Idle resources can be put in non-operational sleep states.

Applying a power optimization policy means making power related decisions which affects the utilization of hardware resources. Some policies try to adapt resource utilization by exploiting information about the workload, system state (e.g. battery level, wireless channel conditions) and required QoS, so that the power con-

Artist FP5 Consortium: Embedded Systems Design, LNCS 3436, 450–478, 2005.
© Springer-Verlag Berlin Heidelberg 2005

sumption is minimized. Closed loop policies may be adopted as they exploit output information to adjust power-related parameters. For instance, PSNR feedback can be used to avoid strong variations in video quality.

Interaction with the user is also possible. In an energy constrained environment, *a user can decide to trade off quality of service with power to increase battery lifetime and thus service duration.* As an example, consider a video telephone application. The user may decide to lower the image quality to extend battery lifetime and conversation duration. Algorithms that allows to gradually trade off quality of service/performance for energy can be defined as energy scalable [Sinha02]. Not all the algorithms are energy scalable and different algorithms have different energy-quality behaviour. Algorithms can be modified to achieve better energy scalability [Sinha00, Sinha02, Bhardwaj01].

In an application-centric view, decisions depend only on the single application, with the additional option of exploiting information from the surrounding environment, represented by local or remote entities interacting with application, like network conditions or the state of a remote content provider. *In this case techniques are said to be collaborative.* For instance, a remote server may provide workload information to aid a dynamic processor voltage scaling (DVS) algorithm [Chung02] or perform energy efficient traffic reshaping to save power spent by a wireless network interface (WNIC) [Acquaviva03].

It is important to notice that application-centric techniques are applicable only in application-specific systems. *OS-collaborative techniques are mandatory in a multi-processing environment* to perform explicit management of shared system resources like processor, network interfaces, video displays. For instance, scaling the processor speed affects all the applications running on the system. As a consequence, the scaling decision cannot be made by a single application but must be coordinated by the operating system. In this case applications may give information about their resource usage or quality of service requirements to an under-laying power manager acting at the OS-level [Yuan01a, Min02].

The state of the art in the area of power aware middleware is surveyed in the *Assessment* section, moving from an application-centric view to more general, OS-collaborative techniques. As a preliminary step, the key concept of energy-scalability is introduced. Energy-scalability is a highly desirable characteristic for applications in an energy-aware environment, since it is an indicator of the potential for smoothly trading off quality of service for power savings. In other words, if the application workload is highly energy scalable, the power management middleware layer has ample opportunities for saving power in a robust fashion (i.e., under a wide spectrum of environmental conditions) without severely compromising quality of service.

Assessment

Application Scalability
The concept of scalability is first introduced with examples taken from the multimedia domain. Then relationship between energy and power consumption is analysed by introdcing a quantitative technique for assessing energy scalability, namely, *Energy – Quality curves (E – Q).* Finally, it is discussed how E – Q behaviour can be improved.

Many embedded applications provide services that must reach several users characterized by diverse local resources (display size, storage and processing capabilities, interconnection bandwidth), often located in a highly mobile scenario, where environmental conditions are strongly variable. A high adaptation capability is required in such a context. Adaptability is obtained by exploiting the concept of scalability. An application of this concept can be found for example in encoding-transmission-decoding applications. The data stream is packetized according to the content of the data, in order to enable fast transmission of low-resolution but critical information, followed by progressive transmission of additional details carried by additional data packets. The described mechanism provides means for recovering the audio-visual information at its highest quality under the imposed system resource constraints.

Different scalability options can be available depending on the algorithm characteristics and implementations like spatial resolution, quality level and temporal resolution of video and audio sequences. This enables a variety of trade-offs between QoS and resource costs such as memory size, processing requirements, power consumption.

As a complex application example, MPEG-4 supports scalability. MPEG4 is an ISO/IEC standard being developed by MPEG (Moving Picture Experts Group). While MPEG-1 standard was mainly targeted to CD-ROM applications, and the MPEG-2 for digital TV and HDTV, with higher quality as well as bandwidth requirements (2Mb/s – 30Mb/s), the MPEG-4 standard primarily focuses on interactivity, higher compression, universal accessibility and portability of video content., with rates between 5 –64Kb/s for mobile applications and up to 2Mb/s for TV/film applications.

MPEG-4 supports scalable coding, the technique allowing access or transmission of Video Objects (VO's) at various spatial and temporal resolutions. This allows to support receivers with different bandwidth or to provide a layered video bit stream amenable to prioritised transmission. Receivers can choose not to reconstruct the full resolution VOs by decoding subsets of the layered bit stream to display the VOs at lower spatial or temporal resolution or with lower quality [Zhao02]. Both spatial and temporal scalability are supported by MPEG-4. For the sake of illustration, we focus on temporal scalability.

Temporal scalability involves partitioning the video object planes (VOPs) that can be defined as the VO in a determined time instant. VOPs are partitioned into layers, where the lower layer is coded by itself to provide the basic temporal rate and the enhancement layer is coded with temporal prediction w.r.t. the lower layer. Similar to spatial scalability, temporal scalability has an additional advantage in that it provides resilience to transmission errors. Object based temporal scalability can also be exploited to allow control of picture quality by controlling temporal rate of each video object under the constraint of a given bit-budget [Zhao02].

Energy Scalability
The scalability property of an application allows for adaptation of service levels to the characteristics of hardware devices. These characteristics can be intended as computational and bandwidth capabilities, but also energy requirements. Hence, scalability can be exploited to achieve a good trade-off between battery lifetime and quality of service: energy consumption can be reduced at the cost of a degradation of quality.

It is important to notice that, not all algorithms scale well w.r.t. energy. This observation leads to the concept of energy scalability, that has been introduced in [Sinha02] as the properties of algorithms to trade off computational accuracy (or quality, Q) with energy requirement (E). More precisely, an algorithm is said to be energy scalable if, when the available computational energy is reduced, the impact on quality gradually reduces. The concept can be extended to the total system energy. Algorithms evidencing this property have a good E – Q behaviour. The E – Q behaviour of an application can be modified to increase energy scalability through algorithmic transformations. Clearly, energy overhead due to these transformations must be small w.r.t. total energy consumption.

The formalization of the concept of desirable E – Q behaviour can be easily introduced through the E-Q graph, which represents the function Q(E), as shown in the figure below. Here Q represents some quality metric (e.g. PNSR, mean square error, etc.) as a function of the system energy. Consider two algorithms (I and II) that performs the same function: II would be more scalable compared to I if $Q_{II}(E) > Q_I(E)$, $\forall$ E. The desired E – Q behaviour described above can be easily expressed through the Q(E) function. In fact, we would like a curve maximally concave downwards (with respect to the energy axis). This is not always obtainable globally (i.e. across $0 \leq E \leq E_{max}$), however, on an average case, for a given energy availability, E, we would like the obtainable quality $Q(E)$ to be as high as possible.

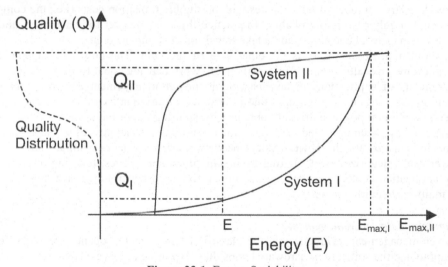

Figure 33.1. Energy Scalability

Energy Controllability and Observability
Most power optimisation strategies are aimed at trading off quality of service for computational or communication power by tuning power – related parameters. Computational power is saved by reducing the number of operations to be performed, while communication power is reduced by acting on the bit rate. The rationale behind these techniques is to adapt to characteristics of the workload to reduce the quality penalty caused by parameter tuning. In essence, they try to act on those parameters

that show good energy scalability. If an application is designed for good energy scalability, the power control middleware is given the potential to achieve substantial power savings without degrading quality of service metrics beyond acceptable levels. Currently, many applications in the embedded multimedia domain are developed taking scalability into the due consideration (refer to the MPEG4 example above). However, two key additional requirements must be met to obtain significant power savings; namely a good degree of *energy controllability* of hardware components and sufficient *observability* on resource requirements on the application side

To understand the notion of energy controllability, observe that resource power management requires hardware knobs allowing reconfiguration via software. For example, processor frequency and voltage can be adjusted to save system energy. Recent processors for embedded systems have been designed in a power-conscious way. As a result, several today's cores support different software-tuneable frequency and voltage levels. Moreover, peripherals are often characterized by multiple power states. For example, wireless network interfaces can be configured in power save mode and their transmission energy can be modulated upon software commands. Recent studies showed that also LCD displays are power manageable [Gatti02] [Choi02]. In an abstract sense a power manageable device can be seen as a state machine, where states correspond to different modes of operation with different power-performance characteristics. Transitions in the state machine are under external control and have a cost both in terms of time and power. Ideally, a components should provide a large number of power states with negligible transition costs (i.e., the component is highly power-controllable). In practice this goal is never fully achieved, and power management decisions should take transition cost into account.

Application observability is the other side of the coin. The power management middleware critically requires information on workload and quality of service requirements of applications to take acceptable power management decisions. As a limiting case, it is easy to observe that in absence of any quality of service requirements, minimum power is trivially obtained by shutting down the system. Many approaches have been proposed to increase the quantity and timeliness of workload and QoS information for the power management middleware. These techniques are surveyed and categorized next, starting from standalone approaches, focusing on a single-application context, and moving to cooperative (synergistic) approaches suitable to multi-task environments.

Standalone Power Management
Power management techniques can be classified based on the quantity they try to adapt to and the software or hardware knobs they exploit to achieve adaptation. Adaptation can be performed on workload (image size, resolution, video/audio content), network conditions (distance range, fading, multipath), user terminal characteristics (battery level, display size, processing capabilities), required QoS. Once established an adaptation parameter, achieving power efficiency through adaptation is not straightforward because of: 1) the intrinsic difficulty to choose an adaptation step (it is obviously not possible to continuously look at the adaptation parameter), 2) a fine tuning of the regulation variable is not always possible, and 3) the effects of the regulation on power consumption may be contrasting. To clarify the last point, let us consider the case of a compression algorithm. Improving communication energy – effi-

ciency by reducing the amount of data to be transmitted requires more computational energy spent by the processor to perform the compression task. The total energy balance must be evaluated in this case if we are interested in increasing the battery lifetime of a mobile device.

Workload adaptation is usually exploited to achieve a better usage of communication or computational resources while matching some constraints on the output (bandwidth or QoS requirements). For instance, several adaptive source coding algorithms look at the variable nature of input data (image and audio characteristics, required QoS) to reduce the amount of processing (which saves computational power), or to reduce the bit rate (which saves communication power) while keeping the required QoS level. Two key ideas in this area are: (1) *use application-provided workload information to operate the hardware resources in the least power consuming state allowed by the workload, (2) exploit application-level buffering for reducing the QoS degradation produced by power state transitions.*

In order to reduce CPU power, applications can exploit speed/voltage scaling capabilities of modern microprocessors. Clock speed reduction by a factor of s allows scaling down voltage as well thus leading to energy reduction by a factor of s^3 [Chandrakasan92]. The minimum power consumption is achieved when voltage is lowered so much that the operation speed is barely sufficient to meet the deadlines imposed by QoS requirements (just in time computation). This must be done in a workload adaptive way to avoid deadline misses impact quality. In the context of MPEG audio streaming, Acquaviva et al. [Acquaviva01] showed that the sample rate and bit rate information contained in the header of an MPEG stream can be exploited to estimate the workload at the beginning of an audio streaming session. This is an example of energy-aware application-level action. Workload information is forwarded to the power management middleware to help precise setting of the CPU power state. Similar approaches are described in [Simunic01, Delaney02].

It has also been observed that a speed setting approach with no voltage scaling can also lead to consistent energy reductions [Acquaviva01]. This is in contrast with the common assumption that speed-setting is effective only accompanied by an adequate voltage-setting policy. Of course, if voltage is scaled with frequency, more power can be saved, but the point here is that this is not a forced choice. Furthermore, even in presence of speed and voltage setting, significant opportunities remain for shutdown-based power management. In fact, in many cases the system or some of its components becomes idle even if execution time is ideally stretched. Consider for instance the case on an MPEG player. Even assuming that processor speed is set to the optimal frequency that guarantees minimum power as well as acceptable audio quality, when an audio stream terminates, the system becomes idle and it should be shut down to prolong battery life.

More in general, idleness can be classified as *implicit idleness* and *explicit idleness*. The first identifies CPU idleness dispersed among useful operations (mainly during memory wait cycles on cache misses). This term varies with frequency: since memory access time is fixed, adjusting the frequency involves variations in number of wait states in a bus cycle. This happens when (as usual) the CPU is not the speed limiting element. The second is due to coarsely clustered idle cycles. Explicit idleness is quite common in practice. When the execution time is fixed, as in the case of real-time constrained algorithms, making a computation faster involves the need of storing the results of computation in a buffer waiting for some event external at the CPU. During that time, the CPU experience idleness, that can be eliminated without affecting the algorithm effectiveness by increasing the time spent in useful operations, that is, by lowering the CPU frequency. Explicit idleness can be reduced by putting the processor in a low-power state while waiting and restoring the running state when the external event arrives (i.e. an external interrupt). The time and energy overhead needed to shut down and wake up the CPU should be taken into account when taking a shut down decision: even in this case, application hints can be extremely useful to decide on the duration of an idle time.

To reduce power even more aggressively, applications can be modified to better exploit clock scaling capabilities of the hardware, and to amortize the performance overhead caused by power state transitions. As an example, we examine the approach taken by Lu et al. They presented a design approach for a multimedia application that require constant output rates and sporadic jobs that need prompt responses. The method is based on splitting the application into stages and inserting data buffers between them [Lu02]. Data buffering has three purposes: 1) to support constant output rates; 2) to allow frequency scaling for energy reduction; and 3) to shorten the response times of sporadic jobs.

The proposed technique is aimed at reducing power by dynamic frequency scaling on processors that have only finite frequencies through data buffer insertion in multimedia programs. Data are processed and stored in the buffers when processor runs at higher frequency. Later, the processor runs at a lower frequency to reduce power and data are taken from the buffer to maintain the same output rate. Before the buffers become empty, the processor begins to run at a higher frequency again. Buffering can also shorten the response time of a sporadic job, if there are enough data in the buffers. In fact, the processor can handle a sporadic job without affecting the output rate of the multimedia program.

Collaborative Power Management
Even if single applications can be designed to address low-power requirements, often a stand-alone approach is not enough to satisfy tight power constraints imposed by battery-operated devices. Collaborative techniques, middleware-centric techniques, may be used in more aggressive power management techniques. In addition, collaborative techniques are mandatory in some cases. Consider for example the approach that perform dynamic voltage/clock processor scaling based on workload information. Application workload information is completely unaware of other applications that may be running on the same hardware platform. Applications often run in a multiprocessing environment, where hardware resources are shared among different processes. In such a context, resources management must be coordinated by the operating system that knows the needs of all active application in the system.

Collaboration can be used also to enhance the adaptation by exploiting workload knowledge provided by surrounding systems interacting with the device running the application. In particular, often mobile devices communicate with a remote machine, i.e. an application server. The remote server application can provide workload information allowing for effective power management decision at the client side. In a multiclient environment, the server can also implement a power aware scheduling strategy. These kinds of techniques are well suitable for hot spot servers that must handle connection with several clients providing them heterogeneous data streams. Collaborative policies may target the reduction of both communication and computational power.

The operating system coordinates resource access (peripherals, CPU and memories) for all the applications. Since a multimedia workload translates in application resource requirements, the OS can perform adaptation by monitoring the usage of resources and by selectively configuring their power states. Current operating systems implement simple policies based on timeout triggered by user interactions or on CPU current utilization. Many energy-aware OS-based collaborative techniques have been proposed in the recent past. They can be divided in three coarse classes, depending on the amount of application-level knowledge they assume: *(i) zero application knowledge, (ii) run-time application knowledge, (iii) design-time application knowledge* (see [Benini00, Pouwelse01, Gruian02] for representative examples of each class).

Zero application knowledge techniques do not require any information flow between applications and operating system. In other words, the OS takes power management decisions by observing the state of system resources, and, possibly, of autonomously collected system monitoring information. These approaches have the key advantage of being completely independent from application-level support, but they operate with very limited information, hence they either cause a measurable performance degradation, or they must be extremely conservative (and generally they save very little power). For this reason, zero-knowledge techniques are not suited for real-time workloads, where deadline misses are either not tolerable or they seriously compromise quality of service. Most of zero-knowledge techniques are based on some workload prediction mechanism: they try to predict future workloads by collecting statistics on past workloads. Power management decisions are then taken based on predictions, and the quality of results strongly depends on prediction quality. Many prediction techniques have been proposed, ranging from conservative timeout setting, to stochastic parameter estimation to various forms of regression. A review of zero-knowledge techniques can be found in [Benini00]. In the following, we describe in some details a representative zero-knowledge approach.

Kumar et al. proposed a modification of an RTOS kernel to perform power-aware scheduling of multimedia tasks that exploits the inherent tolerance of many multimedia applications to lost data samples due to factors like communication noise or network congestion [Kumar01]. This tolerance is used as an immunity noise margin that mitigates the effects of a wrong adaptation. In fact, the proposed strategy is based on a dynamic voltage scaling technique that uses a history of the actual computation requirements of the previous instances of a task to predict the computation required by the next instance. The prediction may have an error that may results in an underestimation that may lead to a deadline miss. The tolerance to a small percentage of missed deadlines can be exploited to do an aggressive DVS.

Table 33.1. Power reduction obtained with the predictive policy

Row No	Power Reduction Compared to Full Power Mode	Power Reduction Compared to Low Mode without Prediction	Number of Deadline Missed
I	95%	60%	33%
II	90%	30%	10%

Results of the application of the prediction strategy on an MPEG player are shown in Table 1. Power reduction achieved by two prediction strategies are shown. The number of frames missing their deadlines for the second strategy (row II) is much smaller compared to those of the first strategy (row I). This enhancement has been obtained by considering that I frames in MPEG are important parts of the sequence, so the prediction has been restricted to when P frames are about to be decoded. I frames are assumed to take always their worst case time to decode. Refer to [Kumar01] for a more detailed explanation of the prediction strategies. This example demonstrates also that better performance can be achieved when increasing the amount of application-level information provided to the OS (in this case, the type of MPEG frames), i.e., when moving toward run-time application knowledge.

Run-time application knowledge approaches assume that applications explicitly provide resource needs, which can be negotiated [Pouwelse01]. The middleware co-ordinates the Processor/Power Resource Management (PPRM) and has four major characteristics: (1) provides a power-aware resource reservation mechanism, where admission control is based on the processor utilization and power availability; (2) adjusts the speed and corresponding power consumption of the processor upon events, triggered by the change of the system workload or power availability; (3) updates reservation contracts of multimedia applications to maintain their resource requirements while adjusting the processor speed; and (4) notifies applications about the change of resource status to enable them to adapt their behaviour and complete tasks before power runs out.

Yuan and Nahrsted that propose a run-time application knowledge middleware framework which will be used as a representative example [Yuan01a]. The architecture of the middleware is shown in Figure 33.2. The operating system exports hardware resource (such as processor and power) status to the middleware layer, which receives resource request from applications. The middleware layer consists of three major components: the *Dynamic Soft Real-Time (DSRT)* processor scheduler [Yavatkar95], the power manager and the coordinating PPRM framework.

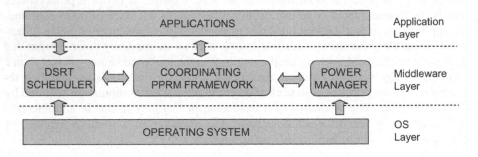

Figure 33.2. Middleware architecture of PPRM framework

The DSRT scheduler allows multimedia applications to reserve processor resource and corresponding power resource, and monitors the system workload. The power manager monitors the power availability (i.e., remaining battery lifetime) and the processor power consumption. The coordinating PPRM framework (1) determines polices on how to adjust reservations according to power availability, (2) uses the corresponding polices to differentiate applications in case of low power availability, (3) adjusts the processor speed to achieve minimum wasted energy, and (4) notifies application, if it cannot extend the battery life and meet the processor resource requirements of applications under low power availability.

The main characteristic of the DSRT scheduler is that it provides a power – aware resource reservation mechanism that separates soft or adaptive real-time multimedia applications from best effort applications, and statistically multiplexes processor resource between them. Each real-time application reserves a certain amount of processor resource, *required capacity, CRE* (as explained below), and the real-time workload is the sum of the *required capacity* of all admitted real-time applications in the system. The best-effort workload is limited by the available unreserved processor resource.

The other important component of this approach is the coordinating algorithm. It dynamically adjusts the speed of the processor to meet the following goals: (1) Ensuring enough power availability for all admitted multimedia applications (that is, the battery can last for the maximum duration of all multimedia applications). (2) Allocating the *required capacity* of processor resource to each multimedia application under high power availability. (2) Reducing the *required capacity* C_{RE} to *weight*C_{RE}* for each multimedia application, and notifying applications under low power availability. The processor is then run as slowly as possible to save energy while meeting the above goals.

Meeting the processor/power resource requirement of an adaptive real-time application means that (1) the *required capacity* of processor resource can be allocated to the application; and (2) the power availability is enough for the duration of the application. Note that a certain amount of processor resources is shared among all best-effort applications to protect starvation for best-effort applications. In Figure 33.3, adapted by [Yuan01a], is reported the utilization and the required capacity as a function of time for the proposed example. Summarizing, authors show that a percentage of *39.5%* of energy can be saved.

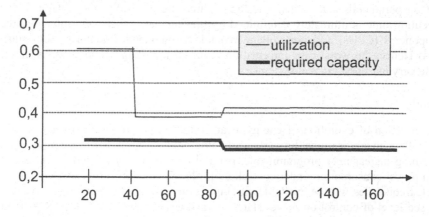

Figure 33.3. Example of application of PPRM framework

The presented technique represent a good evidence that when application provide their resource requirements to power – aware OSes, better power efficiency can be achieved with respect to predictive techniques.

Design-time application knowledge techniques assume a significant amount of knowledge on application knowledge at design time (refer to [Gruian02] for an extensive review). A typical assumption is the knowledge of the worst case execution time (WCET) of all tasks which can be run by a variable-voltage processor. In this setting, it is possible to assign priorities to all tasks and to set the CPU frequency and voltage to be used for each task. Typically, variations of well know real-time scheduling and schedulability analysis algorithms are used (e.g. EDS, RMS), followed by a voltage (and frequency) assignment step. The run-time of the voltage assignment algorithm can be high because the decision is taken at design time. Hence, computationally intensive techniques have been proposed to solve the scheduling and voltage assignment problem (which is NP-complete in all but some highly-simplified cases). This is in sharp contrast with run-time application knowledge policies, which must be run online with minimal performance impact.

Design time application knowledge techniques can benefit substantially from run-time information collection. This is because many conservative design time decisions can be refined when run-time information is available. For instance, design-time scheduling and voltage assignment are based on WCET values for all tasks, and it is well known that task runtime is often much shorter than the WCET. If a task runs in a time shorter than the WCET, the schedule has now some slack, which can be turned into power savings by immediately reducing the processor speed. Many slack reclamation strategies have been proposed, as outlined in [Gruian03]. Another hybrid design time and run time technique exploits intra-task compiler analysis to insert power management commands in correspondence of control flow arcs in the application [Shin02]. In this way, slowdown is subordinate to specific control-flow conditions which cannot be detected at run time only.

Even though most of the publications on power management are concerned with design-time techniques, their usefulness in practice is quite limited. This is because in many practical cases, it is not possible to characterize the workload with the required level of precision. Furthermore, processor voltage and frequency setting have an impact on peripherals and memory systems which are generally not voltage scalable. Execution time is ultimately determined by the interaction between voltage-scalable components (CPUs) and non-voltage scalable components (memories, I/O subsystems) Hence, the worst-case information required for design time analysis may become very inaccurate in real systems.

Trends

The direction of evolution of energy-aware middleware are driven by the trends in technology an applications. From the technological viewpoint, hardware platforms are becoming increasingly programmable, parallel and highly integrated. In an effort to keep power consumption under control, multiple dynamically adjustable voltages and clock frequencies will be available on chip. Hence, the middleware will have an increased level of control on power states of various subsystems. On the other hand, it will be extremely hard to maintain a centralized orchestration of power management decisions, because the various system components will be increasingly decoupled.

From an application-level viewpoint, the main trend is toward distributed application architectures. At the system level, most applications involve interaction between multiple actors (e.g. peer-to-peer, client sever), and the system state and workload can be much better characterized in a distributed fashion, in contrast on focusing on single components. Distributed techniques for power awareness appear therefore extremely promising. Approaches of this type have recently been explored in the context of wireless multimedia systems. These techniques are the first representative examples of the above mentioned trend, and will be described in some detail.

Wireless Mobile devices are often used as playback clients connected by a wireless link to a remote content provider (application server). The application server, based on its knowledge of workload and traffic shape, may provide information to the clients to selectively shut down their network interfaces. The effectiveness of such an approach has been recently explored in a wireless LAN environment [Acquaviva03]. In this work, authors present a power management infrastructure composed by couple of power manager modules, local and remote. The local power manager provides an application program interface to power related parameters of the system. In particular, it can control WLAN power states (off, doze, active), CPU speed and power states (active, idle, sleep). This interface can be exploited to implement a server controlled power management strategy. The proposed technique exploits the server knowledge of the workload, traffic conditions and feedback information from the client in order to minimize WLAN power consumption. Two entities are defined: a server power manager (server PM) and a client power manager (client PM). Both are implemented as a part of the Linux OS and they provide the power control interface to the applications. Server PM uses the information obtained from the client and the network to perform energy efficient traffic reshaping so that WLAN can be turned off. Client PM communicates through a dedicated low-bandwidth link with the server PM and implements the power controls by interfacing with the device drivers. It also provides a set of APIs that client applications can use to provide extra information back to the server.

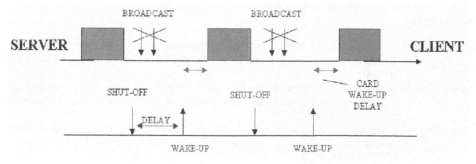

Figure 33.4. Example of application of the server assisted policy

The server PM achieves energy reduction at the wireless interface card of the client by means of traffic reshaping and controlling power states of the card. It schedules the transmission to the client in bursts in order to compensate for the client's performance and energy overheads during the transitions between card's on and off states. The client's WLAN card is switched off once the server has sent a burst of data that will keep the client application busy until the next communication burst. Burst size and delay between bursts must be pre-computed at the server. The goal is to have a delay large enough to almost empty the client input buffer and small enough burst size to avoid overflow while keeping the buffer sufficiently filled. An illustration of the shut-off policy is shown in Figure 33.4. The horizontal axes represent the time. In the upper axis the network traffic is represented, while in the lower axis are represented the power management decisions made by the server.

When the server decides to transmit (gray boxes) the WLAN is switched on, while when the server stops the transmission the WLAN is switched off (down arrow in the lower axis), thus discarding the broadcast traffic (down arrows in the upper axis). Before beginning a new transmission time interval, the server wakes up the WLAN (up arrow in the lower axis). The only parameters needed by the server to implement this policy are the burst size and time between bursts, which determines the time the card is in off state. The burst size has been established as the largest value as possible to avoid overflow conditions in the access point (AP) buffer or the application buffer, whichever the smaller. The burst delay can be computed by exploiting server's knowledge of frame composition, i.e. the number of packets needed to compose a video frame. This number may be strongly variable depending on the characteristics of the video sequence.

While this server-driven network interface power reduction technique is just a representative example, it demonstrates the potential and the key characteristics of distributed power management. First, by collecting and communicating data across multiple devices, more complete information on workloads and their evolution over time can be obtained. Second, energy-aware traffic re-shaping, which is possible only in a distributed approach, can greatly enhance power management opportunities. Third, complex power management decisions can be offloaded (possibly, in a dynamic fashion) to less energy constrained system components. Opportunities abound, but several challenges still remain open, and the evolution of distributed power management middleware is still at a preliminary stage.

References

[Acquaviva01] A. Acquaviva, L. Benini, B. Riccò, "Software Controlled Processor Speed-Setting for Low-Power Streaming Multimedia," Transaction on CAD, Novembre 2001.

[Acquaviva03] A. Acquaviva, T. Simunic, V. Deolalikar, S. Roy, "Remote Power Control of Wireless Network Interfaces," Proceedings of PATMOS, Turin, September 2003.

[Benini00] L. Benini, A. Bogliolo, and G. De Micheli. "A survey of design techniques for system-level dynamic power management". IEEE Trans. on VLSI Systems, 8(3):299--316, 2000.

[Yuan01a] W. Yuan, K. Nahrstedt, "A Middleware Framework Coordinating Processor/Power Resource Management for Multimedia Applications," Proceedings of IEEE GLOBECOM, November 2001.

[Lu02] Y.H. Lu, L. Benini, G. De Micheli, "Dynamic Frequency Scaling with Buffer Insertion for Mixed Workloads," IEEE Transaction on CAD, November 2002.

[Zhao02]   J. Zhao, R. Chandramouli, N. Vijaykrishnan, M.J. Irwin, B. Kang, S. Soma-
              sundaram, "Influence of MPEG-4 Parameters on System Energy," Proceedings
              of IEEE ASIC/SOC, 2002.

[Chung02]   E.Y. Chung, L. Benini, G. De Micheli, "Contents Provider-Assisted Dynamic
              Voltage Scaling for Low Energy Multimedia Applications," Proceedings of
              IEEE ISLPED, August 2002.

[Delaney02]   B. Delaney, N. Jayant, M. Hans, T. Simunic, A. Acquaviva, "A low-power,
              fixed-point, front-end feature extraction for a distributed speech recognition
              system," IEEE Proceedings of ICASSP, May 2002.

[Sinha02]   A.Sinha, A. Wang, A. Chandrakasan, "Energy Scalable System Design," IEEE
              Transaction on VLSI, Vol 10, No. 2, April 2002.

[He97a]   Z.L. He, K.K. Chan, C.Y. Tsui, M.L.Liou, "Low-Power Motion Estimation
              Design Using Adaptive Pixel Truncation," IEEE Proceedings of ISLPED, 1997.

[He97b]   Z.L. He, M.L. Liou, "Reducing Hardware Complexity of Motion Estimation
              Algorithms using Truncated Pixels," Proceedings of IEEE ISCAS, June 1997.

[Yuan01b]   W. Yuan, K. Nahrstedt, K. Kim, "R-EDF: A Reservation Based EDF Schedul-
              ing Algorithm for Multiple Multimedia Task Classes," IEEE Real-Time Tech-
              nology and Applications Symposium, May 2001.

[Kumar01]   P.Kumar, M. Srivastava, "Power Aware Multimedia Systems using Run-Time
              Prediction," Proceedings of IEEE VLSI Design, January 2001.

[Yavatkar95] R. Yavatkar, K. Laksman, "A CPU Scheduling Algorithm for Continuous Me-
              dia Applications," Workshop on Network and OS Support for Digital Audio
              and Video, April 1995.

[Gatti02]   F. Gatti, A. Acquaviva, L. Benini, B. Riccò, "Power Control Techniques for
              TFT LCD Displays," Procedings of ACM CASES, Grenoble, 2002.

[Gruian02]   F. Gruian, "Energy-Centric Scheduling for Real-Time Systems", Doctoral
              Dissertation, Lund University, Faculty of technology, 2002.

[Min02]   R. Min, A. Chandrakasan, "A Framework for Energy-Scalable Communication
              in High Density Wireless Networks," Proceedings of IEEE ISLPED, August
              2002.

[Sinha00]   A.Sinha, A. Wang, A. Chandrakasan, "Algorithmic Transforms for Efficient
              Energy Scalable Computation," Proceedings of IEEE ISLPED, August 2000.

[Simunic01]   T. Simunic, L. Benini, A. Acquaviva, P. Glynn, G. de Micheli, "Dynamic volt-
              age scaling and power management for portable systems," IEEE Proceedings of
              DAC, June 2001.

[Chandrasena00] L. H. Chandrasena, M. J. Liebelt, "A comprehensive analysis of energy sav-
              ings in dynamic supply voltage scaling systems using data dependent voltage
              level selection," Proceedings of IEEE International Conference on Multimedia
              and Expo, July-August 2000.

[Pouwelsc01] J. Pouwelse, K. Langendoen, H. Sips, "Energy priority scheduling for variable
              voltage processors," IEEE Proceedings of ISLPED, August 2001.

[Chandrakasan92] A. P. Chandrakasan, S. Sheng, R. W. Brodersen, "Low Power CMOS Digital
              Design," IEEE Journal of Solid State Circuits, Vol. 27 No. 4 , April 1992.

[Choi02]   I. Choi, H. Shim, N. Chang, "Low-Power Color TFT LCD Display for Hand-
              Held Embedded Systems," IEEE Proceedings of ISLPED, August 2002.

[Qu00]   G. Qu, M. Potkonjak, "Energy minimization with guaranteed quality of ser-
              vice," Proceedigns of IEEE ISLPED, July 2000.

30.2   Memory Hierarchy and Low Power Embedded Processors

Memory aspects of low power embedded processors cover two aspects corresponding to the two memory hierarchies in the processor: low power instruction memory and low power data memory. Power estimation techniques of embedded processors show that both parts are important to reduce the total processor power consumption. The data memory consumes up to 43% of the total power and the instruction memory up to 30% [15]. The section on data memory is partially based on [24].

Landscape

Data Memory Aspects
- **Code and Data Flow Transformations**: It has been recognized quite early in compiler theory (for an overview see [9]) and high-level synthesis that in front of the memory organization related tasks, it is necessary to perform transformations which optimize mainly the loop control flow. Otherwise, the memory organisation will be heavily suboptimal with respect to power.

  Interactive loop transformations: Most existing work focuses on the loop control flow. Work to support this crucial transformation task has been especially targeted to interactive systems of which only few *support* sufficiently general loop transformations. Very early work on this has started already at the end of the 70's [73] but that was only a classification of the possible loop transformations.

  In the *parallel compiler domain*, interactive environments like Tiny [121], Omega at U. Maryland [61], SUIF at Stanford [49], the Paradigm compiler 1 at Univ. of Illinois [8] and the ParaScope Editor [78] at Univ. of Rice have been presented. Also non-singular transformations have been investigated in this context [69]. These provide very powerful environments for interactive loop transformations as long as no other transformations are required.

  Automated loop transformation steering: In addition, research has been performed on (partly) automating the steering of these loop transformations. Many transformations and methods to steer them have been proposed which *increase the parallelism*, in several contexts. This has happened in the array synthesis community (e.g. at Saarbrucken [111], mainly intended for interconnect reduction in practice, at Versailles [41] and E.N.S. Lyon [34] and at the Univ. of SW Louisiana [103]) in the parallelizing compiler community (e.g. at Cornell [69], at Illinois [84], at Stanford [5], at Santa Clara [102], and more individual efforts like [115] and [28]) and finally also in the high-level synthesis community (at Univ. of Minnesota [92] and Univ. of Notre-Dame [94]). None of these approaches work globally across the entire system, which is required to obtain the largest impact for multimedia algorithms.

  Efficient parallelism is however partly coupled to *locality of data access* and this has been incorporated in a number of approaches. Therefore, within the parallel compiler community, work has been performed on improving data locality. Most effort has been oriented to dealing with *pseudo-scalars* or signal streams to be stored in local caches and register-files. Examples of this are the work at INRIA [39] in register-file use, and at Rice for vector registers [4].

Some approaches are dealing with *array signals* in loop nests. Examples are the work on data and control-flow transformations for distributed shared-memory machines at the Univ. of Rochester [29], or heuristics to improve the cache hit ratio and execution time at the Univ. of Amherst [79]. At Cornell, access normalisation strategies for NUMA machines have been proposed [70]. Rice Univ. has also looked at the actual memory bandwidth issues and the relation to loop fusion [37]. At E.N.S. Lyon the effect of several loop transformation on memory access has been studied too [42]. A quite broad transformation framework including interprocedural analysis has been proposed in [77]. It is focused on parallelization on a shared memory multiprocessor. The memory related optimizations are still performed on a loop nest basis (so still "local") but the loops in that loop nest may span different procedures and a fusing preprocessing step tries to combine all compatible loop nests that do not have dependencies blocking their fusing.

Some work is however also directly oriented to storage or transfer optimization *between the processor(s) and their memories* to reduce the memory related cost (mainly in terms of area and power). Very early work in the compiler community has focused on loop fusion and distribution of the arrays over multiple pages in the memories [1]. That was intended to numerical loop nests with limited indexing.

The work at Ecole des Mines de Paris [6] on data mapping is also relevant in the context of multimedia applications. It tries to derive a good memory allocation in addition to the transformation (affine scheduling and tiling) of loop nests on a distributed memory MIMD processor. It does not support optimizations inside the processor memory however, so the possibility to map signals in-place on top of one another in the memory is not available. In *the high-level and embedded system-level synthesis community*, also some other work has been done in this direction. An example is the research at U.C. Irvine on local loop transformations to reduce the memory access in procedural descriptions [66]. In addition, at the Univ. of Notre Dame, work has addressed multi-dimensional loop scheduling for buffer reduction [95]. The link with the required compile- and run-time data dependence analysis to avoid false dependencies leading to unnecessary memory accesses has been addressed in [99]. Within the Phideo context at Philips and T.U. Eindhoven, loop transformations on periodic streams have been applied to reduce an abstract storage and transfer cost [119]. At Penn State [52] work on power oriented loop transformations has started. In the same context, at Louisiana State Univ., improving data locality by unimodular transformations is addressed in [98].

At IMEC, contributions have been made to a global loop transformation steering methodology and automatable techniques, using a Polyhedral Dependency Graph (PDG) model [23]. Later on a more accurate cost function [33] was added, and a constraint-based exploration method [33] was presented. To provide feedback to the system designer or to the loop transformation and data reuse decision steps, array-oriented memory size estimation techniques are required [65].

*   **Platform Dependent Memory Issues**: The memory interaction has been identified as a crucial bottleneck [96]. Still, the amount of effort at the compiler level to address this bottleneck shows a focus on a number of areas while leaving big holes in other (equally important) research issues. A summary about the different issues is provided in [22, 83].

Memory organization issues: Several papers have analyzed memory organization issues in processors, like the number of memory ports in multipleinstruction machines [81], or the processor and memory utilization [113]. This is however only seldom resulting in a formalizable method to guide the memory organization issues. Moreover, the few approaches are usually addressing the "foreground" memory organization issues, i.e. how scalar data is organized in the local register files.

Some approaches address the data organization in processors for programs with loop nests. Examples include a quantitative approach based on life-time window calculations to determine register allocation and cache usage at IRISA [19], a study at McMaster Univ. for the optimization of multiple streams in heavily pipelined data-path processors [76], and work at Rice on vector register allocation [4].

In a high-level or system synthesis context also several approaches have been introduced. A multimedia stream caching oriented approach is proposed in [50]. Interleaved memory organizations for custom memories are addressed in [26]. Memory bank assignment is addressed in [86].

Recently, this area has been the focus of much more effort, due to the growing importance of embedded software systems and their sensitivity to cost efficiency. As a result, the pure performance oriented approaches that had been the main focus for many decades are now augmented also with cost-aware approaches. A nice overview of the state-of-the-art related to the low power cost aspect can be found in section 30.2 of [16].

At IMEC, formalized techniques have been proposed to decide on the exploitation of the memory hierarchy [123]. Important considerations here are the distribution of the data (copies) over the hierarchy levels as these determine the access frequency and the size of each resulting memory. Once the memory hierarchy is defined globally, it can be further optimized by minimizing the storage bandwidth [124] and optimizing the signal to memory assignment [116].

Data locality and cache organisation related issues: Data (re)placement policies in caches have been studied for a long time, especially the theoretically optimal ones [11]. Most of this work however requires a-priori knowledge of the data sequence and hardware overhead.

Also data locality optimizing algorithm transformations have been studied relatively well already in the past, e.g. at Illinois/INRIA [43] and Stanford [120]. The focus lies on the detection of spatial and temporal data reuse exploitation in a given procedural code. Tiling (blocking) combined with some local (applied within a single loop nest) uniform loop transformations are then used to improve the locality. Partitioning or blocking strategies for loops to optimize the use of caches have been studied in several flavors and contexts, in particular at HP [40] and at Toronto [75]. The explicit analysis of caches is usually done by simulation leading to traces (see e.g. [38]), but some analytical approaches to model the sources of cache misses have been presented also [58]. This allows to more efficiently steering the transformations. Also software approaches to analyze the spatial cache alignment and its possible improvement have been proposed [122].

This has been extended and implemented in the SUIF compiler project at Stanford [49] to deal with multiple levels of memory hierarchy but it still is based on conventional loop nest models. Multi-level caches have also been investigated in [56]. The work at IRISA, Rennes [114] which distributes data over cache blocks is relevant here too. It uses a temporal correlation based heuristic for this but relies mostly on the hardware cache management still and is oriented mostly to scalars (or indivisible array units). The effect of spatial locality is studied e.g. in [59]. Prefetching (both in hardware and software) is also employed to achieve a better cache performance (see e.g. [71]). Program and related data layout optimizations based on a branch-and-bound search for the possible cache offsets (including "padding") have been proposed in [10].

Relevant work has also focused on the multimedia and communication application domain related memory organization issues in an embedded processor context. This is the case for especially U.C. Irvine. At U.C. Irvine, the focus has been initially on [85]: distributing arrays over multiple memories with clique partitioning and bin packing [90], optimizing the main memory data layout for improved caching based on padding and clustering signals in the main memory to partly reduce conflict misses [87], selecting an optimal data cache size based on conflict miss estimates [88] and distributing data between the cache and a scratch-pad memory based on life-time analysis to determine access conflicts in a loop context [89]. All of this is starting from a given algorithm code and the array signals are treated as indivisible units (i.e. similar as scalars but with a weight corresponding to their size). More recently they have added reordering of the accesses to reduce the misses [47]. This is based on accurate memory access models [46]. The exploration of the effect of the cache size and associativity and the related code transformations has been studied in [105].

In addition, there is a very large literature on code transformations which can potentially optimize this cache behaviour for a given cache organization which is usually restricted to one level of hardware caching (see other section). Architecture level low-power or high-performance caching issues have been addressed in other work also. Modified data caching architectures have been explored, such as victim buffers [3]. Both for instructions and data these are actually successors of the original idea of adding a small fully associative cache [57] to the memory hierarchy.

Instruction Memory Aspects

Although at a lower level of abstraction, data and instructions are essentially bits stored in memories, a distinction between the two has proved useful for optimizations at higher levels of abstraction. At such higher levels, different techniques are used to optimize instruction memory and data memory. Several features of the platform are found to heavily influence the interactions with the instruction memories. Many techniques can be found in the literature that exploit these features in order to reduce power consumption in instruction memories.

- **Code Compression**: Smaller memories are known to be faster and consume less power. Hence generating compact programs of the application has been desirable for both performance and energy reasons. For a given instruction set architecture, the techniques described in [14, 13, 25, 54] explicitly use some form of compression algorithm on the binary image to reduce the static code size. Additionally, compile-time [35] and link-time optimization techniques exist to generate compact code. Certain processors provide two instruction set, one normal and one reduced instruction set. Compiler techniques to exploit this dual instruction in order to produce compact code have been proposed [48].

Essentially, the bits in the program are the ones that ultimately cause switching in the physical system. Hence, reducing the number of bits and the modifying the way the bits cause the switching is one of the prime concerns to reduce energy. Several instruction encoding schemes [74, 67, 27, 13, 14] have been applied to reduce the effective switching on the (instruction and address) buses. Some of these techniques in addition to reduce to the effective switching also reduce the effective memory size. An exhaustive survey of various code compaction techniques can be found in [17].

- **Memory Organization**: Power and performance of the system is heavily influenced by the memory organization for a given memory access pattern. By adopting the memory organization to suit the access pattern, power can be reduced. Partitioning memories is an effective scheme to reduce power. Essentially, a block of memory is partitioned into smaller blocks and accesses to these blocks are restricted. Reduction in the number of accesses to memories reduces power consumption. In a n-way set-associative cache, each way can be considered as a partition. By using some way-prediction schemes, accesses to different partitions can be reduced. Several variants of this prediction scheme exist [2, 97, 21]. Alternatively, the caches themselves are partitioned into multiple caches and similar prediction schemes can be adopted [62, 53, 63]. In comparison with data memory accesses, instruction memory accesses have higher locality. This observation has led to some prediction schemes specific to instruction memories [53]. This aspect of high instruction locality has been used in direct mapped caches to reduce the number of accesses to the tag memory [51].

  Since memory accesses to larger memories consume more power, accesses can be filtered through a smaller buffer or a cache. This idea of an L0 buffer was first proposed in [57]. Since the locality of instructions is high the instruction accesses can be restricted to this small buffer to a large extent, thus reducing power. This scheme has proved to be very effective for many signal processing applications which are dominated by small loops. Many variants of this scheme have been proposed [64, 7, 109, 108, 110, 45, 31, 32, 44]. Most of these schemes are primarily hardware controlled. However, recently software controlled buffers have shown to be much more effective in embedded system domain [12, 118, 107, 91].

  For a certain class of embedded processors, very long instruction word (VLIW) processors, special cache designs exist. Flexible silo cache is one such design specifically designed for VLIW processors [30]. Similar to the L0 buffer, scheme for general purpose embedded processors clustered L0 buffers are shown to be power efficient for VLIW processors [55].

- **Software Transformations**: Furthermore, the memory access pattern influences the way the memory is organized. This access pattern can be changed by doing transformations at the mapping level or at the source code level. Several techniques exist to influence the memory access patterns through scheduling of operations [104, 20, 93]. Higher level loop transformations, like loop peeling and code hoisting also exist to exploit the L0 buffer [106, 117]. Optimization techniques based on high-level code transformations like function inlining, dead code removal, loop splitting and function call insertion, have also been proposed [72].

Assessment

In many different domains (compilation for parallel machines, high level synthesis, etc.), techniques have been developed that can be reused in the context of data access and storage optimization for low power embedded processors.

A low power *data* memory hierarchy has been a research issue much longer than *instruction* memory hierarchy, and therefore it is much more mature. But since in modern low power processors, e.g. VLIWs, the instruction part has become almost as important as the data part, the former has been the subject of intense research recently. Because behaviour of instructions and data memory is fundamentally different, the data memory techniques cannot be applied directly to the instruction side of the processor.

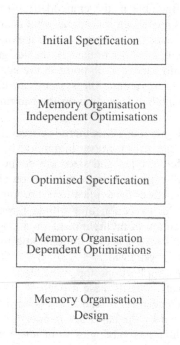

Figure 33.5. Memory optimization stages in an embedded system

Methodologies in this area tend to be split up in two stages: a platform-independent stage followed by a memory platform-dependent one (Figure 33.5). The first of the stages is nearly independent of the target architecture. The advantage of this stage is therefore that it has to be executed only once during the complete design trajectory irrespective of the number of mplementation platforms that is considered. The results obtained by the platform independent stage can be further improved. That is done by adapting the source code to the characteristics of the underlying (platform) memory organization. Its advantage is mainly the possibility of exploring platform specific trade-offs (e.g., speed versus power) that add crucial gains to the target cost function (e.g., power). Loop and data flow transformations play an important role in the platform independent optimizations.

Trends

We foresee that in future low power embedded systems, the components will be *i)* software controlled and *ii)* reconfigurable (either at design time, at run time or a combination of both). Because the components are software controlled, their power consumption can be optimized using characteristics of the running application without the overhead of hardware detection of these characteristics. Configuration at design time can lead to a certain optimal design for a certain application domain. Reconfiguration at runtime can lead to efficient utilization for a certain application.

These two aspects will influence future research issues related to memories. Some of the issues are as follows:

- **Design Space Exploration (DSE)**: Efficient exploration of the parameters that are configurable and reconfigurable in the embedded systems. Questions to be answered here are: What is the design space, and what is an efficient way to explore it? Typically the design space is too big to explore it exhaustively. In systems with multiple objectives (power, area, performance), the design time exploration results can be expressed in Pareto curves. Each point in the curve is Pareto optimal with respect to the objectives. At runtime the system can be reconfigured from one Pareto optimal point to another depending on the runtime behaviour of the application.
- **Platform**: Related to the previous issue, there is a trend to go from one instruction memory hierarchy and one data memory hierarchy, to a more hybrid approach where memories of different types and sizes are connected to the other components (e.g. computational engines) using a network on chip. The network on chip will be adaptable to the needs of the application(s) running on the platform.
- **Concurrency:** Support for execution of multiple threads in an SMT-like, low power fashion. The execution of multiple tasks on a single processor with shared memory will have significant impact on the data and instruction memory hierarchy. This will have to be investigated.
- **Runtime Management:** Applications for embedded systems are showing more and more dynamic aspects. One of these aspects is the use of dynamically allocated data structures. Management of allocation is normally done in the operating system (software), assisted by the hardware memory management unit. Foreseen future research will include methodologies to efficient manage dynamic memory completely in software.
- **Unified Methodologies:** Currently there is not integrated flow that combines the optimizations for data memory with those for instruction memory in an efficient way. Recent work has shown that a trade-off can exist between data and instruction memory optimizations for low power.
- **Tool Support:** For software controlled hardware, the compiler is responsible for inserting the special control instruction in the program. Support for these hardware features will need to be integrated in the current compilers. Additionally, the compiler also needs to be extended to take advantage of the configurable aspect of the system.

Another major evolution in low power memory is the growing importance of the *leakage power*. Leakage power can be avoided by shutting down parts of the memory that are not used. This way, however, the contents will be lost. Intermediate solutions exist that remain the contents, will still reducing the power consumption (e.g. drowsy mode for caches). All future optimization methods for low power need to take into account this power component.

References

[1]   W.Abu-Sufah, D.Kuck, D.Lawrie, "On the performance enhancement of paging systems through program analysis and transformations", *IEEE Trans. on Computers*, Vol.C-30, No.5, pp.341-355, May 1981.

[2]   D. H. Albenosi. Selective cache ways: On-demand cache resource allocation. *Journal of Instruction-Level Parallelism*, 2:1–6, 2000.

[3]   G.Albera, I.Bahar, "Power/performance advantages of victim bu®er in highperformance processors", *IEEE Alessandro Volta Memorial Intnl. Wsh. on Low Power Design (VOLTA)*, Como, Italy, pp.43-51, March 1999.

[4]   R.Allen, K.Kennedy, "Vector register allocation," *IEEE Trans. on Computers*, Vol.41, No.10, pp.1290-1316, Oct. 1992.

[5]   S.Amarasinghe, J.Anderson, M.Lam, and C.Tseng, "The SUIF compiler for scalable parallel machines", in *Proc. of the 7th SIAM Conf. on Parallel Proc. for Scientific Computing*, 1995.

[6]   C.Ancourt, D.Barthou, C.Guettier, F.Irigoin, B.Jeannet, J.Jourdan, J.Mattioli, "Automatic data mapping of signal processing applications", *Proc. Intnl. Conf. on Applic.-Spec. Array Processors*, Zurich, Switzerland, pp.350-362, July 1997.

[7]   R. S. Bajwa, M. Hiraki, H. Kojima, D. J. Gorny, K. Nitta, A. Shridhar, K. Seki, and K. Sasaki. Instruction bu®ering to reduce power in processors for signal processing. *IEEE Transactions on Very Large Scale Integration (VLSI) Systems*, 5(4):417–424, December 1997.

[8]   P.Banerjee, J.Chandy, M.Gupta, E.Hodges, J.Holm, A.Lain, D.Palermo, S.Ramaswamy, E.Su, "The Paradigm compiler for distributed-memory multicomputers", *IEEE Computer Magazine*, Vol.28, No.10, pp.37-47, Oct. 1995.

[9]   U.Banerjee, R.Eigenmann, A.Nicolau, D.Padua, "Automatic program parallelisation", *Proc. of the IEEE*, invited paper, Vol.81, No.2, pp.211-243, Feb. 1993.

[10]   S.Bartolini, C.A.Prete, "A software strategy to improve cache performance", *IEEE TC on Computer Architecture Newsletter*, pp.35-40, Jan. 2001.

[11]   L.A.Belady, "A study of replacement algorithms for a virtual-storage computer", *IBM Systems J.*, Vol.5, No.6, pp.78-101, 1966.

[12]   N. Bellas, I. Hajj, C. Polychronopoulos, and G. Stamoulis. Architectural and compiler support for energy reduction in the memory hierarchy of high performance microprocessors. In *Proc of International Symposium on Low Power Electronic Design (ISLPED)*, August 1998.

[13]   L. Benini, A. Macii, E. Macii, and M. Poncino. Selective instruction compression for memory energy reduction in embedded systems. In *Proc of International Symposium on Low Power Electronic Design (ISLPED)*, August 1999.

[14]   L. Benini, A. Macii, and A. Nannarelli. Cached-code compression for energy minimization in embedded processors. In *Proc of Interational Symposium on Low Power Electronic Design (ISLPED)*, August 2001.

[15]   L.Benini, D. Bruni, M. Chinosi,C. Silvano, V. Zaccaria, "A Power Modeling and Estimation Framework for VLIW-Based Embedded System", *ST Journal of System Research*, Vol.3, No.1, pp.110-118, April 2002.

[16]   L.Benini, G.De Micheli, "System-level power optimization techniques and tools", *ACM Trans. on Design Automation for Embedded Systems (TODAES)*, Vol.5, No.2, pp.115-192, April 2000.

[17]   A. Besd'ez, R. Ferenc, T. Gyimtthy, A. Dolenc, and K. Karsisto. Survey of code-size reduction methods. *ACM Computing Surveys (CSUR)*, 35(3):223–267, September 2003.

[18]   S.Bhattacharyya, P.Murthy, E.Lee, "Optimal parenthesization of lexical orderings for DSP block diagrams", *IEEE Wsh. on VLSI signal processing*, Osaka, Japan, Oct. 1995. Also in *VLSI Signal Processing VIII*, I.Kuroda, T.Nishitani, (eds.), IEEE Press, New York, pp.177-186, 1995.

[19]   F.Bodin, W.Jalby, D.Windheiser, C.Eisenbeis, "A quantitative algorithm for data locality optimization", Technical Report IRISA/INRIA, Rennes, France, 1992.

[20]   A. Bona, M. Sami, D. Sciuto, V. Zaccaria, C. Silvano, and R. Zafalon. An instruction-level methodology for power estimation and optimization of embedded vliw cores. In *Proc of Design Automation and Test in Europe(DATE)*, March 2002.

[21]   B. Calder, D. Grunwald, and J. Emer. Predictive sequential associative cache. In *Proc of 2nd International Symposium on High Performance Computer Architecture (HPCA)*, February 1996.

[22]   F.Catthoor, "Energy-delay e±cient data storage and transfer architectures and methodologies: current solutions and remaining problems", special issue on "IEEE CS Annual Wsh. on VLSI" (eds. A.Smailagic, R.Brodersen, H.De Man) in *J. of VLSI Signal Processing*, Vol.21, No.3, Kluwer, Boston, pp.219-232, July 1999.

[23]   F.Catthoor, S.Wuytack, E.De Greef, F.Balasa, L.Nachtergaele, A.Vandecappelle, "Custom Memory Management Methodology – Exploration of Memory Organisation for Embedded Multimedia System Design", ISBN 0-7923-8288-9, Kluwer Acad. Publ., Boston, 1998.

[24]   F.Catthoor, K. Danckaert, C. Kulkarni, E. Brockmeyer, P. G. Kjeldsberg, T. Van Achteren, T. Omnes, "Data Access and Storage Management for Embedded Programmable Processors", ISBN 0-7923-7689-7, Kluwer Acad. Publ., Boston, 2002.

[25]   P. Centoducatte, G. Araujo, and R. Pannain. Compressed code execution on dsp architectures. In *Proc of International Symposium on System Synthesis (ISSS)*, November 1999.

[26]   S.Chen, A.Postula, "Synthesis of custom interleaved memory systems", *IEEE Trans. on VLSI Systems*, Vol.8, No.1, pp.74-83, Feb. 2000.

[27]   W.C. Cheng and M. Pedram. Power-aware bus encoding techniques for i/o and data busses in an embedded system. *Journal of Circuits, Systems, and Computers*, 11(4):351–364, August 2002.

[28]   W.Chin, J.Darlington, Y.Guo, "Parallelizing conditional recurrences", *Proc. EuroPar Conf.*, Lyon, France, Aug. 1996. "Lecture notes in computer science" series, Springer Verlag, pp.579-586, 1996.

[29]   M.Cierniak, W.Li, "Unifying Data and Control Transformations for Distributed Shared-Memory Machines", *Proc. of the SIGPLAN'95 Conf. on Programming Language Design and Implementation*, La Jolla, pp.205-217, Feb. 1995.

[30]   T. M. Conte, S. Banerjia, S. Y. Larin, and K. N. Menezes. Instruction fetch mechanisms for vliw architectures with compressed encodings. In *Proc of 29th International Symposium on Microarchitecture (MICRO)*, December 1996.

[31]   S. Cotterell and F. Vahid. Synthesis of customized loop caches for core-based embedded systems. In *Proc of International Conference on Computer Aided Design (ICCAD)*, November 2002.

[32]   S. Cotterell and F. Vahid. Tuning of loop cache architectures to programs in embedded system design. In *Proc of International Symposium on System Synthesis (ISSS)*, October 2002.

[33]   K.Danckaert, F.Catthoor, H.De Man, "A preprocessing step for global loop transformations for data transfer and storage optimization", *Proc. Intnl. Conf. on Compilers, Arch. and Synth. for Emb. Sys.*, San Jose CA, pp.34-40, Nov. 2000.

[34]   A.Darte, T.Risset, Y.Robert, "Loop nest scheduling and transformations", in *Environments and Tools for Parallel Scientific Computing*, J.J.Dongarra et al. (eds.), Advances in Parallel Computing 6, North Holland, Amsterdam, pp.309- 332, 1993.

[35]   S. Debray, W. Evans, R. Muth, and B. D. Sutter. Compiler techniques for code compaction. *ACM Transactions on Programming Languages and Systems (TOPLAS)*, 22(2):378–415, March 2000.

[36]   C.Dezan, H.Le Verge, P.Quinton, and Y.Saouter, "The Alpha du CENTAUR experiment", in *Algorithms and parallel VLSI architectures II*, P.Quinton and Y.Robert (eds.), Elsevier, Amsterdam, pp.325-334, 1992.

[37]   C.Ding, K.Kennedy, "The memory bandwidth bottleneck and its amelioration by a compiler", *Proc. Intnl. Parallel and Distr. Proc. Symp.(IPDPS)* in Cancun, Mexico, pp.181-189, May 2000.

[38]   R.Doalla, B.Fraguela, E.Zapata, "Set associative cache behaviour optimization", *Proc. EuroPar Conf.*, Toulouse, France, pp.229-238, Sep. 1999.

[39]   C.Eisenbeis, W.Jalby, D.Windheiser, F.Bodin, "A Strategy for Array Management in Local Memory", *Proc. of the 4th Wsh. on Languages and Compilers for Parallel Computing*, Aug. 1991.

[40]   J.Z.Fang, M.Lu, "An iteration partition approach for cache or local memory thrashing on parallel processing", *IEEE Trans. on Computers*, Vol.C-42, No.5, pp.529-546, May 1993.

[41]   P.Feautrier, "Compiling for massively parallel architectures: a perspective", *Intnl. Wsh. on Algorithms and Parallel VLSI Architectures*, Leuven, Belgium, Aug. 1994. Also in "Algorithms and Parallel VLSI Architectures III" (eds. M.Moonen, F.Catthoor), Elsevier, pp.259-270, 1995.

[42]   A.Fraboulet, G.Huard, A.Mignotte, "Loop alignment for memory access optimisation", *Proc. 12th ACM/IEEE Intnl. Symp. on System-Level Synthesis* (ISSS), San Jose CA, pp.71-70, Dec. 1999.

[43]   D.Gannon, W.Jalby, K.Gallivan, "Strategies for cache and local memory management by global program transformations", *J. of Parallel and Distributed Computing*, Vol.5, pp.568-586, 1988.

[44]   A. Gordon-Ross and F. Vahid. Dynamic loop caching meets preloaded loop caching – a hybrid approach. In *Proc of International Conference on Computer Design (ICCD)*, September 2002.

[45]   A. Gordon-Ross, S. Cotterell, and F. Vahid. Exploiting fixed programs in embedded systems: A loop cache example. In *Proc of IEEE Computer Architecture Letters*, Jan 2002.

[46]   P.Grun, N.Dutt, and A.Nicolau, "Memory aware compilation through accurate timing extraction", *Proc. 37th ACM/IEEE Design Automation Conf.*, Los Angeles CA, pp.316-321, June 2000.

[47]   P.Grun, N.Dutt, and A.Nicolau, "MIST: an algorithm for memory miss tra±c management", *Proc. IEEE Intnl. Conf. on Comp. Aided Design*, Santa Clara CA, pp.431-437, Nov. 2000.

[48]   A. Halambi, A. Shrivastava, P. Biswas, N. Dutt, and A. Nicolau. An e±cient compiler technique for code size reduction using reduced bit-width isas. In *Proc of Design Automation Conference (DAC)*, March 2002.

[49]   M.Hall, J.Anderson, S.Amarasinghe, B.Murphy, S.Liao, E.Bugnion, M.Lam, "Maximizing multiprocessor performance with the SUIF compiler", *IEEE Computer Magazine*, Vol.30, No.12, pp.84-89, Dec. 1996.

[50]   F.Harmsze, A.Timmer, J.van Meerbergen, "Memory arbitration and cache management in stream-based systems", *Proc. 3rd ACM/IEEE Design and Test in Europe Conf.* (DATE), Paris, France, pp.257-262, April 2000.

[51]   K. Inoue, V. G. Moshnyaga, and K. Murakami. A history-based i-cache for low-energy multimedia applications. In *Proc of ACM/IEEE International Symposium on Low Power Electronics (ISLPED)*, August 2002.

[52]   M.J.Irwin, M.Kandemir, N.Vijaykrishnan, A.Sivasubramaniam, "A holistic approach to system level energy optimisation", *Proc. IEEE Wsh. on Power and Timing Modeling, Optimization and Simulation (PATMOS)*, Goettingen, Germany, pp.88-107, Oct. 2000.

[53]   J. Irwin, M. D. May, H. L. Muller, and D. Page. Predictable instruction caching for media processors. In *Proc of Internation Conference on Application-Specific Systems, Architectures and processors (ASAP)*, July 2002.

[54]   T. Ishihara and H. Yasuura. A power reduction technique with object code merging for application specific embedded processors. In *Proc of Design Automation and Test in Europe (DATE)*, March 2000.

[55]   M. Jayapala, F. Barat, P. OpDeBeeck, F. Catthoor, G. Deconinck, and H. Corporaal. A low energy clustered instruction memory hierarchy for long instruction word processors. In *Proc of 12th International Workshop on Power And Timing Modeling, Optimization and Simulation (PATMOS)*, September 2002.

[56]   M.Jimenez, J.Llaberia, A.Fernandez, E.Morancho, "A unified transformation technique for multi-level blocking" *Proc. EuroPar Conf.*, Lyon, France, Aug. 1996. "Lecture notes in computer science" series, Springer Verlag, pp.402-405, 1996.

[57]   N.Jouppi, "Improving direct-mapped cache performance by the addition of a small fully-associative cache and prefetch bu®ers", *Proc. ACM Intnl. Symp. on Computer Arch.*, pp.364-373, May 1990.

[58]   M.Kamble, K.Ghose, "Analytical Energy Dissipation Models for Low Power Caches", *Proc. IEEE Intnl. Symp. on Low Power Design*, Monterey CA, pp.143-148, Aug. 1997.

[59]   M.Kampe, F.Dahlgren, "Exploration of spatial locality on emerging applications and the consequences for cache performance", *Proc. Intnl. Parallel and Distr. Proc. Symp.(IPDPS)* in Cancun, Mexico, pp.163-170, May 2000.

[60]   J.Kang, A.van der Werf, P.Lippens, "Mapping array communication onto FIFO communication – towards an implementation", *Proc. 13th ACM/IEEE Intnl. Symp. on System-Level Synthesis* (ISSS), Madrid, Spain, pp.207-213, Sep. 2000.

[61]   W.Kelly, W.Pugh, "Generating schedules and code within a unified reordering transformation framework", Technical Report UMIACS-TR-92-126, CS-TR-2995, Institute for Advanced Computer Studies Dept. of Computer Science, Univ. of Maryland, College Park, MD 20742, 1992.

[62]   S. Kim, N. Vijaykrishnan, M. Kandemir, A. Sivasubramaniam, M. J. Irwin, and E. Geethanjali. Power-aware partitioned cache architectures. In *Proc of ACM/IEEE International Symposium on Low Power Electronics (ISLPED)*, August 2001.

[63]   S. Kim, N. Vijaykrishnan, M. Kandemir, A. Sivasubramaniam, and M. J. Irwin. Partitioned instruction cache architecture for energy e±ciency. *ACM Transactions on Embedded Computing Systems(TECS)*, July 2002.

[64]   J. Kin, M. Gupta, and W. H. Mangione-Smith. Filtering memory references to increase energy e±ciency. *IEEE Transactions on Computers*, 49(1):1–15, January 2000.

[65]   P.G.Kjeldsberg, "Storage requirement estimation and optimisation for datainten-sive applications", *Doctoral dissertation*, Norwegian Univ. of Science and Technology, Trondheim, Norway, March 2001.

[66]   D.Kolson, A.Nicolau, N.Dutt, "Minimization of memory tra±c in high-level synthesis", *Proc. 31st ACM/IEEE Design Automation Conf.*, San Diego, CA, pp.149-154, June 1994.

[67]   H. Lekatsas, J. Henkel, and W. Wolf. Code compression for low power embedded system design. In *Proc of Design Automation Conference (DAC)*, June 2000.

[68]   S.T.Leung, J.Zahorjan, "Restructuring arrays for e±cient parallel loop execution", Technical Report, Dep. of CSE, Univ. of Washington, Feb. 1994.

[69]   W.Li, K.Pingali. "A singular loop transformation framework based on nonsingular matrices", *Proc. 5th Annual Wsh. on Languages and Compilers for Parallelism*, New Haven CN, Aug. 1992.

[70]   W.Li, K.Pingali. "Access normalization: loop restructuring for NUMA compilers", *Proc. 5th Intnl. Conf. on Architectural Support for Prog. Lang. and Operating Systems (ASPLOS)*, April 1992.

[71]   H.B.Lim, P-C.Yew, "Efficient integration of compiler-directed cache coherence and data prefetching", *Proc. Intnl. Parallel and Distr. Proc. Symp.(IPDPS)* in Cancun, Mexico, pp.331-339, May 2000.

[72]   N. Liveris, N. D. Zervas, D. Soudris, and C. E. Goutis. A code transformation-based methodology for improving i-cache performance of dsp applications, March 2002.

[73]   D.B.Loveman, "Program improvement by source-to-source transformation", *J. of the ACM*, Vol.24, No.1, pp.121-145, 1977.

[74]   M. Mahendale, S. D. Sherlekar, and G. Venkatesh. Extensions to programmable dsp architectures for reduced power dissipation. In *Proc of VLSI Design*, January 1998.

[75]   N.Manjiakian, T.Abdelrahman, "Array data layout for reduction of cache conflicts", *Intnl. Conf. on Parallel and Distributed Computing Systems*, 1995.

[76]   D.McCrackin, "Eliminating interlocks in deeply pipelined processors by delay enforced multistreaming", *IEEE Trans. on Computers*, Vol.C-40, No.10, pp.1125-1132, Oct. 1991.

[77]   K.McKinley, "A compiler optimization algorithm for shared-memory multiprocessors", *IEEE Trans. on Parallel and Distributed Systems*, Vol.9, No.8, pp.769-787, Aug. 1998.

[78]   K.McKinley, M.Hall, T.Harvey, K.Kennedy, N.McIntosh, J.Oldham, M.Paleczny, and G.Roth, "Experiences using the ParaScope editor: an interactive parallel programming tool", in *4th ACM SIGPLAN Symp. on Principles and Practice of Parallel Programming*, San Diego, USA, May 1993.

[79]   K.McKinley, S.Carr, C-W.Tseng, "Improving data locality with loop transformations", *ACM Trans. on Programming Languages and Systems*, Vol.18, No.4, pp.424-453, July 1996.

[80]   P.Middelhoek, G.Mekenkamp, B.Molenkamp, T.Krol, "A transformational approach to VHDL and CDFG based high-level synthesis: a case study", *Proc. IEEE Custom Integrated Circuits Conf.*, Santa Clara CA, pp.37-40, May 1995.

[81]   S.M.Moon, K.Ebcioglu, "A study on the number of memory ports in multiple instruction issue machines", *Micro'26*, pp.49-58, Nov. 1993.

[82]   P.Murthy, S.Bhattacharyya, "A bu®er merging technique for reducing memory requirements of synchronous dataflow specifications", *Proc. 12th ACM/IEEE Intnl. Symp. on System-Level Synthesis (ISSS)*, San Jose CA, pp.78-84, Dec. 1999.

[83]   L.Nachtergaele, V.Tiwari, N.Dutt, "System and architecture-level power reduction of microprocessor-based communication and multi-media applications", *Proc. IEEE Intnl. Conf. on Comp. Aided Design*, Santa Clara CA, pp.569-573, Nov. 2000.

[84]   D.A.Padua, M.J.Wolfe. "Advanced compiler optimizations for supercomputers", *Communications of the ACM*, Vol.29, No.12, pp.1184-1201, 1986.

[85]   P.R.Panda, "Memory optimizations and exploration for embedded systems", *Doctoral Dissertation*, U.C.Irvine, April 1998.

[86]   P.R.Panda, "Memory bank customization and assignment in behavioural synthe-
         sis", *Proc. IEEE Intnl. Conf. Comp. Aided Design*, Santa Clara CA, pp.477-481,
         Nov. 1999.
[87]   P.R.Panda, H.Nakamura, N.D.Dutt, A.Nicolau, "Augmenting loop tiling with data
         alignment for improved cache performance", *IEEE Trans. on Computers*, Vol.48,
         No.2, pp.142-149, Feb. 1999.
[88]   P.R.Panda, N.D.Dutt, A.Nicolau, "Data cache sizing for embedded processor ap-
         plications", *Proc. 1st ACM/IEEE Design and Test in Europe Conf.* (DATE), Paris,
         France, pp.925-926, Feb. 1998.
[89]   P.R.Panda, N.D.Dutt, A.Nicolau, "Local memory exploration and optimization in
         embedded systems", *IEEE Trans. on Comp.-aided Design*, Vol.CAD-18, No.1,
         pp.3-13, Jan. 1999.
[90]   P.Panda, N.Dutt, "Low power mapping of behavioural arrays to multiple memo-
         ries", *Proc. IEEE Intnl. Symp. on Low Power Design*, Monterey CA, pp.289-292,
         Aug. 1996.
[91]   S. Parameswaran and J. Henkel. I-copes: Fast instruction code placement for em-
         bedded systems to improve performance and energy e±ciency. In *Proc of Interna-
         tion Conference on Computer Aided Design (ICCAD)*, November 2001.
[92]   K.Parhi, "Algorithmic transformation techniques for concurrent processors", *Proc.
         of the IEEE*, Vol.77, No.12, pp.1879-1895, Dec. 1989.
[93]   A. Parikh, M. Kandemir, N. Vijaykrishnan, and M. J. Irwin. Instruction scheduling
         based on energy and performance constraints. In *Proc of IEEE Computer Society
         Annual Workshop on VLSI (WVLSI)*, April 2000.
[94]   N.Passos, E.Sha, "Full parallelism of uniform nested loops by multi-dimensional
         retiming", *Proc. Intnl. Conf. on Parallel Processing*, Vol.2, pp.130-133, Aug.
         1994.
[95]   N.Passos, E.Sha, L-F.Chao, "Multi-dimensional interleaving for time-andmemory
         design optimization", *Proc. IEEE Intnl. Conf. on Computer Design*, Austin TX,
         pp.440-445, Oct. 1995.
[96]   D.Patterson, J.Hennessey, "Computer architecture : A quantitative approach",
         Morgan Kaufmann Publ., San Francisco, 1996.
[97]   M. D. Powell and et al. Reducing set-associative cache energy via way-prediction
         and selective direct-mapping. In *Proc of 34th International Symposium on Mi-
         croarchitecture (MICRO)*, November 2001.
[98]   J.Ramanujam, J.Hong, M.Kandemir, A.Narayan, "Reducing memory requirements
         of nested loops for embedded systems", *38th ACM/IEEE Design Automation
         Conf.*, Las Vegas NV, pp.359-364, June 2001.
[99]   S.Ravi, G.Lakshminarayana, N.Jha, "Removal of memory access bottlenecks for
         scheduling control-flow intensive behavioural descriptions", *Proc. IEEE Intnl.
         Conf. Comp. Aided Design*, Santa Clara CA, pp.577-584, Nov. 1998.
[100]   J.Saltz, H.Berrymann, J.Wu, "Multiprocessors and runtime compilation", *Proc.
         Intnl. Wsh. on Compilers for Parallel Computers*, Paris, France, 1990.
[101]   H.Samsom, L.Claesen, H.De Man, "SynGuide: an environment for doing interac-
         tive correctness preserving transformations", *IEEE Wsh. on VLSI signal process-
         ing*, Veldhoven, The Netherlands, Oct. 1993. Also in *VLSI Signal Processing VI*,
         L.Eggermont, P.Dewilde, E.Deprettere, J.van Meerbergen (eds.), IEEE Press, New
         York, pp.269-277, 1993.
[102]   W.Shang, E.Hodzic, Z.Chen, "On uniformization of a±ne dependence algorithms",
         IEEE Trans. on Computers, Vol.45, No.7, pp.827-839, July 1996.

[103]   W.Shang, M.O'Keefe, J.Fortes, "Generalized cycle shrinking", presented at Wsh. on "Algorithms and Parallel VLSI Architectures II", Bonas, France, June 1991. Also in *Algorithms and parallel VLSI architectures II*, P.Quinton and Y.Robert (eds.), Elsevier, Amsterdam, pp.131-144, 1992.

[104]   D. Shin and J. Kim. An operation rearrangement technique for low power vliw instruction fetch. In *Proc of Workshop on Complexity-E®ective Design*, 2000.

[105]   W.T.Shiue, C.Chakrabarti, "Memory exploration for low power embedded systems", *Proc. 36th ACM/IEEE Design Automation Conf.*, New Orleans LA, pp.140-145, June 1999.

[106]   J. W. Sias, H. C. Hunter, and W. mei W. Hwu. Enhancing loop bu®ering of media and telecommunications applications using low-overhead predication. In *Proc of 34th Annual International Symposium on Microarchitecture (MICRO)*, December 2001.

[107]   S. Steinke, L. Wehmeyer, B.-S. Lee, and P. Marwedel. Assigning program and data objects to scratchpad for energy reduction. In *Proc of Design Automation and Test in Europe (DATE)*, March 2002.

[108]   W. Tang, R. Gupta, and A. Nicolau. Design of a predictive filter cache for energy savings in high performance processor architectures. In *Proc of Internal Conference on Computer Design (ICCD)*, September 2001.

[109]   W. Tang, R. Gupta, and A. Nicolau. Power savings in embedded processors through decode filter cache. In *Proc of Design Automation and Test in Europe (DATE)*, March 2002.

[110]   W. Tang, R. Gupta, and A. Nicolau. Reducing power with an l0 instruction cache using history-based prediction. In *Proc of Internal Workshop on Innovative Architecture for Future Generation High-Performance processors and Systems (IWIA)*, January 2002.

[111]   L.Thiele, "On the design of piecewise regular processor arrays", *Proc. IEEE Intnl. Symp. on Circuits and Systems*, Portland OR, pp.2239-2242, May 1989.

[112]   D.E.Thomas, E.Dirkes, R.Walker, J.Rajan, J.Nestor, R.Blackburn, "The system architect's workbench", *Proc. 25th ACM/IEEE Design Automation Conf.*, San Francisco CA, pp.337-343, June 1988.

[113]   E.Torrie, M.Martonosi, C-W.Tseng, M.Hall, "Characterizing the memory behaviour of compiler-parallelized applications", *IEEE Trans. on Parallel and Distributed Systems*, Vol.7, No.12, pp.1224-1236, Dec. 1996.

[114]   D.N.Truong, F.Bodin, A.Seznec, "Accurate data distribution into blocks may boost cache performance", *IEEE TC on Computer Architecture Newsletter*, special issue on "Interaction between Compilers and Computer Architectures", pp.55-57, June 1997.

[115]   T.Tzen, L.Ni, "Dependence uniformization: a loop parallelization technique", *IEEE Trans. on Parallel and Distributed Systems*, Vol.4, No.5, pp.547-557, May 1993.

[116]   A.Vandecappelle, M.Miranda, E.Brockmeyer, F.Catthoor, D.Verkest, "Global Multimedia System Design Exploration using Accurate Memory Organization Feedback" *Proc. 36th ACM/IEEE Design Automation Conf.*, New Orleans LA, pp.327-332, June 1999.

[117]   T. Vander Aa, M. Jayapala, F. Barat, G. Deconinck, R. Lauwereins, F. Catthoor, and H. Corporaal. Instruction bu®ering exploration for low energy vliws with instruction clusters. In *Proc. of the Asian Pacific Design and Automation Conference 2004 (ASPDAC'2004)*, Yokohama, Japan, January 2004.

[118]   T. Vander Aa, M. Jayapala, F. Barat, G. Deconinck, R. Lauwereins, H. Corporaal, and F. Catthoor. Instruction bu®ering exploration for low energy embedded processors. In *Proc of 13th International Workshop on Power And Timing Modeling, Optimization and Simulation (PATMOS)*, September 2003.

[119]   W.Verhaegh, E.Aarts, P.Van Gorp, "Period assignment in multi-dimensional periodic scheduling", *Proc. IEEE Intnl. Conf. Comp. Aided Design*, Santa Clara CA, pp.585-592, Nov. 1998.

[120]   M.Wolf, M.Lam, "A data locality optimizing algorithm", *Proc. of the SIGPLAN' 91 Conf. on Programming Language Design and Implementation*, Toronto ON, Canada, pp.30-43, June 1991.

[121]   M.Wolfe, "The Tiny loop restructuring tool", *Proc. of Intnl. Conf. on Parallel Processing*, pp.II.46-II.53, 1991.

[122]   D.Wong, E.Davis, J.Young, "A software approach to avoiding spatial cache collisions in parallel processor systems", *IEEE Trans. on Parallel and Distributed Systems*, Vol.9, No.6, pp.601-608, June 1998.

[123]   S.Wuytack, F.Catthoor, G.De Jong, B.Lin, H.De Man, "Flow Graph Balancing for Minimizing the Required Memory Bandwidth", *Proc. 9th ACM/IEEE Intnl. Symp. on System-Level Synthesis* (ISSS), La Jolla CA, pp.127-132, Nov. 1996.

[124]   S.Wuytack, F.Catthoor, G.De Jong, H.De Man, "Minimizing the Required Memory Bandwidth in VLSI System Realizations", *IEEE Trans. on VLSI Systems*, Vol.7, No.4, pp.433-441, Dec. 1999.

Index

.NET
II. 10, 10.2, 12.2, 13.3, 14.1, 15.1
III. 17.4, 22.1, 23, 23.1, 23.2, 23.3

109 Challenge
I. 4.1

A380
I. 3.2

AAA
I. 5

AADL (Avionics Architecture
Description Language):
II. 12.5, 14.3
See also: ADL

Ada
I. 4.3, 6, 6.1, 6.3, 7.1, 7.3
II. 14.3
III. 17.4, 21.1, 23.1, 25.1, 25.2,
25.3, 25.4, 26.5
IV. 29.1

Adaptive
See: Adaptive Embedded System,
Adaptive Real Time, QoS Adapta-
tion, Reconfigurable

Adaptive Embedded System
III. 17.2, 17.4

Adaptive Real Time
III. *entire section*
See also: Adaptive Scheduling,
Soft Real Time

Adaptive Scheduling
III. 20.4
See also: Load Adaptation

ADL: (Architecture Description
Language)
I. 6.3
II. 10.2, 12.1, 12.3, 12.5, 14,
14.2, 14.3, 15.1
See also: AADL, Meta-H

AEE Project
I. 3.1

Aeronautics
I. 3.2, 4.2, 5, 6

Aerospace
I. 9.1, 9.2
II. 12.5
III. 21.1, 21.3, 24.4
IV. 28.2, 29.1, 29.4

AIL Language
I. 3.1, 5

aiT WCET Analyser
I. 7.3
III. 21.1
IV. 29.2

Analysis
See: Fault Analysis, Schedulability Analysis, Static Analysis

APEX
III. 21.1, 21.2, 21.3

Application Areas
See: Aeronautics, Aerospace,
Automation, Automotive, Avionics, Consumer Electronics, Control, Multimedia, Space, Telecommunications, Transport, Wireless Communication

Architecture
See: Hardware Architecture, Jini,
Reconfigurable Architecture,
Software Architecture

ARINC
I. 3.2
III. 21.1, 21.2, 21.3, 21.4, 24.1

ASIC
I. 2.2, 3.1, 3.2, 5
IV. 27, 29.2, 29.3

Lecture Notes in Computer Science

For information about Vols. 1–3315

please contact your bookseller or Springer

Vol. 3361: S. Bengio, H. Bourlard (Eds.), Machine Learning for Multimodal Interaction. XII, 362 pages. 2005.

Vol. 3360: S. Spaccapietra, E. Bertino, S. Jajodia, R. King, D. McLeod, M.E. Orlowska, L. Strous (Eds.), Journal on Data Semantics II. XI, 223 pages. 2005.

Vol. 3359: G. Grieser, Y. Tanaka (Eds.), Intuitive Human Interfaces for Organizing and Accessing Intellectual Assets. XIV, 257 pages. 2005. (Subseries LNAI).

Vol. 3358: J. Cao, L.T. Yang, M. Guo, F. Lau (Eds.), Parallel and Distributed Processing and Applications. XXIV, 1058 pages. 2004.

Vol. 3357: H. Handschuh, M.A. Hasan (Eds.), Selected Areas in Cryptography. XI, 354 pages. 2004.

Vol. 3356: G. Das, V.P. Gulati (Eds.), Intelligent Information Technology. XII, 428 pages. 2004.

Vol. 3355: R. Murray-Smith, R. Shorten (Eds.), Switching and Learning in Feedback Systems. X, 343 pages. 2005.

Vol. 3353: J. Hromkovič, M. Nagl, B. Westfechtel (Eds.), Graph-Theoretic Concepts in Computer Science. XI, 404 pages. 2004.

Vol. 3352: C. Blundo, S. Cimato (Eds.), Security in Communication Networks. XI, 381 pages. 2005.

Vol. 3351: G. Persiano, R. Solis-Oba (Eds.), Approximation and Online Algorithms. VIII, 295 pages. 2005.

Vol. 3350: M. Hermenegildo, D. Cabeza (Eds.), Practical Aspects of Declarative Languages. VIII, 269 pages. 2005.

Vol. 3349: B.M. Chapman (Ed.), Shared Memory Parallel Programming with Open MP. X, 149 pages. 2005.

Vol. 3348: A. Canteaut, K. Viswanathan (Eds.), Progress in Cryptology - INDOCRYPT 2004. XIV, 431 pages. 2004.

Vol. 3347: R.K. Ghosh, H. Mohanty (Eds.), Distributed Computing and Internet Technology. XX, 472 pages. 2004.

Vol. 3346: R.H. Bordini, M. Dastani, J. Dix, A.E.F. Seghrouchni (Eds.), Programming Multi-Agent Systems. XIV, 249 pages. 2005. (Subseries LNAI).

Vol. 3345: Y. Cai (Ed.), Ambient Intelligence for Scientific Discovery. XII, 311 pages. 2005. (Subseries LNAI).

Vol. 3344: J. Malenfant, B.M. Østvold (Eds.), Object-Oriented Technology. ECOOP 2004 Workshop Reader. VIII, 215 pages. 2005.

Vol. 3343: C. Freksa, M. Knauff, B. Krieg-Brückner, B. Nebel, T. Barkowsky (Eds.), Spatial Cognition IV. Reasoning, Action, and Interaction. XIII, 519 pages. 2005. (Subseries LNAI).

Vol. 3342: E. Şahin, W.M. Spears (Eds.), Swarm Robotics. IX, 175 pages. 2005.

Vol. 3341: R. Fleischer, G. Trippen (Eds.), Algorithms and Computation. XVII, 935 pages. 2004.

Vol. 3340: C.S. Calude, E. Calude, M.J. Dinneen (Eds.), Developments in Language Theory. XI, 431 pages. 2004.

Vol. 3339: G.I. Webb, X. Yu (Eds.), AI 2004: Advances in Artificial Intelligence. XXII, 1272 pages. 2004. (Subseries LNAI).

Vol. 3338: S.Z. Li, J. Lai, T. Tan, G. Feng, Y. Wang (Eds.), Advances in Biometric Person Authentication. XVIII, 699 pages. 2004.

Vol. 3337: J.M. Barreiro, F. Martin-Sanchez, V. Maojo, F. Sanz (Eds.), Biological and Medical Data Analysis. XI, 508 pages. 2004.

Vol. 3336: D. Karagiannis, U. Reimer (Eds.), Practical Aspects of Knowledge Management. X, 523 pages. 2004. (Subseries LNAI).

Vol. 3335: M. Malek, M. Reitenspieß, J. Kaiser (Eds.), Service Availability. X, 213 pages. 2005.

Vol. 3334: Z. Chen, H. Chen, Q. Miao, Y. Fu, E. Fox, E.-p. Lim (Eds.), Digital Libraries: International Collaboration and Cross-Fertilization. XX, 690 pages. 2004.

Vol. 3333: K. Aizawa, Y. Nakamura, S. Satoh (Eds.), Advances in Multimedia Information Processing - PCM 2004, Part III. XXXV, 785 pages. 2004.

Vol. 3332: K. Aizawa, Y. Nakamura, S. Satoh (Eds.), Advances in Multimedia Information Processing - PCM 2004, Part II. XXXVI, 1051 pages. 2004.

Vol. 3331: K. Aizawa, Y. Nakamura, S. Satoh (Eds.), Advances in Multimedia Information Processing - PCM 2004, Part I. XXXVI, 667 pages. 2004.

Vol. 3330: J. Akiyama, E.T. Baskoro, M. Kano (Eds.), Combinatorial Geometry and Graph Theory. VIII, 227 pages. 2005.

Vol. 3329: P.J. Lee (Ed.), Advances in Cryptology - ASIACRYPT 2004. XVI, 546 pages. 2004.

Vol. 3328: K. Lodaya, M. Mahajan (Eds.), FSTTCS 2004: Foundations of Software Technology and Theoretical Computer Science. XVI, 532 pages. 2004.

Vol. 3327: Y. Shi, W. Xu, Z. Chen (Eds.), Data Mining and Knowledge Management. XIII, 263 pages. 2005. (Subseries LNAI).

Vol. 3326: A. Sen, N. Das, S.K. Das, B.P. Sinha (Eds.), Distributed Computing - IWDC 2004. XIX, 546 pages. 2004.

Vol. 3325: C.H. Lim, M. Yung (Eds.), Information Security Applications. XI, 472 pages. 2005.

Vol. 3323: G. Antoniou, H. Boley (Eds.), Rules and Rule Markup Languages for the Semantic Web. X, 215 pages. 2004.

Vol. 3322: R. Klette, J. Žunić (Eds.), Combinatorial Image Analysis. XII, 760 pages. 2004.

Vol. 3321: M.J. Maher (Ed.), Advances in Computer Science - ASIAN 2004. Higher-Level Decision Making. XII, 510 pages. 2004.

Vol. 3320: K.-M. Liew, H. Shen, S. See, W. Cai (Eds.), Parallel and Distributed Computing: Applications and Technologies. XXIV, 891 pages. 2004.

Vol. 3319: D. Amyot, A.W. Williams (Eds.), System Analysis and Modeling. XII, 301 pages. 2005.

Vol. 3318: E. Eskin, C. Workman (Eds.), Regulatory Genomics. VII, 115 pages. 2005. (Subseries LNBI).

Vol. 3317: M. Domaratzki, A. Okhotin, K. Salomaa, S. Yu (Eds.), Implementation and Application of Automata. XII, 336 pages. 2005.

Vol. 3316: N.R. Pal, N.K. Kasabov, R.K. Mudi, S. Pal, S.K. Parui (Eds.), Neural Information Processing. XXX, 1368 pages. 2004.